Taste of Home's
Complete
guide to
Baking

Editor: Julie Schnittka

Food Editor: Janaan Cunningham

Associate Food Editors: Coleen Martin, Diane Werner

Cookbook Project and Recipe Editor: Janet Briggs

Senior Art Director: Linda Dzik

Associate Editors: Heidi Reuter Lloyd, Jean Steiner, Beth Wittlinger

Test Kitchen Director: Karen Johnson

Test Kitchen Assistants: Rita Krajcir, Sue Megonigle, Megan Taylor

Food Stylists: Kristin Arnett, Joylyn Trickel

Food Photography: Rob Hagen, Dan Roberts

Senior Food Photography Artist: Stephanie Marchese

Food Photography Artist: Julie Ferron

Photo Studio Manager: Anne Schimmel

Graphic Art Associates: Ellen Lloyd, Catherine Fletcher

Chairman and Founder: Roy Reiman

President: Barbara Newton

Taste of Home Books
©2004 Reiman Media Group, Inc.
5400 S. 60th St., Greendale WI 53129

International Standard Book Number: 0-89821-416-5
Library of Congress Control Number: 2004094977

To order additional copies of this book, write *Taste of Home* Books, P.O. Box 908, Greendale WI 53129. To order with a credit card, call toll-free 1-800/344-2560 or visit our Web site at **www.reimanpub.com**.

Pictured on front cover. Sour Cream Chocolate Cake (page 100).

Taste of Home's
Complete guide to
Baking

Tried-and-True Recipes Take The Guesswork Out of Baking

THANKS to over 1 million cooks who share thousands of fabulous recipes with us each year, *Taste of Home* has become an authority on cooking. (We have the No. 1 food magazine in the country to prove it!)

So when we published *The Complete Guide to Country Cooking* in 1998, people were thrilled! They *finally* had a cookbook focusing on the basics of delicious, down-home cooking from the folks who've always known the kitchen is the heart of every household.

It wasn't long before readers started requesting a cookbook dedicated to the time-honored tradition of baking. Our home economists got to work sifting through thousands of unbeatable recipes for baked goods that have appeared in *Taste of Home*, *Quick Cooking*, *Country Woman*, *Country* and *Reminisce* magazines through the years.

We compiled 513 fresh-from-the-oven favorites and put them into this instructional, recipe-packed and colorful cookbook—*Taste of Home's Complete Guide to Baking*! The following fantastic features will have you turning to this timeless treasury for years to come:

Baking Basics. *Taste of Home's Complete Guide to Baking* begins with the basics—measuring and mixing techniques...a pan size substitution chart...tips for buying appliances and bakeware...an explanation of common baking ingredients and terms...and more!

People who are new to baking will find this information indispensable. It's a good refresher course for the more experienced bakers as well.

Guaranteed-to-be-Good Recipes. As is true with all of our publications, this book's recipes have been tested at least once...and often two or three times! So you can try your hand at any of the 513 foolproof dishes with confidence. Plus, the recipes come from everyday cooks coast to coast and are favorites of families *just like yours!*

From cookies, cakes, brownies, pies and desserts to quick breads, biscuits, yeast breads, muffins and more, *Taste of Home's Complete Guide to Baking* provides a variety of sweet and savory goodies fit for any time of day or any kind of occasion.

Want to round out family meals around the clock? Whip up early-morning treats like Cinnamon Swirl Quick Bread and Apricot Cheese Danish. At dinner, pass a basket brimming with Crusty French Bread and Caraway Rye Rolls.

Entertaining guests? Dazzling desserts like Brownie Baked Alaska, Royal Raspberry Cheesecake and Traditional Caramel Flan will leave a lasting impression.

Need to pass a pan of bars or brownies at an upcoming potluck? Peppermint Crumb Squares and Fudge-Topped Brownies are real crowd pleasers.

Step-by-Step Recipe Directions. We've taken the worry out of baking by breaking down the recipe directions into numbered steps. It's like having your own personal home economist guiding you along the way!

Helpful How-to Photos. Because some baking recipes can be a little more involved, *Taste of Home's Complete Guide to Baking* is packed with hundreds of how-to photos and captions to clearly demonstrate certain techniques.

Beginner bakers can learn how to easily mix moist muffins, prepare perfect pie pastries and master classic cutout cookies. With just a little experience, you'll be baking impressive cake rolls, making marvelous meringues and whipping up spectacular souffles!

Colorful Photos. We know you're more likely to make a recipe if you see a photo of the finished food. So this big book features colorful photos of *more than 300* baked goods.

Handy Indexes. We offer three separate indexes— an alphabetical listing of recipes, a reference index for the book's *over 200* handy tips and a general index that lists each recipe by food category and major ingredient.

With tried-and-true recipes, time-saving tips and helpful how-to instructions, *Taste of Home's Complete Guide to Baking* makes baking a breeze for novice and experienced bakers alike.

Now it's time to turn the page, head to the kitchen, tie on an apron and begin baking. The wonderful aroma will beckon family and friends, who'll thank you *mmm*any times over for your efforts!

Janaan Cunningham

Food Editor, *Taste of Home*

Here's a Sample of What You'll See Inside

The pages of this classic cookbook (like the example below) are packed with mouth-watering recipes, colorful photos, handy how-to instructions and helpful hints.

Photo of finished food.

Description of the baked good, including preparation pointers and serving suggestions.

Numbered paragraphs to guide you through the recipe directions step by step.

Name of the cook contributing the family-favorite baked good.

A variety of useful baking, cooking and kitchen tips.

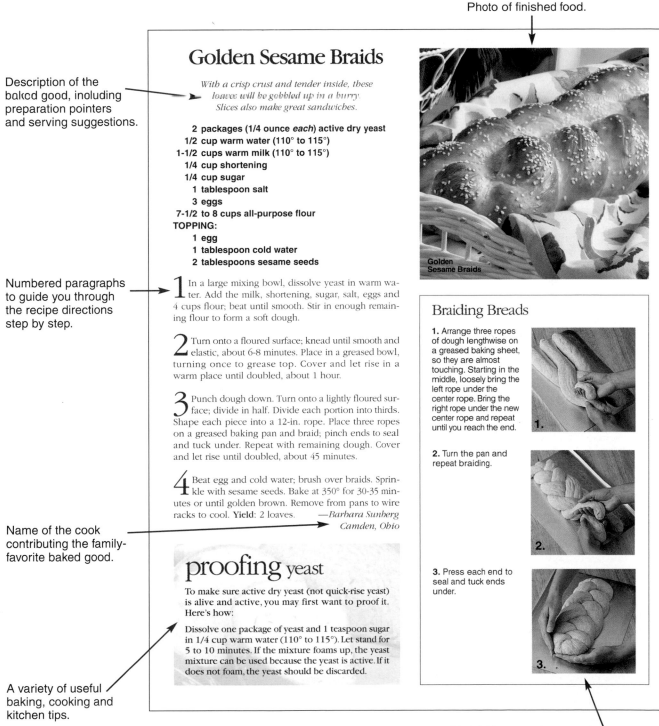

Golden Sesame Braids

With a crisp crust and tender inside, these loaves will be gobbled up in a hurry. Slices also make great sandwiches.

- 2 packages (1/4 ounce *each*) active dry yeast
- 1/2 cup warm water (110° to 115°)
- 1-1/2 cups warm milk (110° to 115°)
- 1/4 cup shortening
- 1/4 cup sugar
- 1 tablespoon salt
- 3 eggs
- 7-1/2 to 8 cups all-purpose flour
- **TOPPING:**
- 1 egg
- 1 tablespoon cold water
- 2 tablespoons sesame seeds

1 In a large mixing bowl, dissolve yeast in warm water. Add the milk, shortening, sugar, salt, eggs and 4 cups flour; beat until smooth. Stir in enough remaining flour to form a soft dough.

2 Turn onto a floured surface; knead until smooth and elastic, about 6-8 minutes. Place in a greased bowl, turning once to grease top. Cover and let rise in a warm place until doubled, about 1 hour.

3 Punch dough down. Turn onto a lightly floured surface; divide in half. Divide each portion into thirds. Shape each piece into a 12-in. rope. Place three ropes on a greased baking pan and braid; pinch ends to seal and tuck under. Repeat with remaining dough. Cover and let rise until doubled, about 45 minutes.

4 Beat egg and cold water; brush over braids. Sprinkle with sesame seeds. Bake at 350° for 30-35 minutes or until golden brown. Remove from pans to wire racks to cool. **Yield:** 2 loaves.
—*Barbara Sunberg*
Camden, Ohio

Golden
Sesame Braids

Braiding Breads

1. Arrange three ropes of dough lengthwise on a greased baking sheet, so they are almost touching. Starting in the middle, loosely bring the left rope under the center rope. Bring the right rope under the new center rope and repeat until you reach the end.

1.

2. Turn the pan and repeat braiding.

2.

3. Press each end to seal and tuck ends under.

3.

proofing yeast

To make sure active dry yeast (not quick-rise yeast) is alive and active, you may first want to proof it. Here's how:

Dissolve one package of yeast and 1 teaspoon sugar in 1/4 cup warm water (110° to 115°). Let stand for 5 to 10 minutes. If the mixture foams up, the yeast mixture can be used because the yeast is active. If it does not foam, the yeast should be discarded.

Helpful how-to photos and captions that clearly demonstrate the techniques for successfully making the recipe.

baking Basics

Measuring tools and techniques, tips for buying appliances and bakeware, and an explanation of common baking ingredients are just some of the basics in this chapter that will make baking fun and easy for you!

secrets for successful baking

- Read the entire recipe before you begin. Make sure you understand the cooking techniques.

- Check to see that you have all the ingredients for the recipe.

- Prepare the ingredients before you start mixing. Let the butter soften, toast the coconut, chop the nuts, etc.

- Measure the ingredients correctly, using proper techniques and measuring utensils.

- Prepare the recipe according to directions. It's best to use the baking pan or dish called for in the recipe.

- Preheat the oven before baking.

- Use a kitchen timer to accurately time the recipe. If you use a pan size other than the one called for in the recipe, you may need to adjust the baking time.

- Use an oven thermometer to verify the accuracy of your oven. To check the accuracy of your oven, preheat it to the desired temperature. Place an oven thermometer on the center rack. Close the oven door and leave the oven on at the set temperature. Keep the thermometer in the oven for 15 minutes, then check. If the thermometer does not agree with the set oven temperature, the oven temperature is inaccurate. Adjust the oven temperature accordingly.

- Cool baked goods on a wire rack to allow air to circulate around the food.

Measuring tools

To ensure good and consistent baking results, every cook needs to know how to accurately and correctly measure ingredients. Not all measuring cups are the same and not all ingredients are measured in the same manner.

- A liquid measuring cup is either clear glass or transparent plastic with a handle and a pour spout. They are available in 1-cup, 2-cup, 4-cup and 8-cup sizes. Liquid measures are used for milk, honey, molasses, corn syrup, water and oil.

- A dry measuring cup is made from metal or plastic and has a handle. The food to be measured should be even with the rim of the cup. Dry measuring cups usually come in a set with 1/4-cup, 1/3-cup, 1/2-cup and 1-cup sizes. Some sets may have additional sizes such as 1/8 cup or 2/3 cup. Dry measures are used for flour and sugar. They also are

used to measure shortening, sour cream, yogurt and applesauce. While these ingredients are not "dry", they can mound when measured. The dry measure allows you to level the ingredient at the top of the cup for an accurate measurement.

- Standard measuring spoons are used to measure both liquid and dry ingredients. Sets include a 1/4 teaspoon, 1/2 teaspoon, 1 teaspoon and 1 tablespoon. Some sets are available with a 1/8 teaspoon.

Proper Measuring Techniques

Measuring Liquids

Place liquid measuring cup on a level surface. For a traditional liquid measuring cup, view the amount at eye level to be sure of an accurate measure. Do not lift cup to check the level. Some newer liquid measuring cups are designed so that they can be accurately read from above.

For sticky liquids such as molasses, corn syrup or honey, spray the measuring cup with nonstick cooking spray before adding the liquid. This will make it easier to pour out the liquid and clean the cup.

Measuring Dry Ingredients

For dry ingredients such as flour, sugar or cornmeal, spoon ingredients into a dry measuring cup over a canister or waxed paper. Fill cup to overflowing, then level by sweeping a metal spatula or flat side of a knife across the top.

Measuring Bulk Dry Ingredients

Spoon bulky dry ingredients such as cranberries, raisins, chocolate chips or oats into the measuring cup. If necessary, level the top with a spatula or flat side of knife.

Measuring Brown Sugar

Since brown sugar has a unique moist texture, it needs to be packed into a dry measuring cup. Firmly press brown sugar into the cup with your fingers or the back of a spoon. Level with the rim of the cup. Brown sugar should hold the shape of the cup when it is turned out.

Measuring Sour Cream and Yogurt

Spoon sour cream and yogurt into a dry measuring cup, then level top by sweeping a metal spatula or flat side of a knife across the top of the cup.

Measuring Shortening

Press shortening into a dry measuring cup with a spatula to make sure it is solidly packed without air pockets. With a metal spatula or flat side of a knife, level with the rim. Some shortenings come in sticks and may be measured like butter (see below).

Measuring Butter

The wrappers for sticks of butter come with markings for tablespoons, 1/4 cup, 1/3 cup and 1/2 cup. Use a knife to cut off the desired amount.

Using Measuring Spoons

For dry ingredients such as flour, sugar or spices, heap the ingredient into the spoon over a canister or waxed paper. With a metal spatula or the flat side of a knife, level with the rim of the spoon.

For shortening or butter, spread into spoon and level off. For liquids, pour into measuring spoon over a bowl or custard cup. Never measure over the batter, because some may spill and you may end up with too much in the batter.

Choosing bakeware

The recipes in this book call for standard-size baking pans and baking dishes. For best results, use the pan size called for in the recipe. However, there are some practical substitutions (see chart below).

- Baking pans are made of metal. Aluminum pans with dull finishes give the best overall baking results. Pans with dark finishes often cook and brown foods more quickly. If you use pans with dark finishes, you may need to adjust the baking time and cover tops of baked goods with foil to prevent overbrowning. Insulated pans generally take longer to bake and brown foods.

- Baking dishes are made of ovenproof glass or ceramic. If you substitute a glass baking dish in a recipe calling for a metal baking pan, reduce the oven temperature by 25° to avoid overbaking and over-browning.

- To measure your bakeware's diameter, length or width, use a ruler and measure from one inside top edge to the opposite inside top edge. To measure the height, place a ruler on the outside of the dish and measure from the bottom to a top edge. For volume, fill the pan or dish full to the rim with water.

Bakeware Substitution

If you don't have the right pan for a recipe, here are a few substitutions. (Smaller pans will require less baking time.)

If you don't have this pan(s):	Use this pan(s) instead:
One 9-in. x 5-in. x 3-in. loaf pan	Three 5-3/4-in. x 3-in. x 2-in. loaf pans
One 8-in. x 4-in. x 2-in. loaf pan	Two 5-3/4-in. x 3-in. x 2-in. loaf pans
One 9-in. round baking pan	One 8-in. square baking dish
Two 9-in. round baking pans	One 13-in. x 9-in. x 2-in. baking pan
One 10-in. fluted tube pan	One 10-in. tube pan *or* two 9-in. x 5-in. x 3-in. loaf pans
One 13-in. x 9-in. x 2-in. baking pan	Two 9-in. round baking pans *or* two 8-in. square baking dishes

Basic Bakeware

A well-stocked kitchen should have the following items:

1. 9-in. x 1-1/2-in. round baking pan (two to three)
2. 13-in. x 9-in. x 2-in. baking pan and/or dish (3 qt.)
3. 10-in. fluted tube pan
4. 15-in. x 10-in. x 1-in. baking pan (jelly-roll pan)
5. Baking sheets (without sides) in assorted sizes
6. 9-in. springform pan
7. 9-in. pie plate
8. 12-cup muffin pan (standard size)
9. 6-oz. custard cups (set of six)
10. 9-in. x 5-in. x 3-in. loaf pan (two) and 8-in. x 4-in. x 2-in. loaf pan (two)
11. 9-in. x 9-in. x 2-in. and 8-in. x 8-in. x 2-in. square baking dishes and/or pans
12. 10-in. tube pan

These other items are also nice to have on hand:

11-in. x 7-in. x 2-in. baking pan and/or dish (2 qt.)
9-in. deep-dish pie plate
9-in. fluted tart pan with removable bottom
10-in. springform pan
5-3/4-in. x 3-in. x 2-in. loaf pan (three to four)
Miniature muffin pans
10-oz. custard cups (set of six)
8-in. fluted tube pan

Mixing tools and appliances

When baking, it's nice to have a variety of tools to make the job easier.

1. Blender
2. Food processor
3. Dough cutter/scraper
4. Grater
5. Juicer
6. Measuring cups (dry and liquid)
7. Measuring spoons
8. Metal spatulas
9. Mixer (portable)
10. Mixer (stand)
11. Mixing bowls
12. Pastry bag and tips
13. Pastry blender
14. Pastry brushes
15. Rolling pin
16. Sieve
17. Spatulas (rubber or plastic)
18. Timers
19. Wire rack
20. Wire whisk
21. Wooden spoons

Common baking ingredients

Chocolate

Chocolate is one of the most popular flavorings in baked goods. Chocolate comes from cocoa beans, which are processed to produce cocoa powder, cocoa butter and chocolate liquor (the liquid created when the meat of the cocoa bean "nibs" are crushed). The various forms and flavors of chocolate products are a combination of these products and other ingredients. For best results, we recommend using the type of chocolate listed in the recipe.

Baking cocoa is the powdery residue that remains after the cocoa butter is removed from the chocolate liquor. This form of chocolate contains the least amount of fat. Dutch-processed cocoa has been treated during processing with an alkalizing agent, which produces a smoother flavor and darker color than untreated baking cocoa.

Candy coating or almond bark is not considered true chocolate because it uses other vegetable fats instead of cocoa butter. Candy coatings come in a variety of flavors. They are mainly used as a coating on cookies, fruits or nuts or in candy making. Candy coatings are rarely used as a baking ingredient.

Chocolate chips are available in standard, miniature and larger "chunk" sizes. Chocolate chips come in a variety of flavors: semisweet, milk and vanilla or white. Specialty flavors such as raspberry or mint are sometimes available.

Chocolate syrup is a liquid made from cocoa, corn syrup and flavorings.

German sweet chocolate comes in a bar and is a sweeter chocolate than semisweet.

Milk chocolate contains cocoa butter, sugar, vanilla, chocolate liquor and 12% milk solids. It's available in chips and candy bars.

Semisweet and bittersweet chocolate are sometimes used interchangeably. However, bittersweet chocolate is less sweet than semisweet chocolate. Semisweet chocolate is made with chocolate liquor, additional cocoa butter, sugar and vanilla. It is available in packages of 1 ounce squares, chips and candy bars.

Unsweetened chocolate may also be referred to as baking chocolate. It is solidified chocolate liquor and does not contain sugar. It is available in packages of 1-ounce squares.

White chocolate is not a true chocolate because it does not contain chocolate liquor. White chocolate is made with cocoa butter, sugar, milk solids and vanilla. It is available in packages of 1-ounce squares and chips.

Storing Chocolate

Store chocolate tightly wrapped in a cool dry place. If stored improperly, the appearance of the chocolate will change. When chocolate is stored at too warm a temperature, a fat bloom occurs, causing grayish-white streaks or blotches in the chocolate. When chocolate is stored in a damp place, a sugar bloom occurs, giving a rough feel to the chocolate. You can still melt chocolate with blooms and incorporate it into batter or dough for baked goods.

Melting Chocolate

Break or chop large pieces of chocolate so it will melt more evenly. Melt chocolate in a dry heavy saucepan over low heat and stir until smooth. Even small amounts of water will cause the chocolate to seize (become thick and lumpy), making it unusable. If the chocolate needs to set up after melting (such as when it's used for dipping or garnishes), add 1/4 to 1/2 teaspoon of shortening for every 6 ounces of chocolate.

To melt chocolate in the microwave, place chocolate in a microwave-safe bowl. Melt semisweet chocolate at 50% power, and milk chocolate and vanilla or white chocolate at 30% power. Stir frequently until the chocolate is melted; do not overheat.

Dairy Products

Dairy products add moisture to bake goods. They also impart flavor and tenderness and aid in browning. Unless otherwise stated, the recipes in this book were tested with whole milk. You may substitute reduced-fat or fat-free milk for the whole milk, but the texture and richness of the final product may be affected.

Buttermilk is made by adding a bacteria to fat-free or reduced-fat milk. The result is a tangy flavor and a slightly thicker consistency. Buttermilk was originally the low-fat liquid that remained when cream was churned into butter.

Evaporated milk is whole milk with 60% of the water removed and contains about 7.9% milk fat. An unopened can of evaporated milk is shelf stable. Do not use evaporated milk as a substitute for sweetened condensed milk. Reduced-fat and fat-free evaporated milk are also available.

Fat-free milk, also called skim or nonfat milk, contains no more than 1/2% milk fat.

Half-and-half cream is a blend of whole milk and cream that contains from 10-1/2% to 18% milk fat.

Heavy whipping cream contains at least 36% milk fat. When whipped, it should double in volume and hold stiff peaks.

Nonfat dry milk powder is fat-free milk with all the moisture removed. It is reconstituted with water.

Reduced-fat milk has 2% milk fat.

Sour cream is half-and-half cream that has been soured by using a lactic acid-producing bacteria or acidifiers. It has a tangy flavor and a thick texture.

Sweetened condensed milk is made from whole milk with about 50% of the water removed and has added sugar. It is a thick, sweet product. An unopened can of sweetened condensed milk is shelf stable. Do not use sweetened condensed milk as a substitute for evaporated milk. Reduced-fat and fat-free sweetened condensed milk are also available.

Whole milk, referred to as milk in this cookbook, has about 3-1/2% milk fat.

Yogurt is made from whole, reduced-fat or fat-free milk. The milk is fermented with lactic acid-producing bacteria. It has a tangy flavor and a thick texture. Yogurt may have added sweeteners, flavorings and fruit.

Eggs

Eggs perform many functions in baking—they add color, flavor, texture (give a tender crumb), structure and help leaven. Egg yolks add fat and act as an emulsifier, which helps blend the shortening or oil into the liquid ingredients. Egg whites are used for their drying properties, especially for meringues.

Purchase eggs with unbroken shells from a refrigerated case. Refrigerate them as soon as possible after purchase. Store eggs in their carton on an inside refrigerator shelf, not in a compartment on the door. The carton cushions the eggs and helps prevent moisture loss and odor adsorption. Use eggs by the expiration date printed on the carton.

Never use a recipe where the eggs will not be thoroughly cooked. Eggs are thoroughly cooked when they reach a temperature of 160°. For food safety reasons, do not leave eggs at room temperature for over 2 hours. Discard any eggs that have cracked or broken shells.

Egg Substitutes are available in cartons in the refrigerated and frozen section of grocery stores. Egg substitutes use egg whites and contain no cholesterol and little or no fat. One-fourth cup of egg substitute is equal to one egg. Do not use egg substitute for items such as cream puffs, popovers and sponge cakes. Baking with egg substitutes may affect the quality of your baked item. Generally, it is best to use egg substitutes for only a portion of the eggs called for in a recipe.

Egg Size Equivalents

The recipes in this cookbook were tested with large eggs. The following are some guidelines for substituting other size eggs for large eggs.

1 large egg = 1 jumbo; 1 extra-large; 1 medium

2 large eggs = 2 jumbo; 2 extra-large; 2 medium; 3 small

3 large eggs = 2 jumbo; 3 extra-large; 3 medium; 4 small

4 large eggs = 3 jumbo; 4 extra-large; 5 medium; 5 small

5 large eggs = 4 jumbo; 4 extra-large; 6 medium; 7 small

6 large eggs = 5 jumbo; 5 extra-large; 7 medium; 8 small

Separating Eggs

Place an egg separator over a custard cup; crack egg into the separator. As each egg is separated, place yolk in another bowl and empty egg whites into a mixing bowl. It is easier to separate eggs when they are cold.

Beating Eggs

Lightly beaten
To beat the egg with a fork until the yolk and white are combined.

Lemon-colored
To beat eggs with an electric mixer on high speed for about 5 minutes. The volume of the beaten eggs will increase, the texture will go from liquid to thick and foamy, and the color will be a light yellow.

Thick and pale yellow
To beat eggs and sugar with an electric mixer on high speed for about 7-8 minutes or until mixture has thickened and turned a very pale yellow. Mixture will fall in ribbons from a spoon.

Soft peaks
To beat egg whites with an electric mixer on medium speed until they are thick and white. To test for soft peaks, lift the beaters from the whites—the egg white peaks should curl down.

For best results, make sure the bowl and beaters are free from oil and the egg whites contain no specks of yolk. Both will prevent the whites from reaching full volume.

Stiff peaks
To continue beating the egg whites after they have reached the soft-peak stage with an electric mixer on high speed until the volume increases more and they are thicker. To test for stiff peaks, lift the beaters from the whites—the egg white peaks should stand straight up and if you tilt the bowl, the whites should not slide around.

Fats

Fats in baked goods can perform many functions—they tenderize, add moisture, carry flavors and give a richness to flavors. Fats act as a leavener when creamed, because the creaming process incorporates air into the batter or dough. They also help keep baked goods fresh.

Butter adds flavor and may add color. In some recipes (such as shortbread) butter is the main or only flavoring component, and the use of butter is essential to that recipe. When creaming butter, it should be softened (a table knife will be able to glide through the butter). When butter is cut into a mixture, it generally should be cold from the refrigerator. Recipes for this cookbook were tested with butter, not margarine.

Margarine is made from a variety of vegetable oils, usually soybean and corn oils. Not all margarines are alike. They vary in oil content and form. For baking, use stick margarine with an 80% fat content. Margarine with lower fat content, usually labeled as margarine spread or whipped margarine, has more water and air in it and will adversely affect the quality of your baked goods.

Shortening is a solid fat (it holds its shape at room temperature) that is made from 100% vegetable oils. Shortening is not as temperature-sensitive as butter and margarine, so shortening makes cookies spread less during baking and makes pastries flakier. Regular vegetable shortening adds no flavor to baked goods. Butter-flavored shortening adds flavor and some color.

Oil is most frequently used in cakes to add tenderness and moistness. Because oil cannot be creamed like butter, margarine and shortening, it does not help in leavening. Oil cannot be used interchangeably with solid shortening.

Flours

Flours are made from the finely ground meal of edible grains. Wheat flour, the most commonly used flour, contains gluten—an elastic protein that traps the gases produced by leaveners. The trapped gases push against the protein, causing the product to rise. During baking, the protein is set by the heat and gives the baked good its structure. The terms soft and hard wheat refer to the amount of protein (gluten) in the flour—soft has less and hard has more. The amount of gluten will affect the texture of the baked product.

Wheat flour will bleach naturally when exposed to air over many weeks. In commercially bleached flour, this whitening process is accelerated with a small amount of bleaching agents. Unbleached flour does not use bleaching agents and may give baked goods an off-white color.

All-purpose flour is a blend of hard (high-gluten) wheat and soft (low-gluten) wheat flours. It is a general-purpose flour, which means it is suitable for all types of baking.

Bread flour is made from hard (high-gluten) wheat and is specifically formulated for yeast breads.

Cake flour is made from soft (low-gluten) wheat and has a fine texture. It gives a tender delicate crumb to cakes.

Rye flour contains less gluten than wheat flours like all-purpose flour and should be used in combination with wheat flour. Rye flour produces breads with a darker color, denser texture and more distinctive flavor. Medium rye flour is available in most grocery stores, but light and dark rye flours are also sold in specialty markets.

Self-rising flour is all-purpose flour to which salt and baking powder have been added. Self-rising flour is used as a shortcut in some biscuit and cake recipes.

Whole wheat flour, also called graham flour, is a wheat flour that is processed from the entire wheat kernel, which contains the bran and the germ. Whole wheat flour has more fiber, nutrition and fat than all-purpose flour. Because of the fat from the bran and germ, whole wheat flour has a shorter shelf life than white flours. Store whole wheat flour in the refrigerator for up to 6 months.

Leaveners

Leaveners cause baked goods to rise and have a light texture. Baking powder, baking soda, yeast and eggs are leavening agents.

Creaming fat also helps leaven baked goods by incorporating air into the batter. The air expands during baking, causing the product to rise. Liquids such as water create steam during baking, which can also cause baked products to rise.

Baking powder is

available in single-acting and double-acting varieties. Double-acting baking powder is the most readily available type and is the type used in this cookbook. Double-acting baking powder produces carbon dioxide gas in two stages: when it is mixed with liquid and when it is heated. Single-acting baking powder creates carbon dioxide gas only when it is mixed with liquid. Baking powder can lose its ability to leaven. Discard any baking powder that is past the expiration date on the can.

Baking soda is an alkaline substance used in batters that have acidic ingredients such as buttermilk, molasses and sour cream. When the baking soda is mixed with the acidic ingredient, there is an immediate release of carbon dioxide gas. Batters and doughs that only use baking soda as a leavening agent should be baked immediately. Otherwise, the baked product might not rise as high and the texture won't be as light.

Yeast is a microorganism that becomes activated when combined with warm water and sugar. It consumes the sugars in sweeteners and flours and produces carbon dioxide gas that helps give bread its light airy texture. There are several different types of yeast and each is handled differently. Check the expiration date on the package before using and discard yeast if it is past the date.

Active dry yeast is available in 1/4-ounce foil packages or 4-ounce jars. With the Traditional Mixing Method on page 284, the active yeast is dissolved in liquid that has been warmed to 110° to 115°. If the liquid temperature is too low, the yeast will not be activated. If the liquid temperature is too high, the yeast will be killed, preventing the bread from rising.

With the Rapid Mixing Method on page 292, the active dry yeast is added directly to the flour and other dry ingredients. Then warm liquid (120° to 130°) is added.

Quick-rise yeast is available in 1/4-ounce foil packages or 4-ounce jars. Quick-rise yeast is finely granulated and should only be combined with the other ingredients using the Rapid Mixing Method on page 292. Quick-rise yeast will raise bread dough in about a third to half the traditional time.

Bread machine yeast is available in 4-ounce jars. This is an instant yeast with finer granules. The smaller granules allow the yeast to mix into the dough more evenly.

Fresh or cake yeast is most commonly available in 2-ounce cakes, which is equivalent to three 1/4-ounce packages of active dry yeast. A third of the fresh yeast cake (about .6 ounce) is equal to one packet of active dry yeast. Older bread recipes often call for a "cake of yeast".

Cake yeast is a fresh product found in your grocer's dairy case. It should be used within 10 days of purchase. To use, crumble the yeast into dry ingredients or soften in tepid water (70° to 80°).

Eggs are whipped to incorporate air to create a foam. The incorporated air expands when heated, causing the baked product to rise. Foam cakes such as angel foods and chiffon use egg whites as a leavening agent.

Salt

Salt helps round out flavors. In bread making, salt also controls the growth of the yeast. Too much salt in the bread dough will inhibit the growth of the yeast, resulting in a dense loaf.

Sugars and Other Sweeteners

Sugars and other sweeteners perform many functions in baked goods. They tenderize, add sweetness and flavor, promote browning and enhance the keeping quality. Sugar is used in meringues for stability. Sweeteners are used in small amounts to feed the yeast when making bread.

Brown sugar is a combination of granulated sugar and molasses. Available in light and dark, brown sugars can be used interchangeably. Dark brown sugar has more molasses and therefore, a more distinctive molasses flavor than light brown sugar. Dark brown sugar will also cause the color of the baked good to be slightly darker.

Equivalents and Substitutions

Confectioners' sugar, also known as powdered sugar, is granulated sugar that has been ground into a fine powder and mixed with a little cornstarch to prevent clumping. It is mainly used for frostings and glazes. For smooth frostings without any lumps, sift confectioners' sugar after measuring.

Granulated sugar, also know as sugar or white sugar, is made from refined sugarcane or beets. In this cookbook, it's simply referred to as sugar.

Corn syrup is made from corn. It helps keep baked goods moist. It is available in light and dark. Dark corn syrup has caramel color and flavor added to it, so it will cause baked goods to be darker in color.

Honey adds a distinct flavor and sweetness to baked items and also keeps them moist. Honey's flavor is affected by the type of flowers the bees collect nectar from. Honey caramelizes at a lower temperature than sugar and may cause baked good to brown more quickly. Honey is available in liquid and whipped form. The recipes in this cookbook were tested with liquid honey.

Molasses is the by-product of refining sugarcane. It adds sweetness, a distinct flavor and color to baked goods. It is available in light, dark and black strap. As you would expect, the light has the mildest flavor and the lightest color and black strap has the strongest flavor and darkest color.

Weight and Measure Equivalents

Dash or pinch = less than 1/8 teaspoon

1-1/2 teaspoons = 1/2 tablespoon

3 teaspoons = 1 tablespoon; 1/2 fluid ounce

4-1/2 teaspoons = 1-1/2 tablespoons

2 tablespoons = 1/8 cup; 1 fluid ounce

4 tablespoons = 1/4 cup; 2 fluid ounces

5-1/3 tablespoons = 1/3 cup; 5 tablespoons plus 1 teaspoon

8 tablespoons = 1/2 cup; 4 fluid ounces

10-2/3 tablespoons = 2/3 cup; 10 tablespoons plus 2 teaspoons

12 tablespoons = 3/4 cup; 6 fluid ounces

16 tablespoons = 1 cup; 8 fluid ounces; 1/2 pint

1/8 cup = 2 tablespoons; 1 fluid ounce

1/4 cup = 4 tablespoons; 2 fluid ounces

1/3 cup = 5-1/3 tablespoons

1/2 cup = 8 tablespoons; 4 fluid ounces

2/3 cup = 10-2/3 tablespoons

3/4 cup = 12 tablespoons; 6 fluid ounces

7/8 cup = 3/4 cup plus 2 tablespoons

1 cup = 16 tablespoons; 8 fluid ounces; 1/2 pint

2 cups = 1 pint; 16 fluid ounces

4 cups = 2 pints; 1 quart; 32 fluid ounces

1/2 pint = 1 cup; 8 fluid ounces

1 pint = 2 cups; 16 fluid ounces

1 quart = 4 cups; 32 fluid ounces

4 quarts = 16 cups; 1 gallon

16 ounces = 1 pound

Emergency Ingredient Substitutions

Ingredient	Amount	Substitution
Apple pie spice	1 teaspoon	1/2 teaspoon ground cinnamon plus 1/4 teaspoon ground nutmeg, 1/8 teaspoon ground allspice and dash ground cloves *or* cardamom
Baking powder	1 teaspoon	1/2 teaspoon cream of tartar plus 1/4 teaspoon baking soda
Buttermilk	1 cup	1 tablespoon lemon juice *or* white vinegar plus enough milk to measure 1 cup. Stir and let stand for 5 minutes before using. *Or* 1 cup plain yogurt
Chocolate, semisweet	1 square (1 ounce)	3 tablespoons semisweet chocolate chips *or* 1 square (1 ounce) unsweetened chocolate plus 1 tablespoon sugar
Chocolate, unsweetened	1 square (1 ounce)	3 tablespoons baking cocoa plus 1 tablespoon shortening *or* vegetable oil
Corn syrup, light	1 cup	1 cup sugar plus 1/4 cup water
Corn syrup, dark	1 cup	3/4 cup light corn syrup plus 1/4 cup molasses
Cream, half-and-half	1 cup	1 tablespoon melted butter plus enough whole milk to measure 1 cup
Egg	1 whole	2 egg whites *or* 2 egg yolks *or* 1/4 cup egg substitute
Flour, cake	1 cup	1 cup minus 2 tablespoons (7/8 cup) all-purpose flour
Flour, self-rising	1 cup	Place 1-1/2 teaspoons baking powder and 1/2 teaspoon salt in a measuring cup. Add all-purpose flour to measure 1 cup.
Fruit liqueur	1 tablespoon	1 tablespoon fruit juice
Honey	1 cup	1-1/4 cups sugar plus 1/4 cup water
Lemon juice	1 teaspoon	1 teaspoon cider vinegar
Lemon peel	1 teaspoon	1/2 teaspoon lemon extract
Milk, whole	1 cup	1/2 cup evaporated milk plus 1/2 cup water *or* 1 cup water plus 1/3 cup nonfat dry milk powder
Molasses	1 cup	1 cup honey
Pumpkin pie spice	1 teaspoon	1/2 teaspoon ground cinnamon plus 1/4 teaspoon ground ginger, 1/4 teaspoon ground allspice and 1/8 teaspoon ground nutmeg *or* cloves
Sour cream	1 cup	1 cup plain yogurt
Sugar	1 cup	1 cup packed brown sugar *or* 2 cups sifted confectioners' sugar

Common baking terms

Bake—To cook in an oven surrounded by dry heat. When baking, it's important to preheat the oven before placing the food inside.

Batter—A mixture made of flour and a liquid such as milk. It may also include ingredients such as sugar, butter, shortening or oil, eggs, leaveners and flavorings. The consistency of batters range from thin to thick. Thin batters are pourable such as pancakes or cakes. Thick batters can be dropped from a spoon such as quick breads or muffins.

Beat—To rapidly mix with a spoon, fork, wire whisk or electric mixer.

Blend—To combine several ingredients with a spoon, electric mixer, blender or food processor.

Boil—To heat liquids until bubbles form that cannot be stirred down. In the case of water, the temperature will reach 212° at sea level.

Caramelize—To heat sugar in a skillet or saucepan over low heat until melted and golden brown in color.

Chill—To cool foods to below room temperature (40° or less) by placing in the refrigerator, freezer or an ice bath.

Chop—To cut foods into 1/4-inch to 1/2-inch pieces.

Coats Spoon—To leave a thin even smooth film on the back of a metal spoon. This is a doneness test for stirred custards.

Combine—To place several ingredients in a single bowl or container and thoroughly mix.

Cool—To bring foods to room temperature (about 70°).

Core—To remove the seed area of an apple or pear using a coring tool or a small knife.

Cream—To beat softened butter, margarine or shortening alone or with sugar using a spoon or mixer until light and fluffy.

Crimp—To seal the edge of a double-crust pie by pinching or pressing the bottom and top pastry together with your fingers, fork or other utensil.

Cube—To cut foods into 1/2-inch to 1-inch square pieces.

Cut in—To break down and distribute cold butter, margarine or shortening into a flour mixture using a pastry blender or two knives.

Dash—A measurement less than 1/8 teaspoon that is used for herbs, spices or hot pepper sauce. This is not an accurate measurement.

Dice—To cut foods into 1/8-inch to 1/4-inch cubes.

Dissolve—To stir a solid food with a liquid until none of the solid remains, such as yeast with warm water or gelatin in boiling water.

Dot—To break up small pieces of butter and distribute over the top of pie filling or dough.

Dough—A thick mixture made of flour and a liquid that is not pourable. It may also include ingredients such as sugar, butter, shortening or oil, eggs, leaveners and flavorings. It is stiff enough to be worked with by hand, for example, kneading bread dough.

Drizzle—To slowly spoon or pour a thin stream of icing, melted butter or other liquid.

Dust—To lightly sprinkle confectioners' sugar, baking cocoa or flour.

Egg Wash—A mixture of beaten egg, egg yolk or egg white and water that is brushed over breads, rolls, pastries or pie crusts before baking. Egg washes give the final baked product a shiny brown finish.

Extracts—The distilled essential oils from plant materials, which are then dissolved in alcohol. Common examples are vanilla and almond.

Flavorings—Chemical compounds that replicate the flavor of a particular food or plant and do not originate from the plant material. Common examples are maple, banana and coconut.

Flute—To make a V shape or scalloped edge on pie crust with your thumb and fingers.

Fold—A method of mixing to combine light or delicate ingredients such as whipped cream or egg whites with other ingredients without beating. A rubber spatula is used to gently cut down through the ingredients, move across the bottom of the bowl and bring up part of the mixture.

Food Coloring—Used to tint foods and available in liquid, gel or paste.

Frost—To cover a cake, cupcake or cookie with a spreadable frosting.

Glaze—To coat the exterior of sweet or savory foods with a thin glossy mixture.

Grate—To rub ingredients such as citrus peel, spices and chocolate over a grater to produce very fine particles.

Grease—To rub the inside of a baking dish or pan with shortening, butter or oil or to coat with nonstick cooking spray to keep the contents from sticking.

Grease and Flour—To rub a thin layer of shortening, butter or oil over the inside of a baking pan or dish and then dust with flour. The excess flour is shaken out of the pan. Cakes baked in round baking pans or fluted tube pans generally require that the pan be greased and floured.

Grind—To transform a solid piece of food into smaller pieces using a food processor, blender or a mortar and pestle.

Ice—To spread a thin icing over cakes or cookies.

Jelly Roll—A dessert made by spreading a filling of jelly, cream or whipped cream over a sponge cake baked in a 15-inch x 10-inch x 1-inch pan and rolling into a log. Jelly-roll style is used when any food is filled and rolled into a log shape.

Knead—To work dough by using a pressing and folding action to make it smooth and elastic.

Line—To cover a baking sheet with a piece of parchment paper, waxed paper or foil to prevent sticking.

Marble—To swirl light and dark batters for a cake, bar, pie or cheesecake. The batters should not be combined into one color; there should still be two distinctive batters after marbling.

Mince—To cut foods into very fine pieces no larger than 1/8 inch.

Mix—To stir or beat two or more ingredients together with a spoon or a fork until well combined.

Moisten—To add enough liquid to dry ingredients while stirring gently to make a wet but not runny mixture. Often used in the preparation of muffins.

Peel—To remove the skin from fruits and vegetables. Also, the outer portion of a citrus fruit is known as peel. To remove the peel, use small sharp knife, grater, vegetable peeler or zester.

Pinch—A small amount (less than 1/8 teaspoon) of a seasoning or spice that is easily held between the thumb and index finger. This is not an accurate measurement.

Pipe—To force a soft mixture such as whipped cream, frosting or meringue through a pastry bag or tip for a fancy shape.

Plump—To soak dried fruit such as raisins and cherries in liquid until softened.

Press—Often called a cookie press. Used to form cookie dough into decorative shapes.

Prick—To pierce food or pastry with the tines of a fork to prevent them from bursting or rising during baking.

Proof—To check the quality of yeast before using in bread making. To proof yeast, dissolve yeast and a little sugar in warm water (110° to 115°) and let stand for 5 minutes. If the yeast is alive, there will be a thick foam on the surface. To proof also refers to letting yeast dough rise after it's been shaped and before baking.

Punch Down—To use a fist to deflate risen yeast dough after the first rising.

Puree—To mash solid foods into a smooth mixture using a food processor, food mill, blender or sieve.

Refrigerate—To place in the refrigerator to chill.

Rounded Teaspoon or Tablespoon—To mound dough slightly in the measuring spoon.

Score—To make thin slashes on the surface of breads to decorate and allow steam to escape during baking.

Seize—To become thick and lumpy. Seizing refers to when a small amount of liquid comes in contact with melted chocolate.

Separate—To remove the egg white from the egg yolk.

Sift—To pass dry ingredients such as flour or confectioners' sugar through a fine-mesh strainer to remove lumps, add air and combine several dry ingredients.

Soften—To bring butter, margarine or cream cheese to a soft consistency by letting it stand at room temperature for a short time.

Soft Peaks—The stage when beating egg whites or heavy whipping cream when the beater is lifted from the mixture and points of the peaks curl over.

Stiff Peaks—The stage when beating egg whites or heavy whipping cream when the beater is lifted from the mixture and points of the peaks stand straight up.

Stir—To blend a combination of ingredients by hand using a spoon in a circular motion.

Strain—To separate solids from liquid by pouring through a sieve or colander.

Toss—To quickly and gently mix ingredients with a spoon or fork. Often done with flour and candied fruit in baked goods.

Whip—To beat rapidly by hand or with an electric mixer to add air and increase volume.

Whisk—A multi-looped wire mixing utensil with a handle used to whip sauces, eggs, cream, etc. to a smooth, airy consistency. To whisk means to whip ingredients together.

Zest—See Peel.

homemade Cookies make tasty treats

From drop cookies and refrigerator favorites to shaped specialties and cutout classics, cookies appeal to novices and experienced bakers alike. Nothing can beat a treat like Peanut Butter Sandwich Cookies (p. 51), Neapolitan Cookies (p. 36) and Cherry Almond Chews (p. 35) served alongside a cold glass of milk.

the basics of Cookies

Cookies are grouped into five categories according to how they're shaped: drop, refrigerator, shaped, cutout and bars. (Bars and brownies appear in the next chapter.)

- The consistency of drop cookie dough allows it to simply be dropped from a spoon onto a baking sheet, making it the easiest kind of cookie to bake.

- For refrigerator cookies (also known as icebox cookies), the dough is shaped into logs, wrapped in plastic, then refrigerated until firm enough to slice and bake.

- Shaped cookies are formed by hand into various shapes (such as balls, logs and crescents) or are pressed through a cookie press (such as spritz).

- Cutout cookies have a firmer dough. To make it easier to handle, the dough may need to be chilled before being rolled out and cut into shapes with a cookie cutter.

secrets for successful cookies

- Use butter, stick margarine (with at least 80% oil) or shortening. Whipped, tub, soft, liquid or reduced-fat products contain air and water and will produce flat, tough, underbrowned cookies.

- Measure ingredients accurately, using the measuring tools and techniques on pages 8 and 9.

- Avoid overmixing the dough. If it's handled too much, the cookies will be tough.

- Use heavy-gauge dull aluminum baking sheets with one or two low sides. When a recipe calls for greased baking sheets, use shortening or non-stick cooking spray. Dark finishes may cause the cookies to become overly browned.

- Preheat the oven for 10 to 15 minutes.

- For even baking, make cookies the same size and thickness.

- Unless the recipe states otherwise, place cookie dough 2 to 3 in. apart on a cool baking sheet.

- Leave at least 2 in. around the baking sheet and the oven walls for good heat circulation. For best results, bake only one sheet of cookies at a time. If you need to bake two sheets at once, switch the position of the baking sheets halfway through the baking time.

- Check the cookies when the minimum baking time has been reached, baking longer if needed. Follow doneness tests given in individual recipes.

- Unless otherwise directed, let cookies cool for 1 minute on the baking sheet before removing to a wire rack. Cool completely before storing.

- Let baking sheets cool before placing the next batch of cookie dough on it. Otherwise, the heat from the baking sheet will soften the dough and cause it to spread.

problem-Solving pointers for Cookies

If this happens to your cookies:	Try one of these solutions:
Cookies are spreading too much.	Place the dough on a cool baking sheet. Chill the dough before baking. Next time, replace part of the butter in the recipe with shortening. If using margarine, check the label and make sure it contains 80% vegetable oil.
Cookies are not spreading enough.	Add 1 to 2 tablespoons of liquid, such as milk or water, to the remaining dough. Let the dough stand at room temperature before baking. Next time use butter, not margarine or shortening.
Cookies are tough.	Too much flour was worked into the dough. Add 1 or 2 tablespoons of shortening, butter or sugar to the remaining dough. The dough was overhandled or overmixed. Next time, use a lighter touch when mixing.
Cookies are too brown.	Oven temperature is too high. Check with an oven thermometer. Use heavy-gauge dull aluminum baking sheets. Dark baking sheets will cause the cookies to become overly browned.
Cookies are too pale.	Oven temperature is too low. Check with an oven thermometer. Use heavy-gauged dull aluminum baking sheets. Insulated baking sheets cause cookies to be pale in color. Next time use butter, not margarine or shortening. Or substitute 1 to 2 tablespoons corn syrup for the sugar.

Drop cookies

tips for making drop cookies

- If your mixer begins to strain because the cookie dough is too thick, use a wooden spoon to stir in the last of the flour or ingredients such as nuts, chips or dried fruit.

- For even baking, it's important that you make cookies the same size. Use a teaspoon or tablespoon from your flatware set (see Shaping Drop Cookies above right) or a small ice cream scoop (see Using an Ice Cream Scoop to Make Drop Cookies on page 27).

- Drop cookies generally melt and spread during baking. But sometimes a recipe may instruct you to flatten the cookies with the bottom of a glass dipped in sugar or with a fork making a crisscross pattern.

Shaping Drop Cookies

Fill a teaspoon or tablespoon with dough. Use another spoon or small rubber spatula to push the mound of dough off the spoon onto a cool baking sheet. Place dough 2 to 3 in. apart or as recipe directs.

Chocolate Chip Cookies

(Also pictured on back cover)

Chocolate chip cookies are a mainstay in every cookie jar. They have mass appeal, making them perfect for gifts, bake sales or everyday snacking.

- 1 cup butter, softened
- 1 cup shortening
- 2 cups packed light brown sugar
- 1 cup sugar
- 4 eggs
- 2 teaspoons vanilla extract
- 4-1/2 cups all-purpose flour
- 2 teaspoons baking soda
- 2 teaspoons salt
- 2 cups (12 ounces) semisweet chocolate chips
- 1 cup chopped pecans

1 In a large mixing bowl, cream the butter, shortening and sugars until light and fluffy. Beat in eggs and vanilla. Combine the flour, baking soda and salt; add to creamed mixture and mix well. Stir in chocolate chips and nuts (dough will be slightly sticky).

2 Drop by tablespoonfuls 2 in. apart onto greased baking sheets. Bake at 350° for 10-12 minutes or until lightly browned. Remove to wire racks to cool. **Yield:** about 11 dozen.
—*Cindy Utter*
Jacksonville, Illinois

Chocolate Chip Cookies

Whoopie Pies

This confection features an irresistible cream filling sandwiched between two chocolate cupcake-like cookies. Enlist the kids to help assemble these old-fashioned favorites.

      1 cup butter, softened
1-1/2 cups sugar
      2 eggs
      2 teaspoons vanilla extract
      4 cups all-purpose flour
   3/4 cup baking cocoa
      2 teaspoons baking soda
   1/2 teaspoon salt
      1 cup water
      1 cup buttermilk
FILLING:
      2 cups marshmallow creme
      2 cups confectioners' sugar
   1/2 cup butter, softened
      2 teaspoons vanilla extract

1 In a large mixing bowl, cream butter and sugar until light and fluffy. Add the eggs and vanilla; mix well. Combine the flour, cocoa, baking soda and salt; add to creamed mixture alternately with water and buttermilk, beating well after each addition.

2 Drop by teaspoonfuls 2 in. apart onto greased baking sheets. Bake at 375° for 5-7 minutes or until set. Remove to wire racks to cool completely.

3 In a small mixing bowl, beat filling ingredients until fluffy. Spread filling on the bottom of half of the cookies; top with remaining cookies. **Yield:** about 3 dozen. —*Ruth Ann Stelfox, Raymond, Alberta*

Using an Ice Cream Scoop to Make Drop Cookies

An ice cream scoop is the perfect utensil for making uniformly sized drop cookies. (A 1 tablespoon-size ice cream scoop will result in a standard-size 2-in. cookie.) Just scoop the dough, even off the top with a flat-edge metal spatula and release onto a baking sheet.

Double Chocolate Crisps

Double Chocolate Crisps

Chock-full of chocolate, these crispy cookies have a tantalizing aroma while baking. They'll surely satisfy a sweet tooth.

      1 cup butter, softened
      2 cups sugar
      2 eggs
      4 squares (1 ounce *each*) unsweetened chocolate, melted and cooled
      2 teaspoons vanilla extract
2-1/4 cups all-purpose flour
      1 teaspoon baking soda
      1 teaspoon salt
   1/4 teaspoon ground cinnamon
      1 cup (6 ounces) semisweet chocolate chips
      1 cup chopped pecans

1 In a large mixing bowl, cream butter and sugar until light and fluffy. Add eggs, one at time, beating well after each addition. Beat in chocolate and vanilla. Combine the flour, baking soda, salt and cinnamon; gradually add to the creamed mixture. Stir in chocolate chips and pecans.

2 Drop by tablespoonfuls 2 in. apart onto ungreased baking sheets. Bake at 375° for 10-12 minutes or until tops are cracked. Remove to wire racks to cool. **Yield:** 4 dozen. —*Marilyn Spangler, Oak Creek, Wisconsin*

Toffee Chip Thins

Every bite of these crisp cookies is bursting with the flavors of toffee, chocolate and coconut. Graham cracker crumbs add to their deliciously different flavor.

       1/2 cup butter, softened
         1 can (14 ounces) sweetened condensed milk
         2 cups graham cracker crumbs (about 32 squares)
       3/4 cup all-purpose flour
         2 teaspoons baking powder
         2 cups (12 ounces) semisweet chocolate chips
         1 cup English toffee bits *or* almond brickle chips
   1-1/2 cups flaked coconut, optional

1 In a large mixing bowl, combine the butter and milk; mix well. Combine the graham cracker crumbs, flour and baking powder; gradually add to the butter mixture. Stir in chocolate chips, toffee bits and coconut if desired.

2 Drop by rounded tablespoonfuls 2 in. apart onto greased baking sheets. Bake at 375° for 10-12 minutes or until edges are lightly browned. Cool for 2 minutes before removing to wire racks to cool completely. **Yield:** about 4-1/2 dozen. —*Lynae Lang Wolf Point, Montana*

Nutty Sugar Crisps

These slightly crisp drop cookies are especially appealing to folks who don't want to hassle with cutout sugar cookies.

       1 cup butter, softened
   1/2 cup vegetable oil
       1 cup sugar
       1 cup confectioners' sugar
       2 eggs
       1 teaspoon vanilla extract
   4-1/2 cups all-purpose flour
       1 teaspoon baking soda
       1 teaspoon cream of tartar
       1 cup chopped walnuts

1 In a large mixing bowl, cream the butter, oil and sugars until light and fluffy. Add eggs, one at a time, beating well after each addition. Beat in vanilla. Combine the flour, baking soda and cream of tartar; gradually add to the creamed mixture. Stir in walnuts.

2 Drop by teaspoonfuls 2 in. apart onto ungreased baking sheets. Flatten slightly with a glass dipped in sugar. Bake at 375° for 10-12 minutes or until edges are golden brown. Remove to wire racks to cool. **Yield:** 8-1/2 dozen. —*Eleanore Kovach, Lakeview, Oregon*

German Chocolate Cookies

A handy boxed cake mix hurries along the preparation of chewy cookies studded with chips and raisins. Even with only six ingredients, they have wonderful bakery-shop flavor.

       1 package (18-1/4 ounces) German chocolate cake mix
       2 eggs
   1/2 cup butter, melted
   1/2 cup quick-cooking oats
       1 cup (6 ounces) semisweet chocolate chips
   1/2 cup raisins

1 In a large mixing bowl, combine the dry cake mix, eggs, butter and oats; mix well. Stir in the chocolate chips and raisins.

2 Drop by rounded tablespoonfuls 3 in. apart onto ungreased baking sheets. Bake at 350° for 9-11 minutes or until set. Cool for 5 minutes before removing to wire racks to cool completely. **Yield:** about 3-1/2 dozen. —*Leslie Henke, Louisville, Colorado*

German Chocolate Cookies

Chocolate Marshmallow Cookies

Chocolate Marshmallow Cookies

These double-chocolaty delights have a surprise inside. Atop the chocolate cookie base, marshmallow peeks out under chocolate icing. Kids love them!

    1/2 cup butter, softened
      1 cup sugar
      1 egg
    1/4 cup milk
      1 teaspoon vanilla extract
  1-3/4 cups all-purpose flour
    1/3 cup baking cocoa
    1/2 teaspoon baking soda
    1/2 teaspoon salt
     16 to 18 large marshmallows
ICING:
      6 tablespoons butter
      2 tablespoons baking cocoa
    1/4 cup milk
  1-3/4 cups confectioners' sugar
    1/2 teaspoon vanilla extract
Pecan halves

1 In a large mixing bowl, cream butter and sugar until light and fluffy. Beat in the egg, milk and vanilla. Combine the flour, cocoa, baking soda and salt; beat into creamed mixture.

2 Drop by rounded teaspoonfuls 2 in. apart onto ungreased baking sheets. Bake at 350° for 8 minutes. Meanwhile, cut marshmallows in half. Press a marshmallow half cut side down onto each cookie. Bake 2 minutes longer. Remove to wire racks to cool.

3 For icing, combine the butter, cocoa and milk in a saucepan. Bring to a boil; boil for 1 minute, stirring constantly. Cool slightly; transfer to a small mixing bowl. Add confectioners' sugar and vanilla; beat well. Spread over the cooled cookies. Top each with a pecan half. **Yield:** about 3 dozen.

—*June Formanek*
Belle Plaine, Iowa

Frosted Pineapple Cookies

Never thought of using pineapple to make cookies? We encourage you to give this recipe a try! Sweet and moist with real tropical flavor, these cookies will be a hit whenever you serve them.

  1 **can (8 ounces) crushed pineapple**
1/2 **cup shortening**
  1 **cup packed brown sugar**
  1 **egg**
  1 **teaspoon vanilla extract**
  2 **cups all-purpose flour**
1-1/2 **teaspoons baking powder**
1/4 **teaspoon baking soda**
1/4 **teaspoon salt**
1-1/2 **cups confectioners' sugar**

1 Drain pineapple, reserving 3 tablespoons juice. Set pineapple aside; set reserved juice aside for frosting. In a large mixing bowl, cream shortening and brown sugar until light and fluffy. Beat in egg. Add pineapple and vanilla; mix well. Combine the flour, baking powder, baking soda and salt; gradually add to the creamed mixture.

2 Drop by tablespoonfuls 2 in. apart onto greased baking sheets. Bake at 325° for 17-20 minutes or until golden. Remove to wire racks to cool.

3 For frosting, in a small bowl, combine confectioners' sugar with enough of the reserved pineapple juice to achieve spreading consistency. Frost cooled cookies. **Yield:** 3 dozen.

—Mary DeVoe
Bradenton, Florida

Frosted Pineapple Cookies

Chocolate Raspberry Cookies

The combination of raspberries and chocolate gives each bite of these cookies an elegant feel. Serve them for special occasions or "just because"!

  1 **cup butter, softened**
3/4 **cup sugar**
3/4 **cup packed brown sugar**
  2 **eggs**
3/4 **cup semisweet chocolate chips, melted and cooled**
1/2 **cup fresh raspberries, pureed**
  3 **cups all-purpose flour**
3/4 **teaspoon baking soda**
3/4 **teaspoon salt**
  1 **cup vanilla *or* white chips**

1 In a large mixing bowl, cream butter and sugars until light and fluffy. Add eggs, one at a time, beating well after each addition. Beat in melted chocolate and raspberries. Combine the flour, baking soda and salt; gradually add to the creamed mixture. Stir in vanilla chips.

2 Drop by teaspoonfuls 2 in. apart onto ungreased baking sheets. Bake at 375° for 10-12 minutes or until edges begin to brown. Remove to wire racks to cool. **Yield:** 6 dozen.

—Sherri Crotwell
Shasta Lake, California

Oatmeal Sandwich Cremes

Sandwich cookies can be a little time-consuming but are well worth it. To save some time, bake the cookies, cool and freeze. When ready to serve, thaw the cookies, make the filling and assemble the sandwiches.

3/4 **cup shortening**
1 **cup sugar**
1 **cup packed brown sugar**
1 **egg**
1/4 **cup water**
1 **teaspoon vanilla extract**
1-1/2 **cups self-rising flour***
1 **teaspoon baking soda**
1 **teaspoon ground cinnamon**
3 **cups quick-cooking oats**
3/4 **cup raisins**
FILLING:
1/2 **cup butter, softened**
1/2 **cup shortening**
3-3/4 **cups confectioners' sugar**
2 **tablespoons milk**
1 **teaspoon vanilla extract**
Dash salt

1 In a large mixing bowl, cream shortening and sugars until light and fluffy. Beat in the egg, water and vanilla. Combine the flour, baking soda and cinnamon; gradually add to the creamed mixture. Stir in oats and raisins.

2 Drop by tablespoonfuls 2 in. apart onto ungreased baking sheets. Flatten with a greased glass. Bake at 325° for 13-14 minutes or until lightly browned. Remove to wire racks to cool.

3 Combine filling ingredients in a large mixing bowl; beat until smooth. Spread on the bottom of half of the cookies; top with remaining cookies. **Yield:** 3 dozen.
—*Lesley Mansfield, Monroe, North Carolina*

*Editor's Note: As a substitute for 1 cup self-rising flour, place 1-1/2 teaspoons baking powder and 1/2 teaspoon salt in a 1-cup measuring cup; add all-purpose flour to measure 1 cup. For 1/2 cup, place 3/4 teaspoon baking powder and 1/4 teaspoon salt in a 1/2-cup measuring cup; add all-purpose flour to measure 1/2 cup.

Banana Oatmeal Cookies

Banana Oatmeal Cookies

Bananas and chocolate chips give ordinary oatmeal cookies a flavorful twist. Keep some ripe bananas in the freezer to make these treats on a moment's notice.

1 **cup butter-flavored shortening**
1 **cup sugar**
2 **eggs**
1 **teaspoon vanilla extract**
2 **cups all-purpose flour**
1 **teaspoon baking soda**
1 **teaspoon ground cinnamon**
1 **teaspoon ground cloves**
3 **medium bananas, mashed**
2 **cups quick-cooking oats**
1 **cup (6 ounces) semisweet chocolate chips**

1 In a large mixing bowl, cream shortening and sugar until light and fluffy. Beat in eggs and vanilla. Combine the flour, baking soda, cinnamon and cloves; add to creamed mixture and mix well. Stir in the bananas, oats and chocolate chips.

2 Drop by rounded teaspoonfuls 2 in. apart onto greased baking sheets. Bake at 375° for 10-12 minutes. Immediately remove to wire racks to cool. **Yield:** about 4 dozen.
—*Yvonne Miller Chenango Forks, New York*

Some kids' idea of a seven-course meal is six cookies and a glass of milk.

Iced Orange Cookies

Orange juice in both the dough and icing lends to the tropical flavor of these bite-size cookies.

    1/2 cup shortening
      1 cup sugar
      2 eggs
    1/2 cup orange juice
      1 tablespoon grated orange peel
  2-1/2 cups all-purpose flour
  1-1/2 teaspoons baking powder
    1/2 teaspoon salt
ICING:
      2 cups confectioners' sugar
    1/4 cup orange juice
      2 tablespoons butter, melted

1 In a large mixing bowl, cream shortening and sugar until light and fluffy. Add eggs, one at a time, beating well after each addition. Beat in orange juice and peel. Combine the flour, baking powder and salt; gradually add to the creamed mixture.

2 Drop by rounded teaspoonfuls 2 in. apart onto ungreased baking sheets. Bake at 350° for 10-12 minutes or until edges begin to brown. Remove to wire racks to cool. In a small bowl, combine icing ingredients until smooth; drizzle over cooled cookies. **Yield:** about 5-1/2 dozen. *—Lori DiPietro, New Port Richey, Florida*

Chewy Macaroons

A perfectly prepared macaroon will be lightly crisp on the outside and chewy on the inside. Macaroons are primarily made with coconut, but some varieties feature nuts.

      2 egg whites
    1/2 teaspoon vanilla extract
Pinch salt
      6 tablespoons sugar
      1 cup flaked coconut

1 In a small mixing bowl, beat egg whites, vanilla and salt on medium speed until soft peaks form. Gradually add sugar, one tablespoon at a time, beating on high until stiff peaks form. Fold in the coconut.

2 Drop by tablespoonfuls 2 in. apart onto wellgreased baking sheets. Bake at 300° for 25 minutes or until lightly browned. Immediately remove to wire racks to cool. **Yield:** about 2 dozen.
—Herbert Borland, Des Moines, Washington

Chewy Macaroons

Lace Cookies

Light and crispy, these cookies melt in your mouth, while the plump pecan perched on top provides a little crunch. They're delicate when they come out of the oven, so keep them on the foil until completely cool, then carefully remove.

Lace Cookies

     1 **cup chopped pecans**
     1 **cup sugar**
  1/4 **cup all-purpose flour**
  1/4 **teaspoon baking powder**
  1/8 **teaspoon salt**
     1 **egg**
  1/2 **cup butter, melted**
     1 **teaspoon vanilla extract**
Pecan halves

1 In a food processor, combine chopped pecans and sugar; cover and process until nuts are ground. Transfer to a small mixing bowl; add the flour, baking powder and salt. In a bowl, beat egg; add butter and vanilla. Stir into pecan mixture.

2 Drop by teaspoonfuls about 3 in. apart onto lightly greased foil-lined baking sheets. Place a pecan half in the center of each cookie. Bake at 325° for 8-10 minutes or until golden brown and lacy. Allow cookies to cool completely before carefully removing from foil. **Yield:** about 4-1/2 dozen. —*Bonnie Thompson Cave City, Kentucky*

removing cookies from a baking sheet

If cookies seem to crumble when you remove them from the baking sheet, let them cool for 1 to 2 minutes first.

But be aware that if cookies cool too long, they become hard and can break when removed. If this happens, return the baking sheet to the oven to warm the cookies slightly so they'll release more easily.

Pumpkin Raisin Cookies

Fall is the perfect time to turn on the oven and bake up a batch of nicely spiced pumpkin cookies.

  1/2 **cup shortening**
     1 **cup sugar**
     1 **cup canned pumpkin**
     1 **teaspoon vanilla extract**
     2 **cups all-purpose flour**
     1 **teaspoon baking powder**
     1 **teaspoon baking soda**
     1 **teaspoon ground cinnamon**
Dash salt
     1 **cup raisins**
FROSTING:
     2 **tablespoons butter**
1-1/2 **cups confectioners' sugar**
     2 **tablespoons milk**
     1 **teaspoon vanilla extract**

1 In a large mixing bowl, cream shortening and sugar until light and fluffy. Add pumpkin and vanilla. Combine the flour, baking powder, baking soda, cinnamon and salt; add to the creamed mixture and mix well. Fold in the raisins.

2 Drop by teaspoonfuls 2 in. apart onto greased baking sheets. Bake at 350° for 12-14 minutes or until lightly browned. Remove to wire racks to cool.

3 For frosting, melt butter in a saucepan. Stir in the sugar, milk and vanilla until smooth. Frost cooled cookies. **Yield:** about 3 dozen. —*Carol Preston Bloomington, Indiana*

German Chocolate Toffee Cookies

the **history**
of cookies

Cookies started out as little cakes used to test the oven temperature before the larger cake was baked. In fact, the word cookie is derived from the Dutch word "koekje", meaning little cake.

German Chocolate Toffee Cookies

German sweet chocolate gives these crisp cookies a unique twist. Don't be surprised if the big batch disappears quickly!

       1 cup butter, softened
       1 cup shortening
   2-1/2 cups sugar
     1/2 cup packed brown sugar
       1 package (4 ounces) German sweet chocolate, melted and cooled
       4 eggs
       2 teaspoons water
       2 teaspoons vanilla extract
   6-1/2 cups all-purpose flour
       2 teaspoons baking soda
   1-1/2 teaspoons salt
   1-1/2 cups English toffee bits *or* almond brickle chips
   1-1/2 cups chopped walnuts

1 In a large mixing bowl, cream the butter, shortening and sugars until light and fluffy. Beat in chocolate. Add eggs, one at a time, beating well after each addition. Beat in water and vanilla. Combine the flour, baking soda and salt; gradually add to the creamed mixture. Stir in toffee bits and walnuts.

2 Drop by tablespoonfuls 2 in. apart onto greased baking sheets. Bake at 350° for 12-15 minutes or until golden brown. Remove to wire racks to cool. **Yield:** 13 dozen.
— *Joyce Robb, Dillon, Montana*

Soft Lemonade Cookies

These lovely lemon cookies are so moist, you won't be able to stop eating them! Frozen lemonade concentrate is the surprise ingredient.

   1 cup butter, softened
   1 cup sugar
   2 eggs
   3 cups all-purpose flour
   1 teaspoon baking soda
   1 can (6 ounces) frozen lemonade concentrate, thawed, *divided*
Additional sugar

1 In a large mixing bowl, cream butter and sugar until light and fluffy. Add eggs, one at a time, beating well after each addition. Combine flour and baking soda; add to the creamed mixture alternately with 1/3 cup of lemonade concentrate, beating well after each addition.

2 Drop by rounded teaspoonfuls 2 in. apart onto ungreased baking sheets. Bake at 400° for 8-10 minutes. Remove to wire racks. Brush warm cookies with remaining lemonade concentrate; sprinkle with sugar. Cool. **Yield:** 6 dozen.
— *Margo Neuhauser, Bakersfield, California*

Sour Cream Drops

This unique frosting combines melted butter and confectioners' sugar for rich flavor.

1/4 cup shortening
3/4 cup sugar
  1 egg
1/2 cup sour cream
1/2 teaspoon vanilla extract
1-1/3 cups all-purpose flour
1/4 teaspoon baking powder
1/4 teaspoon baking soda
1/4 teaspoon salt
FROSTING:
  2 tablespoons butter
1/2 cup confectioners' sugar
1/4 teaspoon vanilla extract
  3 to 4 teaspoons hot water

1 In a large mixing bowl, cream shortening and sugar until light and fluffy. Beat in the egg, sour cream and vanilla. Combine the flour, baking powder, baking soda and salt; add to the creamed mixture. Cover and refrigerate for at least 1 hour.

2 Drop by tablespoonfuls 2 in. apart onto greased baking sheets. Bake at 425° for 7-8 minutes or until lightly browned. Remove to wire racks to cool.

3 For frosting, melt butter in a saucepan until golden brown; stir in the confectioners' sugar, vanilla and enough water to achieve a spreading consistency. Frost cooled cookies. **Yield:** about 2-1/2 dozen.
—*Tracy Betzler, Reston, Virginia*

Sour Cream Drops

Cherry Almond Chews

(Pictured on page 22 and on back cover)

Topped with a bright red cherry, coconut cookies are terrific for the holidays. During that busy time of year, you'll appreciate the fact that these freeze well, so you can make them ahead.

1 cup shortening
1 cup sugar
1 cup packed brown sugar
2 eggs
3/4 teaspoon almond extract
2-1/2 cups all-purpose flour
1 teaspoon baking soda
1 teaspoon salt
2-1/2 cups flaked coconut
3/4 cup chopped almonds *or* pecans, optional
1 jar (16 ounces) maraschino cherries, drained and halved

1 In a large mixing bowl, cream shortening and sugars until light and fluffy. Add eggs, one at a time, beating well after each addition. Beat in extract. Combine the flour, baking soda and salt; gradually add to the creamed mixture. Stir in coconut and nuts if desired.

2 Drop by rounded teaspoonfuls 2 in. apart onto lightly greased baking sheets. Place a cherry half in the center of each. Bake at 350° for 12-14 minutes or until lightly browned. Remove to wire racks to cool. **Yield:** about 7 dozen. —*Alma Chaney, Trenton, Ohio*

Refrigerator cookies

refrigerator cookie facts

- To make refrigerator cookie dough easier to slice, use nuts and fruits that are finely chopped. If the nuts and fruit are too large, the cookie dough may break apart when sliced.

- Wrap dough tightly to prevent it from drying out in the refrigerator. Refrigerate dough until firm.

- Generally, the dough can be refrigerated up to 1 week or frozen up to 6 months.

- To keep a nice round shape for refrigerated cookie dough, place each roll inside a tall glass and place the glass on its side in the refrigerator. The rounded glass will prevent the bottom of the roll from flattening out.

- Use a thin sharp knife to slice through the dough. Cut one roll at a time, keeping additional rolls refrigerated until ready to use. After each slice, rotate the roll to avoid having one side that's flat.

Neapolitan Cookies

(Pictured on page 23)

These eye-catching cookies may look complicated, but they're actually easy to prepare. The flavor is reminiscent of Neapolitan ice cream.

```
    1  cup butter, softened
1-1/2  cups sugar
    1  egg
    1  teaspoon vanilla extract
2-1/2  cups all-purpose flour
1-1/2  teaspoons baking powder
  1/2  teaspoon salt
  1/2  teaspoon almond extract
    6  drops red liquid food coloring
  1/2  cup chopped walnuts
    1  square (1 ounce) unsweetened baking
       chocolate, melted and cooled
```

1 Line a 9-in. x 5-in. x 3-in. loaf pan with waxed paper; set aside. In a large mixing bowl, cream butter and sugar until light and fluffy. Beat in egg and vanilla. Combine the flour, baking powder and salt; gradually add to the creamed mixture. Divide the dough into thirds. Add almond extract and food coloring to one portion; spread evenly into prepared pan. Add nuts to second portion; spread evenly over first layer. Add melted chocolate to third portion; spread over second layer. Cover with waxed paper; refrigerate overnight.

2 Unwrap dough; cut loaf in half lengthwise. Cut each portion into 1/8-in. slices. Place 1 in. apart on ungreased baking sheets. Bake at 350° for 10-12 minutes or until edges are firm. Remove to wire racks to cool. **Yield:** 12 dozen. —*Jan Mallo, White Pigeon, Michigan*

Cute Kitty Cookies

Here's a fun dessert idea to serve children. Half of the dough is chocolate, which frames the playful cat faces.

```
  1/2  cup butter, softened
  1/4  cup shortening
    1  cup sugar
    2  eggs
    1  teaspoon vanilla extract
2-1/4  cups all-purpose flour
  3/4  teaspoon baking powder
  1/2  teaspoon salt
    1  cup quick-cooking oats
    2  squares (1 ounce each) unsweetened
       chocolate, melted and cooled
```
Semisweet chocolate chips
Red-hot candies
Black shoestring licorice, cut into 1-1/2-inch pieces

1 In a large mixing bowl, cream the butter, shortening and sugar until light and fluffy. Add eggs, one at a time, beating well after each addition. Beat in vanilla. Combine the flour, baking powder and salt; gradually add to the creamed mixture. Stir in oats. Divide dough in half. Add melted chocolate to one portion.

Cute Kitty
Cookies

Cream Cheese-Filled Cookies

With a cream cheese filling and chocolate topping, these rich cookies are more fancy than others. Their eye-catching appeal makes them perfect for special occasions.

1/3 cup butter, softened
1/3 cup shortening
3/4 cup sugar
1 egg
1 teaspoon vanilla extract
1-3/4 cups all-purpose flour
1 teaspoon baking powder
1/2 teaspoon salt

FILLING:
2 packages (3 ounces *each*) cream cheese, softened
1-1/2 cups confectioners' sugar
2 tablespoons all-purpose flour
1 teaspoon vanilla extract
1 drop yellow food coloring, optional

TOPPING:
3/4 cup semisweet chocolate chips
3 tablespoons butter

2 Shape the plain dough into an 8-in. roll. Roll chocolate dough between waxed paper into an 8-in. square. Place plain dough roll at one end of square; roll up. Seal seam. Wrap in plastic wrap; refrigerate for 3 hours or overnight.

3 Unwrap dough; cut into 1/4-in. slices. Place 2 in. apart on ungreased baking sheets. To form ears, pinch two triangles on the top of each cookie. Bake at 350° for 8-10 minutes or until lightly browned. Immediately place two chocolate chips for eyes, a red-hot for the nose and six pieces of licorice on each for whiskers. Remove to wire racks to cool. **Yield:** 3 dozen.
—*Kay Curtis*
Guthrie, Oklahoma

1 In a large mixing bowl, cream the butter, shortening and sugar until light and fluffy. Beat in egg and vanilla. Combine the flour, baking powder and salt; gradually add to the creamed mixture. Shape into two 12-in. rolls; wrap each in plastic wrap. Refrigerate for 4 hours or overnight.

2 Unwrap dough; cut into 3/4-in. slices. Place 1 in. apart on greased baking sheets. Bake at 375° for 10-12 minutes or until lightly browned. Remove to wire racks to cool.

3 In a mixing bowl, combine the filling ingredients; mix well. Place 2 teaspoonfuls in the center of each cookie. Let stand until set. In a heavy saucepan or microwave, melt chocolate chips and butter; stir until smooth. Drizzle over cookies. Store in the refrigerator. **Yield:** about 2-1/2 dozen. —*Ruth Glick*
New Holland, Pennsylvania

Making Cute Kitty Cookies

Cute Kitty Cookies have a solid center of vanilla dough encased in a chocolate dough. To make these two-toned cookies, shape the vanilla dough into an 8-in. roll. Roll out the chocolate dough into an 8-in. square between two sheets of waxed paper. Remove the top sheet of waxed paper and place the vanilla roll at one edge of the square. Trim if necessary. Roll up jelly-roll style, peeling waxed paper away while rolling. Seal seam. Wrap the roll in plastic wrap and refrigerate.

Black Walnut Cookies

3-1/2 cups all-purpose flour
1 teaspoon baking soda
1/4 teaspoon salt
2 cups chopped black walnuts *or* walnuts, *divided*

1 In a large mixing bowl, cream the butter and brown sugar until light and fluffy. Beat in the eggs and vanilla. Combine the flour, baking soda and salt; gradually add to the creamed mixture. Stir in 1-1/4 cups of walnuts. Finely chop the remaining nuts. Shape dough into two 15-in. rolls. Roll in chopped nuts, pressing gently. Wrap each in plastic wrap. Refrigerate for 2 hours or until firm.

2 Unwrap dough; cut into 1/4-in. slices. Place 2 in. apart on greased baking sheets. Bake at 350° for 8-11 minutes. Remove to wire racks to cool. **Yield:** 10 dozen.　—*Mrs. Doug Black, Conover, North Carolina*

Coating the Edge of Refrigerated Cookies

To give a little twist to refrigerated cookies, coat the edge in nuts, colored sugar, jimmies, nonpareils, coconut or cinnamon-sugar. Spread the coating lengthwise down a piece of waxed paper. Place the roll of dough on top of the coating and roll gently, pressing coating onto dough with your hands.

Black Walnut Cookies

Like most nuts, walnuts can be stored in a cool dark place for several months. An open bag of shelled chopped nuts can become rancid quickly and should be used within a week. For long-term storage, refrigerate them for up to 6 months or freeze for up to 1 year.

1 cup butter, softened
2 cups packed brown sugar
2 eggs
1 teaspoon vanilla extract

Simple Sugar Cookies

Confectioners' sugar takes the place of granulated sugar in this sweet standby. They're a nice alternative to traditional cutout sugar cookies.

1 cup butter, softened
1-1/4 cups confectioners' sugar
1 egg
1 teaspoon vanilla extract
2 cups all-purpose flour
1 teaspoon baking soda
1 teaspoon cream of tartar
1/8 teaspoon salt

1 In a large mixing bowl, cream butter and confectioners' sugar until light and fluffy. Beat in egg and vanilla. Combine the flour, baking soda, cream of tartar

and salt; gradually add to the creamed mixture. Shape into two 5-in. rolls; wrap each in plastic wrap. Refrigerate for 1 hour or until firm.

2 Unwrap dough; cut into 1/4-in. slices. Place 2 in. apart on ungreased baking sheets. Bake at 350° for 8-10 minutes. Remove to wire racks to cool. **Yield:** 3-1/2 dozen. —*Maxine Guin, Barnhart, Missouri*

Chewy Date Pinwheels

(Pictured on back cover)

For a lovely look on your holiday cookie tray, make a batch of these pretty pinwheel cookies. The date and pecan filling gives them old-fashioned flavor.

FILLING:
 1-1/2 **cups chopped dates**
    1 **cup sugar**
    1 **cup water**
  1/2 **cup chopped pecans**
DOUGH:
    1 **cup butter, softened**
    2 **cups packed brown sugar**
  1/2 **cup sugar**
    3 **eggs**
 4-1/2 **cups all-purpose flour**
    1 **teaspoon baking soda**
    1 **teaspoon salt**
    1 **teaspoon ground cinnamon**

1 In a large saucepan, combine the dates, sugar and water. Cook and stir over medium heat for 8 minutes or until thick. Add nuts; cool. In a large mixing bowl, cream butter and sugars until light and fluffy. Add eggs, one at a time, beating well after each addition. Combine the flour, baking soda, salt and cinnamon; gradually add to creamed mixture. Divide dough in half.

2 On a floured surface, roll out one portion of dough into a 1/4-in.-thick rectangle. Spread with half of the filling. Roll up jelly-roll style, starting with a long side. Repeat with remaining dough and filling. Wrap each roll in plastic wrap; refrigerate overnight.

3 Unwrap dough; cut into 1/2-in. slices. Place 2 in. apart on greased baking sheets. Bake at 375° for 12-14 minutes. Remove to wire racks to cool. **Yield:** about 4 dozen. —*Naomi Cross, Goshen, Indiana*

Fruit 'n' Nut Cookies

Dotted with red and green maraschino cherries, these soft colorful cookies are a nice addition to a Christmas dessert tray.

  3/4 **cup butter, softened**
  3/4 **cup shortening**
 1-1/4 **cups packed brown sugar**
    2 **eggs**
    1 **teaspoon vanilla extract**
    4 **cups all-purpose flour**
    2 **teaspoons baking powder**
  1/2 **teaspoon salt**
    1 **can (8 ounces) crushed pineapple, drained**
  1/2 **cup chopped dates**
  1/2 **cup chopped red maraschino cherries**
  1/2 **cup chopped green maraschino cherries**
  1/2 **cup flaked coconut**
  1/2 **cup chopped pecans** *or* **walnuts**

1 In a large mixing bowl, cream the butter, shortening and brown sugar until light and fluffy. Add eggs, one at a time, beating well after each addition. Beat in vanilla. Combine the flour, baking powder and salt; gradually add to the creamed mixture. Stir in the remaining ingredients. Shape into three 10-in. rolls; wrap each in plastic wrap. Refrigerate for 2 hours or until firm.

2 Unwrap dough; cut into 1/4-in. slices. Place 2 in. apart on ungreased baking sheets. Bake at 375° for 8-10 minutes or until golden brown. Remove to wire racks to cool. **Yield:** 7 dozen. —*Jennie Loftus Gasport, New York*

Fruit 'n' Nut Cookies

Chocolate Almond Cookies

These sandwich cookies are not only jam-filled but also dipped in chocolate for a doubly delicious treat. Raspberry jam and chocolate pair well together, but feel free to use whatever flavor jam you prefer.

- 1/2 **cup butter, softened**
- 6 **tablespoons sugar**
- 1-1/2 **teaspoons vanilla extract**
- 1 **cup all-purpose flour**
- 1 **cup finely chopped blanched almonds**
- 1/4 to 1/2 **cup raspberry jam** *or* **jam of your choice**
- 3 **squares (1 ounce** *each***) semisweet chocolate**

1 In a large mixing bowl, cream the butter, sugar and vanilla until light and fluffy. Combine flour and almonds; gradually add to the creamed mixture. Shape into a 12-in. roll; wrap in plastic wrap. Refrigerate for 4 hours or until firm.

2 Unwrap dough; cut into 1/4-in. slices. Place 2 in. apart on ungreased baking sheets. Bake at 350° for 8-10 minutes or until lightly browned. Remove to wire racks to cool.

3 Spread 1 teaspoon jam on the bottom of half of the cookies; top with remaining cookies. Melt chocolate. Dip cookies halfway into chocolate; shake off excess. Place on waxed paper until chocolate is set. **Yield:** 2 dozen.
—Kathryn Werner
Peterborough, Ontario

removing skins from hazelnuts

To easily remove skins from shelled hazelnuts—and, in the process, to enrich their flavor by toasting—try this trick:

Spread the nuts in a single layer in a baking pan. Bake at 350° for 10 to 15 minutes or until the nuts are toasted and the skins begin to flake. Transfer nuts to a clean kitchen towel; rub against the towel to remove skins.

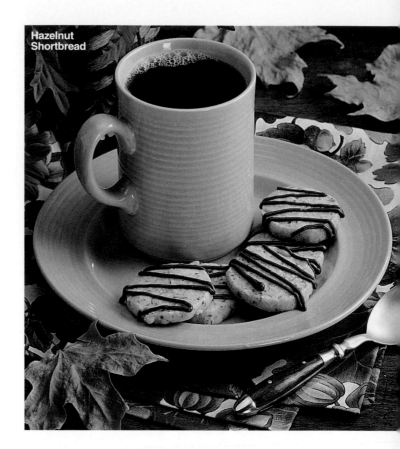

Hazelnut Shortbread

Hazelnut Shortbread

Traditional shortbread only contains flour, sugar and butter, resulting in a rich crumbly cookie. This version gets added flavor from chopped hazelnuts, some maple syrup and a touch of chocolate.

- 1 **cup butter, softened**
- 1/2 **cup sugar**
- 2 **tablespoons maple syrup** *or* **honey**
- 2 **teaspoons vanilla extract**
- 2 **cups all-purpose flour**
- 1-1/4 **cups finely chopped hazelnuts**
- 1/2 **cup semisweet chocolate chips**

1 In a large mixing bowl, cream butter and sugar until light and fluffy. Add syrup and vanilla. Add flour; mix just until combined. Fold in the nuts. Shape into two 1-1/2-in. rolls; wrap each in plastic wrap. Refrigerate for 2 hours or until firm.

2 Unwrap dough; cut into 1/4-in. slices. Place 2 in. apart on ungreased baking sheets. Bake at 325° for 14-16 minutes or until edges begin to brown. Remove to wire racks to cool. Melt chocolate chips; drizzle over cookies. Let stand until chocolate is set. **Yield:** about 6 dozen.
—Karen Morrell, Canby, Oregon

Double Peanut Butter Cookies

The extra taste of peanut butter in the middle of the cookie is a delicious surprise the first time you bite into one. It's a nice soft cookie and fun to make with little helpers. Kids love to put that extra dab of peanut butter in the middle and snitch some at the same time.

      1-1/2 cups all-purpose flour
    1/2 cup sugar
    1/2 teaspoon baking soda
    1/4 teaspoon salt
    1/2 cup shortening
    1/2 cup creamy peanut butter
    1/4 cup light corn syrup
      1 tablespoon milk
Additional peanut butter

1 In a large bowl, combine the flour, sugar, baking soda and salt. Cut in shortening and peanut butter until mixture resembles coarse crumbs. Stir in the corn syrup and milk; mix well. Shape into a 10-in. roll; wrap in plastic wrap. Refrigerate for 3 hours or overnight.

2 Unwrap dough; cut into 1/4-in. slices. Place half of the slices 2 in. apart on ungreased baking sheets. Top each with 1/2 teaspoon of peanut butter. Top with remaining slices; seal edges with a fork. Bake at 350° for 12-14 minutes or until lightly browned. Cool for 2 minutes before removing to wire racks to cool completely. **Yield:** 20 cookies. —*Jeannette Mack, Rushville, New York*

Orange Pecan Cookies

This cookie is pure heaven with a subtle orange flavor and just a sprinkling of chopped pecans throughout.

      1 cup butter, softened
    1/2 cup sugar
    1/2 cup packed brown sugar
      1 egg
      2 tablespoons orange juice
      1 tablespoon grated orange peel
2-1/2 cups all-purpose flour
    1/2 teaspoon baking soda
    1/2 teaspoon salt
    1/2 cup chopped pecans

1 In a large mixing bowl, cream butter and sugars until light and fluffy. Beat in the egg, orange juice and peel. Combine the flour, baking soda and salt; gradually add to creamed mixture and mix well. Stir in pecans. Shape into two 11-1/2-in. rolls; wrap each in plastic wrap. Refrigerate for 4 hours or overnight.

2 Unwrap dough; cut into 1/4-in. slices. Place 2 in. apart on lightly greased baking sheets. Bake at 400° for 7-8 minutes or until golden brown. Remove to wire racks to cool. **Yield:** 6 dozen. —*Eleanor Henry Derry, New Hampshire*

Double Peanut Butter Cookies

Shaped cookies

tips for making shaped cookies

- Refrigerate the dough until it is chilled for easier handling. If there is a high butter content in the dough, the heat from your hands can soften the butter in the dough, making it harder to shape.

- Dust hands lightly with flour to prevent dough from sticking while shaping it.

Chocolate Thumbprints

Stunning shaped cookies like this are a real standout on any cookie tray. A chocolate cookie base is a nice change of pace.

    1/2 cup butter, softened
    2/3 cup sugar
      1 egg, *separated*
      2 tablespoons milk
      1 teaspoon vanilla extract
      1 cup all-purpose flour
    1/3 cup baking cocoa
    1/4 teaspoon salt
      1 cup finely chopped walnuts
FILLING:
    1/2 cup confectioners' sugar
      1 tablespoon butter, softened
      2 teaspoons milk
    1/4 teaspoon vanilla extract
     26 milk chocolate kisses

1 In a large mixing bowl, cream butter and sugar until light and fluffy. Beat in the egg yolk, milk and vanilla. Combine the flour, cocoa and salt; gradually add to creamed mixture and mix well. Cover and refrigerate for 1 hour or until firm enough to roll into balls.

2 In a small bowl, lightly beat egg white. Shape dough into 1-in. balls; dip in egg white, then roll in nuts.

Place on greased baking sheets. Using a wooden spoon handle, make an indentation in the center of each cookie. Bake at 350° for 10-12 minutes or until center is set.

3 For filling, combine the confectioners' sugar, butter, milk and vanilla in a small bowl; stir until smooth. Spoon 1/4 teaspoon into each warm cookie; gently press a chocolate kiss in the center. Carefully remove from pans to wire racks to cool. **Yield:** about 2 dozen.
—*Laura Bryant German*
West Warren, Massachusetts

Shaping Cookie Dough into Balls

Roll the dough between your palms until it forms a ball. A 1-in. ball requires about 2 teaspoons of dough. If the dough is sticky, you can refrigerate it until it is easy to handle, lightly flour your hands or spray your hands with nonstick cooking spray.

Chocolate Thumbprints

Cinnamon
Crackle Cookies

Shape into 1-in. balls; roll in sugar. Place 2 in. apart on ungreased baking sheets. Bake at 350° for 10-15 minutes or until lightly browned. Remove to wire racks to cool. **Yield:** about 6 dozen.

—*Vicki Lair, Apple Valley, Minnesota*

Snickerdoodles

The history of this whimsically named treat is widely disputed, but the popularity of this classic cinnamon-sugar-coated cookie is undeniable!

- 1/2 **cup butter, softened**
- 1 **cup plus 2 tablespoons sugar,** *divided*
- 1 **egg**
- 1/2 **teaspoon vanilla extract**
- 1-1/2 **cups all-purpose flour**
- 1/4 **teaspoon baking soda**
- 1/4 **teaspoon cream of tartar**
- 1 **teaspoon ground cinnamon**

1 In a large mixing bowl, cream butter and 1 cup sugar until light and fluffy. Beat in egg and vanilla. Combine the flour, baking soda and cream of tartar; gradually add to the creamed mixture. In a small bowl, combine cinnamon and remaining sugar.

2 Shape dough into 1-in. balls; roll in cinnamon-sugar. Place 2 in. apart on ungreased baking sheets. Bake at 375° for 10-12 minutes or until lightly browned. Remove to wire racks to cool. **Yield:** 2-1/2 dozen.

Cinnamon Crackle Cookies

A blend of cinnamon, nutmeg and orange and lemon peel gives these sugar cookies excellent flavor. Keep a batch in the freezer for a speedy snack.

- 1/2 **cup butter, softened**
- 1/2 **cup shortening**
- 1 **cup sugar**
- 1/2 **cup packed brown sugar**
- 1 **egg**
- 1 **teaspoon vanilla extract**
- 1/2 **teaspoon almond extract**
- 2-1/2 **cups all-purpose flour**
- 3 **teaspoons ground cinnamon**
- 2 **teaspoons baking soda**
- 2 **teaspoons cream of tartar**
- 2 **teaspoons ground nutmeg**
- 2 **teaspoons grated orange peel**
- 1 **teaspoon grated lemon peel**
- 1/2 **teaspoon salt**

Additional sugar

1 In a large mixing bowl, cream the butter, shortening and sugars until light and fluffy. Beat in egg and extracts. Combine the flour, cinnamon, baking soda, cream of tartar, nutmeg, orange and lemon peel and salt; gradually add to the creamed mixture.

While it isn't necessary to have a cookie jar to be a good grandmother, it doesn't hurt.

Chocolate-Tipped
Butter Cookies

Chocolate-Tipped Butter Cookies

After dipping these cookies in melted chocolate and coating with chopped nuts, let them stand at room temperature until set before you stack them on a platter.

    1 cup plus 3 tablespoons butter, softened,
      divided
1/2 cup confectioners' sugar
    2 cups all-purpose flour
    1 teaspoon vanilla extract
    1 cup (6 ounces) semisweet chocolate chips
1/2 cup finely chopped pecans *or* walnuts

1 In a large mixing bowl, cream 1 cup butter and confectioners' sugar until light and fluffy. Add flour and vanilla; mix well. Cover and refrigerate for 1 hour.

2 Shape 1/4 cupfuls of dough into 1/2-in.-thick logs. Cut logs into 2-1/2-in. pieces; place 1 in. apart on ungreased baking sheets. Bake at 350° for 12-14 minutes or until lightly browned. Remove to wire racks to cool.

3 In a heavy saucepan or microwave, melt chocolate and remaining butter; stir until smooth. Dip one end of each cookie into chocolate, then dip into nuts. Place on waxed paper until chocolate is set. **Yield:** about 5 dozen. —*Thara Baker-Alley, Columbia, Missouri*

Shaping Chocolate-Tipped Butter Cookies

Shape 1/4 cupfuls of dough into logs that are 1/2 in. thick. Cut the logs into 2-1/2-in. pieces, using a ruler as your guide.

Dipping Cookies in Chocolate

Melt the chocolate chips, baking chocolate or candy coating according to recipe directions. If necessary, transfer chocolate to a narrow container.

Dip cookie partway into chocolate and scrape bottom of the cookie across the edge of the container to remove excess chocolate. Place on a baking sheet lined with waxed paper and allow to set at room temperature.

Toward the end of the process, when the chocolate is running low, it might be necessary to spoon the chocolate over the cookies.

If chocolate cools too much to coat the cookies properly, rewarm before finishing dipping.

Cookie Jar Gingersnaps

*Each time you take a bite of these crisp
and chewy gingersnaps, you'll be reminded
of your grandma's cozy kitchen.*

3/4 **cup shortening**
1 **cup sugar**
1 **egg**
1/4 **cup molasses**
2 **cups all-purpose flour**
2 **teaspoons baking soda**
1-1/2 **teaspoons ground ginger**
1 **teaspoon ground cinnamon**
1/2 **teaspoon salt**
Additional sugar

1 In a large mixing bowl, cream the shortening and sugar until light and fluffy. Beat in egg and molasses. Combine the flour, baking soda, ginger, cinnamon and salt; gradually add to creamed mixture and mix well.

2 Shape teaspoonfuls of dough into balls. Dip one side into sugar; place sugar side up 2 in. apart on greased baking sheets. Bake at 350° for 12-15 minutes or until lightly browned and crinkly. Remove to wire racks to cool. **Yield:** 3-4 dozen. —*Deb Handy
Pomona, Kansas*

Split-Second Cookies

*These easy-to-bake cookies feature flavorful
raspberry jam. Their rectangular shape
makes them a nice addition to the traditional
round varieties found on most cookie trays.*

3/4 **cup butter, softened**
2/3 **cup sugar**
1 **egg**
1 **teaspoon vanilla extract**
2 **cups all-purpose flour**
1/2 **teaspoon baking powder**
1/2 **teaspoon salt**
1/3 **cup raspberry jam**

1 In a large mixing bowl, cream butter and sugar until light and fluffy. Beat in egg and vanilla. Combine the flour, baking powder and salt; gradually add to creamed mixture and mix well.

2 Divide dough into four equal portions; shape each into a 12-in. x 3/4-in. roll. Place 4 in. apart on two greased baking sheets. Make a 1/2-in. depression down center of logs; fill with jam. Bake at 350° for 15-20 minutes or until lightly browned. Cool for 2 minutes; cut diagonally into 3/4-in. slices. Remove to wire racks to cool. **Yield:** about 5 dozen. —*Mrs. Richard Foust
Stoneboro, Pennsylvania*

**Cookie Jar
Gingersnaps**

Lemon Crisp Cookies

*The sunny yellow color and big
lemon flavor of these quick-to-fix
cookies are sure to bring smiles.*

1 **package (18-1/4 ounces) lemon cake mix**
1 **cup crisp rice cereal**
1/2 **cup butter, melted**
1 **egg, beaten**
1 **teaspoon grated lemon peel**

1 In a large bowl, combine all ingredients until well mixed (dough will be crumbly). Shape into 1-in. balls. Place 2 in. apart on ungreased baking sheets.

2 Bake at 350° for 10-12 minutes or until set. Cool for 1 minute before removing from wire racks to cool completely. **Yield:** about 4 dozen.

—*Julia Livingston, Frostproof, Florida*

Pecan Crescent Cookies

Pecan Crescent Cookies

Dust these rich buttery cookies with confectioners' sugar just before serving; otherwise, it will be absorbed into the cookie.

1 cup butter, softened
1/2 cup sugar
1 teaspoon vanilla extract
2 cups all-purpose flour
1 cup finely chopped pecans
Confectioners' sugar

1 In a large mixing bowl, cream the butter, sugar and vanilla until light and fluffy. Gradually add flour. Stir in pecans.

2 Shape rounded teaspoonfuls of dough into 2-1/2-in. logs and shape into crescents. Place 1 in. apart on ungreased baking sheets. Bake at 325° for 20-22 minutes

or until set and bottoms are lightly browned. Let stand for 2-3 minutes before removing to wire racks to cool completely. Dust with confectioners' sugar before serving. **Yield:** 6 dozen. *—Grace Yaskovic Branchville, New Jersey*

Almond Biscotti

In Italian, biscotti means twice-baked. The dough is first formed into a rectangle and baked. Then it's cut into slices, which are baked again. A crisp texture makes them great dunking cookies.

1/2 cup butter, softened
1-1/4 cups sugar, *divided*
3 eggs
1 teaspoon anise *or* vanilla extract
2 cups all-purpose flour
2 teaspoons baking powder
Dash salt
1/2 cup chopped almonds
2 teaspoons milk

1 In a large mixing bowl, cream butter and 1 cup sugar until light and fluffy. Add eggs, one at a time, beating well after each addition. Stir in extract. Combine the flour, baking powder and salt; add to creamed mixture and mix well. Stir in almonds.

2 Line a baking sheet with parchment paper and grease the paper. Divide dough in half; spread each portion into a 12-in. x 3-in. rectangle on prepared pan. Brush with milk and sprinkle with remaining sugar. Bake at 375° for 15-20 minutes or until golden brown and firm to the touch.

3 Remove from oven and reduce heat to 300°. Lift rectangles with paper onto a wire rack; cool for 15 minutes. Place on a cutting board; cut with a serrated knife at a 45° angle into 1/2-in.-thick slices. Place slices cut side down on ungreased baking sheets. Bake for 10 minutes on each side. Turn oven off; leave cookies in oven with door ajar to cool. **Yield:** 3-1/2 dozen.
—Mrs. H. Michaelsen, St. Charles, Illinois

Making Crescent-Shaped Cookies

Shape rounded teaspoonfuls of dough into 2-1/2-in. logs, then bend slightly to form the crescent shape.

Brownie Alpine Biscotti

Brownie mix makes these biscotti cookies easy to stir up, and a white chocolate and almond topping adds a special touch.

1 package fudge brownie mix (13-inch x 9-inch size)
3/4 cup ground almonds
1/2 cup all-purpose flour
3/4 teaspoon baking powder
1 egg
3 egg whites
1 teaspoon almond extract
1/4 cup sliced almonds, optional
3 squares (1 ounce *each*) white baking chocolate, melted, optional

1 In a large bowl, combine dry brownie mix, ground almonds, flour and baking powder; mix well. In a small bowl, whisk egg, egg whites and extract. Add to brownie mixture; stir until combined. Divide dough into thirds.

2 On a greased baking sheet and using greased hands, shape each portion of dough into a 7-in. x 3-1/2-in. rectangle. Bake at 350° for 24 minutes. Remove from the oven; cool on baking sheet for 5 minutes. Transfer to a cutting board; cut with a serrated knife at a 45° angle into 3/4-in.-thick slices. Place cut side down on greased baking sheets. Bake for 6-7 minutes on each side or until firm. Remove to wire racks to cool.

3 If desired, sprinkle with sliced almonds and drizzle with white chocolate. Let stand until chocolate is set.
Yield: 2-1/2 dozen.
—*Jeanie Williams*
Minnetonka, Minnesota

Cutting Biscotti

After the rectangular biscotti dough is baked, it needs to be cut into slices, which will be baked longer.

With a serrated knife, cut the cookie diagonally into 1/2- or 3/4-in.-thick slices. Place the sliced cookies cut side down on a baking sheet and bake as directed.

Brownie Alpine Biscotti

Coconut Washboards

This simple yet satisfying coconut cookie recipe has been around for generations. Pressing a fork into the top gives the look of an old-fashioned washboard.

   1/2 **cup butter, softened**
   1/2 **cup shortening**
     2 **cups packed brown sugar**
     2 **eggs**
   1/4 **cup water**
     1 **teaspoon vanilla extract**
     4 **cups all-purpose flour**
1-1/2 **teaspoons baking powder**
   1/2 **teaspoon baking soda**
   1/4 **teaspoon salt**
     1 **cup flaked coconut**

1 In a large mixing bowl, cream the butter, shortening and brown sugar until light and fluffy. Beat in eggs. Gradually add water and vanilla. Combine the flour, baking powder, baking soda and salt; add to the creamed mixture and mix well. Fold in coconut. Cover and refrigerate for 2-4 hours.

2 Shape into 1-in. balls. Place 2 in. apart on greased baking sheets; flatten with fingers into 2-1/2-in. x 1-in. rectangular shapes. Press lengthwise with a floured fork. Bake at 400° for 8-10 minutes or until lightly browned. Cool for 2 minutes before removing to a wire rack to cool completely. **Yield:** about 9 dozen.

—Tommie Sue Shaw, McAlester, Oklahoma

Coconut Washboards

Forming Coconut Washboard Cookies

With your hands, shape 1-in. balls of dough into 2-1/2-in. x 1-in. rectangles. Using a floured fork, press the tines lengthwise across the dough, giving it a washboard look.

Brown Sugar Cookies

Dark brown sugar and ground pecans give these cookies added richness. They're sure to solicit recipe requests!

  1 **cup butter, softened**
3/4 **cup sugar,** *divided*
1/2 **cup packed dark brown sugar**
  1 **egg**
  1 **teaspoon vanilla extract**
  2 **cups all-purpose flour**
1/2 **cup finely ground pecans**
  1 **teaspoon salt**
1/2 **teaspoon baking soda**
ICING:
  1 **cup packed dark brown sugar**
1/2 **cup half-and-half cream**
  1 **cup confectioners' sugar**

1 In a large mixing bowl, cream the butter, 1/2 cup sugar and brown sugar until light and fluffy. Beat in egg and vanilla. Combine the flour, pecans, salt and baking soda; gradually add to creamed mixture and mix well. Cover and refrigerate for 20 minutes or until easy to handle.

2 Shape into 1-in. balls; roll in remaining sugar. Place 2 in. apart on ungreased baking sheets. Flatten with a glass dipped in sugar. Bake at 350° for 10-12 minutes or until edges are lightly browned. Remove to wire racks to cool.

3 For icing, combine brown sugar and cream in a saucepan. Bring to a boil; boil and stir for 4 minutes. Remove from the heat. Sift confectioners' sugar into the hot mixture; stir until combined. Drizzle over cookies. **Yield:** 5-1/2 dozen.

—Leonora Cloon
Ironwood, Michigan

Chocolate Pretzel Cookies

1 In a large mixing bowl, cream butter and sugar until light and fluffy. Add the egg, chocolate and vanilla; mix well. Combine flour and salt; gradually add to creamed mixture and mix well. Cover and refrigerate for 1 hour or until firm.

2 Divide dough into fourths; shape each portion into a 6-in. roll. Cut each roll into 1/2-in. slices; roll each into a 9-in. rope. Place ropes on greased baking sheets; form into pretzel shapes and space 2 in. apart. Bake at 400° for 5-7 minutes or until firm. Cool for 1 minute before removing to wire racks to cool completely.

3 For glaze, melt the chocolate chips and shortening with corn syrup in a heavy saucepan or microwave; stir until smooth. Stir in confectioners' sugar and enough coffee to make a smooth glaze. Dip pretzels in glaze; place on waxed paper until set. Melt white chocolate; drizzle over pretzels. Let stand until completely set. Store in an airtight container. **Yield:** 4 dozen. —*Priscilla Anderson, Salt Lake City, Utah*

Chocolate Pretzel Cookies

These pretzel-shaped buttery cookies are covered in a rich mocha glaze and drizzled with white chocolate. Your family will go wild over their chocolaty crunch.

   1/2 **cup butter, softened**
   2/3 **cup sugar**
     1 **egg**
     2 **squares (1 ounce** *each***) unsweetened chocolate, melted and cooled**
     2 **teaspoons vanilla extract**
1-3/4 **cups all-purpose flour**
   1/2 **teaspoon salt**
MOCHA GLAZE:
     1 **cup (6 ounces) semisweet chocolate chips**
     1 **teaspoon shortening**
     1 **teaspoon light corn syrup**
     1 **cup confectioners' sugar**
     4 **to 5 tablespoons strong brewed coffee**
     2 **squares (1 ounce** *each***) white baking chocolate**

storing
cookies

- Allow cookies to cool completely before storing.

- Store soft cookies and crisp cookies in separate airtight containers. If stored together, the moisture from the soft cookies will soften the crisp cookies, making them lose their crunch.

- Flavors can also blend during storage, so don't store strong-flavored cookies with delicate-flavored ones.

- Layer cookies in a container, separating each layer with waxed paper.

- Allow icing on cookies to completely dry before storing.

- Unfrosted cookies can be stored in a cool dry place in airtight containers for about 3 days. Cookies topped with a cream cheese frosting should be stored in the refrigerator.

- For longer storage, wrap unfrosted cookies in plastic wrap, stack in an airtight container, seal and freeze for up to 3 months. Thaw wrapped cookies at room temperature before frosting and serving.

- If your crisp cookies became soft during storage, crisp them up by heating in a 300° oven for 5 minutes.

Chocolate
Meringue Stars

Chocolate Meringue Stars

These light, delicate cookies sure make for merry munching. Their big chocolate flavor makes it difficult to keep the kids away from them long enough to get any on the cookie tray.

  3 egg whites
3/4 teaspoon vanilla extract
3/4 cup sugar
1/4 cup baking cocoa
GLAZE:
  3 squares (1 ounce *each*) semisweet chocolate
  1 tablespoon shortening

1 In a large mixing bowl, beat egg whites and vanilla on medium speed until soft peaks form. Gradually add sugar, about 2 tablespoons at a time, beating on high until stiff peaks form. Gently fold in cocoa.

2 Insert a #8b large open star tip into a pastry bag; fill half full with meringue. Pipe stars, about 1-1/4-in. diameter, or drop by rounded teaspoonfuls onto parchment paper-lined baking sheets. Bake at 300° for 30-35 minutes or until lightly browned. Remove from paper; cool on wire racks.

3 In a heavy saucepan or microwave, melt chocolate and shortening; stir until smooth. Dip the cookies halfway into glaze; place on waxed paper until set. **Yield:** about 4 dozen. —*Edna Lee, Greeley, Colorado*

Piping Meringue Cookies

Insert a decorating tip that has a large opening into a pastry bag or heavy-duty resealable plastic bag. (If using a plastic bag, first cut a small hole in the corner of the bag.)
  Fill the bag about half full with meringue. Smooth the meringue down toward the decorating tip to remove any air bubbles that could cause breaks in the design when piping. Twist the top of the bag shut.
  Line a baking sheet with parchment paper. Hold the pastry bag straight up and position the tip about 1/8 to 1/4 in. above the baking sheet. Hold the tip with one hand and squeeze the pastry bag with other. Stop squeezing before you lift up the decorating tip.

Shaping Peanut Butter Cookies

Peanut butter cookie dough is generally a stiff dough and needs to be flattened before baking. Using a floured fork, press the balls of dough until 3/8 in. thick. Press again in the opposite direction to make a crisscross pattern.

Peanut Butter Sandwich Cookies

(Pictured on page 23)

A creamy filling gives traditional peanut butter cookies a new twist.

- 1 cup butter-flavored shortening
- 1 cup creamy peanut butter
- 1 cup sugar
- 1 cup packed brown sugar
- 3 eggs
- 1 teaspoon vanilla extract
- 3 cups all-purpose flour
- 2 teaspoons baking soda
- 1/4 teaspoon salt

FILLING:
- 1/2 cup creamy peanut butter
- 3 cups confectioners' sugar
- 1 teaspoon vanilla extract
- 5 to 6 tablespoons milk

1 In a large mixing bowl, cream the shortening, peanut butter and sugars until light and fluffy. Add eggs, one at a time, beating well after each addition. Beat in vanilla. Combine the flour, baking soda and salt; gradually add to the creamed mixture.

2 Shape into 1-in. balls. Place 2 in. apart on ungreased baking sheets. Flatten to 3/8-in. thickness with a fork. Bake at 375° for 7-8 minutes or until golden. Remove to wire racks to cool.

3 In a large mixing bowl, combine filling ingredients; beat until smooth. Spread on the bottom of half of the cookies; top with remaining cookies. **Yield:** about 4 dozen.
—*Debbie Kokes*
Tabor, South Dakota

Chocolate Truffle Cookies

Chocolate lovers will gobble up these sweet treats featuring baking cocoa, chocolate chips and chocolate sprinkles. Pair them with a mug of coffee or cup of milk for an afternoon snack.

- 1-1/4 cups butter, softened
- 2-1/4 cups confectioners' sugar
- 1/3 cup baking cocoa
- 1/4 cup sour cream
- 1 tablespoon vanilla extract
- 2-1/4 cups all-purpose flour
- 2 cups (12 ounces) semisweet chocolate chips
- 1/4 cup chocolate sprinkles

1 In a large mixing bowl, cream the butter, confectioners' sugar and cocoa until light and fluffy. Beat in sour cream and vanilla. Add flour; mix well. Stir in chocolate chips. Cover and refrigerate for 1 hour.

2 Shape into 1-in. balls; dip one side in chocolate sprinkles. Place sprinkled side up 2 in. apart on ungreased baking sheets. Bake at 325° for 10-12 minutes or until set. Cool for 5 minutes before removing to wire racks to cool completely. **Yield:** about 5-1/2 dozen.
—*Sharon Miller, Thousand Oaks, California*

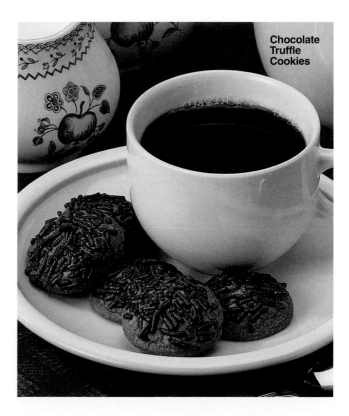

Chocolate Truffle Cookies

success with spritz cookies

- Be sure your butter or cream cheese is softened before beginning.

- Always press cookies onto a cool baking sheet.

- Hold the cookie press so that it is upright and touching the baking sheet. Force the dough through the press until you see it at the end of the rim of the cookie press. Lift the press straight up when the shape is formed.

- If the dough is too soft and not making a sharp design, refrigerate briefly. If the dough is too stiff and won't move through the press, let the dough stand at room temperature briefly until it is the right consistency.

Perfectly Shaped Spritz

If you are making spritz cookies for the first time, it may take a little practice with the cookie press to make perfectly shaped cookies.

Just Right. When just the right amount of dough is pressed out, the baked cookie will have a uniform design and crisp indentations.

Too Small. When too little dough is pressed out, the design will not meet at all the indentations. The cookie will be too small and break easily.

Too Big. When too much dough is pressed out, the design will lose its form.

Swedish Spritz

A touch of almond extract gives these spritz wonderful flavor. For Christmas, you could tint half of the dough with red food coloring and the other half with green.

    1 cup butter, softened
  2/3 cup sugar
    1 egg
  1/2 teaspoon almond extract
  1/2 teaspoon vanilla extract
2-1/4 cups all-purpose flour
    1 teaspoon baking powder
Prepared frosting

1 In a large mixing bowl, cream butter and sugar until light and fluffy. Beat in egg and extracts. Combine the flour and baking powder; gradually add to the creamed mixture.

2 Using a cookie press fitted with the disk of your choice, press dough 1 in. apart onto ungreased baking sheets. Bake at 400° for 7-9 minutes or until edges are firm and lightly browned. Remove to wire racks to cool. Frost as desired. **Yield:** 4-5 dozen.

—*Irmgard Sinn, Sherwood Park, Alberta*

Lemon-Butter Spritz

Using a cookie press may be too difficult for children to master. Instead, have them help sprinkle spritz with colored sugar before baking.

    2 cups butter, softened
1-1/4 cups sugar
    2 eggs
Grated peel of 1 lemon
    2 teaspoons lemon juice
    1 teaspoon vanilla extract
5-1/4 cups all-purpose flour
  1/4 teaspoon salt
Colored sugar

1 In a large mixing bowl, cream butter and sugar until light and fluffy. Beat in the eggs, lemon peel, lemon juice and vanilla. Combine flour and salt; gradually add to the creamed mixture.

2 Using a cookie press fitted with the disk of your choice, press dough 1 in. apart onto ungreased baking sheets. Sprinkle with colored sugar. Bake at 400° for 8-10 minutes or until lightly browned around the edges. **Yield:** about 12 dozen. —*Paula Pelis*
Rocky Point, New York

Chocolate-Dipped Spritz

Give traditional spritz cookies a tasty twist by dipping them in chocolate. Tuck some in a coffee mug, add a ribbon and use it as a holiday gift for a neighbor, teacher or friend.

     1 **cup butter, softened**
  3/4 **cup sugar**
     1 **egg**
     1 **teaspoon vanilla extract**
2-1/4 **cups all-purpose flour**
  1/2 **teaspoon salt**
  1/4 **teaspoon baking powder**
    11 **ounces dark, white *or* milk chocolate candy coating**
Finely chopped walnuts *or* colored sprinkles, optional

Chocolate-Dipped Spritz

1 In a large mixing bowl, cream butter and sugar until light and fluffy. Beat in egg and vanilla. Combine the flour, salt and baking powder; gradually add to the creamed mixture.

2 Using a cookie press fitted with the disk of your choice, press dough 1 in. apart onto ungreased baking sheets. Bake at 375° for 7-9 minutes or until set (do not brown). Remove to wire racks to cool.

3 In a heavy saucepan or microwave, melt candy coating; stir until smooth. Dip each cookie halfway into coating. If desired, sprinkle walnuts or sprinkles over chocolate. Place on waxed paper until set. **Yield:** about 6 dozen. —*Nancy Ross, Alvordton, Ohio*

Cinnamon Almond Strips

These rich buttery cookies are proof that sometimes the most simple ingredients can result in the most delicious foods.

1-1/2 **cups butter, softened**
    1 **cup sugar**
    3 **eggs, *separated***
    3 **cups all-purpose flour**
TOPPING:
1-1/2 **cups sugar**
    1 **cup finely chopped almonds**
1-1/2 **teaspoons ground cinnamon**

1 In a large mixing bowl, cream butter and sugar until light and fluffy. Beat in egg yolks. Gradually add flour; mix well.

2 Using a cookie press fitted with a bar disk, press dough 1 in. apart into long strips onto ungreased baking sheets. In a small mixing bowl, beat egg whites until stiff peaks form; brush over dough. Combine topping ingredients; sprinkle over strips. Cut each strip into 2-in. pieces (there is no need to separate the pieces).

3 Bake at 350° for 8-10 minutes or until edges are firm (do not brown). Cut into pieces again if necessary. Remove to wire racks to cool. **Yield:** about 10 dozen. —*Fred Grover*
Lake Havasu City, Arizona

Cutout cookies

tips for cutout cookies

- Use a light touch when handling the dough; over-handling will cause the cookies to be tough.

- For easier handling, refrigerate the dough before rolling. This is especially true if the dough was made with butter rather than shortening.

- Lightly dust the rolling pin and work surface with flour to prevent sticking. Working too much extra flour into the dough will result in tough cookies.

- Roll out a portion of the dough at a time and keep the remaining dough in the refrigerator. Roll out from the center to the edge, keeping a uniform thickness and checking the thickness with a ruler. If the thickness of the dough is uneven, the cookies will bake unevenly. Thinner cookies will be crisp and may burn, while thicker cookies will be chewy.

- To prevent the dough from sticking to the cookie cutter, dip the cutter in flour or spray it with nonstick cooking spray.

- After the dough is rolled out, position the shapes from the cookie cutters close together to avoid having too many scraps. Save all the scraps and reroll them just once to prevent tough cookies.

- To keep the cutouts intact before and after baking, transfer them to and from the baking sheet with a large metal spatula or pancake turner that supports the entire cutout.

Lemon Sugar Cookies

These light cookies are crisp on the outside and soft inside. Each bite has an appealing hint of lemon.

  2 cups butter, softened
  4 cups confectioners' sugar
  4 eggs
  3 tablespoons lemon juice
  3 tablespoons half-and-half cream
  2 teaspoons grated lemon peel
6-1/2 cups all-purpose flour
  1 teaspoon baking soda
  1/4 teaspoon salt
Sugar

1 In a large mixing bowl, cream butter and confectioners' sugar until light and fluffy. Add the eggs, one at a time, beating well after each addition. Beat in the lemon juice, cream and lemon peel. Combine the flour, baking soda and salt; gradually add to the creamed mixture. Cover and refrigerate for 2 hours or until easy to handle.

2 On a lightly floured surface, roll out dough to 1/8-in. thickness. Cut with floured 2-1/2-in. cookie cutters. Place 1 in. apart on ungreased baking sheets. Sprinkle with sugar. Bake at 350° for 8-10 minutes or until lightly browned. Remove to wire racks to cool. **Yield:** about 13 dozen.
—Vivian Hines
New Philadelphia, Ohio

Maple Leaf Cookies

The shape of these cutout cookies hints at the maple syrup in the frosting. If you don't have a leaf cookie cutter, use whatever shape you have on hand.

1 cup butter, softened
1 cup sugar
2 eggs
1 teaspoon vanilla extract
3 cups all-purpose flour
2 teaspoons cream of tartar
1 teaspoon baking soda
Dash salt
FROSTING:
4 cups confectioners' sugar
2 tablespoons butter, softened
1 teaspoon vanilla extract
1/2 teaspoon salt
3/4 cup maple syrup
Red paste *or* liquid food coloring

1 In a large mixing bowl, cream butter and sugar until light and fluffy. Beat in eggs and vanilla. Combine the flour, cream of tartar, baking soda and salt; add to creamed mixture and mix well. Cover and refrigerate for at least 1 hour or until easy to handle.

2 On a floured surface, roll out dough to 1/8-in. thickness. Cut with a floured 2-3/4-in. maple leaf-shape cookie cutter. Place 1 in. apart on ungreased baking sheets. Bake at 350° for 8-10 minutes or until edges are lightly browned (do not overbake). Remove to wire racks to cool.

3 For frosting, beat the confectioners' sugar, butter, vanilla and salt in a mixing bowl. Add syrup; beat until smooth. If leaf veins are desired, set aside 1/2 cup; add food coloring to remaining frosting. Spread red frosting on cookies. Cut a small hole in the corner of a pastry or plastic bag; insert a #3 round tip into bag. Fill bag with reserved frosting; pipe veins on leaves. **Yield:** about 6 dozen. —*Lynda Harnish*
Pembroke, Ontario

Gingerbread Cutouts

For the young and young at heart, Christmas isn't complete without Gingerbread Cutouts adorning a holiday table. You can make them like a pro with this wonderful recipe.

   1 cup butter, softened
   1 cup sugar
1/2 cup dark corn syrup
   1 teaspoon *each* ground cinnamon, nutmeg, cloves and ginger
   2 eggs, beaten
   1 teaspoon white vinegar
   5 cups all-purpose flour
   1 teaspoon baking soda
Red-hot candies

1 In a large saucepan, combine the butter, sugar, corn syrup and spices; bring to a boil, stirring constantly. Remove from the heat and cool to lukewarm. Stir in eggs and vinegar. Combine the flour and baking soda; stir into sugar mixture to form a soft dough. Cover and refrigerate for several hours or until easy to handle.

2 On a lightly floured surface, roll dough to 1/4-in. thickness. Cut with a floured 2-1/2-in. gingerbread man cookie cutter. Place 2 in. apart on greased baking sheets. Use red-hots for eyes and buttons. Bake at 350° for 8-10 minutes. Remove to wire racks to cool. **Yield:** about 6 dozen. —*LaJunta Malone*
Camden, Alabama

Making Cutout Cookies

1. For easier handling, chill dough for 1 to 2 hours before rolling out. Lightly flour the surface and rolling pin. Roll out dough as evenly as possible to the recommended thickness.

2. Dip the cutter in flour, then press into the dough. With a large metal spatula or pancake turner, move cookies to baking sheet.

3. Bake according to recipe directions. Remove cookies from the baking sheet to a wire rack, being careful to support the entire cookie. Cool completely before frosting and/or storing.

Gingerbread Cutouts

Deluxe Sugar Cookies

on ungreased baking sheets. Repeat with the remaining dough. Bake at 350° for 7-8 minutes or until the edges begin to brown. Remove to wire racks to cool. **Yield:** 5 dozen. —*Dawn Fagerstrom, Warren, Michigan*

Holiday Ginger Cutouts

Looking to get a little creative with your cookie decorating? Paint your own masterpiece on a ginger cookie canvas!

  1 **cup shortening**
  1 **cup sugar**
  1 **egg**
  1 **cup molasses**
  2 **tablespoons white vinegar**
4-1/2 **cups all-purpose flour**
  2 **teaspoons ground ginger**
1-1/2 **teaspoons baking soda**
  1 **teaspoon ground cinnamon**
3/4 **teaspoon ground cloves**
1/2 **teaspoon salt**
ROYAL ICING:
  4 **cups confectioners' sugar**
  2 **tablespoons meringue powder***
1/2 **cup warm water**
Assorted colors of liquid food coloring

1 In a large mixing bowl, cream shortening and sugar until light and fluffy. Add the egg, molasses and vinegar; mix well. Combine the flour, ginger, baking soda, cinnamon, cloves and salt; add to creamed mixture and mix well. Cover and refrigerate for 3 hours or overnight.

2 On a lightly floured surface, roll out dough to 1/8-in. thickness. Cut into desired shapes with floured cookie cutters. Place 1 in. apart on lightly greased baking sheets. Bake at 350° for 7-9 minutes or until set. Remove to wire racks to cool.

Deluxe Sugar Cookies

Christmas cutouts signal the holiday season. For variety, sprinkle half of the cookies with colored sugar before baking and frost the remaining ones after they've cooled.

  1 **cup butter, softened**
1-1/2 **cups confectioners' sugar**
  1 **egg**
  1 **teaspoon vanilla extract**
1/2 **teaspoon almond extract**
2-1/2 **cups all-purpose flour**
  1 **teaspoon baking soda**
  1 **teaspoon cream of tartar**

1 In a large mixing bowl, cream butter and sugar until light and fluffy. Beat in egg and extracts. Combine the flour, baking soda and cream of tartar; gradually add to the creamed mixture and mix well. Cover and refrigerate for at least 1 hour or until easy to handle.

2 Divide dough into fourths. On a surface lightly sprinkled with confectioners' sugar, roll out one portion of dough to 1/8-in. thickness. Cut into desired shapes with floured 2-in. cookie cutters. Place 1 in. apart

3 For icing, sift confectioners' sugar and meringue powder into a large mixing bowl. Add water; beat on low speed until blended. Beat on high for 5-6 minutes or until soft peaks form. Place a damp paper towel over bowl and cover tightly until ready to use.

4 Cut a small hole in the corner of a pastry or plastic bag; insert a small round tip. Fill bag with 1 cup icing. Outline each cookie with icing. Tint remaining icing with food coloring if desired. Add water, a few drops at a time, until mixture is thin enough to flow smoothly. Prepare additional pastry or plastic bags

with thinned icing. Fill in cookies, letting icing flow up to the outline. Let cookies dry at room temperature overnight. With food coloring and small new paintbrushes, paint designs on dry icing. Store cookies in airtight containers. **Yield:** about 6 dozen.

—*Joanne MacVey, Blue Grass, Iowa*

*Editor's Note: Meringue powder can be ordered by mail from Wilton Industries, Inc. Call 1-800/794-5866 or visit their Web site, *www.wilton.com.*

Holiday Ginger Cutouts

Decorating Cookies with Royal Icing

1. Cut a small hole in the corner of a pastry or plastic bag. Insert a round tip; fill bag with icing. Hold bag at a 45° angle to the cookie, and pipe a bead of icing around the edge. Stop squeezing the bag before you lift the tip from the cookie.

2. Thin remaining icing so that it will flow smoothly. Fill another bag with thinned icing. Starting in the middle, fill in the cookie with the thinned icing, letting icing flow up to the outline. Let cookies dry overnight.

3. With a new small paintbrush, paint your own designs on the cookies with liquid food coloring.

Making Sandwich Cookies

Spread filling over the bottoms of half of the cookies. Place another cookie over the filling, bottom side down.

Apricot-Filled Cookies

Canned apricots are a versatile ingredient all year long. One delicious way to take advantage of their goodness is in these sandwich cookies.

- 1/2 cup shortening
- 1 cup sugar
- 2 eggs
- 1 teaspoon vanilla extract
- 2-1/2 cups all-purpose flour
- 1/2 teaspoon salt
- 1/4 teaspoon baking soda

FILLING:
- 2 cups canned apricots, mashed
- 2/3 cup sugar
- 2/3 cup water
- 1/2 cup finely chopped almonds
- 1 teaspoon lemon juice

1 In a large mixing bowl, cream shortening and sugar until light and fluffy. Beat in eggs and vanilla. Combine the flour, salt and baking soda; gradually add to the creamed mixture. Cover and refrigerate for 1 hour. Meanwhile, in a large saucepan, combine filling ingredients. Cook and stir until thickened, about 15 minutes. Cool completely.

2 Divide the dough in half. On a lightly floured surface, roll out each portion to 1/8-in. thickness. Cut half of the dough with a floured 2-1/2-in. round cookie cutter. Cut the other half with a floured 2-1/2-in. doughnut cutter. Place 1 in. apart on ungreased baking sheets.

3 Bake at 375° for 8-10 minutes or until edges are very lightly browned. Remove to wire racks to cool. To assemble, spread bottom of solid cookies with filling; top with cutout cookies. **Yield:** about 1-1/2 dozen.
—*Bonnie Waliezer, Brush Prairie, Washington*

Almond Raspberry Stars

Guests will think you bought these impressive-looking cookies at a gourmet bakery. They may take some time to prepare, but the oohs and aahs you'll hear make it well worth it!

- 3/4 cup butter, softened
- 1/2 cup confectioners' sugar
- 1 teaspoon vanilla extract
- 1/2 teaspoon almond extract
- 1-3/4 cups plus 2 tablespoons all-purpose flour
- 2 tablespoons finely chopped almonds
- 1 tablespoon sugar
- 1/2 teaspoon ground cinnamon
- 1 egg white, lightly beaten
- 1/3 cup raspberry jam

1 In a large mixing bowl, cream the butter and confectioners' sugar until light and fluffy. Beat in extracts. Stir in flour. Shape into a ball; cover and refrigerate for 15 minutes.

2 On a lightly floured surface, roll out dough to 1/4-in. thickness. Cut into about 72 stars, half 2-1/2 in. and half 1-1/2 in. Combine the almonds, sugar and cinnamon. Brush small stars with egg white and immediately sprinkle with almond mixture. Leave large stars plain.

3 Place 1 in. apart on ungreased baking sheets. Bake small stars at 350° for 10 minutes and large stars for 12 minutes or until the tips just begin to brown. Remove to wire racks to cool.

Apricot-Filled Cookies

4 To assemble, spread enough jam over large stars to cover the centers. Top with small stars; press lightly (jam should show around edge of small stars). Let jam set before storing. **Yield:** about 3 dozen.
— *Darlene Weaver, Lebanon, Pennsylvania*

Chocolate Orange Cookies

Cutout cookies are a time-honored holiday tradition for most every family. This version combines the fabulous flavors of orange and chocolate.

       1 **cup butter, softened**
    3/4 **cup sugar,** *divided*
       1 **egg**
       1 **teaspoon vanilla extract**
 2-1/2 **cups all-purpose flour**
    1/2 **teaspoon salt**
    1/4 **cup finely grated orange peel**
       1 **cup (6 ounces) semisweet chocolate chips**

1 In a large mixing bowl, cream butter and 1/2 cup sugar until light and fluffy. Beat in egg and vanilla. Gradually add flour and salt; mix well. Cover and refrigerate for 15 minutes.

Chocolate Orange Cookies

2 On a floured surface, roll out dough to 1/4-in. thickness. Cut with a floured 2-in. cookie cutter or shape into 2-in. x 1-in. rectangles. Place 2 in. apart on ungreased baking sheets. Combine orange peel and remaining sugar; sprinkle over cookies.

3 Bake at 350° for 14-16 minutes or until the edges just begin to brown. Remove to wire racks to cool. Melt chocolate chips; decorate cookies. **Yield:** about 3 dozen.
— *Ruth Rumple, Rockford, Ohio*

packing and shipping cookies

Here are some pointers to ensure that cookies arrive at their destination as delicious and attractive as when you baked them.

- First, select cookies that are sturdy and will travel well, such as bars and brownies, drop, icebox and sandwich cookies. Cutouts and other thin cookies might break or crumble during shipping. Cookies requiring refrigeration are a poor choice for shipping because they'll spoil.

- Bake and completely cool cookies just before packing and shipping so they arrive as fresh as possible.

- Wrap them in bundles of two (for drop cookies, place their bottoms together) with plastic wrap. Wrap bars individually. Pack crisp and soft cookies in separate tins and pack strong-flavored cookies, such as gingersnaps, separate from mild-flavored cookies.

- Line a tin or box with crumpled waxed paper to cushion the cookies. Snugly pack the cookies to within 1 inch of the top. Use crumpled waxed paper or bubble wrap to fill in any gaps between cookies and side of container and to cover tops of cookies. Close box or tin.

- Wrap the cookie container in a slightly larger cardboard box and cushion with bubble wrap, crumpled paper or shipping peanuts. Seal box and label it as "Fragile and Perishable".

Pineapple Star Cookies

1 In a large mixing bowl, cream the butter and cream cheese until light and fluffy. Add flour and mix well. Cover and refrigerate for 2 hours or until easy to handle. Meanwhile, in a saucepan, combine sugar and flour; add pineapple and stir until blended. Cook over low heat until mixture comes to a boil and is thickened, stirring frequently. Cover and refrigerate.

2 Divide dough in half. On a lightly floured surface, roll out each portion to 1/8-in. thickness. Cut into 3-in. squares. Place 1 in. apart on ungreased baking sheets. To form star, make a 1-1/4-in. cut from each corner toward center (do not cut through center). Place 1/4 teaspoon of pineapple filling in the center of each. Fold every other point toward the center, overlapping pieces; press lightly to seal. Bake at 375° for 8-10 minutes or until set. Remove to wire racks to cool.

3 For frosting, combine the confectioners' sugar, butter, milk and vanilla in a bowl until smooth. Drizzle over cookies; sprinkle with walnuts. **Yield:** 5 dozen.
—*Sarah Lukaszewicz, Batavia, New York*

Feathered Friend Cookies

Let your imagination soar as an egg yolk glaze transforms plain sugar cookies into fanciful winged wonders. Use paste food coloring instead of liquid for more intense color.

  1/2 **cup butter, softened**
  1/4 **cup shortening**
    1 **cup sugar**
    2 **eggs**
    2 **tablespoons sour cream**
    1 **teaspoon vanilla extract**
  1/4 **teaspoon almond extract**
2-3/4 **cups all-purpose flour**
1-1/2 **teaspoons baking powder**
    1 **teaspoon salt**
GLAZE:
  4 to 6 **egg yolks**
  1 to 1-1/2 **teaspoons water**
Paste *or* gel food coloring

1 In a large mixing bowl, cream the butter, shortening and sugar until light and fluffy. Beat in the eggs, sour cream and extracts. Combine the flour, baking powder and salt; add to the creamed mixture and mix well. Cover and refrigerate for about 1 hour or until easy to handle.

Pineapple Star Cookies

When you see the pretty shape of these treats and savor the pineapple filling and sweet frosting, you'll know they're worth the effort.

  1 **cup butter, softened**
  1 **package (8 ounces) cream cheese, softened**
  2 **cups all-purpose flour**
FILLING:
  3/4 **cup sugar**
4-1/2 **teaspoons all-purpose flour**
  1 **can (8 ounces) crushed pineapple, drained**
FROSTING:
  1 **cup confectioners' sugar**
  2 **tablespoons butter, melted**
  2 **tablespoons milk**
  1/2 **teaspoon vanilla extract**
  1/2 **cup chopped walnuts**

Feathered Friend Cookies

2 On a floured surface, roll out dough to 1/4-in. thickness. Cut with a floured 4-in. bird-shaped cookie cutter. Place 1 in. apart on ungreased baking sheets.

3 For each color of glaze, beat 1 egg yolk and 1/4 teaspoon water in a custard cup; tint with food coloring. Decorate cookies as desired. Bake at 375° for 7-9 minutes or until edges are lightly browned. Cool for 1-2 minutes before removing to wire racks to cool completely. **Yield:** 3-1/2 dozen.

1/2 teaspoon baking soda
1/4 teaspoon salt
FILLING:
 2-3/4 cups confectioners' sugar
 1/4 cup half-and-half cream
 1/4 teaspoon peppermint extract
 1/4 teaspoon salt
Green food coloring

1 In a large mixing bowl, cream butter and sugars until light and fluffy. Add milk and egg; mix well. Combine the flour, cocoa, baking powder, baking soda and salt; gradually add to creamed mixture and mix well. Cover and refrigerate for 2 hours or until firm.

2 On a floured surface, roll out dough to 1/8-in. thickness. Cut with a floured 1-1/2-in. cookie cutter. Place 1 in. apart on greased baking sheets. Bake at 375° for 5-6 minutes or until edges are lightly browned. Remove to wire racks to cool.

3 Combine filling ingredients; spread on the bottom of half of the cookies; top with remaining cookies. **Yield:** about 7-1/2 dozen. —*Annette Esau*
Durham, Ontario

'Painting' with Egg Yolks

In a small bowl combine egg yolk, water and food coloring. With a small new paintbrush, decorate the unbaked cookies, then bake as directed. If the glaze thickens, stir in a few drops of water.

Chocolate Mint Wafers

We guarantee a batch of these chocolaty treats with cool mint filling won't last long around your house. They're so pretty piled high on a glass plate.

 2/3 cup butter, softened
 1/2 cup sugar
 1/2 cup packed brown sugar
 1/4 cup milk
 1 egg
 2 cups all-purpose flour
 3/4 cup baking cocoa
 1 teaspoon baking powder

Chocolate Mint Wafers

Bars & Brownies
can't be beat

For quick, convenient and tasty treats, nothing compares to
a bounty of bars and brownies, whether you're baking for a
potluck or at-home snacking. The only thing that rivals the
wonderful flavor of Lattice Fruit Bars (p. 66),
Shortbread Lemon Bars (p. 67)
and Fudgy Nut Brownies (p. 82) will be
the smiles on your family's faces!

the basics of Bars & Brownies

*B*ars and brownies are easy to make but difficult to define since they can be made in endless variations. They can be crisp with a rich buttery shortbread crust, cake-like or fudgy. They can have layers, fruit, jam or a cooked filling and be topped with frosting, glaze or icing. Or, they can be deliciously humble like a chocolate chip cookie bar.

- Bar cookies may be made with a pourable batter, spreadable dough or a crumbly crust that needs to be patted into the pan. The one thing they all have in common is that they are baked in a pan, rather than on a baking sheet. After cooling, they are cut into bars, squares, fingers, triangles or diamonds.

- Brownies are generally chocolate, flour, sugar and eggs with or without nuts. They may be cake-like, fudgy, chewy, dense or moist. They may also be frosted or plain. Brownies are usually baked in a square or rectangular pan. Those with a butterscotch or vanilla flavor are called blondies. Most people have a preference as to the type of brownie they think is the best.

secrets for successful bars & brownies

- Use butter, stick margarine (with at least 80% oil) or shortening. Whipped, tub, soft, liquid or reduced-fat products contain air and water and will produce flat, tough bars or brownies.

- Measure ingredients accurately, using the measuring tools and techniques suggested on pages 8 and 9.

- Avoid overmixing the batter. If it's handled too much, the gluten in the flour will be developed and the bars or brownies will be tough.

- Use dull aluminum baking pans or glass dishes. Dark-colored pans may cause overbrowning.

- Grease the pan with shortening or coat with nonstick cooking spray.

- To easily remove bars and brownies from a pan, line the bottom of the pan with foil, then grease. Add the batter and bake as directed. (See Lining a Baking Pan with Foil on page 70.)

- Preheat oven for 10 to 15 minutes before baking.

- It's important to evenly spread batter in the pan. If one corner is thinner than another, it will bake faster and be overbaked when the rest of the pan is done.

- Center the pan in the middle of the oven.

- Use a kitchen timer. Check bars when the minimum baking time has been reached, baking longer if needed. Follow doneness tests given in individual recipes.

- Generally, bars and brownies should cool completely on a wire rack before being cut. However, crisp bars should be cut while still slightly warm.

problem-Solving pointers for Bars & Brownies

If your bars or brownies:	This could be the reason:
Baked unevenly.	The batter wasn't spread evenly in the pan.
	The oven rack wasn't level.
Are overbaked.	A pan larger than called for in the recipe was used, causing the batter to be thin and dry.
	Oven temperature is too high. Check with an oven thermometer.
	Next time, check the bars 5 minutes sooner than the baking time given in the recipe.
Are gummy.	A pan smaller than called for in the recipe was used.
Are tough.	Stir in dry ingredients with a wooden spoon and don't overmix, which can develop the gluten in the flour and cause the bars to be tough.
Have a soggy crust.	The crust was not baked long enough before placing the filling on top.
Have a crumbly crust.	Next time, cut in a little more butter so that the crust will stick together.
Crumble when they are cut.	Cool the bars completely before cutting.
	Use a sawing motion when cutting.
	Warm the blade of knife in hot water, dry, then cut. Clean and rewarm the knife after each cut.

One of the secrets
of a happy life
is continuous
small treats.

Best bars

Lattice Fruit Bars

(Pictured on page 62)

A pretty lattice top makes these an eye-catching addition to any table. You'll like the fact that one batch goes a long way.

- 3 cups all-purpose flour
- 1 cup sugar
- 1 teaspoon baking powder
- 1/2 teaspoon salt
- 1 cup cold butter
- 2 eggs
- 2 teaspoons vanilla extract
- 3/4 cup apricot preserves
- 3/4 cup raspberry preserves

1 In a bowl, combine the flour, sugar, baking powder and salt; cut in butter until the mixture is crumbly. Combine eggs and vanilla; stir into crumb mixture until blended. Cover and refrigerate a fourth of the dough for at least 45 minutes.

2 Press remaining dough into an ungreased 15-in. x 10-in. x 1-in. baking pan. Spread 1/4 cup apricot preserves in a 1-3/4-in. strip over one long side of crust. Spread 1/4 cup of raspberry preserves in a 1-3/4-in. strip adjoining the apricot strip. Repeat twice.

3 Roll out chilled dough to 1/8-in. thickness. Cut into 1/2-in. strips; place over filling to make a lattice top. Bake at 325° for 30-35 minutes or until lightly browned. Cool on a wire rack. Cut into bars. **Yield:** about 3-1/2 dozen. —*Betty Keisling, Knoxville, Tennessee*

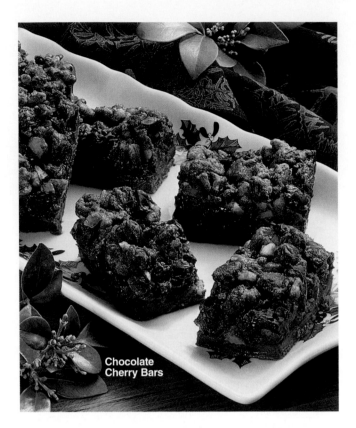

Chocolate Cherry Bars

Chocolate Cherry Bars

These tempting bars are simple to make with cherry pie filling, crunchy almonds and chocolate chips. The taste is reminiscent of chocolate-covered cherries.

- 1-3/4 cups all-purpose flour
- 1 cup sugar
- 1/4 cup baking cocoa
- 1 cup cold butter
- 1 egg, lightly beaten
- 1 teaspoon almond extract
- 1 can (21 ounces) cherry pie filling
- 2 cups (12 ounces) semisweet chocolate chips
- 1 cup chopped almonds

1 In a bowl, combine the flour, sugar and cocoa. Cut in butter until the mixture is crumbly. Add egg and almond extract until blended. Set aside 1 cup for topping. Press remaining crumb mixture into a greased 13-in. x 9-in. x 2-in. baking pan. Carefully top with pie filling. Combine chocolate chips, almonds and reserved crumb mixture; sprinkle over pie filling.

2 Bake at 350° for 35-40 minutes or until a toothpick inserted near the center comes out clean. Cool on a wire rack. Refrigerate for at least 2 hours before cutting into bars. **Yield:** 3 dozen. —*Tina Dierking Canaan, Maine*

Shortbread Lemon Bars

(Pictured on page 62)

A yummy shortbread crust puts a special spin on these lemon bars. You don't need to be afraid to make this dessert for guests...it's bound to be a hit!

- 1-1/2 cups all-purpose flour
- 1/2 cup confectioners' sugar
- 1 teaspoon grated lemon peel
- 1 teaspoon grated orange peel
- 3/4 cup cold butter
- FILLING:
- 4 eggs
- 2 cups sugar
- 1/3 cup lemon juice
- 1/4 cup all-purpose flour
- 2 teaspoons grated lemon peel
- 2 teaspoons grated orange peel
- 1 teaspoon baking powder
- TOPPING:
- 2 cups (16 ounces) sour cream
- 1/3 cup sugar
- 1/2 teaspoon vanilla extract

1 In a food processor, combine the flour, confectioners' sugar, lemon peel and orange peel. Cut in butter until the mixture is crumbly; process until mixture forms a ball. Pat into a greased 13-in. x 9-in. x 2-in. baking pan. Bake at 350° for 12-14 minutes or until set and edges are lightly browned.

2 In a large mixing bowl, combine the filling ingredients; mix well. Pour over hot crust. Bake for 14-16 minutes or until set and lightly browned.

3 In a bowl, combine the topping ingredients. Spread over filling. Bake 7-9 minutes longer or until topping is set. Cool on a wire rack. Refrigerate overnight. Cut into bars just before serving. Store in the refrigerator. **Yield:** 3 dozen.

—*Margaret Peterson*
Forest City, Iowa

Polka-Dot Cookie Bars

When you're serving a group, these lightly sweet bars are a lot easier to make than fussing with individual cookies. For the true chocolate lover, substitute semisweet chips for the vanilla chips.

- 1 cup butter, softened
- 3/4 cup sugar
- 3/4 cup packed brown sugar
- 2 eggs
- 1/2 teaspoon almond extract
- 2-1/4 cups all-purpose flour
- 1/3 cup baking cocoa
- 1 teaspoon baking soda
- 1/2 teaspoon salt
- 1 package (10 to 12 ounces) vanilla *or* white chips

1 In a large mixing bowl, cream butter and sugars until light and fluffy. Add eggs, one at a time, beating well after each addition. Beat in extract. Combine the flour, cocoa, baking soda and salt; gradually add to the creamed mixture. Set aside 1/4 cup vanilla chips; stir remaining chips into batter. Spread into a greased 15-in. x 10-in. x 1-in. baking pan. Sprinkle with the reserved chips.

2 Bake at 375° for 18-23 minutes or until a toothpick inserted near the center comes out clean. Cool on a wire rack. Cut into bars. **Yield:** 4 dozen.

—*Elizabeth Poire*
Kailua-Kona, Hawaii

Polka-Dot Cookie Bars

Scotch
Shortbread

1 cup butter, softened
1 cup packed brown sugar
1 egg yolk
1 teaspoon vanilla extract
2 cups all-purpose flour
1/4 teaspoon salt
2 packages (4 ounces *each*) German sweet
   chocolate
1/2 cup chopped nuts

1 In a large mixing bowl, cream butter and brown sugar until light and fluffy. Add the egg yolk, vanilla, flour and salt; mix well. Spread into a greased 13-in. x 9-in. x 2-in. baking pan.

2 Bake at 350° for 20-25 minutes or until golden brown. In a heavy saucepan or microwave, melt chocolate; stir until smooth. Spread over hot bars. Immediately sprinkle with nuts. Cool on a wire rack. Cut into 1-1/4-in. squares. **Yield:** 4-1/2 dozen.
—*Judy Scholovich, Waukesha, Wisconsin*

Scotch Shortbread

This simple three-ingredient recipe makes wonderfully rich, buttery bars. Serve with fresh berries of the season for a simply delicious dessert.

4 cups all-purpose flour
1 cup sugar
1 pound cold butter

1 In a large mixing bowl, combine flour and sugar. Cut in butter until mixture resembles fine crumbs. Knead dough until smooth, about 6-10 minutes. Pat into an ungreased 15-in. x 10-in. x 1-in. baking pan. Pierce with a fork.

2 Bake at 325° for 25-30 minutes or until lightly browned. Cut into squares while warm. Cool on a wire rack. **Yield:** 4 dozen. —*Marlene Hellickson Big Bear City, California*

Editor's Note: This recipe makes a dense, crisp bar, so it does not call for baking powder or soda.

Toffee Squares

These candy-like bars are very rich, so cut them into smaller bars. Using German sweet chocolate gives them a delightfully different taste.

Double Chip Meringue Bars

The meringue topping and blend of chocolate and peanut butter chips makes these bars extra special. Keep a pan in your refrigerator for late-night snacking.

1 cup butter, melted
1/2 cup sugar
1/2 cup packed brown sugar
2 egg yolks
1 teaspoon water
1 teaspoon vanilla extract
2 cups all-purpose flour
1 teaspoon baking powder
1/4 teaspoon baking soda
1/4 teaspoon salt
1 cup semisweet chocolate chips
1 cup peanut butter chips
TOPPING:
2 egg whites
1 cup packed brown sugar

1 In a large mixing bowl, cream butter and sugars until light and fluffy. Beat in the egg yolks, water and vanilla; mix well. Combine the flour, baking powder, baking soda and salt; gradually add to creamed mixture.

2 Spread into a greased 13-in. x 9-in. x 2-in. baking pan. Sprinkle with chips and pat lightly. For topping, in a small mixing bowl, beat egg whites on medium speed until soft peaks form. Gradually beat in brown sugar, 2 tablespoons at a time, on high until stiff peaks form. Spread evenly over chips.

3 Bake at 350° for 25-30 minutes or until golden brown. Cool on a wire rack. Cut into bars. Store in the refrigerator. **Yield**: 4 dozen. —*Dawn Onuffer Freeport, Florida*

Pecan Squares

These bars are good for snacking when you're on the road or for taking to gatherings. They're different from ordinary dessert bars…if you love pecan pie, you'll likely find them irresistible!

        2 cups all-purpose flour
    1/3 cup sugar
    3/4 cup butter, softened
    1/4 teaspoon salt
FILLING:
        4 eggs
    1-1/2 cups corn syrup
    1-1/2 cups sugar
        3 tablespoons butter, melted
    1-1/2 teaspoons vanilla extract
    2-1/2 cups chopped pecans

Pecan Squares

1 In a large mixing bowl, combine the flour, sugar, butter and salt until the mixture resembles coarse crumbs. Press firmly and evenly into a greased 15-in. x 10-in. x 1-in. baking pan. Bake at 350° for 20 minutes.

2 For filling, combine the eggs, corn syrup, sugar, butter and vanilla in a bowl. Stir in the pecans. Spread evenly over hot crust. Bake 25-30 minutes longer or until set. Cool on a wire rack. Cut into squares. **Yield**: 4 dozen. —*Sylvia Ford, Kennett, Missouri*

Patting a Crust into a Pan

Transfer the dough or crumb mixture to a greased pan and spread evenly. Press into the pan, using your fingers. Make sure to go into the corners and along the sides.

Rich 'n' Buttery Bars

You'll keep a cake mix on hand just to make these rich bars. They're fancy enough to serve company, yet easy enough to stir up for a bake sale.

    1/2 cup cold butter
        1 package (18-1/4 ounces) yellow cake mix
        1 egg, beaten
FILLING:
        1 package (8 ounces) cream cheese, softened
        2 cups confectioners' sugar
        2 eggs
        1 teaspoon vanilla extract
Additional confectioners' sugar

1 In a bowl, cut butter into cake mix until crumbly. Add egg and mix well. Press into a greased 13-in. x 9-in. x 2-in. baking pan. For filling, in a small mixing bowl, beat cream cheese and sugar. Add eggs and vanilla; beat until smooth. Spread evenly over crust.

2 Bake at 325° for 35-40 minutes or until the center is just set. Dust with confectioners' sugar while warm. Cool to room temperature before cutting. Store in the refrigerator. **Yield**: 4 dozen. —*Ann Horst Boonsboro, Maryland*

Triple-Layer Cookie Bars

With chocolate, coconut and peanut butter,
these bars are the perfect treat when
you crave something sweet.

1-1/4 cups all-purpose flour
  2/3 cup sugar
  1/3 cup baking cocoa
  1/4 cup packed brown sugar
    1 teaspoon baking powder
  1/4 teaspoon salt
  1/2 cup cold butter
    2 eggs
TOPPING:
    1 package (7 ounces) flaked coconut
    1 can (14 ounces) sweetened condensed milk
    2 cups (12 ounces) semisweet chocolate chips
  1/2 cup creamy peanut butter

1 In a large mixing bowl, combine the first six ingredients. Cut in butter until mixture is crumbly. Add eggs; mix well. Spread into a greased 13-in. x 9-in. x 2-in. baking pan.

2 Bake at 350° for 8 minutes. Sprinkle coconut over crust; drizzle with milk. Bake 20-25 minutes longer or until lightly browned. In a heavy saucepan or microwave, melt chocolate chips and peanut butter; stir until smooth. Spread over top. Cool on a wire rack. Cut into bars. **Yield:** 2-3 dozen.
—*Diane Bradley*
Sparta, Michigan

Jewel Nut Bars

With the eye-catching appeal of candied
cherries and the crunchy goodness of mixed nuts,
these colorful bars are certain to become
a holiday favorite year after year.

1-1/4 cups all-purpose flour
  2/3 cup packed brown sugar, *divided*
  3/4 cup cold butter
    1 egg
  1/2 teaspoon salt
1-1/2 cups salted mixed nuts
1-1/2 cups halved green and red candied cherries
    1 cup (6 ounces) semisweet chocolate chips

1 In a bowl, combine flour and 1/3 cup brown sugar; cut in butter until the mixture resembles coarse crumbs. Press into a lightly greased 13-in. x 9-in. x 2-in. baking pan. Bake at 350° for 15 minutes.

2 In a large mixing bowl, beat the egg. Add salt and remaining brown sugar. Stir in the nuts, cherries and chocolate chips. Spoon evenly over crust. Bake 20-25 minutes longer or until set. Cool on a wire rack. Cut into bars. **Yield:** 3 dozen.
—*Joyce Fitt*
Listowel, Ontario

Lining a Baking Pan with Foil

To easily remove bars and brownies from the pan, first line it with foil. Cut a piece of foil that is larger than the pan. Turn the pan upside down and mold the foil around the bottom and sides of the pan. Remove the foil, turn the pan right side up and place the formed foil in the pan, allowing the foil to extend beyond the edges of the pan.

    Grease the foil, add the batter and bake as directed. After bars or brownies are completely cooled, lift the foil out of the pan.

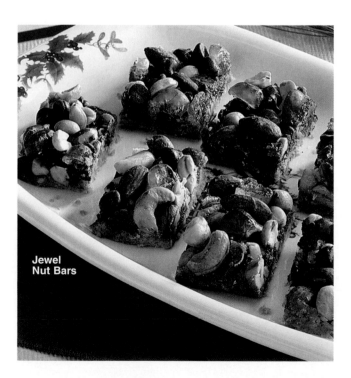

Jewel
Nut Bars

Chocolate Raspberry Bars

Chocolate and raspberry jam go together so well in these rich, sweet bars. Their make-ahead convenience is perfect for hectic days.

1 cup all-purpose flour
1/4 cup confectioners' sugar
1/2 cup cold butter
FILLING:
1/2 cup seedless raspberry jam
4 ounces cream cheese, softened
2 tablespoons milk
1 cup vanilla *or* white chips, melted
GLAZE:
3/4 cup semisweet chocolate chips
2 tablespoons shortening

1 In a bowl, combine flour and confectioners' sugar; cut in butter until mixture is crumbly. Press into an ungreased 9-in. square baking pan. Bake at 375° for 15-18 minutes or until browned.

2 Spread jam over warm crust. In a small mixing bowl, beat cream cheese and milk until smooth. Add vanilla chips; beat until smooth. Spread carefully over jam layer. Cool completely. Refrigerate for 1 hour or until set.

3 For glaze, melt chocolate chips and shortening in a heavy saucepan or microwave; stir until smooth. Spread over filling. Refrigerate for 10 minutes. Cut into bars; chill 1 hour longer. Store in the refrigerator. **Yield:** 3 dozen. —*Kathy Smedstad, Silverton, Oregon*

Best Date Bars

These date treats are very easy to bake, and one pan will yield 48 good-size bars to share at a church bazaar or any group function.

2-1/2 cups pitted dates, cut up
1/4 cup sugar

Chocolate Raspberry Bars

1-1/2 cups water
1/3 cup coarsely chopped walnuts, optional
1-1/4 cups all-purpose flour
1 teaspoon salt
1/2 teaspoon baking soda
1-1/2 cups quick-cooking oats
1 cup packed brown sugar
1/2 cup cold butter
1 tablespoon water

1 In a saucepan, combine the dates, sugar and water. Cook, stirring frequently, until very thick. Stir in walnuts if desired; cool.

2 Sift the flour, salt and baking soda together in a large bowl; add oats and brown sugar. Cut in butter until mixture is crumbly. Sprinkle water over mixture; stir lightly. Pat half into a greased 13-in. x 9-in. x 2-in. baking pan. Spread with date mixture; cover with remaining oat mixture and pat lightly.

3 Bake at 350° for 35-40 minutes or until lightly browned. Cool on a wire rack. Cut into bars. **Yield:** 4 dozen. —*Dorothy DeLeske, Scottsdale, Arizona*

Diamond Bars

You'll need just seven basic ingredients to stir up a batch of these delicious bars. Cutting them into diamonds makes for an interesting presentation.

1 cup butter, softened
1 cup packed brown sugar
2 egg yolks
2 cups all-purpose flour
2 cups (12 ounces) semisweet chocolate chips
1 cup chopped walnuts
1 cup flaked coconut

1 In a large mixing bowl, cream the butter and brown sugar until light and fluffy. Beat in egg yolks. Add flour and mix well. Spread into a greased 15-in. x 10-in. x 1-in. baking pan. Bake at 325° for 20-25 minutes or until golden brown.

2 Sprinkle with chocolate chips. Bake 1 minute longer or until chips are melted. Spread chocolate over crust. Sprinkle with walnuts and coconut. Cool on a wire rack. Cut into diamond shapes. **Yield:** 5 dozen.
—*Lois Lipker, Ormond Beach, Florida*

Diamond
Bars

Cutting Bars into Diamond Shapes

With a large knife, make a diagonal cut from one corner of the pan to the opposite corner; repeat, forming an "X". Make diagonal cuts at 1-1/2-in. intervals parallel to the lines of the "X", forming a diamond pattern.

Frosted Cinnamon Zucchini Bars

When your garden is at its peak, you can never have enough recipes calling for zucchini! These cake-like bars with a cinnamon-flavored frosting are unbelievably good.

3/4 cup butter, softened
1/2 cup sugar
1/2 cup packed brown sugar
2 eggs
1 teaspoon vanilla extract
1-3/4 cups all-purpose flour
1-1/2 teaspoons baking powder
2 cups shredded zucchini
1 cup flaked coconut
3/4 cup chopped walnuts
FROSTING:
2 cups confectioners' sugar
1 teaspoon ground cinnamon
2 tablespoons butter, melted
1 teaspoon vanilla extract
2 to 3 tablespoons milk

1 In a large mixing bowl, cream butter and sugars until light and fluffy. Add eggs, one at a time, beating well after each addition. Beat in vanilla. Combine flour and baking powder; gradually add to the creamed mixture. Stir in zucchini, coconut and nuts. Spread into a greased 15-in. x 10-in. x 1-in. baking pan.

2 Bake at 350° for 25-30 minutes or until a toothpick inserted near the center comes out clean. Cool on a wire rack. For frosting, combine confectioners' sugar and cinnamon in a bowl. Stir in the butter, vanilla and enough milk to achieve spreading consistency. Frost bars before cutting. **Yield:** about 5 dozen.
—*Bonita Holzbacher, Batesville, Indiana*

tips for cutting bars & brownies

- With a knife, use a gentle sawing motion. Remove the corner piece first. Then the rest will be easier to remove.

- For perfectly sized bars, lay a clean ruler on top of the bars and make cut marks with the point of a knife. Use the edge of the ruler as a cutting guide.

- For basic bars and brownies (those without soft fillings or toppings), line the pan with foil before baking. (See page 70.) When cool, lift the foil from the pan. Trim the edges of the bars or brownies, then cut into bars, squares or diamonds. The scraps can be crumbled and used as a topping for ice cream or pudding.

- An 8-in. square pan will yield 16 (2-in.) squares or 64 (1-in.) squares. A 9-in. square pan will yield 54 (1-1/2-in. x 1-in.) bars or 81 (1-in.) squares. A 13-in. x 9-in. x 2-in. pan will yield 78 (1-1/2-in. x 1-in.) bars.

Apple-Berry Streusel Bars

sprinkle over fruit mixture. Bake 30-35 minutes longer or until lightly browned. Cool completely on a wire rack. Cut into bars. **Yield:** 4 dozen. —*Jane Acree Holcomb, Illinois*

Apple-Berry Streusel Bars

Raspberry preserves add a special touch to a basic apple bar. The wonderful aroma while baking invokes fabulous images of fall!

2-1/2 cups plus 2 tablespoons all-purpose flour, *divided*
   2 cups old-fashioned oats
1-1/4 cups sugar
   2 teaspoons baking powder
   1 teaspoon ground cinnamon
   1 cup butter, melted
   3 cups thinly sliced peeled tart apples
   1 jar (12 ounces) raspberry preserves
1/2 cup finely chopped walnuts

1 In a large mixing bowl, combine 2-1/2 cups flour, oats, sugar, baking powder and cinnamon. Beat in butter just until moistened. Set aside 2 cups for topping. Pat remaining oat mixture into a greased 13-in. x 9-in. x 2-in. baking pan. Bake at 375° for 15 minutes.

2 In a bowl, toss apples with remaining flour; stir in the preserves. Spread over hot crust to within 1/2 in. of edges. Combine nuts and reserved oat mixture;

Easy Company Bars

Keep ingredients on hand for this fast-to-fix dessert, so you can easily make a treat for unexpected company.

   2 tablespoons butter, melted
   2 eggs
   1 cup packed brown sugar
   1 teaspoon vanilla extract
1/3 cup all-purpose flour
1/8 teaspoon baking soda
   1 cup finely chopped nuts
Confectioners' sugar

1 Coat the bottom of an 8-in. square baking dish with melted butter. In a large mixing bowl, beat eggs. Gradually beat in brown sugar and vanilla just until combined. Combine flour and baking soda; stir into the egg mixture. Fold in nuts. Pour batter evenly over butter; do not stir.

2 Bake at 350° for 25 minutes or until a toothpick inserted near the center comes out clean. Cool slightly on a wire rack. Dust with confectioners' sugar; cut into bars. Cool completely. **Yield:** 1-1/2 dozen.
—*Ruby Lee Hughes, Lynchburg, Virginia*

Cool Lime Triangles

Folks will enjoy this variation on the popular lemon bars. Lime juice adds fresh flavor while nuts add some crunch. They're especially refreshing during the warm summer months.

**2 cups all-purpose flour
1/2 cup confectioners' sugar
1/2 cup ground almonds
1 cup butter, melted
FILLING:
4 eggs
2 cups sugar
1/3 cup lime juice
1/4 cup all-purpose flour
1 teaspoon baking powder
1/2 teaspoon grated lime peel
1 to 2 drops green food coloring, optional
1/2 cup sliced almonds
Confectioners' sugar**

1 In a large mixing bowl, combine the first four ingredients; mix well. Press into a greased 13-in. x 9-in. x 2-in. baking pan. Bake at 350° for 13-15 minutes or just until edges are lightly browned.

2 For filling, in a large mixing bowl, combine eggs, sugar, lime juice, flour, baking powder, lime peel and food coloring if desired; beat until frothy. Pour over hot crust. Sprinkle with almonds.

3 Bake 20-25 minutes longer or until light golden brown. Cool on a wire rack. Dust with confectioners' sugar. Cut into triangles. **Yield:** 4 dozen.
—*TerryAnn Moore, Oaklyn, New Jersey*

Cutting Bars into Triangles

Triangle-shaped bars give a festive look to a cookie platter. Simply cut the bars into squares, then cut each square in half diagonally.

Fun Marshmallow Bars

These colorful kid-tested treats will go fast at bake sales. Cake mix really cuts your prep time.

**1 package (18-1/4 ounces) devil's food cake mix
1/4 cup butter, melted
1/4 cup water
1 egg
3 cups miniature marshmallows
1 cup milk chocolate M&M's
1/2 cup chopped peanuts**

1 In a large mixing bowl, combine the dry cake mix, butter, water and egg; mix well. Press into a greased 13-in. x 9-in. x 2-in. baking pan. Bake at 375° for 20-22 minutes or until a toothpick inserted near the center comes out clean.

2 Sprinkle with marshmallows, M&M's and peanuts. Bake 2-3 minutes longer or until the marshmallows begin to melt. Cool on a wire rack. Cut into bars. **Yield:** 3-1/2 dozen. —*Debbie Brunssen, Randolph, Nebraska*

Peanut Butter Bars

These bars can be dressed up for festive occasions by substituting colored icing for the peanut butter frosting. Drizzle them with pastel colors for Easter...red, white and blue for the Fourth of July...and orange and chocolate for Halloween.

1/2 **cup butter, softened**
1/2 **cup sugar**
1/2 **cup packed brown sugar**
1/2 **cup creamy peanut butter**
  1 **egg**
  1 **teaspoon vanilla extract**
  1 **cup all-purpose flour**
1/2 **cup quick-cooking oats**
  1 **teaspoon baking soda**
1/4 **teaspoon salt**
  1 **cup (6 ounces) semisweet chocolate chips**
ICING:
1/2 **cup confectioners' sugar**
  2 **tablespoons creamy peanut butter**
  2 **tablespoons milk**

1 In a large mixing bowl, cream the butter, sugars and peanut butter until light and fluffy. Beat in egg and vanilla. Combine the flour, oats, baking soda and salt; stir into the creamed mixture. Spread into a greased 13-in. x 9-in. x 2-in. baking pan. Sprinkle with chocolate chips.

2 Bake at 350° for 20-25 minutes or until lightly browned. Cool on a wire rack for 10 minutes. Combine icing ingredients; drizzle over the top. Cool completely. Cut into bars. **Yield:** 3-4 dozen.
— *Patricia Staudt, Marble Rock, Iowa*

Lemon Bars

Basic lemon bars have been popular for years. The wonderful tangy flavor is a nice change from chocolate-laden desserts.

  1 **cup all-purpose flour**
1/2 **cup butter, softened**
1/4 **cup confectioners' sugar**

FILLING:
  2 **eggs**
  1 **cup sugar**
  2 **tablespoons all-purpose flour**
1/2 **teaspoon baking powder**
  2 **tablespoons lemon juice**
  1 **teaspoon grated lemon peel**
Additional confectioners' sugar

1 In a bowl, combine the flour, butter and confectioners' sugar. Pat into an ungreased 8-in. square baking dish. Bake at 350° for 20 minutes.

2 For filling, in a small mixing bowl, beat eggs. Add the sugar, flour, baking powder, lemon juice and peel; beat until frothy. Pour over the crust. Bake 25 minutes longer or until light golden brown. Cool on a wire rack. Dust with confectioners' sugar. Cut into bars. **Yield:** 9 servings. — *Etta Soucy, Mesa, Arizona*

Lemon Bars

Chewy Peanut Butter Bars

This mouth-watering dessert is very rich and filling, so a small piece usually satisfies even a real sweet tooth.

   1 cup all-purpose flour
   1/3 cup sugar
   1/2 cup cold butter
FILLING:
   2 eggs
   1/2 cup sugar
   1/2 cup corn syrup
   1/4 cup crunchy peanut butter
   1/4 teaspoon salt
   1/2 cup flaked coconut
   1/2 cup semisweet chocolate chips

1 In a bowl, combine flour and sugar; cut in the butter until mixture is crumbly. Press into a greased 13-in. x 9-in. x 2-in. baking pan. Bake at 350° for 14-16 minutes or until lightly browned.

2 For filling, in a large mixing bowl, beat the eggs, sugar, corn syrup, peanut butter and salt until smooth. Fold in coconut and chocolate chips. Pour over crust. Bake 15-20 minutes longer or until golden. Cool on a wire rack. Cut into bars. **Yield:** 3 dozen.
   —*Mrs. Sanford Wickham, Holbrook, Nebraska*

Cranberry Bars

Keep some cranberries in the freezer all year so you can make these bars whenever you get a craving for their tart flavor.

FILLING:
   3/4 cup sugar
   1/2 cup water
   2 cups fresh *or* frozen cranberries
   1/4 cup orange juice
   1 tablespoon grated orange peel
   1 tablespoon butter
   1/2 teaspoon ground cinnamon
   1/4 teaspoon salt
   1 cup chopped walnuts
CRUST:
   2 cups all-purpose flour
   1/4 teaspoon salt
   1-1/4 cups cold butter
   1 cup sugar
   3 cups quick-cooking oats

1 In a saucepan, bring sugar and water to a boil. Add cranberries and cook until they pop, about 4-6 minutes. Add the orange juice, orange peel, butter, cinnamon and salt. Cook 5 minutes longer or until mixture thickens. Remove from the heat; stir in walnuts and set aside.

2 For crust, combine the flour and salt in a bowl; cut in butter until mixture is crumbly. Add sugar and oats; mix well. Spoon half into an ungreased 13-in. x 9-in. x 2-in. baking pan; pat firmly into pan. Spread filling evenly over crust. Top with remaining crumb mixture; pat lightly.

3 Bake at 400° for 30-35 minutes. Cool on a wire rack. Cut into bars. **Yield:** about 2-1/2 dozen.
   —*Betty Noga, Milwaukie, Oregon*

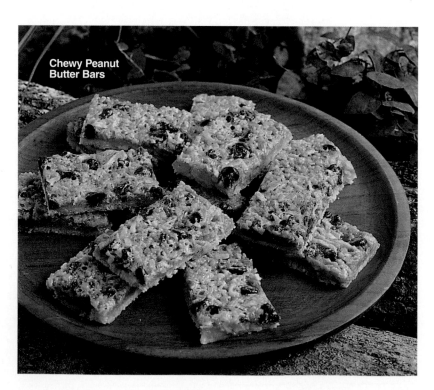

Chewy Peanut Butter Bars

Fruitcake Bars

These bars are so easy to make…and they're colorful, too—chock-full of candied pineapple and red and green cherries.

  3/4 **cup butter, softened**
1-3/4 **cups packed brown sugar**
   3 **eggs**
   1 **tablespoon vanilla extract**
1-1/2 **cups all-purpose flour**
   3 **cups coarsely chopped walnuts**
1-1/2 **cups coarsely chopped candied pineapple**
1-3/4 **cups red and green candied cherries, halved**
   2 **cups pitted dates, halved**

1 In a large mixing bowl, cream the butter and brown sugar until light and fluffy. Add eggs, one at time, beating well after each addition. Stir in vanilla. Add flour and walnuts; mix well. Spread evenly into a greased and floured 15-in. x 10-in. x 1-in. baking pan. Sprinkle with pineapple, cherries and dates; press lightly into dough.

2 Bake at 325° for 45-50 minutes or until lightly browned. Cool on a wire rack. Cut into bars. **Yield:** 8 dozen.   —*Terry Mercede, Danbury, Connecticut*

Celestial Bars

With their marbled base, fluffy icing and pretty chocolate glaze, these nutty bars will be the stars of bake sales, cookie gift packs and parties.

  1/2 **cup butter, softened**
   2 **cups packed brown sugar**
   3 **eggs**
   1 **teaspoon vanilla extract**
  1/2 **teaspoon almond extract**
   2 **cups all-purpose flour**
  1/2 **teaspoon salt**
1-1/2 **cups chopped pecans**
   2 **squares (1 ounce** *each***) unsweetened chocolate, melted and cooled**
ICING:
  1/2 **cup butter, softened**
   3 **cups confectioners' sugar**
   3 **to 4 tablespoons milk**
   1 **teaspoon vanilla extract**
GLAZE:
  1/2 **cup semisweet chocolate chips**
   2 **teaspoons shortening**

Celestial Bars

1 In a large mixing bowl, cream butter and brown sugar until light and fluffy. Add eggs, one at a time, beating well after each addition. Add extracts; beat well. Combine flour and salt; add to creamed mixture. Stir in pecans (batter will be thick). Divide batter in half; stir chocolate into one portion. Alternately spoon plain and chocolate batters into a greased 13-in. x 9-in. x 2-in. baking pan. Swirl with a knife.

2 Bake at 350° for 16-20 minutes or until a toothpick inserted near the center comes out clean. Cool completely on a wire rack.

3 For icing, in a large mixing bowl, cream butter and confectioners' sugar. Add milk and vanilla; beat until smooth. Spread over bars.

4 For glaze, melt chocolate chips and shortening in a heavy saucepan or microwave; stir until smooth. Drizzle over bars. Let stand until chocolate is completely set before cutting into bars. **Yield:** 4 dozen.
                —*Maribeth Gregg, Cable, Ohio*

A day without something sweet is like a day without sunshine.

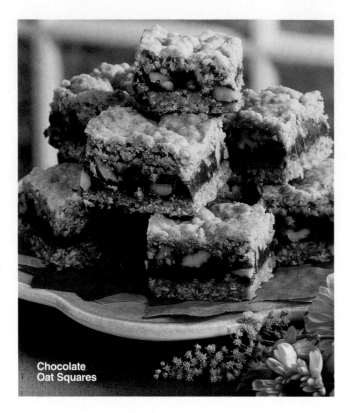

Chocolate
Oat Squares

Chocolate Oat Squares

*When you bring these chewy treats to a group meal,
guests will be tempted to start at the dessert table.
Chock-full of chocolate and walnuts,
they'll satisfy any sweet tooth.*

   1 cup plus 2 tablespoons butter, softened,
     divided
   2 cups packed brown sugar
   2 eggs
   4 teaspoons vanilla extract, *divided*
   3 cups quick-cooking oats
2-1/2 cups all-purpose flour
1-1/2 teaspoons salt, *divided*
   1 teaspoon baking soda
   1 can (14 ounces) sweetened condensed milk
   2 cups (12 ounces) semisweet chocolate chips
   1 cup chopped walnuts

1 In a large mixing bowl, cream 1 cup butter and brown sugar until light and fluffy. Beat in eggs and 2 teaspoons vanilla. Combine the oats, flour, 1 teaspoon salt and baking soda; stir into creamed mixture. Press two-thirds of oat mixture into a greased 15-in. x 10-in. x 1-in. baking pan.

2 In a saucepan, combine the milk, chocolate chips and remaining butter and salt. Cook and stir over low heat until chocolate is melted. Remove from the heat; stir in walnuts and remaining vanilla. Spread over crust. Sprinkle with remaining oat mixture.

3 Bake at 350° for 25 minutes or until golden brown. Cool on a wire rack. Cut into squares. **Yield:** 4 dozen.   *—Jennifer Eilts, Central City, Nebraska*

Butterscotch Bars

*A cream cheese filling sets these apart from other
butterscotch bars. They'd be a cool summer
treat served from the refrigerator.*

   1 cup butter-flavored shortening
   1 cup sugar
   1 cup packed brown sugar
   2 eggs
   1 teaspoon vanilla extract
   2 cups all-purpose flour
   1 cup old-fashioned oats
1/2 teaspoon baking soda
   1 package (10 ounces) butterscotch chips
   1 cup chopped pecans
FILLING:
   1 package (3 ounces) cream cheese, softened
   2 tablespoons butter, softened
1/4 cup sugar
   1 egg
   1 tablespoon all-purpose flour

1 In a large mixing bowl, cream the shortening and sugars until light and fluffy. Add eggs, one at a time, beating well after each addition. Beat in vanilla. Combine the flour, oats and baking soda; gradually add to the creamed mixture. Stir in chips and pecans. Reserve 2 cups. Spread remaining dough into a greased 13-in. x 9-in. x 2-in. baking pan.

2 In a small mixing bowl, combine filling ingredients; beat until smooth. Spread evenly over crust. Crumble reserved dough over filling.

3 Bake at 375° for 40-42 minutes or until golden brown. Cool on a wire rack. Cut into bars. Store in the refrigerator. **Yield:** about 1-1/2 dozen.
   —Romagene Deuel, Clarkston, Michigan

Triple-Nut Diamonds

Every delectable bite of these rich nutty bars is like a slice of pecan pie. One pan makes a nice size batch.

   1 **cup all-purpose flour**
 1/2 **cup sugar**
 1/2 **cup cold butter,** *divided*
 1/2 **cup packed brown sugar**
   2 **tablespoons honey**
 1/4 **cup heavy whipping cream**
 2/3 **cup** *each* **chopped pecans, walnuts and almonds**

1 Line a greased 9-in. square baking pan with foil; grease the foil and set aside. In a bowl, combine the flour and sugar. Cut in 1/4 cup butter until mixture resembles coarse crumbs. Press into prepared pan. Bake at 350° for 10 minutes.

2 In a saucepan, heat the brown sugar, honey and remaining butter until bubbly. Boil for 1 minute. Remove from the heat; stir in cream and nuts. Pour over crust. Bake 16-20 minutes longer or until surface is bubbly. Cool on a wire rack.

3 Refrigerate for 30 minutes. Using foil, lift bars out of the pan; cut into diamonds. **Yield:** 4 dozen.
　　　　　　　—*Darlene King, Estevan, Saskatchewan*

Strawberry Jam Bars

A golden crust nicely seasoned with nutmeg, allspice and honey complements these sweet bars. You can replace the strawberry jam with any flavor you prefer.

 1/2 **cup butter, softened**
 3/4 **cup sugar**
   1 **egg**
   1 **tablespoon honey**
 1-1/4 **cups all-purpose flour**
 1/4 **teaspoon baking powder**
 1/8 **teaspoon ground allspice**
 1/8 **teaspoon ground nutmeg**
 2/3 **cup strawberry jam**
 1/2 **cup chopped walnuts**

1 In a large mixing bowl, cream butter and sugar until light and fluffy. Beat in egg and honey. Combine the flour, baking powder, allspice and nutmeg; gradually add to the creamed mixture.

2 Divide the dough in half; spread one portion into a lightly greased 9-in. square baking pan. Spread with jam. Drop remaining dough by teaspoonfuls over jam. Sprinkle with walnuts.

3 Bake at 350° for 25-30 minutes or until top is golden brown. Cool on a wire rack. Cut into bars. **Yield:** 16 bars.
　　　　　　　—*Patricia Olson Barstow, California*

Triple-Nut Diamonds

storing
bars & brownies

- Cover a pan of uncut brownies and bars with foil—or put the pan in a large resealable plastic bag. (If made with perishable ingredients, like cream cheese, they should be covered and refrigerated.) Once the bars are cut, store them in an airtight container.

- Most bars and brownies freeze well for up to 3 months. To freeze a pan of uncut bars, place in an airtight container or resealable plastic bag. Or wrap individual bars in plastic wrap and stack in an airtight container. Thaw at room temperature before serving.

Chewy Granola Bars

For a satisfying snack that's both soft and crispy, try this recipe. These bars are a tempting, nutritious treat.

  1/2 cup butter, softened
    1 cup packed brown sugar
  1/4 cup sugar
    2 tablespoons honey
  1/2 teaspoon vanilla extract
    1 egg
    1 cup all-purpose flour
    1 teaspoon ground cinnamon
  1/2 teaspoon baking powder
  1/4 teaspoon salt
1-1/2 cups quick-cooking oats
1-1/4 cups crisp rice cereal
    1 cup chopped nuts
    1 cup raisins *or* semisweet chocolate chips, optional

1 In a large mixing bowl, cream butter and sugars until light and fluffy. Add the honey, vanilla and egg; mix well. Combine the flour, cinnamon, baking powder and salt; gradually add to creamed mixture. Stir in the oats, cereal, nuts and raisins if desired.

2 Press into a greased 13-in. x 9-in. x 2-in. baking pan. Bake at 350° for 25-30 minutes or until the top is lightly browned. Cool on a wire rack. Cut into bars. **Yield:** 2 dozen.
—*Virginia Krites*
Cridersville, Ohio

Chocolate Chip Cookie Bars

When you have a craving for chocolate chip cookies but don't have time to spend in the kitchen, reach for this bar recipe. The big batch is great for potlucks.

    2 cups butter, softened
1-1/2 cups sugar
1-1/2 cups packed brown sugar
    4 eggs
    2 teaspoons vanilla extract
    1 teaspoon water
4-1/2 cups all-purpose flour
    2 teaspoons baking soda
1-1/2 teaspoons salt
    3 cups (18 ounces) semisweet chocolate chips
    1 cup chopped walnuts

1 In a large mixing bowl, cream butter and sugars until light and fluffy. Beat in the eggs, vanilla and water. Combine the flour, baking soda and salt; gradually add to creamed mixture and mix well. Fold in chocolate chips and nuts.

2 Press into three greased 15-in. x 10-in. x 1-in. baking pans. Bake at 375° for 15-18 minutes or until golden brown. Cool on wire racks. Cut into bars. **Yield:** 8 dozen.
—*Barbara Witte, Irving, Texas*

Soft Spice Bars

These bars have the old-fashioned taste of gingersnaps, but they're chewy and very easy to make.

  3/4 cup butter, melted
    1 cup plus 2 tablespoons sugar, *divided*
  1/4 cup molasses
    1 egg
    2 cups all-purpose flour
    2 teaspoons baking soda
    1 teaspoon ground cinnamon
  1/2 teaspoon salt
  1/2 teaspoon ground ginger
  1/2 teaspoon ground cloves

1 In a large mixing bowl, combine butter, 1 cup of sugar and molasses. Beat in egg until smooth. Combine the flour, baking soda, cinnamon, salt, ginger and cloves; stir into the molasses mixture.

2 Spread into a greased 15-in. x 10-in. x 1-in. baking pan. Sprinkle with remaining sugar. Bake at 375° for 10-12 minutes or until lightly browned (do not overbake). Cool on a wire rack. Cut into bars. **Yield:** 2-1/2 dozen.
—Sharon Nichols
Brookings, South Dakota

Peppermint Crumb Squares

To crush the peppermint candy for this recipe, place the candy in a resealable plastic bag and seal. With the flat side of a meat mallet, pound the candy until crushed.

3/4 **cup butter, softened**
1/2 **cup packed brown sugar**
  2 **cups all-purpose flour**
  1 **can (14 ounces) sweetened condensed milk**
  1 **package (10 to 12 ounces) vanilla *or* white chips**
2/3 **cup crushed peppermint candy**

1 In a large mixing bowl, cream butter and brown sugar until light and fluffy. Add flour; beat until crumbly. Press 2 cups into a greased 13-in. x 9-in. x 2-in. baking pan; set remaining crumb mixture aside. Bake the crust at 350° for 8-10 minutes.

2 In a heavy saucepan or microwave, heat milk and vanilla chips until the chips are melted; stir until smooth. Pour over hot crust and spread evenly. Combine the candy and reserved crumb mixture; sprinkle over the top.

3 Bake 18-22 minutes longer or until lightly browned. Cool on a wire rack. Cut into squares. **Yield:** 4 dozen.
—Martha Kerr, Abilene, Texas

Caramel
Peanut Bars

Caramel Peanut Bars

With chocolate, peanuts and caramel between golden oat and crumb layers, these bars are very popular. They taste like candy bars but with homemade goodness.

1-1/2 **cups quick-cooking oats**
1-1/2 **cups all-purpose flour**
1-1/4 **cups packed brown sugar**
  3/4 **teaspoon baking soda**
  1/4 **teaspoon salt**
  3/4 **cup butter, melted**
    1 **package (14 ounces) caramels***
  1/2 **cup heavy whipping cream**
1-1/2 **cups semisweet chocolate chips**
  3/4 **cup chopped peanuts**

1 In a bowl, combine the first five ingredients; stir in the butter. Set aside 1 cup for topping. Press the remaining oat mixture into a greased 13-in. x 9-in. x 2-in. baking pan. Bake at 350° for 10 minutes or until lightly browned.

2 In a heavy saucepan or microwave, melt caramels with cream, stirring often. Sprinkle chocolate chips and peanuts over the crust; top with the caramel mixture. Sprinkle with reserved oat mixture. Bake 15-20 minutes longer or until topping is golden brown. Cool completely on a wire rack. Cut into bars. **Yield:** 3 dozen.
—Ardyce Piehl, Wisconsin Dells, Wisconsin

*Editor's Note: This recipe was tested with Hershey's caramels.

Brownie bonanza

Fudgy Nut Brownies

(Pictured on page 63)

A brownie like this never goes out of style. A semisweet chocolate frosting and white chocolate drizzle make every bite irresistible.

2-1/2 **cups semisweet chocolate chips**
   1 **cup butter**
   1 **cup sugar**
 1/4 **teaspoon salt**
   4 **eggs**
   2 **teaspoons vanilla extract**
 3/4 **cup all-purpose flour**
   1 **cup coarsely chopped hazelnuts *or* almonds, toasted**
TOPPING:
  12 **squares (1 ounce *each*) semisweet chocolate**
   1 **tablespoon shortening**
   3 **squares (1 ounce *each*) white baking chocolate**

1 In a heavy saucepan or microwave, melt chocolate chips and butter; stir until smooth. Add sugar and salt; stir until dissolved. Cool for 10 minutes. Stir in the eggs, vanilla, flour and nuts.

2 Spread into a greased 15-in. x 10-in. x 1-in. baking pan. Bake at 350° for 25-30 minutes or until a toothpick inserted near the center comes out with moist crumbs (do not overbake). Cool completely on a wire rack.

3 For topping, melt semisweet chocolate and shortening in a heavy saucepan or microwave; stir until smooth. Spread over brownies. Melt white chocolate; cool slightly. Pour into a small heavy-duty resealable plastic bag; cut a small hole in corner of bag. Pipe thin lines 1 in. apart widthwise. Beginning about 1 in. from a long side, gently pull a toothpick lengthwise through the lines to the opposite side. Wipe toothpick clean. Pull toothpick through lines in opposite direction. Repeat over entire top at 1-in. intervals. Cut into bars. **Yield:** about 2-1/2 dozen. —*Ruth Sparer Stern Shadow Hills, California*

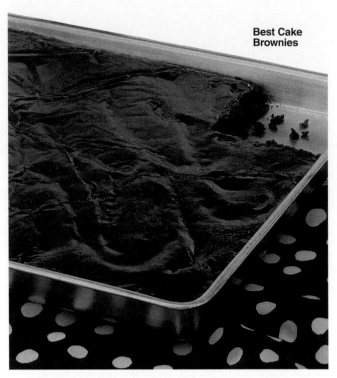

Best Cake Brownies

Best Cake Brownies

Chocolate lovers will be delighted to know this recipe calls for a whole can of chocolate syrup! Plus, the smooth chocolate glaze features creamy marshmallows.

1/2 **cup butter, softened**
  1 **cup sugar**
  4 **eggs**
  1 **can (16 ounces) chocolate syrup**
  1 **teaspoon vanilla extract**
  1 **cup all-purpose flour**
1/2 **teaspoon salt**
GLAZE:
  1 **cup sugar**
1/3 **cup butter**
1/3 **cup milk**
2/3 **cup semisweet chocolate chips**
2/3 **cup miniature marshmallows**

1 In a large mixing bowl, cream butter and sugar until light and fluffy. Add the eggs, one at a time, beating well after each addition. Beat in chocolate syrup and vanilla. Add the flour and salt until blended.

2 Pour into a greased 15-in. x 10-in. x 1-in. baking pan. Bake at 350° for 20-25 minutes or until a toothpick inserted near the center comes out clean (top of brownies will still appear wet). Cool on a wire rack for 15-20 minutes.

3 For glaze, combine sugar, butter and milk in a saucepan. Bring to a boil; boil until the sugar is dissolved. Remove from the heat; stir in chocolate chips and marshmallows until melted. Pour over the brownies and spread evenly. Refrigerate for 5 minutes before cutting. **Yield:** about 3 dozen. *—Jean Kennedy Springfield, Oregon*

Chocolate-Dipped Brownies

Dipping brownies in melted chocolate just might make these the world's most chocolaty brownies! It's best to store them in a single layer.

3/4 cup sugar
1/3 cup butter
2 tablespoons water
4 cups (24 ounces) semisweet chocolate chips, divided
1 teaspoon vanilla extract
2 eggs
3/4 cup all-purpose flour
1/2 teaspoon salt
1/4 teaspoon baking soda
2 tablespoons shortening
1/2 cup chopped pecans, toasted

1 In a saucepan, bring the sugar, butter and water to a boil over medium heat; remove from the heat. Stir in 1 cup chocolate chips and vanilla; stir until smooth. Cool for 5 minutes. Add eggs, one at a time, beating well after each addition. Combine the flour, salt and baking soda; stir into the chocolate mixture. Stir in 1 cup chocolate chips.

2 Pour into a greased 9-in. square baking pan. Bake at 325° for 35 minutes or until set. Cool completely on a wire rack. Place in the freezer for 30-40 minutes (do not freeze completely). Cut into bars.

3 In a heavy saucepan or microwave, melt remaining chips with shortening; stir until smooth. Using a small fork, dip brownies in chocolate to completely coat; shake off excess. Place on waxed paper; immediately sprinkle with pecans. Let stand until set. Store in an airtight container in a cool dry place. **Yield:** 3 dozen. *—Jackie Archer, Clinton, Iowa*

Chocolate-Dipped Brownies

Dipping Bars in Chocolate

Melt the chocolate chips, baking chocolate or candy coating according to recipe directions. If necessary, transfer chocolate to a narrow container.

To cover an entire bar in chocolate, use two forks to dip the bar into the chocolate and lift up. Gently shake the bar to remove excess chocolate. Place on a waxed paper-lined baking sheet to set at room temperature.

If the chocolate cools too much to coat the bars properly, rewarm and continue dipping.

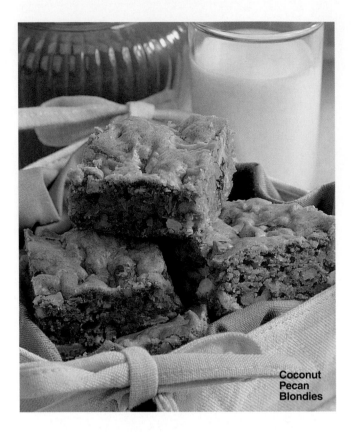

Coconut
Pecan
Blondies

Coconut Pecan Blondies

*Here's a classic white chocolate brownie that's
perfect when feeding a smaller group.*

    1 egg
  3/4 cup plus 2 tablespoons packed brown sugar
  1/2 cup butter, melted and cooled
1-1/2 teaspoons vanilla extract
  3/4 cup plus 2 tablespoons all-purpose flour
  1/2 teaspoon baking soda
  1/8 teaspoon salt
  3/4 cup coarsely chopped pecans, toasted
  2/3 cup flaked coconut
    4 squares (1 ounce *each*) white baking
      chocolate, coarsely chopped

1 In a large mixing bowl, beat egg and brown sugar
for 3 minutes. Add butter and vanilla; mix well. Combine the flour, baking soda and salt; gradually add to the brown sugar mixture, beating just until blended. Stir in the pecans, coconut and white chocolate.

2 Spread into a greased 8-in. square baking dish. Bake at 325° for 30-40 minutes or until a toothpick inserted near the center comes out with moist crumbs (do not overbake). Cool on a wire rack. Cut into bars. **Yield:** 16 brownies. —*Anna Tokash Henry, Keller, Texas*

Black Forest Brownies

*This chocolate and cherry treat tastes just like a
traditional Black Forest Cake but with less work.*

1-1/3 cups all-purpose flour
    1 teaspoon baking powder
  1/2 teaspoon salt
    1 cup butter
    1 cup baking cocoa
    4 eggs
    2 cups sugar
1-1/2 teaspoons vanilla extract
    1 teaspoon almond extract
    1 cup chopped maraschino cherries
  1/2 cup chopped nuts
ICING:
  1/4 cup butter, softened
    1 teaspoon vanilla extract
    2 cups confectioners' sugar
    6 tablespoons baking cocoa
  1/4 cup milk
  1/4 cup chopped nuts

1 Combine the flour, baking powder and salt; set aside. In a saucepan, melt butter. Remove from the heat and stir in cocoa until smooth. Blend in the eggs, sugar and extracts. Stir in the flour mixture, cherries and nuts. Pour into a greased 13-in. x 9-in. x 2-in. baking pan. Bake at 350° for 30-35 minutes or until a toothpick inserted near the center comes out clean.

2 For icing, in a bowl, blend the butter, vanilla, confectioners' sugar, cocoa and milk until smooth; spread over hot brownies. Sprinkle with nuts. Cool on a wire rack. Cut into bars. **Yield:** 3 dozen.
—*Toni Reeves, Medicine Hat, Alberta*

Butterscotch Brownies

*Brownies get an extra-special, rich flavor from
butterscotch chips and marshmallows in this recipe.*

  3/4 cup butter
    1 cup butterscotch chips
1-1/2 cups all-purpose flour
  2/3 cup packed brown sugar
    2 teaspoons baking powder
  1/4 teaspoon salt
    2 eggs
    2 teaspoons vanilla extract
    2 cups miniature marshmallows

2 cups semisweet chocolate chips
1/2 cup chopped walnuts

1 In a saucepan, melt butter and butterscotch chips; stir until smooth. Cool. In a large mixing bowl, combine the flour, brown sugar, baking powder and salt. Add the eggs, vanilla and butterscotch mixture; mix well (batter will be thick). Fold in the marshmallows, chocolate chips and walnuts.

2 Spread into a well-greased 15-in. x 10-in. x 1-in. baking pan. Bake at 350° for 20-25 minutes or until a toothpick inserted near the center comes out clean. Cool on a wire rack. Cut into bars. **Yield:** about 2 dozen. —*Lois Culberson, Pana, Illinois*

Chocolate Cream Cheese Brownies

This is a good brownie to take to gatherings because it won't crumble in your hand. It's easy to achieve the attractive marbled effect.

1 package (4 ounces) German sweet chocolate, broken into squares
3 tablespoons butter

Chocolate Cream Cheese Brownies

2 eggs
3/4 cup sugar
1/2 cup all-purpose flour
1/2 teaspoon baking powder
1/4 teaspoon salt
1 teaspoon vanilla extract
1/4 teaspoon almond extract
1/2 cup chopped nuts
FILLING:
2 tablespoons butter, softened
1 package (3 ounces) cream cheese, softened
1/4 cup sugar
1 egg
1 tablespoon all-purpose flour
1/2 teaspoon vanilla extract

1 In a saucepan or microwave, melt chocolate and butter; stir until smooth. Cool. In a large mixing bowl, beat the eggs. Gradually add sugar, beating until thick and pale yellow. Combine the flour, baking powder and salt; add to egg mixture. Stir in melted chocolate, extracts and nuts. Pour half of the batter into a greased 8-in. square baking dish; set aside.

2 For filling, in a small mixing bowl, beat butter and cream cheese until light and fluffy. Gradually add sugar, beating until fluffy. Blend in the egg, flour and vanilla; mix well. Pour over batter in pan. Spoon remaining batter over filling. With a knife, cut through batter to create a marbled effect.

3 Bake at 325° for 35-40 minutes or until a toothpick inserted near the center comes out clean. Cool on a wire rack. Cut into bars. Store in the refrigerator. **Yield:** about 2 dozen. —*Lisa Godfrey, Temple, Georgia*

Marbling Batters

To give batters a marbled look, spoon one batter in a random pattern over the other batter. Cut through the batter with a knife. Be careful not to overdo it, or the two batters will blend together and you'll lose the effect.

Fudge Ripple Brownies

These brownies have a rich chocolate taste and yummy browned butter frosting. Chocolate topping drizzled over them adds to the appeal.

  1 **cup butter, softened**
  2 **cups sugar**
  4 **eggs**
  2 **squares (1 ounce** *each***) unsweetened chocolate, melted and cooled**
  2 **teaspoons vanilla extract**
1-1/2 **cups all-purpose flour**
  1 **teaspoon baking powder**
  1 **teaspoon salt**
  1 **cup chopped walnuts**
FROSTING:
  1/3 **cup butter**
  3 **cups confectioners' sugar**
1-1/2 **teaspoons vanilla extract**
  4 **to 5 tablespoons heavy whipping cream**
TOPPING:
  1 **square (1 ounce) unsweetened chocolate**
  1 **tablespoon butter**
  1 **tablespoon confectioners' sugar**

1 In a large mixing bowl, cream butter and sugar until light and fluffy. Add eggs, one at a time, beating well after each addition. Add chocolate and vanilla; mix well. Combine the flour, baking powder and salt; add to creamed mixture and mix well. Stir in nuts.

2 Spread into a greased 15-in. x 10-in. x 1-in. baking pan. Bake at 350° for 25-30 minutes or until a toothpick inserted near the center comes out clean. Cool on a wire rack.

Fudge Ripple Brownies

3 For frosting, cook and stir butter in a saucepan over medium heat for 6-7 minutes or until golden brown. Pour into a large mixing bowl; add the confectioners' sugar, vanilla and enough cream to achieve spreading consistency. Frost cooled brownies.

4 For topping, melt chocolate and butter in a heavy saucepan or microwave; stir until smooth. Add confectioners' sugar; stir until smooth. Drizzle over frosting. Cut into bars. **Yield:** 4 dozen.
       —Bobi Raab
       St. Paul, Minnesota

Drizzling Chocolate over Bars

Melt chocolate according to recipe directions. Transfer to a resealable plastic bag and cut a small hole in one corner. While moving the bag back and forth over the bars gently squeeze out the melted chocolate.

    You can also put the melted chocolate in a small bowl and use a spoon or fork to drizzle it.

Mocha Truffle Brownies

Even folks who don't care for coffee can't resist these mocha morsels. For a little more visual appeal, use vanilla or white chips instead of chocolate chips when making the glaze.

1-1/4 **cups semisweet chocolate chips**
  1/2 **cup butter**
  1 **teaspoon instant coffee granules**
  2 **tablespoons hot water**
  2 **eggs**
  3/4 **cup packed brown sugar**
  3/4 **cup all-purpose flour**
  1/2 **teaspoon baking powder**
FILLING:
  1 **tablespoon instant coffee granules**
  1 **tablespoon hot water**

1 **package (8 ounces) cream cheese, softened**
1/3 **cup confectioners' sugar**
1 **cup (6 ounces) semisweet chocolate chips,
    melted**
GLAZE:
1/4 **cup semisweet chocolate chips**
1 **teaspoon shortening**

1 In a heavy saucepan or microwave, melt chocolate chips and butter; stir until smooth. Cool for 5 minutes. Dissolve coffee granules in hot water; set aside. In a large mixing bowl, beat eggs and brown sugar on medium speed for 1 minute. Stir in chocolate mixture and coffee. Combine flour and baking powder; gradually add to chocolate mixture.

2 Transfer to a greased 9-in. square baking pan. Bake at 350° for 30-35 minutes or until a toothpick inserted near the center comes out with moist crumbs. Cool completely on a wire rack.

3 For filling, dissolve coffee granules in water; set aside. In a small mixing bowl, beat cream cheese until smooth. Beat in the confectioners' sugar, melted chocolate and coffee. Spread over brownies.

4 For glaze, melt the chocolate chips and shortening in a heavy saucepan or microwave; stir until smooth. Drizzle over filling. Refrigerate for at least 2 hours before cutting. Store in the refrigerator. **Yield:** about 6-1/2 dozen. —*Margaret Roberts, Kuna, Idaho*

Cookies 'n' Cream Brownies

You won't want to frost these brownies, since the marbled top is too pretty to cover up. Besides, the tasty cream cheese layer makes them taste like they're already frosted. The crushed cookies add extra chocolate flavor and a fun crunch.

1 **package (8 ounces) cream cheese, softened**
1/4 **cup sugar**
1 **egg**
1/2 **teaspoon vanilla extract**
BROWNIE LAYER:
1/2 **cup butter, melted**
1/2 **cup sugar**
1/2 **cup packed brown sugar**
1/2 **cup baking cocoa**

2 **eggs**
1/2 **cup all-purpose flour**
1 **teaspoon baking powder**
1 **teaspoon vanilla extract**
12 **cream-filled chocolate sandwich cookies,
    crushed**

1 In a small mixing bowl, beat the cream cheese, sugar, egg and vanilla until smooth; set aside. For brownie layer, combine the butter, sugars and cocoa in a large mixing bowl; blend well. Add eggs, one at a time, beating well after each addition. Combine flour and baking powder; stir into the cocoa mixture. Stir in vanilla and cookie crumbs.

2 Pour into a greased 11-in. x 7-in. x 2-in. baking pan. Spoon cream cheese mixture over batter; cut through batter with a knife to swirl. Bake at 350° for 25-30 minutes or until a toothpick inserted near the center comes out with moist crumbs. Cool completely on a wire rack. Cut into bars. Store in the refrigerator. **Yield:** 2 dozen. —*Darlene Markel, Sublimity, Oregon*

Cookies 'n' Cream Brownies

Chunky Blond Brownies

Every bite of these chewy blond brownies is packed with chunks of white and semisweet chocolate and macadamia nuts. It's a potluck offering that stands out.

 1/2 **cup butter, softened**
 3/4 **cup sugar**
 3/4 **cup packed brown sugar**
   2 **eggs**
   2 **teaspoons vanilla extract**
1-1/2 **cups all-purpose flour**
   1 **teaspoon baking powder**
 1/2 **teaspoon salt**
   1 **cup vanilla *or* white chips**
   1 **cup semisweet chocolate chunks**
   1 **jar (3-1/2 ounces) macadamia nuts *or* 3/4 cup blanched almonds, chopped, *divided***

1 In a large mixing bowl, cream butter and sugars until light and fluffy. Add eggs and vanilla; mix well. Combine the flour, baking powder and salt; add to creamed mixture and mix well. Stir in the vanilla chips, chocolate chunks and 1/2 cup nuts.

2 Spoon into a greased 13-in. x 9-in. x 2-in. baking pan; spread to evenly cover bottom of pan. Sprinkle with the remaining nuts. Bake at 350° for 25-30 minutes or until top begins to crack and is golden brown. Cool on a wire rack. Cut into bars. **Yield:** 2 dozen.
—*Rosemary Dreiske, Keldron, South Dakota*

Maple Butterscotch Brownies

Here's a great treat when cooking for a smaller group. But with these brownies' terrific maple flavor, don't be surprised if you're asked to make more!

1-1/4 **cups packed brown sugar**
 1/2 **cup butter, melted**
1-1/2 **teaspoons maple flavoring**
   2 **eggs**
1-1/2 **cups all-purpose flour**
   1 **teaspoon baking powder**
   1 **cup chopped walnuts**
Confectioners' sugar, optional

1 In a bowl, combine the brown sugar, butter and maple flavoring. Add the eggs, one at a time, beating well after each addition. Combine flour and baking powder; add to egg mixture. Stir in nuts.

2 Pour into a greased 9-in. square baking pan. Bake at 350° for 27-32 minutes or until a toothpick inserted near the center comes out clean. Cool on a wire rack. Dust with confectioners' sugar if desired. Cut into bars. **Yield:** 16 brownies.
—*Grace Vanhold, Rochester, New York*

Chunky Blond Brownies

Peppermint Patty Brownies

A layer of chocolate-covered mint patties provides a rich, refreshing surprise.

1-1/2 cups butter, softened
   3 cups sugar
   5 eggs
   1 tablespoon vanilla extract
   2 cups all-purpose flour
   1 cup baking cocoa
   1 teaspoon baking powder
   1 teaspoon salt
   1 package (13 ounces) chocolate-covered peppermint patties

Peppermint Patty Brownies

1 In a large mixing bowl, cream butter and sugar until light and fluffy. Add eggs, one at a time, beating well after each addition. Beat in vanilla. Combine the flour, cocoa, baking powder and salt; add to creamed mixture and mix well.

2 Spread about two-thirds of the batter into a greased 13-in. x 9-in. x 2-in. baking pan. Arrange peppermint patties over top. Carefully spread remaining batter over patties. Bake at 350° for 35-40 minutes or until edges begin to pull away from sides of pan and a toothpick inserted near the center comes out clean (top will appear uneven). Cool completely on a wire rack. Cut into bars. **Yield:** 2 to 2-1/2 dozen.
—*Clara Bakke, Coon Rapids, Minnesota*

Macaroon Brownies

These three-layer brownies make for a pretty presentation on any dessert table.

   1 cup butter, softened
   2 cups sugar
   4 eggs
   1 teaspoon vanilla extract
   2 cups all-purpose flour
1/2 cup baking cocoa
1/2 teaspoon cream of tartar
1/2 cup chopped walnuts

MACAROON FILLING:
   1 package (14 ounces) flaked coconut
   1 can (14 ounces) sweetened condensed milk
   2 teaspoons vanilla extract
FROSTING:
3/4 cup sugar
1/4 cup milk
   2 tablespoons butter
   1 cup miniature marshmallows
   1 cup (6 ounces) semisweet chocolate chips
   1 teaspoon vanilla extract

1 In a large mixing bowl, cream butter and sugar until light and fluffy. Add eggs and vanilla; mix well. Combine the flour, cocoa and cream of tartar; gradually add to creamed mixture. Stir in nuts. Spread half into a greased 13-in. x 9-in. x 2-in. baking pan.

2 For filling, combine the coconut, condensed milk and vanilla; carefully spread over batter in pan. Top with the remaining batter. Bake at 350° for 40-45 minutes or until a toothpick inserted near the center comes out clean. Cool on a wire rack.

3 For frosting, combine the sugar, milk and butter in a saucepan; cook and stir until sugar is dissolved. Add the marshmallows and chocolate chips; cook and stir until melted. Remove from the heat; stir in vanilla. Cool until frosting reaches spreading consistency, about 25 minutes. Spread over the cooled brownies. Cut into bars. **Yield:** 4 dozen.
—*Christine Foust Stoneboro, Pennsylvania*

Apricot Angel Brownies

*With white chocolate and apricots,
these brownies are just right for folks who prefer
fruit desserts over chocolate creations.*

- 4 squares (1 ounce *each*) white baking chocolate
- 1/3 cup butter
- 1/2 cup packed brown sugar
- 2 eggs
- 1/4 teaspoon vanilla extract
- 3/4 cup all-purpose flour
- 1/2 teaspoon baking powder
- 1/4 teaspoon salt
- 1 cup finely chopped dried apricots
- 1/4 cup sliced almonds
- 1/4 cup flaked coconut

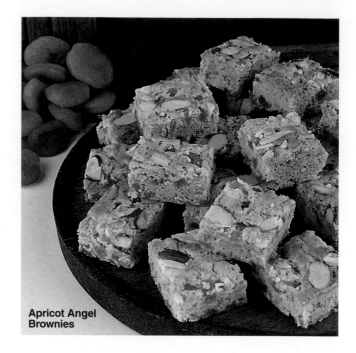

Apricot Angel
Brownies

1 In a saucepan, melt chocolate and butter over low heat, stirring constantly. Remove from the heat; stir in the brown sugar, eggs and vanilla until blended. Set aside. In a bowl, combine the flour, baking powder and salt. Stir in chocolate mixture. Combine the apricots, almonds and coconut; stir half into the batter.

2 Pour into a greased 9-in. square baking pan. Sprinkle remaining apricot mixture on top. Bake at 350° for 25 minutes or until golden brown. Cool on a wire rack. Cut into bars. **Yield:** about 2 dozen.

—*Tamara Sellman, Barrington, Illinois*

1 In a heavy saucepan or microwave, melt chocolate and butter; stir until smooth. Cool slightly. In a large mixing bowl, beat eggs for 2 minutes. Gradually add sugar, beating until thick and pale yellow, about 3 minutes. Stir in chocolate mixture and vanilla. Fold in flour and nuts if desired.

2 Pour into two greased and floured 9-in. square baking pans. Bake at 350° for 25-30 minutes or until a toothpick inserted in the center comes out with moist crumbs (do not overbake). Sprinkle each pan with 1 cup of marshmallows. Broil until marshmallows are golden brown, about 30-60 seconds. Drizzle with melted chocolate. Cool on a wire rack. Refrigerate for several hours before cutting. **Yield:** 4 dozen.   —*Brenda Wood Egbert, Ontario*

Really Rocky Road Brownies

Rocky road refers to any kind of dessert featuring nuts, marshmallows and chocolate. It's so named because of the bumpy "rocky road" appearance.

- 8 squares (1 ounce *each*) unsweetened chocolate
- 1-1/2 cups butter
- 6 eggs
- 3 cups sugar
- 1 tablespoon vanilla extract
- 1-1/2 cups all-purpose flour
- 1 cup chopped walnuts, optional

TOPPING:
- 2 cups miniature marshmallows
- 1 square (1 ounce) unsweetened chocolate, melted

Fudge-Topped Brownies

Why have only brownies or fudge when you can combine them? These exquisite brownies are the ultimate chocolate dessert.

- 1 cup butter
- 4 squares (1 ounce *each*) unsweetened chocolate
- 2 cups sugar
- 2 teaspoons vanilla extract
- 4 eggs, beaten
- 1-1/2 cups all-purpose flour
- 1 teaspoon baking powder

1/2 teaspoon salt

1 cup chopped walnuts

TOPPING:

4-1/2 cups sugar

1 can (12 ounces) evaporated milk

1/2 cup butter

1 package (12 ounces) semisweet chocolate chips

1 package (11-1/2 ounces) milk chocolate chips

1 jar (7 ounces) marshmallow creme

2 teaspoons vanilla extract

2 cups coarsely chopped walnuts

1 In a heavy saucepan or microwave, melt butter and chocolate; stir until smooth. Remove from the heat; blend in sugar and vanilla. Add eggs; mix well. Combine the flour, baking powder and salt; add to chocolate mixture. Stir in walnuts. Pour into a greased 13-in. x 9-in. x 2-in. baking pan. Bake at 350° for 25-30 minutes or until top springs back when lightly touched.

2 For topping, combine the sugar, milk and butter in a large heavy saucepan; bring to a boil over medium heat. Reduce heat; simmer, uncovered, for 5 minutes, stirring constantly. Remove from the heat. Stir in the chocolate chips, marshmallow creme and vanilla until smooth. Add nuts. Spread over warm brownies. Freeze for 3 hours or until firm. Cut into 1-in. squares. Store in the refrigerator. **Yield:** about 10 dozen.

—*Judy Olson, Whitecourt, Alberta*

German Chocolate Brownies

These saucepan brownies capture the rich flavor of a favorite cake with a few easy steps. Broiling the sweet coconut topping makes it gooey and good!

1/2 cup butter

1 package (4 ounces) German sweet chocolate, broken into squares

1/2 cup sugar

1 teaspoon vanilla extract

2 eggs, beaten

1 cup all-purpose flour

1/2 teaspoon baking powder

1/4 teaspoon salt

TOPPING:

2 tablespoons butter, melted

1/2 cup packed brown sugar

1 cup flaked coconut

1/2 cup chopped pecans

2 tablespoons corn syrup

2 tablespoons milk

1 In a heavy saucepan or microwave, melt butter and chocolate; stir until smooth. Remove from the heat; cool slightly. Stir in sugar and vanilla. Add eggs; mix well. Combine the flour, baking powder and salt; add to chocolate mixture. Pour into a greased 9-in. square baking pan. Bake at 350° for 18-22 minutes or until a toothpick inserted near the center comes out clean.

2 For topping, combine butter and brown sugar in a bowl. Add the coconut, pecans, corn syrup and milk; mix well. Drop by teaspoonfuls onto warm brownies; spread evenly. Broil several inches from the heat for 2-4 minutes or until top is browned and bubbly. Cool on a wire rack. Cut into bars. **Yield:** 16 brownies.

—*Karen Grimes, Stephens City, Virginia*

Fudge-Topped Brownies

great endings begin with Cakes

From single-layer sensations like Plum Upside-Down Cake (p. 108) to layered beauties such as Pretty Pineapple Torte (p. 121) and Sour Cream Chocolate Cake (p. 100), this chapter offers cakes for everyday and special occasions. Experienced bakers as well as novices will find an assortment of recipes to suit their skills.

the basics of Cakes

Cakes add a festive air to any meal and usually make an appearance at special-occasion dinners. Cakes can be rich and moist, dense, buttery or airy and are divided into two basic categories:

- Butter cakes get their name because the batter is made from creaming fat—such as butter or shortening—with sugar. The creaming traps air in the batter; this trapped air expands during baking and gives the cake its height. Butter cakes have a fine moist texture and a tender crumb.

- Foam cakes contain a high proportion of eggs or egg whites to flour. Beaten eggs give foam cakes their light, fluffy texture.

There are three kinds of foam cakes: angel food, sponge and chiffon. Angel food is made with whipped egg whites but without fat and has a delicate crumb. Sponge cake also is made without fat but contains both egg whites and yolks (the fat in the cake comes only from egg yolks). Sponge cakes have a richer texture than angel food. Chiffon cake, which has the richest texture of the three types, is made with fat and both egg whites and yolks.

Preparing a Cake Pan

1. Grease the sides and bottom of the pan by spreading shortening with a paper towel over the interior of the pan.

2. Sprinkle 1 to 2 tablespoons of flour into the greased pan; tilt the pan to coat bottom and sides. Turn pan over and tap to remove excess flour.

Butter cakes

Yellow Layer Cake

Instead of turning to a boxed cake mix, why not try your hand at this easy recipe for a basic yellow cake? You just can't beat the homemade goodness!

> 2/3 cup butter, softened
> 1-3/4 cups sugar
> 2 eggs
> 1-1/2 teaspoons vanilla extract
> 2-1/2 cups all-purpose flour
> 2-1/2 teaspoons baking powder
> 1/2 teaspoon salt
> 1-1/4 cups milk
> 2-1/2 cups frosting of your choice

1 In a large mixing bowl, cream butter and sugar until light and fluffy. Add eggs, one at a time, beating well after each addition. Stir in vanilla. Combine the flour, baking powder and salt; add to the creamed mixture alternately with milk, beating well after each addition.

2 Pour into two greased and floured 9-in. round baking pans. Bake at 350° for 25-30 minutes or until a toothpick inserted near the center comes out clean. Cool for 10 minutes before removing from pans to wire racks to cool completely. Spread frosting between layers and over the top and sides of cake. **Yield:** 10-12 servings.

White Layer Cake

Every recipe file should contain a standard delicious cake like this. Topped with your favorite flavor of frosting, it's great for any occasion.

    1/2 cup butter, softened
  1-1/2 cups sugar
      4 egg whites
      2 teaspoons vanilla extract
      2 cups all-purpose flour
      1 teaspoon baking powder
    1/2 teaspoon baking soda
    1/4 teaspoon salt
  1-1/3 cups buttermilk
  2-1/2 cups frosting of your choice

1 In a large mixing bowl, cream butter and sugar until light and fluffy. Add egg whites, one at a time, beating well after each addition. Beat in vanilla. Combine the flour, baking powder, baking soda and salt; add to creamed mixture alternately with buttermilk, beating well after each addition.

2 Spread evenly into two greased and floured 9-in. round baking pans. Bake at 350° for 30-35 minutes or until a toothpick inserted near the center comes out clean. Cool for 10 minutes before removing from pans to wire racks to cool completely. Spread frosting between layers and over the top and sides of cake. **Yield:** 10-12 servings.

Zucchini Fudge Cake

Zucchini makes each bite of this fudgy cake moist and delicious. Chocolate provides the perfect disguise!

      1 cup butter, softened
  2-1/2 cups sugar
      4 eggs
      2 teaspoons vanilla extract
      3 cups all-purpose flour
    1/2 cup baking cocoa
      2 teaspoons baking powder
      1 teaspoon baking soda
    3/4 teaspoon salt
      1 cup buttermilk
      3 cups shredded zucchini
  3-1/2 cups prepared chocolate frosting

1 In a large mixing bowl, cream butter and sugar until light and fluffy. Add the eggs, one at a time, beating well after each addition. Beat in vanilla. Combine the flour, cocoa, baking powder, baking soda and salt; add to the creamed mixture alternately with buttermilk, beating well after each addition. Stir in zucchini.

2 Pour into three greased and floured 9-in. round baking pans. Bake at 350° for 25-30 minutes or until a toothpick inserted near the center comes out clean. Cool for 10 minutes before removing from pans to wire racks to cool completely. Spread frosting between layers and over the top and sides of cake. **Yield:** 10-12 servings.

—*Robert Keith, Rochester, Minnesota*

Compromise is the art of cutting a cake so that everyone believes he or she got the biggest piece.

secrets for successful butter cakes

- Use butter, stick margarine (with at least 80% oil) or shortening. The fat should be softened (at room temperature), meaning it is pliable when touched. Whipped, tub, soft, liquid or reduced-fat products should not be used.

- Measure ingredients accurately, using the measuring tools and techniques suggested on pages 8 and 9.

- Arrange the oven racks so that the cake will bake in the center of the oven.

- Preheat oven for 10 to 15 minutes before baking.

- Most butter cake recipes call for creaming the butter and sugar. Beat the softened butter or shortening and sugar with an electric mixer or wooden spoon to a light and fluffy consistency, about 5 minutes.

- For better volume, allow eggs to stand at room temperature for 30 minutes before using. Or, place eggs in their shell in a bowl of warm water while assembling the remaining ingredients.

- Mix dry ingredients together to evenly distribute the leavener throughout the flour. This will ensure that it's evenly incorporated into the batter.

- Stop the mixer occasionally—or between additions of ingredients—and scrape the batter down sides of bowl with a rubber or plastic spatula.

- It's best to use the pan size recommended in the recipe. For substitutions, check the Bakeware Substitution Chart on page 10. Baking times may need to be adjusted.

- For a tender golden crust, use aluminum pans with a dull rather than shiny or dark finish. If using glass baking dishes, reduce the oven temperature 25°.

- Grease and flour baking pans for butter cakes that will be removed from the pans. Cakes that will be served from the pans should be greased but not floured. Some cake recipes call for the pan to be lined with waxed paper for easier removal of the cake from the pan. (See Lining a Baking Pan with Waxed Paper on page 100.)

- Fill pans half to three-fourths full. A thin batter will rise more than a heavy batter, so allow more room for thin batters to rise.

- Pour thinner batters into pans, then tap pans on the countertop to remove air bubbles. Spoon firmer batters into pans, then spread gently to even out the batter.

- Leave at least 1 in. of space between pans and between pans and sides of oven for good heat circulation. If using two oven racks, stagger pans in the oven so that they are not directly over one another. Switch pan positions and rotate pans from front to back halfway through baking.

- Use a kitchen timer. Check for doneness at the minimum recommended baking time, then check every 2 minutes after that. Butter cakes are done when a toothpick inserted near the center of the cake comes out clean. (See Testing Butter Cakes for Doneness on page 102.)

- Cool cakes for 10 minutes in the pan, unless recipe directs otherwise. Loosen the cake by running a knife around the edge of the pan. Turn out onto a wire rack, place another rack over the cake and flip right side up. Cool completely before filling or frosting unless directed otherwise by recipe.

- If a cake sticks to the pan and will not come out when inverted, return to a heated oven for 1 minute, then try again to turn it out.

- Use a serrated knife or use a sawing motion when cutting. Warm the blade of knife in hot water, then dry and make a cut. Clean and rewarm knife before each cut.

Strawberry Cake

When you cut into this cake, people will be delighted to see the pretty pink tint. To hint at the flavor before cutting, garnish the top with whole strawberries.

> 1 package (18-1/4 ounces) white cake mix
> 1 package (3 ounces) strawberry gelatin
> 1 cup water
> 1/2 cup vegetable oil
> 4 egg whites
> 1/2 cup mashed unsweetened strawberries
> 3-1/2 cups whipped cream *or* frosting of your choice

1 In a large mixing bowl, combine the dry cake mix, gelatin powder, water and oil. Beat on low speed for 1 minute or until moistened; beat on medium for 4 minutes. In a small mixing bowl and with clean beaters, beat egg whites on high speed until stiff peaks form. Fold egg whites and mashed strawberries into cake batter.

2 Pour into three greased and floured 9-in. round baking pans. Bake at 350° for 20-25 minutes or until a toothpick inserted near the center comes out clean. Cool for 10 minutes before removing from pans to wire racks to cool completely. Frost with whipped cream or frosting. If frosted with whipped cream, store in the refrigerator. **Yield:** 12-16 servings.

—*Pam Anderson, Billings, Montana*

Butter Pecan Cake

Pecans and butter give this cake the same irresistible flavor as the popular ice cream.

2-2/3 cups chopped pecans
1-1/4 cups butter, softened, *divided*
2 cups sugar
4 eggs
2 teaspoons vanilla extract
3 cups all-purpose flour
2 teaspoons baking powder
1/2 teaspoon salt
1 cup milk

FROSTING:
1 cup butter, softened
8 to 8-1/2 cups confectioners' sugar
1 can (5 ounces) evaporated milk
2 teaspoons vanilla extract

1 Place pecans and 1/4 cup of butter in a baking pan. Bake at 350° for 20-25 minutes or until toasted, stirring frequently; set aside. In a large mixing bowl, cream sugar and remaining butter until light and fluffy. Add eggs, one at a time, beating well after each addition. Stir in vanilla. Combine the flour, baking powder and salt; add to the creamed mixture alternately with milk, beating well after each addition. Stir in 1-1/3 cups of toasted pecans.

2 Pour into three greased and floured 9-in. round baking pans. Bake at 350° for 25-30 minutes or until a toothpick inserted near the center comes out clean. Cool for 10 minutes before removing from pans to wire racks to cool completely.

3 For frosting, cream butter and confectioners' sugar in a large mixing bowl until light and fluffy. Add milk and vanilla; beat until smooth. Stir in remaining toasted pecans. Spread frosting between layers and over top and sides of cake. **Yield:** 12-16 servings.

—*Becky Miller, Tallahassee, Florida*

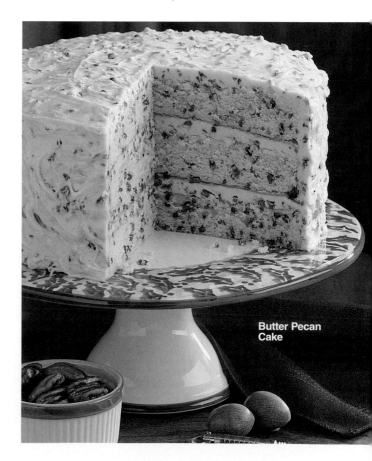

Butter Pecan Cake

Triple-Layer Brownie Cake

A little of this rich brownie cake goes a long way, so you'll have plenty to share with grateful family members and friends. It's a sure way to satisfy chocolate lovers.

1-1/2 cups butter
   6 squares (1 ounce *each*) unsweetened chocolate
   3 cups sugar
   5 eggs
1-1/2 teaspoons vanilla extract
1-1/2 cups all-purpose flour
  3/4 teaspoon salt
FROSTING:
   2 packages (8 ounces *each*) semisweet baking chocolate
   3 cups heavy whipping cream
   2 milk chocolate candy bars (1.55 ounces *each*), grated

1 In a heavy saucepan or microwave, melt butter and chocolate; stir until smooth. Stir in sugar. Transfer to a large mixing bowl. Add eggs, one at a time, beating well after each addition. Stir in vanilla. Combine flour and salt; stir into chocolate mixture.

2 Pour into three greased and floured 9-in. round baking pans. Bake at 350° for 23-25 minutes or until a toothpick inserted near the center comes out clean. Cool for 10 minutes before removing from pans to wire racks to cool completely.

3 For frosting, melt semisweet chocolate in a heavy saucepan over medium heat. Gradually stir in cream until well blended. Heat to a gentle boil; boil and stir for 1 minute. Transfer to a large mixing bowl. Refrigerate for 2-3 hours or until mixture reaches a pudding-like consistency, stirring occasionally. Beat until soft peaks form. Immediately spread between layers and over top and sides of cake. Sprinkle with grated chocolate. Store in the refrigerator. **Yield:** 16-20 servings.
—*Barbara Dean, Littleton, Colorado*

White Chocolate Holiday Cake

This white frosted cake looks stunning on a holiday table. For extra impact, garnish with chocolate curls.

   4 eggs, *separated*
   1 cup butter, softened
   2 cups sugar, *divided*
1-1/2 cups buttermilk
   1 package (6 ounces) white baking chocolate, melted and cooled
   1 teaspoon vanilla extract
2-1/2 cups cake flour
1-1/2 teaspoons baking powder
  1/2 teaspoon salt
  1/4 teaspoon baking soda
   1 cup chopped pecans
   1 cup flaked coconut
FROSTING:
1-1/2 cups butter, softened
   6 cups confectioners' sugar
   1 tablespoon vanilla extract
   3 to 4 tablespoons milk

1 Let eggs stand at room temperature for 30 minutes. In a large mixing bowl, cream butter and 1-1/2 cups sugar until light and fluffy. Add egg yolks, one at a time, beating well after each addition; set aside. Gradually stir buttermilk into white chocolate; add vanilla. Combine the flour, baking powder, salt and baking soda; add to creamed mixture alternately with chocolate mixture, beating well after each addition. In a small mixing bowl and with clean beaters, beat egg whites on medium speed until soft peaks

Triple-Layer Brownie Cake

form. Gradually beat in remaining sugar, a tablespoon at a time, on high until stiff peaks form. Fold into batter. Fold in pecans and coconut.

2 Pour into three greased and floured 9-in. round baking pans. Bake at 350° for 30-35 minutes or until a toothpick inserted near the center comes out clean. Cool for 10 minutes before removing from pans to wire racks to cool completely.

3 For frosting, beat butter, confectioners' sugar, vanilla and 3 tablespoons milk on low speed in a large mixing bowl until moistened. Beat on medium for 1-1/2 minutes, adding additional milk to achieve spreading consistency. Spread between layers and over the top and sides of cake. **Yield:** 12-16 servings.

—*Kim Van Rheenen, Mendota, Illinois*

Buttermilk Banana Cake

Buttermilk Banana Cake

A rich fluffy frosting tastefully tops off this moist banana cake.

3/4 **cup butter, softened**
  1 **cup sugar**
1/2 **cup packed brown sugar**
  2 **eggs**
  1 **cup mashed ripe bananas (about 2 medium)**
  1 **teaspoon vanilla extract**
  2 **cups cake flour**
  1 **teaspoon baking powder**
  1 **teaspoon baking soda**
1/2 **teaspoon salt**
1/2 **cup buttermilk**

FILLING:
1/2 **cup sugar**
  2 **tablespoons all-purpose flour**
1/4 **teaspoon salt**
1/2 **cup half-and-half cream**
  2 **tablespoons butter**
  1 **teaspoon vanilla extract**
1/2 **cup chopped pecans**
FROSTING:
  2 **cups heavy whipping cream**
1/4 **cup confectioners' sugar**

1 In a large mixing bowl, cream butter and sugars until light and fluffy. Add eggs; beat for 2 minutes. Add bananas and vanilla; beat for 2 minutes. Combine the flour, baking powder, baking soda and salt; add to creamed mixture alternately with buttermilk, beating well after each addition.

2 Pour into two greased and floured 9-in. round baking pans. Bake at 375° for 25-30 minutes or until a toothpick inserted near the center comes out clean. Cool for 10 minutes before removing from pans to wire racks to cool completely.

3 For filling, combine the sugar, flour and salt in a saucepan. Stir in half-and-half cream until smooth; add butter. Bring to a boil; cook and stir for 2 minutes. Remove from the heat; stir in vanilla and pecans. Cool. Spread between cake layers.

4 For frosting, beat heavy whipping cream in a chilled large mixing bowl until soft peaks form. Gradually add confectioners' sugar, a tablespoon at a time, beating until stiff peaks form. Spread over top and sides of cake. Store in the refrigerator. **Yield:** 12-16 servings.

—*Arlene Grenz, Linton, North Dakota*

Leveling Cake Layers

Stacking layers for a layered cake is easier when the layers are level. When the cake is cool, use a long serrated knife to slice the high spot from the bottom layer of a two-layer cake or the bottom and middle layers of a three-layer cake. You can trim off the crown of the top layer or leave it for a domed effect.

Lining a Baking Pan with Waxed Paper

To easily remove cakes from the pan, consider lining the pan with waxed paper. Place pan on a piece of waxed paper. Trace the shape of the pan onto the waxed paper, then cut out. Grease the pan; place the waxed paper in the pan and grease it. Remove the paper as soon as the baked cake is inverted onto a wire rack to cool.

2 Pour into two greased and floured 9-in. round baking pans. Bake at 350° for 30-35 minutes or until a toothpick inserted near the center comes out clean. Cool for 10 minutes before removing from pans to wire racks to cool completely.

3 In a large mixing bowl, combine frosting ingredients. Beat until smooth and creamy. Spread between layers and over top and sides of cake. Store in the refrigerator. **Yield:** 12-16 servings.

—Patsy Foster
Marion, Arkansas

Sour Cream Chocolate Cake

(Pictured on page 92 and on the cover)

For a special touch, top this classic with chocolate curls, raspberries and fresh mint sprigs.

      4 squares (1 ounce *each*) unsweetened chocolate, melted and cooled
      1 cup water
    3/4 cup sour cream
    1/4 cup shortening
      1 teaspoon vanilla extract
      2 eggs
      2 cups all-purpose flour
      2 cups sugar
  1-1/4 teaspoons baking soda
      1 teaspoon salt
    1/2 teaspoon baking powder
FROSTING:
    1/2 cup butter, softened
      6 squares (1 ounce *each*) unsweetened chocolate, melted and cooled
      6 cups confectioners' sugar
    1/2 cup sour cream
      6 to 8 tablespoons milk
      2 teaspoons vanilla extract
    1/8 teaspoon salt

1 In a large mixing bowl, combine the chocolate, water, sour cream, shortening, vanilla and eggs; mix well. Combine the flour, sugar, baking soda, salt and baking powder; gradually add to chocolate mixture. Beat on low speed just until moistened. Beat on high for 3 minutes.

Apple Spice Cake

Look no further than this cake when you need a dessert to celebrate someone's birthday. With walnuts and apples, this spice cake is especially fitting for fall.

  2-2/3 cups all-purpose flour
  1-2/3 cups sugar
    3/4 teaspoon baking soda
      1 teaspoon salt
    3/4 teaspoon ground cinnamon
      3 eggs

Apple Spice Cake

1 cup vegetable oil
2 teaspoons vanilla extract
2 cups chopped peeled baking apples
3/4 cup chopped walnuts
FROSTING:
5 tablespoons all-purpose flour
1 cup milk
1 cup butter, softened
2 cups confectioners' sugar
1 teaspoon vanilla extract
1/4 teaspoon salt
Red food coloring, optional
1 to 1-1/4 cups chopped walnuts

1 In a large mixing bowl, combine the flour, sugar, baking soda, salt and cinnamon. In a bowl, whisk the eggs, oil and vanilla; add to dry ingredients and beat well. Fold in apples and walnuts (batter will be thick).

2 Spread into two greased 9-in. round baking pans. Bake at 350° for 35-40 minutes or until a toothpick inserted near the center comes out clean. Cool for 10 minutes before removing from pans to wire racks to cool completely.

3 For frosting, combine flour and milk in a saucepan until smooth. Bring to a boil; cook and stir for 1 minute. Set aside, uncovered, at room temperature for 20 minutes. In a large mixing bowl, cream butter, confectioners' sugar and vanilla until light and fluffy. Add salt and cooked flour mixture; beat until smooth. If you wish to "write" on the cake with frosting, reserve 1/4 cup and tint with red food coloring; set aside. Use remaining frosting to frost between layers and over top and sides of cake. If desired, use the red frosting and a round decorator's tip to add "Happy Birthday" on top. Carefully press walnuts around sides. Store in the refrigerator. **Yield:** 10-12 servings. —*Alberta McKay*
Bartlesville, Oklahoma

Sunny Coconut Cake

For a refreshing finale to any dinner, present this appealing cake. Orange gelatin in the batter and mandarin oranges on top give it beautiful color.

2 cups (16 ounces) sour cream
2 cups sugar
1/4 cup orange juice

Sunny Coconut Cake

1 package (14 ounces) flaked coconut
1 package (18-1/4 ounces) yellow cake mix
1 package (3 ounces) orange gelatin
1 cup water
1/3 cup vegetable oil
2 eggs
1 cup heavy whipping cream
1 can (11 ounces) mandarin oranges, well drained

1 In a small mixing bowl, combine the sour cream, sugar and orange juice. Beat in coconut. Cover and refrigerate. In a large mixing bowl, combine the dry cake mix, gelatin powder, water, oil and eggs; mix well.

2 Pour into two greased and floured 9-in. round baking pans. Bake at 350° for 30-35 minutes or until a toothpick inserted near the center comes out clean. Cool for 10 minutes before removing from pans to wire racks to cool completely.

3 Split each cake into two horizontal layers. Set aside 1 cup of the coconut filling; spread remaining filling between cake layers. Refrigerate. In a chilled large mixing bowl, beat cream until stiff peaks form; fold into reserved filling. Frost the top and sides of cake. Garnish with oranges. Store in the refrigerator. **Yield:** 12-14 servings. —*Annette Buckner, Charlotte, North Carolina*

Peanut Butter Lover's Cake

The combination of chocolate and peanut butter gives this cake the flavor of a popular candy bar. Folks will be impressed when you serve this cake.

Peanut Butter Lover's Cake

3 eggs
1-2/3 cups sugar, *divided*
1-1/2 cups milk, *divided*
3 squares (1 ounce *each*) unsweetened chocolate, finely chopped
1/2 cup shortening
1 teaspoon vanilla extract
2 cups cake flour
1 teaspoon baking soda
1/2 teaspoon salt
PEANUT BUTTER FROSTING:
2 packages (8 ounces *each*) cream cheese, softened
1 can (14 ounces) sweetened condensed milk
1-1/2 cups peanut butter
1/4 cup salted peanuts, chopped
3 milk chocolate candy bars (1.55 ounces *each*), broken into squares

1 In a saucepan, whisk one egg until blended. Stir in 2/3 cup sugar, 1/2 cup milk and chocolate. Cook and stir over medium heat until chocolate is melted and mixture just comes to a boil. Remove from the heat; cool to room temperature.

2 In a large mixing bowl, cream shortening and remaining sugar until light and fluffy. Add remaining eggs, one at a time, beating well after each addition. Beat in vanilla. Combine the flour, baking soda and salt; add to creamed mixture alternately with remaining milk, beating well after each addition. Add chocolate mixture; mix well.

3 Pour into three greased and floured 9-in. round baking pans. Bake at 325° for 25-30 minutes or until a toothpick inserted near the center comes out clean. Cool for 10 minutes before removing from pans to wire racks to cool completely.

4 For frosting, beat cream cheese in a large mixing bowl until light and fluffy. Gradually add milk and peanut butter, beating well after each addition. Spread between layers and over top and sides of cake. Sprinkle with peanuts. Garnish with candy bars. Store in the refrigerator. **Yield:** 12-14 servings.
—*Teresa Mozingo, Camden, South Carolina*

Testing Butter Cakes for Doneness

Insert a toothpick in several spots near the center of the cake. If the toothpick comes out clean, the cake is done.

If the toothpick comes out with crumbs, the cake needs to bake longer.

Victorian Strawberry Chocolate Cake

With its alternating light and dark layers, rich chocolate frosting and fresh strawberry garnishes, this heart-shaped cake will be a hit for any occasion.

2 cups boiling water
1 cup baking cocoa
1 cup butter, softened
2-1/2 cups sugar
4 eggs
1-1/2 teaspoons vanilla extract
2-3/4 cups all-purpose flour
2 teaspoons baking powder
2 teaspoons baking soda
1 quart fresh strawberries
1 cup (6 ounces) semisweet chocolate chips, melted

FROSTING:
2/3 cup shortening
1 package (32 ounces) confectioners' sugar
1/2 cup water

ICING:
1-1/2 cups semisweet chocolate chips
1/3 cup heavy whipping cream
Chocolate shavings and additional confectioners' sugar, optional

1 In a small bowl, stir water into cocoa until blended; set aside. In a large mixing bowl, cream butter and sugar until light and fluffy. Add eggs, one at a time, beating well after each addition. Beat in vanilla. Combine the flour, baking powder and baking soda; add to the creamed mixture alternately with cocoa mixture, beating well after each addition.

2 Pour into two greased and floured 9-in. heart-shaped pans. Bake at 350° for 35-40 minutes or until a toothpick inserted near the center comes out clean. Cool for 10 minutes before removing from pans to wire racks to cool completely.

3 Slice 10 strawberries; set aside. Dip remaining whole strawberries into melted chocolate, about three-fourths to top. Place on a waxed paper-lined baking sheet; refrigerate until set.

4 For frosting, cream shortening and confectioners' sugar in a large mixing bowl until light and fluffy; gradually add water, beating until smooth. Spread between layers and over top and sides of cake. Set aside to dry, about 30 minutes.

5 For icing, heat chocolate chips and cream in a saucepan over medium heat until chocolate is melted, stirring occasionally. Spread over frosted cake until smooth. Refrigerate until set. Before serving, arrange two rows of sliced strawberries on top of cake in a heart shape. Fill center with chocolate shavings and dust with confectioners' sugar if desired. Place dipped strawberries around base. Store in the refrigerator. **Yield:** 10-12 servings. *—Amy Parker Ponca City, Oklahoma*

Editor's Note: Cake may also be baked in two greased and floured 9-in. square pans.

Victorian Strawberry Chocolate Cake

cupcake capers

- Batter for a two-layer 9-in. cake can be used to make 2 to 2-1/2 dozen cupcakes. Fill greased or paper-lined muffin cups two-thirds full. Bake at 350° for 20 to 30 minutes or until a toothpick comes out clean. Cool cupcakes for 10 minutes before removing from pans to wire racks to cool completely. Frost as desired.

- To make cupcakes of the same size, use a solid plastic ice cream scoop to measure out the batter and fill the muffin cups.

Lemon Cream Cupcakes

Delicate cupcakes like these are sure to disappear at your next potluck or bake sale.

      1 **cup butter, softened**
      2 **cups sugar**
      3 **eggs**
      2 **teaspoons grated lemon peel**
      1 **teaspoon vanilla extract**
3-1/2 **cups all-purpose flour**
      1 **teaspoon baking soda**
  1/2 **teaspoon baking powder**
  1/2 **teaspoon salt**
      2 **cups (16 ounces) sour cream**
FROSTING:
      3 **tablespoons butter, softened**
2-1/4 **cups confectioners' sugar**
      2 **tablespoons lemon juice**
  3/4 **teaspoon vanilla extract**
  1/4 **teaspoon grated lemon peel**
      1 **to 2 tablespoons milk**

1 In a large mixing bowl, cream butter and sugar until light and fluffy. Add eggs, one at a time, beating well after each addition. Beat in lemon peel and vanilla. Combine the flour, baking soda, baking powder and salt; add to creamed mixture alternately with sour cream, beating well after each addition (batter will be thick).

2 Fill greased or paper-lined muffin cups with 1/4 cup of batter. Bake at 350° for 25-30 minutes or until a toothpick comes out clean. Cool for 10 minutes before removing from pans to wire racks to cool completely.

3 For the frosting, cream butter and confectioners' sugar in a small mixing bowl until light and fluffy. Add the lemon juice, vanilla, lemon peel and milk; beat until smooth. Frost cupcakes. **Yield:** about 2-1/2 dozen.
—Ruth Ann Stelfox, Raymond, Alberta

**Lemon Cream
Cupcakes**

Frosting Cupcakes in a Flash

To quickly frost cupcakes, place frosting in a bowl. The frosting should be a soft spreadable consistency. If it is too stiff, add milk a teaspoon at a time until it reaches desired consistency. Dip top of the cupcake into the frosting, twist slightly and lift up.

Fancy Cream Cupcakes

These cute filled cupcakes are creamy and not too sweet. They look fancy but are actually quick to fix.

  1/2 **cup shortening**
1-1/2 **cups sugar**

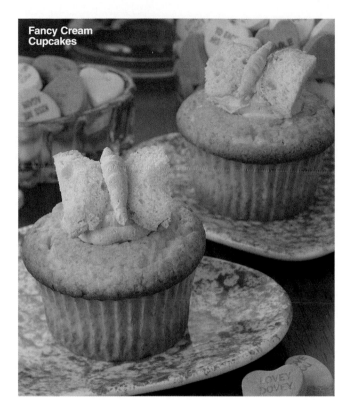

Fancy Cream Cupcakes

4 egg whites
1 teaspoon vanilla extract
2 cups all-purpose flour
3-1/2 teaspoons baking powder
1 teaspoon salt
1 cup milk
FILLING:
1 cup heavy whipping cream
2 tablespoons confectioners' sugar
4 to 5 drops red food coloring, optional
1/4 teaspoon almond extract

1 In a large mixing bowl, cream shortening and sugar until light and fluffy. Add egg whites, one at a time, beating well after each addition. Beat in vanilla. Combine flour, baking powder and salt; add to creamed mixture alternately with milk, beating well after each addition.

2 Fill paper- or foil-lined muffin cups two-thirds full. Bake at 350° for 20-25 minutes or until a toothpick comes out clean. Cool for 10 minutes before removing from pans to wire racks to cool completely.

3 For filling, beat cream in a chilled small mixing bowl until it begins to thicken. Gradually beat in confectioners' sugar and food coloring if desired until stiff peaks form. Beat in almond extract. Cut a 1-in. cone shape from the center of each cupcake; set cone aside.

Fill indentation with filling. Cut each cone in half from top to bottom; place two halves on filling for butterfly wings. If desired, pipe a thin strip of filling between wings for butterfly body. **Yield:** 22 cupcakes.
—*Merrilee Chambers*
Haines Junction, Yukon Territory

Mocha Cupcakes

Instant coffee granules add the right amount of mocha flavor to the chocolate frosting.

1 cup boiling water
1 cup mayonnaise*
1 teaspoon vanilla extract
2 cups all-purpose flour
1 cup sugar
1/2 cup baking cocoa
2 teaspoons baking soda
MOCHA FROSTING:
3/4 cup confectioners' sugar
1/4 cup baking cocoa
1/2 to 1 teaspoon instant coffee granules
Pinch salt
1-1/2 cups heavy whipping cream

1 In a large mixing bowl, combine the water, mayonnaise and vanilla. Combine the flour, sugar, cocoa and baking soda; add to the mayonnaise mixture and beat until well mixed.

2 Fill greased or paper-lined muffin cups two-thirds full. Bake at 350° for 20-25 minutes or until a toothpick comes out clean. Cool for 10 minutes before removing from pans to wire racks to cool completely.

3 For frosting, combine the confectioners' sugar, cocoa, coffee granules and salt in a large mixing bowl. Stir in cream. Place mixer beaters in bowl; cover and chill for 30 minutes. Beat frosting until stiff peaks form. Frost the cupcakes. **Yield:** about 1-1/2 dozen.
—*Lorna Smith, New Hazelton, British Columbia*

*Editor's Note: Reduced-fat or fat-free mayonnaise may not be substituted for regular mayonnaise in this recipe.

Chocolate Chip Cake

A delightful chocolate and cinnamon filling is sandwiched between tender white cake layers. It's the perfect size for a smaller group.

> 1/2 cup butter, softened
> 1-1/2 cups sugar, *divided*
> 2 eggs
> 1 teaspoon vanilla extract
> 2 cups all-purpose flour
> 1 teaspoon baking powder
> 1/2 teaspoon baking soda
> 1 cup (8 ounces) sour cream
> 3/4 cup semisweet chocolate chips
> 1 teaspoon ground cinnamon

1 In a large mixing bowl, cream butter and 1 cup sugar until light and fluffy. Add eggs, one at a time, beating well after each addition. Beat in vanilla. Combine the flour, baking powder and baking soda; add to the creamed mixture alternately with sour cream, beating well after each addition.

2 Spread half of the batter into a greased 9-in. square baking pan. Sprinkle with chocolate chips. Combine cinnamon and remaining sugar; sprinkle over chips. Spread with remaining batter. Bake at 350° for 40-45 minutes or until a toothpick inserted near the center comes out clean. Cool on a wire rack. **Yield:** 9 servings.
— *Sue Reichenbach, Langhorne, Pennsylvania*

Moist Chocolate Cake

Moist Chocolate Cake

This cake is so moist it doesn't need frosting. Simply sprinkle confectioners' sugar over the top.

> 1-1/2 cups all-purpose flour
> 1 cup sugar
> 3 tablespoons baking cocoa
> 1 teaspoon baking soda
> 1/2 teaspoon salt
> 6 tablespoons vegetable oil
> 1 tablespoon white vinegar
> 1 teaspoon vanilla extract
> 1 cup cold water
> Confectioners' sugar

1 In a large mixing bowl, combine the flour, sugar, cocoa, baking soda and salt. Using a spoon, make three wells in the dry ingredients. Pour oil into one, vinegar into another and vanilla into the third. Slowly pour water over all. Beat on low speed until thoroughly combined (batter will be thin).

2 Pour into a greased 8-in. square baking dish. Bake at 350° for 30-35 minutes or until a toothpick inserted near the center comes out clean. Cool on a wire rack. Dust with confectioners' sugar. **Yield:** 9 servings.
— *Beulah Sak, Fairport, New York*

Dusting Cakes with Confectioners' Sugar

Place confectioners' sugar in a small metal sieve or sifter; shake or sift over the top of the baked and cooled cake. To make a pattern, lay a doily over the cake; sift an even layer of sugar over all. Lift the doily straight up, leaving the pattern on the cake.

3 For filling, combine sugar and flour in a heavy saucepan. Stir in water until smooth. Cook and stir over medium-high heat until thickened and bubbly. Reduce heat; cook and stir 2 minutes longer. Remove from the heat. Stir a small amount of hot filling into egg yolks; return all to the pan, stirring constantly. Bring to a gentle boil; cook and stir 2 minutes longer. Remove from the heat. Gently stir in lemon juice, butter and lemon peel. Cool to room temperature without stirring. Place cake on a baking sheet, spoon filling on top of cake to within 1/2 in. of edge.

4 For meringue, let egg whites stand at room temperature for 30 minutes. In a small mixing bowl and with clean beaters, beat egg whites and cream of tartar on medium speed until soft peaks form. Gradually add sugar, 1 tablespoon at a time, beating on high until stiff peaks form. Carefully spread over filling, sealing to edges of cake. Bake at 350° for 12-15 minutes or until lightly browned. **Yield:** 6-8 servings. —*Debra Blair*
Glenwood, Minnesota

Lemon Meringue Cake

When you can't decide whether to make a cake or pie, reach for this unique recipe and make both!

> 1/4 **cup butter, softened**
> 1/2 **cup sugar**
> 1 **egg**
> 2 **egg yolks**
> 1/2 **teaspoon vanilla extract**
> 1 **cup all-purpose flour**
> 1 **teaspoon baking powder**
> 1/3 **cup milk**
> **FILLING:**
> 3/4 **cup sugar**
> 1/3 **cup all-purpose flour**
> 1 **cup water**
> 2 **egg yolks, lightly beaten**
> 1/4 **cup lemon juice**
> 1 **tablespoon butter**
> 1/2 **teaspoon grated lemon peel**
> **MERINGUE:**
> 4 **egg whites**
> 1/2 **teaspoon cream of tartar**
> 1/2 **cup sugar**

1 In a large mixing bowl, cream butter and sugar until light and fluffy. Add the egg and yolks; mix well. Beat in vanilla. Combine the flour and baking powder; add to the creamed mixture alternately with milk, beating well after each addition.

2 Pour into a greased and floured 9-in. round baking pan. Bake at 350° for 25-30 minutes or until a toothpick inserted near the center comes out clean. Cool for 10 minutes before removing to a wire rack to cool completely.

Lemon Meringue Cake

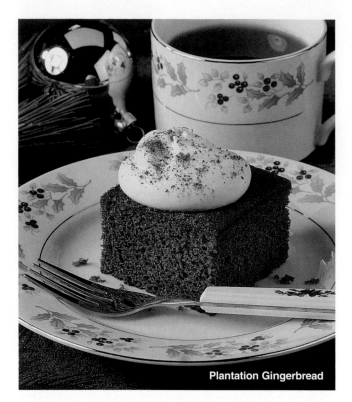

Plantation Gingerbread

Plantation Gingerbread

The wonderful aroma of gingerbread will fill the house when you make this dessert. A dollop of sweetened whipped cream crowns each piece.

      1 cup butter, softened
      1 cup sugar
      3 eggs
      1 cup molasses
   3/4 cup hot water
  2-1/2 cups all-purpose flour
  1-1/2 teaspoons ground ginger
      1 teaspoon baking soda
      1 teaspoon ground cinnamon
   1/2 teaspoon salt
   1/2 teaspoon ground nutmeg
      1 cup heavy whipping cream
      1 to 2 tablespoons confectioners' sugar
Additional nutmeg, optional

1 In a large mixing bowl, cream butter and sugar until light and fluffy. Add eggs; beat on low speed for 2 minutes. Gradually add the molasses and hot water. Combine the flour, ginger, baking soda, cinnamon, salt and nutmeg; gradually add to creamed mixture. Beat on low for 1 minute.

2 Pour into a greased 13-in. x 9-in. x 2-in. baking pan. Bake at 350° for 30-35 minutes or until a toothpick inserted near the center comes out clean. Cool on a wire rack.

3 In a chilled small mixing bowl, beat cream until it begins to thicken. Add confectioners' sugar; beat until soft peaks form. Serve with the gingerbread. Sprinkle with nutmeg if desired. **Yield:** 12-16 servings.
— *Wanda Burchell, Lynnville, Tennessee*

Plum Upside-Down Cake

(Pictured on page 93)

The delicate flavor of plums is a pleasing change of pace in this upside-down cake.

   1/3 cup butter
   1/2 cup packed brown sugar
      2 pounds fresh plums, pitted and halved
      2 eggs
   2/3 cup sugar
      1 cup all-purpose flour
      1 teaspoon baking powder
   1/4 teaspoon salt
   1/3 cup hot water
   1/2 teaspoon lemon extract
Whipped cream, optional

1 Melt butter in a 10-in. cast-iron or ovenproof skillet. Sprinkle brown sugar over butter. Arrange plum halves cut side down in a single layer over sugar; set aside.

2 In a large mixing bowl, beat eggs until thick and lemon-colored; gradually beat in sugar. Combine the flour, baking powder and salt; add to egg mixture and mix well. Blend water and lemon extract; beat into batter. Pour over plums.

3 Bake at 350° for 40-45 minutes or until a toothpick inserted near the center comes out clean. Immediately invert onto a serving plate. Serve warm with whipped cream if desired. **Yield:** 8-10 servings.
— *Bobbie Talbott, Veneta, Oregon*

Spiced Pineapple Upside-Down Cake

Upside-down cakes, which have been around since the 1800s, were once called skillet cakes because they were cooked in cast-iron skillets on the stovetop.

1-1/3 cups butter, softened, *divided*
   1 cup packed brown sugar
   1 can (20 ounces) pineapple slices, drained
 10 to 12 maraschino cherries
 1/2 cup chopped pecans
1-1/2 cups sugar
   2 eggs
   1 teaspoon vanilla extract
   2 cups all-purpose flour
   2 teaspoons baking powder
 1/2 teaspoon baking soda
 1/2 teaspoon salt
 1/2 teaspoon ground cinnamon
 1/2 teaspoon ground nutmeg
   1 cup buttermilk

1 In a saucepan, melt 2/3 cup butter; stir in brown sugar. Spread on the bottom of an ungreased heavy 12-in. ovenproof skillet or a 13-in. x 9-in. x 2-in. baking pan. Arrange pineapple in a single layer over sugar mixture; place a cherry in the center of each slice. Sprinkle with pecans; set aside.

2 In a large mixing bowl, cream sugar and remaining butter until light and fluffy. Beat in eggs and vanilla. Combine the flour, baking powder, baking soda, salt, cinnamon and nutmeg; add to creamed mixture alternately with buttermilk, beating well after each addition. Carefully pour over the pineapple.

3 Bake at 350° for 40 minutes for skillet (50-60 minutes for baking pan) or until a toothpick inserted near the center comes out clean. Immediately invert onto a serving platter. Serve warm. **Yield:** 12 servings.
—*Jennifer Sergesketter, Newburgh, Indiana*

properly storing cakes

- Cover and store butter cakes for 2 to 3 days and foam cakes for 2 days at room temperature. Cakes with fillings or frosting that contain perishable ingredients (such as cream cheese, yogurt, whipping cream, sour cream and eggs) should be stored in the refrigerator.

- Unfrosted butter cakes and ones frosted with a simple buttercream frosting can be frozen. Place individual cake layers on a baking sheet and freeze. Once frozen, wrap in plastic wrap or place in resealable plastic freezer bags. Freeze unfrosted butter cakes for up to 4 months and frosted butter cakes for up to 2 months. Not all frostings are suitable for freezing. Freeze unfrosted foam cakes in their pan or in plastic bags for up to 2 months. Thaw cakes in the refrigerator.

Spiced Pineapple Upside-Down Cake

German Chocolate Cake

Despite its name, this recipe didn't come from Germany. It refers to the type of chocolate called for. German chocolate is similar to milk chocolate and sweeter than regular baking chocolate.

    4 eggs, *separated*
    1 package (4 ounces) German sweet chocolate
1/2 cup water
    1 cup butter, softened
    2 cups sugar
    1 teaspoon vanilla extract
2-1/2 cups cake flour
    1 teaspoon baking soda
1/2 teaspoon salt
    1 cup buttermilk
COCONUT-PECAN FROSTING:
    1 cup evaporated milk
    1 cup sugar
    3 egg yolks, lightly beaten
1/2 cup butter
1-1/3 cups flaked coconut
    1 cup chopped pecans
    1 teaspoon vanilla extract

1 Let eggs stand at room temperature for 30 minutes. Line a greased 13-in. x 9-in. x 2-in. baking pan with waxed paper. Grease and flour the paper; set aside.

2 In a saucepan, melt chocolate in water over low heat; cool. In a large mixing bowl, cream butter and sugar until light and fluffy. Add egg yolks, one at a time, beating well after each addition. Add chocolate mixture and vanilla; mix well. Combine the flour, baking soda and salt; add to creamed mixture alternately with buttermilk, beating well after each addition. In a small mixing bowl and with clean beaters, beat egg whites until stiff peaks form; fold into batter.

3 Spread batter evenly into prepared pan. Bake at 350° for 50-55 minutes or until a toothpick inserted near the center comes out clean. Cool for 10 minutes before inverting onto a wire rack to cool completely. Remove waxed paper.

4 For frosting, combine the milk, sugar, egg yolks and butter in a large saucepan; cook and stir over medium heat until thickened. Remove from the heat; stir in coconut, pecans and vanilla. Beat until frosting is cool and achieves spreading consistency. Place cake on a serving platter; spread frosting over top and sides. **Yield:** 12-15 servings. —*Lisa Andis, Morristown, Indiana*

flour facts

All-purpose flour is the most commonly used flour and creates a good cake. Cake flour gives a more tender and delicate crumb. Self-rising flour contains the leavening agent and salt, so you only need to measure one ingredient. While you can substitute one flour for another, you will need to make some adjustments to the recipe.

- For 1 cup cake flour, use 3/4 cup plus 2 tablespoons all-purpose flour.

- For 1 cup all-purpose flour, use 1 cup plus 2 tablespoons cake flour.

- For 1 cup self-rising flour, place 1-1/2 teaspoons baking powder and 1/2 teaspoon salt in a measuring cup. Add all-purpose flour to measure 1 cup.

Beware of the person who likes to have their cake— and yours, too.

Apple Cake

Every bite of this perfectly sized cake is packed with tender and juicy apples. Served warm or cold, with or without cream or ice cream, it's a treat every time.

    3 tablespoons butter, softened
    1 cup sugar
    1 egg
    1 teaspoon vanilla extract
    1 cup all-purpose flour
    1 teaspoon baking soda
1/2 teaspoon salt
1/2 teaspoon ground cinnamon
1/2 teaspoon ground nutmeg
    3 cups diced peeled apples
1/4 cup chopped nuts
Whipped cream *or* ice cream, optional

1 In a large mixing bowl, cream butter and sugar until light and fluffy. Beat in egg and vanilla. Combine the flour, baking soda, salt, cinnamon and nutmeg; add to creamed mixture (batter will be thick). Stir in apples and nuts.

2 Spread into a greased 8-in. square baking dish. Bake at 350° for 35-45 minutes or until a toothpick inserted near the center comes out with just a few crumbs. Serve warm or cold with whipped cream or ice cream if desired. **Yield:** 9 servings. —*Iona Redemer*
Calumet, Oklahoma

Grandma's
Blackberry Cake

Boston Cream Cake

Boston Cream Pie (which is truly more like a cake) is believed to have originated at Boston's Parker House restaurant in 1856. A boxed cake mix makes this version easy to prepare.

- 1 **package (9 ounces) yellow cake mix**
- 1/2 **teaspoon lemon extract**
- 2 **cups cold milk**
- 1 **package (3.4 ounces) instant vanilla pudding mix**
- 1 **square (1 ounce) semisweet chocolate**
- 1 **tablespoon butter**
- 1/2 **cup confectioners' sugar**
- 2 **to 3 teaspoons hot water**

1 Prepare cake batter according to package directions, adding lemon extract. Pour into a greased and floured 9-in. round baking pan. Bake at 350° for 25 minutes or until a toothpick inserted near the center comes out clean. Cool for 10 minutes before removing from pan to a wire rack to cool completely.

2 In a bowl, whisk milk and pudding mix for 2 minutes; refrigerate. In a heavy saucepan or microwave, melt chocolate and butter; stir until smooth. Stir in confectioners' sugar until crumbly. Stir in hot water, 1 teaspoon at a time, until smooth. Split cake into two horizontal layers. Spread pudding on bottom layer. Place second layer over pudding. Pour chocolate glaze over top, letting it drizzle down the sides. Store in the refrigerator. **Yield:** 6-8 servings. —*Michelle Mirich*
Youngstown, Ohio

Grandma's Blackberry Cake

A lightly seasoned spice cake lets the wonderful flavor of blackberries shine through.

- 1 **cup fresh blackberries**
- 2 **cups all-purpose flour,** *divided*
- 1/2 **cup butter, softened**
- 1 **cup sugar**
- 2 **eggs**
- 1 **teaspoon baking soda**
- 1 **teaspoon ground cinnamon**
- 1 **teaspoon ground nutmeg**
- 1/2 **teaspoon salt**
- 1/4 **teaspoon ground cloves**
- 1/4 **teaspoon ground allspice**
- 3/4 **cup buttermilk**
- **Whipped cream, optional**

1 Toss blackberries with 2 tablespoons of flour; set aside. In a large mixing bowl, cream butter and sugar until light and fluffy. Add eggs; beat well. Combine the baking soda, cinnamon, nutmeg, salt, cloves, allspice and remaining flour; add to creamed mixture alternately with buttermilk, beating well after each addition. Fold in blackberries.

2 Pour into a greased 9-in. square baking pan. Bake at 350° for 45-50 minutes or until a toothpick inserted near the center comes out clean. Cool on a wire rack. Serve cake with whipped cream if desired. **Yield:** 9 servings. —*Diana Martin*
Moundsville, West Virginia

Carrot Cake

You'll love the texture this pretty, moist cake gets from pineapple, coconut and, of course, carrots. Its traditional cream cheese frosting adds just the right amount of sweetness.

2 cups all-purpose flour
2 cups sugar
2 teaspoons ground cinnamon
1 teaspoon baking soda
1/2 teaspoon salt
3 eggs
1-1/2 cups vegetable oil
2 cups finely grated carrots
1 teaspoon vanilla extract
1 cup well-drained crushed pineapple
1 cup flaked coconut
1/2 cup chopped nuts
CREAM CHEESE FROSTING:
2 packages (3 ounces *each*) cream cheese, softened
3 cups confectioners' sugar
6 tablespoons butter, softened
1 teaspoon vanilla extract
1/2 cup chopped nuts

1 In a large mixing bowl, combine the flour, sugar, cinnamon, baking soda and salt. Add the eggs, oil, carrots and vanilla; beat until combined. Stir in the pineapple, coconut and nuts.

2 Pour into a greased 13-in. x 9-in. x 2-in. baking pan. Bake at 350° for 50-60 minutes or until a toothpick inserted near the center comes out clean. Cool on a wire rack.

3 For frosting, beat cream cheese in a small mixing bowl until fluffy. Add the confectioners' sugar, butter and vanilla; beat until smooth. Frost cake. Sprinkle with nuts. Store in the refrigerator. **Yield:** 12-16 servings.
—*Debbie Jones, California, Maryland*

Hawaiian Cake

Pineapple, coconut and a delightful blend of instant pudding, cream cheese and whipped topping dress up a yellow cake mix. This is a favorite dessert that suits any occasion.

1 package (18-1/4 ounces) yellow cake mix
2 cups cold milk
2 packages (3.4 ounces *each*) instant vanilla pudding mix
1 package (8 ounces) cream cheese, softened
1 carton (8 ounces) frozen whipped topping, thawed
1 can (20 ounces) crushed pineapple, drained
1/2 cup chopped maraschino cherries, drained
1/2 cup flaked coconut
1/2 cup chopped walnuts

1 Prepare cake batter according to package directions. Pour into a greased 15-in. x 10-in. x 1-in. baking pan. Bake at 350° for 20-25 minutes or until a toothpick inserted near the center comes out clean. Cool on a wire rack.

2 In a large mixing bowl, combine milk and pudding mixes; beat in cream cheese until smooth. Fold in whipped topping. Spread over cooled cake. Top with pineapple, cherries, coconut and walnuts. Store in the refrigerator. **Yield:** 16-20 servings. —*Estella Traeger Milwaukee, Wisconsin*

Carrot Cake

ture alternately with sour cream, stirring just until combined. Stir in walnuts.

2 Pour into a greased and floured 10-in. fluted tube pan. Bake at 350° for 50-55 minutes or until a toothpick inserted near the center comes out clean. Cool for 10 minutes before removing from pan to a wire rack to cool completely. Dust with confectioners' sugar. **Yield:** 12-16 servings. —*Oma Rollison*
El Cajon, California

Pumpkin Spice Cake

Canned pumpkin and pudding mix dress up a boxed spice cake and make every bite moist and mouth-watering! This cake is a nice alternative to pumpkin pie.

  1 package (18-1/4 ounces) spice cake mix
  3 eggs
  1 cup canned pumpkin
1/2 cup water
1/2 cup vegetable oil
  1 package (3.4 ounces) instant vanilla pudding mix
  1 teaspoon ground cinnamon
1/2 cup chopped pecans
Cream Cheese Frosting (page 143) *or* **whipped cream**

1 In a large mixing bowl, combine the dry cake mix, eggs, pumpkin, water, oil, pudding mix and cinnamon. Beat on medium speed for 5 minutes. Stir in pecans.

2 Pour into a greased and floured 10-in. fluted tube pan. Bake at 350° for 45-55 minutes or until a toothpick inserted near the center comes out clean. Cool for 10 minutes before removing from pan to a wire rack to cool completely. Frost cake or serve with whipped cream. Store in the refrigerator. **Yield:** 12-16 servings.
—*Kathy Rhoads, Circleville, Ohio*

Bananas 'n' Cream
Bundt Cake

Bananas 'n' Cream Bundt Cake

This absolutely scrumptious cake needs no icing…just a dusting of confectioners' sugar. Ripe bananas will provide the most intense flavor.

  1/3 cup shortening
1-1/4 cups sugar
    2 eggs
    1 teaspoon vanilla extract
1-1/4 cups mashed ripe bananas (2 to 3 medium)
    2 cups all-purpose flour
1-1/4 teaspoons baking powder
    1 teaspoon baking soda
  1/2 teaspoon salt
    1 cup (8 ounces) sour cream
  3/4 cup chopped walnuts
Confectioners' sugar

1 In a large mixing bowl, cream the shortening and sugar until light and fluffy. Add the eggs, one at a time, beating well after each addition. Beat in vanilla. Add bananas and mix well. Combine the flour, baking powder, baking soda and salt; add to the creamed mix-

Packable Chocolate Chip Cake

This recipe doesn't call for frosting, so it travels well to potlucks and in brown-bag lunches. Sour cream in the batter makes the cake deliciously moist.

> 1 package (18-1/4 ounces) yellow cake mix
> 1 cup (8 ounces) sour cream
> 1/2 cup vegetable oil
> 1/4 cup water
> 4 eggs
> 1 to 1-1/2 cups semisweet chocolate chips
> Confectioners' sugar

1 In a large mixing bowl, combine the dry cake mix, sour cream, oil, water and eggs. Beat on medium speed for 2 minutes. Fold in the chocolate chips.

2 Pour into a greased and floured 10-in. fluted tube pan. Bake at 350° for 45-50 minutes or until a toothpick inserted near the center comes out clean. Cool for 20 minutes before removing from pan to a wire rack to cool completely. Just before serving, dust with confectioners' sugar. **Yield:** 12-16 servings.

—*Barbara Hofstede, Waukesha, Wisconsin*

Chocolate Almond Cake

Folks will be pleasantly surprised to see a rich chocolate cake beneath the fluffy white frosting. Sliced toasted almonds on top add a little crunch.

> 3/4 cup butter, softened
> 1-2/3 cups sugar
> 2 eggs
> 3/4 cup sour cream
> 1 teaspoon vanilla extract
> 1 teaspoon almond extract
> 2 cups all-purpose flour
> 2/3 cup baking cocoa
> 2 teaspoons baking soda
> 1/2 teaspoon salt
> 1 cup buttermilk
> FROSTING:
> 5 tablespoons butter, softened
> 2-1/2 cups confectioners' sugar
> 1 teaspoon vanilla extract
> 1/2 teaspoon almond extract
> 3 to 4 tablespoons milk
> Sliced almonds, toasted

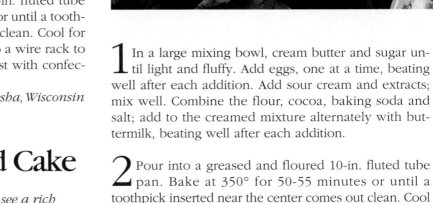

Chocolate Almond Cake

1 In a large mixing bowl, cream butter and sugar until light and fluffy. Add eggs, one at a time, beating well after each addition. Add sour cream and extracts; mix well. Combine the flour, cocoa, baking soda and salt; add to the creamed mixture alternately with buttermilk, beating well after each addition.

2 Pour into a greased and floured 10-in. fluted tube pan. Bake at 350° for 50-55 minutes or until a toothpick inserted near the center comes out clean. Cool for 10 minutes before removing from pan to a wire rack to cool completely.

3 For frosting, beat butter, sugar and extracts in a small mixing bowl until smooth. Add enough milk until frosting achieves desired spreading consistency. Spread over cake. Decorate with almonds. **Yield:** 12-16 servings.

—*Sherri Gentry, Dallas, Oregon*

Adams County Apple Cake

Cinnamon-sugar coated apples are tucked inside this tempting tube cake. Granny Smith, Cortland, Jonathan, Rome Beauty, McIntosh and Lady Apple are just a few varieties of tart apples that are great for baking.

> 3 cups all-purpose flour
> 3 teaspoons baking powder
> 2 cups plus 5 tablespoons sugar, *divided*
> 1 cup vegetable oil
> 4 eggs
> 1/3 cup orange juice
> 1/2 teaspoon salt
> 2-1/2 teaspoons vanilla extract
> 4 medium baking apples, peeled and thinly sliced
> 2 teaspoons ground cinnamon
> Confectioners' sugar, optional

1 In a large mixing bowl, combine the flour, baking powder, 2 cups sugar, oil, eggs, orange juice, salt and vanilla. Beat until thoroughly combined. In another bowl, toss apples with cinnamon and remaining sugar. Spread a third of the batter into a greased and floured 10-in. tube pan. Cover with half of the apples. Repeat layers. Spoon remaining batter over top.

2 Bake at 350° for 1-1/2 hours or until a toothpick inserted near the center comes out clean. Cool for 20 minutes before removing from pan to a wire rack to cool completely. Just before serving, dust with confectioners' sugar if desired. **Yield:** 12-16 servings.
—*Gretchen Berendt, Carroll Valley, Pennsylvania*

Cherry Chocolate Marble Cake

Cherries and chocolate are natural partners that make desserts such as this simply scrumptious! The marbled effect is easily achieved by layering the two different batters.

> 1 cup butter, softened
> 2 cups sugar
> 3 eggs
> 6 tablespoons maraschino cherry juice
> 6 tablespoons water
> 1 teaspoon almond extract
> 3-3/4 cups all-purpose flour
> 2-1/4 teaspoons baking soda
> 3/4 teaspoon salt
> 1-1/2 cups (12 ounces) sour cream
> 3/4 cup chopped maraschino cherries, drained
> 3/4 cup chopped walnuts, toasted
> 3 squares (1 ounce *each*) unsweetened chocolate, melted
> Confectioners' sugar, optional

1 In a large mixing bowl, cream butter and sugar until light and fluffy. Add the eggs, one at a time, beating well after each addition. Add the cherry juice, water and extract; mix well. Combine the flour, baking soda and salt; add to creamed mixture alternately with sour cream, beating well after each addition. Divide batter in half. To one portion, add cherries and walnuts; mix well. To the second portion, add chocolate; mix well. Spoon half of the cherry mixture into a greased and floured 10-in. fluted tube pan. Cover with half of the chocolate mixture. Repeat layers.

2 Bake at 350° for 1 hour and 15 minutes or until a toothpick inserted near the center comes out clean. Cool for 15 minutes before removing from pan to a wire rack to cool completely. Dust with confectioners' sugar if desired. **Yield:** 12-16 servings. —*Sandra Campbell Chase Mills, New York*

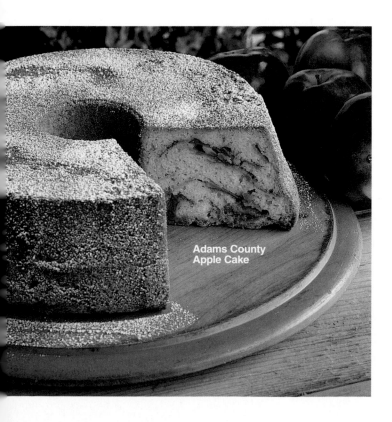

Adams County Apple Cake

Glazed Lemon Bundt Cake

A sunny lemon-flavored cake brightens up any day. Lemon peel provides a nice zing, and a light glaze gives the golden cake a delicate crust.

         1 cup butter, softened
         2 cups sugar
         4 eggs
    1-1/2 teaspoons lemon extract
    1-1/2 teaspoons vanilla extract
         3 cups all-purpose flour
         2 teaspoons baking powder
      1/2 teaspoon salt
         1 cup milk
         1 tablespoon grated lemon peel
GLAZE:
      1/4 cup lemon juice
         1 tablespoon water
      1/2 teaspoon lemon extract
      3/4 cup sugar

1 In a large mixing bowl, cream butter and sugar until light and fluffy. Add the eggs, one at a time, beating well after each addition. Beat in extracts. Combine the flour, baking powder and salt; add to the creamed mixture alternately with milk, beating well after each addition. Stir in lemon peel.

2 Pour into a greased and floured 10-in. fluted tube pan. Bake at 350° for 60-70 minutes or until a toothpick inserted near the center comes out clean. Cool for 10 minutes before removing from pan to a wire rack. Cool 10 minutes longer.

3 Place waxed paper under rack. Combine glaze ingredients; drizzle over the warm cake. Cool completely before serving. **Yield:** 12-16 servings.

—John Thompson, Vandalia, Illinois

baking cakes at high altitudes

High altitude (over 3,000 feet) has less air pressure and drier air. These conditions affect baked goods. The lower air pressure allows the gases created by the leavening agents to expand more quickly and causes liquids to evaporate and boil at lower temperatures. The drier air also dries out the flour.

For cakes, this means that there might be excessive rising from the gases the leavening produced. This would cause the texture to be coarse or may even cause the cake to fall before the structure of the cake can be set by baking. Faster evaporation of the liquid, due to lower boiling point, would reduce the amount of liquid and increase the concentration of sugar. This higher sugar concentration may also weaken the structure of the cake.

Some measures to take for butter cakes are to increase the oven temperature 15° to 25°, which will allow cakes to set faster and prevent falling. Fill baking pans half full not two-thirds full, since cakes rise higher. Reduce the leavener, reduce the sugar and increase the liquid. Here are some general guidelines for adjusting ingredients for butter cakes.

Adjustment	3,000 Feet	5,000 Feet	7,000 Feet
For each teaspoon of baking powder, reduce by:	1/8 teaspoon	1/8-1/4 teaspoon	1/4 teaspoon
For each cup of sugar, reduce by:	0-1 tablespoon	0-2 tablespoons	1-3 tablespoons
For each cup of liquid, increase by:	1-2 tablespoons	2-4 tablespoons	3-4 tablespoons

For foam cakes, only beat the egg whites until soft peaks form (see page 15). To strengthen the structure of the cake, decrease the amount of sugar by a tablespoon or two and increase the amount of flour or egg component of the cake a little. Increasing the oven temperature by 15° to 25° will also help set the cake structure sooner.

Blueberry Sour Cream Pound Cake

Original recipes for pound cake called for a pound each of butter, sugar, eggs and flour! Through the years, recipes have been adjusted to be a little lighter yet still have outstanding results.

　6　**eggs,** *separated*
　1　**cup butter, softened**
　3　**cups sugar**
　1　**teaspoon almond extract**
　1　**teaspoon vanilla extract**
　1　**teaspoon butter flavoring**
　3　**cups all-purpose flour**
1/4　**teaspoon baking soda**
　1　**cup (8 ounces) sour cream**
1-1/2　**cups fresh** *or* **frozen blueberries***

1 Let eggs stand at room temperature for 30 minutes. In a large mixing bowl, cream butter and sugar until light and fluffy. Add egg yolks, one at a time, beating well after each addition. Add the extracts and butter flavoring. Combine flour and baking soda; add to creamed mixture alternately with sour cream, beating well after each addition. In another mixing bowl and with clean beaters, beat egg whites on high speed until stiff peaks form. Fold into batter. Fold in blueberries.

2 Spoon into a greased and floured 10-in. tube pan. Bake at 350° for 60-70 minutes or until a toothpick inserted near the center comes out clean. Cool for 10 minutes before removing from pan to a wire rack to cool completely. **Yield:** 12-16 servings.　—*Juanita Miller Arnett, Oklahoma*

***Editor's Note:** If using frozen blueberries, do not thaw before adding to batter.

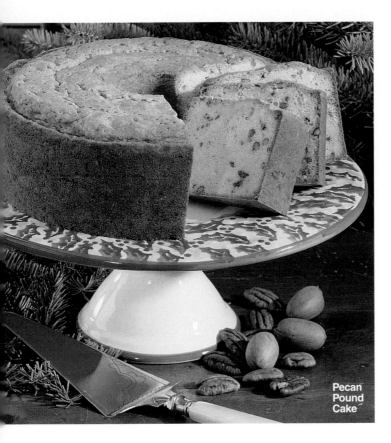

Pecan Pound Cake

Pecan Pound Cake

This cake always turns out great. It's wonderful with a steaming cup of coffee on a chilly winter day.

1-1/2　**cups butter, softened**
3-3/4　**cups confectioners' sugar**
　6　**eggs**
　1　**tablespoon vanilla extract**
2-1/2　**cups all-purpose flour**
1/2　**teaspoon salt**
　1　**cup flaked coconut**
2/3　**cup chopped pecans, toasted**

1 In a large mixing bowl, cream butter and confectioners' sugar until light and fluffy. Add eggs, one at a time, beating well after each addition. Add vanilla. Combine flour and salt; add to creamed mixture just until combined. Stir in coconut and pecans.

2 Pour into a greased and floured 10-in. tube pan; spread evenly. Bake at 325° for 60-65 minutes or until a toothpick inserted near the center comes out clean. Cool for 10 minutes before removing from pan to a wire rack to cool completely. **Yield:** 12-16 servings.
　—*Fleta West, Hayes, Virginia*

problem-Solving pointers for Butter Cakes

If this happens to your cake:	This could be the reason:
Cake has a sunken center.	Oven temperature was too low. Check temperature with an oven thermometer.
	Cake was underbaked, resulting in a sticky layer in the center of the cake under the top crust.
	Too much sugar was used, resulting in a thick, firm and overly brown crust.
	Too much liquid was used, resulting in a sticky layer above the bottom crust.
	Too much leavener was used, resulting in a chemical or bitter taste.
Cake has a peaked or cracked center.	Oven temperature was too high.
	Batter was overbeaten after the flour was added, causing the gluten in the flour to be developed.
	A hard wheat (high-gluten) flour was used. Next time, try a soft wheat flour like cake flour.
Cake is heavy.	The fat and sugar were not creamed long enough.
	Either too much sugar, flour or fat was used or not enough leavener was used.
Cake has tunnels.	Oven temperature was too high.
	Batter was overbeaten after the flour was added, causing the gluten in the flour to be developed.
Cake is dry.	Oven temperature was too high.
	Too small a baking pan was used. The pan should be filled from half to three-fourths full.
Cake overflowed pan.	The cake was overbaked.
	Too small a baking pan was used. The pan should be filled from half to three-fourths full.
Cake has a dark crust.	The baking pan was a dark color. For best results, use aluminum pans with a dull finish.
	Too much sugar was used, resulting in a thick, firm and overly brown crust.

CREAM FILLING:
- 2 cups heavy whipping cream
- 1 tablespoon confectioners' sugar
- 1 teaspoon vanilla extract

1 Line two greased 9-in. round baking pans with waxed paper; set aside. In a heavy saucepan or microwave, melt butter and chocolate; stir until smooth and cool. In a large mixing bowl, combine the flour, sugar, baking soda and baking powder. Add the chocolate mixture, water and vanilla. Beat on low speed for 1 minute; beat on medium for 2 minutes. Add eggs, one at a time, beating well after each addition.

2 Pour into the prepared pans. Bake at 350° for 25-30 minutes or until a toothpick inserted near the center comes out clean. Cool for 10 minutes before removing from pans to wire racks to cool completely.

3 For chocolate filling, melt 1-1/2 bars of German chocolate in a heavy saucepan or microwave; stir until smooth. Stir in butter and nuts. Watching closely, cool filling just until it reaches spreading consistency. For cream filling, beat cream in a chilled large mixing bowl until it begins to thicken. Add confectioners' sugar and vanilla; beat until stiff peaks form.

4 Split each cake into two horizontal layers. Place one layer on a serving plate; cover with half of the chocolate filling. Top with a second cake layer; spread with half of the cream filling. Repeat layers. Grate remaining German chocolate; sprinkle on the top. Store in the refrigerator. **Yield:** 12-16 servings.

— *Glatis McNiel, Constantine, Michigan*

Black Forest Torte

Black Forest Torte

Looking for a surefire way to impress guests? Present this eye-catching torte! It features a moist chocolate cake and both a rich chocolate filling and a smooth cream filling.

- 2/3 cup butter
- 4 squares (1 ounce *each*) unsweetened chocolate
- 1-1/3 cups all-purpose flour
- 1-3/4 cups sugar
- 1 teaspoon baking soda
- 1/4 teaspoon baking powder
- 1-1/4 cups water
- 1 teaspoon vanilla extract
- 3 eggs

CHOCOLATE FILLING:
- 2 bars (4 ounces *each*) German sweet chocolate, *divided*
- 3/4 cup butter
- 1/2 cup chopped pecans

Splitting Cakes into Layers

Using a ruler, mark the center of the side of the cake with a toothpick. Continue inserting toothpicks around the cake. Using the toothpicks as a guide, cut the cake horizontally in half with a long serrated knife. Carefully remove the top half. Frost or fill the bottom half as recipe instructs and replace the top cut side down.

Apricot Hazelnut Torte

This pretty torte is a nice change from the usual chocolate desserts.

- 4 **eggs, *separated***
- 1 **cup ground hazelnuts**
- 3/4 **cup all-purpose flour**
- 2 **teaspoons baking powder**
- 1/2 **teaspoon salt**
- 2 **tablespoons water**
- 1 **teaspoon vanilla extract**
- 1 **cup sugar, *divided***
- 2 **cups heavy whipping cream**
- 1/4 **cup confectioners' sugar**
- 2/3 **cup pureed canned apricots**
- 1/2 **cup apricot jam, warmed**

Whipped cream, sliced apricots and whole *or* chopped hazelnuts, optional

1 Let eggs stand at room temperature for 30 minutes. Line two greased 9-in. round baking pans with waxed paper; grease the paper and set aside. In a bowl, combine the hazelnuts, flour, baking powder and salt; set aside. In a large mixing bowl, beat the egg yolks, water and vanilla until lemon-colored. Gradually add 3/4 cup sugar; set aside. In a small mixing bowl and with clean beaters, beat egg whites on medium speed until soft peaks form. Gradually add remaining sugar, 1 tablespoon at a time, beating on high until stiff peaks form. Fold a fourth of the dry ingredients into egg yolk mixture. Repeat three times. Fold in egg white mixture.

2 Spread batter evenly into prepared pans. Bake at 350° for 20-25 minutes or until cake springs back when lightly touched. Cool for 10 minutes before removing from pans to wire racks to cool completely.

3 In a chilled large mixing bowl, beat cream until it begins to thicken. Add confectioners' sugar; beat until stiff peaks form. Fold in apricots. Split each cake into two horizontal layers. Spread filling between layers and over sides of torte. Spread jam over the top. Garnish with whipped cream, apricots and hazelnuts if desired. Store in the refrigerator. **Yield:** 12-14 servings.

—*Enid Stoehr, Emsdale, Ontario*

Apricot Hazelnut Torte

Chocolate Whipping Cream Torte

This recipe uses unsweetened chocolate, which is also called baking or bitter chocolate.

- 1/2 **cup butter**
- 3 **squares (1 ounce *each*) unsweetened chocolate**
- 1-1/2 **cups heavy whipping cream**
- 4 **eggs, lightly beaten**
- 1 **teaspoon vanilla extract**
- 2 **cups all-purpose flour**
- 1-1/2 **cups sugar**
- 2 **teaspoons baking powder**
- 1/2 **teaspoon salt**

FILLING:
- 1 **cup heavy whipping cream**
- 1 **package (8 ounces) cream cheese, softened**
- 1 **cup confectioners' sugar**
- 1 **teaspoon vanilla extract**

FROSTING:
- 1/4 **cup butter**
- 2 **squares (1 ounce *each*) unsweetened chocolate**
- 1/2 **cup heavy whipping cream**

1 teaspoon vanilla extract
3 cups confectioners' sugar
Fresh strawberries, optional

1 In a heavy saucepan or microwave, melt butter and chocolate; stir until smooth. Cool. In a chilled large mixing bowl, beat cream until soft peaks form. Add the eggs, vanilla and cooled chocolate mixture; beat on low speed just until combined. Combine the flour, sugar, baking powder and salt; add to chocolate mixture just until combined.

2 Pour into three greased and floured 9-in. round baking pans. Bake at 350° for 20-25 minutes or until a toothpick inserted near the center comes out clean. Cool for 10 minutes before removing from pans to wire racks to cool completely. Wrap cakes in plastic wrap; refrigerate for 1 hour or until chilled.

3 For filling, beat cream in a chilled small mixing bowl until soft peaks form; set aside. In a large mixing bowl, beat cream cheese until smooth. Beat in confectioners' sugar and vanilla. Add whipped cream; beat until smooth.

4 Split each cake into two horizontal layers. Place one layer on a serving plate; top with about 1/2 cup filling. Repeat four times. Top with remaining cake layer. Cover and refrigerate.

5 For frosting, melt butter and chocolate in a heavy saucepan or microwave; stir until smooth. Cool to room temperature; transfer to a large mixing bowl. Add cream and vanilla; mix well. Beat in confectioners' sugar. Spread over top and sides of cake. Garnish with strawberries if desired. Store in the refrigerator. **Yield:** 12-14 servings. —*Rita Futral*
Ocean Springs, Mississippi

Pretty Pineapple Torte

(Also pictured on page 92)

Pineapple stars in both the cake and filling in this tall, beautiful dessert.

3 eggs, *separated*
1/2 cup butter, softened
1 cup sugar, *divided*
1 can (20 ounces) crushed pineapple
1 teaspoon vanilla extract
2-1/2 cups cake flour
2 teaspoons baking powder
1/2 teaspoon baking soda

Pretty Pineapple Torte

1/2 teaspoon salt
FILLING:
1-1/2 cups heavy whipping cream
1/4 cup confectioners' sugar
1/2 teaspoon almond extract
2 tablespoons slivered almonds, toasted

1 Let eggs stand at room temperature for 30 minutes. In a large mixing bowl, cream butter and 3/4 cup sugar until light and fluffy. Beat in egg yolks. Drain pineapple, reserving 2/3 cup juice. In a bowl, combine the juice, 3/4 cup pineapple and vanilla (set remaining pineapple aside for the filling). Combine the flour, baking powder, baking soda and salt; add to the creamed mixture alternately with pineapple mixture, beating well after each addition. In a small mixing bowl and with clean beaters, beat egg whites on medium speed until soft peaks form. Gradually add remaining sugar, 1 tablespoon at a time, beating on high until stiff peaks form. Fold a fourth of the egg whites into batter; fold in remaining whites.

2 Spoon into two greased and floured 9-in. round baking pans. Bake at 350° for 28-32 minutes or until cake springs back when lightly touched. Cool for 10 minutes before removing from pans to wire racks to cool completely.

3 For filling, beat the cream, confectioners' sugar and extract in a chilled large mixing bowl until stiff peaks form. Fold in reserved pineapple. Split each cake into two horizontal layers. Spread about 3/4 cup filling between each layer; spread remaining filling over top. Sprinkle with almonds. Store in the refrigerator. **Yield:** 10-12 servings. —*Iola Egle, McCook, Nebraska*

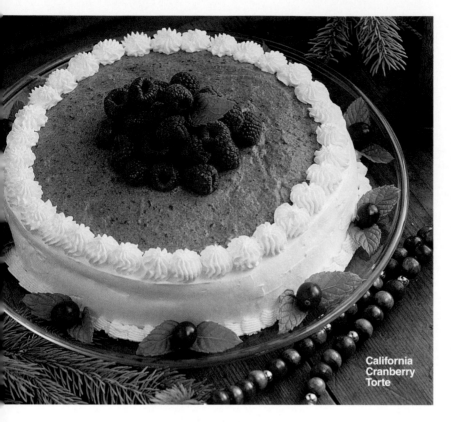

California
Cranberry
Torte

3 Insert a 1/2-in. round pastry tip, #A1, in a pastry bag or heavy-duty plastic bag. Fill bag with meringue. Starting in the center of each circle on prepared sheets, pipe meringue in a spiral pattern until circle is completely filled. Bake at 250° for 1 hour. Turn oven off and let meringue dry in oven for 1 hour with door closed.

4 Meanwhile, in a saucepan, melt cranberry sauce over medium heat. Add gelatin powder; stir until dissolved. Cool. In a chilled large mixing bowl, beat cream and confectioners' sugar; fold 1 cup into cranberry mixture.

5 To assemble, place 1 tablespoon of whipped cream in the center of serving plate to hold meringue in place. Top with a meringue shell; spread a third of the cranberry mixture on top. Repeat with remaining meringues and cranberry mixture. Frost sides with reserved whipped cream. If desired, a pastry bag can be used to decorate edges of torte. Refrigerate for 6 hours or overnight. Garnish with berries and mint just before serving. Refrigerate leftovers. **Yield:** 12-16 servings. —*Pat Parsons Bakersfield, California*

California Cranberry Torte

Three meringue layers serve as the "cake" in this pretty dessert. A cool cranberry filling is just right for the holidays.

>   6 **egg whites**
> **Pinch salt**
>   1/4 **teaspoon cream of tartar**
>   1-1/2 **cups sugar**
>   1 **teaspoon vanilla extract**
>   1 **can (16 ounces) jellied cranberry sauce**
>   2 **tablespoons raspberry gelatin powder**
>   1-1/2 **cups heavy whipping cream**
>   2 **tablespoons confectioners' sugar**
> **Fresh cranberries, raspberries and mint**

1 Let egg whites stand at room temperature for 30 minutes. Line baking sheets with parchment paper. Draw three 8 in. circles on the paper; set aside.

2 In a large mixing bowl, beat the egg whites, salt and cream of tartar on medium speed until soft peaks form. Gradually add sugar, 2 tablespoons at a time, beating on high for 5 minutes or until stiff peaks form. Add vanilla.

Piping Meringue into a Disk

Make meringue according to recipe directions. Cut a small hole in the corner of a pastry or resealable plastic bag. Insert a 1/2-in. round decorating tip (#A1).

Fill bag about half full with meringue. Smooth filling down toward the decorating tip to eliminate air bubbles, which will cause breaks in the design when piping. Twist top of bag shut.

Line a baking sheet with parchment or waxed paper and draw 8-in. circles on paper. Hold the pastry bag straight up and position the tip about 1/8 to 1/4 in. above the baking sheet. Starting at the middle of a circle, pipe meringue in a spiral until the circle is completely filled. Stop squeezing before you lift the tip from the baking sheet.

California
Cranberry
Torte

Southern Fruitcake

One story of fruitcake dates back to the 1700s and the nut harvests in Europe. After the harvest, some nuts were used to make a fruitcake, which was saved until the next year. Then it would be eaten to bring good luck for another successful harvest.

       4 **cups chopped pecans**
1-3/4 **cups chopped candied pineapple**
1-1/2 **cups chopped dried peaches *or* apricots**
1-1/2 **cups golden raisins**
       2 **cups all-purpose flour, *divided***
       1 **cup butter, softened**
       1 **cup packed brown sugar**
       5 **eggs**
       1 **cup peach *or* apricot nectar, *divided***
   1/2 **cup honey**
   1/4 **cup milk**
1-1/2 **teaspoons ground cinnamon**
   3/4 **teaspoon baking powder**
   1/2 **teaspoon salt**
   1/2 **teaspoon ground allspice**

1 Grease and flour two 9-in. x 5-in. x 3-in. loaf pans. Line the bottoms with waxed paper; grease and flour the paper. Set aside. Combine the pecans, pineapple, peaches, raisins and 1/2 cup flour; set aside.

2 In a large mixing bowl, cream butter and brown sugar until light and fluffy. Add eggs, one at a time, beating well after each addition. Add 1/2 cup peach nectar, honey and milk; beat well (mixture will appear curdled). Combine the cinnamon, baking powder, salt, allspice and remaining flour; add to creamed mixture and mix well. Add pecan mixture; stir well.

3 Pour into prepared pans. Bake at 325° for 1-1/2 hours or until a toothpick inserted near the center comes out clean. Cool for 10 minutes. With a skewer, poke holes in the loaves. Spoon remaining nectar over loaves. Cool

10 minutes longer before removing from pans to a wire rack to cool completely. Wrap tightly and store in a cool place. Slice and bring to room temperature before serving. **Yield:** 2 loaves.
—Ruth Marie Lyons
Boulder, Colorado

Cherry Date Fruitcake

Brushing the baked fruitcakes with corn syrup adds a little extra sweetness, making each slice finger-licking good!

1-1/2 **cups all-purpose flour**
1-1/2 **cups sugar**
       1 **teaspoon baking powder**
       1 **teaspoon salt**
5-1/2 **cups pecan halves**
       2 **jars (16 ounces *each*) maraschino cherries, drained and halved**
       1 **pound diced candied pineapple**
       2 **packages (8 ounces *each*) chopped pitted dates**
       6 **eggs**
   1/2 **cup apple juice**
   1/4 **cup light corn syrup**

1 Line two 9-in. x 5-in. x 3-in. loaf pans with foil; grease the foil and set aside. In a large bowl, combine the flour, sugar, baking powder and salt. Add the pecans, cherries, pineapple and dates; toss to coat. Beat eggs and apple juice; add to fruit mixture and mix well.

2 Pat into prepared pans. Bake at 300° for 1-3/4 to 2 hours or until a toothpick inserted near the center comes out clean. Cool for 10 minutes before removing from pans to wire racks. Carefully peel off foil. Brush each loaf with corn syrup. Cool completely. **Yield:** 2 loaves.
—Judy Schultz, Jamestown, New York

Southern
Fruitcake

Foam cakes

secrets for successful foam cakes

- Measure ingredients accurately, using the measuring tools and techniques suggested on pages 8 and 9.

- When baking foam cakes in tube pans, set the oven rack in the lowest position.

- Preheat oven for 10 to 15 minutes before baking.

- Separate eggs when they are cold. (See Separating Eggs on page 15.)

- To ensure egg whites reach their maximum volume, they should stand at room temperature no more than 30 minutes before beating. Also, make sure there are no specks of egg yolk in the white.

- Before beating egg whites, make sure your mixing bowl and beaters are clean by washing them thoroughly in hot soap water and drying with a clean kitchen towel. Use metal or glass mixing bowls. Plastic bowls, even freshly washed and dried ones, may have an oily film on them.

- Beat whole eggs or egg yolks until they are thick and lemon-colored.

- Gently fold in the ingredients. Using a rubber spatula, gently cut down through the ingredients/batter, move across the bottom of the bowl and bring up part of the mixture. (See Folding in Ingredients on page 136.)

- Use only the pan size recommended in the recipe.

- For a tender golden crust, use aluminum pans with a dull rather than a shiny or dark finish.

- Do not grease or flour tube pans when baking foam cakes. To rise properly, the batter needs to cling to the sides of the pan.

- To avoid large air pockets in a baked cake, cut through the batter with a knife to break air bubbles.

- Use a kitchen timer. Foam cakes are done when the top springs back when touched and the cracks at the top of the cake look and feel dry. (See Testing Foam Cakes for Doneness on page 125.)

- It's important to cool foam cakes upside down in the pan, otherwise they will collapse and flatten. If using a tube pan with legs, invert the pan onto its legs. If using a tube pan without legs, invert the pan and place the neck over a funnel or narrow bottle. (See Cooling a Foam Cake on page 127.)

- Cool cakes completely in the pan before removing. To loosen from the pan, run a thin metal spatula around the edge of the pan and around the center tube using a sawing motion. Gently press the metal spatula between the pan and the cake to loosen more. If the cake pan has a removable bottom, lift out the cake and run a knife along the bottom of the cake. If the pan is one piece, invert the pan onto a plate; tap the side of the pan with the flat side of a knife and lift the pan away from the cake.

- Cool the cake completely before filling or frosting.

- Cut foam cakes with a serrated knife or electric knife with a sawing motion.

Lemon Angel Food Supreme

1 Let egg whites stand at room temperature for 30 minutes. Sift cake flour and 3/4 cup plus 2 tablespoons sugar together twice; set aside. In a large mixing bowl, beat egg whites, cream of tartar, extracts and salt on medium speed until soft peaks form. Gradually add remaining sugar, 2 tablespoons at a time, beating on high until stiff peaks form. Gradually fold in flour mixture, about a fourth at a time.

2 Gently spoon into an ungreased 10-in. tube pan. Cut through the batter with a knife to remove air pockets. Bake on the lowest rack at 375° for 30-35 minutes or until top springs back when lightly touched and cracks feel dry. Immediately invert baking pan; cool completely. Run a knife around sides and center tube of pan. Invert cake onto a serving plate.

3 For sauce, beat eggs and sugar in a heavy saucepan over low heat. Stir in the lemon juice, butter and lemon peel. Cook until the mixture thickens and reaches 160°, about 15 minutes; chill. Fold in whipped cream and food coloring if desired. Serve with cake. Store sauce in the refrigerator. **Yield:** 12-16 servings.

—*Linda Blaska, Dunwoody, Georgia*

Lemon Angel Food Supreme

This delicate cake topped with a tart, creamy lemon sauce is perfect for folks who want a little lighter dessert.

1-1/2 cups egg whites (about 12)
   1 cup cake flour
1-1/2 cups plus 2 tablespoons sugar, *divided*
1-1/2 teaspoons cream of tartar
1-1/2 teaspoons vanilla extract
  1/2 teaspoon lemon extract
  1/4 teaspoon salt
LEMON SAUCE:
   3 eggs
   1 cup sugar
  1/2 cup lemon juice
  1/4 cup butter, melted
   1 tablespoon grated lemon peel
  1/2 cup heavy whipping cream, whipped
Yellow food coloring, optional

Testing Foam Cakes for Doneness

Foam cakes are done when the top springs back when touched with your finger and the cracks at the top of the cake look and feel dry.

Homemade Angel Food Cake

Nothing can compare to the heavenly taste of homemade angel food cake. You can skip the frosting and serve slices with fresh fruit and sweetened whipped cream.

- 1-1/2 **cups egg whites (about 12)**
- 1 **cup cake flour**
- 1 **cup confectioners' sugar**
- 1 **teaspoon cream of tartar**
- 1 **teaspoon vanilla extract**

Pinch salt

- 1-1/4 **cups sugar**

FROSTING:

- 1 **plain milk chocolate candy bar (7 ounces)**
- 2 **cups heavy whipping cream**
- 3 **tablespoons confectioners' sugar**
- 1 **teaspoon vanilla extract**

Chocolate shavings, optional

1 Let egg whites stand at room temperature for 30 minutes. Sift flour and confectioners' sugar together twice; set aside. In a large mixing bowl, beat the egg whites, cream of tartar, vanilla and salt on medium speed until soft peaks form. Gradually add sugar, about 2 tablespoons at a time, beating on high until stiff glossy peaks form and sugar is dissolved. Gradually fold in flour mixture, about 1/2 cup at a time.

2 Gently spoon into an ungreased 10-in. tube pan. Cut through the batter with a knife to remove air pockets. Bake on the lowest rack at 325° for 50-60 minutes or until top springs back when lightly touched and cracks feel dry. Immediately invert baking pan; cool completely.

3 For frosting, melt the candy bar in a heavy saucepan or microwave; stir until smooth. Cool for 5 minutes. In a chilled large mixing bowl, beat cream until it begins to thicken. Add confectioners' sugar; beat until stiff peaks form. Stir in vanilla. Fold in melted chocolate.

4 Run a knife around sides and center tube of pan. Invert cake onto a serving plate; frost top and sides. Garnish with chocolate shavings if desired. Store in the refrigerator. **Yield:** 12-16 servings. —*Joan Schroeder Pinedale, Wyoming*

Chocolate Angel Food Cake

Chocolate Angel Food Cake

To achieve the look of the frosting in the photo above, refer to the cake comb technique in Simple Frosting Finishes on page 141.

- 1-1/2 **cups egg whites (about 12)**
- 3/4 **cup cake flour**
- 1-1/2 **cups plus 2 tablespoons sugar,** *divided*
- 1/4 **cup baking cocoa**
- 1-1/2 **teaspoons cream of tartar**
- 1-1/2 **teaspoons vanilla extract**
- 1/4 **teaspoon salt**

Rich 'n' Fluffy Chocolate Frosting (page 140), optional

1 Let egg whites stand at room temperature for 30 minutes. Sift flour, 3/4 cup plus 2 tablespoons sugar and cocoa together twice; set aside. In a large mixing bowl, beat the egg whites, cream of tartar, vanilla and salt on medium speed until soft peaks form. Gradually add remaining sugar, about 2 tablespoons at a time, beating on high until stiff glossy peaks form and sugar is dissolved. Gradually fold in the flour mixture, about 1/2 cup at a time.

2 Gently spoon into an ungreased 10-in. tube pan. Cut through the batter with a knife to remove air pockets. Bake on the lowest rack at 350° for 45-50 minutes or until the top springs back when lightly touched and cracks feel dry. Immediately invert baking pan; cool completely.

3 Run a knife around the sides and center tube of pan. Invert cake onto a serving plate. Frost if desired. If frosted, store in the refrigerator. **Yield:** 12-16 servings.
—Mary Ann Iverson, Woodville, Wisconsin

yellow batter over orange layer (do not mix). Spoon green batter over yellow layer. Bake on the lowest rack at 375° for 30-35 minutes or until top springs back when lightly touched and cracks feel dry. Immediately invert baking pan; cool completely. Run a knife around sides and center tube of pan. Invert cake onto a serving plate. Combine confectioners' sugar and milk until smooth; drizzle over cake. **Yield:** 12-16 servings.
—Pat Habiger, Spearville, Kansas

Rainbow Angel Food Cake

Bring the colors of spring flowers to your table with this attractive angel food cake. On the Fourth of July, keep a third of the batter plain, then tint one third red and another third blue.

1-1/2 cups egg whites (about 12)
    1 cup cake flour
1-1/2 cups sugar, *divided*
1-1/2 teaspoons cream of tartar
1-1/2 teaspoons vanilla extract
    1/2 teaspoon almond extract
    1/4 teaspoon salt
Red, yellow and green food coloring
1-1/2 cups confectioners' sugar
    2 to 3 tablespoons milk

1 Let egg whites stand at room temperature for 30 minutes. Sift flour and 3/4 cup sugar together twice; set aside. In a large mixing bowl, beat the egg whites, cream of tartar, extracts and salt on medium speed until soft peaks form. Gradually add remaining sugar, 2 tablespoons at a time, beating on high until stiff glossy peaks form and sugar is dissolved. Gradually fold in flour mixture, a fourth at a time.

2 Divide batter into three bowls. To the first bowl, add 1 drop red and 1 drop yellow food coloring. To the second bowl, add 2 drops yellow food coloring. To the third bowl, add 2 drops green food coloring. Fold food coloring into each batter.

3 Spoon orange batter into an ungreased 10-in. tube pan; carefully spread to cover bottom. Spoon

Cooling a Foam Cake

If your tube pan has legs, invert the pan onto its legs until the cake is completely cool.

If your tube pan does not have legs, place pan over a funnel or the neck of a narrow bottle until cake is completely cool.

Rainbow Angel Food Cake

Lemon Daffodil Cake

You're sure to impress dinner guests when you present this eye-catching sponge cake. A light lemon filling and frosting make it a perfect springtime dessert.

1-1/4 **cups egg whites (about 10)**
   1 **teaspoon cream of tartar**
1/2 **teaspoon salt**
1-1/3 **cups sugar**
   1 **cup all-purpose flour**
1/2 **teaspoon vanilla extract**
   4 **egg yolks**
1/4 **teaspoon almond extract**
LEMON FILLING:
   1 **tablespoon unflavored gelatin**
3/4 **cup cold water,** *divided*
   1 **cup sugar**
   3 **tablespoons cornstarch**
   4 **egg yolks, beaten**
1/3 **cup butter**
   2 **tablespoons grated lemon peel**
1/2 **cup lemon juice**
   1 **cup heavy whipping cream, whipped**

1 Let egg whites stand at room temperature for 30 minutes. In a large mixing bowl, beat the egg whites, cream of tartar and salt on medium speed until soft peaks form. Gradually add sugar, 2 tablespoons at a time, beating on high until stiff glossy peaks form and sugar is dissolved. Fold in flour, 1/4 cup at a time. Divide mix-ture in half. Fold vanilla into one portion; set aside. In another large mixing bowl, beat egg yolks on high speed until thick and lemon-colored. Stir in almond extract. Fold in unflavored egg white batter.

2 Alternately spoon batters into an ungreased 10-in. tube pan. Gently cut through batter with a knife to swirl. Bake on the lowest rack at 325° for 50-60 minutes or until top springs back when lightly touched. Immediately invert pan; cool completely.

3 For filling, soften gelatin in 1/4 cup cold water; let stand for 1 minute. In a heavy saucepan, combine the sugar, cornstarch and remaining water until smooth. Bring to a boil over medium heat; cook and stir 2 minutes longer. Remove from the heat. Gradually stir 1/2 cup hot filling into egg yolks; return all to the pan, stirring constantly. Bring to a gentle boil, stirring constantly. Cook and stir 2 minutes longer. Remove from the heat; stir in butter and lemon peel. Gently stir in lemon juice and softened gelatin until gelatin is dissolved.

4 Cool to room temperature without stirring. Fold in whipped cream. Refrigerate until mixture achieves spreading consistency, about 40-50 minutes.

5 Run a knife around sides and center tube of pan. Remove cake; split into two horizontal layers. Spread filling between layers and over top of cake. Store in the refrigerator. **Yield:** 12 servings. —*Eunice Richardson Shullsburg, Wisconsin*

**Lemon
Daffodil
Cake**

Confetti Cream Cake

Luscious layers of cake and creamy filling form this attractive dessert. If you're short on time, ready the filling ingredients a day ahead. Then assemble and frost right before serving.

   5 **eggs**
   1 **teaspoon vanilla extract**
   1 **cup sugar**
   1 **cup all-purpose flour**
1/2 **teaspoon baking powder**
1/2 **teaspoon salt**
FILLING:
   1 **package (8 ounces) cream cheese, softened**
   1 **cup sugar,** *divided*
   1 **teaspoon vanilla extract**
1/4 **teaspoon ground cinnamon**
   1 **cup (8 ounces) sour cream**
1/2 **cup finely chopped walnuts**

1/2 cup flaked coconut, optional
1/3 cup chopped maraschino cherries
2 milk chocolate candy bars (1.55 ounces *each*), shaved or finely chopped
1-1/2 cups heavy whipping cream

1 In a large mixing bowl, beat eggs and vanilla on high speed until foamy. Add sugar; beat until thick and lemon-colored. Combine the flour, baking powder and salt; fold into egg mixture, a third at a time.

2 Pour into two greased and floured 9-in. round baking pans. Bake at 350° for 25-30 minutes or until top springs back when lightly touched. Cool for 5 minutes before removing from pans to wire racks to cool completely.

3 In a large mixing bowl, beat the cream cheese, 2/3 cup sugar, vanilla and cinnamon until smooth. Stir in the sour cream, walnuts, coconut if desired and cherries. Fold in chocolate. In a chilled large mixing bowl, beat cream until it begins to thicken. Add remaining sugar; beat until soft peaks form. Fold half of the whipped cream into the cream cheese mixture. Set remaining whipped cream aside.

4 Split each cake into two horizontal layers; spread a fourth of the cream cheese mixture on one layer. Repeat. Frost sides with reserved whipped cream. Store in the refrigerator. **Yield:** 10-12 servings.
—*Jennie Moshier, Fresno, California*

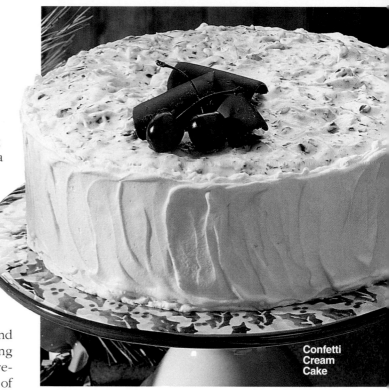

Confetti Cream Cake

Chocolate Sponge Cake

Every bite of this cake has a mild chocolate flavor that will appeal to all palates. Enjoy it dusted with confectioners' sugar or topped with Rich 'n' Fluffy Chocolate Frosting on page 140.

6 eggs, *separated*
1/2 cup orange juice
1 teaspoon vanilla extract
1-1/2 cups sugar, *divided*
1 cup all-purpose flour
1/3 cup baking cocoa
1/2 teaspoon cream of tartar

1 Let eggs stand at room temperature for 30 minutes. In a large mixing bowl, beat egg yolks until slightly thickened and lemon-colored, about 5 minutes. Stir in orange juice and vanilla until combined. Gradually beat in 1 cup sugar on low speed, about 2 tablespoons at a time, beating well after each addition. Beat on high until mixture thickens and nearly doubles in volume. Combine the flour and cocoa. Fold a fourth of the flour mixture into the yolk mixture. Repeat with remaining flour mixture; set aside.

2 In a large mixing bowl and with clean beaters, beat egg whites and cream of tartar on medium speed until soft peaks form. Gradually beat in remaining sugar, about 1 tablespoon at a time, on high until stiff glossy peaks form and sugar is dissolved. Fold a fourth of the egg whites into the yolk mixture; fold in remaining whites.

3 Pour into an ungreased 10-in. tube pan. Bake at 325° for 55-60 minutes or until top springs back when lightly touched. Immediately invert pan; cool completely. Run a knife around sides and center tube of pan; remove cake. **Yield:** 12 servings.

Flourless Chocolate Cake

*One bite of fudgy Flourless Chocolate Cake and you'll
see why it's pure pleasure for confirmed chocoholics! A
small slice of this rich, dense dessert goes a long way.*

    4 eggs, *separated*
   10 tablespoons butter
  1/2 cup sugar, *divided*
    6 squares (1 ounce *each*) semisweet chocolate,
      chopped
    3 squares (1 ounce *each*) unsweetened
      chocolate, chopped
    2 teaspoons vanilla extract
  1/4 cup finely ground pecans, toasted
Chocolate Ganache (page 139), optional
Sliced strawberries and fresh mint, optional

1 Let eggs stand at room temperature for 30 minutes.
In a heavy saucepan, melt butter, 1/4 cup sugar
and chocolate over low heat, stirring constantly. Cool
until mixture is lukewarm. In a large mixing bowl, beat
egg yolks until thick and lemon-colored, about 3 minutes. Beat in vanilla. Gradually beat in pecans and
chocolate mixture. In a small mixing bowl and with
clean beaters, beat egg whites on medium speed until
soft peaks form. Gradually add remaining sugar, 1 tablespoon at a time, beating on high speed until stiff peaks
form. Stir a small amount of whites into chocolate mixture. Fold in remaining whites.

2 Pour into a greased 9-in. springform pan. Place on
a baking sheet. Bake at 350° for 40-50 minutes or
until a toothpick inserted near the center comes out with
a few moist crumbs. Cool on a wire rack for 20 minutes.
Carefully run a knife around edge of pan to loosen; remove sides of pan and cool completely. Frost with
Chocolate Ganache if desired. Garnish with strawberries
and mint if desired. **Yield:** 16 servings.

**Flourless
Chocolate Cake**

Classic Sponge Torte

*Sponge cakes call for both egg whites and egg
yolks, giving them a richer texture than angel food
cakes. Here, the layered cake is topped
with a delightful chocolate frosting.*

  6 eggs, *separated*
  1 cup sugar, *divided*
  2 teaspoons vanilla extract

Pinch salt
  1 cup cake flour
FROSTING:
  1 cup butter, softened
  2 cups confectioners' sugar
  4 squares (1 ounce *each*) semisweet chocolate,
    melted
  3 tablespoons milk
  1 teaspoon vanilla extract

1 cup heavy whipping cream
Grated chocolate, optional

1 Let eggs stand at room temperature for 30 minutes. Line two greased 9-in. round baking pans with waxed paper; grease and flour the waxed paper. Set aside. In a large mixing bowl, beat egg yolks for 2 minutes. Add 3/4 cup sugar; beat for 3 minutes or until mixture is thick and lemon-colored and falls in a ribbon from beaters. Beat in vanilla.

2 In another large mixing bowl and with clean beaters, beat egg whites and salt on medium speed until soft peaks form. Gradually add remaining sugar, 1 tablespoon at a time, beating on high until stiff peaks form. Fold flour into egg yolk a third at a time. Stir in a third of the whites. Fold in remaining whites.

3 Spread batter into prepared pans. Bake at 350° for 15-18 minutes or until top springs back when lightly touched. Cool for 10 minutes before removing from pans to wire racks to cool completely.

4 For frosting, in a large mixing bowl, beat the butter, confectioners' sugar, chocolate, milk and vanilla until smooth. In a chilled small mixing bowl, beat cream until stiff peaks form; fold into chocolate mixture.

5 To assemble, split each cake into two horizontal layers. Spread frosting between layers and over top and sides of cake. Sprinkle with grated chocolate if desired. Store in the refrigerator. **Yield:** 12 servings.

—Kathy Wells, Brodhead, Wisconsin

Making a Sponge Cake

1. Beat egg yolks in a mixing bowl until they begin to thicken. Gradually add 3/4 cup sugar, beating until the mixture is lemon-colored (shown at right). Blend in flavorings. Sift together flour and salt; beat into egg yolk mixture.

2. In another mixing bowl, beat egg whites on medium speed until soft peaks form. Gradually add sugar, beating on high until stiff peaks form.

3. Spoon a fourth of the egg white mixture into the yolk mixture; carefully fold in with a rubber spatula. Fold in the remaining egg white mixture just until combined. Don't overmix. Proceed with the recipe as directed.

Rainbow Sherbet Cake Roll

A cake roll doesn't have to be complicated, especially when you start out with an angel food cake mix. For added convenience, this sherbet-filled dessert can be kept in the freezer for weeks.

1 package (16 ounces) one-step angel food
cake mix
1 to 2 tablespoons confectioners' sugar
1/2 gallon berry rainbow sherbet

1 Coat two 15-in. x 10-in. x 1-in. baking pans with nonstick cooking spray; line pans with waxed paper and spray the paper. Prepare cake mix according to package directions; spread batter into prepared pans. Bake at 375° for 18-22 minutes or until the top springs back when lightly touched. Cool in pans for 5 minutes.

2 Turn each cake onto a kitchen towel dusted with confectioners' sugar. Gently peel off waxed paper. Roll up cakes in the towels jelly-roll style, starting with a short side. Cool completely on a wire rack.

3 Unroll cakes; spread each with 4 cups sherbet to within 1/2 in. of edges. Roll up again. Place seam side down on plastic wrap. Wrap securely; freeze until firm, about 6 hours. Remove from the freezer 15 minutes before serving. Cut into 1-in. slices. Freeze leftovers. **Yield:** 2 cake rolls (10 servings each). *—Karen Edland McHenry, North Dakota*

Gingerbread Cake Roll

Instead of making ordinary gingerbread, turn it into this awesome cake roll. The creamy spiced filling is a delightful complement to the moist cake.

  3 eggs, *separated*
1/2 cup molasses
  1 tablespoon butter, melted
1/4 cup sugar
  1 cup all-purpose flour
1/4 teaspoon baking soda
1/2 teaspoon *each* ground cinnamon, ginger and
     cloves
1/8 teaspoon salt
  1 to 2 tablespoons confectioners' sugar
SPICED CREAM FILLING:
1-1/2 cups heavy whipping cream
1/3 cup confectioners' sugar
  1 teaspoon ground cinnamon
  1 teaspoon vanilla extract
1/4 teaspoon ground cloves
Additional ground cinnamon, optional

1 Let eggs stand at room temperature for 30 minutes. Line a greased 15-in. x 10-in. x 1-in. baking pan with waxed paper; grease and flour the paper. Set aside. In a large mixing bowl, beat egg yolks on high speed until thickened, about 3 minutes. Beat in molasses and butter. In a small mixing bowl and with clean beaters, beat egg whites on medium speed until foamy. Gradually add sugar, 1 tablespoon at a time, beating on high

Making a Cake Roll

1. Cool cake in the pan for 5 minutes. Turn out onto a kitchen towel dusted with confectioners' sugar; gently peel off waxed paper. Roll up cake in the towel jelly-roll style, starting with a short side. Cool completely on a wire rack.

2. Unroll cake and spread filling evenly over cake to within 1/2 in. of edges.

3. Starting with a short side, roll up the cake loosely, pulling away the towel. Place seam side down on a serving platter.

Gingerbread
Cake Roll

until soft peaks form. Fold into yolk mixture. Combine the flour, baking soda, spices and salt; gently fold into egg mixture until combined.

2 Spread batter into prepared pan. Bake at 375° for 9-12 minutes or until top springs back when lightly touched. Cool in pan for 5 minutes. Turn cake onto a kitchen towel dusted with confectioners' sugar. Gently peel off waxed paper. Roll up cake in the towel jelly-roll style, starting with a short side. Cool completely on a wire rack.

3 In a chilled large mixing bowl, combine the first five filling ingredients; beat until soft peaks form. Unroll cake; spread half of the filling evenly over cake to within 1/2 in. of edges. Roll up again. Spread remaining filling over cake. Sprinkle with cinnamon if desired. **Yield:** 10 servings.

—Bernadette Colvin, Houston, Texas

Yule Log

This tasty cake stems from a long-standing Christmas tradition. During the Middle Ages, people would cut down a huge tree to burn throughout the holiday season. Later on, folks sweetened the idea by making cakes that resembled the logs.

    4 eggs, *separated*
  1/3 cup sugar
    1 teaspoon vanilla extract
    4 squares (1 ounce *each*)
      semisweet chocolate,
      melted and cooled
  1/3 cup water
  1/2 cup all-purpose flour
    1 teaspoon baking soda
    1 to 2 tablespoons
      confectioners' sugar
    1 can (16 ounces)
      coconut-pecan frosting
    1 can (16 ounces) milk
      chocolate frosting,
      divided
Large marshmallows
Baking cocoa

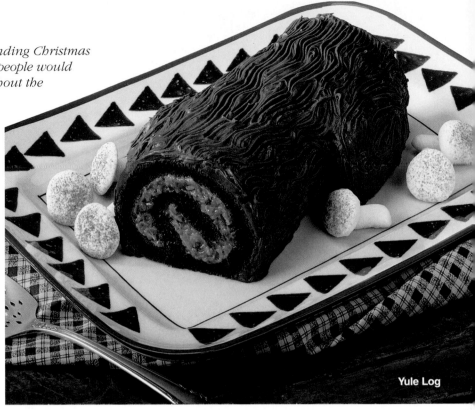

Yule Log

1 Let eggs stand at room temperature for 30 minutes. Line a greased 15-in. x 10-in. x 1-in. baking pan with waxed paper; grease and flour the paper. Set aside. In a large mixing bowl, beat egg yolks, sugar and vanilla on high speed until thick and lemon-colored, about 5 minutes. Beat in chocolate and water on low until blended. Add flour and baking soda; mix well. In a small mixing bowl and with clean beaters, beat egg whites on high speed until stiff peaks form. Fold into the chocolate mixture.

2 Spread evenly into prepared pan. Bake at 375° for 15 minutes or until a toothpick inserted near the center comes out clean. Cool in pan for 5 minutes. Turn cake onto a kitchen towel dusted with confectioners' sugar. Gently peel off waxed paper. Roll up cake in the towel jelly-roll style, starting with a short side. Cool completely on a wire rack.

3 Unroll cake; spread coconut-pecan frosting to within 1 in. of edges. Roll up again. Cut a 3-in. piece from one end of cake roll. Cut the piece diagonally in half. Reserve 2 tablespoons chocolate frosting for mushrooms. Attach diagonal cake slices with a little of the frosting to opposite sides of cake to resemble stumps. Frost entire cake with remaining chocolate frosting. With the tines of a fork, make strokes in the frosting to resemble bark on a tree trunk.

4 For the mushrooms, halve marshmallows crosswise. Flatten half of each marshmallow for cap of mushroom; roll other half between palms of hands for stem. Attach caps to stems with the reserved frosting. Dust tops of mushrooms with cocoa; place around the log. **Yield:** 8 servings.

It's hard to convince a child that in meeting a day's requirement for vegetables, carrot cake doesn't count.

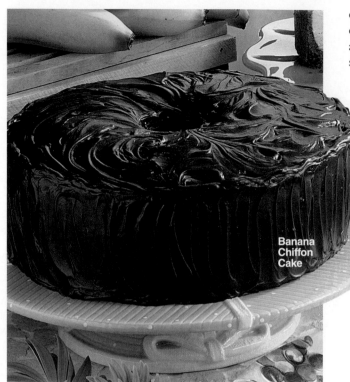

Banana Chiffon Cake

or until top springs back when lightly touched. Immediately invert baking pan; cool completely. Run a knife around sides and center tube of pan. Invert cake onto serving plate; frost top and sides. **Yield:** 12-16 servings.
—*Nancy Horsburgh, Everett, Ontario*

Orange Chiffon Cake

The delicate orange flavor of this simply delicious cake is perfect for rounding out a rich meal. The orange glaze would also be a nice way to top off slices of your favorite angel food cake.

　6 eggs, *separated*
　2 cups all-purpose flour
1-1/2 cups sugar
　1 teaspoon salt
1/2 teaspoon baking soda
3/4 cup fresh orange juice
1/2 cup vegetable oil
　2 tablespoons grated orange peel
1/2 teaspoon cream of tartar
ORANGE GLAZE:
1/2 cup butter
　2 cups confectioners' sugar
　2 to 4 tablespoons fresh orange juice
1/2 teaspoon grated orange peel

1 Let eggs stand at room temperature for 30 minutes. In a large mixing bowl, combine the flour, sugar, salt, and baking soda. In a bowl, whisk the egg yolks, orange juice, oil and orange peel; add to dry ingredients. Beat until well blended. In another large mixing bowl and with clean beaters, beat egg whites and cream of tartar on high speed until stiff peaks form. Fold into orange mixture.

2 Gently spoon batter into an ungreased 10-in. tube pan. Cut through the batter with a knife to remove air pockets. Bake on the lowest rack at 350° for 45-50 minutes or until top springs back when lightly touched. Immediately invert pan; cool completely. Run a knife around sides and center tube of pan. Invert cake onto a serving plate.

3 For glaze, melt butter in a saucepan; add remaining glaze ingredients. Stir until smooth. Pour over the top of cake, allowing it to drizzle down sides. **Yield:** 12-16 servings.　—*Marjorie Ebert, South Dayton, New York*

Banana Chiffon Cake

Stock up on overripe bananas when they're on sale. Freeze them whole and unpeeled in a large resealable plastic bag. Take out what you need from the freezer, then thaw and peel before mashing.

　5 eggs, *separated*
2-1/4 cups cake flour
1-1/2 cups sugar
　1 tablespoon baking powder
　1 teaspoon salt
1/3 cup vegetable oil
1/3 cup water
　1 teaspoon vanilla extract
　1 cup mashed ripe bananas (about 2 medium)
Chocolate frosting *or* frosting of your choice

1 Let eggs stand at room temperature for 30 minutes. In a large mixing bowl, combine the flour, sugar, baking powder and salt. In a bowl, whisk the egg yolks, oil, water and vanilla; add to dry ingredients along with bananas. Beat until well blended. In another large mixing bowl and with clean beaters, beat egg whites on high speed until stiff peaks form. Fold into yolk mixture.

2 Gently spoon batter into an ungreased 10-in. tube pan. Cut through batter with a knife to remove air pockets. Bake on lowest rack at 325° for 60-65 minutes

Tunnel of Berries Cake

A tunnel of strawberries is tucked inside this frosted chiffon cake. Although not overly sweet or heavy, its rich taste makes just one piece satisfying.

      6 eggs, *separated*
2-1/4 cups cake flour
      2 cups sugar, *divided*
      1 tablespoon baking powder
      1 teaspoon ground cinnamon
   3/4 teaspoon salt
   3/4 cup water
   1/2 cup vegetable oil
1-1/2 teaspoons vanilla extract, *divided*
   1/4 teaspoon cream of tartar
      4 cups fresh whole strawberries, *divided*
2-1/2 cups heavy whipping cream

1 Let eggs stand at room temperature for 30 minutes. In a large mixing bowl, combine flour, 1 cup sugar, baking powder, cinnamon and salt. In a bowl, whisk the egg yolks, water, oil and 1 teaspoon vanilla; add to dry ingredients. Beat until well blended. In another large mixing bowl and with clean beaters, beat egg whites and cream of tartar on medium speed until soft peaks form. Fold into yolk mixture.

2 Gently spoon batter into an ungreased 10-in. tube pan. Cut through the batter with a knife to remove air pockets. Bake on the lowest rack at 325° for 60-70

minutes or until top springs back when lightly touched. Immediately invert pan; cool completely. Run a knife around sides and center tube of pan. Invert cake onto a serving plate.

3 Slice off the top 1 in. of the cake; set aside. With a knife, cut a tunnel about 1-1/2 in. deep in bottom of cake, leaving a 3/4-in. shell. Remove cake from tunnel and save for another use. Chop half of the strawberries; set aside. In a chilled large mixing bowl, beat cream until it begins to thicken. Gradually add the remaining sugar and vanilla, beating until stiff peaks form. Combine 1-1/2 cups cream mixture and chopped berries.

4 Fill the tunnel with strawberry mixture. Replace cake top. Frost cake with the remaining cream mixture. Refrigerate. Just before serving, cut the remaining strawberries in half for garnish. Refrigerate leftovers. **Yield:** 12-16 servings.

—Shirley Noe
Lebanon Junction, Kentucky

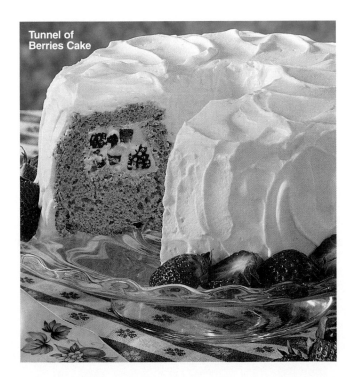

Tunnel of Berries Cake

Filling and Frosting a Tube Cake

1. Cut a 1-in. slice off the top of the cake; carefully set aside. Using a very sharp knife, carve a 1-1/2-in. deep tunnel in the cake, leaving a 3/4-in. wall on all sides. Carefully remove cake and save for another use.

2. Spoon filling into the tunnel.

3. Carefully replace cake top. Frost top and sides of cake. Chill for 2 to 8 hours before serving.

Chocolate Chiffon Cake

If you want to offer family and friends a dessert that really stands out from the rest, this is the cake to make. Beautiful high layers of rich sponge cake are drizzled with a succulent chocolate glaze.

      7 eggs, *separated*
    1/2 cup baking cocoa
    3/4 cup boiling water
  1-3/4 cups cake flour
  1-3/4 cups sugar
    1/2 teaspoon baking soda
      1 teaspoon salt
    1/2 cup vegetable oil
      2 teaspoons vanilla extract
    1/4 teaspoon cream of tartar
ICING:
    1/3 cup butter
      2 cups confectioners' sugar
      2 squares (1 ounce *each*) unsweetened
         chocolate, melted and cooled
  1-1/2 teaspoons vanilla extract
      3 to 4 tablespoons hot water
Chopped nuts, optional

Chocolate Chiffon Cake

1 Let eggs stand at room temperature for 30 minutes. In a bowl, combine the cocoa and water until smooth; cool for 20 minutes. In a large mixing bowl, combine the flour, sugar, baking soda and salt. In a bowl, whisk the egg yolks, oil and vanilla; add to dry ingredients along with the cocoa mixture. Beat until well blended. In another large mixing bowl and with clean beaters, beat egg whites and cream of tartar on high speed until stiff peaks form. Gradually fold into egg yolk mixture.

2 Gently spoon batter into an ungreased 10-in. tube pan. Cut through the batter with a knife to remove air pockets. Bake on lowest rack at 325° for 60-65 minutes or until top springs back when lightly touched. Immediately invert pan; cool completely. Run a knife around sides and center tube of pan. Invert cake onto a serving plate.

3 For icing, melt butter in a saucepan. Remove from the heat; stir in the confectioners' sugar, chocolate, vanilla and water. Drizzle over cake. Sprinkle with nuts if desired. **Yield:** 12-16 servings.
                                                    —*Erma Fox*
                                                Memphis, Missouri

Folding in Ingredients

To fold a lighter mixture into a heavier one, use a rubber spatula to gently cut down through the middle of the ingredients. Move the spatula across the bottom of the bowl and bring up part of the heavier mixture. Repeat this circular motion just until mixture is combined.

Poppy Seed Chiffon Cake

There's just something about the combination of poppy seeds and lemon that people can't resist. With a flavorful frosting, this cake melts in your mouth.

    7 egg whites
2-1/2 cups all-purpose flour
    1 cup sugar
    1 tablespoon baking
      powder
  1/2 teaspoon salt
    5 egg yolks
  3/4 cup water
  1/2 cup vegetable oil
    1 teaspoon lemon
      extract
    1 teaspoon grated lemon
      peel
    1 can (12-1/2 ounces) poppy seed
      filling
  1/2 teaspoon cream of tartar
LEMON BUTTER FROSTING:
    6 tablespoons butter, softened
    4 cups confectioners' sugar
    3 to 5 tablespoons milk
    1 tablespoon lemon juice
    1 teaspoon lemon extract

1 Let egg whites stand at room temperature for 30 minutes. In a large mixing bowl, combine the flour, sugar, baking powder and salt. In a bowl, whisk the egg yolks, water, oil, lemon extract, lemon peel and poppy seed filling. Add to dry ingredients; beat until well blended. In another mixing bowl and with clean beaters, beat egg whites and cream of tartar on high speed until stiff peaks form. Fold into egg yolk mixture.

2 Gently spoon batter into an ungreased 10-in. tube pan. Cut through the batter with a knife to remove air pockets. Bake on the lowest rack at 350° for 55-60 minutes or until top springs back when lightly touched. Immediately invert pan; cool completely. Run a knife around edge and center tube of pan. Invert cake onto a serving plate.

3 For frosting, beat butter and confectioners' sugar in a large mixing bowl. Add the milk, lemon juice and extract; beat until smooth. Frost cake. **Yield:** 12-16 servings.
— *Irene Hirsch, Tustin, California*

problem-Solving pointers for Foam Cakes

If this happens to your cake:	This could be the reason:
Cake is heavy and dense.	Oven temperature was too low. Check temperature with an oven thermometer.
	Didn't use large eggs.
	Ingredients were folded in too vigorously.
	Eggs were underbeaten.
	There was egg yolk in the egg whites before beating.
	Egg whites were beaten in a bowl with a greasy film.
Cake top has sunk.	Oven temperature was too high. Check temperature with an oven thermometer.
	Cake was underbaked.

Flavorful frostings

secrets for successful frosting

- Always sift confectioners' sugar before using it for frosting. If there are any lumps in the sugar, there will be lumps in the frosting, which will clog decorating tips.

- Frosting needs to be just the right consistency for spreading and decorating. If it's too thin, add a little confectioners' sugar. If it's too thick, add a little milk.

- Tint white frosting with liquid, gel or paste food coloring. Liquid will give a pastel color; gel and paste give a deeper color. Add a little at a time, stir in and check the color. You can always add more, but it's hard to lighten the color. The color generally darkens as the frosting dries.

Fluffy White Frosting

Classic Vanilla Buttercream Frosting

This rich, buttery frosting has just the right amount of sweetness. So it's a perfect complement to any flavor of cake.

2/3 cup sugar
1/4 cup water
4 egg yolks, lightly beaten
1 teaspoon vanilla extract
1 cup butter, softened
1/4 cup confectioners' sugar

1 In a heavy saucepan, bring sugar and water to a boil; cook over medium-high heat until sugar is dissolved. Remove from the heat. Add a small amount of hot mixture to egg yolks; return all to the pan, stirring constantly. Cook 2 minutes longer or until mixture thickens, stirring constantly. Remove from the heat; stir in vanilla. Cool to room temperature.

2 In a mixing bowl, cream butter until fluffy. Gradually beat in cooked sugar mixture. Beat in confec-

tioners' sugar. If necessary, refrigerate until frosting reaches spreading consistency. Store in the refrigerator. **Yield:** 2-1/4 cups. —*Elizabeth Blondefield San Jose, California*

Classic Chocolate Buttercream Frosting: Prepare buttercream frosting as directed above and set aside. In a saucepan or microwave, melt 1 cup semisweet chocolate chips with 3 tablespoons water; stir until smooth. Remove from the heat; cool to room temperature. Stir into buttercream frosting. **Yield:** 2-1/4 cups.

Fluffy White Frosting

For a heavenly light and fluffy frosting, you can't top this variation of the classic 7-minute frosting.

1-1/2 cups sugar
2 egg whites
1/3 cup water
1/4 teaspoon cream of tartar
1 teaspoon vanilla extract

In a large heavy saucepan over low heat or double boiler over simmering water, combine the sugar, egg whites, water and cream of tartar. With a portable mixer, beat mixture on low speed for 1 minute. Continue beating on low speed over low heat until frosting reaches 160°, about 8-10 minutes. Pour into a large mixing bowl; add

Filling and Frosting a Layer Cake

1. After the cake layers have completely cooled to room temperature, use a soft pastry brush to carefully remove any loose crumbs on the top and sides of each layer. Trim off any crisp edges with a knife or kitchen scissors.

2. To keep crumbs from loosening from the cake and mixing into the frosting, first spread a very thin layer of frosting over the top and sides. If the frosting is very thick, it may need to be thinned with a teaspoon or two of milk or cream.

3. To keep the serving plate clean, line it with 3-in. strips of waxed paper. Center the first cake layer over the strips. To use frosting as the cake filling, dollop about 1/2 cup frosting over the top of the cake and spread to the edges. Repeat with the second layer, if frosting a three-layer cake.

4. If your cake filling is different from the frosting, it might spill out the edges and discolor the frosting. To prevent this, pipe or spread a 1/2-in. strip of icing around the top edge of each layer before spreading the filling in the center. This keeps the filling inside.

5. Top with the last layer. Frost the sides of the cake, building up the top edge of the cake slightly. Make large swirling strokes in a vertical pattern.

6. Spread remaining frosting over the top of the cake, smoothing right to the edges of the cake. Swirl top to match sides. Garnish or decorate if desired. Carefully remove waxed paper by pulling one piece at a time out from under the cake.

vanilla. Beat on high speed until stiff peaks form, about 7 minutes. **Yield:** about 5 cups.

— *Georgie Bohmann, West Allis, Wisconsin*

Editor's Note: A stand mixer is recommended for beating the frosting after it reaches 160°.

Chocolate Ganache

This smooth satin chocolate frosting will bring a touch of elegance to even the most basic cake. A simple garnish such as fresh fruit, mint leaves or edible flowers adds the finishing touch.

1 cup (6 ounces) semisweet chocolate chips
2/3 cup heavy whipping cream

1 In a heavy saucepan, melt chocolate chips with cream over low heat. Remove from the heat. Refrigerate, stirring occasionally.

2 For a pourable ganache, cool until mixture reaches 85°-90° and is slightly thickened, about 40 minutes. Pour over cake, allowing some to flow down the edges to completely coat. Spread ganache with a spatula if necessary to evenly coat, working quickly before it thickens. Chill until set.

3 For a spreadable ganache, chill until mixture reaches a spreading consistency. Spread over cake. Chill until set. **Yield:** 1-1/4 cups.

frosting amounts for Cakes

	For cooked fluffy frostings, double the amounts needed. Plan on an extra 1/2 to 1 cup frosting to use for decorating.			
Pan Size and Shape	**Between Each Layer**	**Sides**	**Top**	**Total**
8- or 9-in. round, two layers	1/2 cup	1-1/4 cups	3/4 cup	2-1/2 cups
8- or 9-in. square, one layer	—	1 cup	3/4 cup	1-3/4 cups
8- or 9-in. square, two layers	3/4 cup	1-1/2 cups	3/4 cup	3 cups
13- x 9-in. rectangle	—	1 cup	1-1/4 cups	2-1/4 cups
10-in. tube pan (angel food) or 10-in. fluted tube pan (bundt)	—	1-1/2 cups	3/4 cup	2-1/4 cups
24 cupcakes	—	—	2-1/4 cups	2-1/4 cups

Easy Vanilla Buttercream Frosting

This basic buttery frosting has unmatchable homemade taste. With a few simple variations, you can come up with different colors and flavors.

1/2 cup butter, softened
4-1/2 cups confectioners' sugar
1-1/2 teaspoons vanilla extract
5 to 6 tablespoons milk

In a large mixing bowl, cream butter until light and fluffy. Beat in confectioners' sugar and vanilla. Add enough milk to achieve desired consistency. **Yield:** about 3 cups. —*Diana Wilson, Denver, Colorado*

Easy Chocolate Buttercream Frosting: Prepare as directed above, except use 4 cups confectioners' sugar, 1/2 cup baking cocoa and 6-7 tablespoons milk. **Yield:** about 3 cups.

Easy Peanut Butter Frosting: Prepare as directed above, except use 1/2 cup peanut butter instead of the butter and use 6-8 tablespoons milk. **Yield:** about 3 cups.

Easy Lemon Buttercream Frosting: Prepare as directed above, except use 5-6 tablespoons lemon juice instead of the milk and add 1 teaspoon grated lemon peel. **Yield:** about 3 cups.

Easy Orange Buttercream Frosting: Prepare as directed above, except use 5-6 tablespoons orange juice instead of the milk and add 1 teaspoon grated orange peel. **Yield:** about 3 cups.

Easy Almond Buttercream Frosting: Prepare as directed at left, except use 1/2 to 3/4 teaspoon almond extract instead of the vanilla. **Yield:** about 3 cups.

Easy Peppermint Buttercream Frosting: Prepare as directed at left, except use 1/2 to 3/4 teaspoon peppermint extract instead of the vanilla. **Yield:** about 3 cups.

Rich 'n' Fluffy Chocolate Frosting

Whisking up a batch of smooth-as-silk fudgy chocolate icing is a snap using this short recipe and your favorite flavor of baking chips.

1 cup heavy whipping cream
1 cup semisweet chocolate, milk chocolate *or* vanilla *or* white chips
3-3/4 to 4-1/4 cups confectioners' sugar

In a saucepan, bring cream to a simmer, about 180°; remove from the heat. Stir in chips until melted. Place pan in a bowl of ice water; stir constantly until cooled. Gradually whisk in confectioners' sugar until smooth and thick. Store in the refrigerator. **Yield:** 2-1/2 cups. —*Jeanette Mack, Rushville, New York*

Simple Frosting Finishes

To give a little pizzazz without a lot of fuss, try these easy decorating techniques. For the best results, use a fluffy creamy frosting, such as Easy Vanilla Buttercream Frosting (page 140) or Bakery Frosting (below).

Scallops. Smooth frosting over top of cake. Turn a teaspoon tip side down and press the tip in rows across the top of the cake, making scallop marks in frosting.

Waves. Run the tines of a table fork through the frosting in a wavy motion. You can also use a cake comb.

Peaks. Smooth frosting over top and sides of cake. With an icing spatula or small flat metal spatula, press a flat side of the spatula tip in frosting and pull straight up, forming a peak. Repeat over top and sides of cake.

Cake Comb. Smooth frosting over top and sides of cake. It is easier if you can place the cake on a turntable. Hold a cake comb at a 45° angle to the side of the cake and rotate the turntable until entire side of the cake is scored. If a turntable is not available, just sweep the comb around the side of the cake.

For the top of the cake, sweep the comb over the top in a circular pattern.

Swirls. Smooth frosting over top and sides of cake. With the tip of an icing spatula or small flat metal spatula, make a swirling or waving movement over top and sides of cake.

For more texture, use the back of a tablespoon or teaspoon to make a small twisting motion in one direction. Then move the spoon over a little and make another twist in the opposite direction. Repeat until entire cake is covered.

Bakery Frosting

This recipe makes it easy to capture the fabulous flavor of cakes from the best bakeries. A big batch of this sweet frosting keeps for 3 months in the refrigerator.

2 cups shortening
1/2 cup nondairy creamer
1 teaspoon almond extract
1 package (32 ounces) confectioners' sugar
1/2 to 3/4 cup water
Food coloring, optional

In a large mixing bowl, beat the shortening, creamer and extract. Gradually beat in confectioners' sugar. Add enough water until frosting reaches desired consistency. If desired, add food coloring. Store in the refrigerator for up to 3 months. Bring to room temperature before spreading. **Yield:** 8 cups.
—*Barbara Jones*
Pana, Illinois

Fancy Frosting Patterns

Decorate cakes like a pro with decorating tips and pastry or resealable plastic bags. Cut a small hole in the corner of the bag and insert a decorating tip. Reinforce the seal between the bag and tip with tape or use a plastic coupler. The coupler lets you easily change decorating tips. For very simple decorations, you can just snip the corner off of a heavy-duty resealable plastic bag.

   To fill a pastry or resealable plastic bag with frosting, insert a decorating tip if desired and place bag in a measuring cup. Roll down top edge to make a cuff. Fill about half full with frosting. Roll up cuff. Smooth filling down toward tip to remove air bubbles, which will cause breaks in the design when piping. Twist top of bag shut.

Writing, Printing, Vines.
Use a small round tip and hold the bag at a 45° angle. Touch the surface lightly with the tip and squeeze frosting out evenly as you go. Release pressure and touch the cake surface to stop each line, letter or vine.

Drop Flowers or Stars.
Use a flower or star tip and hold the bag at a 90° angle. Position tip just above the surface, and holding tip in place, squeeze bag as flower or star is formed. Stop pressure and pull tip up. Increase or decrease pressure to slightly change the size.

Shell Border. Use a star tip and hold the bag at a 45° angle. Squeeze bag and slightly lift tip as frosting builds and fans out. Relax pressure as you lower tip to make the tail. Stop pressure completely and pull tip away. Work from left to right, resting the head of one shell on the tail of the previous shell.

Leaves. Use a leaf tip and hold the bag at a 45° angle. Touch the surface lightly with the tip, and holding tip in place, squeeze bag to let frosting fan out to create wide base of leaf. Relax and stop pressure as you pull tip away from leaf and draw it up to a point.

Basket Weave Pattern.
With serrated side of a basket weave tip facing up, pipe a vertical line of frosting. Squeeze out a short horizontal bar over the top of the vertical line. Add additional bars, each about a tip width apart, to cover line.

   Make another vertical line of frosting to the right of first one, a tip width apart, overlapping ends of horizontal bars. Repeat the procedure of covering lines with bars by gently tucking tip under the line first to create a basket weave effect.

Favorite White Frosting

This buttery frosting is light enough so it doesn't overpower the fabulous flavor of the cake.

- **2 tablespoons cornstarch**
- **1 cup cold water**
- **1 cup butter, softened**
- **1 cup sugar**
- **1/2 teaspoon almond extract**

1 In a saucepan, combine cornstarch and water until smooth. Bring to a boil over medium heat; cook and stir for 2 minutes or until thickened. Refrigerate for 1 hour.

2 In a large mixing bowl, cream butter and sugar until light and fluffy. Beat in almond extract. Add cornstarch mixture and beat until sugar is dissolved and frosting is fluffy, about 4 minutes. Store in the refrigerator. **Yield:** about 3-1/3 cups.
                                          —*Martha Mills*
                                    Walterboro, South Carolina

Chocolate Mousse Frosting

This smooth, fluffy frosting is a real treat for cake lovers. You can also use it as a dip for fresh fruit.

- **1 cup cold milk**
- **1 package (3.9 ounces) instant chocolate fudge pudding mix**
- **1 carton (8 ounces) frozen whipped topping, thawed**

In a large mixing bowl, whisk milk and pudding mix for 2 minutes. Fold in whipped topping. Store in the refrigerator. **Yield:** 3-1/2 cups.

— *Kim Marie Van Rheenen, Mendota, Illinois*

Chocolate Mousse Frosting

Sweetened Whipping Cream

Sometimes a dollop of sweetened whipped cream is all you need to top your favorite cake or other dessert. To make ahead, slightly underwhip the cream, then cover and refrigerate for several hours. Beat briefly just before using.

- **1 cup heavy whipping cream**
- **3 tablespoons confectioners' sugar**
- **1/2 teaspoon vanilla extract**

In a chilled small mixing bowl and with chilled beaters, beat cream until it begins to thicken. Add confectioners' sugar and vanilla; beat until soft peaks form. Store in the refrigerator. **Yield:** 2 cups.

Soft Lemon Frosting

This fresh-tasting citrus icing makes a pretty topping for white cake or cupcakes, especially when garnished with grated lemon peel. Plus, it's a snap to stir up in a jiffy.

- **1 can (14 ounces) sweetened condensed milk**
- **3/4 cup lemonade concentrate**
- **1 carton (8 ounces) frozen whipped topping, thawed**

In a bowl, combine milk and lemonade concentrate. Fold in whipped topping. Store in the refrigerator. **Yield:** about 4 cups.

— *Madge Robertson Murfreesboro, Arkansas*

Cream Cheese Frosting

This smooth, versatile frosting has a delicate vanilla flavor. Most folks agree carrot cake and pumpkin bars wouldn't be complete without it!

- **2 packages (3 ounces *each*) cream cheese, softened**
- **1/2 cup butter, softened**
- **2 teaspoons vanilla extract**
- **1/4 teaspoon salt**
- **5 to 6 cups confectioners' sugar**

In a large mixing bowl, beat cream cheese, butter, vanilla and salt until smooth. Gradually beat in confectioners' sugar. Store in the refrigerator. **Yield:** about 3 cups.

— *Sharon Lugdon, Costigan, Maine*

creamy
Cheesecakes
will impress
guests

The ultimate in dessert indulgence, cheesecakes elicit oohs and aahs whenever they're presented to guests. This chapter offers classic cheesecakes like Caramel Fudge Cheesecake (p. 157) and Golden Lemon-Glazed Cheesecake (p. 152) as well as choice cheese pies and bars plus savory appetizer cheesecakes.

the basics of Cheesecakes

Whether served as an appetizer or a dessert, cheesecakes are a real crowd-pleaser. Their eye-catching look will give folks the impression that you spent hours in the kitchen! While cheesecakes do require advance planning to allow for chilling, they are actually easy to make.

Cream cheese is the foundation of the cheesecakes featured here. Sometimes, cream cheese is paired with other cheeses such as ricotta or cottage cheese. For appetizer cheesecakes, cream cheese is often combined with a savory cheese like Swiss or blue.

Loosening Cheesecake from Sides of Pan

To prevent cracks during cooling, it's important to loosen the cheesecake from the sides of the pan after baking.

First cool the cheesecake on a wire rack for 10 minutes. Then carefully run a table knife or small metal spatula between the cheesecake and the inside of the pan. Cool 1 hour longer. Refrigerate overnight before removing the sides of the pan.

problem-Solving pointers for Cheesecakes

If this happens to your cheesecake:	This could be the reason:
The cheesecake has lumps.	The cream cheese was not softened before mixing and/or was not thoroughly blended before adding the eggs.
The cheesecake has a cracked top.	The batter was overbeaten.
	The oven temperature was too high. Check temperature with an oven thermometer.
	The cheesecake was overbaked.
	You checked for doneness with a knife or toothpick.
	The cheesecake was cooled in a drafty area or the oven door was opened during baking.
	Next time, try baking the cheesecake in a water bath. (See page 156.)
The top cracked when the sides of the pan were removed.	You didn't loosen the cheesecake from the sides of the pan with a knife while it was cooling.

secrets for
successful cheesecakes

- Measure ingredients accurately, using the measuring tools and techniques suggested on pages 8 and 9.

- Before preheating the oven, arrange the oven racks so that the cheesecake will bake in the center of the oven.

- Preheat the oven for 10 to 15 minutes before baking.

- Grease the bottom and sides of the springform pan to help prevent the filling from cracking when the cheesecake cools. It will naturally pull away from the sides.

- For best results, we recommend using regular cream cheese and sour cream, unless a recipe specifically calls for reduced-fat or fat-free products.

- To avoid lumps, always soften cream cheese at room temperature for about 30 minutes before mixing. To soften in the microwave, place an unwrapped 8-ounce package of cream cheese on a microwave-safe plate; microwave on medium for about 30 to 60 seconds or until softened. If cream cheese is not softened before mixing, it cannot be smoothed after blending.

- Make sure the batter is completely smooth and free of lumps before adding eggs. Add the eggs all at once and beat on low speed just until blended. Avoid overbeating at this step. If too much air is beaten into the mixture, the cheesecake will puff during baking, then collapse and split when cooled.

- Stop the mixer occasionally and scrape the batter down from the sides of the bowl with a rubber spatula.

- Open the oven door as little as possible while baking the cheesecake, especially during the first 30 minutes. Drafts can cause a cheesecake to crack.

- For best results, the springform pan should not be warped and should seal tightly. If in doubt about the tightness of the seal, tightly wrap heavy-duty foil around the outside of the pan to prevent butter in the crust from leaking out. Place on a baking sheet.

- Use a kitchen timer. Check for doneness at the minimum recommended baking time. A cheesecake is done when the edges are slightly puffed and when the center (about 1 in. in diameter) jiggles slightly when the side of the pan is tapped with a spoon. The retained heat will continue to cook the center while the cheesecake is cooling. A cheesecake cooked in a water bath will be just set across the top. The top will look dull, not shiny. Don't use a knife to test for doneness…doing so will cause the top to crack.

- Cool the cheesecake for 10 minutes on a wire rack, then run a knife around the inside edge to loosen the cheesecake from the springform pan. Don't remove the sides of the pan yet.

- Cool the cheesecake on a wire rack in a draft-free location for 1 hour. Refrigerate, uncovered, for at least 3 to 4 hours. When the cheesecake is cold, cover it with a piece of foil or plastic wrap across the top of the pan and refrigerate for at least 6 hours or overnight. This allows the cheesecake to set and will make it easier to cut.

- When ready to serve, loosen the latch of the springform and carefully lift the rim of the pan straight up. Slice the cheesecake chilled. But for maximum flavor, allow slices to stand at room temperature for 15 to 30 minutes before serving.

- Use a straight-edge knife to cut a cheesecake. Warm the blade in hot water, dry and slice. Clean and rewarm the knife after each cut.

Classic cheesecakes

Luscious Almond Cheesecake

Almonds and almond extract give a traditional sour cream-topped cheesecake a tasty twist.

- 1-1/4 **cups crushed vanilla wafers (about 28 wafers)**
- 3/4 **cup finely chopped almonds**
- 1/4 **cup sugar**
- 1/3 **cup butter, melted**

FILLING:
- 4 **packages (8 ounces *each*) cream cheese, softened**
- 1-1/4 **cups sugar**
- 4 **eggs, lightly beaten**
- 1-1/2 **teaspoons almond extract**
- 1 **teaspoon vanilla extract**

Topping a Cheesecake with Sour Cream

Sour cream toppings are frequently spread over cheesecakes a few minutes before the end of baking. Remove the cheesecake from oven and let stand for 5 to 15 minutes. Spoon sour cream topping around the edge of the cheesecake, then carefully spread toward the center.

TOPPING:
- 2 **cups (16 ounces) sour cream**
- 1/4 **cup sugar**
- 1 **teaspoon vanilla extract**
- 2 **tablespoons sliced almonds, toasted**

1 In a bowl, combine the wafer crumbs, almonds and sugar; stir in butter. Press onto the bottom of a greased 10-in. springform pan; set aside.

2 In a large mixing bowl, beat cream cheese and sugar until smooth. Add eggs; beat on low speed just until combined. Stir in extracts. Pour into crust. Place pan on a baking sheet.

3 Bake at 350° for 50-55 minutes or until center is almost set. Remove from the oven; let stand for 5 minutes (leave oven on). Combine the sour cream, sugar and vanilla. Spoon around edge of cheesecake; carefully spread over filling. Bake 5 minutes longer. Cool pan on a wire rack for 10 minutes. Carefully run a knife around edge of pan to loosen; cool 1 hour longer. Refrigerate overnight.

4 Just before serving, sprinkle with almonds and remove sides of pan. Refrigerate leftovers. **Yield:** 14-16 servings.
—*Brenda Clifford, Overland Park, Kansas*

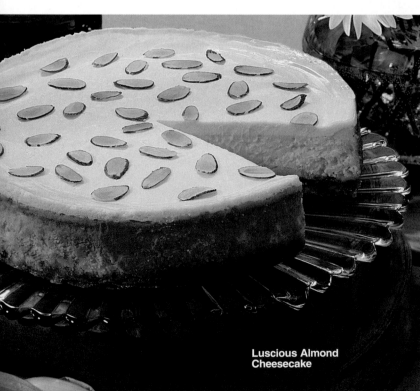

Luscious Almond Cheesecake

Old-World Ricotta Cheesecake

The subtle cinnamon flavor of the zwieback crust and the dense texture of the ricotta cheese are reminiscent of old-fashioned cheesecakes.

  1-2/3 **cups zwieback crumbs**
      3 **tablespoons sugar**
    1/2 **teaspoon ground cinnamon**
    1/3 **cup butter, softened**
FILLING:
      2 **cartons (15 ounces *each*) ricotta cheese**
    1/2 **cup sugar**
    1/2 **cup half-and-half cream**
      2 **tablespoons all-purpose flour**
      1 **tablespoon lemon juice**
      1 **teaspoon finely grated lemon peel**
    1/4 **teaspoon salt**
      2 **eggs, lightly beaten**
TOPPING:
      1 **cup (8 ounces) sour cream**
      2 **tablespoons sugar**
      1 **teaspoon vanilla extract**

1 In a bowl, combine the zwieback crumbs, sugar and cinnamon; mix in butter until mixture is crumbly. Press onto the bottom and 1-1/2 in. up the sides of a greased 9-in. springform pan. Refrigerate until chilled.

2 For filling, beat the ricotta cheese, sugar, cream, flour, lemon juice, lemon peel and salt in a large mixing bowl. Blend until smooth. Add eggs; beat on low speed just until combined. Pour into crust. Place pan on a baking sheet.

Swirling Filling into a Cheesecake

Spoon small amounts of the filling to be swirled in a random pattern onto cheesecake batter. Cut through cheesecake batter with a knife to swirl in the filling. Be careful not to draw the blade through the filling too often, or the filling will blend into the rest of the batter and you'll lose the pretty pattern.

---

3 Bake at 350° for 50-55 minutes or until center is almost set. Remove from the oven; let stand for 15 minutes (leave oven on). Combine topping ingredients; spoon around edge of cheesecake. Carefully spread over filling. Bake 10 minutes longer. Cool pan on a wire rack for 10 minutes. Carefully run a knife around edge of pan to loosen; cool 1 hour longer. Refrigerate for 3 hours or overnight. Remove sides of pan. Refrigerate leftovers. **Yield:** 12-14 servings.

Chocolate Swirl Cheesecake

The wonderful flavors of orange and chocolate combine in this creamy cheesecake.

    1/3 **cup graham cracker crumbs (about 6 squares)**
      4 **packages (8 ounces *each*) cream cheese, softened**
  1-1/3 **cups sugar**
      4 **eggs, lightly beaten**
      2 **tablespoons orange juice**
      2 **teaspoons grated orange peel**
      2 **squares (1 ounce *each*) semisweet chocolate, melted and cooled**
Whipped cream, optional

1 Sprinkle cracker crumbs over bottom and sides of a lightly greased 9-in. springform pan; set aside. In a large mixing bowl, beat cream cheese until smooth. Add sugar; beat for 1 minute. Add eggs; beat on low speed just until combined. Add orange juice and peel; beat on medium for 2-3 minutes. Set aside 3/4 cup; pour remaining filling into pan. Combine chocolate and reserved filling. Drop by spoonfuls over filling in pan and swirl with a knife. Place pan on a double thickness of heavy-duty foil (about 16 in. x 16 in.). Securely wrap foil around pan.

2 Place pan in a large baking pan. Fill larger pan with hot water to a depth of 1 in. (Refer to Preparing a Water Bath for Cheesecakes on page 156.) Bake at 350° for 75-80 minutes or until center is just set. Remove springform pan from water bath. Cool on a wire rack for 10 minutes. Carefully run a knife around edge of pan to loosen; cool 1 hour longer. Remove foil. Refrigerate 3-4 hours or overnight.

3 Remove sides of pan. Serve with whipped cream if desired. Refrigerate leftovers. **Yield:** 12-14 servings.
—*Aida Babbel, Coquitlam, British Columbia*

Royal Raspberry Cheesecake

Every bite of this creamy cheesecake is bursting with a succulent raspberry topping. Instead of the usual cracker crust, it features a rich pastry crust.

        3/4 cup all-purpose flour
          3 tablespoons sugar
        1/2 teaspoon finely grated lemon peel
          6 tablespoons butter, softened
          1 egg yolk, lightly beaten
        1/4 teaspoon vanilla extract

FILLING:

          3 packages (8 ounces *each*) cream cheese,
            softened
        1/2 teaspoon finely grated lemon peel
        1/4 teaspoon vanilla extract
          1 cup sugar
          2 tablespoons all-purpose flour
        1/4 teaspoon salt
          2 eggs, lightly beaten
          1 egg yolk, lightly beaten
        1/4 cup milk

RASPBERRY SAUCE:

          1 tablespoon cornstarch
          1 package (10 ounces) frozen sweetened
            raspberries, thawed and crushed
        1/2 cup currant jelly
          3 cups whole raspberries

1 In a bowl, combine the flour, sugar and lemon peel. Cut in butter until mixture is crumbly. Stir in egg yolk and vanilla. Pat half of the dough onto the bottom of a greased 9-in. springform pan with the sides removed. Bake at 400° for 7 minutes or until golden. Cool completely on a wire rack. Attach the sides of the pan and grease sides. Pat remaining dough 1-1/2 in. up the sides and press onto the bottom crust along the sides of pan. Set aside.

2 For filling, in a large mixing bowl, beat the cream cheese, lemon peel and vanilla until smooth. Combine the sugar, flour and salt; add to cream cheese mixture, beating until smooth. Add eggs and yolk; beat on low speed just until combined. Stir in milk. Pour into crust. Place pan on a baking sheet.

3 Bake at 375° for 35-40 minutes or until center is almost set. Cool pan on a wire rack for 10 minutes. Carefully run a knife around edge of pan to loosen; cool 1 hour longer. Refrigerate overnight.

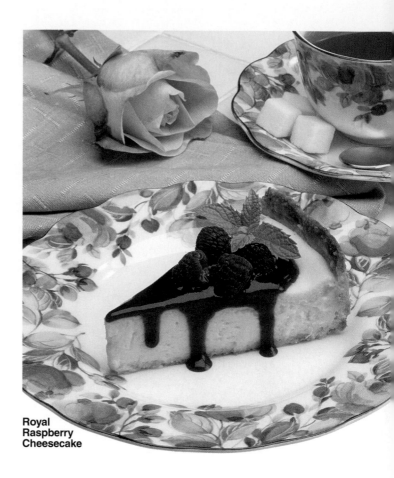

Royal
Raspberry
Cheesecake

4 For sauce, combine the cornstarch and crushed raspberries in a saucepan until blended. Stir in jelly. Bring to a boil over medium heat; cook and stir for 1 minute or until thickened. Remove from the heat; strain to remove berry seeds. Discard seeds. Cool sauce; refrigerate until serving.

5 Just before serving, remove sides of pan. Cut cheesecake into slices; garnish with sauce and fresh berries. Refrigerate leftovers. **Yield:** 12-14 servings.
—*Lori Monthorpe, Ile Bizard, Quebec*

disguise
a cracked cheesecake

If the top of your cheesecake has a crack in it, just cover it up! Topping the cheesecake with fruit, a sour cream topping or your favorite jam will offer a delectable disguise.

Making a Pastry Crust for Cheesecakes

1. Prepare crust according to recipe directions. Remove the bottom from a springform pan. Pat about one-half of the dough onto the bottom of a springform pan. Bake as directed.

2. Cool completely. Attach sides of pan and grease sides. Pat remaining dough 1-1/2 in. up the sides of the pan and press onto the bottom crust along the sides of the pan.

1 In a small bowl, combine the flour, sugar and cocoa; cut in butter until mixture is crumbly. Gradually add water, tossing with a fork until dough forms a ball. Shape into 24 balls. Place in greased miniature muffin cups; press dough onto the bottom and up the sides of each cup.

2 In a large mixing bowl, beat cream cheese and sugar until smooth. Beat in milk and vanilla. Add egg; beat on low speed just until combined. Spoon about 1 tablespoonful into each cup.

3 Bake at 325° for 15-18 minutes or until set. Cool on a wire rack for 30 minutes. Carefully remove from pans to cool completely. Top with pie filling. Store in the refrigerator. **Yield:** 2 dozen. —*Janice Hertlein Esterhazy, Saskatchewan*

Tiny Cherry Cheesecakes

Individual cheesecakes are a nice alternative to a large cheesecake because they take less time to bake. Plus, they're a pretty addition to any dessert tray.

    1 **cup all-purpose flour**
1/3 **cup sugar**
1/4 **cup baking cocoa**
1/2 **cup cold butter**
    2 **tablespoons cold water**
FILLING:
    2 **packages (3 ounces** *each***) cream cheese, softened**
1/4 **cup sugar**
    2 **tablespoons milk**
    1 **teaspoon vanilla extract**
    1 **egg, lightly beaten**
    1 **can (21 ounces) cherry** *or* **strawberry pie filling**

Tiny Cherry Cheesecakes

Golden Lemon-Glazed Cheesecake

(Pictured on page 145)

A light lemon glaze adds the perfect finishing touch to a rich and creamy cheesecake.

- 2-1/2 cups graham cracker crumbs (about 40 squares)
- 1/4 cup sugar
- 2/3 cup butter, melted

FILLING:
- 3 packages (8 ounces *each*) cream cheese, softened
- 1-1/4 cups sugar
- 3 eggs, lightly beaten
- 3 tablespoons lemon juice
- 1 tablespoon grated lemon peel
- 1 teaspoon vanilla extract

GLAZE:
- 1 small lemon, thinly sliced, *divided*
- 3 cups water, *divided*
- 1 cup sugar
- 3 tablespoons cornstarch
- 1/3 cup lemon juice

1 In a bowl, combine cracker crumbs and sugar; stir in butter. Press onto the bottom and 2 in. up the sides of a greased 9-in. springform pan. Place pan on a baking sheet. Bake at 350° for 10 minutes or until set. Place pan on a wire rack (leave oven on).

2 In a large mixing bowl, beat the cream cheese and sugar until smooth. Add eggs; beat on low speed just until combined. Stir in the lemon juice, lemon peel and vanilla just until blended. Pour into the crust. Return pan to baking sheet.

3 Bake for 40-45 minutes or until center is almost set. Cool pan on a wire rack for 10 minutes. Carefully run a knife around edge of pan to loosen; cool 1 hour longer. Refrigerate overnight.

4 Set aside 1 lemon slice; coarsely chop the remaining lemon slices. In a saucepan, combine the chopped lemon and 2 cups water; bring to a boil. Reduce heat; simmer, uncovered, for 15 minutes. Drain and discard the liquid. In another saucepan, combine the sugar and cornstarch; stir in the remaining water until smooth. Add lemon juice and lemon pulp. Bring to a boil; cook and stir for 3 minutes or until thickened. Refrigerate until cooled, stirring occasionally.

5 Remove sides of pan. Pour the lemon glaze over the cheesecake; garnish with the reserved lemon slice. Refrigerate leftovers. **Yield:** 12-14 servings.
—*Betty Jacques, Hemet, California*

Making a Cheesecake Crumb Crust

1. Place cookies or crackers in a heavy-duty resealable plastic bag. Seal bag, pushing out as much air as possible. Press a rolling pin over the bag, crushing the cookies or crackers into fine crumbs. Or, process cookies and crackers in a food processor.

2. Use a flat-bottomed measuring cup or glass to firmly press the prepared crumb mixture onto the bottom (and up the sides if recipe directs) of a springform pan.

Strawberry Cheesecake

Juicy whole strawberries top off this impressive dessert.

- 3/4 cup ground pecans
- 3/4 cup graham cracker crumbs (about 12 squares)
- 3 tablespoons butter, melted

FILLING:
- 4 packages (8 ounces *each*) cream cheese, softened
- 1-1/4 cups sugar
- 1 tablespoon lemon juice
- 2 teaspoons vanilla extract
- 4 eggs, lightly beaten

TOPPING:
- 2 cups (16 ounces) sour cream
- 1/4 cup sugar
- 1 teaspoon vanilla extract

STRAWBERRY GLAZE:
- 2 tablespoons cornstarch
- 1/4 cup water

1 jar (12 ounces) strawberry jelly
3 tablespoons orange juice
Red food coloring, optional
1 quart whole fresh strawberries

1 In a bowl, combine the pecans and cracker crumbs; stir in butter. Press onto the bottom of a greased 10-in. springform pan; set aside.

2 In a large mixing bowl, beat the cream cheese until smooth. Add the sugar, lemon juice and vanilla; beat well. Add eggs; beat on low speed just until combined. Spoon over crust. Place pan on a baking sheet.

3 Bake at 350° for 45-50 minutes or until center is almost set. Remove from the oven; let stand for 15 minutes (leave oven on). For topping, combine all the ingredients; spoon around edge of cheesecake. Carefully spread over filling. Bake 5 minutes longer. Cool pan on a wire rack for 10 minutes. Carefully run a knife around the edge of pan to loosen; cool 1 hour longer. Refrigerate overnight.

4 Several hours before serving, prepare glaze. In a saucepan, combine cornstarch and water until smooth; add jelly. Bring to a boil over medium-high heat; cook and stir for 1-2 minutes or until jelly is melted and glaze is thickened. Remove from the heat; stir in orange juice and food coloring if desired. Cool to room temperature.

5 Just before serving, remove sides of pan. Arrange strawberries on top of cheesecake with pointed ends up. Spoon glaze over berries, allowing some to drip down sides of cake. Refrigerate leftovers. **Yield:** 14-16 servings.
—*L.C. Herschap, Luling, Texas*

Chocolate Chip Cookie Dough Cheesecake

This recipe captures the flavor of a popular ice cream.

**1-3/4 cups crushed chocolate chip cookies *or*
chocolate wafer crumbs**
1/4 cup sugar
1/3 cup butter, melted
FILLING:
3 packages (8 ounces *each*) cream cheese,
softened
1 cup sugar
3 eggs, lightly beaten

Chocolate Chip
Cookie Dough Cheesecake

1 cup (8 ounces) sour cream
1/2 teaspoon vanilla extract
COOKIE DOUGH:
1/4 cup butter, softened
1/4 cup sugar
1/4 cup packed brown sugar
1 tablespoon water
1 teaspoon vanilla extract
1/2 cup all-purpose flour
**1-1/2 cups miniature semisweet chocolate chips,
*divided***

1 In a small bowl, combine cookie crumbs and sugar; stir in butter. Press onto the bottom and 1 in. up the sides of a greased 9-in. springform pan; set aside.

2 In a large mixing bowl, beat the cream cheese and sugar until smooth. Add eggs; beat on low just until combined. Add sour cream and vanilla; beat just until blended. Pour over crust; set aside. In another large mixing bowl, cream butter and sugars until light and fluffy. Add water and vanilla. Gradually add flour. Stir in 1 cup chocolate chips. Drop dough by teaspoonfuls over filling, gently pushing dough below surface (dough should be completely covered by filling). Place pan on a baking sheet.

3 Bake at 350° for 45-55 minutes or until center is almost set. Cool pan on a wire rack for 10 minutes. Carefully run a knife around edge of pan to loosen; cool 1 hour longer. Refrigerate overnight. Remove sides of pan. Sprinkle with remaining chips. Refrigerate leftovers. **Yield:** 12-14 servings.
—*Julie Craig
Jackson, Wisconsin*

Chocolate Truffle Cheesecake

If you delight in the taste of chocolate, this is the cheesecake for you! Every creamy bite melts in your mouth. It looks elegant yet is so easy to prepare.

- 1-1/2 cups chocolate wafer crumbs (about 27 wafers)
- 2 tablespoons sugar
- 1/4 cup butter, melted

FILLING:
- 1/4 cup semisweet chocolate chips
- 1/4 cup heavy whipping cream
- 3 packages (8 ounces *each*) cream cheese, softened
- 1 cup sugar
- 1/3 cup baking cocoa
- 3 eggs, lightly beaten
- 1 teaspoon vanilla extract

Anything is good if it's made of chocolate.

TOPPING:
- 1-1/2 cups semisweet chocolate chips
- 1/4 cup heavy whipping cream
- 1 teaspoon vanilla extract

Whipped cream and miniature chocolate kisses, optional

1 In a small bowl, combine wafer crumbs and sugar; stir in butter. Press onto the bottom and 1-1/2 in. up the sides of a greased 9-in. springform pan. Place pan on a baking sheet. Bake at 350° for 10 minutes. Place pan on a wire rack. Reduce heat to 325°.

2 For filling, melt chocolate chips in a small heavy saucepan or microwave; stir until smooth. Remove from the heat; add cream and mix well. Set aside. In a large mixing bowl, beat cream cheese and sugar until smooth. Add cocoa and beat well. Add eggs; beat on low just until combined. Stir in vanilla and reserved chocolate mixture just until blended. Pour over crust. Return pan to baking sheet.

3 Bake for 45-50 minutes or until center is almost set. For topping, melt chocolate chips in a heavy saucepan or microwave; stir until smooth. Stir in cream and vanilla; mix well. Spread over filling. Cool pan on a wire rack for 10 minutes. Carefully run a knife around edge of pan to loosen; cool 1 hour longer. Refrigerate overnight.

4 Remove sides of pan. Just before serving, garnish with whipped cream and miniature chocolate kisses if desired. Refrigerate leftovers. **Yield:** 12-14 servings.

—*Mary Jones, Cumberland, Maine*

Chocolate Truffle Cheesecake

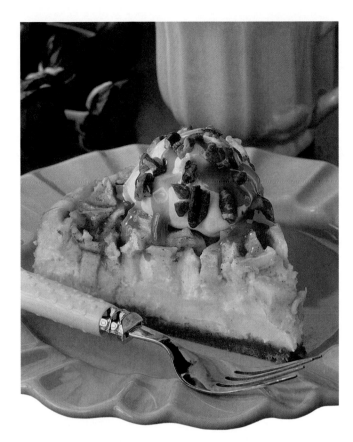

1. In a bowl, combine the cracker crumbs, sugar, pecans and cinnamon; stir in butter. Press onto the bottom of a lightly greased 9-in. springform pan. Place pan on a baking sheet. Bake at 350° for 10 minutes. Place pan on a wire rack (leave oven on).

2. In a large mixing bowl, beat cream cheese and sugar until smooth. Add eggs; beat on low speed just until combined. Stir in vanilla. Pour over crust. Toss apples with lemon juice, sugar and cinnamon; spoon over filling. Return pan to baking sheet.

3. Bake for 55-60 minutes or until center is almost set. Cool pan on a wire rack for 10 minutes. Carefully run a knife around edge of pan to loosen. Drizzle with 4 tablespoons caramel topping. Cool 1 hour longer. Refrigerate overnight.

4. Remove sides of pan. Garnish with whipped cream. Drizzle with remaining caramel topping; sprinkle with pecans. Refrigerate leftovers. **Yield:** 12-14 servings.
—*Debbie Wilson, Sellersburg, Indiana*

Apple-of-Your-Eye Cheesecake

With apples, caramel and pecans, this exquisite cheesecake will win you many compliments.

> 1 cup graham cracker crumbs (about 16 squares)
> 3 tablespoons sugar
> 2 tablespoons finely chopped pecans
> 1/2 teaspoon ground cinnamon
> 1/4 cup butter, melted

FILLING:
> 3 packages (8 ounces *each*) cream cheese, softened
> 3/4 cup sugar
> 3 eggs, lightly beaten
> 3/4 teaspoon vanilla extract

TOPPING:
> 2-1/2 cups chopped peeled apples
> 1 tablespoon lemon juice
> 1/4 cup sugar
> 1/2 teaspoon ground cinnamon
> 6 tablespoons caramel ice cream topping, *divided*

Sweetened whipped cream
> 2 tablespoons chopped pecans

Mini Apricot Cheesecakes

Vanilla wafers are used to create the no-fuss crusts for these darling bite-size treats. For a different look and taste, vary the kind of preserves on top.

> 24 vanilla wafers
> 2 packages (8 ounces *each*) cream cheese, softened
> 3/4 cup sugar
> 2 eggs, lightly beaten
> 1 tablespoon lemon juice
> 1 teaspoon vanilla extract
> 1 cup apricot preserves

1. Place wafers flat side down in paper- or foil-lined muffin cups; set aside. In a large mixing bowl, beat cream cheese and sugar until smooth. Add the eggs, lemon juice and vanilla; beat well. Fill muffin cups three-fourths full.

2. Bake at 375° for 17-20 minutes or until top is set. Cool on a wire rack for 20 minutes. Carefully remove from pans to cool completely. Top each cheesecake with 2 teaspoons preserves. Store in the refrigerator. **Yield:** 2 dozen.
—*Carol Twardzik*
Spy Hill, Saskatchewan

Chocolate-Covered White Cheesecake

The inside scoop on this tasty treat is the white chocolate center. Drizzling melted vanilla chips on top of the chocolate glaze makes for a pretty presentation.

1-1/2 cups chocolate wafer crumbs (about 27 wafers)
   3 tablespoons butter, melted
FILLING:
   3 packages (8 ounces *each*) cream cheese, softened
 1/2 cup sugar
 1/4 cup heavy whipping cream
   1 teaspoon vanilla extract
   3 eggs, lightly beaten
1-1/2 cups vanilla *or* white chips, melted and cooled
GLAZE:
   2 cups (12 ounces) semisweet chocolate chips
   1 cup heavy whipping cream
   2 tablespoons butter
   2 tablespoons sugar
   1 cup vanilla *or* white chips
Striped chocolate kisses, optional
Raspberries, optional

1 In a small bowl, combine wafer crumbs and butter; press onto the bottom of a greased 9-in. springform pan. Place pan on a baking sheet. Bake at 350° for 10 minutes. Place pan on a wire rack (leave oven on).

2 In a large mixing bowl, beat the cream cheese, sugar, cream and vanilla until well blended. Add eggs; beat on low speed just until combined. Stir in melted vanilla chips. Pour into crust. Place pan on a double thickness of heavy-duty foil (about 16 in. x 16 in.). Securely wrap foil around pan.

3 Place springform pan in a larger baking pan. Fill larger pan with hot water to a depth of 1 in. Bake for 65-70 minutes until center is just set. Remove springform pan from water bath. Cool on a wire rack for 10 minutes. Carefully run a knife around edge of pan to loosen; cool 1 hour longer. Refrigerate for 4 hours or overnight.

4 For glaze, place chocolate chips in a bowl; set aside. In a heavy saucepan, bring the cream, butter and sugar to a boil over medium-high heat, stirring constantly. Pour over chocolate chips. Cool for 3 minutes;

stir until smooth and cooled. Remove sides of pan. Spread glaze over top and sides of cheesecake. Refrigerate for 2 hours. Melt remaining vanilla chips; drizzle over cheesecake. Garnish with kisses and raspberries if desired. Refrigerate leftovers. **Yield:** 12-14 servings.

—Carol Staniger, Springdale, Arkansas

Preparing a Water Bath for Cheesecakes

1. Using a double thickness of heavy-duty foil, make a 16-in. square. Center springform pan on foil, then tightly mold foil around pan.

2. Place springform pan in a larger pan, such as a large shallow baking dish or roasting pan. Set dish on rack in oven. Using a kettle or large measuring cup, carefully pour hot water into larger pan to a depth of 1 in.

Chocolate-Covered White Cheesecake

Caramel Fudge Cheesecake

(Pictured on page 144)

It's hard to resist this chocolaty cheesecake with its fudgy crust, crunchy pecans and gooey layer of caramel. It satisfies both chocolate and cheesecake lovers.

- 1 package fudge brownie mix (8-inch square pan size)
- 1 package (14 ounces) caramels*
- 1/4 cup evaporated milk
- 1-1/4 cups coarsely chopped pecans
- 2 packages (8 ounces *each*) cream cheese, softened
- 1/2 cup sugar
- 2 eggs, lightly beaten
- 2 squares (1 ounce *each*) semisweet chocolate, melted and cooled
- 2 squares (1 ounce *each*) unsweetened chocolate, melted and cooled

1 Prepare brownie batter according to package directions. Spread into a greased 9-in. springform pan. Place pan on a baking sheet. Bake at 350° for 20 minutes. Place pan on a wire rack for 10 minutes (leave oven on).

2 Meanwhile, in a microwave-safe bowl, melt the caramels with milk. Pour over brownie crust; sprinkle with pecans. In a large mixing bowl, beat cream cheese and sugar. Add eggs; beat on low speed just until combined. Stir in melted chocolate. Pour over pecans. Return pan to baking sheet.

3 Bake for 35-40 minutes or until center is almost set. Cool pan on a wire rack for 10 minutes. Run a knife around edge of pan to loosen; cool 1 hour longer. Refrigerate overnight. Remove sides of pan. Refrigerate leftovers. **Yield:** 12-14 servings. —*Brenda Ruse Truro, Nova Scotia*

***Editor's Note:** This recipe was tested with Hershey caramels.

Cool Lime Cheesecake

The mixture of tart lime and sweet creamy cheesecake is absolutely scrumptious. At any get-together, it's a show-stopping dessert that's always enjoyed.

Cool Lime Cheesecake

- 2-1/4 cups graham cracker crumbs (about 36 squares)
- 1/3 cup sugar
- 1/2 cup butter, melted

FILLING:
- 20 ounces cream cheese, softened
- 3/4 cup sugar
- 1 cup (8 ounces) sour cream
- 3 tablespoons all-purpose flour
- 3 eggs, lightly beaten
- 2/3 cup lime juice
- 1 teaspoon vanilla extract
- 1 drop green food coloring, optional

Whipped cream and lime slices

1 In a bowl, combine cookie crumbs and sugar; stir in butter. Press onto the bottom and 1 in. up the sides of a greased 10-in. springform pan. Place pan on a baking sheet. Bake at 375° for 8 minutes. Place pan on a wire rack. Reduce heat to 325°.

2 In a large mixing bowl, beat cream cheese and sugar until smooth. Add sour cream and flour; beat well. Add eggs; beat on low speed just until combined. Stir in the lime juice, vanilla and food coloring if desired just until mixed. Pour into crust. Return pan to baking sheet.

3 Bake for 50-55 minutes or until center is almost set. Cool pan on a wire rack for 10 minutes. Carefully run a knife around edge of pan to loosen; cool 1 hour longer. Refrigerate overnight. Remove sides of pan. Garnish with whipped cream and lime. Refrigerate leftovers. **Yield:** 14-16 servings. —*Karen Donhauser Frazer, Pennsylvania*

Layered
Vegetable
Cheesecake

combined. Add the sour cream, flour, onion, salt and pepper; beat just until combined. Pour 1 cup into crust; sprinkle with carrots. Continue layering 1 cup cream cheese mixture, green pepper, 1 cup cream cheese mixture, red pepper, then remaining cream cheese mixture. Place pan on a baking sheet.

3 Bake at 325° for 1 hour or until center is almost set. Cool pan on a wire rack for 10 minutes. Carefully run a knife around edge of pan to loosen; cool 1 hour longer. Refrigerate overnight. In a small bowl, combine sauce ingredients; refrigerate.

4 Remove sides of pan. Serve chilled or warm with cucumber dill sauce.

5 To serve warm, remove from the refrigerator 1 hour before serving. Let cheesecake come to room temperature for 30 minutes, then reheat at 300° for 20-25 minutes or until warm. Refrigerate leftovers. **Yield:** 20 appetizer servings. —*Donna Cline, Pensacola, Florida*

Layered Vegetable Cheesecake

Everyone who tastes this cheesy concoction, topped with a dilly of a cucumber sauce, will relish its richness and come back for more.

- 1-1/3 **cups dry bread crumbs**
- 1/3 **cup butter, melted**

FILLING:
- 2 **packages (8 ounces** *each***) cream cheese, softened**
- 2 **eggs, lightly beaten**
- 1 **cup (8 ounces) sour cream**
- 1/3 **cup all-purpose flour**
- 1/4 **cup finely chopped onion**
- 1/4 **teaspoon salt**
- 1/4 **teaspoon white pepper**
- 3/4 **cup shredded carrots**
- 3/4 **cup diced green pepper**
- 3/4 **cup diced sweet red pepper**

CUCUMBER DILL SAUCE:
- 1 **cup (8 ounces) plain yogurt**
- 1/3 **cup mayonnaise**
- 1/2 **cup finely chopped unpeeled cucumber**
- 1/4 **teaspoon salt**
- 1/4 **teaspoon dill weed**

1 Combine bread crumbs and butter; press onto the bottom and 1 in. up the sides of a greased 9-in. springform pan. Set aside.

2 In a large mixing bowl, beat cream cheese until smooth. Add eggs; beat on low speed just until

Savory Appetizer Cheesecake

Unlike most other appetizer cheesecakes, this version is best served warm from the oven.

- 6 **bacon strips, diced**
- 1 **large onion, chopped**
- 1 **garlic clove, minced**
- 1 **carton (15 ounces) ricotta cheese**
- 1/2 **cup half-and-half cream**
- 2 **tablespoons all-purpose flour**
- 1/2 **teaspoon salt**
- 1/8 to 1/4 **teaspoon cayenne pepper**

2 eggs, lightly beaten
1/2 cup sliced green onions
Assorted crackers and fresh fruit

1 In a skillet, cook bacon over medium heat until crisp. Remove with a slotted spoon to paper towels. In the drippings, saute onion and garlic until tender; remove with a slotted spoon.

2 In a large mixing bowl, beat the ricotta cheese, cream, flour, salt and cayenne until smooth. Add eggs; beat on low speed just until combined. Set aside 3 tablespoons bacon for garnish. Stir green onions, sauteed onion and remaining bacon into egg mixture. Pour into a greased 8-in. springform pan. Place pan on a baking sheet.

3 Bake at 350° for 35-40 minutes or until center is almost set. Cool pan on a wire rack for 10 minutes. Carefully run a knife around the edge of pan to loosen. Remove sides of pan. Sprinkle with reserved bacon. Serve warm with crackers and fruit. Refrigerate leftovers. **Yield**: 16-20 appetizer servings. —*Joy Burke Punxsutawney, Pennsylvania*

1 In a small bowl, combine the cracker crumbs and butter. Press onto the bottom of a greased 9-in. springform pan. Place pan on a baking sheet. Bake at 350° for 10 minutes. Place pan on a wire rack. Reduce heat to 325°.

2 In a large mixing bowl, beat cream cheese and 1/4 cup sour cream until smooth. Add eggs; beat on low speed just until combined. Add the onion, lemon juice, seafood seasoning, hot pepper sauce and pepper; beat just until blended. Fold in crab. Pour over crust. Return pan to baking sheet.

3 Bake for 35-40 minutes or until center is almost set. Cool pan on a wire rack for 10 minutes. Carefully run a knife around edge of pan to loosen; cool 1 hour longer. Carefully spread remaining sour cream over top. Refrigerate overnight.

4 Remove sides of pan. Let cheesecake stand at room temperature for 30 minutes before serving. Sprinkle with additional seafood seasoning if desired. Refrigerate leftovers. **Yield**: 20-24 appetizer servings. —*Cathy Sarrels, Tucson, Arizona*

Creamy Crab Cheesecake

A savory appetizer cheesecake such as this one, dotted with tender crabmeat, is sure to grab the attention and tempt the taste buds of guests. It's an elegant spread that you make ahead, so there's no last-minute fuss.

1 cup crushed butter-flavored crackers (about 25 crackers)
3 tablespoons butter, melted
2 packages (8 ounces *each*) cream cheese, softened
3/4 cup sour cream, *divided*
3 eggs, lightly beaten
2 teaspoons grated onion
1 teaspoon lemon juice
1/4 teaspoon seafood seasoning
2 drops hot pepper sauce
1/8 teaspoon pepper
1 cup crabmeat, drained, flaked and cartilage removed
Additional seafood seasoning, optional

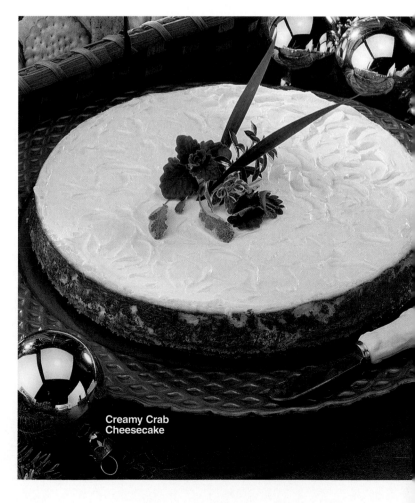

Creamy Crab Cheesecake

Cheese Pies & Bars

Raspberry Swirl Cheesecake Pie

Raspberry jam gives this attractive dessert its marbled effect. While the cheesecake refrigerates overnight, its flavors blend beautifully.

Pastry for single-crust pie (9 inches)
  2 packages (8 ounces *each*) cream cheese, softened
  1/2 cup sugar
  1/2 teaspoon vanilla extract
  2 eggs, lightly beaten
  3 tablespoons raspberry jam
Whipped topping, optional

1 Line unpricked pastry shell with a double thickness of heavy-duty foil. Bake at 450° for 5 minutes; remove foil. Bake 5 minutes longer. Place on a wire rack. Reduce heat to 350°.

2 In a large mixing bowl, beat the cream cheese, sugar and vanilla until smooth. Add eggs; beat on low speed just until combined. Pour into pastry shell.

Stir jam; drizzle over the filling. Cut through filling with a knife to swirl the jam.

3 Bake for 25-30 minutes or until center is almost set. Cool on a wire rack for 1 hour. Refrigerate overnight. Let stand at room temperature for 30 minutes before slicing. If desired, pipe whipped topping around pie. Refrigerate leftovers. **Yield:** 8 servings.
—*Sandra McKenzie, Braham, Minnesota*

Chocolate Cheese Pie

A chocolate "chain of hearts" on top of this cheesecake makes it a lovely dessert on Valentine's Day. Or skip the chocolate step and top plain pieces with cherry or blueberry pie filling.

  3 cups graham cracker crumbs (about 48 squares)
  1/2 cup sugar
  2/3 cup butter, melted
FILLING:
  3 packages (8 ounces *each*) cream cheese, softened
  1 cup sugar
  5 eggs, lightly beaten
  1 tablespoon vanilla extract
  1 package (4 ounces) German sweet chocolate, melted and cooled

1 In a bowl, combine cracker crumbs and sugar; stir in butter. Divide in half and press onto the bottom and up the sides of two ungreased 9-in. pie plates. Refrigerate while preparing filling.

2 In a large mixing bowl, beat cream cheese until fluffy. Gradually add sugar, beating until smooth. Add eggs; beat on low speed just until combined. Beat in vanilla. Remove 1-1/2 cups to a small bowl; fold in melted chocolate. Divide remaining filling mixture between crusts.

3 To make the chain of hearts on each pie, drop teaspoonfuls of chocolate filling, forming eight drops equally spaced around outside edges and four drops in center. Starting in the center of one outer drop, run a knife through the center of each to connect the drops and form a circle of hearts. Repeat with center drops.

Raspberry Swirl Cheesecake Pie

4 Bake at 350° for 40-45 minutes or until center is almost set. Cool on wire racks for 1 hour. Refrigerate for at least 6 hours or overnight. Refrigerate leftovers. **Yield:** 2 pies (8 servings each). —*Lorra Rhyner Poynette, Wisconsin*

storing *cheesecakes*

Cover and refrigerate cheesecake for up to 3 days. To freeze, place entire cheesecake or individual slices on a baking sheet and freeze until firm. Wrap in heavy-duty plastic wrap and place in a freezer bag. Freeze for up to 2 months. Thaw in the refrigerator.

Blueberry Swirl Cheesecake

Blueberry Swirl Cheesecake

Convenient canned blueberry pie filling and a prepared graham cracker crust make this dessert extra easy.

   2 packages (8 ounces *each*) cream cheese, softened
1/2 cup sugar
1/4 teaspoon vanilla extract
   2 eggs, lightly beaten
   1 graham cracker crust (9 inches)
   1 can (21 ounces) blueberry pie filling, *divided*

1 In a large mixing bowl, beat cream cheese, sugar and vanilla until smooth. Add eggs; beat on low speed just until combined. Pour into crust. Drop 1/2 cup of pie filling by heaping teaspoonfuls onto the cream cheese mixture; cut through with a knife to swirl the pie filling.

2 Bake at 350° for 35-40 minutes or until center is almost set. Cool on a wire rack for 1 hour. Refrigerate for 2 hours. Top with remaining pie filling. Refrigerate leftovers. **Yield:** 8 servings. —*Suzanne Cleveland Lyons, Georgia*

Lemon Cheesecake Pie

Lemon peel lightly flavors this smaller-serving version of a traditional cheesecake.

1-1/4 cups graham cracker crumbs (about 20 squares)
   1/3 cup butter, melted
FILLING:
      2 packages (8 ounces *each*) cream cheese, softened
   1/2 cup sugar
      2 eggs, lightly beaten
      1 teaspoon vanilla extract
   1/2 teaspoon finely grated lemon peel
TOPPING:
      1 cup (8 ounces) sour cream
      2 tablespoons sugar
   1/2 teaspoon vanilla extract
Fresh mint and lemon peel strips, optional

1 In a bowl, combine cracker crumbs and butter; press onto the bottom and up the sides of an ungreased 9-in. pie plate. Cover and refrigerate for 30 minutes.

2 In a large mixing bowl, beat the cream cheese and sugar until smooth. Add eggs; beat on low speed just until combined. Stir in vanilla and lemon peel just until blended. Pour into prepared crust.

3 Bake at 325° for 20-25 minutes or until center is almost set. Remove from the oven; let stand for 5 minutes (leave oven on). Combine the sour cream, sugar and vanilla; spread carefully over pie. Bake 5 minutes longer. Cool on a wire rack for 1 hour. Refrigerate overnight. Garnish with mint and lemon peel if desired. Refrigerate leftovers. **Yield:** 8 servings.

—*Hope Huggins, Santa Cruz, California*

Pineapple
Cheesecake Squares

3 Bake at 325° for 1 hour or until a knife inserted near the center comes out clean. Cool on a wire rack for 1 hour. Store in the refrigerator. **Yield:** 9 servings.
—*Elisabeth Garrison, Elmer, New Jersey*

Cinnamon Cherry Cheesecake Squares

This recipe calls for cinnamon graham crackers instead of the regular variety, which gives each bite a deliciously different taste.

1-3/4 **cups crushed cinnamon graham crackers (about 28 crackers)**
1/4 **cup sugar**
1/2 **cup butter, melted**
FILLING:
2 **packages (8 ounces *each*) cream cheese, softened**
1/2 **cup sugar**
3 **eggs, lightly beaten**
1 **teaspoon vanilla extract**
TOPPING:
2 **cups (16 ounces) sour cream**
1/4 **cup sugar**
1 **teaspoon vanilla**
1 **can (16 ounces) cherry pie filling**

1 In a bowl, combine graham crackers and sugar; stir in butter. Press onto the bottom of a greased 11-in. x 7-in. x 2-in. baking dish. Set aside.

2 For filling, beat cream cheese and sugar in a large mixing bowl until smooth. Add eggs; beat on low speed until just combined. Add vanilla. Pour into the crust.

3 Bake at 350° for 25 minutes. Remove from the oven; let stand for 5 minutes (leave oven on). For topping, combine the sour cream, sugar and vanilla; carefully spread over pie. Bake 5 minutes longer. Cool on a wire rack for 1 hour. Refrigerate for 4 hours or overnight. Cut into squares; top each with a spoonful of cherry pie filling. Refrigerate leftovers. **Yield:** 12-15 servings.
—*Vera Kramer, Jenera, Ohio*

Pineapple Cheesecake Squares

For a fun, tropical twist, prepare these cheese bars starring crushed pineapple. Because they're not too sweet, it's hard to eat just one!

1/2 **cup all-purpose flour**
3 **tablespoons sugar**
1/4 **teaspoon salt**
1/4 **cup cold butter**
FILLING:
1 **can (8 ounces) crushed pineapple**
1 **package (8 ounces) cream cheese, softened**
3 **tablespoons sugar**
1 **tablespoon all-purpose flour**
1 **egg, lightly beaten**
1 **cup milk**
1 **teaspoon vanilla extract**
Ground cinnamon

1 In a bowl, combine the flour, sugar and salt; cut in butter until mixture is crumbly. Press onto the bottom of an ungreased 8-in. square baking dish. Bake at 325° for 12 minutes. Cool on a wire rack.

2 For filling, drain pineapple, reserving the juice; set pineapple and juice aside. In a large mixing bowl, beat the cream cheese, sugar and flour until smooth. Add egg; beat on low speed just until combined. Add pineapple juice. Gradually add milk and vanilla. Sprinkle pineapple over the crust. Slowly pour filling over pineapple. Sprinkle with cinnamon.

Nutty Cheesecake Squares

These bars are easy enough to make for everyday occasions but special enough to serve company. They also travel well to potlucks and picnics.

  2 cups all-purpose flour
  1 cup finely chopped walnuts
  2/3 cup packed brown sugar
  1/2 teaspoon salt
  2/3 cup cold butter
FILLING:
  2 packages (8 ounces *each*) cream cheese, softened
  1/2 cup sugar
  2 eggs, lightly beaten
  1/4 cup milk
  1 teaspoon vanilla extract

1 In a bowl, combine the flour, walnuts, brown sugar and salt; cut in butter until the mixture resembles coarse crumbs. Set half aside; press remaining crumb mixture onto the bottom of a greased 13-in. x 9-in. x 2-in. baking pan. Bake at 350° for 10-15 minutes or until lightly browned.

2 In a large mixing bowl, beat filling ingredients until smooth; pour over crust. Sprinkle with reserved crumb mixture. Bake for 20-25 minutes or until a knife inserted near the center comes out clean. Cool on a wire rack for 1 hour. Store in the refrigerator. **Yield:** 16-20 servings.
— *Ruth Simon, Buffalo, New York*

Rhubarb Cheesecake Dessert

These pretty rhubarb-topped squares will signal the arrival of spring!

  1 cup all-purpose flour
1/2 cup packed brown sugar
1/4 teaspoon salt
1/4 cup cold butter
1/2 cup chopped walnuts
  1 teaspoon vanilla extract
FILLING:
  2 packages (8 ounces *each*) cream cheese, softened
3/4 cup sugar

  3 eggs, lightly beaten
  1 teaspoon vanilla extract
TOPPING:
  1 cup sugar
  1 tablespoon cornstarch
1/4 teaspoon ground cinnamon
1/4 cup water
  3 cups chopped fresh *or* frozen rhubarb*

1 In a bowl, combine the flour, brown sugar and salt; cut in butter until mixture resembles coarse crumbs. Stir in walnuts and vanilla. Press into a greased 13-in. x 9-in. x 2-in. baking dish. Bake at 375° for 10 minutes. Cool slightly.

2 In a large mixing bowl, beat cream cheese and sugar until smooth. Add eggs; beat on low speed just until combined. Add vanilla. Pour over crust. Bake at 375° for 20-25 minutes or until center is almost set and edges are light brown. Cool on a wire rack for 1 hour.

3 In a large saucepan, combine the sugar, cornstarch and cinnamon. Gradually stir in water until smooth. Add rhubarb. Bring to a boil over medium heat; cook and stir until for 5 minutes or until thickened. Cool. Pour over filling. Refrigerate at least 1 hour. Refrigerate leftovers. **Yield:** 12-15 servings.
— *Joyce Krumwiede Mankato, Minnesota*

***Editor's Note:** If using frozen rhubarb, measure rhubarb while still frozen, then thaw completely. Drain in a colander, but do not press liquid out.

Rhubarb Cheesecake Dessert

Pies & Tarts are a slice of paradise

Do you favor fruit-filled favorites like Golden Apple Pie (p. 172) and Apple Cranberry Tart (p. 189)? Or maybe a creamy confection like Chocolate Almond Silk Pie (p. 182) is more your style. No matter the craving, this chapter offers a host of pleasing pies and tasty tarts to satisfy any sweet tooth.

the basics of Pies & Tarts

*M*eat pies have been around for centuries, but England often gets the credit for creating fruit pies during the reign of Queen Elizabeth I in the 1500s.

The early crusts were frequently tough and inedible and were designed more to hold the filling together during baking than to actually be eaten. Most historians agree that fruit pies as Americans now know them were invented by the Pennsylvania Dutch in the 1700s.

While pies conjure up a homey image and tarts feel a little more elegant, they both have a sweetened filling. The main difference is that tarts are more shallow than pies (typically about 1 inch high). Tarts can be full size, bite size or individual tartlets.

helpful hints for baking and storing pies

- A pastry shell is thoroughly baked when it is a light golden brown. Fruit pies are done when the filling bubbles and the crust is light golden brown. (The filling should be clear, not cloudy.) Meringues are properly baked when the top has set and the tips of the meringue peaks are light golden brown. Custard pies are done when a knife inserted near the center comes out clean. A small area in the center of pie should still be soft. The center will continue to cook and set up during cooling.

- Cool fruit pies for at least 1 hour before serving. They can be kept at room temperature for 1 day. For longer storage, cover and refrigerate for up to 5 days. Cool meringue-topped and custard pies on a wire rack for 1 hour, then chill for at least 3 hours before serving. Store custard and cream pies in the refrigerator for up to 3 days.

Prebaking a Pastry Shell

1. After placing pastry in the pie plate and fluting edges, line unpricked shell with a double thickness of heavy-duty foil. If desired, fill with dried beans, uncooked rice or pie weights. The weight will keep the crust from puffing up, shrinking and slipping down the pie plate during baking.

2. Bake at 450° for 8 minutes. With oven mitts, carefully remove the foil and beans, rice or weights. Bake 5-6 minutes longer or until light golden brown. Cool on a wire rack. Let beans or rice cool, then store. They may be reused for pie weights, but cannot be cooked and used in recipes.

problem-Solving pointers for Pies

If this happens to your pie:	This could be the reason:
Crust is not flaky.	The shortening was cut in too much. Cut in shortening so it resembles coarse crumbs, not any smaller.
Crust is tough and/or has shrunk.	The pastry was overhandled.
	Too much water was used. Stir in only enough water to moisten the flour so a ball forms.
Crust is soggy.	Next time, bake the crust longer or at a higher temperature.
	Before adding the filling, brush the crust with a beaten egg white.
	Add the filling to the crust right before baking.
Crust is burnt in spots.	Make sure the crust is rolled out evenly.
	Your oven may bake unevenly. Next time, rotate the pie during baking.
Pie bubbles over.	Too much filling was used. Reduce the amount of filling or use a deep-dish pie plate.
There's a watery layer between the meringue and filling.	Keep the filling warm while making the meringue. Then spread the meringue over hot filling.
Meringue has shrunk during baking.	Be sure to seal the meringue to the edge of the pastry before baking.
Beads formed on the top of the meringue and/or the meringue is sticky.	Meringue was baked at too high a temperature or was underbaked.
	For best results, meringue should not be made on a humid or rainy day.
Bubbles formed in a custard-type pie.	Beat the filling only until combined.

Pie Pastries

Classic Pie Pastry

Just four ingredients are all you need to create a fabulous flaky pie crust. The double-crust recipe should be used when making a lattice-topped pie.

INGREDIENTS FOR SINGLE-CRUST PIE:
 1-1/4 **cups all-purpose flour**
  1/2 **teaspoon salt**
  1/3 **cup shortening**
    4 **to 5 tablespoons cold water**

INGREDIENTS FOR DOUBLE-CRUST PIE:
    2 **cups all-purpose flour**
  3/4 **teaspoon salt**
  2/3 **cup shortening**
    6 **to 7 tablespoons cold water**

1 In a small bowl, combine the flour and salt; cut in shortening until mixture is crumbly. Gradually add the milk, tossing with a fork until a ball forms. Cover and refrigerate for 30 minutes or until easy to handle.

2 For a single crust, roll out pastry to fit a 9-in. or 10-in. pie plate. Transfer pastry to pie plate. Trim pastry to 1/2 in. beyond edge of plate; flute edges. Fill or bake shell according to recipe directions. **Yield:** pastry for single-crust pie (9 or 10 inches).

3 For a double crust, divide dough in half so that one ball is slightly larger than the other. Roll out larger ball to fit a 9-in. or 10-in. pie plate. Transfer pastry to pie plate. Trim pastry even with edge of plate. Add filling. Roll out remaining pastry to fit top of pie; place over filling. Trim, seal and flute edges. Cut slits in top. Bake according to recipe directions. **Yield:** pastry for double-crust pie (9 or 10 inches).

secrets for successful pie pastry

- Classic pie pastry recipes are prepared with solid shortening. Lard or butter-flavored shortening can be substituted for plain shortening if desired.

- Measure ingredients accurately, using the measuring tools and techniques suggested on pages 8 and 9.

- Combine flour and salt thoroughly before adding the shortening and water.

- Be sure to use ice-cold water. Add an ice cube to water and measure before adding to the flour mixture.

- The key to producing a flaky crust is to avoid overmixing when adding the water to the flour and shortening mixture. Overmixing will cause the gluten in the flour to develop and the pastry to be tough.

- A floured surface is essential to prevent sticking when rolling out pastry. A pastry cloth and rolling pin cover are good investments—they will keep the pastry from sticking and minimize the amount of flour used. The less flour you add while rolling, the flakier and lighter the pastry will be.

- Chill pie pastry dough for 30 minutes before rolling to make it easier to handle.

- Choose dull-finish aluminum or glass pie plates for crisp golden crusts. Shiny pans can produce soggy crusts.

- Because of the high fat content in a pastry, do not grease the pie plate unless the recipe directs.

- Never prick the bottom of a pastry crust when the filling and crust are to be baked together.

- Arrange the oven racks so that the pie will bake in the center of the oven.

- Preheat the oven for 10-15 minutes before baking.

Making and Shaping Single- and Double-Crust Pie Pastry

1. Combine flour and salt in a bowl. With a pastry blender or two knives, cut in shortening until the mixture resembles coarse crumbs (the size of small peas).

2. Sprinkle 1 tablespoon of cold water at a time over the mixture and toss gently with a fork. Repeat until the dry ingredients are moist and mixture forms a ball. Use only as much water as necessary to moisten the flour.

3. Shape into a ball. (For a double-crust pie, divide pastry in half so that one ball is slightly larger than the other.) On a floured surface or floured pastry cloth, flatten the ball (the larger one, if making a double-crust pie) into a circle, pressing together any cracks or breaks.

4. Roll with a floured rolling pin from the center of the pastry to the edges, forming a circle 2 in. larger than the pie plate. The pastry should be about 1/8 in. thick.

5. To move pastry to the pie plate, roll up onto the rolling pin. Position over the edge of pie plate and unroll. Let the pastry ease into the plate. Do not stretch the pastry to fit.
　　For a single-crust pie, trim pastry with a scissors to 1/2 in. beyond plate edge; turn under and flute as in step 8. For a double-crust pie, trim pastry even with the edge of plate. For a lattice-crust pie, trim pastry to 1 in. beyond plate edge. Either bake the shell or fill according to recipe directions.

6. For a double-crust pie, roll out second ball into a 12-in. circle about 1/8 in. thick. Roll up pastry onto the rolling pin; position over filling. With a knife, cut several slits in top to allow steam to escape while baking.

7. With scissors, trim top pastry to 1 in. beyond plate edge. Fold top pastry over bottom pastry.

8. To flute the edge as shown at left, position your thumb on the inside of the crust. Place the thumb and index finger of your other hand on the outside edge and pinch pastry around the thumb to form a V shape and seal dough together. Continue around the edge.

Decorative Pie Crust Edges

Ruffle edge is used for a single- or double-crust pie. Trim pastry 1/2 in. beyond edge of pie plate (1 in. for a double-crust pie). Turn the overhanging pastry under to form the rolled edge. Position your thumb and index finger about 1 in. apart on the edge of the crust, pointing out.

Position the index finger on your other hand between the two fingers and gently push the pastry toward the center in an upward direction. Continue around the edge.

Rope edge is used for a single- or double-crust pie. Trim pastry 1/2 in. beyond edge of pie plate (1 in. for a double-crust pie). Turn the overhanging pastry under to form the rolled edge. Make a fist with one hand and press your thumb at an angle into the pastry. Pinch some of the pastry between your thumb and index finger.

Repeat at about 1/2-in. intervals around the crust. For a looser-looking rope, position your thumb at a wider angle and repeat at 1-in. intervals.

Cut scalloped edge is used for a single-crust pie. Line a 9-in. pie plate with the bottom pastry and trim pastry even with edge of pie plate. Hold a teaspoon or tablespoon upside down and roll the tip of the spoon around the edge of the pastry, cutting it. Remove and discard the cut pieces to create a scalloped look. Remember—the larger the spoon, the bigger the scallops.

Braided edge is used for a single-crust pie. Make enough pastry for a double crust. Line a 9-in. pie plate with the bottom pastry and trim pastry even with edge of pie plate.

Roll remaining pastry into a 10-in. x 8-in. rectangle. With a sharp knife, cut twelve 1/4-in.-wide strips; gently braid three strips. Brush edge of crust with water; place braid on edge and press lightly to secure.

Repeat with remaining strips, attaching additional braids until entire edge is covered. Cover with foil to protect edges from overbrowning.

Leaf trim is used for a single-crust pie. Make enough pastry for a double crust. Line a 9-in. pie plate with the bottom pastry and trim pastry even with edge of pie plate. Roll out remaining pastry to 1/8-in. thickness.

Cut out leaf shapes, using 1-in. to 1-1/2-in. cookie cutters. With a sharp knife, score pastry to create leaf veins. Brush bottom of each leaf with water. Place one or two layers of leaves around the edge of crust; press lightly to secure. Cover with foil to protect edges from overbrowning.

You can also use this technique with other cookie cutter designs such as stars, hearts and apples. Vary them to suit the occasion or season you are celebrating.

The proof in the pie is in the amount of crust that is eaten.

Never-Fail Pie Crust

Even novice bakers who normally shy away from homemade pie pastry can't go wrong with this recipe. It's so easy to roll out and produces a tender, flaky crust every time.

INGREDIENTS FOR SINGLE-CRUST PIE:
- 1 cup all-purpose flour
- 1/4 teaspoon salt
- 1/3 cup shortening
- 1-1/2 teaspoons white vinegar
- 2 to 3 tablespoons milk

INGREDIENTS FOR DOUBLE-CRUST PIE:
- 2 cups all-purpose flour
- 1/2 teaspoon salt
- 2/3 cup shortening
- 1 tablespoon white vinegar
- 5 to 6 tablespoons milk

1 In a small bowl, combine the flour and salt; cut in shortening until mixture is crumbly. Sprinkle with vinegar. Gradually add the milk, tossing with a fork until a ball forms. Cover and refrigerate for 30 minutes or until easy to handle.

2 For a single crust, roll out pastry to fit a 9-in. or 10-in. pie plate. Transfer pastry to pie plate. Trim pastry to 1/2 in. beyond edge of plate; flute edges. Fill or bake shell according to recipe directions. **Yield:** pastry for single-crust pie (9 or 10 inches).

3 For a double crust, divide pastry in half so that one ball is slightly larger than the other. Roll out larger ball to fit a 9-in. or 10-in. pie plate. Transfer pastry to pie plate. Trim pastry even with edge of plate. Add filling. Roll out remaining pastry to fit top of pie; place over filling. Trim, seal and flute edges. Cut slits in top. Bake according to recipe directions. **Yield:** pastry for double-crust pie (9 or 10 inches). —*Ruth Gritter Grand Rapids, Michigan*

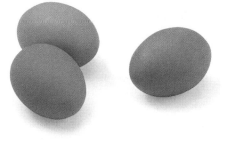

Egg Yolk Pastry

Egg yolk lends an attractive golden color to this pie pastry. The recipe makes enough for one double-crust pie or two single-crust pies.

- 2-1/2 cups all-purpose flour
- 2 teaspoons sugar
- 1/4 teaspoon baking powder
- 1/4 teaspoon salt
- 3/4 cup shortening
- 1 egg yolk, lightly beaten
- 5 to 6 tablespoons cold water

1 In a small bowl, combine the flour, sugar, baking powder and salt; cut in shortening until mixture is crumbly. Combine the egg yolk and water; gradually add to flour mixture, tossing with a fork until a ball forms. Cover and refrigerate for 30 minutes or until easy to handle.

2 For a double crust, divide pastry in half so that one ball is slightly larger than the other. Roll out larger ball to fit a 9-in. pie plate. Transfer pastry to pie plate. Trim pastry even with edge of plate. Add filling. Roll out remaining pastry to fit top of pie; place over filling. Trim, seal and flute edges. Cut slits in top. Bake according to recipe directions. **Yield:** pastry for double-crust pie (9 inches).

3 For two single crusts, divide pastry in half. Roll out each portion to fit a 9-in. pie plate. Transfer pastry to pie plate. Trim pastry to 1/2 in. beyond edge of plate; flute edges. Fill or bake shell according to recipe directions. **Yield:** pastry for 2 single-crust pies (9 inches). —*Dolores Skrout, Summerhill, Pennsylvania*

Pleasing pies

thickeners for fruit pies

- Thickeners help prevent fruit pies from being too runny. All-purpose flour, cornstarch and quick-cooking tapioca are the thickeners commonly used in fruit pies. Flour gives the filling an opaque appearance, cornstarch gives a clear appearance and tapioca gives a clear to almost gel-like appearance.

- One thickener can be substituted for another; however, the thickening power of each is different and you may need to make adjustments. Equal amounts of quick-cooking tapioca and cornstarch can be substituted for each other. When replacing flour in a recipe, use half the amount of cornstarch or use 2 teaspoons of quick-cooking tapioca for every 1 tablespoon of flour.

- When using tapioca, mix it with the filling ingredients and allow the mixture to stand for 15 minutes before proceeding with the recipe.

1 In a large mixing bowl, combine the sugar, flour and salt. Stir in the egg, vanilla and sour cream until smooth. Add apples; mix well. Pour into pastry shell. Bake at 375° for 15 minutes. Reduce heat to 325°; bake for 30 minutes.

2 For topping, combine flour and sugar in a small bowl. Cut in butter until mixture is crumbly. Sprinkle over pie; bake 20 minutes longer or until filling is bubbly and topping is browned. Cool on a wire rack. Serve warm or chilled. Store in the refrigerator. **Yield:** 6-8 servings. —*Eugenia McQueen, Tampa, Florida*

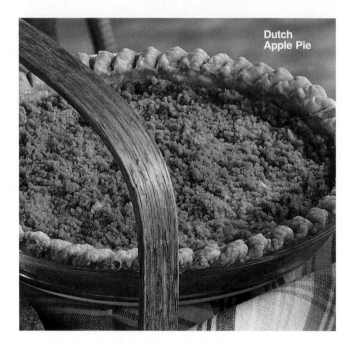

Dutch Apple Pie

Dutch Apple Pie

Sour cream adds extra richness to this classic pie's unbeatable crust. A not-too-sweet streusel topping provides the finishing touch.

  3/4 **cup sugar**
    2 **tablespoons all-purpose flour**
Pinch salt
    1 **egg, beaten**
  1/2 **teaspoon vanilla extract**
    1 **cup (8 ounces) sour cream**
    2 **cups chopped peeled tart apples (about 3 medium)**
    1 **unbaked pastry shell (9 inches)**
STREUSEL TOPPING:
  1/3 **cup all-purpose flour**
  1/3 **cup packed brown sugar**
    2 **tablespoons cold butter**

Golden Apple Pie

(Pictured on page 164)

A classic double-crust apple pie like this never goes out of fashion. Serve slices alone or a la mode.

    6 **cups sliced peeled Golden Delicious apples (about 7 medium)**
  3/4 **cup plus 2 tablespoons apple juice, *divided***
  3/4 **cup sugar**
    1 **teaspoon ground cinnamon**
  1/2 **teaspoon apple pie spice**
    2 **tablespoons cornstarch**
  1/4 **teaspoon vanilla extract**
CRUST:
2-1/2 **cups all-purpose flour**
    1 **teaspoon salt**
    1 **cup cold butter**
    6 **to 8 tablespoons cold water**

1 In a large saucepan, combine the apples, 3/4 cup apple juice, sugar, cinnamon and apple pie spice; bring to a boil over medium heat, stirring occasionally. Combine cornstarch and remaining apple juice until smooth; stir into apple mixture. Bring to a boil; cook and stir for 1 minute or until thickened. Remove from the heat. Stir in vanilla. Cool to room temperature, stirring occasionally.

2 For crust, combine flour and salt in a bowl; cut in butter until mixture is crumbly. Gradually add water, tossing with a fork until mixture forms a ball. Divide in half, making one half slightly larger. On a lightly floured surface, roll out large portion.

3 Line a 9-in. pie plate with bottom pastry; trim even with edge of plate. Add filling. Roll out remaining pastry to fit top of pie; place over filling. Trim, seal and flute edges. Cut slits in top.

4 Bake at 400° for 40-45 minutes or until crust is golden brown and apples are tender. Cool on a wire rack. **Yield:** 6-8 servings. —*Theresa Brazil Petaluma, California*

Meringue Berry Pie

A hot day calls for a cool dessert like this tempting pie. Fresh berries and a sweet raspberry sauce over ice cream in a meringue crust make each slice absolutely irresistible.

1/2 cup sugar, *divided*
1/4 cup slivered almonds, toasted and ground
2 tablespoons cornstarch
2 egg whites
1/8 teaspoon cream of tartar
SAUCE AND TOPPING:
1/2 cup sugar
1 tablespoon cornstarch
1/3 cup water
1 pint fresh raspberries
1 quart vanilla ice cream
2 cups fresh mixed berries

1 In a small bowl, combine 1/4 cup sugar, almonds and cornstarch. In a small mixing bowl, beat egg whites and cream of tartar on medium speed until soft peaks form. Gradually beat in remaining sugar, 1 tablespoon at a time, on high until stiff glossy peaks form and sugar is dissolved. Fold in almond mixture. Spread evenly over the bottom and up the sides of a greased 9-in. pie plate.

2 Bake at 275° for 1 to 1-1/2 hours or until light golden brown. Turn off oven and do not open door; let crust dry for 1 hour. Cool on a wire rack.

3 For sauce, combine sugar and cornstarch in a saucepan. Gradually stir in water until smooth; add raspberries. Bring to a boil over medium heat; cook and stir for 1 minute or until thickened. Set aside to cool.

4 To serve, scoop ice cream into crust; top with mixed berries and sauce. Serve immediately. Freeze leftovers. **Yield:** 6-8 servings.

Meringue Berry Pie

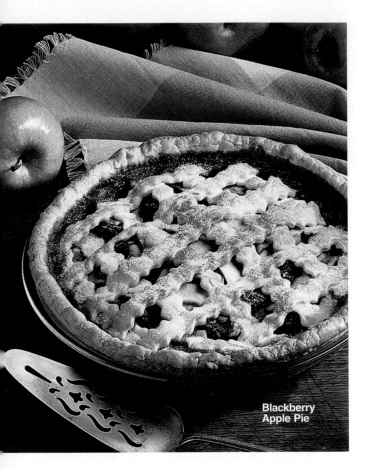

Blackberry Apple Pie

Blackberry Apple Pie

One pint of fresh blackberries yields 1-1/2 to 2 cups.
They'll keep in the refrigerator for 2 days.

Pastry for double-crust pie (9 inches)
    **5 cups thinly sliced peeled tart apples (about 5
      medium)**
    1 pint fresh blackberries
    1 tablespoon lemon juice
  3/4 cup sugar
    2 tablespoons cornstarch
    2 tablespoons butter
    1 egg
    1 tablespoon water *or* milk
Additional sugar

1 Line a 9-in. pie plate with bottom pastry; trim to 1 in. beyond edge of plate. Top with a thin layer of apples. In a large bowl, combine blackberries and remaining apples; sprinkle with lemon juice. Combine sugar and cornstarch. Add to fruit mixture; toss gently to coat. Spoon into pie shell; dot with butter.

2 Roll out remaining pastry; make a lattice crust. Trim, seal and flute edges. Beat egg with water or milk; brush over lattice top and pie edges.

3 Bake at 375° for 50 minutes or until filling is bubbly and apples are tender. Cool on a wire rack. Sprinkle with additional sugar. Serve warm or at room temperature. **Yield:** 6-8 servings.
                      —Fran Stanfield
                      Blanchester, Ohio

Creating a Lattice-Topped Pie

Make pastry for a double-crust pie. Line a 9-in. pie plate with the bottom pastry and trim to 1 in. beyond edge of plate. Roll out remaining pastry to a 12-in. circle. With a fluted pastry wheel, pizza cutter or sharp knife, cut pastry into 1/2-in.- to 1-in.-wide strips. Lay strips in rows about 1/2 in. to 3/4 in. apart. (Use longer strips for the center of the pie and shorter strips for the sides.)

Fold every other strip halfway back. Starting at the center, add strips at right angles, lifting every other strip as the cross strips are put down. Continue to add strips, lifting and weaving until lattice top is completed.

Trim strips even with pastry edge. Fold bottom pastry up and over ends of strips and seal. Flute edges.

Apple Praline Pie

After this double-crust pie is baked, it's covered with
a deliciously rich brown sugar, butter and pecan
topping. Then the pie is returned to the oven so the
topping can bubble and bake onto the crust.

    **7 cups thinly sliced peeled tart apples (about 8
      medium)**
    1 cup sugar
    6 tablespoons all-purpose flour
    1 teaspoon ground cinnamon
    1 teaspoon ground nutmeg
Pastry for double-crust pie (9 inches)
    3 tablespoons apple cider *or* apple juice
    2 tablespoons butter, melted

PRALINE TOPPING:
- 2 tablespoons butter
- 1/4 cup packed brown sugar
- 2 tablespoons apple cider *or* apple juice
- 1 tablespoon half-and-half cream
- 1/2 cup chopped pecans

1 In a large bowl, combine the apples, sugar, flour, cinnamon and nutmeg; toss gently to coat. Line a 9-in. pie plate with bottom pastry; trim even with edge of plate. Brush well with apple cider. Add apple mixture; pour any remaining cider over top. Drizzle with butter. Roll out remaining pastry to fit top of pie; place over filling. Trim, seal and flute edges. Cut slits in top. Bake at 350° for 50 minutes.

2 For topping, melt butter in a small saucepan. Add the brown sugar, cider and cream. Bring to a full rolling boil over low heat, stirring occasionally. Remove from the heat. Stir in pecans.

3 Remove pie from the oven (leave oven on) and place on a baking sheet. Slowly pour topping over pie. Bake 5-10 minutes longer or until topping bubbles. Cool on a wire rack for at least 1 hour before serving. **Yield:** 6-8 servings.
—Bev Higley
Londonderry, Ohio

Purple Plum Pie

This pie is a terrific way to put bountiful summer plums to use. Look for plums that are free of blemishes like cracks, soft spots and brown discoloration. The skin's light gray cast is natural and doesn't affect quality.

- 4 cups sliced fresh plums (about 1-1/2 pounds)
- 1 tablespoon lemon juice
- 1/2 cup sugar
- 1/4 cup all-purpose flour
- 1/4 teaspoon salt

- 1/4 teaspoon ground cinnamon
- 1 unbaked deep-dish pastry shell (9 inches)

TOPPING:
- 1/2 cup sugar
- 1/2 cup all-purpose flour
- 1/4 teaspoon ground cinnamon
- 1/4 teaspoon ground nutmeg
- 3 tablespoons cold butter

1 In a large bowl, sprinkle the plums with lemon juice. Combine the sugar, flour, salt and cinnamon. Add to plums; toss gently to coat. Pour into the pastry shell.

2 For topping, combine the sugar, flour, cinnamon and nutmeg in a small bowl; cut in butter until mixture is crumbly. Sprinkle over filling. Bake at 375° for 50-60 minutes or until filling is bubbly. Cover edges of crust with foil during the last 20 minutes to prevent overbrowning. Cool on a wire rack. **Yield:** 6-8 servings.
—Michelle Beran, Claflin, Kansas

Purple Plum Pie

Making Pastry Cutouts for a Pie

Pastry cutouts can be used for a single- or double-crust pie. To make cutouts, roll out dough to 1/8-in. thickness. Cut out with 1-in. to 1-1/2-in. cookie cutters of desired shape. With a sharp knife, score designs (if desired) on cutouts.

For a single-crust pie, bake cutouts on an ungreased baking sheet at 400° for 6-8 minutes or until golden brown. Remove to a wire rack to cool. Arrange over cooled filling on baked pie.

For a double-crust pie, brush bottom of each unbaked cutout with water or milk and arrange over top crust of an unbaked pie. Press lightly to secure. Bake pie according to recipe.

Golden
Peach Pie

Golden Peach Pie

Here's an easy way to peel a peach: With a slotted spoon, dip the peach into boiling water for 20 to 30 seconds. Remove and immediately place in a bowl of ice water. Peel off the skin with a paring knife.

Pastry for double-crust pie (9 inches)
- **5 cups sliced peeled fresh peaches (about 7 medium)**
- **2 teaspoons lemon juice**
- **1/2 teaspoon grated orange peel**
- **1/8 teaspoon almond extract**
- **1 cup sugar**
- **1/4 cup cornstarch**
- **1/4 teaspoon ground nutmeg**
- **1/8 teaspoon salt**
- **2 tablespoons butter**

Milk

1 Line a 9-in. pie plate with bottom pastry; trim even with edge of plate. Set aside. In a large bowl, combine the peaches, lemon juice, orange peel and extract. Combine the sugar, cornstarch, nutmeg and salt. Add to peach mixture; toss gently to coat. Pour into crust; dot with butter.

2 Roll out remaining pastry to fit top of pie; make decorative cutouts in pastry. Set cutouts aside. Place top crust over filling. Trim, seal and flute edges. Brush pastry and cutouts with milk; place cutouts on top of pie. Cover the edges loosely with foil.

3 Bake at 400° for 40 minutes. Remove the foil; bake 10-15 minutes longer or until the crust is golden brown and filling is bubbly. Cool on a wire rack. **Yield:** 6-8 servings. —*Shirley Olson, Polson, Montana*

Strawberry Meringue Pie

This recipe is simple, so don't be put off by the long directions. The meringue crust filled with chocolate and berries makes an impressive dessert to dress up any meal.

- **3 egg whites**
- **1/3 cup finely crushed saltines (about 12 crackers), *divided***
- **1 teaspoon vanilla extract**
- **1/4 teaspoon cream of tartar**
- **1/8 teaspoon salt**
- **1 cup sugar**
- **1/2 cup chopped pecans, toasted**
- **1 package (4 ounces) German sweet chocolate**
- **2 tablespoons butter**
- **4 cups fresh strawberries, halved**
- **1 cup heavy whipping cream**
- **2 tablespoons confectioners' sugar**

1 Let egg whites stand at room temperature for 30 minutes. Sprinkle 2 tablespoons of cracker crumbs into a greased 9-in. pie plate; set aside. In a large mixing bowl, beat the egg whites, vanilla, cream of tartar and salt on medium speed until soft peaks form. Gradually add sugar, 2 tablespoons at a time, beating on high until stiff glossy peaks form and sugar is dissolved. Fold in pecans and remaining cracker crumbs.

2 Spread evenly onto the bottom and up the sides of prepared pan. Bake at 300° for 45 minutes. Turn off oven and do not open door; let crust cool in oven overnight.

3 In a small heavy saucepan or microwave, melt chocolate and butter; stir until smooth. Drizzle over crust. Let stand for 15 minutes or until set. Top with strawberries. In a chilled small mixing bowl, beat cream until it begins to thicken. Add confectioners' sugar; beat until soft peaks form. Spoon over berries. Refrigerate leftovers. **Yield:** 6-8 servings. —*Kathleen Mercier Orrington, Maine*

Cran-Raspberry Pie

Jewel-toned fruits team up to pack this lattice-topped pie. It's a lovely addition to holiday meals.

- **1-1/2 cups chopped fresh *or* frozen cranberries, thawed**
- **1 package (12 ounces) unsweetened frozen raspberries, thawed**
- **1/2 teaspoon almond extract**
- **1 to 1-1/4 cups sugar**
- **1/4 cup quick-cooking tapioca**
- **1/4 teaspoon salt**
- **Pastry for double-crust pie (9 inches)**

1 In a large bowl, combine the cranberries, raspberries and almond extract. Combine the sugar, tapioca and salt. Add to fruit mixture; toss gently to coat. Let stand for 15 minutes.

2 Line a 9-in. pie plate with bottom pastry; trim to 1 in. beyond edge of plate. Add filling. Roll out remaining pastry; make a lattice crust. Trim, seal and flute edges. Cover edges loosely with foil.

3 Bake at 375° for 40-45 minutes or crust is golden brown and filling is bubbly. Cool on a wire rack. **Yield:** 6-8 servings. —*Verona Koehlmoss Pilger, Nebraska*

Fresh Apricot Pie

This is a nice change of pace from the more traditional apple or cherry pies.

- **4 cups sliced fresh apricots (about 1-3/4 pounds)**
- **1 tablespoon lemon juice**
- **1 cup sugar**
- **1/3 cup all-purpose flour**
- **Pinch ground nutmeg**
- **Pastry for double-crust pie (9 inches)**
- **Milk**
- **Additional sugar**

1 In a large bowl, sprinkle apricots with lemon juice. Combine the sugar, flour and nutmeg. Add to apricots; toss gently to coat.

2 Line a 9-in. pie plate with bottom pastry; trim to 1 in. beyond edge of pie plate. Add filling. Roll out remaining pastry; make a lattice crust. Trim, seal and flute edges. Brush with milk and sprinkle with additional sugar.

3 Cover the edges loosely with foil. Bake at 375° for 45-55 minutes or until crust is golden brown and filling is bubbly. Cool on a wire rack. **Yield:** 6-8 servings. —*Ruth Peterson, Jenison, Michigan*

finishing touches for pie crusts

To top off double-crust pies before baking, use a pastry brush to lightly and evenly apply one of the following washes to the top crust, avoiding the edges:

- For a shine and light browning, brush with an egg white that was lightly beaten with 1 teaspoon of water.
- For a glossy golden appearance, brush with an egg yolk that was beaten with 1 teaspoon of water.
- For a slight shine, brush with half-and-half cream or heavy whipping cream.
- For a crisp brown crust, brush with water.
- For a little sparkle, sprinkle with sugar or decorator sugar after brushing with one of the washes.

To give a little more shine to a baked double-crust pie, warm 1 tablespoon of light corn syrup. Gently brush over the baked warm crust.

homemade crumb crusts

In a mixing bowl, combine the crumbs and sugar; add the melted butter and blend well. Press the mixture onto the bottom and up the sides of an ungreased 9-in. pie plate. Refrigerate for 30 minutes before filling, or bake at 375° for 8-10 minutes or until crust is lightly browned. Cool on a wire rack before filling.

Editor's Note: For desserts made in a 9-in. springform pan (such as cheesecakes), you may need to add 1/4 to 1/2 cup crumbs and 1 tablespoon butter.

Type of Crust	Amount of Crumbs	Sugar	Butter, Melted
Graham Cracker	1-1/2 cups (24 squares)	1/4 cup	1/3 cup
Chocolate Wafer	1-1/4 cups (20 wafers)	1/4 cup	1/4 cup
Vanilla Wafer	1-1/2 cups (30 wafers)	none	1/4 cup
Cream-Filled Chocolate	1-1/2 cups (15 cookies)	none	1/4 cup
Gingersnap	1-1/2 cups (24 cookies)	none	1/4 cup
Macaroon	1-1/2 cups	none	1/4 cup
Pretzel (use a greased pie plate)	1-1/4 cups	1/4 cup	1/2 cup

Spectacular Ice Cream Pie

You can prepare this ice cream pie ahead of time and store it in the freezer until ready to serve, making it great for unexpected guests. Use whatever flavor of ice cream you prefer.

  1 cup graham cracker crumbs (about 16 squares)
1/2 cup finely chopped walnuts
1/3 cup butter, melted
  1 pint coffee ice cream *or* flavor of your choice, softened
  1 pint vanilla ice cream, softened
SAUCE:
  3 tablespoons butter
  1 cup packed brown sugar
1/2 cup half-and-half cream
  1 cup finely chopped walnuts
  1 teaspoon vanilla extract

1 In a small bowl, combine cracker crumbs and walnuts; stir in butter. Press onto the bottom and up the sides of a greased 9-in. pie plate. Bake at 375° for 8-10 minutes. Cool on a wire rack.

2 Spread coffee ice cream over crust. Freeze for 2 hours or until firm. Repeat with vanilla ice cream. Remove pie from the freezer 15 minutes before serving.

3 For sauce, combine butter and brown sugar in a saucepan; cook and stir over low heat for 5-6 minutes. Remove from the heat; slowly stir in cream. Cook and stir for 1 minute. Remove from the heat; stir in walnuts and vanilla. Serve warm over slices of pie. **Yield:** 8-10 servings.
—*Gladys McCollum Abee*
McKee, Kentucky

Peach-Pear Pie

namon and allspice. Add to fruit; toss gently to coat. Pour into pastry shell.

2 For streusel, combine the flour, sugars, cinnamon and nutmeg in a small bowl; cut in butter until mixture is crumbly. Stir in walnuts. Sprinkle over filling. Cover edges loosely with foil. Bake at 375° for 1 hour or until bubbly. Cool on a wire rack. **Yield:** 6-8 servings. —*Jayne Littlefield, Ft. Morgan, Colorado*

Deep-Dish Cherry Pie

This unique dessert is baked in a shallow 1-1/2-quart baking dish. Plus it only has a crust on the top, not the bottom.

 6 cups fresh *or* frozen pitted tart red cherries, thawed, drained and patted dry
 3/4 cup sugar
 3/4 cup packed brown sugar
 1/4 cup cornstarch
 1 teaspoon almond extract
Dash salt
Red food coloring, optional
 3 to 4 tablespoons butter
CRUST:
 1-1/2 cups all-purpose flour
 1 tablespoon sugar
 1/2 teaspoon salt
 1/2 teaspoon ground nutmeg
 1/2 cup shortening
 4 to 5 tablespoons cold water
Milk *or* cream
Additional sugar

1 In a large bowl, combine the cherries, sugars, cornstarch, extract, salt and a few drops of food coloring if desired. Pour into a shallow greased 1-1/2-qt. or 2-qt. baking dish. Dot with butter. Set aside.

2 For crust, combine the flour, sugar, salt and nutmeg in a small bowl. Cut in shortening until mixture is crumbly. Gradually add water, tossing with a fork until a ball forms. On a lightly floured surface, roll out pastry to fit top of baking dish. Place over filling, pressing against the sides of the dish. Cut slits in center of crust. Brush with milk or cream and sprinkle with additional sugar.

3 Bake at 350° for 50-55 minutes or until crust is golden brown and filling is bubbly. Cool on a wire rack for at least 15 minutes before serving. **Yield:** 8-10 servings. —*Lilliam Heston, Warren, New Jersey*

Peach-Pear Pie

With both peaches and pears, this special pie is twice as pleasing. A nutty streusel topping gives each bite a little crunch.

 2-1/2 cups sliced peeled fresh peaches (about 3 medium)
 2-1/2 cups sliced peeled fresh pears (about 3 medium)
 1 tablespoon lemon juice
 1/3 cup packed brown sugar
 1/4 cup sugar
 3 tablespoons cornstarch
 1/2 teaspoon ground cinnamon
 1/4 teaspoon ground allspice
 1 unbaked pastry shell (9 inches)
WALNUT STREUSEL:
 1/2 cup all-purpose flour
 1/4 cup sugar
 3 tablespoons brown sugar
 1/4 teaspoon ground cinnamon
 1/4 teaspoon ground nutmeg
 1/4 cup cold butter
 1/3 cup chopped walnuts

1 In a large bowl, sprinkle the peaches and pears with lemon juice. Combine the sugars, cornstarch, cin-

Old-Fashioned Raisin Pie

The wonderful flavor of this old-fashioned pie will take you back in taste and time to Grandma's kitchen.

    3/4 cup sugar
      2 tablespoons cornstarch
    1/4 teaspoon salt
      1 cup water
    1/2 cup dark corn syrup
  1-1/2 cups raisins
      1 tablespoon lemon juice
      2 teaspoons butter
Pastry for double-crust pie (9 inches)

Old-Fashioned
Raisin Pie

1 In a saucepan, combine the sugar, cornstarch and salt. Stir in the water and corn syrup until blended. Add raisins. Bring to a boil over medium heat; cook and stir for 2 minutes or until thickened. Remove from the heat; stir in lemon juice and butter (filling will be thin).

2 Line a 9-in. pie plate with bottom pastry; trim even with edge of plate. Add filling. Roll out remaining pastry to fit top of pie; place over filling. Trim, seal and flute edges. Cut slits in top.

3 Bake at 425° for 10 minutes. Reduce heat to 375°; bake 30 minutes longer or until crust is golden brown. Cool on a wire rack. **Yield:** 8 servings. *—Pat Sisk, South Elgin, Illinois*

1 In a large bowl, combine the flour, oats, pecans, sugar and salt; stir in the butter until blended. Press onto the bottom and up the sides of a 9-in. pie plate. Bake at 400° for 12-15 minutes or until lightly browned. Cool on a wire rack.

2 For filling, combine sugar and cornstarch in a saucepan. Gradually stir in water and corn syrup until smooth. Bring to a boil over medium heat; cook and stir for 2 minutes or until thickened. Remove from the heat; stir in gelatin until dissolved. Cool to room temperature.

3 Arrange berries in the crust. Carefully pour gelatin mixture over berries. Refrigerate for 2 hours or until set. Refrigerate leftovers. **Yield:** 6-8 servings. *—Florence Robinson, Lenox, Iowa*

Fresh Strawberry Pie

A pretty pie like this will elicit many compliments when you present it to family and friends. Serve with whipped cream or ice cream.

    3/4 cup all-purpose flour
    1/2 cup quick-cooking oats
    1/2 cup chopped pecans
      2 tablespoons sugar
    1/8 teaspoon salt
    1/2 cup butter, melted
FILLING:
    3/4 cup sugar
      2 tablespoons cornstarch
      1 cup water
      2 tablespoons light corn syrup
      2 tablespoons strawberry gelatin powder
      1 quart fresh strawberries

Protecting Pastry Edges from Overbrowning

The edges of a pie pastry often brown before the rest of the pie is thoroughly baked. To protect the edges, fold a 12-in. piece of foil in quarters. Place the folded corner toward you. Measure 3-3/4 in. up each adjacent side and cut out an arc joining the two sides. Discard the center.

Unfold the remaining foil and place it over the unbaked pie. Trim corners if necessary. Gently crimp foil around edge of crust to secure. Bake the pie for 20 to 30 minutes before removing the foil. Or add during the final 10 to 20 minutes of baking.

Chocolate Chip Pecan Pie

Chocolate chips give ordinary pecan pie a tasty twist. Top with a scoop of vanilla ice cream for added indulgence.

        4 eggs
        1 cup sugar
        1 cup light corn syrup
        1 teaspoon vanilla extract
    1/2 cup butter, melted
        1 cup chopped pecans
    1/2 cup semisweet chocolate chips
        1 unbaked pastry shell (10 inches)

1 In a large mixing bowl, beat the eggs, sugar, corn syrup and vanilla. Add butter and mix well. Stir in pecans and chocolate chips. Pour into pie shell.

2 Bake at 350° for 50-55 minutes or until set. Cool on a wire rack. **Yield:** 10-12 servings.
—*Maggie Garrett, Kosciusko, Mississippi*

Traditional Pumpkin Pie

Most families would agree that Thanksgiving dinner isn't complete until slices of pumpkin pie are passed. Here, brown sugar, cinnamon, cloves, nutmeg and ginger add spark to canned pumpkin.

        2 cups all-purpose flour
    3/4 teaspoon salt
    2/3 cup shortening
        4 to 6 tablespoons cold water
FILLING:
        6 eggs
        1 can (29 ounces) solid-pack pumpkin
        2 cups packed brown sugar
        2 teaspoons ground cinnamon
        1 teaspoon salt

    1/2 teaspoon *each* ground cloves, nutmeg and ginger
        2 cups evaporated milk

1 In a large bowl, combine the flour and salt; cut in shortening until mixture is crumbly. Gradually add water, tossing with a fork until a ball forms. Divide pastry in half. On a floured surface, roll out each portion to fit a 9-in. pie plate. Place pastry in pie plates; trim to 1/2 in. beyond edge of plate. Flute edges. Set aside.

2 For filling, beat eggs in a large mixing bowl. Add the pumpkin, brown sugar, cinnamon, salt, cloves, nutmeg and ginger; beat just until smooth. Gradually stir in milk. Pour into pastry shells.

3 Bake at 450° for 10 minutes. Reduce heat to 350°; bake 40-45 minutes longer or until a knife inserted near the center comes out clean. Cool on wire racks for 1 hour. Refrigerate for at least 3 hours before serving. Refrigerate leftovers. **Yield:** 2 pies (6-8 servings each). —*Gloria Warczak, Cedarburg, Wisconsin*

Editor's Note: To decorate the top of a single-crust pie with cutouts as shown below, see page 176.

Traditional Pumpkin Pie

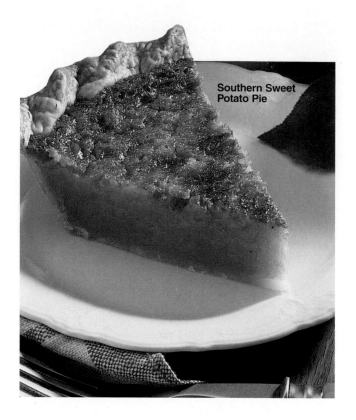

Southern Sweet Potato Pie

Southern Sweet Potato Pie

To prevent sweet potatoes from sprouting, store them in a basket or paper bag in a dark, cool, well-ventilated place for up to 2 weeks. One pound of sweet potatoes (about 3 medium) equals approximately 2 cups mashed.

   3 tablespoons all-purpose flour
1-2/3 cups sugar
   1 cup mashed sweet potatoes
   2 eggs
1/4 cup light corn syrup
1/4 teaspoon ground nutmeg
Pinch salt
1/2 cup butter, softened
3/4 cup evaporated milk
   1 unbaked pastry shell (9 inches)

1 In a large mixing bowl, combine flour and sugar. Add the sweet potatoes, eggs, corn syrup, nutmeg, salt, butter and evaporated milk; beat well. Pour into pastry shell.

2 Bake at 350° for 55-60 minutes. Cool on a wire rack for 1 hour. Refrigerate for at least 3 hours before serving. Refrigerate leftovers. **Yield:** 6-8 servings.
—*Bonnie Holcomb, Fulton, Mississippi*

Chocolate Almond Silk Pie

(Pictured on page 164)

Looking for a special dessert for the chocolate lovers in your family? Try this pie! With a rich, velvet-like texture, even a small slice will satisfy.

2/3 cup all-purpose flour
1/4 cup butter, softened
   3 tablespoons finely chopped almonds, toasted
   2 tablespoons confectioners' sugar
1/8 teaspoon vanilla extract
FILLING:
3/4 cup sugar
   3 eggs
   3 squares (1 ounce *each*) unsweetened chocolate, coarsely chopped
1/8 teaspoon almond extract
1/2 cup butter, softened
Sweetened whipped cream and toasted sliced almonds, optional

1 In a small mixing bowl, combine the first five ingredients. Beat on low speed until well combined, about 2-3 minutes. Press onto the bottom and up the sides of a greased 9-in. pie plate. Bake at 400° for 8-10 minutes or until golden. Cool on a wire rack.

2 For filling, combine sugar and eggs in a small saucepan until well blended. Cook over low heat, stirring constantly, until mixture coats the back of a metal spoon and reaches 160°. Remove from the heat. Stir in chocolate and almond extract until smooth. Cool to lukewarm (90°), stirring occasionally.

3 In a large mixing bowl, cream butter until light and fluffy. Add cooled egg mixture; beat on high speed for 5 minutes. Pour into cooled pie shell. Refrigerate for at least 6 hours before serving. Garnish with whipped cream and almonds if desired. Refrigerate leftovers. **Yield:** 8-10 servings.
—*Diane Larson Roland, Iowa*

Coconut Banana Cream Pie

This pie features the perfect pairing of bananas and coconut, giving it a slightly tropical taste.

      3 **cups flaked coconut**
      7 **tablespoons butter**
    3/4 **cup sugar**
    1/4 **cup all-purpose flour**
      3 **tablespoons cornstarch**
    1/4 **teaspoon salt**
      3 **cups half-and-half cream**
      4 **egg yolks, lightly beaten**
      2 **teaspoons vanilla extract**
      2 **large firm bananas, sliced**
Whipped cream and sliced bananas, optional

1 In a large skillet, saute coconut in butter until golden. Reserve 2 tablespoons for garnish. Press remaining toasted coconut onto the bottom and up the sides of a greased 9-in. pie plate. Bake at 350° for 7 minutes. Cool on a wire rack.

2 For filling, combine the sugar, flour, cornstarch and salt in a large saucepan. Stir in cream until smooth. Cook and stir over medium-high heat until thickened and bubbly. Reduce heat; cook and stir 2 minutes longer. Remove from the heat. Stir a small amount of hot filling into egg yolks; return all to the pan, stirring constantly. Bring to a gentle boil; cook and stir 2 minutes longer. Remove from the heat. Gently stir in vanilla. Cool to room temperature without stirring.

3 Place bananas in the crust. Cover with cream mixture. Refrigerate until set, about 2 hours. Sprinkle with reserved toasted coconut. If desired, garnish with whipped cream and bananas. Refrigerate leftovers.
Yield: 6-8 servings.
—*Tammy Olson*
Bruce, South Dakota

Creamy Maple Pie

Every bite of this cool and creamy pie is bursting with rich maple flavor. It slices well for pretty presentation.

Pastry for single-crust pie (9 inches)
    1/4 **cup cornstarch**
    1/4 **teaspoon salt**
  1-3/4 **cups milk**
    3/4 **cup plus 1 tablespoon maple syrup, *divided***
      2 **egg yolks, lightly beaten**
      2 **tablespoons butter, cubed**
      1 **cup heavy whipping cream**
Toasted sliced almonds

1 Line a 9-in. pie plate with pastry; trim to 1/2 in. beyond edge of plate. Flute edges. Line unpricked pastry shell with a double thickness of heavy-duty foil. Bake at 450° for 8 minutes. Remove foil; bake 5 minutes longer. Cool on a wire rack.

2 For filling, combine cornstarch and salt in a large saucepan. Stir in 1/2 cup milk until smooth. Gradually stir in remaining milk and 3/4 cup maple syrup. Cook and stir over medium heat until thickened and bubbly. Reduce heat; cook and stir 2 minutes longer. Remove from the heat. Stir a small amount of hot filling into egg yolks; return all to the pan, stirring constantly. Bring to a gentle boil; cook and stir 2 minutes longer. Remove from the heat. Gently stir in butter. Cool to room temperature without stirring.

3 In a chilled small mixing bowl, beat cream on high speed until stiff peaks form. Fold 1 cup cream into cooled filling; spoon into crust. Fold remaining syrup into remaining cream; frost top of pie. Refrigerate overnight. Garnish with toasted almonds. Refrigerate leftovers. **Yield:** 8 servings.
—*Emma Magielda*
Amsterdam, New York

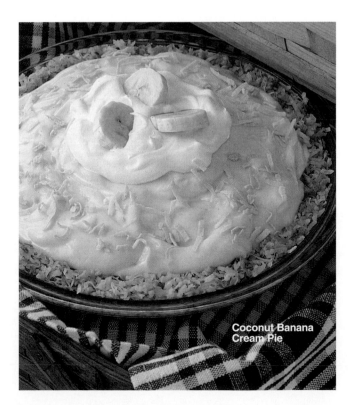

Coconut Banana Cream Pie

Grandma's Lemon Meringue Pie

For a refreshing change from heavier desserts, nothing can compare to lemon meringue pie. Meringues take some time to prepare, but it's a surefire way to impress dinner guests.

  1-1/4 **cups sugar**
    6 **tablespoons cornstarch**
    2 **cups water**
    3 **egg yolks, beaten**
    3 **tablespoons butter, cubed**
  1/3 **cup lemon juice**
    2 **teaspoons white vinegar**
  1-1/2 **teaspoons lemon extract**
    1 **pastry shell (9 inches), baked**
MERINGUE:
  1/2 **cup plus 2 tablespoons water**
    1 **tablespoon cornstarch**
    3 **egg whites**
    1 **teaspoon vanilla extract**
Pinch salt
    6 **tablespoons sugar**

1 In a large saucepan, combine sugar and cornstarch. Stir in water until smooth. Cook and stir over medium-high heat until thickened and bubbly. Reduce heat to low; cook and stir 2 minutes longer. Remove from the heat. Stir 1 cup of hot filling into egg yolks; return all to the pan, stirring constantly. Bring to a gentle boil; cook and stir 2 minutes longer. Remove from the heat. Stir in butter. Gently stir in the lemon juice, vinegar and extract. Pour hot filling into pastry shell.

2 For meringue, combine water and cornstarch in a saucepan until smooth. Cook and stir until thickened and clear, about 2 minutes. Meanwhile, beat the egg whites, vanilla and salt in a large mixing bowl on medium speed until soft peaks form. Gradually beat in sugar, 1 tablespoon at a time, on high until stiff glossy peaks form and sugar is dissolved. Gradually add cornstarch mixture, beating well on high. Immediately spread evenly over hot filling, sealing edges to crust.

3 Bake at 350° for 10-12 minutes or until meringue is golden brown. Cool on a wire rack for 1 hour. Refrigerate for at least 3 hours before serving. Refrigerate leftovers. **Yield:** 6-8 servings.
—*Gwen Johnson*
Medford, Oregon

tips for making meringue

- Since humidity is the most critical factor in making a successful meringue, choose a dry day. Meringues can absorb moisture on a humid day and become limp or sticky.

- Separate the eggs while they are still cold from the refrigerator, then allow the egg whites to stand at room temperature for 30 minutes before beating.

- For the greatest volume, place whites in a small clean metal or glass mixing bowl. Even a drop of fat from the egg yolk or a film sometimes found on plastic bowls will prevent egg whites from foaming. For this reason, be sure to use clean beaters.

- After stiff peaks form, check that the sugar is dissolved. It should feel silky smooth when rubbed between your thumb and index finger.

- Spread the meringue over hot filling to minimize "weeping" (the watery layer between the meringue and filling) and seal to the edges of pastry.

- Cool the pie away from drafts on a wire rack at room temperature for 1 hour. Refrigerate for at least 3 hours before cutting and serving. Store leftovers in the refrigerator.

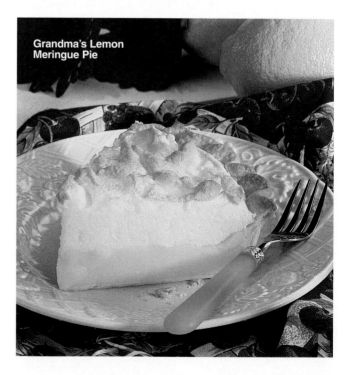

Grandma's Lemon Meringue Pie

Orange Meringue Pie

Most folks are accustomed to lemon meringue pie. So surprise them with this taste twist. It's colorful, refreshing and looks so pretty on the plate.

1-1/2 cups graham cracker crumbs
(about 24 squares)
1/4 cup sugar
1/3 cup butter, melted
FILLING:
  1 cup sugar
1/4 cup cornstarch
1/4 teaspoon salt
  1 cup orange juice
1/2 cup water
  3 egg yolks, beaten
  2 tablespoons lime juice
  4 teaspoons grated orange peel
  1 tablespoon butter
MERINGUE:
  3 egg whites
1/8 teaspoon cream of tartar
  6 tablespoons sugar

Orange Meringue Pie

1 In a small bowl, combine cracker crumbs and sugar; stir in butter. Press onto the bottom and up the sides of a 9-in. pie plate. Bake at 375° for 8-10 minutes or until lightly browned. Cool on a wire rack.

2 For filling, combine the sugar, cornstarch and salt in a small saucepan. Stir in orange juice and water until smooth. Cook and stir over medium heat until thickened and bubbly. Reduce heat; cook and stir 2 minutes longer. Remove from the heat. Stir 1 cup hot filling into egg yolks; return all to the pan, stirring constantly. Bring to a gentle boil; cook and stir 2 minutes longer. Remove from the heat; stir in the lime juice, orange peel and butter. Pour hot filling into pie crust.

3 For meringue, beat egg whites and cream of tartar in a small mixing bowl on medium speed until soft peaks form. Gradually beat in sugar, 1 tablespoon at a time, on high until stiff glossy peaks form and sugar is dissolved. Spread evenly over hot filling, sealing edges to crust.

4 Bake at 350° for 12-15 minutes or until meringue is golden brown. Cool on a wire rack for 1 hour. Refrigerate for at least 3 hours before serving. Refrigerate leftovers. **Yield:** 6-8 servings.

—June Nehmer
Las Vegas, Nevada

Topping a Pie with Meringue

Use a metal spatula to spread meringue over hot filling. Be sure to seal meringue to edges of the pastry to prevent shrinkage while baking.

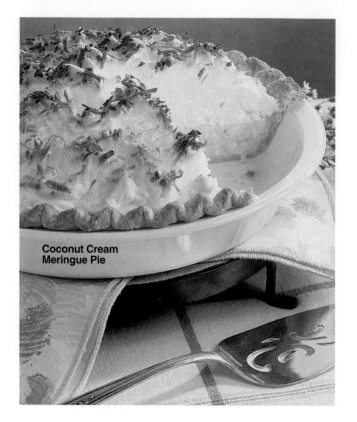

**Coconut Cream
Meringue Pie**

small amount of hot filling into egg yolks; return all to the pan, stirring constantly. Bring to a gentle boil; cook and stir 2 minutes longer. Remove from the heat. Gently stir in vanilla and coconut. Pour into crust.

3 For meringue, beat egg whites and cream of tartar in a small mixing bowl on medium speed until soft peaks form. Gradually beat in sugar, 1 tablespoon at a time, on high until stiff glossy peaks form and sugar is dissolved. Spread evenly over hot filling, sealing edges to crust. Sprinkle with coconut.

4 Bake at 350° for 12-15 minutes or until meringue is golden brown. Cool on a wire rack for 1 hour. Refrigerate for 3 hours before serving. Refrigerate leftovers.
Yield: 6-8 servings.   —*Joyce Reece, Mena, Arkansas*

Coconut Cream Meringue Pie

*Coconut not only appears in this pie's filling
but on top of the meringue as well.*

- 1 **unbaked pastry shell (9 inches)**
- 6 **tablespoons sugar**
- 5 **tablespoons all-purpose flour**
- 1/4 **teaspoon salt**
- 2 **cups milk**
- 3 **egg yolks, beaten**
- 2 **teaspoons vanilla extract**
- 1 **cup flaked coconut**
MERINGUE:
- 3 **egg whites**
- 1/4 **teaspoon cream of tartar**
- 6 **tablespoons sugar**
- 1/2 **cup flaked coconut**

1 Line unpricked pastry shell with a double thickness of heavy-duty foil. Bake at 450° for 8 minutes. Remove foil; bake 5 minutes longer. Cool on a wire rack.

2 In a saucepan, combine the sugar, flour and salt. Stir in milk until smooth. Cook and stir over medium-high heat until thickened and bubbly. Reduce heat; cook and stir 2 minutes longer. Remove from the heat. Stir a

Cream Cheese Lime Pie

*The shortbread cookie crust and lime filling are
delicious changes from the typical lemon pie.
You can substitute graham cracker crumbs
for the cookie crumbs.*

- 1-1/2 **cups shortbread cookie crumbs**
- 3 **tablespoons butter, melted**
LIME FILLING:
- 1 **cup sugar**
- 1/4 **cup cornstarch**
- 3 **tablespoons all-purpose flour**
- 1/4 **teaspoon salt**
- 2 **cups water**
- 3 **egg yolks, beaten**
- 1 **tablespoon butter**
- 1 **teaspoon grated lime peel**
Green liquid food coloring, optional
- 1/4 **cup lime juice**
CREAM CHEESE FILLING:
- 1 **package (8 ounces) cream cheese, softened**
- 1/2 **cup confectioners' sugar**
- 2 **teaspoons lime juice**
- 1 **cup whipped topping**

1 Combine cookie crumbs and butter; press onto the bottom and up the sides of an ungreased 9-in. pie plate. Bake at 375° for 8-10 minutes or until crust just begins to brown. Cool on a wire rack.

2 For lime filling, combine the sugar, cornstarch, flour and salt in a saucepan. Stir in water until smooth. Cook and stir over medium-high heat until thickened and bubbly. Reduce heat; cook and stir 2 minutes longer. Remove from the heat. Stir a small amount of hot filling into egg yolks; return all to the pan, stirring constantly. Bring to a gentle boil; cook and stir 2 minutes longer. Remove from the heat. Stir in butter, lime peel and food coloring if desired. Gently stir in lime juice. Cool to room temperature without stirring.

3 For cream cheese filling, beat cream cheese, confectioners' sugar and lime juice in a small mixing bowl until smooth. Fold in whipped topping. Spread evenly in crust; top with lime filling. Refrigerate for 3 hours or until firm. Refrigerate leftovers. **Yield:** 6-8 servings.

Old-Fashioned Custard Pie

You will need to prepare a double-crust pastry if you wish to make a braided crust edge (see page 170). Otherwise, simply prepare a single-crust pie and flute in the traditional manner.

Pastry for single- *or* double-crust pie (9 inches)
- 4 eggs
- 2-1/2 cups milk
- 1/2 cup sugar
- 1 teaspoon salt
- 1 teaspoon ground nutmeg
- 1 teaspoon vanilla extract
- 1 teaspoon almond extract

1 Line a 9-in. pie plate with bottom pastry; trim to 1/2 in. beyond edge of plate; flute edges or prepare a braided crust. Bake at 400° for 10 minutes.

2 In a large mixing bowl, beat eggs. Add remaining ingredients; mix well. Pour into crust. Cover edges loosely with foil. Bake for 20-25 minutes or until a knife inserted near the center comes out clean. Cool on a wire rack for 1 hour. Refrigerate for at least 3 hours before serving. Refrigerate leftovers. **Yield:** 6-8 servings.
—Maxine Linkenauger, Montverde, Florida

Creamy Banana Pecan Pie

You'll get many compliments when you serve this layered banana beauty. It's a snap to prepare because the filling starts with instant pudding mix.

- 1 cup all-purpose flour
- 1 cup finely chopped pecans
- 1/2 cup butter, softened
- 1 package (8 ounces) cream cheese, softened
- 1 cup confectioners' sugar
- 1 carton (8 ounces) frozen whipped topping, thawed, *divided*
- 3 large firm bananas, sliced
- 1-1/3 cups cold milk
- 1 package (3.4 ounces) instant vanilla pudding mix
Additional chopped pecans, optional

1 In a small bowl, combine the flour, pecans and butter. Press onto the bottom and up the sides of a greased 9-in. pie plate. Bake at 350° for 25 minutes. Cool completely on a wire rack.

2 In a small mixing bowl, beat cream cheese and confectioners' sugar. Fold in 1 cup whipped topping. Spread over crust. Arrange bananas on top. In another bowl, whisk milk and pudding mix for 2 minutes. Immediately pour over bananas. Top with remaining whipped topping. Garnish with pecans if desired. Refrigerate for at least 3 hours before serving. Refrigerate leftovers. **Yield:** 6-8 servings.
—Isabel Fowler
Fairbanks, Alaska

Old-Fashioned Custard Pie

Rhubarb Custard Pie

Although rhubarb is technically a vegetable, it's usually viewed as a fruit to be used in desserts. "Pieplant" is an appropriate nickname for rhubarb because it frequently stars in pies.

> 3 **eggs**
> 3 **tablespoons milk**
> 2 **cups sugar**
> 3 **tablespoons quick-cooking tapioca**
> **Pastry for double-crust pie (9 inches)**
> 4 **cups diced fresh *or* frozen rhubarb***
> 2 **teaspoons butter**
> **Half-and-half cream, optional**
> **Cinnamon-sugar, optional**

1 In a small mixing bowl, lightly beat eggs; blend in milk. Combine sugar and tapioca; stir into egg mixture. Let stand for 15 minutes. Line a 9-in. pie plate with bottom pastry; trim even with edge of plate. Add rhubarb. Pour egg mixture over rhubarb. Dot with butter.

2 Roll out remaining pastry to fit top of pie; place over filling. Trim, seal and flute edges. Cut slits in top. Brush pastry with cream if desired.

3 Bake at 425° for 15 minutes. Reduce heat to 350°; bake 35-40 minutes longer or until lightly browned. Sprinkle with cinnamon-sugar if desired. Cool on a wire rack for 1 hour. Refrigerate for at least 3 hours before serving. Refrigerate leftovers. **Yield:** 6-8 servings.
> —*Lucile Proctor, Panguitch, Utah*

*Editor's Note: If using frozen rhubarb, measure rhubarb while still frozen, then thaw completely. Drain in a colander, but do not press liquid out.

Peanut Butter Pie

Who can resist a tempting chocolate crumb crust and a creamy filling with big peanut butter taste? Be prepared to take an empty plate home when you serve this pie at your next potluck.

> 1-1/4 **cups chocolate wafer crumbs (20 wafers)**
> 1/4 **cup sugar**
> 1/4 **cup butter, melted**

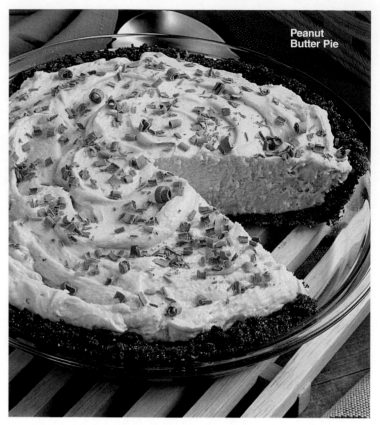

Peanut Butter Pie

> **FILLING:**
> 1 **package (8 ounces) cream cheese, softened**
> 1 **cup creamy peanut butter**
> 1 **cup sugar**
> 1 **tablespoon butter, softened**
> 1 **teaspoon vanilla extract**
> 1 **cup heavy whipping cream, whipped**
> **Grated chocolate *or* chocolate wafer crumbs, optional**

1 In a small bowl, combine cookie crumbs and sugar; stir in butter. Press onto the bottom and up the sides of a 9-in. pie plate. Bake at 375° for 10 minutes. Cool on a wire rack.

2 For filling, beat the cream cheese, peanut butter, sugar, butter and vanilla in a large mixing bowl until smooth. Fold in whipped cream. Gently spoon into crust. Garnish with chocolate or cookie crumbs if desired. Store in the refrigerator. **Yield:** 8-10 servings.
> —*Doris Doherty, Albany, Oregon*

tasty Tarts

Apple Cranberry Tart

(Pictured on page 165)

You'll love the tangy sweetness of this quick but elegant-looking dessert. For directions on creating the pastry cutouts as shown in the photo, see page 176.

Pastry for double-crust pie (9 inches)
    2 cups fresh *or* frozen cranberries, coarsely chopped
    2 medium tart apples, peeled and coarsely chopped
1-1/4 cups packed brown sugar
    2 tablespoons all-purpose flour
    1/2 teaspoon ground cinnamon
    1 to 2 tablespoons butter

1 On a lightly floured surface, roll out half of the pastry into a 13-in. circle. Press onto the bottom and up the sides of an ungreased 11-in. fluted tart pan with removable bottom, or press into the bottom and 1 in. up the sides of a 10-in. springform pan.

2 In a large bowl, combine the cranberries, apples, brown sugar, flour and cinnamon; pour into crust. Dot with butter. Cut remaining pastry with a 1-in. apple cookie cutter. Place over filling.

3 Place pan on a baking sheet. Bake at 425° for 35-40 minutes or until filling is bubbly and crust is golden. Cool on a wire rack. Serve warm. **Yield:** 12-16 servings. —*Suzanne Strocsher, Bothell, Washington*

Rustic Apple Raspberry Tart

This free-form tart requires no pie plate. Just roll out the dough and place on a pizza pan or baking sheet. Place the filling in center of dough and fold up the edge of the pastry to hold in the fruit and juices.

1-1/3 cups all-purpose flour
    1/4 cup sugar
    1/8 teaspoon salt

    6 tablespoons cold butter
    1 egg yolk
    3 tablespoons cold water
FILLING:
 2-1/2 cups thinly sliced peeled tart apples (about 2 medium)
    1 cup fresh *or* frozen raspberries
    1/4 cup sugar
    1 tablespoon cornstarch
    3/4 teaspoon ground cinnamon
    1 tablespoon milk
Coarse decorating sugar

1 In a small bowl, combine the flour, sugar and salt; cut in butter until mixture is crumbly. Gradually add egg yolk and water, tossing with a fork until a ball forms. Shape into a disk; wrap in plastic wrap and refrigerate for at least 1 hour.

2 On a lightly floured surface, roll out pastry into a 14-in. circle. Transfer to a parchment paper-lined 14-in. pizza pan.

3 For filling, combine apples and raspberries in a large bowl. Combine the sugar, cornstarch and cinnamon. Add to the fruit; toss gently to coat. Spoon over pastry to within 2 in. of edges. Fold up edges of pastry over filling, leaving center uncovered. Brush folded pastry with milk; sprinkle with coarse sugar. Bake at 375° for 35-40 minutes or until crust is golden and filling is bubbly. Using parchment paper, slide tart onto a wire rack to cool. **Yield:** 6 servings.

Rustic Apple Raspberry Tart

2 In a chilled small mixing bowl, beat cream until soft peaks form; set aside. In another small mixing bowl, beat the cream cheese and sugar until fluffy. Add extracts and orange peel; mix well. Beat in the whipped cream on low speed. Spoon into crust. Refrigerate for 2-4 hours.

3 Just before serving, arrange peaches and raspberries over filling. In a small saucepan or microwave, melt preserves and honey; mix well. Carefully spoon or brush over fruit. Cut into wedges to serve. Refrigerate leftovers. **Yield:** 6-8 servings.
—*Mary Ann Kosmas, Minneapolis, Minnesota*

Peaches 'n' Cream Tart

Nectarine Blueberry Tart

To ripen nectarines, place in a brown paper bag along with an apple. Store at room temperature for several days.

   1/2 cup butter, softened
   1/3 cup sugar
     1 cup all-purpose flour
Dash salt
PASTRY CREAM:
   1/2 cup sugar
     2 tablespoons plus 2 teaspoons cornstarch
Dash salt
 1-1/2 cups milk
     2 egg yolks
     1 teaspoon vanilla extract
 1-1/2 cups sliced fresh nectarines
   1/2 cup fresh blueberries

1 In a small mixing bowl, cream the butter and sugar until light and fluffy. Add the flour and salt; mix until a ball forms. Cover and refrigerate for 1 hour. Press pastry onto the bottom and up the sides of a greased 9-in. tart pan with removable bottom. Place pan on a baking sheet. Bake at 350° for 18-20 minutes or until golden brown. Cool on a wire rack.

Peaches 'n' Cream Tart

You'll find this luscious dessert as easy as it is elegant. You can bake the crust ahead, then whip together the filling later.

     1 cup finely chopped pecans
   2/3 cup all-purpose flour
   1/2 cup butter, melted
   1/2 cup heavy whipping cream
     1 package (8 ounces) cream cheese, softened
   1/3 cup sugar
     1 teaspoon vanilla extract
   1/2 teaspoon almond extract
     1 teaspoon grated orange peel
     1 can (16 ounces) sliced peaches, well drained
   1/2 cup fresh raspberries
   1/4 cup apricot preserves
     2 tablespoons honey

1 In a small bowl, combine the pecans, flour and butter; press onto the bottom and up the sides of an ungreased 9-in. tart pan with removable bottom. Place pan on a baking sheet. Bake at 350° for 25-30 minutes or until golden brown. Cool completely on a wire rack.

2 For pastry cream, combine the sugar, cornstarch and salt in a saucepan. Stir in milk until smooth. Cook and stir over medium heat until thickened and bubbly. Reduce heat; cook and stir 2 minutes longer. Remove from the heat. Beat a small amount of hot filling into egg yolks; return all to the pan, stirring constantly. Bring to a gentle boil; cook and stir 2 minutes longer. Remove from the heat. Pour into another small bowl; cover with plastic wrap and refrigerate, without stirring, until chilled.

3 Just before serving, pour pastry cream into tart shell. Arrange nectarines and blueberries on top. Refrigerate leftovers. **Yield:** 10-12 servings.

1 tablespoon butter, melted
1 teaspoon vanilla extract
2/3 cup chopped pecans
Maraschino cherry halves, optional

1 In a small mixing bowl, beat cream cheese and butter until fluffy; blend in flour and salt. Refrigerate for 1 hour. Shape into 1-in. balls; press onto the bottom and up the sides of greased miniature muffin cups.

2 For filling, in a small mixing bowl, beat the egg. Add the brown sugar, butter and vanilla; mix well. Stir in pecans. Spoon into tart shells. Bake at 325° for 25-30 minutes. Cool for 15 minutes before carefully removing from pans. Decorate with maraschino cherries if desired. **Yield:** about 20.
—Jean Rhodes
Tignall, Georgia

Pecan Tartlets

preventing soggy tart crusts

Brush tart crusts with melted jelly before layering with fruit. That will help seal the crust and keep the fruit juices from absorbing into the crust.

Tiny Shortbread Tarts

To save time when making these bite-size treats, bake the crusts the day before, cool and store in an airtight container. Top with your favorite filling just before serving.

1 cup butter, softened
1/2 cup confectioners' sugar
2 cups all-purpose flour
1 can (21 ounces) raspberry, cherry *or* strawberry pie filling

1 In a large mixing bowl, cream butter and confectioners' sugar until light and fluffy. Add flour; mix well. Shape into 1-in. balls; press onto the bottom and up the sides of greased miniature muffin cups.

2 Bake at 300° for 17-22 minutes. Cool for 15 minutes before carefully removing from pans to wire racks. Spoon 1 teaspoon of pie filling into each tart. **Yield:** about 3 dozen.
—Kim Marie Van Rheenen
Mendota, Illinois

Pecan Tartlets

The flaky crust combined with a rich center makes these little tarts a satisfying snack. They look so appealing on a pretty platter and make a great finger-food dessert when you're entertaining. They also freeze well.

1 package (3 ounces) cream cheese, softened
1/2 cup butter, softened
1 cup all-purpose flour
1/4 teaspoon salt
FILLING:
1 egg
3/4 cup packed dark brown sugar

White Chocolate Fruit Tart

It takes a little time to make, but this tart is absolutely marvelous, especially in summer when fresh fruit is in abundance.

3/4 cup butter, softened
1/2 cup confectioners' sugar
1-1/2 cups all-purpose flour
FILLING:
   1 package (10 to 12 ounces) vanilla *or* white chips, melted and cooled
1/4 cup heavy whipping cream
   1 package (8 ounces) cream cheese, softened
   1 can (20 ounces) pineapple chunks
   1 pint fresh strawberries, sliced
   1 can (11 ounces) mandarin oranges, drained
   2 kiwifruit, peeled and sliced
GLAZE:
   3 tablespoons sugar
   2 teaspoons cornstarch
1/2 teaspoon lemon juice

1 In a small mixing bowl, cream butter and confectioners' sugar until light and fluffy. Gradually add flour; mix well. Press into an ungreased 11-in. tart pan with removable bottom or 12-in. pizza pan with sides. Place pan on a baking sheet. Bake at 300° for 25-30 minutes or until lightly browned. Cool on a wire rack.

2 For filling, beat melted chips and cream in a small mixing bowl. Add cream cheese; beat until smooth. Spread over crust. Refrigerate for 30 minutes. Drain the pineapple, reserving 1/2 cup juice; set juice aside.

Arrange pineapple, strawberries, oranges and kiwi over filling.

3 For glaze, combine sugar and cornstarch in a small saucepan. Stir in lemon juice and reserved pineapple juice until smooth. Bring to a boil over medium heat; cook and stir for 2 minutes or until thickened. Cool; brush over fruit. Refrigerate for 1 hour before serving. Refrigerate leftovers. **Yield:** 12-16 servings.
   —*Claire Darby, New Castle, Delaware*

Mini Apricot Tarts

These are a wonderful addition to a dessert buffet, which features an assortment of treats.

1/2 cup butter, softened
   1 package (3 ounces) cream cheese, softened
   1 cup all-purpose flour
3/4 cup finely chopped dried apricots
3/4 cup water
1/3 cup chopped pecans
1/4 cup sugar
   2 tablespoons orange marmalade
1/2 teaspoon ground cinnamon
1/8 teaspoon ground cloves
TOPPING:
   2 tablespoons cream cheese, softened
   1 tablespoon butter, softened
1/2 teaspoon vanilla extract
1/2 cup confectioners' sugar

1 In a small mixing bowl, blend butter, cream cheese and flour. Refrigerate for 1 hour.

2 In a small saucepan, bring apricots and water to a boil. Reduce heat; simmer, uncovered, for 5 minutes. Drain. Add the pecans, sugar, marmalade, cinnamon and cloves; set aside.

3 Shape dough into 24 balls. Press onto the bottom and up the sides of greased miniature muffin cups. Spoon apricot mixture into cups. Bake at 350° for 25-30 minutes or until browned. Cool for 10 minutes before removing from pans to wire racks to cool completely.

4 For topping, combine cream cheese and butter in a small mixing bowl. Stir in vanilla until smooth. Beat in confectioners' sugar. Spoon a dollop onto each tart. Store in the refrigerator. **Yield:** 2 dozen.
   —*Phyllis Hickey Bedford, New Hampshire*

White Chocolate Fruit Tart

Raspberry Curd Tartlets

*If you're pressed for time, use purchased lemon curd
in place of the homemade raspberry curd
and garnish with fresh raspberries.*

> 1 cup butter, softened
> 1/2 cup confectioners' sugar
> 1 teaspoon vanilla extract
> 2 cups all-purpose flour
> Dash salt
> 1/2 cup finely chopped almonds
> RASPBERRY CURD:
> 1 package (10 ounces) frozen unsweetened
>   raspberries, thawed
> 3 tablespoons lemon juice
> 1/2 cup butter
> 3 tablespoons sugar
> 4 eggs
> Red liquid food coloring, optional
> Whipped cream, fresh raspberries and mint

Raspberry Curd
Tartlets

1 In a large mixing bowl, cream butter and confectioners' sugar until light and fluffy. Add the vanilla. Combine flour and salt; add to creamed mixture and beat until smooth. Stir in almonds. Press into 2-1/2-in. tartlet pans; trim edges. Place pans on a baking sheet. Bake at 375° for 20-25 minutes or until golden brown. Cool on a wire rack. Remove from pans.

2 For raspberry curd, combine raspberries and lemon juice in a blender or food processor; cover and process until pureed. Press through a strainer to remove seeds.

3 In a saucepan, melt butter over medium heat. Reduce heat to low; add the raspberry puree, sugar and eggs. Cook and stir for 10-15 minutes or until mixture is smooth and thickened and reaches 160°. Remove from the heat. Add food coloring if desired. Press plastic wrap on surface of curd. Refrigerate for several hours or overnight.

4 Spoon about 3 tablespoons of curd into each tart shell; top with whipped cream, raspberries and mint. Refrigerate leftovers. **Yield:** about 2 dozen.

Walnut Tart

*Don't have a tart pan? No problem!
This dessert can be prepared in an
11-in. x 7-in. x 2-in. baking pan instead.*

> 1/3 cup butter, softened
> 1/4 cup sugar
> 1 egg yolk
> 1 cup all-purpose flour
> FILLING:
> 2 cups coarsely chopped walnuts
> 2/3 cup packed brown sugar
> 1/4 cup butter
> 1/4 cup dark corn syrup
> 1/2 cup heavy whipping cream, *divided*

1 In a small mixing bowl, cream butter and sugar until light and fluffy. Add egg yolk; mix well. Add flour just until blended (mixture will be crumbly). Press onto the bottom and up the sides of an ungreased 9-in. tart pan with removable bottom. Place pan on a baking sheet. Bake at 375° for 12-14 minutes. Cool on a wire rack.

2 Sprinkle nuts over crust. In a small heavy saucepan, combine the brown sugar, butter, corn syrup and 2 tablespoons cream. Bring to a boil over medium heat; cook and stir 1 minute longer. Pour over walnuts.

3 Return pan to baking sheet. Bake at 375° for 10-12 minutes or until bubbly. Cool on a wire rack. In a chilled small mixing bowl, beat remaining cream until stiff peaks form. Serve tart at room temperature with whipped cream. **Yield:** 10-12 servings.

—Rovena Wallace, Trafford, Pennsylvania

delectable Desserts
for every occasion

Most folks would agree that a meal isn't complete without something sweet. From Elegant Raspberry Dessert (p. 200) and Lemon Schaum Torte (p. 213) to down-home bread pudding and apple crisp, this chapter features a variety of delectable desserts for any occasion.

Dessert pastries

Work is the main course... pleasure is the dessert.

secrets for successful cream puffs and eclairs

Cream puffs and eclairs are airy pastries made from a French dough called pate a choux or choux pastry. The pastry can be formed into a variety of sizes by being dropped from a spoon or by being piped from a pastry bag. The baked puffs are used for desserts as well as appetizers. Cream puffs and eclairs get their puff from the steam that is produced from the water, eggs and fat in the batter. Follow these guidelines for foolproof cream puffs and eclairs:

- When baking the dough, it's important not to crowd the baking pan. Leave about 3 inches of space around each puff or eclair. The dough needs room to expand during baking and needs air to circulate so the steam it gives off can evaporate.

- Cream puffs and eclairs are done when they are golden brown and have a dry crisp exterior.

For the best flavor, serve cream puffs and eclairs the same day they're made. If necessary, they can be prepared a day in advance. Store the unfilled pastries in a plastic bag in the refrigerator and fill just before serving.

- For longer storage, arrange unfilled pastries in a single layer on a baking sheet and freeze. Once they're frozen, transfer to heavy-duty resealable plastic bags and freeze for up to 2 months. Thaw at room temperature for 15-20 minutes before using. If the thawed pastries are a little soggy, reheat them in the oven for a few minutes.

problem-Solving pointers for Cream Puffs & Eclairs

If this happens with your cream puffs or eclairs:	This could be the reason:
Dough is dry.	The water was boiled too long, causing too much liquid to be evaporated.
Bottoms are soggy.	Puffs or eclairs were filled too soon. Fill just before serving or no sooner than 2 hours beforehand.
Puffs are not crisp.	Puffs are underbaked. They should be golden brown, crisp and dry.

en brown. Remove to wire racks. Immediately cut a slit in each for steam to escape; cool.

3 In a chilled large mixing bowl, beat cream until it begins to thicken. Add sugar and vanilla; beat until almost stiff. Split cream puffs open; discard soft dough from inside. Fill the cream puffs just before serving. Dust with confectioners' sugar. Refrigerate leftovers. **Yield:** 10 servings.   —*Ruth Jungbluth, Dodgeville, Wisconsin*

**State Fair
Cream Puffs**

State Fair Cream Puffs

The Wisconsin Bakers Association has been serving these treats at the Wisconsin State Fair since 1924. In recent years, more than 300,000 are sold annually!

      1 **cup water**
  1/2 **cup butter**
  1/4 **teaspoon salt**
      1 **cup all-purpose flour**
      4 **eggs**
      2 **tablespoons milk**
      1 **egg yolk, lightly beaten**
      2 **cups heavy whipping cream**
  1/4 **cup confectioners' sugar**
  1/2 **teaspoon vanilla extract**
Additional confectioners' sugar

1 In a large saucepan, bring the water, butter and salt to a boil over medium heat. Add flour all at once and stir until a smooth ball forms. Remove from the heat; let stand for 5 minutes. Add eggs, one at a time, beating well after each addition. Continue beating until mixture is smooth and shiny.

2 Drop by 1/4 cupfuls 3 in. apart onto greased baking sheets. Combine milk and egg yolk; brush over puffs. Bake at 400° for 30-35 minutes or until gold-

Making Cream Puffs

1. Bring water, butter and salt to a boil in a saucepan. Add the flour all at once; stir briskly until the mixture leaves the sides of the pan and forms a ball.

2. Remove from the heat and let stand for 5 minutes to allow mixture to cool before adding the eggs. Beat well after adding each egg. Continue beating until mixture is smooth and shiny.

3. Drop dough 3 in. apart onto a greased baking sheet. Bake as directed.

4. Remove puffs from pan to a wire rack. Immediately cut a slit in each puff to allow steam to escape; cool. Split puffs and set tops aside; remove soft dough from inside with a fork and discard. Fill as directed.

Traditional Eclairs

sheet. Bake at 400° for 30-35 minutes or until golden brown. Remove to a wire rack. Immediately cut a slit in each for steam to escape; cool.

3 For filling, combine the sugar and cornstarch in a small saucepan; gradually stir in milk until smooth. Bring to a boil over medium heat until thickened and bubbly, stirring constantly. Reduce heat; cook and stir 2 minutes longer. Remove from the heat. Stir 1 cup hot filling into egg yolks; return all to pan, stirring constantly. Bring to a gentle boil; cook and stir 2 minutes longer. Remove from the heat; stir in butter and vanilla. Cool.

4 Split eclairs open; discard soft dough from inside. Fill eclairs just before serving. Replace tops; dust with confectioners' sugar or spread with frosting. Refrigerate leftovers. **Yield:** 1 dozen.

Traditional Eclairs

Do you recall the old-fashioned sweet eclairs like Grandma used to make? She baked the puffed pastries to a beautiful golden brown, filled them with creamy vanilla pudding and frosted them with chocolaty icing. Now you can make them in your own home!

- 1 cup water
- 1/2 cup butter
- 1 teaspoon sugar
- 1/4 teaspoon salt
- 1 cup all-purpose flour
- 4 eggs

FILLING:

- 1/3 cup sugar
- 3 tablespoons cornstarch
- 2-1/2 cups milk
- 2 egg yolks
- 1 tablespoon butter
- 1-1/2 teaspoons vanilla extract

Confectioners' sugar *or* chocolate frosting

1 In a large saucepan, bring water, butter, sugar and salt to a boil over medium heat. Add flour all at once; stir until a smooth ball forms. Remove from the heat; let stand for 5 minutes. Add eggs, one at a time, beating well after each addition. Continue beating until mixture is smooth and shiny.

2 Insert a 3/4-in. round tip into a pastry bag or heavy-duty resealable plastic bag; add batter. Pipe into 12 strips (about 3 in. long) 3 in. apart on a greased baking

Piping Eclairs

Cut a small hole in the corner of a disposable pastry bag or heavy-duty resealable plastic bag. Place a large round tip (about 3/4 in. in diameter) in bag. Fill bag with dough. Pipe 3-in.-long strips on a greased baking sheet, leaving 3 in. of space between each strip.

Banana Split Cream Puffs

These cream puffs cleverly sandwich banana split ingredients. You can use whatever ice cream and toppings your family prefers.

- 1 cup water
- 1/2 cup butter
- 1/4 teaspoon salt
- 1 cup all-purpose flour
- 4 eggs
- 12 scoops vanilla ice cream
- 1 cup sliced fresh strawberries
- 1 large *or* 2 medium bananas, thinly sliced
- 3/4 cup pineapple tidbits, drained
- 1/2 cup hot fudge ice cream topping

1 In a large saucepan, bring the water, butter and salt to a boil over medium heat. Add flour all at once and stir until a smooth ball forms. Remove from the heat; let stand for 5 minutes. Add eggs, one at a time, beating well after each addition. Continue beating until mixture is smooth and shiny.

2 Drop by rounded tablespoonfuls 3 in. apart onto a greased baking sheet. Bake at 400° for 30-35 minutes or until golden brown. Remove to a wire rack. Immediately cut a slit in each to allow steam to escape; cool. Split puffs open; remove tops and set aside. Discard soft dough from inside.

3 Fill each puff with a scoop of ice cream and top with fruit. Drizzle with hot fudge topping; replace tops. Serve immediately. **Yield:** 12 servings.
—*Sandra McKenzie, Braham, Minnesota*

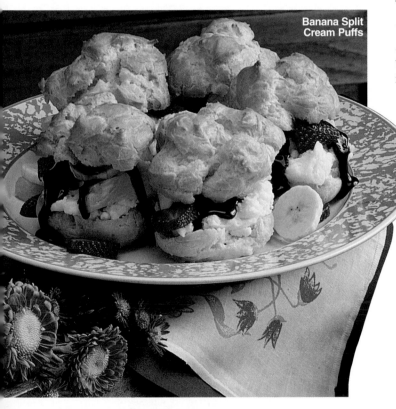
Banana Split Cream Puffs

Almond Puffs

This old-fashioned Danish has a tender crust, a cream puff layer and an almond glaze. Serve it for breakfast or as a dessert.

1/2 cup cold butter
1 cup all-purpose flour
1 to 2 tablespoons water

PUFF LAYER:
1 cup water
1/2 cup butter
1 cup all-purpose flour
1 teaspoon almond extract
3 eggs
GLAZE:
1-1/2 cups confectioners' sugar
2 tablespoons butter, softened
1/2 teaspoon almond extract
1 to 2 tablespoons warm water
2 tablespoons sliced almonds, toasted and chopped

1 In a bowl, cut butter into flour until mixture resembles coarse crumbs. Add water and toss with a fork. Shape into a ball. Divide in half. Pat into two 12-in. x 3-in. strips, 2 in. apart on an ungreased baking sheet. Set aside.

2 In a large saucepan, bring the water and butter to a boil over medium heat. Add flour all at once; stir until a smooth ball forms. Remove from the heat; stir in extract. Let stand for 5 minutes. Add eggs, one at a time, beating well after each addition. Continue beating until mixture is smooth and shiny. Spread over crusts, covering completely.

3 Bake at 325° for 50-55 minutes or until puffed and lightly browned. Cool on a wire rack for 5 minutes. In a bowl, combine the confectioners' sugar, butter, extract and enough water to achieve spreading consistency. Spread over warm puffs. Sprinkle with almonds. Cut into 1-in. strips. Refrigerate leftovers. **Yield:** 24 servings.
—*Mary Ims, Yankton, South Dakota*

problem-
Solving pointers for Puff Pastry

If this happens with your puff pastry:	This could be the reason:
Dough did not bake up puffy.	The cut edges were brushed with an egg wash, preventing the dough from rising.
Sides did not rise evenly.	Edges were not trimmed with a sharp knife.
Dough baked unevenly.	Pastry was overhandled before baking.

tips for
working with
puff pastry

Frozen puff pastry dough is available in sheets or individual shells. It has dozens of paper-thin layers of dough separated by butter. As the pastry bakes, steam created from water in the dough makes the layers rise up and pull apart, resulting in a crisp, flaky pastry. Here are some tips for working with frozen puff pastry:

- Thaw pastry at room temperature for about 20 minutes before handling. Handle as little as possible to avoid stretching and tearing.

- Preheat the oven as directed.

- Cut pastry with a sharp knife or cutter to get a clean edge.

- Only brush an egg wash on the top of the dough, not the edges. If the edges are brushed, they will stick together and the pastry won't rise during baking.

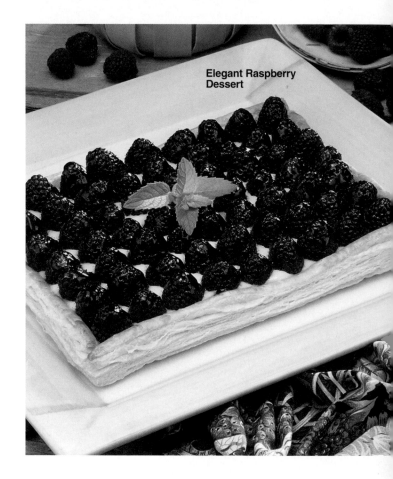

Elegant Raspberry Dessert

Elegant
Raspberry Dessert

(Also pictured on page 194)

If the eye-catching appearance of this dessert doesn't impress guests, the wonderful flavor will! The homemade pastry cream is rich and smooth.

PASTRY CREAM:
1/4 cup sugar
4 teaspoons cornstarch
Dash salt
3/4 cup milk
1 egg yolk, beaten
1/2 teaspoon vanilla extract
CRUST:
1 sheet frozen puff pastry, thawed
1 egg
1 tablespoon water
TOPPING:
1-1/2 cups fresh raspberries *or* other berries
2 tablespoons seedless raspberry jam, warmed

1 In a saucepan, combine the sugar, cornstarch and salt. Stir in milk until smooth. Cook and stir over medium-high heat until thickened and bubbly. Reduce heat; cook and stir 2 minutes longer. Remove from the heat. Stir a small amount of hot filling into yolk; return all to the pan, stirring constantly. Bring to a gentle boil; cook and stir 2 minutes longer. Remove from the heat; stir in vanilla. Pour into a small bowl; cover surface with plastic wrap. Refrigerate, without stirring, until chilled.

2 On a large parchment paper-lined baking sheet, unfold puff pastry sheet and form a 10-in. square (lightly use a rolling pin if necessary). With a large sharp knife or pastry wheel, cut a strip of dough 2-in. wide, leaving a 10-in. x 8-in. rectangle. From the 2-in. strip, cut two 10-in. x 1/2-in. strips and two 7-in. x 1/2-in. strips. Discard trimmings.

3 Prick the 10-in. x 8-in. rectangle (pastry base) with a fork. Brush water 1/2 in. around edges. Place the 10-in. x 1/2-in. and 7-in. x 1/2-in. strips along edge of base to form the sides; press lightly.

4 In a small bowl, beat egg and water; brush over top of pastry. Bake at 400° for 15-20 minutes or until golden brown and puffed. Cool on a wire rack. To serve, place tart on a serving plate. Spread with pastry cream. Top with raspberries; brush with jam. **Yield:** 8 servings.

storing puff pastry

Unbaked puff pastry dough may be wrapped tightly in plastic wrap and stored in the refrigerator for 2 or 3 days or frozen for up to 1 month. Baked pastries are best enjoyed the day they are made and don't refrigerate well. Baked unfilled pastry may be frozen in airtight containers for up to 6 weeks.

Forming a Puff Pastry Crust

1. On a parchment paper-lined baking sheet, unfold puff pastry sheet and form a 10-in. square, using a rolling pin if necessary.

With a ruler, measure 2 in. from one edge in several places and mark with toothpicks. Using the toothpicks as guides, cut a 10-in. x 2-in. rectangle with a long sharp knife or pastry wheel.

2. From the 10-in. x 2-in. strip, cut two 10-in. x 1/2-in. strips and two 7-in. x 1/2-in. strips. Remove and discard trimmings.

3. Prick the 10-in. x 8-in. pastry base all over with a fork.

4. Brush water 1/2 in. around edges of pastry base. Place the 10-in. x 1/2-in. and 7-in. x 1/2-in. strips along edges to form sides. Press lightly.

Palmiers

Blueberry Turnovers

While you can make them a little in advance, these pastries are best served the day they're made.

- **2 cups fresh *or* frozen blueberries, *divided***
- **2 tablespoons sugar**
- **1 tablespoon cornstarch**
- **2 teaspoons grated lemon peel**
- **2 tablespoons butter**
- **1 package (17.3 ounces) frozen puff pastry, thawed**
- **1 egg**
- **1 tablespoon water**
- **1/2 cup confectioners' sugar**
- **1 tablespoon milk**

1 In a saucepan, combine 1/2 cup blueberries, sugar, cornstarch and lemon peel. Mash well with a fork. Bring to a boil over low heat; cook and stir for 2 minutes or until thickened. Remove from the heat. Stir in butter and remaining blueberries.

2 On a lightly floured surface, roll out each pastry sheet into a 12-in. square. Cut each into four squares. Spoon 3 tablespoons of filling into the center of each square; fold diagonally in half and press edges to seal. Place on an ungreased baking sheet.

3 Beat egg and water; brush over pastry. Bake at 450° for 15 minutes or until golden brown. Combine confectioners' sugar and milk; drizzle over turnovers. Serve warm or at room temperature. **Yield:** 8 servings.

Palmiers

It takes just two ingredients to make these impressive but easy-to-do French pastries, which are often called palm leaves.

- **1 cup sugar, *divided***
- **1 sheet frozen puff pastry, thawed**

1 Sprinkle a surface with 1/4 cup sugar; open puff pastry sheet on surface. Sprinkle with 2 tablespoons sugar. Roll into a 14-in. x 10-in. rectangle. Sprinkle with 1/2 cup sugar to within 1/2 in. of edges. Lightly press into pastry.

2 With a knife, very lightly score a line widthwise across the middle of the pastry. Starting at one short side, roll up jelly-roll style, stopping at the score mark in the middle. Starting at the other side, roll up pastry jelly-roll style to score mark. Cut into 3/8-in. slices.

3 Place cut side up 2 in. apart on parchment paper-lined baking sheets. Sprinkle lightly with 1 tablespoon sugar. Bake at 425° for 12 minutes. Turn pastries over and sprinkle with remaining sugar. Bake 5 minutes longer or until golden brown and glazed. Remove to wire racks to cool completely. Store in airtight containers. **Yield:** about 2 dozen.

Making Palmiers

Roll out dough into a 14-in. x 10-in. rectangle. Sprinkle sugar over dough to within 1/2 in. of edges. Lightly press into pastry. With a knife, very lightly score a line widthwise across the middle of the pastry. Starting at one short side, roll up pastry jelly-roll style, stopping at the score mark in the middle. Starting at the other short side, roll up pastry jelly-roll style to the score mark. Cut into 3/8-in. slices.

Heart's Delight Dessert

This lovely and luscious treat will win the hearts of everyone you make it for. If you prefer, skip the step of cutting a heart shape in each pastry sheet and bake them as 12-inch squares.

- 1 package (17.3 ounces) frozen puff pastry, thawed
- 3 cups cold milk
- 1 package (5.1 ounces) instant vanilla pudding mix
- 2 cups heavy whipping cream
- 1 teaspoon vanilla extract, *divided*
- 1 cup confectioners' sugar
- 1 tablespoon water
- 1/4 teaspoon almond extract
- 1/2 cup semisweet chocolate chips
- 1 teaspoon shortening

1 On a lightly floured surface, roll each puff pastry sheet into a 12-in. square. Using an 11-in. heart pattern, cut each square into a heart shape. Place on greased baking sheets. Discard trimmings. Bake at 400° for 12-15 minutes or until golden brown. Remove to wire racks to cool.

2 In a bowl, whisk milk and pudding mix for 2 minutes. Let stand for 2 minutes or until soft-set. In a chilled large mixing bowl, beat cream and 1/2 teaspoon vanilla until stiff peaks form. Carefully fold into pudding.

3 Split puff pastry hearts in half. Place one layer on a serving plate. Top with a third of the pudding mixture. Repeat twice. Top with remaining pastry.

4 In a bowl, combine the confectioners' sugar, water, almond extract and remaining vanilla until smooth. Spread over top pastry. In a heavy saucepan or microwave, melt chocolate chips and shortening; stir until smooth. Pipe in diagonal lines in one direction over frosting. Beginning 1 in. from side of heart, use a sharp knife to draw right angles across the piped lines. Refrigerate until set. Refrigerate leftovers. **Yield:** 10-12 servings.
—*Lorene Milligan, Chemainus, British Columbia*

Cherry Cheesecake Tarts

Frozen puff pastry shells, cream cheese and cherry pie filling make these attractive tarts simple to prepare. The recipe can easily be doubled if you're entertaining a larger group.

- 1 package (10 ounces) frozen puff pastry shells
- 2 packages (3 ounces *each*) cream cheese, softened
- 1/4 cup confectioners' sugar
- 1/2 teaspoon almond extract
- 1 can (21 ounces) cherry pie filling

Additional confectioners' sugar

1 Bake pastry shells according to package directions. In a small mixing bowl, beat the cream cheese, sugar and extract. With a fork, carefully remove the circular top of each baked shell and set aside. Discard any soft pastry from inside shells.

2 Spoon the cream cheese filling into shells; place on a baking sheet. Bake at 400° for 5 minutes. Remove to a wire rack; cool for 1 hour. Refrigerate until serving.

3 Just before serving, spoon pie filling into shells. Top with reserved pastry circles. Dust with confectioners' sugar. Refrigerate leftovers. **Yield:** 6 servings.
—*Mary Lindell, Sanford, Michigan*

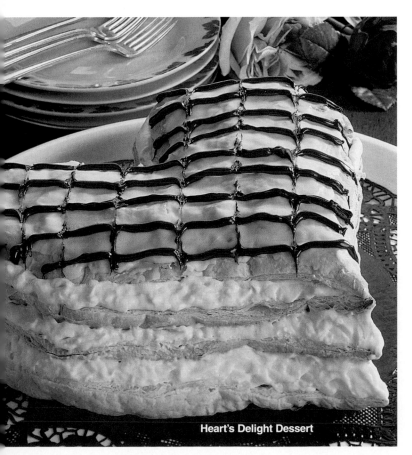
Heart's Delight Dessert

problem-Solving pointers for Phyllo Dough

If this happens with your phyllo dough:	This could be the reason:
Dough is crumbly.	The dough was not thawed completely at room temperature before using.
	The dough was kept in the freezer too long.
Dough is brittle.	The dough became dry. Be sure to properly keep it covered. (See Tips for Working with Phyllo Dough on the opposite page.)

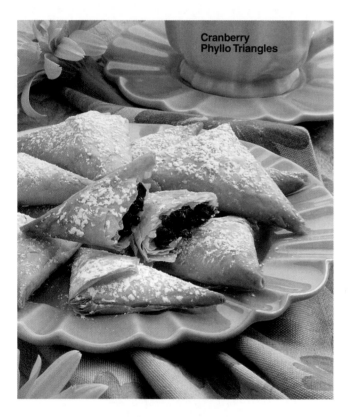

Cranberry Phyllo Triangles

Cranberry Phyllo Triangles

It's hard to eat just one of these crispy cranberry-filled triangles. If you prefer, make the chocolate version instead.

1/2 cup chopped fresh *or* frozen cranberries
3 tablespoons sugar
2 tablespoons raisins
2 tablespoons chopped pecans
1 tablespoon honey
1/4 teaspoon shredded orange peel
20 sheets phyllo dough (14 inches x 9 inches)
1/2 cup butter, melted
Confectioners' sugar

1 In a saucepan, combine the cranberries, sugar, raisins, pecans, honey and orange peel; bring to a boil. Reduce heat; simmer, uncovered, for 5 minutes, stirring occasionally. Drain and discard any juice. Cool to room temperature.

2 Lightly brush one sheet of phyllo with butter; place another sheet of phyllo on top and brush with butter. Keep remaining phyllo covered with plastic wrap and a damp towel to prevent drying. Cut the two layered sheets into three 14-in. x 3-in. strips. Place a teaspoon of cranberry filling in lower corner on each strip. Fold dough over filling, forming a triangle. Fold triangle up, then fold triangle over, forming another triangle. Continue folding, like a flag, until you come to the end of the strip. Brush end of dough with butter and press onto triangle to seal. Turn triangle and brush top with melted butter. Repeat with remaining strips of dough and remaining sheets of phyllo.

3 Place triangles on a greased baking sheet. Bake at 375° for 15-17 minutes or until golden brown. Cool on a wire rack. Sprinkle with confectioners' sugar. **Yield:** 30 triangles.

For Chocolate Phyllo Triangles: In a microwave or heavy saucepan, melt 8 oz. of chopped semisweet chocolate. Stir in 3/4 cup toasted chopped pecans. Place a heaping teaspoonful on phyllo strip. Fold up as directed above.

Making Phyllo Triangles

1. Place 1 teaspoon of filling in lower corner on each strip. Fold dough over filling, forming a triangle.

2. Fold triangle up.

3. Fold triangle over, forming another triangle.

4. Continue folding like a flag, until you come to the end of the strip. Brush end of dough with melted butter and press onto triangle to seal. Turn triangle and brush top with melted butter.

Lime Mousse in Phyllo Cups

Lime gives a tart refreshing flavor to sweetened whipped cream. You can also use the lime mousse to fill individual purchased tart cups.

tips for working with phyllo dough

Phyllo (pronounced FEE-lo) is a tissue-thin dough, generally sold in the freezer section of grocery stores. Phyllo dough is liberally basted with melted butter between each sheet so that it bakes up crisp and flaky. Phyllo dough is used for desserts, appetizers and savory main dishes. Follow these pointers for perfect phyllo:

- Thaw phyllo according to package directions. Always have all the other ingredients assembled and ready to go before unwrapping the dough.

- Because phyllo is thin, fragile and tears easily, work on a smooth dry surface.

- Phyllo dries out quickly. So once the dough is unwrapped and unrolled, cover it with plastic wrap, then a damp kitchen towel. Work with one sheet at a time and keep the other sheets covered.

- Preheat the oven as directed.

12 sheets phyllo dough (14 inches x 9 inches)
 3 tablespoons butter, melted
 1 cup heavy whipping cream
 2 tablespoons sugar
 2 tablespoons lime juice
1-1/2 teaspoons grated lime peel
 1 drop green food coloring, optional
Fresh lime slices, optional

1 Place two sheets of phyllo dough on top of each other. Keep remaining phyllo covered with plastic wrap and a damp towel to prevent drying. Cut layered sheets in half widthwise. Brush top sheet of each with butter. Lightly press one stack into a 6-oz. custard cup coated with nonstick cooking spray. Lightly press second stack on top. Repeat with five more cups.

2 Bake at 375° for 8-10 minutes or until golden brown. Cool for 5 minutes before carefully removing pastry to a wire rack to cool completely.

3 For mousse, beat cream in a chilled small mixing bowl until thickened. Add the sugar, lime juice, lime peel and food coloring if desired; beat until soft peaks form. Just before serving, fill phyllo cups with mousse. Garnish with lime slices if desired. **Yield:** 6 servings.

Hazelnut Apricot Strudel

Did you know that strudel is the German word for whirlpool? The swirling layers of this filled and rolled dessert likely led to its unusual name.

> 1 package (6 ounces) dried apricots, chopped
> 1/4 cup sugar
> 1 teaspoon orange peel
> 1/2 cup orange juice
> 1/4 cup water
> 1/3 cup chopped hazelnuts
> 6 sheets phyllo dough (14 inches x 9 inches)
> 2 tablespoons butter, melted
> 1/3 cup graham cracker crumbs (about 5 squares)

1 In a saucepan, combine the apricots, sugar and orange peel. Stir in orange juice and water. Bring to a boil. Reduce heat; simmer, uncovered, for 15 minutes or until liquid is absorbed, stirring occasionally. Remove from the heat; cool to room temperature. Set aside 1 tablespoon nuts; toast the remaining nuts. Stir toasted nuts into apricot mixture.

2 Cover a work surface with a piece of plastic wrap larger than the phyllo sheet. Place one sheet of phyllo on the plastic wrap. Keep remaining phyllo sheets covered with plastic wrap and a damp towel. Working quickly, layer the phyllo sheets over each other, brushing each sheet with butter and sprinkling with a tablespoon of crumbs. Carefully spread apricot filling along one long edge to within 1 in. of short sides. Fold the two short sides over filling. Using the plastic wrap to help lift one long side, roll up jelly-roll style.

3 Use the plastic wrap to help transfer strudel to a greased baking sheet; discard plastic wrap. Brush top with butter; score top lightly at 1-1/2-in. intervals. Sprinkle with reserved nuts. Bake at 375° for 15-18 minutes or until golden brown. Cool on a wire rack. Slice at scored marks. **Yield:** 8 servings.

Hazelnut Apricot Strudel

storing phyllo dough

Refrigerate unopened phyllo dough for up to 3 weeks or freeze for up to 3 months. Opened dough can be refrigerated for up to 3 days. Baked phyllo should be stored in an airtight container for up to 3 days or frozen for up to 3 months.

The most indispensable ingredient of all good home cooking— love for those you are cooking for.

Making Strudel

1. Cover a smooth dry work surface with a piece of plastic wrap that is larger than the phyllo sheets. Place first sheet of phyllo on the plastic wrap. Working quickly, layer the phyllo sheets over each other, brushing with butter between each sheet and sprinkling with cracker crumbs.

2. Carefully spread filling to within 1 in. of edges.

3. Fold one long side over the filling, then the two short sides. Using the plastic wrap to help lift the remaining long side, roll up jelly-roll style.

4. Use the plastic wrap to help transfer strudel to greased baking sheet. Roll strudel off of plastic wrap and center on baking sheet. Discard plastic wrap.

Chocolate Almond Mousse Napoleons

The chocolate almond mousse is creamy and delicious. You can also serve it in parfait glasses with a crisp cookie.

> **6 sheets phyllo dough (14 inches x 9 inches)**
> **1/4 cup butter, melted**
> **2 tablespoons sugar**
> **MOUSSE:**
> **2 cups heavy whipping cream**
> **1 cup (6 ounces) semisweet chocolate chips**
> **1/4 teaspoon almond extract**
> **GLAZE:**
> **1 cup confectioners' sugar**
> **1/4 teaspoon vanilla extract**
> **Dash salt**
> **4 to 5 teaspoons half-and-half cream**
> **3 tablespoons semisweet chocolate chips, melted**

1 Place one phyllo sheet on a work surface; keep remaining phyllo sheets covered with plastic wrap and a damp towel. Brush phyllo with melted butter; sprinkle with 1 teaspoon sugar. Top with second phyllo sheet. Brush with butter; sprinkle with 1 teaspoon sugar. Repeat with third phyllo sheet, butter and sugar. Cut stack into twelve 3-in. squares. Transfer stacks to a greased baking sheet; place about 1 in. apart. Repeat with remaining three phyllo sheets, butter and sugar. Bake at 350° for 8-9 minutes or until golden brown, watching carefully. Cool on wire racks.

2 For mousse, heat heavy cream in a small saucepan over medium heat until cream begins to simmer, about 180°. Remove from the heat. Whisk in chocolate and extract until smooth. Transfer to a mixing bowl and refrigerate until chilled. Beat cream mixture until soft peaks form. Refrigerate until serving.

3 For glaze, combine the confectioners' sugar, vanilla and salt. Add enough half and half to achieve a spreading consistency. Spread over eight squares of phyllo. Drizzle with melted chocolate.

4 To serve, spread about 1/4 cup mousse over a square of phyllo. Add a second phyllo square and more mousse. Top with one of the glazed phyllo squares. Repeat with remaining phyllo, mousse and glazed phyllo. Serve immediately. **Yield: 8 servings.**

Baklava

*Baklava is a traditional Middle Eastern pastry
made with phyllo dough, nuts and honey.
This dessert is very rich, so one pan goes a long way.*

- 1-1/2 **pounds finely chopped walnuts**
- 1/2 **cup sugar**
- 1/2 **teaspoon ground cinnamon**
- 1/8 **teaspoon ground cloves**
- 1 **pound butter, melted, *divided***
- 2 **packages (16 ounces *each*, 18-inch x 14-inch sheet size) phyllo dough**

SYRUP:
- 2 **cups sugar**
- 2 **cups water**
- 1 **cup honey**
- 1 **tablespoon grated lemon *or* orange peel**

1 In a small bowl, combine the walnuts, sugar, cinnamon and cloves; set aside. Brush a 15-in. x 10-in. x 1-in. baking pan with some of the butter. Unroll each package of phyllo sheets; trim each stack to fit into pan. Cover dough with plastic wrap and a damp cloth while assembling. Place one sheet of phyllo in pan; brush with butter. Repeat 14 times.

2 Spread with 2 cups walnut mixture. Layer with five sheets of phyllo, brushing with butter between each. Spread with remaining walnut mixture. Top with one sheet of phyllo; brush with butter. Repeat 14 times. Cut into 2-1/2-in. squares; cut each square in half diagonally. Brush remaining butter over top. Bake at 350° for 40-45 minutes or until golden brown.

3 In a large saucepan, bring the syrup ingredients to a boil. Reduce heat; simmer for 10 minutes. Strain and discard peel; cool to lukewarm. Pour over warm baklava. **Yield:** 4 dozen.
*—Judy Losecco
Buffalo, New York*

Cheese Danish

*To make the cinnamon-sugar topping, combine
1/4 cup sugar and 2 teaspoons cinnamon.*

- 1 **tube (4 ounces) refrigerated crescent rolls**
- 1 **package (3 ounces) cream cheese, softened**
- 1/4 **cup sugar**
- 1/4 **teaspoon vanilla extract**
- 1 **teaspoon butter, melted**

Cinnamon-sugar

Cheese Danish

1 Unroll crescent roll dough and separate into two rectangles; place on an ungreased baking sheet. Press perforations together.

2 In a small mixing bowl, beat cream cheese, sugar and vanilla until smooth. Spread over half of each rectangle; fold dough over filling and pinch to seal. Brush with butter; sprinkle with cinnamon-sugar. Bake at 350° for 15-20 minutes or until golden brown. **Yield:** 2 servings.
*—Mary Margaret Merritt
Washington Court House, Ohio*

Quick Cherry Turnovers

*Refrigerated crescent rolls let you make these
fruit-filled pastries in a hurry. Feel free to
experiment with other pie fillings.*

- 1 **tube (8 ounces) refrigerated crescent rolls**
- 1 **cup cherry pie filling**
- 1/2 **cup confectioners' sugar**
- 1 **to 2 tablespoons milk**

1 Unroll crescent roll dough and separate into four squares; place on an ungreased baking sheet. Press seams and perforations together. Spoon 1/4 cup pie filling in one corner of each square. Fold to make triangles; pinch to seal.

2 Bake at 375° for 10-12 minutes or until golden. Combine sugar and enough milk to achieve drizzling consistency. Drizzle over turnovers; serve warm. **Yield:** 4 servings. *—Elleen Oberrueter, Danbury, Iowa*

Raspberry Custard Kuchen

Kuchen is German for cake and usually refers to a sweet yeast dough coffee cake, often containing fruit and nuts. It can be served for breakfast or as a special dessert.

- 1-1/2 **cups all-purpose flour,** *divided*
- 1/2 **teaspoon salt**
- 1/2 **cup cold butter**
- 2 **tablespoons heavy whipping cream**
- 1/2 **cup sugar**

FILLING:
- 3 **cups fresh raspberries**
- 1 **cup sugar**
- 1 **tablespoon all-purpose flour**
- 2 **eggs, beaten**
- 1 **cup heavy whipping cream**
- 1 **teaspoon vanilla extract**

1 In a bowl, combine 1 cup flour and salt; cut in butter until mixture resembles coarse crumbs. Stir in cream. Pat into a greased 13-in. x 9-in. x 2-in. baking pan. Combine the sugar and remaining flour; sprinkle over crust.

2 Arrange raspberries over crust. In a large bowl, combine sugar and flour. Stir in the eggs, cream and vanilla; pour over berries. Bake at 375° for 40-45 minutes or until lightly browned. Serve warm or chilled. Store in the refrigerator. **Yield:** 10-12 servings.

—Virginia Arndt, Sequim, Washington

Ladyfingers

These light sponge cakes can be served with ice cream or can be used to make tiramisu. A hint of almond flavors them nicely.

- 3 **eggs,** *separated*
- 1/3 **cup sugar**
- 1 **teaspoon almond extract**
- 1/3 **cup all-purpose flour**

Dash salt
- 1/2 **cup confectioners' sugar**

1 Let eggs stand at room temperature for 30 minutes. Grease and lightly flour two baking sheets; set aside. In a large mixing bowl, beat egg yolks on high speed for 3 minutes. Gradually add sugar, beating until thick and pale yellow. Beat in extract. Gradually add flour and salt, beating until well blended. In a small mixing bowl and with clean beaters, beat egg whites on high speed until soft peaks form. Fold into yolk mixture.

2 Cut a 1/2-in. hole in a corner of a heavy-duty plastic bag, or use a pastry bag with round tip #808. Fill bag with batter. Form 4-in.-long finger shapes 1 in. apart on prepared baking sheets. Dust with confectioners' sugar. Bake at 350° for 12-15 minutes or until golden. Remove to wire racks to cool. **Yield:** about 2 dozen.

—Mary Beth de Ribeaux Gaithersburg, Maryland

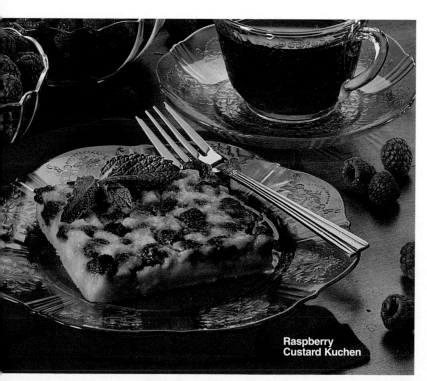

Raspberry Custard Kuchen

Fresh Plum Kuchen

In late summer when plums are in season, this tender fruit-topped cake is delectable! For variety, you can substitute fresh pears or apples instead.

      1/4 cup butter, softened
      3/4 cup sugar
        2 eggs
        1 cup all-purpose flour
        1 teaspoon baking powder
      1/4 cup milk
        1 teaspoon grated lemon peel
        2 cups sliced fresh plums (about 4 medium)
      1/2 cup packed brown sugar
        1 teaspoon ground cinnamon

1 In a small mixing bowl, cream butter and sugar until light and fluffy. Beat in eggs. Combine flour and baking powder; add to the creamed mixture alternately with milk, beating well after each addition. Add lemon peel. Pour into a greased 10-in. springform pan. Arrange plums on top, overlapping slices. Gently press into batter. Sprinkle with brown sugar and cinnamon.

2 Place pan on a baking sheet. Bake at 350° for 40-50 minutes or until top is golden and a toothpick inserted near the center comes out clean. Cool for 10 minutes. Run a knife around edge of pan; remove sides. Cool on a wire rack. **Yield:** 10-12 servings.

—Anna Daley, Montague, Prince Edward Island

Fresh Plum Kuchen

Almond Rhubarb Pastry

Classic desserts like this stand the test of time. The rosy rhubarb filling contrasts beautifully with the golden brown crust.

    1-1/2 cups sugar
      1/4 cup quick-cooking tapioca
        6 cups chopped fresh *or* frozen rhubarb*
PASTRY:
        4 cups all-purpose flour
        4 teaspoons baking powder
    1-1/4 teaspoons salt
    1-1/4 cups shortening
        3 eggs, beaten
      1/3 to 1/2 cup milk, *divided*
TOPPING:
      1/2 cup butter
      3/4 cup sugar
        2 tablespoons milk
      1/2 teaspoon vanilla extract
        1 cup slivered almonds

1 In a large bowl, combine the sugar, tapioca and rhubarb; let stand for 15 minutes. In a large bowl, combine the flour, baking powder and salt; cut in shortening until mixture resembles coarse crumbs. Combine the eggs and 1/3 cup milk; add to crumb mixture, tossing with a fork until dough forms a ball. Add some or all of remaining milk if necessary.

2 Divide dough in half so that one piece is slightly larger than the other. On a lightly floured surface, roll out large half into a 17-in. x 12-in. rectangle. Transfer to a greased 15-in. x 10-in. x 1-in. baking pan.

3 Spoon rhubarb filling into crust. Roll out remaining dough into a 15-in. x 10-in. rectangle. Place over filling. Fold bottom edge of dough over top layer of dough; press edges together to seal.

4 For topping, melt butter in a small saucepan; add sugar and milk. Bring to a gentle boil; cook and stir 2-3 minutes longer or until thickened. Remove from the heat; stir in vanilla. Spread over pastry. Sprinkle almonds on top. Bake at 400° for 20 minutes. Reduce heat to 325°; bake 20-25 minutes longer or until golden brown. Serve warm or cold. **Yield:** 16-20 servings.

—Lois Dyck, Coaldale, Alberta

* **Editor's Note:** If using frozen rhubarb, measure rhubarb while still frozen, then thaw completely. Drain in a colander, but do not press liquid out.

Super
Strawberry Shortcake

Super Strawberry Shortcake

"Wow!" is what people will say when you set this dessert on the table. It's fun to serve since it's attractive, not overly sweet and bursting with flavor.

    1 **quart fresh strawberries, sliced**
    1 **to 2 tablespoons sugar**
SHORTCAKE:
1-3/4 **cups all-purpose flour**
    2 **tablespoons sugar**
    1 **teaspoon baking powder**
1/2 **teaspoon baking soda**
1/2 **teaspoon salt**
1/4 **cup cold butter**
    1 **egg**
3/4 **cup sour cream**
TOPPING:
    1 **cup heavy whipping cream**
    1 **to 2 tablespoons sugar**
    1 **teaspoon vanilla extract**

1 In a large bowl, combine the strawberries and sugar; set aside.

2 For shortcake, combine the flour, sugar, baking powder, baking soda and salt in another large bowl; cut in butter until mixture resembles coarse crumbs. In a small bowl, beat egg; add sour cream. Stir into the crumb mixture just until moistened. Turn onto a floured surface; knead 25 times or until smooth. Roll out into a 7-1/2-in. circle. Cut a 2-in. hole in center to form a ring. Place on a lightly greased baking sheet. Bake at 425° for 12-14 minutes or until golden brown. Remove to wire racks to cool.

3 For topping, beat cream in a chilled small mixing bowl until it begins to thicken. Add sugar and vanilla; beat until stiff peaks form.

4 Just before serving, split shortcake into two horizontal layers. Spoon juice from berries over bottom layer. Spoon half of berries over juice. Spread half of the topping over berries. Add the top cake layer, remaining topping and berries. Cut into wedges. **Yield:** 8 servings.
—*Renee Bisch, Wellesley, Ontario*

Cookie
Sheet Apple Pie

Cookie Sheet Apple Pie

This dessert is a real time-saver when there's a large crowd to be fed. It serves more than a traditional pie with about the same amount of effort.

3-3/4 cups all-purpose flour
1-1/2 teaspoons salt
3/4 cup shortening
3 eggs, lightly beaten
1/3 cup milk
8 cups sliced peeled tart apples (7 to 8 large)
1-1/2 cups sugar
1 cup crushed cornflakes
1 teaspoon ground cinnamon
1/2 teaspoon ground nutmeg
1 egg white, beaten

1 In a bowl, combine flour and salt. Cut in shortening until mixture resembles coarse crumbs. Combine eggs and milk; add to crumb mixture, tossing with a fork until dough forms a ball. Cover and refrigerate for 20 minutes.

2 Divide dough in half so that one piece is slightly larger than the other. On a lightly floured surface, roll out large half to fit the bottom and sides of a greased 15-in. x 10-in. x 1-in. baking pan. Arrange apples over crust. Combine the sugar, cornflakes, cinnamon and nutmeg; sprinkle over apples.

3 Roll out remaining dough to fit top of pan; place over apples. Seal edges; cut slits in top. Brush with egg white. Bake at 400° for 15 minutes. Reduce heat to 350°; bake 25-30 minutes longer or until golden. **Yield:** 16-20 servings. —*Bertha Jeffries, Great Falls, Montana*

Summer Dessert Pizza

This colorful dessert is especially refreshing during the hot months.

1/4 cup butter, softened
1/2 cup sugar
1 egg
1/4 teaspoon lemon extract
1/4 teaspoon vanilla extract
1-1/4 cups all-purpose flour
1/4 teaspoon baking powder
1/4 teaspoon baking soda
1/4 teaspoon salt
GLAZE:
1/4 cup sugar
2 teaspoons cornstarch
1/4 cup water
1/4 cup orange juice
TOPPING:
4 ounces cream cheese, softened
1/4 cup confectioners' sugar
1 cup whipped topping
1 firm banana, sliced
1 cup sliced fresh strawberries
1 can (8 ounces) mandarin oranges, drained
2 kiwifruit, peeled and thinly sliced
1/3 cup fresh blueberries

1 In a small mixing bowl, cream butter and sugar until light and fluffy. Beat in egg and extracts. Combine the flour, baking powder, baking soda and salt; add to creamed mixture and beat well. Cover and refrigerate for 30 minutes.

2 Press dough into a greased 12-in. or 14-in. pizza pan. Bake at 350° for 12-14 minutes or until light golden brown. Cool completely on a wire rack.

3 For glaze, combine sugar and cornstarch in a small saucepan. Stir in the water and orange juice until smooth. Bring to a boil; cook and stir for 1-2 minutes or until thickened. Cool to room temperature, about 30 minutes.

4 For topping, in a small mixing bowl, beat cream cheese and confectioners' sugar until smooth. Add whipped topping; mix well. Spread over crust. Arrange fruit on top. Brush glaze over fruit. Store in the refrigerator. **Yield:** 12-16 servings. —*Ida Ruth Wenger Harrisonburg, Virginia*

Meringue desserts

types of meringue

Meringue is a sweetened egg white foam that can be shaped into cups to hold fruit or mousse or made into a golden crown on Baked Alaska.

Depending on the amount of sugar beaten into the egg whites, meringue is classified as a soft meringue (as used for Baked Alaska or meringue-topped pies) or hard meringue (as used for meringue shells or cookies). For more information on making meringues, see Tips for Making Meringue on page 184.

Lemon Schaum Torte

(Also pictured on page 195)

Schaum Torte is a classic Austrian dessert that consists of meringue layers filled with fruit and topped with whipped cream. This modified version conveniently bakes in a 13-inch x 9-inch pan.

    6 egg whites
    1 teaspoon vanilla extract
1/8 teaspoon cream of tartar
    2 cups sugar, *divided*
    9 egg yolks
1/2 cup lemon juice
    1 tablespoon grated lemon peel
    4 cups heavy whipping cream
2/3 cup confectioners' sugar
Ground cinnamon

1 Place egg whites in a large mixing bowl and let stand at room temperature for 30 minutes. Add vanilla and cream of tartar. Beat on medium speed un-til soft peaks form. Gradually beat in 1 cup sugar, 2 tablespoons at a time, on high until stiff glossy peaks form and sugar is dissolved.

2 Spread meringue over the bottom and up the sides of a greased 13-in. x 9-in. x 2-in. baking dish. Bake at 275° for 1 hour. Turn off oven and do not open door; let meringue dry in oven for at least 1 hour. Remove from the oven; cool on a wire rack.

3 In the top of a double boiler, beat egg yolks and remaining sugar. Stir in lemon juice and peel. Cook and stir over simmering water for 15 minutes or until mixture thickens and reaches 160°. Cover and refrigerate until cool.

4 In a chilled mixing bowl, beat cream until it begins to thicken. Add confectioners' sugar; beat until stiff peaks form. Spread half over meringue; cover with lemon mixture. Top with remaining cream mixture. Sprinkle with cinnamon. Chill overnight. **Yield:** 12-15 servings.
— *Cindy Steffen, Cedarburg, Wisconsin*

Lemon Schaum Torte

makeshift double boiler

If you don't have a double boiler, you can create your own using a metal mixing bowl and a saucepan. The water in the saucepan should not touch the bottom of the bowl.

problem-Solving pointers for Meringue

If this happens with your meringue:	This could be the reason:
Meringue did not reach full volume.	The egg whites were beaten when cold. They should stand at room temperature for 30 minutes before beating. Next time, make sure there are no egg yolks in with the whites and beat in a grease-free bowl.
Beads formed on the top of the meringue and/or the meringue is sticky.	Meringue was made on a humid or rainy day. Meringue was underbaked or overbaked. Meringue was baked at too high a temperature.
Meringue has shrunk during baking.	Seal meringue to edges of the cake or pie before baking.
Meringue has a soft texture.	Meringue was made on a humid or rainy day. Not enough sugar was used. Be sure to use 2 to 4 tablespoons of sugar for each egg white.

Strawberry Schaum Torte

This schaum torte features an easy-to-make strawberry gelatin filling.

- 6 egg whites
- 2 teaspoons water
- 2 teaspoons white vinegar
- 2 teaspoons vanilla extract
- 1 teaspoon baking powder
- 1/4 teaspoon salt
- 2 cups sugar

FILLING:
- 1 package (3 ounces) strawberry gelatin
- 1/2 cup boiling water
- 1 cup fresh *or* frozen sliced strawberries
- 1 teaspoon lemon juice

Dash salt
- 1-1/2 cups whipped cream

1 Place egg whites in a large mixing bowl and let stand at room temperature for 30 minutes. Add the water, vinegar, vanilla, baking powder and salt. Beat on medium speed until soft peaks form. Gradually beat in sugar, 2 tablespoons at a time, on high until stiff glossy peaks form and sugar is dissolved.

2 Spread evenly into a greased 13-in. x 9-in. x 2-in. baking pan. Bake at 300° for 45 minutes. Turn off oven and do not open door; let crust dry in oven overnight.

3 For filling, dissolve gelatin in boiling water in a bowl. Stir in the strawberries, lemon juice and salt (mixture will thicken quickly). Fold in cream. Spread over crust. Store in the refrigerator. **Yield:** 12 servings.
—*Geraldine Sauke, Alberta Lea, Minnesota*

Brownie Baked Alaska

The name Baked Alaska originated at Delmonico's Restaurant in New York City in 1876 and was created in honor of the newly acquired territory of Alaska.

- 2 squares (1 ounce *each*) unsweetened chocolate
- 1/2 cup shortening

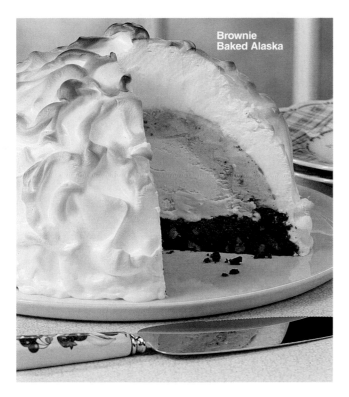

Brownie Baked Alaska

1 cup sugar
1 teaspoon vanilla extract
2 eggs
3/4 cup all-purpose flour
1/2 teaspoon baking powder
1/2 teaspoon salt
1 cup chopped walnuts, optional

FILLING:
1 quart strawberry ice cream, slightly softened
1 quart vanilla ice cream, slightly softened

MERINGUE:
5 egg whites
2/3 cup sugar
1/2 teaspoon cream of tartar
1 teaspoon vanilla extract

1 In a large saucepan, melt chocolate and shortening; remove from the heat. Stir in sugar and vanilla. Add eggs, one at a time, beating well after each addition. Combine the flour, baking powder and salt; stir into chocolate mixture. Add nuts if desired.

2 Spread into a greased 9-in. round baking pan. Bake at 350° for 25-30 minutes or until a toothpick inserted near the center comes out with moist crumbs (do not overbake). Cool for 10 minutes before removing from pan to a wire rack to cool completely.

3 Line an 8 in. or 9 in. round bowl (1-1/2-qts.) with foil. Quickly spread strawberry ice cream over bottom and up sides of bowl, leaving center hollow; cov-

Making a Meringue for Baked Alaska

1. In a double boiler over simmering water, beat egg whites and cream of tartar with a portable mixer on low speed for 1 minute.

2. Continue beating on low speed until meringue reaches 160°, about 12 minutes. Remove from the heat; add vanilla. Beat on high speed until stiff peaks form.

3. Quickly spread over ice cream, sealing meringue to cake layer.

er and freeze for 30 minutes. Pack vanilla ice cream into center; cover and freeze.

4 To assemble, place the brownie base on a 10-in. ovenproof serving plate. Unmold ice cream onto brownie. Return to freezer while preparing meringue.

5 In a heavy saucepan or double boiler over simmering water, combine the eggs whites, sugar and cream of tartar. With a portable mixer; beat on low speed for 1 minute. Continue beating over low heat until egg mixture reaches 160°, about 12 minutes. Remove from the heat; add vanilla. Beat on high speed until stiff peaks form. Quickly spread over ice cream and brownie. Bake at 500° for 2-5 minutes or until meringue is lightly browned. (Or return to freezer until ready to bake.) Transfer to a serving plate; serve immediately.
Yield: 12 servings.
—*Carol Twardzik*
Spy Hill, Saskatchewan

Chocolate-Filled Meringues

Chocolate-Filled Meringues

These lovely delicate meringue shells are easy to make, and their crisp texture is a perfect complement to the creamy chocolate filling. Trace circles onto the parchment paper to use as a guide when making meringue cups.

    2 egg whites
  1/4 teaspoon cream of tartar
  1/4 teaspoon vanilla extract
Dash salt
  1/2 cup sugar
FILLING:
    1 package (8 ounces) cream cheese, softened
    1 cup confectioners' sugar
  1/4 cup baking cocoa
    1 cup whipped topping
    1 package (10 ounces) frozen sweetened sliced strawberries, thawed

1 Place egg whites in a small mixing bowl; let stand at room temperature for 30 minutes. Add the cream of tartar, vanilla and salt; beat on medium speed until

Making Meringue Cups

1. In a mixing bowl, beat egg whites, cream of tartar, vanilla and salt on medium speed until the egg whites begin to increase in volume and soft peaks form.

To test for soft peaks, lift the beaters from the whites, and the peaks of egg white should curl down.

2. Add sugar, 1 tablespoon at a time, beating on high speed until stiff peaks form and sugar is dissolved.

To test for stiff peaks, lift the beaters from the whites, and the peaks of egg white should stand straight up; if you tilt the bowl, the whites should not slide around. Sugar is dissolved when mixture feels silky-smooth between your fingers.

3. Line a baking sheet with parchment paper. Drop meringue into mounds on the paper. Using the back of a spoon, make an indentation in the center of each mound to form a 3-in. cup.

4. Bake as recipe directs. After drying in the oven for 1 hour, remove meringues and cool completely on baking sheet. Carefully remove meringues from paper and store in an airtight container at room temperature for up to 2 days.

soft peaks form. Gradually beat in sugar, 1 tablespoon at a time, on high until stiff glossy peaks form and sugar is dissolved.

2 Line a baking sheet with parchment paper. Spoon meringue into six mounds on paper. Using the back of a spoon, shape into 3-in. cups. Bake at 250° for 35 minutes. Turn off oven and do not open door; let meringues dry in oven for 1 hour. Cool on baking sheet on a wire rack.

3 For filling, in a mixing bowl, beat cream cheese, confectioners' sugar and cocoa until smooth and fluffy. Fold in whipped topping. Place strawberries in a blender or food processor; cover and process until pureed. To serve, spoon filling into meringue shells. Top with strawberry sauce. **Yield:** 6 servings.
—*Mary Lou Wayman, Salt Lake City, Utah*

Special souffles

secrets for successful souffles

Souffles are made from an egg yolk-based custard that is lightened with beaten egg whites. This mixture bakes up into a light airy creation that makes an impressive dessert.

The following guidelines help ensure success when baking a souffle:

- Separate eggs (see page 15) when they are cold. Let the separated eggs or egg whites stand at room temperature for 30 minutes before beating.

- Make sure there are no specks of egg yolk in the white.

- Before beating egg whites, remove all fat residue from your mixing bowl and beaters by washing them thoroughly in hot soapy water and drying with a clean kitchen towel. Use metal or glass mixing bowls. Plastic bowls, even freshly washed and dried ones, may have an oily film on them.

- To lighten the batter, fold about a third of the beaten egg whites into the custard base. Then fold in the remaining egg whites.

- Spoon or pour custard into baking dish. Souffles rise two to three times the volume of the batter. A four-egg souffle should be baked in a 1-1/2- to 2-qt. dish.

- Bake on the middle rack of a preheated oven according to recipe directions.

- A souffle is done when the top feels firm and a knife inserted near the center comes out clean.

- A souffle will fall slightly once it's removed from the oven. For best results, serve the souffle immediately.

- An unbaked souffle may be refrigerated up to 2 hours before baking or frozen for 3 weeks. Thaw a frozen souffle in the refrigerator before baking. A frozen souffle will not bake up as high as a freshly prepared souffle.

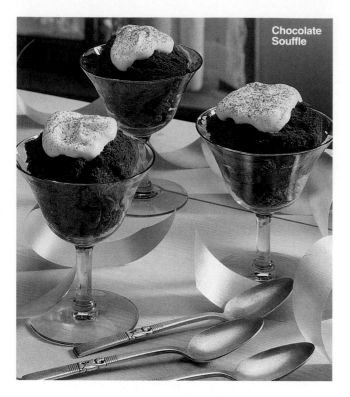

Chocolate Souffle

Chocolate Souffle

Every bite of this creamy souffle will melt in your mouth. The sweetened cream sauce balances the richness of the chocolate.

2 squares (1 ounce *each*) unsweetened chocolate
1/4 cup butter
5 tablespoons all-purpose flour
1/3 cup plus 1 teaspoon sugar, *divided*
1/4 teaspoon salt
1 cup milk
3 eggs, *separated*
1 teaspoon vanilla extract
1/4 teaspoon almond extract
TOPPING:
1 cup heavy whipping cream
1/4 cup confectioners' sugar
1/4 teaspoon vanilla extract
Baking cocoa *or* ground cinnamon, optional

1 In a heavy saucepan, melt chocolate and butter over low heat. In a small bowl, combine the flour, 1/3 cup sugar and salt. Add milk; stir until smooth. Stir into the melted chocolate. Cook and stir over medium heat until thickened and bubbly. Reduce heat; cook and stir 2 minutes longer. Remove from the heat.

2 In a small bowl, beat egg yolks. Stir a small amount of hot filling into yolks; return all to the pan, stirring constantly. Add extracts. In a small mixing bowl and with clean beaters, beat egg whites on medium speed until soft peaks form. Gradually beat in remaining sugar on high until stiff peaks form. With a spatula, stir a

problem-Solving pointers for Souffles

If this happens with your souffle:	This could be the reason:
Souffle did not rise.	Egg whites were overbeaten. Beat just until they reach a stiff peak.
	Ingredients weren't gently folded together.
	The batter wasn't gently spooned into the dish.
	The oven wasn't preheated properly.
Souffle overflowed the dish.	Next time, make a foil collar for the dish or use a larger dish.
Souffle fell.	A souffle will begin to fall shortly after it is removed from the oven. Plan the serving time well and have the guests waiting for the souffle.

fourth of the egg whites into chocolate batter until no white streaks remain, then fold in remaining egg whites.

3 Grease the bottom of a 1-1/2-qt. baking dish; add souffle batter. Place dish in a larger pan. Fill large pan with hot water to a depth of 1 in. Bake at 325° for 1 hour or until a knife inserted near the center comes out clean.

4 For topping, beat the cream in a chilled small mixing bowl until it begins to thicken. Add confectioners' sugar and vanilla; beat until soft peaks form. Serve souffle warm with a dollop of topping. Sprinkle with cocoa or cinnamon if desired. **Yield:** 4-6 servings.
—*Carol Ice, Burlingham, New York*

Baked Orange Souffle

This souffle with a distinctive orange flavor makes a light ending to any meal.

　　1 **teaspoon plus 2 tablespoons butter,** *divided*
　　2 **tablespoons plus 1/2 cup sugar,** *divided*
　　5 **tablespoons all-purpose flour**
1/4 **teaspoon salt**
　　1 **cup milk**
　　4 **eggs,** *separated*
　　2 **tablespoons grated orange peel**
　　1 **to 1-1/4 teaspoons orange extract**
1/8 **teaspoon cream of tartar**

1 Use 1 teaspoon butter to grease bottom and sides of a 6-cup souffle dish. Thoroughly coat inside of dish with 2 tablespoons sugar; tap out excess sugar and discard. In a saucepan, combine flour, salt and 1/4 cup sugar; gradually whisk in milk until smooth. Bring to a boil over medium heat; cook and stir for 2 minutes or until thickened. Transfer to a bowl; whisk in egg yolks, orange peel, extract and remaining butter.

2 In a mixing bowl, beat egg whites and cream of tartar on medium speed until soft peaks begin to form. Gradually add remaining sugar, 1 tablespoon at a time, beating until soft peaks form. With a spatula, stir 1 cup of the whites into the orange batter until no white streaks remain. Fold in remaining egg whites until combined. Gently pour into prepared dish.

3 Bake at 400° for 25-30 minutes or until a knife inserted near the center comes out clean. Serve immediately. **Yield:** 6-8 servings.

Making a Souffle

1. Temper the egg yolks by stirring a small amount of hot filling into egg yolks; return all to the pan, stirring constantly.

2. After adding the sugar, beat egg white mixture on high speed just until stiff peaks form; do not overbeat.

3. Stir about a fourth of the egg whites into the egg yolk mixture to lighten.

4. Fold in remaining egg whites.

5. Transfer to prepared baking dish.

Custards & Puddings

the basics about custards & puddings

- Baked custards are a sweetened mixture of milk, eggs and flavoring. They can be baked individually in custard cups or in one large baking dish. They are usually baked in a water bath to help ensure gentle and even baking. (See Making a Water Bath on page 224.)

- Custards are done when a knife inserted about halfway to the center comes out clean and the top looks set.

- To unmold a cooled custard, carefully run a knife around the edge of dish to loosen. If possible, lift the bottom edge of the custard with the tip of the knife blade to loosen. Place a serving dish over the top of the baking dish. Invert and remove custard dish.

- Bread puddings are made with cubes or slices of bread baked in a custard mixture. They can be enriched with fruits, nuts, chocolate and spices. Bread puddings are served warm or cold and may be accompanied by a sauce. Bread puddings are done when a knife inserted near the center comes out clean.

- Rice puddings are made with cooked rice, a custard mixture, flavoring and spices. They can be served warm or cold. Rice puddings are done when a knife inserted near the center comes out clean.

- Store baked custards and puddings in the refrigerator for 1 to 2 days.

Baked Custard

Adults and kids alike get a kick out of having their own individual custard set before them. Serving them warm or chilled is a matter of preference.

> 2 eggs
> 2 cups milk
> 1/3 cup sugar
> 1/4 teaspoon salt
> **Dash ground cinnamon**
> **Dash ground nutmeg**

1 In a small bowl, whisk the eggs, milk, sugar and salt. Pour into four ungreased 8-oz. custard cups; sprinkle with cinnamon and nutmeg.

2 Place cups in a 13-in. x 9-in. x 2-in. baking pan. Fill pan with hot water to a depth of 3/4 in. Bake, uncovered, at 350° for 50-55 minutes or until a knife inserted near the center comes out clean. Remove cups to a wire rack to cool. Serve warm or chilled. Store in the refrigerator. **Yield:** 4 servings.　　*—Mary Kay Morris Cokato, Minnesota*

Baked Custard

Pumpkin Custard

This dessert is a refreshing departure from pumpkin pie, but it has the same good old-fashioned flavor.

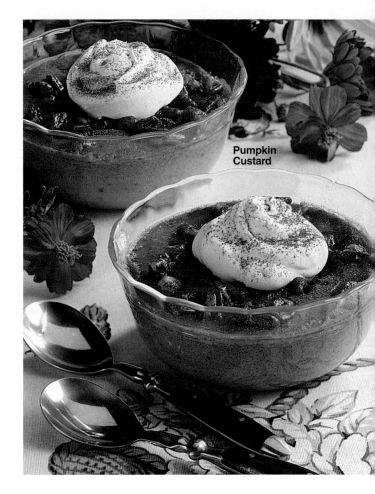

Pumpkin Custard

   1 can (15 ounces) solid-pack pumpkin
   2 eggs
   1 cup half-and-half cream
 2/3 cup packed brown sugar
 1-1/2 teaspoons pumpkin pie spice
   1/2 teaspoon salt
TOPPING:
   1/4 cup packed brown sugar
   1/4 cup chopped pecans
     1 tablespoon butter, melted
Whipped cream and ground cinnamon, optional

1 In a large mixing bowl, combine the first six ingredients; beat until smooth. Pour into four greased 10-oz. custard cups.

2 Place cups in a 13-in. x 9-in. x 2-in. baking pan. Fill pan with hot water to a depth of 1 in. Bake, uncovered, at 350° for 20 minutes.

3 For topping, combine the brown sugar, pecans and butter in a small bowl. Sprinkle over custard. Bake 30-35 minutes longer or until a knife inserted near the center comes out clean. Serve warm or chilled; top with whipped cream and cinnamon if desired. Store in the refrigerator. **Yield:** 4 servings.
   —*Andrea Holcomb, Torrington, Connecticut*

problem-Solving pointers for Custard

If this happens with your custard:	This could be the reason:
Custard is curdled.	It's overbaked. Bake only until a knife inserted about halfway to the center comes out clean, not until the center is completely set. Next time, bake the custard in a water bath. After baking, immediately remove custard from water bath; otherwise, it will continue to cook in the hot water.
Custard has bubbles on the top.	Next time, beat eggs only until they are blended, not foamy.

Traditional
Caramel Flan

Traditional Caramel Flan

*This delectable dessert is baked over a layer
of caramelized sugar. When inverted,
a delicious golden sauce runs down the edges of the
flan and forms a pool on the serving platter.*

1-1/4 cups sugar, *divided*
2-3/4 cups milk
   5 eggs
 1/8 teaspoon salt
   1 teaspoon vanilla extract

1 In a heavy saucepan or skillet over medium-low heat, melt 3/4 cup sugar. Do not stir. When sugar is melted, reduce heat to low; cook until syrup is golden brown, stirring constantly. Quickly pour into an ungreased souffle dish or 2-qt. round baking dish, tilting to coat the bottom of the dish. Let stand for 10 minutes.

2 In a saucepan, heat milk over medium heat until bubbles form around sides of saucepan. Remove from the heat. In a bowl, whisk eggs, salt and remaining sugar. Stir 1 cup of warm milk into egg mixture; return all to the pan, stirring constantly. Add vanilla. Pour into prepared dish.

3 Place dish in a large baking pan. Fill larger pan with boiling water to a depth of 1 in. Bake at 325° for 55-60 minutes or until center is just set (mixture will jiggle). Remove flan dish to a wire rack; cool for 1 hour. Refrigerate for 3-4 hours or until thoroughly chilled. Run a knife around edge and invert onto a rimmed serving platter. Refrigerate leftovers. **Yield:** 6 servings.

—*Mary Ann Kosmas, Minneapolis, Minnesota*

Caramelizing Sugar

In a heavy saucepan or skillet, melt sugar over medium-low heat, about 10 minutes. Do not stir. When sugar is melted, reduce heat to low. Cook for about 5 minutes or until syrup is golden, stirring constantly with a metal spoon.

Coconut Cream Pudding

A golden baked meringue is the crowning touch to this mouth-watering dessert.

1-1/4 cups sugar, *divided*
1/4 cup cornstarch
3 cups milk
4 eggs, *separated*
1 cup flaked coconut
1 teaspoon vanilla extract

1 In a large heavy saucepan, combine 3/4 cup sugar and cornstarch; stir in milk until smooth. Cook and stir over medium heat until thickened and bubbly. Reduce heat; cook and stir 2 minutes longer. Remove from the heat.

2 In a bowl, beat egg yolks. Stir 1 cup hot milk mixture into egg yolks; return to pan, stirring constantly. Bring to a gentle boil over medium heat; cook and stir 2 minutes longer. Remove from the heat. Stir in coconut and vanilla. Cool to lukewarm without stirring.

3 Pour into an ungreased 8-in. square baking dish. In a large mixing bowl and with clean beaters, beat egg whites on medium speed until soft peaks form. Gradually beat in remaining sugar, 1 tablespoon at a time, on high until stiff peaks form. Spread over pudding, sealing to edges. Bake, uncovered, at 350° for 10-15 minutes. Serve warm. **Yield:** 9 servings.
—*Verona Koehlmoos, Pilger, Nebraska*

Bread Pudding

Back in 13th-century England, bread pudding was called poor man's pudding. Leftover bread was simply soaked in water, then seasoned with sugar and spices. Today's version features eggs, milk and butter.

3 eggs
3 cans (12 ounces *each*) evaporated milk
1-1/4 cups sugar
1/4 cup butter, melted
1/2 to 1 cup raisins
2 teaspoons vanilla extract
1 teaspoon ground cinnamon
1/2 teaspoon salt
1 loaf (1 pound) bread, cut into cubes

Testing Bread Puddings for Doneness

Insert a knife near the center of the bread pudding. It's done when the knife comes out clean.

Bread Pudding

1 In a large bowl, beat eggs. Add the milk, sugar, butter, raisins, vanilla, cinnamon and salt; mix well. Add bread cubes; stir gently.

2 Pour into a greased 13-in. x 9-in. x 2-in. baking dish. Bake, uncovered, at 325° for 50-60 minutes or until a knife inserted near the center comes out clean. Serve warm or cold. Refrigerate leftovers. **Yield:** 12-16 servings. —*Evette Rios, Westfield, Massachusetts*

Grandma's Rice Pudding

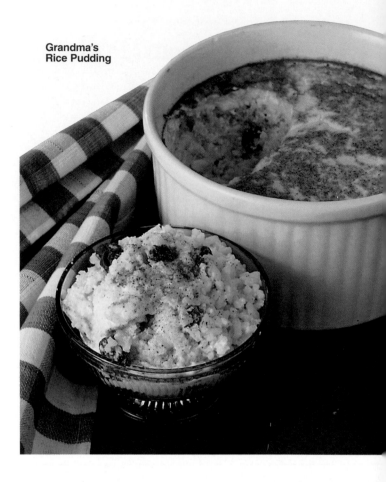

Grandma's
Rice Pudding

You can whip up this classic dessert on short notice if you keep cooked rice on hand. Cooked rice can be frozen in an airtight container for up to 3 months. Thaw in the refrigerator before using.

1-1/2 **cups cooked rice**
  1/4 **cup raisins**
    2 **eggs**
1-1/2 **cups milk**
  1/2 **cup sugar**
  1/2 **teaspoon ground nutmeg**
Additional milk, optional

1 Place the rice and raisins in a greased 1-qt. baking dish. In a small mixing bowl, beat the eggs, milk, sugar and nutmeg; pour over rice.

2 Bake, uncovered, at 375° for 45-50 minutes or until a knife inserted near the center comes out clean. Cool. Pour additional milk over each serving if desired. Refrigerate leftovers. **Yield:** 4-6 servings.
—Margaret DeChant, Newberry, Michigan

Butterscotch Rice Pudding

Brown sugar in this rice pudding's unique meringue topping gives a pretty golden color.

  3 **cups milk, *divided***
1/2 **cup uncooked long grain rice**
1/2 **teaspoon salt**
3/4 **cup packed brown sugar, *divided***
  2 **tablespoons butter**
  2 **eggs, *separated***
  1 **teaspoon vanilla extract**

1 In a large heavy saucepan, bring 2 cups milk to a gentle boil. Stir in rice and salt. Cover and cook over medium-low heat for 45 minutes, stirring occasionally. Remove from the heat; set aside.

2 In a small saucepan, heat 1/2 cup brown sugar, butter and remaining milk until simmering. Remove from the heat. In a small bowl, beat egg yolks. Add a small amount of hot milk mixture to yolks; return to the pan, stirring constantly. Stir into rice mixture; cook and stir over medium heat for 5 minutes. Remove from the heat. Stir in vanilla.

3 Pour into a greased 1-1/2-qt. baking dish; set aside. In a small mixing bowl and with clean beaters, beat egg whites on medium speed until soft peaks form. Gradually beat in remaining brown sugar, 1 tablespoon at a time, on high until stiff peaks form. Spread over rice mixture, sealing to edges. Bake, uncovered, at 300° for 20-25 minutes. **Yield:** 6-8 servings.
—Faye Hintz
Springfield, Missouri

Making a Water Bath for Custards & Puddings

Place baking dish in a larger baking pan or dish, then place on rack in oven. Using a kettle or large measuring cup, carefully pour hot or boiling water into larger pan or dish. Fill according to recipe directions, generally to a depth of 1 in. or halfway up the sides of the larger pan or dish.

Saucy Mocha Pudding Cake

This pudding cake goes great with ice cream and whipped cream, but it's just as scrumptious served alone. It's very easy to prepare. So don't wait for a special occasion to try it...it sweetens any meal.

  1/2 **cup sugar**
  1/2 **cup packed brown sugar**
  1/4 **cup baking cocoa**
1-1/2 **cups strong brewed coffee**
CAKE:
  1/3 **cup butter, softened**
  2/3 **cup sugar**
    1 **egg**
  1/2 **teaspoon vanilla extract**
    1 **cup all-purpose flour**
1-1/2 **teaspoons baking powder**
  1/4 **teaspoon salt**
  1/3 **cup milk**
Fresh raspberries and mint, optional

1 In a saucepan, combine the sugars and cocoa. Stir in coffee; keep warm over low heat. For cake, in a mixing bowl, cream butter and sugar until light and fluffy. Beat in egg and vanilla. Combine the flour, baking powder and salt; add to creamed mixture alternately with milk, beating well after each addition. Spread into a greased 8-in. square baking dish. Pour mocha sauce slowly over batter. Do not stir.

2 Bake, uncovered, at 350° for 45-50 minutes or until a toothpick inserted near the center of the cake comes out clean. When finished, the cake will float in the hot mocha sauce. Garnish with raspberries and mint if desired. **Yield:** 9 servings.
—*Kathy Koch*
Smoky Lake, Alberta

what is a pudding cake?

Pudding cakes offer two treats in one. While baking, the cake portion rises to the top and a creamy pudding-like sauce forms on the bottom.

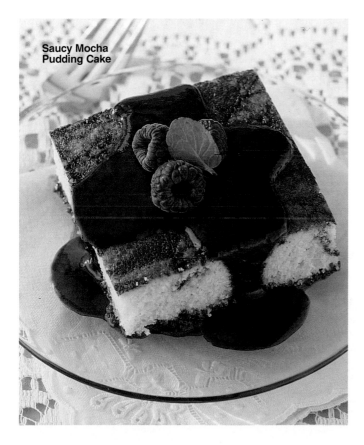

Saucy Mocha Pudding Cake

Lemon Pudding Cake

The tart taste of lemon brings the perfect finish to this meal. The fluffy, light cake texture is appealing.

  2 **eggs, *separated***
  1 **cup sugar**
  3 **tablespoons all-purpose flour**
3/4 **cup milk**
1/4 **cup lemon juice**
  1 **tablespoon butter, melted**
  2 **teaspoons grated lemon peel**

1 Let eggs stand at room temperature for 30 minutes. In a large bowl, combine sugar and flour. Stir in the milk, lemon juice, butter and lemon peel. Beat egg yolks; add to lemon mixture. In a small mixing bowl and with clean beaters, beat egg whites on high speed until stiff peaks form. Fold into lemon mixture.

2 Pour into a greased 1-qt. baking dish. Place in a larger baking pan. Fill larger pan with hot water to a depth of 1 in. Bake, uncovered, at 350° for 45-50 minutes or until a knife inserted near the center comes out clean. Serve warm. Refrigerate leftovers. **Yield:** 4 servings.
—*Ann Berg*
Chesapeake, Virginia

Fruit desserts

facts about fruit desserts

Apple, pears, peaches and berries lend themselves to so many delicious desserts. Here is a description of the old-fashioned desserts featured in this section.

- Betty is made with alternate layers of sweetened fruit and cake, cookie or bread crumbs. The top layer of crumbs brown as it bakes.

- Buckle is a cake-like dessert made with berries and may or may not have a crumb topping. It got its name because the cake sometimes buckles under the weight of the topping.

- Cobbler has a biscuit topping over the fruit. The topping can be either in a single layer or dropped over the fruit to give a cobblestone effect.

- Crisps have a crumb topping over the fruit. The topping has flour, sugar and butter and may or may not have oats, nuts and spices. The topping gets crisp while baking.

- Dessert dumplings use a flaky pastry to enclose the fruit.

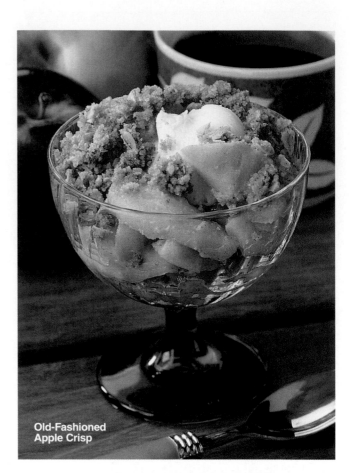

Old-Fashioned Apple Crisp

Old-Fashioned Apple Crisp

Nostalgic, comforting, luscious—call it what you will, this is one of those simple, old-time treats that never goes out of style.

  4 cups sliced peeled tart apples (about 3 medium)
3/4 cup packed brown sugar
1/2 cup all-purpose flour
1/2 cup old-fashioned oats
  1 teaspoon ground cinnamon
1/4 to 1/2 teaspoon ground allspice
1/3 cup cold butter
Vanilla ice cream, optional

1 Place the apples in a greased 8-in. square baking dish. In a small bowl, combine the brown sugar, flour, oats, cinnamon and allspice; cut in butter until mixture is crumbly. Sprinkle over apples.

2 Bake, uncovered, at 375° for 30-35 minutes or until apples are tender. Serve warm with ice cream if desired. **Yield:** 4-6 servings.
          —Grace Yaskovic
Branchville, New Jersey

Cranberry Apple Betty

For a tart autumn dessert, this one is hard to beat. You'll love the way the sweet apples and brown sugar complement the tangy cranberries. Topped off with lemon sauce, it's a winner!

>   4 cups soft bread crumbs
>   6 tablespoons butter, *divided*
>   5 cups sliced peeled tart apples (4 to 5 large)
>   1 cup packed brown sugar
> 3/4 teaspoon ground nutmeg
>   2 cups fresh *or* frozen cranberries, thawed
> **LEMON SAUCE:**
> 1/2 cup sugar
>   1 tablespoon cornstarch
> **Dash salt**
>   1 cup water
>   1 teaspoon grated lemon peel
>   2 tablespoons lemon juice
>   2 tablespoons butter

1 In a skillet, brown the bread crumbs in 3 tablespoons butter. Place half of the apples in a greased 8-in. square baking dish. Combine brown sugar and nutmeg; sprinkle half over the apples. Top with half of the bread crumbs. Dot with half of the remaining butter. Place the cranberries on top. Layer with the remaining apples, brown sugar mixture, bread crumbs and butter.

2 Cover and bake at 350° for 45 minutes. Uncover; bake 15-20 minutes longer or until fruit is tender.

3 For lemon sauce, combine the sugar, cornstarch and salt in a small saucepan. Stir in water and lemon peel until smooth. Bring to a boil; cook and stir for 2 minutes or until thickened. Remove from the heat; stir in lemon juice and butter until butter is melted. Serve over warm betty. **Yield:** 6-8 servings. —*Leona Cullen Melrose, Massachusetts*

Nutty Peach Crisp

A moist bottom layer made with canned peaches and a boxed cake mix is covered with a lovely golden topping of coconut and pecans.

>   1 can (29 ounces) sliced peaches, undrained
>   1 package (18-1/4 ounces) yellow *or* butter pecan cake mix
> 1/2 cup butter, melted
>   1 cup flaked coconut
>   1 cup chopped pecans

1 Arrange peaches in an ungreased 13-in. x 9-in. x 2-in. baking dish. Sprinkle dry cake mix over the top. Drizzle with butter; sprinkle with coconut and pecans.

2 Bake, uncovered, at 325° for 55-60 minutes or until golden brown. Let stand for 15 minutes before serving. Serve warm or cold. **Yield:** 12-15 servings.
—*Nancy Carpenter, Sidney, Montana*

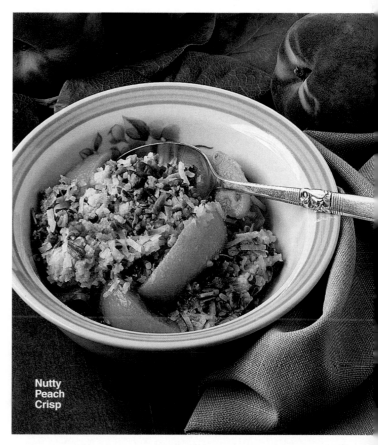

Nutty Peach Crisp

Blackberry Buckle

This homey dessert can be made with blueberries or raspberries instead.

1/2 cup shortening
1 cup sugar, *divided*
1 egg, beaten
2-1/2 cups all-purpose flour, *divided*
2-1/2 teaspoons baking powder
1/2 teaspoon salt
1/2 cup milk
2 cups fresh *or* frozen blackberries*
2 teaspoons lemon juice
1/2 teaspoon ground cinnamon
1/4 cup cold butter

1 In a large mixing bowl, cream the shortening and 1/2 cup sugar until light and fluffy. Add the egg and mix well. Combine 2 cups flour, baking powder and salt; add to the creamed mixture alternately with the milk, beating well after each addition.

2 Spread into a greased 9-in. square baking dish. Toss the blackberries with lemon juice; sprinkle over batter. In a small bowl, combine the cinnamon and remaining sugar and flour; cut in the butter until mixture resembles coarse crumbs. Sprinkle over berries.

3 Bake, uncovered, at 350° for 45-50 minutes or until a toothpick inserted near the center comes out clean. Refrigerate leftovers. **Yield:** 9-12 servings.

*Editor's Note: If using frozen berries, do not thaw before adding to batter.

Praline Peach Cobbler

Cobbler is a delicious dessert for picnics and potluck dinners. It can be served cold or warm and is especially good topped with a generous scoop of vanilla ice cream.

1-1/2 cups plus 2 teaspoons sugar, *divided*
2 tablespoons cornstarch
1 teaspoon ground cinnamon
1 cup water
8 cups sliced peeled fresh peaches
2 cups self-rising flour*
1/2 cup shortening
1/2 cup buttermilk
Additional buttermilk, optional
3 tablespoons butter, melted
1/4 cup packed brown sugar
1 cup chopped pecans

1 In a large saucepan, combine 1-1/2 cups sugar, cornstarch and cinnamon. Stir in water until smooth. Add peaches. Bring to a boil over medium heat; cook and stir for 2 minutes or until thickened. Pour into a lightly greased 13-in. x 9-in. x 2-in. baking dish; set aside.

2 In a bowl, combine the flour and remaining sugar; cut in shortening until mixture resembles coarse crumbs. Add buttermilk and stir just until moistened. If needed, add additional buttermilk, 1 tablespoon at a time, until dough clings together. Turn onto a floured surface; knead gently 6-8 times. Roll into a 12-in. x 8-in. rectangle.

3 Combine the butter, brown sugar and pecans; spread over dough to within 1/2 in. of edges. Roll up jelly-roll style, starting with a long side. Cut into twelve 1-in. pieces. Place over peach mixture. Bake, uncovered, at 400° for 25-30 minutes or until golden brown. **Yield:** 12 servings. *—Maithel Martin Kansas City, Missouri*

*Editor's Note: As a substitute for *each* cup of self-rising flour, place 1-1/2 teaspoons baking powder and 1/2 teaspoon salt in a measuring cup. Add all-purpose flour to measure 1 cup.

Praline
Peach Cobbler

Pumpkin Pie Squares

This dessert has all the spicy pumpkin goodness of the traditional pie without the fuss of a pastry crust.

> 1 cup all-purpose flour
> 1/2 cup quick-cooking oats
> 1/2 cup packed brown sugar
> 1/2 cup cold butter

FILLING:

> 2 cans (15 ounces *each*) solid-pack pumpkin
> 2 cans (12 ounces *each*) evaporated milk
> 4 eggs
> 1-1/2 cups sugar
> 2 teaspoons ground cinnamon
> 1 teaspoon ground ginger
> 1/2 teaspoon ground cloves
> 1 teaspoon salt

TOPPING:

> 1/2 cup packed brown sugar
> 1/2 cup chopped pecans
> 2 tablespoons butter, softened

1 In a small bowl, combine the flour, oats and brown sugar. Cut in butter until mixture is crumbly. Press into a greased 13-in. x 9-in. x 2-in. baking pan. Bake at 350° for 20 minutes or until golden brown.

2 In a large mixing bowl, beat filling ingredients until smooth; pour over crust. Bake for 45 minutes.

3 Combine topping ingredients; sprinkle over filling. Bake 15-20 minutes longer or until a knife inserted near the center comes out clean. Cool on a wire rack. Store in the refrigerator. **Yield:** 16-20 servings.
—*Denise Goedeken, Platte Center, Nebraska*

Apple Dumplings

Apple Dumplings

Instead of an apple pie, why not make these pastry-wrapped apples?

2-1/2 cups water
1-1/4 cups sugar
> 1/2 teaspoon ground cinnamon
> 1/4 cup plus 6 teaspoons butter, *divided*
> 2 cups all-purpose flour
> 2 teaspoons baking powder
> 1 teaspoon salt
> 3/4 cup shortening
> 1/2 cup milk
> 6 small tart apples, peeled and cored

Cinnamon-sugar
Additional milk

1 In a small saucepan, combine the water, sugar and cinnamon. Cook and stir over medium until sugar is dissolved, about 5 minutes. Add 1/4 cup butter; stir until melted. Remove from the heat; set aside.

2 In a bowl, combine the flour, baking powder and salt. Cut in shortening until the mixture resembles coarse crumbs. Stir in milk.

3 Divide pastry into six portions. On a lightly floured surface, roll each portion into a 6-in. square. Place an apple in the center of each. Sprinkle with cinnamon-sugar; dot with remaining butter. Bring corners of pastry to center. Brush edges with milk; pinch edges to seal.

4 Place in a greased 13-in. x 9-in. x 2-in. baking dish; drizzle with reserved syrup. Bake, uncovered, at 375° for 35-40 minutes or until golden brown. **Yield:** 6 servings.
—*Marilyn Strickland*
Williamson, New York

Strawberry Pretzel Dessert

A salty pretzel crust nicely contrasts cream cheese and gelatin layers.

2 cups crushed pretzels (about 8 ounces)
3/4 cup butter, melted
3 tablespoons sugar
FILLING:
   2 cups whipped topping
   1 package (8 ounces) cream cheese, softened
   1 cup sugar
TOPPING:
   1 package (6 ounces) strawberry gelatin
   2 cups boiling water
   2 packages (16 ounces *each*) frozen sliced strawberries with syrup, thawed
Additional whipped topping, optional

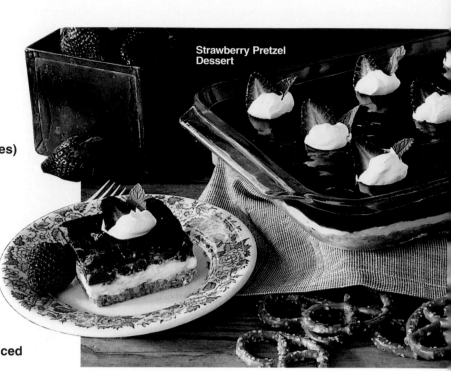

Strawberry Pretzel Dessert

1 In a bowl, combine the pretzels, butter and sugar. Press into the bottom of an ungreased 13-in. x 9-in. x 2-in. baking pan. Bake at 350° for 10 minutes. Cool on a wire rack.

2 For filling, in a mixing bowl, beat the whipped topping, cream cheese and sugar until smooth. Spread over crust. Refrigerate until chilled.

3 For topping, dissolve the gelatin in boiling water in a large bowl. Stir in the strawberries with syrup; refrigerate until partially set. Carefully spoon over filling. Refrigerate for 4-6 hours or until firm. Cut into squares; serve with whipped topping if desired. **Yield:** 12-16 servings.   —*Aldene Belch, Flint, Michigan*

Pear Melba Dumplings

Special meals call for elegant desserts like this. A whole pear is packaged inside a pretty pastry pocket.

2 cups all-purpose flour
1-1/4 teaspoons salt
1/2 teaspoon cornstarch
2/3 cup butter-flavored shortening
4 to 5 tablespoons cold water
6 small ripe pears, peeled and cored
6 tablespoons brown sugar
1/4 teaspoon ground cinnamon

2 tablespoons milk
1 tablespoon sugar
RASPBERRY SAUCE:
   1 tablespoon sugar
   1 tablespoon cornstarch
   2 tablespoons water
   1 package (10 ounces) frozen raspberries, thawed
   1/4 teaspoon almond extract
Ice cream, optional

1 In a large bowl, combine the flour, salt and cornstarch. Cut in shortening until mixture resembles coarse crumbs. Gradually add the water, tossing with a fork until dough forms a ball. On a floured surface, roll out into a 21-in. x 14-in. rectangle. Cut into six squares.

2 Place one pear in the center of each square. Pack centers of pears with brown sugar; sprinkle with cinnamon. Brush edges of pastry with milk; fold up corners to center and pinch to seal. Place in a greased 15-in. x 10-in. x 1-in. baking pan. Brush with milk; sprinkle with sugar. Bake, uncovered, at 375° for 35-40 minutes or until golden brown.

3 For sauce, combine the sugar, cornstarch and water in a small saucepan until smooth. Add raspberries. Bring to a boil; cook and stir for 2 minutes or until thickened. Remove from the heat; stir in almond extract. Serve warm over warm dumplings with ice cream if desired. **Yield:** 6 servings.   —*Doreen Kelly Roslyn, Pennsylvania*

Lemon Whirligigs with Raspberries

Golden pastry swirls with a tart lemon flavor float on a raspberry sauce in this whimsically named dessert. Substitute blackberries for the raspberries if you like.

2/3 **cup sugar**
2 **tablespoons cornstarch**
1/4 **teaspoon ground cinnamon**
1/8 **teaspoon ground nutmeg**
1/8 **teaspoon salt**
1 **cup water**
3 **cups fresh raspberries**
WHIRLIGIGS:
1 **cup all-purpose flour**
2 **teaspoons baking powder**
1/2 **teaspoon salt**
3 **tablespoons shortening**
1 **egg, lightly beaten**
2 **tablespoons half-and-half cream**
1/4 **cup sugar**
2 **tablespoons butter, melted**
1 **teaspoon grated lemon peel**
Heavy whipping cream and additional raspberries, optional

1 In a saucepan, combine the sugar, cornstarch, cinnamon, nutmeg and salt. Stir in water until smooth. Bring to a boil; cook and stir for 2 minutes or until thickened.

2 Place the raspberries in an ungreased 1-1/2-qt. shallow baking dish; pour hot sauce over top. Bake, uncovered, at 400° for 10 minutes; remove from the oven and set aside.

3 For whirligigs, combine the flour, baking powder and salt in a small bowl. Cut in shortening until crumbly. Combine egg and half-and-half; stir into crumb mixture to form a stiff dough.

4 Shape into a ball. On a lightly floured surface, roll out into a 12-in. x 6-in. rectangle. Combine the sugar, butter and lemon peel; spread over dough to within 1/2 in. of edges. Roll up jelly-roll style, starting with a long side. Cut into 10 slices; pat slightly to flatten. Place over berry mixture.

5 Bake, uncovered, at 400° for 15 minutes or until whirligigs are golden. Garnish servings with cream and raspberries if desired. **Yield:** 10 servings.
—*Vicky Ayres, Wappingers Falls, New York*

buying and storing berries

- Purchase brightly colored, plump berries. Discard any that are soft, bruised or moldy.

- Place unwashed raspberries and blackberries in a single layer on a paper towel-lined baking pan and chill. Refrigerate unwashed blueberries and strawberries in a tightly covered container. Most berries should be eaten within a few days. Wash just before using.

- One pint of blackberries, blueberries or raspberries yields 2 cups. One pint of strawberries yields 2 cups sliced.

Lemon Whirligigs with Raspberries

Quick Breads
are a boon to busy bakers

You don't "knead" to spend hours slaving in the kitchen to make homemade bread from scratch. From luscious loaves like Lemon Poppy Seed Bread (p. 235) to coffee cakes such as Raspberry Crumb Cake (p. 249), quick breads are a fast solution for folks on the go.

the basics of Quick Breads

The convenience of quick breads comes from the fact that they're leavened with baking powder and/or baking soda, not yeast. So you can mix, bake and enjoy these baked goods in less time than traditional yeast breads. Like yeast breads, quick breads can be sweet or savory.

> "Bread is like dresses, hats and shoes— in other words, essential!"
>
> —Emily Post

secrets for successful quick breads

- Measure ingredients accurately, using the measuring tools and techniques suggested on pages 8 and 9.

- Before preheating the oven, arrange the oven racks so that the bread will bake in the center of the oven.

- Preheat the oven for 10-15 minutes before baking.

- Be sure your baking powder and baking soda are fresh. (See Testing Baking Powder & Soda for Freshness on page 243.) Always check the expiration date on the packages before using.

- Mix the liquid and dry ingredients only until moistened. A few lumps in the batter is fine. Overmixing causes the gluten in the flour to develop and the texture to be coarse and tough.

- Grease aluminum baking pans and sheets with a dull rather than shiny or dark finish. Fill pans two-thirds full.

- Most quick breads should be baked shortly after dry ingredients and liquid ingredients are combined because the leaveners will begin producing gas once they are moistened. If allowed to stand too long before baking, the bread may have a sunken center.

- To allow for good air circulation while baking, leave at least 1 inch of space between pans and between pans and sides of oven. Switch pan positions and rotate pans halfway through baking.

- Use a kitchen timer. Check for doneness 10-15 minutes before the end of the recommended baking time. The bread is done if a toothpick inserted near the center comes out clean. If it is not done, test again in a few more minutes. The bread may have a split in the center, which is typical of a quick bread.

- Cool in the pan for 10 minutes, unless recipe directs otherwise. Turn loaves out onto a wire rack to cool. Most quick breads should be cooled completely before slicing to prevent crumbling.

- Quick breads such as banana, zucchini and cranberry slice and taste best when served a day after baking. Wrap the cooled bread in foil or plastic wrap; leave at room temperature overnight. Others like corn bread and coffee cakes are best served warm.

- Using a sawing motion, cut loaves with a thin sharp knife. Use a serrated knife for quick breads that have fruits and/or nuts.

problem-Solving pointers for Quick Breads

If this happens with your quick bread:	This could be the reason:
Bread is tough and dense or has tunnels.	Batter was overmixed.
Bread is soggy.	Batter had too much liquid or fat.
Center of bread has sunk.	There was too little or too much leavening.
	Bread was underbaked.
	Batter stood too long before baking.
Bread has a thick brown crust.	Batter had too much sugar.
Bread has a bitter aftertaste.	Batter had too much leavener.
Bread crumbled while being cut.	Bread was still warm. Cool completely before slicing.
Nuts, fruit or chocolate chips sink to the bottom of bread.	Batter was too thin to hold the fruit, nuts or chips. Next time, chop them smaller or use miniature chocolate chips.

Lemon Poppy Seed Bread

Lemon Poppy Seed Bread

(Also pictured on page 232)

If the days that you have time for baking are few and far between, try this extra-quick bread. You'll love the ease of preparation and the delicious flavor.

   1 **package (18-1/4 ounces) white cake mix**
   1 **package (3.4 ounces) instant lemon pudding mix**
   4 **eggs**
   1 **cup warm water**
 1/2 **cup vegetable oil**
   4 **teaspoons poppy seeds**

1 In a large mixing bowl, combine the dry cake and pudding mixes, eggs, water and oil; beat until well mixed. Fold in poppy seeds.

2 Pour into two greased 9-in. x 5-in. x 3-in. loaf pans. Bake at 350° for 35-40 minutes or until a toothpick inserted near the center comes out clean. Cool for 10 minutes before removing from pans to wire racks to cool completely. **Yield:** 2 loaves.

—*Karen Dougherty, Freeport, Illinois*

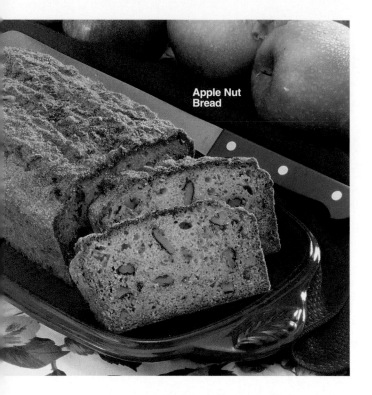

Apple Nut
Bread

Apple Nut Bread

*Your family will love the nutty texture and
fresh apple flavor of this standby.*

1/2 **cup butter, softened**
1 **cup plus 2 tablespoons sugar,** *divided*
2 **eggs**
1/2 **teaspoon vanilla extract**
2 **cups all-purpose flour**
1 **teaspoon baking soda**
1/2 **teaspoon salt**
2 **tablespoons buttermilk**
1 **cup grated peeled apple**
1 **cup chopped nuts**
3/4 **teaspoon ground cinnamon**

1 In a large mixing bowl, cream butter and 1 cup
sugar until light and fluffy. Add eggs, one at a time,
beating well after each addition. Stir in vanilla. Combine
the flour, baking soda and salt; add to the creamed
mixture alternately with buttermilk, beating well after
each addition. Fold in apple and nuts.

2 Pour into a greased 9-in. x 5-in. x 3-in. loaf pan.
Combine cinnamon and remaining sugar; sprinkle
over batter. Bake at 350° for 60-65 minutes or until a
toothpick inserted near the center comes out clean. Cool
for 10 minutes before removing from pan to a wire
rack to cool completely. **Yield:** 1 loaf.   —*June Mullins
Livonia, Missouri*

Making Quick Bread with a Creamed Batter

When a quick bread is made with solid fat, like
softened butter or shortening, the fat and sugar are
first creamed together. Then the eggs, dry ingredients
and any liquids are added. This method incorporates
air bubbles into the fat, resulting in a cake-like texture.
For best results, make sure the butter is softened,
not melted. (A knife should glide through the butter.)

1. In a mixing bowl,
cream butter and
sugar. Add eggs, one
at a time, beating well
after each addition.

2. Combine the dry
ingredients to evenly
distribute the baking
powder or soda.

3. Add the flour
mixture alternately
with milk or other
liquid to the creamed
mixture, beating well
after each addition.

4. Fold in any other
ingredients. Bake as
directed.

Cinnamon Swirl Quick Bread

While cinnamon bread is a natural for breakfast, it's great served around the clock! This is a nice twist on traditional cinnamon swirl yeast breads.

    2 cups all-purpose flour
1-1/2 cups sugar, *divided*
    1 teaspoon baking soda
    1/2 teaspoon salt
    1 cup buttermilk
    1 egg
    1/4 cup vegetable oil
    1 tablespoon ground cinnamon
GLAZE:
    1/4 cup confectioners' sugar
1-1/2 to 2 teaspoons milk

1 In a large bowl, combine the flour, 1 cup sugar, baking soda and salt. Combine the buttermilk, egg and oil; stir into dry ingredients just until moistened. In a small bowl, combine the cinnamon and remaining sugar.

2 Grease the bottom only of a 9-in. x 5-in. x 3-in. loaf pan. Pour half of the batter into pan; sprinkle with half of the cinnamon-sugar. Carefully spread with remaining batter and sprinkle with remaining cinnamon-sugar; swirl a knife through batter. Bake at 350° for 45-50 minutes or until a toothpick inserted near the center comes out clean. Cool for 10 minutes before removing from pan to a wire rack to cool completely.

3 For glaze, combine confectioners' sugar and enough milk to achieve drizzling consistency. Drizzle over bread. **Yield:** 1 loaf.
    —Helen Richardson
    Shelbyville, Michigan

Cinnamon Swirl Quick Bread

Orange Yogurt Bread

This moist bread is complemented by a slightly tangy glaze. It makes a nice addition to a breakfast buffet.

    2/3 cup butter, softened
1-1/4 cups sugar
    2 eggs
    1/2 cup plain yogurt
    1/2 cup orange juice
    1 tablespoon grated orange peel
2-1/2 cups all-purpose flour
    1/2 teaspoon baking powder
    1/2 teaspoon baking soda
    1/2 teaspoon salt
GLAZE:
    1/2 cup confectioners' sugar
    2 to 3 teaspoons orange juice

1 In a large mixing bowl, cream butter and sugar until light and fluffy. Add eggs, one at a time, beating well after each addition. Add the yogurt, orange juice and peel. Combine the flour, baking powder, baking soda and salt; add to the creamed mixture and mix well.

2 Pour into a greased 9-in. x 5-in. x 3-in. loaf pan. Bake at 350° for 55-65 minutes or until a toothpick inserted near the center comes out clean (cover loosely with foil if top browns too quickly). Cool for 10 minutes before removing from pan to a wire rack to cool completely.

3 For glaze, combine confectioners' sugar and enough orange juice to achieve desired consistency. Drizzle over cooled bread. **Yield:** 1 loaf.
    —Nancy Juntunen, Prattville, Alabama

Making Quick Bread with a Stirred Batter

When a quick bread is made with liquid fat (melted butter or oil), the fat, eggs and any liquid are first combined, then stirred into the dry ingredients.

1. In a large bowl, combine dry ingredients to evenly distribute the baking powder or soda. Make a well in the center.

2. Beat eggs and combine with any liquid ingredients.

3. Pour egg mixture into the well all at one time.

4. Stir the ingredients together just until moistened, leaving a few lumps. Overmixing will result in a tough baked product.

5. Fold in any other ingredients. Bake as directed.

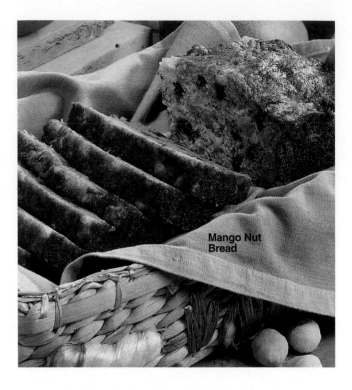

Mango Nut Bread

Mango Nut Bread

It can be difficult to remove the large flat oval pit inside a mango. Try cutting along each side of the mango next to the pit, resulting in two large sections. Then remove the fruit from the peel and chop.

> 2 cups all-purpose flour
> 1-1/2 cups sugar
> 1 teaspoon baking soda
> 1/2 teaspoon salt
> 1/2 teaspoon ground cinnamon
> 3 eggs
> 1/2 cup vegetable oil
> 1 teaspoon vanilla extract
> 2 cups chopped mangoes
> 1/2 cup chopped dates
> 1/2 cup chopped walnuts *or* macadamia nuts

1 In a large bowl, combine the flour, sugar, baking soda, salt and cinnamon. In another bowl, beat the eggs, oil and vanilla; stir into dry ingredients just until moistened. Fold in mangoes, dates and nuts (batter will be stiff).

2 Spoon into two greased 8-in. x 4-in. x 2-in. loaf pans. Bake at 350° for 50-55 minutes or until a toothpick inserted near the center comes out clean. Cool for 10 minutes before removing from pans to wire racks to cool completely. **Yield:** 2 loaves.

—Jo Sherley, Kahului, Hawaii

Autumn Pear Mini Loaves

Pears give these little loaves delicious flavor and help keep them nice and moist. They're great to wrap up in plastic wrap and give as gifts.

   2 cups all-purpose flour
   1 cup sugar
   1 teaspoon baking powder
1/2 teaspoon baking soda
1/2 teaspoon salt
1/8 teaspoon ground nutmeg
1/2 cup cold butter
   2 eggs
1/4 cup buttermilk
   1 teaspoon vanilla extract
   1 cup finely chopped peeled ripe pears

1 In a large bowl, combine the flour, sugar, baking powder, baking soda, salt and nutmeg. Cut in butter until mixture is crumbly. In a small bowl, beat the eggs, buttermilk and vanilla; stir into crumb mixture just until moistened. Fold in the pears.

2 Spoon into two greased 5-3/4-in. x 3-in. x 2-in. loaf pans. Bake at 350° for 35-40 minutes or until a toothpick inserted near the center comes out clean. Cool for 10 minutes before removing from pans to a wire rack to cool completely. **Yield:** 2 loaves.
—*Mary Lynn Wilson, Linden, Texas*

Triple-Chocolate Quick Bread

Chocolate lovers will beg you to bake this bread! Chocolate chips dot the chocolate batter, while melted chips form the glaze.

1-1/2 cups miniature semisweet chocolate chips, *divided*
   1/2 cup butter, softened
   2/3 cup packed brown sugar
      2 eggs
1-1/2 cups applesauce
      2 teaspoons vanilla extract
2-1/2 cups all-purpose flour
      1 teaspoon baking powder
      1 teaspoon baking soda
      1 teaspoon salt

GLAZE:
1/2 cup miniature semisweet chocolate chips
   1 tablespoon butter
   2 to 3 tablespoons half-and-half cream
1/2 cup confectioners' sugar
1/4 teaspoon vanilla extract
Pinch salt

1 In a microwave-safe bowl, melt 1 cup chocolate chips; set aside. In a large mixing bowl, cream butter and brown sugar until light and fluffy. Add eggs and melted chocolate; mix well. Add applesauce and vanilla. Combine the flour, baking powder, baking soda and salt; add to creamed mixture and mix well. Stir in the remaining chocolate chips.

2 Spoon into four greased 5-3/4-in. x 3-in. x 2-in. loaf pans. Bake at 350° for 35-40 minutes or a toothpick inserted near the center comes out clean. Cool for 10 minutes before removing from pans to wire racks.

3 For glaze, melt chocolate chips and butter in a small heavy saucepan; stir in cream. Remove from the heat. Stir in the confectioners' sugar, vanilla and salt. Drizzle over warm bread. Cool completely. **Yield:** 4 mini loaves.
—*Karen Grimes, Stephens City, Virginia*

Triple-Chocolate Quick Bread

Coconut Bread

This bread is easy to make and just a little different from other quick breads. Get ready for recipe requests!

- 2 cups sugar
- 3/4 cup vegetable oil
- 4 eggs
- 2 teaspoons coconut extract
- 3 cups all-purpose flour
- 1 teaspoon baking powder
- 1/2 teaspoon baking soda
- 1/2 teaspoon salt
- 1 cup buttermilk
- 1 cup flaked coconut
- 1 cup chopped walnuts

1 In a large mixing bowl, combine the sugar, oil, eggs and extract. Combine the flour, baking powder, baking soda and salt; add to sugar mixture alternately with buttermilk, stirring just until moistened. Fold in coconut and walnuts.

2 Pour into two greased 8-in. x 4-in. x 2-in. loaf pans. Bake at 325° for 60-65 minutes or until a toothpick inserted near the center comes out clean. Cool for 10 minutes before removing from pans to wire racks to cool completely. **Yield:** 2 loaves.

—Virginia Doyle, Pinedale, Wyoming

Peachy Peach Bread

Since this recipe calls for canned peaches, you can enjoy a taste of summer even when the weather turns cool.

- 2 cups all-purpose flour
- 3/4 cup packed brown sugar
- 2 teaspoons baking powder
- 1/2 teaspoon salt
- 1 can (15-1/4 ounces) sliced peaches
- 2 eggs
- 6 tablespoons butter, melted
- 3/4 cup chopped pecans
- **Peach preserves**

1 In a large bowl, combine the flour, brown sugar, baking powder and salt. Drain peaches, reserving 1/4 cup syrup. Finely chop 1 cup of the peaches; set aside. Place remaining peaches and reserved syrup in a blender or food processor; add eggs and butter. Cover and process until smooth. Stir into dry ingredients just until moistened. Fold in the pecans and chopped peaches.

2 Spoon into two greased 5-3/4-in. x 3-in. x 2-in. loaf pans. Bake at 350° for 40-45 minutes or until a toothpick inserted near the center comes out clean. Cool for 10 minutes before removing from pans to a wire rack to cool completely. Serve with peach preserves. **Yield:** 2 mini loaves.

—Leanne Fried
Bismarck, North Dakota

Coconut Bread

substitute for buttermilk

If you're out of buttermilk, you may substitute soured milk. To sour fresh milk, place 1 tablespoon lemon juice or white vinegar in a liquid measuring cup. Add milk to measure 1 cup. Stir and let stand for 5 minutes to allow milk to thicken.

Checking Quick Breads for Doneness

Insert a toothpick near the center of the bread. If the toothpick comes out clean—without any crumbs—the bread is done.

Mocha Nut Bread

The unbeatable combination of coffee and chocolate is featured in this rich, dark-colored loaf.

     2 cups all-purpose flour
     1 cup sugar
   1/3 cup baking cocoa
     2 tablespoons instant coffee granules
     1 teaspoon baking soda
   1/4 teaspoon salt
     2 eggs
 1-1/4 cups sour cream
   1/3 cup butter, melted
 1-1/2 cups semisweet chocolate chips
   1/2 cup chopped pecans

1 In a large bowl, combine the flour, sugar, cocoa, coffee granules, baking soda and salt. In another bowl, beat the eggs, sour cream and butter until smooth. Stir into dry ingredients just until moistened. Fold in chocolate chips and pecans.

2 Pour into a greased 9-in. x 5-in. x 3-in. loaf pan. Bake at 350° for 55-60 minutes or until a toothpick inserted near the center comes out clean. Cool for 10 minutes before removing from pan to a wire rack to cool completely. **Yield:** 1 loaf.
 —*Winnie Higgins
Salisbury, Maryland*

Pineapple Carrot Bread

This bread has the wonderful flavor of carrot cake but is jazzed up with crushed pineapple.

   3 cups all-purpose flour
   2 cups sugar

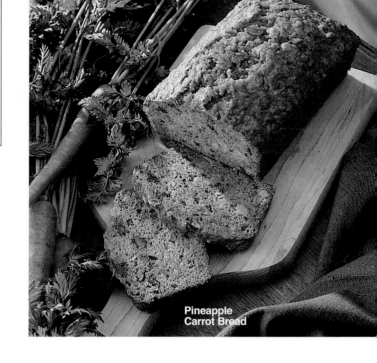

Pineapple Carrot Bread

     1 teaspoon baking soda
     1 teaspoon ground cinnamon
   3/4 teaspoon salt
     3 eggs
     2 cups shredded carrots
     1 cup vegetable oil
     1 can (8 ounces) crushed pineapple, drained
     2 teaspoons vanilla extract
     1 cup chopped pecans *or* walnuts
   3/4 cup confectioners' sugar, optional
     1 to 1-1/2 teaspoons milk, optional

1 In a large bowl, combine the flour, sugar, baking soda, cinnamon and salt. In another bowl, beat the eggs; add carrots, oil, pineapple and vanilla. Stir into dry ingredients just until moistened. Fold in nuts.

2 Spoon into two greased 8-in. x 4-in. x 2-in. loaf pans. Bake at 350° for 65-75 minutes or until a toothpick inserted near the center comes out clean. Cool for 10 minutes before removing from pans to wire racks to cool completely. If glaze is desired, combine confectioners' sugar and milk; drizzle over loaves. **Yield:** 2 loaves.
 —*Paula Spink
Elkins Park, Pennsylvania*

Lemon Blueberry Bread

The lemon glaze adds a lustrous finish and locks in moisture. To have more of the glaze soak into the bread, first prick the top with the tines of a fork.

1/3 cup butter, melted
1 cup sugar
2 eggs
3 tablespoons lemon juice
1-1/2 cups all-purpose flour
1 teaspoon baking powder
1/2 teaspoon salt
1/2 cup milk
2 tablespoons grated lemon peel
1/2 cup chopped nuts
1 cup fresh *or* frozen blueberries*
GLAZE:
2 tablespoons lemon juice
1/4 cup sugar

1 In a large mixing bowl, cream butter and sugar until light and fluffy. Beat in eggs and lemon juice. Combine the flour, baking powder and salt; add to the creamed mixture alternately with milk, beating well after each addition. Fold in the lemon peel, nuts and blueberries.

2 Pour into a greased 8-in. x 4-in. x 2-in. loaf pan. Bake at 350° for 60-70 minutes or until a toothpick inserted near the center comes out clean. Cool for 10 minutes before removing from pan to a wire rack. Combine glaze ingredients; drizzle over warm bread. Cool completely. **Yield:** 1 loaf.   —*Julianne Johnson Grove City, Minnesota*

*Editor's Note: If using frozen blueberries, do not thaw before adding to batter.

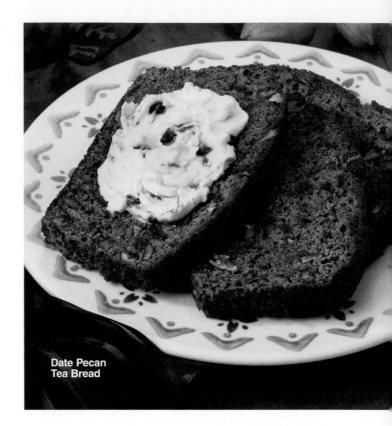

Date Pecan
Tea Bread

Date Pecan Tea Bread

Packed with dates and pecans, this moist sweet bread is excellent on its own and even better topped with the chunky cream cheese spread.

2-1/2 cups chopped dates
1-1/2 cups boiling water
1-1/2 teaspoons baking soda
2 tablespoons butter, softened
1-1/4 cups sugar
1 egg
2 teaspoons vanilla extract
1-3/4 cups all-purpose flour
1/4 teaspoon *each* ground ginger, cinnamon, nutmeg and cloves
1-1/2 cups coarsely chopped pecans
SPREAD:
1 package (3 ounces) cream cheese, softened
2 tablespoons chopped dates
2 tablespoons coarsely chopped pecans
1 tablespoon milk

1 Place dates in a bowl. Combine boiling water and baking soda; pour over dates. In a large mixing bowl, cream butter and sugar until light and fluffy. Beat in egg and vanilla. Combine flour and spices; add to the creamed mixture alternately with date mixture, beating well after each addition. Fold in pecans.

testing baking powder & soda for freshness

Much of a quick bread's success depends upon baking powder and baking soda. So test them for freshness before using.

- For baking powder, mix 1 teaspoon baking powder and 1/3 cup hot water.

- For baking soda, mix 1/4 teaspoon baking soda and 2 teaspoons vinegar.

If bubbling occurs, the products are still fresh. If not, they should be replaced.

2 Pour into a greased 9-in. x 5-in. x 3-in. loaf pan. Bake at 350° for 65-75 minutes or until a toothpick inserted near the center comes out clean. Cool for 10 minutes before removing from pan to a wire rack to cool completely.

3 Combine spread ingredients in a small bowl. Cover and refrigerate for 1 hour. Serve with the bread. **Yield:** 1 loaf (1/2 cup spread).
—*Carole Resnick, Cleveland, Ohio*

1 teaspoon baking soda
1 teaspoon salt
1 teaspoon ground nutmeg
1/2 teaspoon ground cinnamon
1/4 teaspoon baking powder
3 eggs
1/2 cup unsweetened applesauce
1/2 cup vegetable oil
1 tablespoon grated orange peel
2 teaspoons vanilla extract
2 cups shredded zucchini
1 cup chopped walnuts
1 cup (6 ounces) semisweet chocolate chips

1 In a large bowl, combine the flour, sugar, baking soda, salt, nutmeg, cinnamon and baking powder. In another bowl, beat the eggs, applesauce, oil, orange peel and vanilla. Stir into dry ingredients just until moistened. Fold in the zucchini, nuts and chocolate chips.

2 Transfer to two greased 9-in. x 5-in. x 3-in. loaf pans. Bake at 350° for 55-60 minutes or until a toothpick inserted near the center comes out clean. Cool for 10 minutes before removing from pans to wire racks to cool completely. **Yield:** 2 loaves.
—*Edie DeSpain, Logan, Utah*

Zucchini Chip Bread

These mild orange-flavored loaves are chock-full of chocolate chips, nuts and spices.

3 cups all-purpose flour
2 cups sugar

Zucchini Chip Bread

Southern Banana Nut Bread

With bananas and pecans in both the bread and topping, this bread really is unique. Use ripe bananas for the most intense flavor.

- 1/2 cup butter-flavored shortening
- 1-1/2 cups sugar
- 2 eggs
- 1 cup mashed ripe bananas (2 to 3 medium)
- 1 teaspoon vanilla extract
- 2 cups self-rising flour*
- 1/2 cup buttermilk
- 3/4 cup chopped pecans

TOPPING:
- 1/4 to 1/3 cup mashed ripe banana
- 1-1/4 cups confectioners' sugar
- 1 teaspoon lemon juice

Additional chopped pecans

1 In a large mixing bowl, cream shortening and sugar until light and fluffy. Beat in eggs. Blend in bananas and vanilla. Add flour alternately with buttermilk, beating well after each addition. Fold in pecans.

2 Pour into two greased 8-in. x 4-in. x 2-in. loaf pans. Bake at 350° for 45-55 minutes or until a toothpick inserted near the center comes out clean. Cool for 10 minutes before removing from pans to wire racks to cool completely.

3 For topping, combine the banana, confectioners' sugar and lemon juice in a small bowl. Spread over loaves. Sprinkle with pecans. **Yield:** 2 loaves.
— *Viva Forman, Tallahassee, Florida*

*Editor's Note: As a substitute for *each* cup of self-rising flour, place 1-1/2 teaspoons baking powder and 1/2 teaspoon salt in a measuring cup. Add all-purpose flour to equal 1 cup.

Pumpkin Spice Bread

One bite and you'll agree this moist bread tastes just like pumpkin pie without the crust. It will become a family favorite in fall.

- 3 cups sugar
- 1 cup vegetable oil

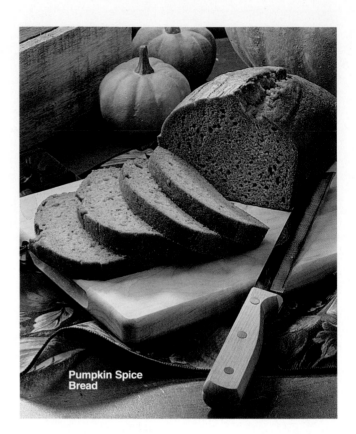

Pumpkin Spice Bread

- 4 eggs, lightly beaten
- 1 can (15 ounces) solid-pack pumpkin
- 3-1/2 cups all-purpose flour
- 1 teaspoon baking soda
- 1 teaspoon salt
- 1 teaspoon ground cinnamon
- 1 teaspoon ground nutmeg
- 1/2 teaspoon baking powder
- 1/2 teaspoon ground cloves
- 1/2 teaspoon ground allspice
- 1/2 cup water

1 In a large bowl, combine the sugar, oil and eggs. Add pumpkin and mix well. Combine the flour, baking soda, salt, cinnamon, nutmeg, baking powder, cloves and allspice; add to the pumpkin mixture alternately with water, beating well after each addition.

2 Pour into two greased 9-in. x 5-in. x 3-in. loaf pans. Bake at 350° for 60-65 minutes or until a toothpick inserted near the center comes out clean. Cool for 10 minutes before removing from pans to wire racks to cool completely. **Yield:** 2 loaves.
— *Delora Lucas, Belle, West Virginia*

Savory quick breads

Jalapeno Corn Bread

With cream-style corn, cheddar cheese and buttermilk, this golden corn bread is more moist than others.

   1 cup cornmeal
1/2 cup shredded cheddar cheese
   2 teaspoons baking powder
3/4 teaspoon salt
   2 eggs
   1 can (8-3/4 ounces) cream-style corn
   1 cup buttermilk
1/4 cup vegetable oil
   1 to 2 tablespoons minced seeded jalapeno peppers*

1 In a large bowl, combine the cornmeal, cheese, baking powder and salt. In another bowl, beat the eggs; add corn, buttermilk, oil and jalapenos. Stir into dry ingredients just until moistened.

2 Transfer to a greased 9-in. square baking pan. Bake at 350° for 50-55 minutes or until a toothpick inserted near the center comes out clean. Cut into squares; serve warm. **Yield:** 9 servings. —*Anita LaRose Benavides, Texas*

*Editor's Note: When cutting or seeding hot peppers, use rubber or plastic gloves to protect your hands. Avoid touching your face.

storing quick breads

- Quick breads may be wrapped in foil or plastic wrap and stored at room temperature for up to 3 days. If made with cheese, cream cheese or other perishable foods, they should be refrigerated.

- For longer storage, place quick breads in heavy-duty resealable plastic bags and freeze for 3 months.

Hearty Oat Loaf

Offer wedges of this bread when making stew or bean soup. Or top with jam and serve alongside your favorite breakfast.

   2 cups all-purpose flour
   1 cup whole wheat flour
1/2 cup plus 2 tablespoons quick-cooking oats, *divided*
1/4 cup sugar
   3 teaspoons baking powder
3/4 teaspoon salt
   1 egg
1-1/2 cups milk
   3 tablespoons vegetable oil

1 In a large bowl, combine the flours, 1/2 cup oats, sugar, baking powder and salt. In another bowl, combine the egg, milk and oil; stir into dry ingredients just until moistened. Spread into a greased 9-in. round baking pan. Sprinkle with remaining oats.

2 Bake at 350° for 40-50 minutes or until a toothpick inserted near the center comes out clean. Cool for 5 minutes before removing from pan to a wire rack. Serve warm. **Yield:** 1 loaf.
—*Judi Havens, Denton, Texas*

Jalapeno Corn Bread

**Round
Cheese Bread**

Round Cheese Bread

*This savory loaf has an Italian flair. Warm buttery
wedges are tasty with a pasta dinner or tossed salad.*

1-1/2 **cups biscuit/baking mix**
   1 **cup (4 ounces) shredded mozzarella cheese**
 1/4 **cup grated Parmesan cheese**
 1/2 **teaspoon dried oregano**
 1/2 **cup milk**
   1 **egg, beaten**
   2 **tablespoons butter, melted**
Additional Parmesan cheese

1 In a bowl, combine the biscuit mix, mozzarella
cheese, Parmesan cheese, oregano, milk and egg
(batter will be thick). Spoon into a greased 9-in. round
baking pan. Drizzle with butter; sprinkle with additional Parmesan cheese.

2 Bake at 400° for 20-25 minutes or until a toothpick
inserted near the center comes out clean. Cool for
10 minutes. Cut into wedges; serve warm. **Yield:** 6-8
servings.   —*Deborah Bitz, Medicine Hat, Alberta*

Boston Brown Bread

*Whole wheat, brown sugar and molasses lend
to the rich brown color of this hearty bread.*

2 **eggs**
2 **cups packed brown sugar**

1 **cup molasses**
4 **cups buttermilk**
4 **cups whole wheat flour**
2 **cups all-purpose flour**
2 **teaspoons salt**
2 **teaspoons baking soda**
1 **cup raisins**
1 **cup chopped walnuts**
Butter *or* cream cheese, optional

1 In a large mixing bowl, beat the eggs
and brown sugar. Add molasses and
buttermilk; mix well. Combine the flours,
salt and baking soda; stir into egg mixture just
until moistened. Fold in raisins and walnuts.

2 Transfer to two greased 9-in. x 5-in. x 3-in. loaf
pans. Bake at 325° for 80-85 minutes or until a
toothpick inserted near the center comes out clean. Cool
for 10 minutes before removing from pans to wire
racks to cool completely. Serve with butter or cream
cheese if desired. **Yield:** 2 loaves.   —*Shellie Robb
Cleveland, Ohio*

Caraway Cheese Bread

*In this savory bread, cheddar cheese blends
beautifully with just the right amount of caraway.*

2-1/2 **cups all-purpose flour**
   2 **cups (8 ounces) shredded cheddar cheese**
1-1/2 **to 2 teaspoons caraway seeds**
 3/4 **teaspoon salt**
 1/2 **teaspoon baking powder**
 1/2 **teaspoon baking soda**
   2 **eggs**
   1 **cup (8 ounces) plain yogurt**
 1/2 **cup butter, melted**
   1 **tablespoon Dijon mustard**

1 In a large bowl, combine the flour, cheese, caraway
seeds, salt, baking powder and baking soda. In another bowl, beat the eggs, yogurt, butter and mustard.
Stir into dry ingredients just until moistened.

2 Pour into a greased 9-in. x 5-in. x 3-in. loaf pan.
Bake at 375° for 30-35 minutes or until a toothpick
inserted near the center comes out clean. Cool for 10
minutes before removing from pan to a wire rack. Serve
warm. Refrigerate leftovers. **Yield:** 1 loaf.
          —*Mrs. Homer Wooten, Ridgetown, Ontario*

Savory Onion Corn Bread

This corn bread is sweet and spicy, thanks to hot pepper sauce. Serve it with chili to warm everyone up on a cold winter evening.

1 medium sweet onion, chopped
1/4 cup butter
1 egg
1 cup cream-style corn
1/3 cup milk
2 drops hot pepper sauce
1 package (8-1/2 ounces) corn bread/muffin mix
1 cup (8 ounces) sour cream
1 cup (4 ounces) shredded cheddar cheese, *divided*
1/4 teaspoon salt
1/4 teaspoon dill weed

1 In a small skillet, saute onion in butter until tender; set aside. In a bowl, combine the egg, corn, milk and hot pepper sauce; stir in muffin mix just until moistened. Pour into a greased 8-in. square baking dish.

2 Combine the sour cream, 1/2 cup cheese, salt, dill and sauteed onion; spoon over batter. Sprinkle with remaining cheese. Bake at 425° for 30-35 minutes or until a toothpick inserted near the center comes out clean. Cut into squares; serve warm. **Yield:** 9 servings.
—*Ruth Chastain, Bellflower, California*

Irish Soda Bread

Legend has it that the cross cut on the top of traditional Irish Soda Bread before baking will ward off evil spirits.

4 cups all-purpose flour
1/4 cup sugar
1 teaspoon baking powder
1 teaspoon baking soda
1/2 teaspoon salt
6 tablespoons shortening
1/2 cup raisins
1 tablespoon caraway seeds
1-1/4 cups buttermilk
1 egg, lightly beaten
2 tablespoons butter, melted
Cinnamon-sugar

1 In a large bowl, combine the flour, sugar, baking powder, baking soda and salt. Cut in shortening until mixture is crumbly. Stir in raisins and caraway seeds. Combine buttermilk and egg; stir into the crumb mixture. Turn onto a lightly floured surface; knead gently 5-6 times.

2 Divide dough in half; shape into two balls. Place on a lightly greased baking sheet. Pat each ball into a 6-in. round loaf. Using a sharp knife, cut a 4-in. cross about 1/4 in. deep on top of each loaf. Brush with butter and sprinkle with cinnamon-sugar. Bake at 375° for 40-45 minutes or until golden brown. **Yield:** 2 loaves.
—*Anne Flanagan, Laguna Hills, California*

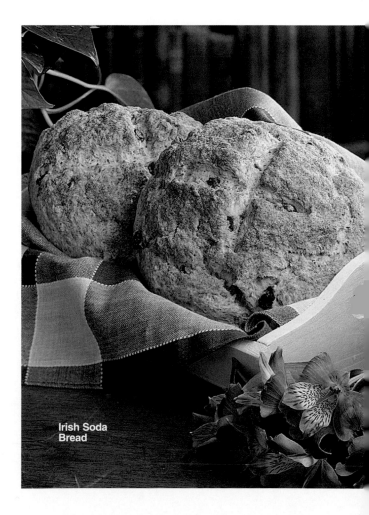

Irish Soda Bread

Pizza Bread

This moist cheesy bread is a fun appetizer. It can also be used to complement Italian meals and main-dish salads.

    2 teaspoons cornmeal
    1 tube (12 ounces) refrigerated biscuits
  1/2 cup pizza sauce
  3/4 cup shredded mozzarella cheese

Sprinkle cornmeal on the bottom of a greased 8-in. square baking dish. Cut each biscuit into quarters; toss with pizza sauce. Place in dish; sprinkle with cheese. Bake at 400° for 14 minutes or until golden brown. **Yield:** 8-10 servings.
—Carla Hodenfield
Mandan, North Dakota

Finnish Flat Bread

It's so nice to have homemade bread with spaghetti, and it's even nicer when you don't have to fuss.

  1-1/2 cups all-purpose flour
    3/4 cup whole wheat flour
      2 tablespoons sugar
  1-1/2 teaspoons baking powder
      1 teaspoon salt
    1/2 teaspoon baking soda
    1/4 cup shortening
      1 cup buttermilk

1 In a large bowl, combine the flours, sugar, baking powder, salt and baking soda. Cut in shortening until mixture is crumbly. Stir in buttermilk just until moistened.

2 Turn dough onto a floured surface; knead for 3-5 minutes. Pat onto an ungreased 12-in. pizza pan. Bake at 350° for 30-35 minutes or until golden. Cool for 10 minutes before removing from pan to a wire rack. **Yield:** 6-8 servings.
—Anne Heinonen
Howell, Michigan

Herbed Monkey Bread

Most folks are familiar with the sweet version of monkey bread. Here a blend of herbs makes a savory bread perfect for pairing with a variety of main courses.

  1/2 cup butter, melted
    1 garlic clove, minced
    2 teaspoons dried parsley flakes
    1 teaspoon dried chives
  1/2 teaspoon dried basil
  1/2 teaspoon dried oregano
    2 packages (12 ounces *each*) refrigerated buttermilk biscuits

In a small bowl, combine the butter, garlic and seasonings. Dip biscuits in butter mixture; place in a greased 10-in. fluted tube pan. Bake at 400° for 18-20 minutes or until golden brown. Cool for 10 minutes before removing from pan to a wire rack. Serve warm. **Yield:** 1 loaf.
—Donna Gordon, Averill Park, New York

Finnish Flat Bread

quick Coffee Cakes

Raspberry Crumb Cake

(Pictured on page 233)

A cake spiced with cinnamon and mace, a yummy raspberry filling and a crunchy almond topping assures this tempting treat will brighten any buffet.

> 2/3 cup sugar
> 1/4 cup cornstarch
> 3/4 cup water
> 2 cups fresh *or* frozen unsweetened raspberries
> 1 tablespoon lemon juice
> **CAKE:**
> 3 cups all-purpose flour
> 1 cup sugar
> 3 teaspoons baking powder
> 1 teaspoon salt
> 1 teaspoon ground cinnamon
> 1/4 teaspoon ground mace
> 1 cup cold butter
> 2 eggs
> 1 cup milk
> 1 teaspoon vanilla extract
> **TOPPING:**
> 1/2 cup all-purpose flour
> 1/2 cup sugar
> 1/4 cup cold butter
> 1/4 cup sliced almonds

1 In a saucepan, combine sugar, cornstarch, water and raspberries. Bring to a boil over medium heat; boil for 5 minutes or until thickened, stirring constantly. Remove from the heat; stir in lemon juice. Cool.

2 In a large bowl, combine the flour, sugar, baking powder, salt, cinnamon and mace. Cut in butter until mixture is crumbly. In another bowl, beat the eggs, milk and vanilla; add to crumb mixture and mix well. Spread two-thirds of the batter into a greased 13-in. x 9-in. x 2-in. baking dish. Spoon raspberry filling over the top to within 1 in. of edges. Top with remaining batter.

3 For topping, combine flour and sugar in a small bowl; cut in butter until mixture is crumbly. Stir in almonds. Sprinkle over the batter. Bake at 350° for 50-55 minutes or until a toothpick inserted near the center comes out clean and top is lightly browned. **Yield:** 12-16 servings. —*Pat Habiger, Spearville, Kansas*

Banana Coffee Cake

You'll go bananas over this yummy coffee cake topped with cinnamon, sugar and pecans! It bakes in a 13-inch x 9-inch pan, so it's easy to transport to potlucks and parties.

> 1 package (8 ounces) cream cheese, softened
> 1/2 cup butter, softened
> 1-1/4 cups sugar
> 2 eggs
> 1 cup mashed ripe bananas (2 to 3 medium)
> 1 teaspoon vanilla extract
> 2-1/4 cups all-purpose flour
> 1-1/2 teaspoons baking powder
> 1/2 teaspoon baking soda
> **TOPPING:**
> 1 cup chopped pecans
> 2 tablespoons sugar
> 1 teaspoon ground cinnamon

1 In a large mixing bowl, beat the cream cheese, butter and sugar until blended. Add eggs, one at a time, beating well after each addition. Add the bananas and vanilla. Combine the flour, baking powder and baking soda; gradually add to the creamed mixture. Combine topping ingredients; stir half into the batter.

2 Transfer to a greased 13-in. x 9-in. x 2-in. baking pan. Sprinkle with the remaining topping. Bake at 350° for 25-30 minutes or until a toothpick inserted near the center comes out clean. Cool on a wire rack. **Yield:** 12-15 servings. —*Georgia Courtney Las Cruces, New Mexico*

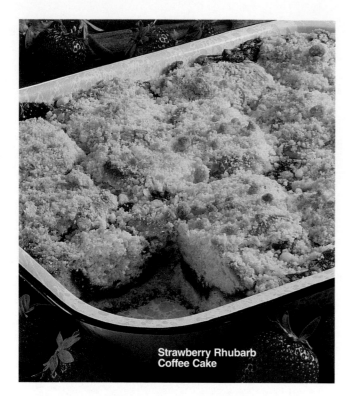
Strawberry Rhubarb
Coffee Cake

Strawberry Rhubarb Coffee Cake

Even people who don't care for rhubarb will find this coffee cake hard to resist.

2/3 cup sugar
1/3 cup cornstarch
  2 cups chopped fresh *or* frozen rhubarb*
  1 package (10 ounces) frozen sweetened sliced strawberries, thawed
  2 tablespoons lemon juice
CAKE:
  3 cups all-purpose flour
  1 cup sugar
  1 teaspoon baking powder
1/2 teaspoon baking soda
  1 cup cold butter
  2 eggs
  1 cup buttermilk
  1 teaspoon vanilla extract
TOPPING:
3/4 cup sugar
1/2 cup all-purpose flour
1/4 cup cold butter

1 In a saucepan, combine sugar and cornstarch; stir in rhubarb and strawberries. Bring to a boil over medium heat; cook for 2 minutes or until thickened. Remove from the heat; stir in lemon juice. Cool.

2 In a large bowl, combine the flour, sugar, baking powder and baking soda; cut in butter until mixture is crumbly. In another bowl, beat the eggs, buttermilk and vanilla; stir into crumb mixture just until moistened. Spoon two-thirds of the batter into a greased 13-in. x 9-in. x 2-in. baking pan. Top with fruit mixture and remaining batter.

3 For topping, combine sugar and flour in a small bowl; cut in butter until mixture is crumbly. Sprinkle over batter. Bake at 350° for 45-50 minutes or until a toothpick inserted near the center comes out clean and cake is golden brown. Cool on a wire rack. **Yield:** 12-16 servings.   —*Benita Thomas, Falcon, Colorado*

*Editor's Note: If using frozen rhubarb, measure rhubarb while still frozen, then thaw completely. Drain in a colander, but do not press liquid out.

Cherry Swirl Coffee Cake

A pretty cherry pie filling peeks out from the golden brown sweet dough in this classic recipe that has mass appeal.

1-1/2 cups sugar
1/2 cup butter, softened
1/2 cup shortening
  1 teaspoon almond extract
  1 teaspoon vanilla extract
1/2 teaspoon baking powder
  4 eggs
  3 cups all-purpose flour
  1 can (21 ounces) cherry pie filling
  1 cup confectioners' sugar
  1 to 2 tablespoons milk

1 In a large mixing bowl, combine the sugar, butter, shortening, extracts, baking powder and eggs. Beat on low speed until blended; beat on high for 3 minutes. Stir in flour.

2 Spread two-thirds of the batter into a greased 15-in. x 10-in. x 1-in. baking pan. Spread pie filling over batter. Drop remaining batter by tablespoonfuls over filling. Bake at 350° for 40-45 minutes or until a toothpick inserted near the center comes out clean and top is golden. Combine the confectioners' sugar and milk; drizzle over coffee cake. Serve warm. **Yield:** 18-20 servings.   —*Charlene Griffin, Minocqua, Wisconsin*

New England Blueberry Coffee Cake

The aroma of this cake is heavenly, and the taste is scrumptious! It's wonderful with mid-morning coffee. You can also serve it at brunch, or with ice cream as a dessert.

- 1-1/2 **cups all-purpose flour**
- 1/2 **cup sugar**
- 3 **teaspoons baking powder**
- 1 **teaspoon ground cinnamon**
- 1/2 **teaspoon salt**
- 1 **egg**
- 1/2 **cup milk**
- 1/4 **cup butter, melted**
- 1-1/2 **cups fresh *or* frozen blueberries***

TOPPING:
- 3/4 **cup packed brown sugar**
- 1 **tablespoon all-purpose flour**
- 1/2 **cup chopped walnuts**
- 1/4 **cup butter, melted**

1 In a large bowl, combine the flour, sugar, baking powder, cinnamon and salt. Combine the egg, milk and butter; stir into dry ingredients just until moistened. Gently fold in blueberries. Spread into a greased 8-in. square baking dish.

2 For topping, combine the brown sugar, flour and walnuts in a small bowl; stir in butter. Sprinkle over batter. Bake at 400° for 20-25 minutes or until top is light golden brown. Serve warm or at room temperature. **Yield:** 12 servings. —*Audrey Thibodeau Lancaster, New Hampshire*

*Editor's Note: If using frozen blueberries, do not thaw before adding to batter.

Cinnamon Coffee Cake

You'll love the texture of this old-fashioned, streusel-topped coffee cake. Always a crowd-pleaser, its sweet vanilla flavor is enriched by sour cream.

- 1 **cup butter, softened**
- 2-3/4 **cups sugar, *divided***
- 4 **eggs**
- 2 **teaspoons vanilla extract**
- 3 **cups all-purpose flour**
- 1 **teaspoon baking soda**
- 1 **teaspoon salt**
- 2 **cups (16 ounces) sour cream**
- 2 **tablespoons ground cinnamon**
- 1/2 **cup chopped walnuts**

1 In a large mixing bowl, cream butter and 2 cups sugar until light and fluffy. Add eggs, one at a time, beating well after each addition. Beat in vanilla. Combine the flour, baking soda and salt; add to the creamed mixture alternately with sour cream, beating just enough after each addition to keep batter smooth.

2 Spoon a third of the batter into a greased 10-in. tube pan. Combine the cinnamon, nuts and remaining sugar; sprinkle a third over batter. Repeat layers twice. Bake at 350° for 60-65 minutes or until a toothpick inserted near the center comes out clean. Cool for 15 minutes before removing from pan to a wire rack to cool completely. **Yield:** 16-20 servings. —*Eleanor Harris Cape Coral, Florida*

Making a Streusel-Filled Coffee Cake

Spoon about a third of the batter into greased pan. Sprinkle with a third of the streusel mixture. Repeat layers twice. Bake as directed.

Cinnamon Coffee Cake

Peachy Sour Cream Coffee Cake

The top of this coffee cake is adorned with fresh peaches.

- 2 cups chopped pecans
- 1/3 cup packed brown sugar
- 3 tablespoons sugar
- 1 teaspoon ground cinnamon

CAKE:
- 1/2 cup butter-flavored shortening
- 1 cup sugar
- 2 eggs
- 1 teaspoon vanilla extract
- 2 cups all-purpose flour
- 1/2 teaspoon baking powder
- 1/2 teaspoon baking soda
- 1/2 teaspoon salt
- 1 cup (8 ounces) sour cream
- 2 cups sliced peeled fresh peaches (about 3 medium)

1 In a small bowl, combine the pecans, sugars and cinnamon; set aside. In a large mixing bowl, cream shortening and sugar until light and fluffy. Add eggs, one at a time, beating well after each addition. Beat in vanilla. Combine the flour, baking powder, baking soda and salt; add to the creamed mixture alternately with sour cream, beating well after each addition.

2 Pour half of the batter into a greased 10-in. tube pan with removable bottom. Sprinkle with 1 cup of the pecan mixture. Top with remaining batter and 1/2 cup pecan mixture. Bake at 350° for 40 minutes.

3 Arrange peaches over cake; sprinkle with remaining pecan mixture. Bake 30-35 minutes longer or until a toothpick inserted near the center comes out clean. Cool for 10 minutes. Carefully run a knife around edge of pan to loosen. Lift cake with removable bottom from pan. Cool completely. Just before serving, carefully remove cake from pan bottom. Store in the refrigerator. **Yield:** 12 servings. *—Alice Brandt Marengo, Illinois*

Cranberry Coffee Cake

This recipe uses cranberry sauce, making it great for when cranberries aren't in season.

- 1/2 cup butter, softened
- 1 cup sugar
- 2 eggs
- 1 teaspoon almond extract
- 2 cups all-purpose flour
- 1 teaspoon baking powder
- 1/2 teaspoon baking soda
- 1/2 teaspoon salt
- 1 cup (8 ounces) sour cream
- 1/3 cup chopped walnuts
- 1 can (16 ounces) whole-berry cranberry sauce

GLAZE:
- 3/4 cup confectioners' sugar
- 2 tablespoons milk
- 1/2 teaspoon vanilla extract

1 In a large mixing bowl, cream butter and sugar until light and fluffy. Add eggs, one at a time, beating well after each addition. Stir in almond extract. Combine the flour, baking powder, baking soda and salt; add to the creamed mixture alternately with sour cream, beating well after each addition.

2 Sprinkle the walnuts into a greased 10-in. fluted tube pan. Spread half of the batter over nuts; top with half of the cranberry sauce. Repeat layers.

3 Bake at 350° for 50-55 minutes or until a toothpick inserted near the center comes out clean. Cool for 10 minutes before removing from pan to a wire rack to cool completely. Combine glaze ingredients; drizzle over coffee cake. **Yield:** 12-16 servings. *—Judith Casserly York Beach, Maine*

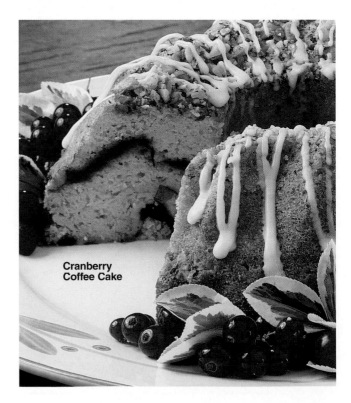

Cranberry Coffee Cake

reheating coffee cakes

If you make a coffee cake in advance but want fresh-from-the-oven flavor when you serve it to guests, try this trick.

Wrap an unfrosted coffee cake in foil. Reheat at 350° for a few minutes or until warm.

Caramel Apple Coffee Cake

Almond Apricot Coffee Cake

The nutty aroma and delicate fruit flavor make this cake special enough to serve to company. Strawberry or raspberry preserves can be used as a tasty variation.

        1 cup butter, softened
        2 cups sugar
        3 eggs
        1 cup (8 ounces) sour cream
        1 teaspoon almond extract
        2 cups all-purpose flour
    1/2 teaspoon baking powder
    1/2 teaspoon baking soda
    1/4 teaspoon salt
    3/4 cup slivered almonds, *divided*
        1 jar (10 to 12 ounces) apricot preserves,
            divided

1 In a large mixing bowl, cream butter and sugar until light and fluffy. Add the eggs, sour cream and extract; mix well. Combine the flour, baking powder, baking soda and salt; add to the creamed mixture and mix well.

2 Spread half of the batter into a greased and floured 10-in. fluted tube pan. Sprinkle with half of the almonds. Spread half of the preserves to within 1/2 in. of the edges. Cover with remaining batter. Spoon remaining preserves over batter to within 1/2 in. of edges. Sprinkle with remaining almonds.

3 Bake at 350° for 55-60 minutes or until a toothpick inserted near the center comes out clean. Cool for 15 minutes before inverting onto a serving plate. **Yield:** 12-16 servings. —*Sharon Mensing, Greenfield, Iowa*

Caramel Apple Coffee Cake

A rich caramel topping is the crowning touch on this delicious apple coffee cake.

        3 eggs
        2 cups sugar
    1-1/2 cups vegetable oil
        2 teaspoons vanilla extract
        3 cups all-purpose flour
        1 teaspoon baking soda
        1 teaspoon salt
        3 cups chopped peeled apples
        1 cup coarsely chopped pecans
TOPPING:
    1/2 cup butter
    1/4 cup milk
        1 cup packed brown sugar
Dash salt

1 In a large mixing bowl, beat the eggs until foamy; gradually add sugar. Blend in oil and vanilla. Combine the flour, baking soda and salt; add to egg mixture. Stir in apples and pecans. Pour into a greased 10-in. tube pan. Bake at 350° for 1-1/4 hours or until a toothpick inserted near the center comes out clean. Cool for 10 minutes before inverting onto a serving plate.

2 In a small saucepan, combine topping ingredients. Bring to a boil; boil for 3 minutes, stirring constantly. Slowly pour over warm cake (some topping will run down onto the plate). **Yield:** 12-16 servings.
—*Ruth Turner, Marinette, Wisconsin*

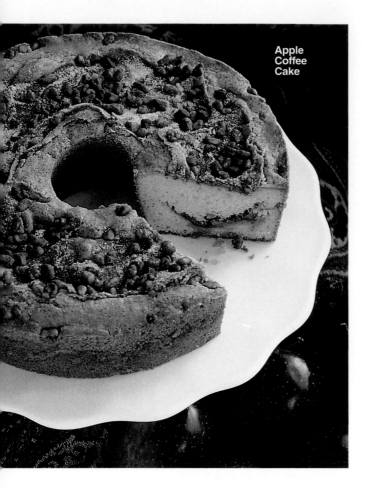

Apple Coffee Cake

to the creamed mixture alternately with sour cream, beating well after each addition. In a small bowl, combine the nuts, cinnamon and remaining sugar.

2 Spread half of the batter into a well-greased 10-in. tube pan with removable bottom. Top with apple slices; sprinkle with half of the nut mixture. Top with remaining batter and nut mixture. Bake at 375° for 40-45 minutes or until a toothpick inserted near the center comes out clean. Cool in pan for 30 minutes.

3 Carefully run a knife around edge of pan to loosen. Lift cake with removable bottom from pan. Cool completely. Before serving, carefully remove cake from pan bottom. **Yield:** 12-16 servings.
—*Oriana Churchill, Londonderry, New Hampshire*

Apple Coffee Cake

This tried-and-true recipe tastes wonderful. The apple filling makes it moist, while the crispy nut mixture adds a bit of crunch.

    1/2 cup butter, softened
1-1/2 cups sugar, *divided*
      2 eggs
      1 teaspoon vanilla extract
      2 cups all-purpose flour
      1 teaspoon baking powder
    1/2 teaspoon baking soda
    1/2 teaspoon salt
      1 cup (8 ounces) sour cream
    1/2 cup chopped walnuts
      2 teaspoons ground cinnamon
      1 medium apple, peeled and thinly sliced

1 In a large mixing bowl, cream the butter and 1 cup sugar until light and fluffy. Add eggs, one at a time, beating well after each addition. Beat in vanilla. Combine the flour, baking powder, baking soda and salt; add

Berry Cream Coffee Cake

For instructions on assembling this coffee cake, see Braiding a Filled Bread on page 331.

      1 package (3 ounces) cream cheese
    1/4 cup cold butter
      2 cups biscuit/baking mix
    1/3 cup milk
    1/2 cup raspberry preserves
GLAZE:
      1 cup confectioners' sugar
      1 to 2 tablespoons milk
    1/2 teaspoon vanilla extract

1 In a bowl, cut cream cheese and butter into biscuit mix until crumbly. Stir in milk just until moistened. Turn onto a floured surface; knead 8-10 times or until dough is smooth. On waxed paper, roll dough into a 12-in. x 8-in. rectangle. Turn onto a greased 15-in. x 10-in. x 1-in. baking pan. Remove waxed paper.

2 Spread preserves down center third of rectangle. On each long side, cut 1-in.-wide strips about 2-1/2 in. into center. Starting at one end, fold alternating strips

at an angle across preserves; seal end. Bake at 425° for 12-15 minutes. Combine the glaze ingredients; drizzle over warm coffee cake. Cool on a wire rack. **Yield:** 8-10 servings. —*Marjorie Miller, Haven, Kansas*

Raspberry Cheese Coffee Cake

Since this recipe calls for raspberry jam and not fresh raspberries, you can make this coffee cake any time of year and bring a touch of spring to your table.

2-1/4 **cups all-purpose flour**
3/4 **cup sugar**
3/4 **cup cold butter**
1/2 **teaspoon baking powder**
1/2 **teaspoon baking soda**
1/2 **teaspoon salt**
3/4 **cup sour cream**
1 **egg, beaten**
1-1/2 **teaspoons almond extract**
FILLING:
1 **package (8 ounces) cream cheese, softened**
1/2 **cup sugar**
1 **egg**
1/2 **cup raspberry jam**
1/2 **cup slivered almonds**

1 In a large mixing bowl, combine flour and sugar; cut in butter until mixture is crumbly. Remove 1 cup and set aside. To the remaining crumb mixture, add baking

powder, baking soda, salt, sour cream, egg and almond extract; mix well. Spread onto the bottom and 2 in. up the sides of a greased 9-in. springform pan.

2 For filling, combine cream cheese, sugar and egg in a small mixing bowl; beat well. Spoon over batter. Top with raspberry jam. Sprinkle with almonds and reserved crumb mixture. Bake at 350° for 55-60 minutes. Cool on a wire rack for 15 minutes. Carefully run a knife around edge of pan to loosen. Remove sides of pan. Cool completely. Store in the refrigerator. **Yield:** 9-12 servings. —*Susan Litwiller, Medford, Oregon*

Chocolate Chip Coffee Cake

With chocolate chips and cinnamon in the middle and on top, this special breakfast treat never fails to please all ages.

1/2 **cup butter, softened**
1-1/2 **cups sugar, *divided***
2 **eggs**
1 **cup (8 ounces) sour cream**
1 **teaspoon vanilla extract**
2-1/2 **cups all-purpose flour**
1-1/2 **teaspoons baking powder**
1 **teaspoon baking soda**
1 **cup (6 ounces) semisweet chocolate chips**
1 **teaspoon ground cinnamon**

1 In a large mixing bowl, cream butter and 1 cup sugar until light and fluffy. Add the eggs, sour cream and vanilla; mix well. Combine the flour, baking powder and baking soda; add to the creamed mixture (batter will be thick).

2 Spread half of the batter into a greased 13-in. x 9-in. x 2-in. baking pan. Combine chocolate chips, cinnamon and remaining sugar; sprinkle half over batter. Drop remaining batter by spoonfuls over the top. Sprinkle with remaining chip mixture. Bake at 350° for 25-30 minutes or until a toothpick inserted near the center comes out clean. Cool on a wire rack. **Yield:** 12-16 servings. —*Trish Quinn, Middletown, Pennsylvania*

Raspberry Cheese Coffee Cake

a medley of Muffins, Biscuits & Scones

Buttermilk Biscuits (p. 269)…Pumpkin Streusel Muffins (p. 260)…
Cranberry Orange Scones (p. 276)…just imagine their
wonderful aroma! These handheld goodies go together in a jiffy
and have a short baking time.

Muffins & more

secrets for successful muffins

- Use butter, stick margarine (with at least 80% oil) or shortening. For best results, do not use whipped, tub, soft, liquid or reduced-fat products. The fat should be softened (at room temperature), meaning it is pliable when touched.

- Measure ingredients accurately, using the measuring tools and techniques suggested on pages 8 and 9.

- Before preheating the oven, arrange the oven racks so that the muffins will bake in the center of the oven.

- Preheat the oven for 10-15 minutes before baking.

- Standard muffin pans come in different sizes, which affect baking time. The muffin pans we used in this book measure 2-1/2 inches across.

- Fill muffin cups from two-thirds to three-fourths full. If your muffin recipe does not fill all the cups in your pan, fill the empty cups with water. The muffins will bake more evenly.

- Unless directed otherwise, muffins should go directly into the oven as soon as the batter is mixed.

- Use a kitchen timer. Check for doneness 5-7 minutes before the end of the recommended baking time to avoid overbaking. Muffins are done when a toothpick inserted near the center comes out clean. For muffins with a filling, make sure the toothpick is inserted into the muffin and not the filling.

- Cool in the pan for 5 minutes, unless the recipe directs otherwise. Muffins are best served warm, fresh from the oven.

Making Muffins

1. In a large bowl, combine dry ingredients with a fork.

2. Beat eggs and combine with liquid ingredients.

3. Make a well in the dry ingredients and pour egg mixture into the well all at one time.

4. With a spoon or spatula, stir the ingredients together just until moistened. Fill greased or paper-lined muffin cups about two-thirds to three-fourths full, wiping off any spills.

5. Bake until golden or test for doneness by inserting a toothpick into the center of the muffin. If the toothpick comes out clean, the muffins are done. Cool for 5 minutes before removing from pan to a wire rack.

problem-Solving pointers for Muffins, Biscuits & Scones

If this happens:	This could be the reason:
Muffins, biscuits or scones are tough.	Batter/dough was overmixed or overhandled. Next time, mix just until combined.
Muffins have tunnels and/or peaks.	Batter was overmixed.
Muffins have a bitter aftertaste.	Too much leavener was used.
Biscuits baked unevenly.	Dough was not patted or rolled out evenly. Next time, use a ruler to measure thickness.

Berry Cream Muffins

If you can't decide which berries to use in these delightful muffins, use half raspberries and half blueberries for a "berry" good treat!

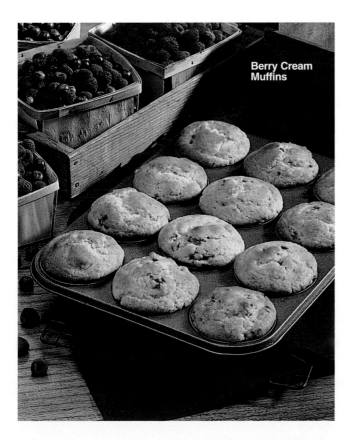

Berry Cream Muffins

4 cups all-purpose flour
2 cups sugar
1 teaspoon baking powder
1 teaspoon baking soda
1 teaspoon salt
3 cups fresh *or* frozen raspberries *or* blueberries*
4 eggs, lightly beaten
2 cups (16 ounces) sour cream
1 cup vegetable oil
1 teaspoon vanilla extract

1 In a large bowl, combine the flour, sugar, baking powder, baking soda and salt. Add berries and toss gently. In another bowl, combine the eggs, sour cream, oil and vanilla; mix well. Stir into dry ingredients just until moistened.

2 Fill greased or paper-lined muffin cups two-thirds full. Bake at 400° for 20-25 minutes or until a toothpick comes out clean. Cool for 5 minutes before removing from pans to wire racks. **Yield:** about 2-1/2 dozen. —*Linda Gilmore, Hampstead, Maryland*

***Editor's Note:** If using frozen berries, do not thaw before adding to batter.

Pumpkin Streusel Muffins

(Pictured on page 257)

Streusel is the German word for "to strew or sprinkle". It often refers to the sweet, crumbly topping sprinkled on top of such baked goods as muffins, quick breads, coffee cakes and pies.

- 1/4 cup butter, softened
- 1/2 cup sugar
- 1/4 cup packed brown sugar
- 2/3 cup canned pumpkin
- 1/2 cup buttermilk
- 2 eggs, lightly beaten
- 2 tablespoons molasses
- 1 teaspoon grated orange peel
- 2 cups all-purpose flour
- 1 teaspoon baking soda
- 1/2 teaspoon baking powder
- 1/2 to 1 teaspoon pumpkin pie spice
- 1/4 teaspoon salt

STREUSEL TOPPING:
- 1/3 cup all-purpose flour
- 3 tablespoons brown sugar
- 2 tablespoons cold butter

1 In a large mixing bowl, cream butter and sugars until light and fluffy. Add the pumpkin, buttermilk, eggs, molasses and orange peel; mix well. Combine the flour, baking soda, baking powder, pumpkin pie spice and salt; gradually add to pumpkin mixture just until blended. Fill greased or paper-lined muffin cups two-thirds full.

2 For topping, combine flour and brown sugar in a bowl; cut in butter until mixture is crumbly. Sprinkle over batter. Bake at 375° for 20-25 minutes or until a toothpick comes out clean. Cool for 5 minutes before removing from pan to a wire rack. **Yield:** 1 dozen.

—*Connie Pietila, Atlantic Mine, Michigan*

filling muffin cups with ease

Using a spoon to fill muffin cups with batter can get messy. To quickly put batter into muffin cups with little mess, use an ice cream scoop with a quick release. Or pour the batter from a measuring cup.

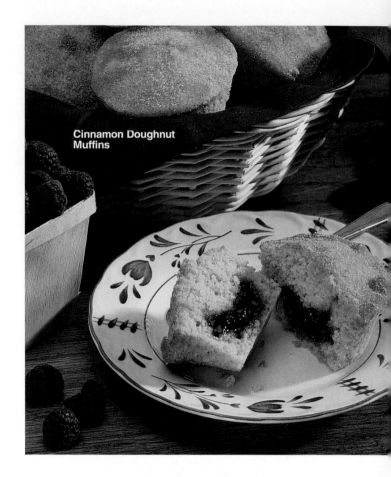

Cinnamon Doughnut Muffins

Cinnamon Doughnut Muffins

With a jam-filled center, these cinnamon-topped muffins are similar to a jelly doughnut. But they are much easier to prepare!

- 1-3/4 cups all-purpose flour
- 1-1/2 teaspoons baking powder
- 1/2 teaspoon salt
- 1/2 teaspoon ground nutmeg
- 1/4 teaspoon ground cinnamon
- 3/4 cup sugar
- 1/3 cup vegetable oil
- 1 egg, lightly beaten
- 3/4 cup milk

Jam

TOPPING:
- 1/4 cup butter, melted
- 1/3 cup sugar
- 1 teaspoon ground cinnamon

1 In a large bowl, combine the flour, baking powder, salt, nutmeg and cinnamon. In a small bowl, combine the sugar, oil, egg and milk. Stir into dry ingredients just until moistened.

2 Fill greased or paper-lined muffin cups half full; place 1 teaspoon of jam on top. Cover jam with enough batter to fill cups three-fourths full. Bake at 350° for 20-25 minutes or until a toothpick inserted 1 in. from the edge comes out clean.

3 Place melted butter in a small bowl; combine sugar and cinnamon in another bowl. Immediately after removing muffins from the oven, dip tops in butter, then in cinnamon-sugar. Serve warm. **Yield:** 10 muffins.
—Sharon Pullen, Alvinston, Ontario

If I had my life to live over, I'd live it over a bakery.

Cappuccino Muffins

Not only are these chocolate and coffee muffins great for breakfast, they make a tasty dessert or midnight snack. Serve them with a cup of coffee or tall glass of cold milk.

ESPRESSO SPREAD:
  4 ounces cream cheese, cubed and softened
  1 tablespoon sugar
1/2 teaspoon instant coffee granules
1/2 teaspoon vanilla extract
1/4 cup miniature semisweet chocolate chips
MUFFINS:
  2 cups all-purpose flour
3/4 cup sugar
2-1/2 teaspoons baking powder
  1 teaspoon ground cinnamon
1/2 teaspoon salt
  1 cup milk

  2 tablespoons instant coffee granules
1/2 cup butter, melted
  1 egg
  1 teaspoon vanilla extract
3/4 cup miniature semisweet chocolate chips

1 In a food processor or blender, combine the spread ingredients; cover and process until well blended. Transfer to a small bowl; cover and refrigerate until serving.

2 In a large bowl, combine the flour, sugar, baking powder, cinnamon and salt. In a small bowl, stir milk and coffee granules until granules are dissolved. Add butter, egg and vanilla; mix well. Stir into dry ingredients just until moistened. Fold in chocolate chips.

3 Fill greased or paper-lined muffin cups two-thirds full. Bake at 375° for 17-20 minutes or until a toothpick comes out clean. Cool for 5 minutes before removing from pans to wire racks. Serve with espresso spread. **Yield:** about 14 muffins (1 cup spread).
—Janice Bassing, Racine, Wisconsin

Cappuccino Muffins

Rhubarb Nut Muffins

moving from pan to a wire rack. **Yield:** about 10 muffins.
—*Mary Kay Morris, Cokato, Minnesota*

*Editor's Note: If using frozen rhubarb, measure rhubarb while still frozen, then thaw completely. Drain in a colander, but do not press liquid out.

Apple Streusel Muffins

You'll find yourself making these fruity muffins often. Their wonderful aroma smacks of fall!

1-1/2 cups all-purpose flour
  1/4 cup sugar
    2 teaspoons baking powder
  1/2 teaspoon ground cinnamon
  1/4 teaspoon salt
  1/8 teaspoon ground nutmeg
    1 egg
  1/2 cup milk
  1/4 cup vegetable oil
    1 cup shredded peeled tart apple
STREUSEL TOPPING:
  1/3 cup packed brown sugar
    2 tablespoons all-purpose flour
  1/2 teaspoon ground cinnamon
    2 tablespoons butter, softened
  1/3 cup chopped pecans

Rhubarb Nut Muffins

A brown sugar topping adds to the richness of these irresistible morsels.

1-1/2 cups all-purpose flour
  3/4 cup packed brown sugar
  1/2 teaspoon baking soda
  1/2 teaspoon salt
    1 egg
  1/3 cup vegetable oil
  1/2 cup buttermilk
    1 teaspoon vanilla extract
    1 cup diced fresh *or* frozen rhubarb*
  1/2 cup chopped walnuts
TOPPING:
  1/4 cup packed brown sugar
  1/4 cup chopped walnuts
  1/2 teaspoon ground cinnamon

1 In a large bowl, combine the flour, brown sugar, baking soda and salt. In a small bowl, whisk the egg, oil, buttermilk and vanilla. Stir into dry ingredients just until moistened. Fold in rhubarb and walnuts.

2 Fill greased or paper-lined muffin cups two-thirds full. Combine the topping ingredients; sprinkle over batter. Bake at 375° for 20-25 minutes or until a toothpick comes out clean. Cool for 5 minutes before re-

1 In a large bowl, combine the flour, sugar, baking powder, cinnamon, salt and nutmeg. In a small bowl, whisk the egg, milk and oil. Stir into dry ingredients just until moistened. Fold in apple. In another small bowl, combine topping ingredients. Set aside 3 tablespoons topping.

2 Spoon half of the batter into 12 greased muffin cups. Sprinkle with the remaining topping. Cover with enough batter to fill muffin cups two-thirds full. Sprinkle with reserved topping. Bake at 400° for 20-25 minutes or until a toothpick comes out clean. Cool for 5 minutes before removing from pan to a wire rack. **Yield:** 1 dozen. —*Cynthia Kolberg, Syracuse, Indiana*

Morning Glory Muffins

For a hearty morning treat, try these muffins full of carrots, raisins, walnuts, coconut and apple.

- 1 cup whole wheat flour
- 3/4 cup sugar
- 1/2 cup all-purpose flour
- 1/2 cup oat bran
- 2 teaspoons baking soda
- 1/2 teaspoon salt
- 3 eggs
- 3/4 cup applesauce
- 1/4 cup vegetable oil
- 1/4 cup molasses
- 2 teaspoons vanilla extract
- 1/4 teaspoon orange extract
- 2 cups grated carrots
- 1/2 cup raisins
- 1/2 cup walnuts
- 1/2 cup flaked coconut
- 1 medium tart apple, peeled and finely chopped

1 In a large bowl, combine the first six ingredients. In a small bowl, combine the eggs, applesauce, oil, molasses and extracts; mix well. Stir into dry ingredients just until moistened. Fold in the carrots, raisins, walnuts, coconut and apple.

2 Fill greased or paper-lined muffin cups three-fourths full. Bake at 350° for 25-30 minutes or until a toothpick comes out clean. Cool for 5 minutes before removing from pans to wire racks. **Yield:** about 1-1/2 dozen. —*Richard Case, Johnstown, Pennsylvania*

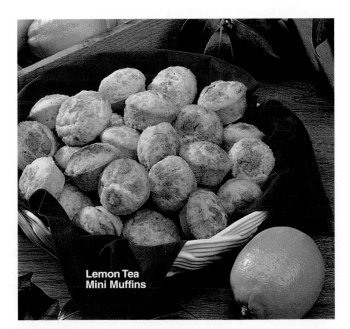

Lemon Tea Mini Muffins

storing muffins, biscuits & scones

- Store muffins, biscuits and scones in an airtight container at room temperature. (If made with cheese, cream cheese or other perishable foods, they should be stored in the refrigerator.)

- Muffins stay fresh for up to 3 days. Biscuits and scones should be eaten within 1 to 2 days.

- You can freeze muffins for up to 1 month and biscuits and scones for up to 3 months.

Lemon Tea Mini Muffins

These light lemon muffins pair well with hot cocoa in winter and cool lemonade in summer.

- 2 eggs, *separated*
- 1/2 cup butter, softened
- 1/2 cup sugar
- 1 cup all-purpose flour
- 1 teaspoon baking powder
- 1/4 teaspoon salt
- 3 tablespoons lemon juice
- 1 teaspoon grated lemon peel

TOPPING:
- 1 tablespoon sugar
- 1/8 teaspoon ground cinnamon

Dash ground nutmeg

1 In a small mixing bowl, beat egg yolks until light and lemon-colored, about 5 minutes. In a large mixing bowl, cream butter and sugar until light and fluffy. Fold in yolks. Combine the flour, baking powder and salt; add to the creamed mixture alternately with lemon juice and peel, stirring just until combined. In another small mixing bowl and with clean beaters, beat egg whites on high speed until stiff peaks form. Fold into batter.

2 Fill greased or paper-lined miniature muffin cups two-thirds full. Combine topping ingredients; sprinkle over batter. Bake at 350° for 16-18 minutes or until a toothpick comes out clean. Cool for 5 minutes before removing from pan to a wire rack. **Yield:** about 2 dozen. —*Terrie Cox, Honeyville, Utah*

*Editor's Note: Batter may be baked in 8 regular-size muffin cups for 20-25 minutes.

Banana Chip Muffins

Mini chocolate chips are just the right size for these muffins. They don't overpower the terrific banana flavor.

  1 **egg**
1/3 **cup vegetable oil**
3/4 **cup sugar**
  3 **medium ripe bananas, mashed (about 1-1/3 cups)**
  2 **cups all-purpose flour**
1/2 **cup old-fashioned oats**
3/4 **teaspoon baking soda**
1/2 **teaspoon baking powder**
1/2 **teaspoon salt**
3/4 **cup miniature semisweet chocolate chips**

1 In a large mixing bowl, beat egg, oil and sugar until smooth. Stir in bananas. Combine the flour, oats, baking soda, baking powder and salt; stir into the banana mixture just until moistened. Stir in chocolate chips.

2 Fill greased muffin cups three-fourths full. Bake at 375° for 18-20 minutes or until a toothpick comes out clean. Cool for 5 minutes before removing from pan to a wire rack. **Yield:** 1 dozen. *—Joanne Shields Olds, Alberta*

Green Chili Corn Muffins

The addition of cake mix makes these corn muffins a little more moist than most. With zesty green chilies, they really round out a Mexican dinner.

  1 **package (8-1/2 ounces) corn bread/muffin mix**
  1 **package (9 ounces) yellow cake mix**
  2 **eggs**
1/2 **cup milk**
1/3 **cup water**
  2 **tablespoons vegetable oil**
  1 **can (4 ounces) chopped green chilies, drained**
  1 **cup (4 ounces) shredded cheddar cheese, *divided***

1 In a large bowl, combine the dry corn bread and cake mixes. In another bowl, combine the eggs, milk, water and oil. Stir into dry ingredients just until moistened. Add the chilies and 3/4 cup cheese.

2 Fill greased or paper-lined muffin cups two-thirds full. Bake at 350° for 20-22 minutes or until a toothpick comes out clean. Immediately sprinkle with the remaining cheese. Cool for 5 minutes before removing from pans to wire racks. Serve warm. **Yield:** 16 muffins. *—Melissa Cook, Chico, California*

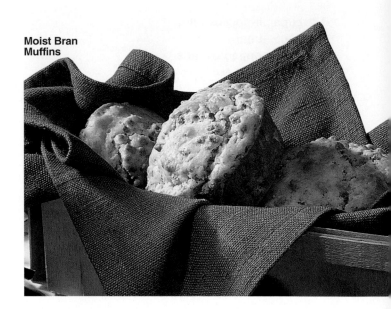

Moist Bran Muffins

Moist Bran Muffins

These tender muffins are a tasty way to complete any meal. The recipe makes a small quantity perfect for a couple or single person.

1/2 **cup All-Bran**
1/2 **cup milk**
  2 **tablespoons vegetable oil**
1/2 **cup all-purpose flour**
  2 **tablespoons sugar**
  1 **teaspoon baking powder**
1/4 **teaspoon salt**

1 In a large bowl, combine the bran and milk; let stand for 5 minutes. Stir in the oil. Combine the flour, sugar, baking powder and salt; stir into bran mixture just until moistened.

2 Fill greased or paper-lined muffin cups half full. Bake at 400° for 18-22 minutes or until a toothpick comes out clean. Cool for 5 minutes before removing from pan to a wire rack. **Yield:** 4 muffins.

—Mildred Ross, Badin, North Carolina

Zucchini Oat Muffins

*Oats and pecans add heartiness
to these slightly sweet muffins. Your
family will never know you're sneaking
a vegetable into these treats!*

2-1/2 cups all-purpose flour
1-1/2 cups sugar
    1 cup chopped pecans
  1/2 cup quick-cooking oats
    3 teaspoons baking powder
    1 teaspoon salt
    1 teaspoon ground cinnamon
    4 eggs
    1 medium zucchini, shredded (about 3/4 cup)
  3/4 cup vegetable oil

1 In a large mixing bowl, combine the flour, sugar, pecans, oats, baking powder, salt and cinnamon. In a small bowl, beat the eggs; add zucchini and oil. Stir into dry ingredients just until moistened (batter will be lumpy).

2 Fill greased muffin cups three-fourths full. Bake at 400° for 20-25 minutes or until a toothpick comes out clean. Cool for 5 minutes before removing from pan to a wire rack. **Yield:** 1 dozen.   *—Janet Bonarski
Perry, New York*

Three-Grain Muffins

*This batter can be stored in the refrigerator for
up to 1 week, so you can whip up a batch
of oven-fresh muffins even on busy mornings!*

    2 cups quick-cooking oats
    2 cups crushed Shredded Wheat (about 5 large)
    2 cups All-Bran
    4 cups buttermilk
    1 cup boiling water
    1 cup vegetable oil
    4 eggs, beaten
2-1/4 cups packed brown sugar
    5 cups all-purpose flour
    5 teaspoons baking soda
    1 teaspoon salt

1 In a large bowl, combine the oats, Shredded Wheat and bran. Add the buttermilk, water, oil and eggs; stir for 1 minute. Stir in the brown sugar. Combine the flour, baking soda and salt; add to the oat mixture and stir well.

2 Fill greased or paper-lined muffin cups two-thirds full. Bake at 400° for 18-20 minutes or until a toothpick comes out clean. Cool for 5 minutes before removing from pans to wire racks. **Yield:** 3-1/2 dozen.
   —Dorothy Collins, Winnsboro, Texas

Three-Grain
Muffins

Cheddar Chive Muffins

Yankee Corn Muffins

The variations of corn bread are endless. Northerners tend to make sweet corn bread with yellow cornmeal. Southerners prefer unsweetened corn bread made with white cornmeal.

    1 cup all-purpose flour
  3/4 cup yellow cornmeal
    3 tablespoons sugar
    2 teaspoons baking powder
    1 teaspoon salt
    1 egg
    1 cup milk
  1/4 cup vegetable oil

1 In a large bowl, combine the flour, cornmeal, sugar, baking powder and salt. In a small bowl, beat the egg, milk and oil. Stir into the dry ingredients just until moistened.

2 Fill greased muffin cups two-thirds full. Bake at 400° for 16-18 minutes or until a toothpick comes out clean. Cool for 5 minutes before removing from pan to a wire rack. **Yield:** 10 muffins. —*Barb Marshall Pickerington, Ohio*

Cheddar Chive Muffins

For a nice change from sweet muffins, try this savory variety. For bite-size morsels, bake the batter in miniature muffin cups for 10 to 12 minutes.

1-1/4 cups milk
  3/4 cup mashed potato flakes
    1 egg
  1/3 cup vegetable oil
    1 cup (4 ounces) shredded cheddar cheese
1-2/3 cups all-purpose flour
    3 tablespoons sugar
    2 tablespoons minced chives
    1 tablespoon dried parsley flakes
    2 teaspoons baking powder
    1 teaspoon salt

1 In a small saucepan, bring milk to a boil. Remove from the heat; stir in potato flakes. Let stand for 2 minutes. Whip with a fork until smooth; cool slightly. Transfer to a large bowl. Beat in the egg, oil and cheese. Combine the flour, sugar, chives, parsley, baking powder and salt; stir into potato mixture just until moistened (batter will be thick).

2 Fill greased muffin cups three-fourths full. Bake at 400° for 20-25 minutes or until a toothpick comes out clean. Cool for 5 minutes before removing from pan to a wire rack. Serve warm. **Yield:** 1 dozen. —*Donna Royer, Largo, Florida*

Maple Bacon Muffins

Great for breakfast on the run, these hearty muffins combine the fabulous flavors of pancakes and bacon.

    1 cup quick-cooking oats
  3/4 cup all-purpose flour
  3/4 cup whole wheat flour
  1/2 cup packed dark brown sugar
    2 teaspoons baking powder
    1 teaspoon baking soda
  1/2 teaspoon salt
    2 eggs
    1 cup buttermilk
    1 cup maple syrup
   10 bacon strips, cooked and crumbled

1 In a large mixing bowl, combine the oats, flours, brown sugar, baking powder, baking soda and salt. In a small bowl, beat the eggs, buttermilk and syrup. Stir into dry ingredients just until moistened. Fold in bacon.

2 Fill greased or paper-lined muffin cups two-thirds full. Bake at 350° for 20-25 minutes or until a toothpick comes out clean. Cool for 5 minutes before removing from pans to wire racks. Serve warm. Refrigerate leftovers. **Yield:** about 1-1/2 dozen. —*Louise Biela Hamburg, New York*

Sweet Onion Mini Muffins

These savory morsels are wonderful alongside any main dish and also make a tasty snack warm or cold. It's hard to stop eating them!

    1-1/2 cups all-purpose flour
      1/2 cup sugar

Sweet Onion Mini Muffins

    1-1/2 teaspoons baking powder
      1/2 teaspoon salt
        2 eggs
        1 cup finely chopped onion
      1/2 cup butter, melted
    1-1/2 cups chopped walnuts

1 In a large bowl, combine the flour, sugar, baking powder and salt. In another bowl, beat the eggs, onion and butter until blended. Stir into dry ingredients just until moistened. Fold in walnuts.

2 Fill greased or paper-lined miniature muffin cups three-fourths full. Bake at 400° for 10-12 minutes or until a toothpick comes out clean. Cool for 5 minutes before removing from pans to wire racks. **Yield:** 3 dozen. —*Mildred Spinn, Cameron, Texas*

Editor's Note: Batter may be baked in 1 dozen regular-size muffin cups for 20-25 minutes.

Dijon Ham Muffins

Easy to fix, these muffins are great for breakfast with scrambled eggs or on a brunch buffet. They're also super with soup for lunch.

    1-2/3 cups all-purpose flour
      1/3 cup cornmeal
      1/4 cup sugar
        1 teaspoon baking powder
        1 to 2 teaspoons ground mustard
      1/2 teaspoon baking soda
      1/2 teaspoon salt
      1/8 teaspoon ground cloves
        2 eggs
        1 cup buttermilk
      1/3 cup vegetable oil
        3 tablespoons Dijon mustard
        1 cup finely chopped fully cooked ham

1 In a large bowl, combine the first eight ingredients. In a small bowl, combine the eggs, buttermilk, oil and mustard. Stir into dry ingredients just until moistened. Fold in the ham.

2 Fill greased muffin cups three-fourths full. Bake at 375° for 20-25 minutes or until a toothpick comes out clean. Cool for 5 minutes before removing from pans to wire racks. **Yield:** 14 muffins. —*Karen Davis Springfield, Missouri*

1 Using 1/2 teaspoon shortening for each cup, grease the bottom and sides of six 6-oz. custard cups or the cups of a popover pan. If using custard cups, place in a 15-in. x 10-in. x 1-in. baking pan.

2 In a small mixing bowl, beat eggs; blend in milk and butter. Beat in flour and salt until smooth (do not overbeat). Fill the cups half full. Bake at 450° for 15 minutes. Reduce heat to 350°; bake 30 minutes longer or until very firm. Remove from the oven and prick each popover to allow steam to escape. Serve immediately. **Yield:** 6 popovers.

—*Lourdes Dewick*
Fort Lauderdale, Florida

Popovers

Popovers

Popovers have a brown crisp exterior with an almost hollow interior. As they bake, the heat causes the liquid in the batter to turn to steam, making the batter pop up. After baking, prick the tops to let the steam escape.

  1 **tablespoon shortening**
  2 **eggs**
  1 **cup milk**
  1 **tablespoon butter, melted**
  1 **cup all-purpose flour**
1/2 **teaspoon salt**

secrets for successful popovers

- Place oven rack in lowest position. Generously grease the muffin pan cups, custard cups or popover pan cups.

- Mix batter until smooth. Batter may be refrigerated for up to 1 day. Pour into cups. Bake according to recipe directions. Don't open the oven door during baking or popovers will fall.

- After removing popovers from the oven, prick with the point of a sharp knife to allow steam to escape. Popovers are best served warm, fresh from the oven.

Soft Breadsticks

You just can't beat the homemade goodness of soft and chewy breadsticks. For variety, skip the sesame seeds and sprinkle with a little garlic salt and Parmesan cheese.

Soft Breadsticks

1-1/4 **cups all-purpose flour**
   2 **teaspoons sugar**
1-1/2 **teaspoons baking powder**
   1/2 **teaspoon salt**
   2/3 **cup milk**
   3 **tablespoons butter, melted**
   2 **teaspoons sesame seeds**

Mozzarella
Puffs

1 In a small bowl, combine the flour, sugar, baking powder and salt. Gradually add milk and stir to form a soft dough. Turn onto a floured surface; knead gently 3-4 times. Roll into a 10-in. x 5-in. x 1/2-in. rectangle; cut into 12 breadsticks.

2 Place butter in a 13-in. x 9-in. x 2-in. baking pan. Place breadsticks in the butter and turn to coat. Sprinkle with sesame seeds. Bake at 450° for 14-18 minutes or until golden brown. Serve warm. **Yield:** 1 dozen.
—*Nancy Johnson, Connersville, Indiana*

Biscuits & Scones

Mozzarella Puffs

Since these cheesy puffs are so quick to make, you can whip up a batch whenever your family asks for them. Serve them alone as a snack or with a meal.

1 **tube (7-1/2 ounces) refrigerated buttermilk biscuits**
1 **teaspoon dried oregano**
1 **block (2 to 3 ounces) mozzarella cheese**
2 **tablespoons pizza sauce**

1 Make an indentation in the center of each biscuit; sprinkle with oregano. Cut the mozzarella into 10 cubes, 3/4 in. each. Place a cube in the center of each biscuit; pinch dough tightly around cheese to seal. Place seam side down on an ungreased baking sheet.

2 Spread pizza sauce over biscuits. Bake at 375° for 10-12 minutes or until golden brown. Serve warm. Refrigerate leftovers. **Yield:** 10 servings.
—*Joan Mousley Dziuba, Waupaca, Wisconsin*

Buttermilk Biscuits

(Pictured on page 257)

You can't go wrong with a basic biscuit like this. Your family will gobble them up when served warm with butter.

2 **cups all-purpose flour**
1 **tablespoon sugar**
1 **teaspoon baking powder**
1/2 **teaspoon salt**
1/2 **teaspoon baking soda**
1/4 **cup shortening**
3/4 **cup buttermilk**

1 In a large bowl, combine the flour, sugar, baking powder, salt and baking soda. Cut in shortening until mixture is crumbly. Add buttermilk; stir just until the dough clings together.

2 Turn dough onto a lightly floured surface; knead gently 10-12 times. Roll out to 1/2-in. thickness. Cut with a floured 2-1/2-in. biscuit cutter. Place 1 in. apart on a greased baking sheet. Bake at 450° for 11-12 minutes or until lightly browned. Serve warm. **Yield:** 1 dozen.
—*Jean Parsons, Sarver, Pennsylvania*

secrets for successful biscuits & scones

- Use cold butter, cold stick margarine (with at least 80% oil) or shortening. Cut in butter or shortening only until mixture resembles coarse crumbs.

- Stir dry ingredients together with a fork to evenly distribute the baking powder or soda.

- For a more tender biscuit or scone, be careful not to overmix or overknead the dough.

- When reworking biscuit trimmings, handle the dough as little as possible and use as little additional flour as needed. Overworking the dough or using too much flour will result in a tough, dry product.

- Dip the biscuit cutter in flour after each cut to prevent sticking.

- Scones are generally patted into a circle and cut into wedges. If the wedges are separated, the scones will have a crisper crust. If the wedges are cut and not separated, the scones will have a softer crust.

- Biscuits and scones are done when they're golden brown on the top and bottom. The sides will always be a little light. Remove to wire racks. Biscuits are best served warm, fresh from the oven. Scones are best on the day they are made.

Baking Powder Biscuits

Baking Powder Biscuits

These flaky biscuits have great flavor and bake to a beautiful golden brown. You'll turn to this foolproof recipe again and again.

   2 cups all-purpose flour
   2 tablespoons sugar
   3 teaspoons baking powder
1/2 teaspoon salt
1/2 cup shortening
   1 egg
2/3 cup milk

1 In a large bowl, combine the flour, sugar, baking powder and salt. Cut in shortening until mixture is crumbly. Beat egg and milk; stir into dry ingredients just until moistened.

2 Turn dough onto a lightly floured surface; roll out to 1/2-in. thickness. Cut with a floured 2-1/2-in. biscuit cutter. Place 1 in. apart on an ungreased baking sheet. Bake at 450° for 10-12 minutes or until golden brown. Serve warm. **Yield:** 10 biscuits.   *—Catherine Yoder Bertha, Minnesota*

Garlic Potato Biscuits

The beauty of biscuits is you can enjoy the aroma of oven-fresh bread with less work than yeast breads.

   1 large potato (1/2 pound), peeled and diced
   3 to 4 garlic cloves, peeled
1/3 cup butter, softened
   1 teaspoon salt
1/4 teaspoon pepper
   2 cups all-purpose flour
   3 teaspoons baking powder
1/3 cup milk

1 Place potato and garlic in a saucepan; cover with water. Bring to a boil. Reduce heat; cover and simmer until potato is tender. Drain. Add butter, salt and pepper to potato and garlic; mash. In a large bowl, combine flour and baking powder; stir in potato mixture until mixture is crumbly. Add milk and stir well.

2 Turn dough onto a lightly floured surface. Roll out to 1/2-in. thickness. Cut with a floured 2-1/2-in. biscuit cutter. Place 1 in. apart on an ungreased baking sheet. Bake at 450° for 10-12 minutes or until golden brown. Serve warm. **Yield:** 12-15 biscuits.   *—Diane Hixon Niceville, Florida*

Making and Shaping Biscuits

1. Combine all dry ingredients with a fork. With a pastry blender or two knives, cut shortening into flour until mixture resembles coarse crumbs.

2. Make a well in the center of the crumb mixture. Pour in the liquid all at once and mix with a fork just until dry ingredients are moistened and the mixture begins to cling together.

3. Turn onto a lightly floured surface and knead gently for as many times as recipe directs.

4. Roll dough evenly to 1/2-in. to 3/4-in. thickness. Cut with a floured biscuit cutter, using a straight downward motion; do not twist cutter.

5. Place biscuits on a baking sheet. Place 1 to 1-1/2 in. apart for biscuits with crusty sides or almost touching for softer-sided biscuits.

6. Gently gather trimmings into a ball. Do not knead. Roll and cut out as in Step 4.

Caraway Wheat Biscuits

Whole wheat flour and caraway make these hearty biscuits terrific for wintertime meals.

- 2-1/2 **cups whole wheat flour**
- 2 **tablespoons caraway seeds**
- 1 **tablespoon baking powder**
- 1/8 **teaspoon salt**
- 1-1/3 **cups grated onions (about 3 medium)**
- 2 **eggs, beaten**
- 1/2 **cup vegetable oil**

1 In a large bowl, combine the flour, caraway seeds, baking powder and salt. In a small bowl, combine the onions, eggs and oil; stir into dry ingredients just until moistened.

2 Turn dough onto a floured surface. Roll out to 3/4-in. thickness. Cut with a floured 2-1/2-in. biscuit cutter. Place 1 in. apart on a greased baking sheet. Bake at 425° for 10-15 minutes or until golden brown. Serve warm. **Yield:** about 1 dozen.
—*Nancy Messmore*
Silver Lake Village, Ohio

Garlic
Cheese
Biscuits

Garlic Cheese Biscuits

Shredded cheddar cheese adds nice color to these biscuits, while a tasty butter mixture brushed on top provides a burst of garlic flavor.

      2 cups all-purpose flour
      3 teaspoons garlic powder, *divided*
2-1/2 teaspoons baking powder
   1/2 teaspoon baking soda
   1/2 teaspoon chicken bouillon granules
   1/2 cup butter-flavored shortening
   3/4 cup shredded cheddar cheese
      1 cup buttermilk
      3 tablespoons butter, melted

1 In a small bowl, combine the flour, 2 teaspoons garlic powder, baking powder, baking soda and bouillon; cut in shortening until mixture is crumbly. Add cheese. Stir in buttermilk just until moistened.

2 Drop by heaping tablespoonfuls 1 in. apart onto a greased baking sheet. Bake at 450° for 10 minutes. Combine the butter and remaining garlic powder; brush over biscuits. Bake 4 minutes longer or until golden brown. Serve warm. **Yield:** about 1-1/2 dozen.
                    —*Gayle Becker, Mt. Clemens, Michigan*

Nutty Cream Cheese Biscuits

Folks are surprised to hear this recipe starts with refrigerated biscuits.

   2 tubes (10 ounces *each*) refrigerated biscuits
   2 packages (3 ounces *each*) cream cheese
1/2 cup sugar
   1 teaspoon ground cinnamon
1/4 teaspoon *each* ground cloves, nutmeg and allspice
   6 tablespoons butter, melted, *divided*
   1 cup chopped pecans

1 Roll each biscuit into a 3-1/2-in. to 4-in. circle. Cut cream cheese into 20 equal cubes; place one cube in the center of each biscuit. Combine the sugar, cinnamon, cloves, nutmeg and allspice; sprinkle 1/2 teaspoon over each biscuit. Set remaining sugar mixture aside. Moisten edges of dough with water; fold over cheese and press edges with a fork to seal.

2 Pour 2 tablespoons butter into each of two 9-in. round baking pans; sprinkle 1 tablespoon of reserved sugar mixture into each pan. Dip one side of each biscuit in remaining butter. Arrange in pans, forming a pinwheel pattern, with butter side up. Sprinkle pecans and remaining sugar mixture on top. Bake at 375° for 20-25 minutes or until golden brown. Serve warm. Refrigerate leftovers. **Yield:** about 1-1/2 dozen.
                    —*Claudia Beene, Bossier, Louisiana*

Shaping Drop Biscuits

Drop dough from a tablespoon or 1/4 cup measure onto a greased baking sheet. Use a rubber spatula, knife or another spoon to push the dough off of the spoon.

Lemon-Berry Biscuits

Lemon and blueberries pair well in a variety of breads and these biscuits are no exception.

  2 cups all-purpose flour
1/3 cup sugar
  2 teaspoons baking powder
1/2 teaspoon baking soda
1/4 teaspoon salt
  1 cup (8 ounces) lemon yogurt
  1 egg, lightly beaten
1/4 cup butter, melted
  1 teaspoon grated lemon peel
  1 cup fresh *or* frozen blueberries*

GLAZE:
1/2 cup confectioners' sugar
  1 tablespoon lemon juice
1/2 teaspoon grated lemon peel

1 In a large bowl, combine the flour, sugar, baking powder, baking soda and salt. In a small bowl, combine the yogurt, egg, butter and lemon peel. Stir into dry ingredients just until moistened. Fold in blueberries.

2 Drop by tablespoonfuls 1 in. apart onto a greased baking sheet. Bake at 400° for 15-18 minutes or until lightly browned. Combine glaze ingredients; drizzle over warm biscuits. **Yield:** 1 dozen.
— *Kristin Dallum, Vancouver, Washington*

*****Editor's Note:** If using frozen blueberries, do not thaw before adding to batter.

Flaky Dill Biscuits

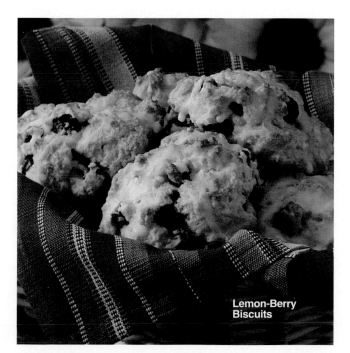

Lemon-Berry Biscuits

Flaky Dill Biscuits

Unlike traditional rolled-out biscuits, this version lets you drop the dough from a spoon. So there's no mess and no fuss.

  2 cups all-purpose flour
  3 teaspoons baking powder
  2 to 3 teaspoons dill weed
3/4 teaspoon salt
1/4 teaspoon pepper
1/2 cup cold butter
  2 eggs, lightly beaten
1/2 cup plus 1 tablespoon half-and-half cream, *divided*

1 In a large bowl, combine the flour, baking powder, dill, salt and pepper. Cut in butter until mixture is crumbly. With a fork, stir in eggs and 1/2 cup cream just until moistened.

2 Drop by 1/4 cupfuls 2 in. apart onto an ungreased baking sheet. Brush tops with remaining cream. Bake at 450° for 10-12 minutes or until golden brown. Serve warm. **Yield:** 9 servings. — *Audrey Lockau, Kitchener, Ontario*

Onion Dill Biscuits

A quick coating in a mixture of melted butter, chopped onion and dill weed dresses up refrigerated biscuits in a hurry. Keep the ingredients on hand for biscuits in a snap.

- 1/4 **cup butter, melted**
- 1 **tablespoon finely chopped onion**
- 1 **teaspoon dill weed**
- 1 **tube (10 ounces) refrigerated buttermilk biscuits**

In a bowl, combine the butter, onion and dill. Cut biscuits in half lengthwise; toss in the butter mixture. Arrange in a single layer in an ungreased 9-in. square baking pan. Bake at 450° for 8-10 minutes or until lightly browned. Serve warm. **Yield:** 6 servings.

—*Marcille Meyer, Battle Creek, Nebraska*

Cornmeal Cheddar Biscuits

These cheesy cornmeal biscuits are a wonderful addition to a chili dinner.

- 1-1/2 **cups all-purpose flour**
- 1/2 **cup cornmeal**
- 3 **teaspoons baking powder**
- 2 **teaspoons sugar**
- 1/4 **to 1/2 teaspoon salt**
- 1/2 **cup cold butter**
- 1/2 **cup shredded cheddar cheese**
- 1 **cup milk**

1 In a large bowl, combine the flour, cornmeal, baking powder, sugar and salt. Cut in butter until mixture is crumbly. Stir in cheese and milk just until moistened.

2 Drop by 1/4 cupfuls 2 in. apart onto an ungreased baking sheet. Bake at 450° for 12-15 minutes or until golden brown. Serve warm. **Yield:** 1 dozen.

Rosemary Buttermilk Biscuits

The delicate herb flavor of these biscuits is special alongside any entree. Use fresh rosemary for the best flavor.

- 2-1/4 **cups all-purpose flour**
- 2 **tablespoons sugar**
- 2 **teaspoons minced fresh rosemary** *or* 3/4 **teaspoon dried rosemary, crushed**
- 1-1/2 **teaspoons baking powder**
- 3/4 **teaspoon salt**
- 1/2 **teaspoon baking soda**
- 1/2 **cup plus 1 tablespoon shortening**
- 3/4 **cup buttermilk**
- 1/4 **cup butter, melted**

1 In a large bowl, combine the flour, sugar, rosemary, baking powder, salt and baking soda. Cut in shortening until mixture is crumbly. Stir in buttermilk just until moistened (dough will be dry).

2 Turn dough onto a lightly floured surface. Roll out to 1/2-in. thickness. Cut with a floured 2-1/2-in. biscuit cutter. Place 1 in. apart on a greased baking sheet. Brush with butter. Bake at 400° for 10-12 minutes or until golden brown. Serve warm. **Yield:** about 1 dozen.

—*Debbie Smith, Crossett, Arkansas*

Cornmeal Cheddar Biscuits

Country Scones

These tempting triangles perfectly balance a light and airy texture with a rich and moist flavor.

3/4 **cup dried currants** *or* **raisins**
2 **cups all-purpose flour**
3 **tablespoons sugar**
2 **teaspoons baking powder**
3/4 **teaspoon salt**
1/2 **teaspoon baking soda**
5 **tablespoons cold butter**
1 **cup (8 ounces) sour cream**
2 **egg yolks**
TOPPING:
1 **egg white**
1 **teaspoon sugar**
1/8 **teaspoon ground cinnamon**

1 Place currants in a bowl; cover with hot water and let stand for 5 minutes. Drain well and set aside. In a bowl, combine the flour, sugar, baking powder, salt and baking soda. Cut in butter until mixture is crumbly. In a small bowl, combine sour cream and egg yolks; add to crumb mixture. Stir in currants just until blended.

2 Turn dough onto a floured surface; knead gently 8-10 times. Pat into a 9-in. circle. Cut into 4-in. circles; place on ungreased baking sheets. Cut each circle into four wedges but do not separate.

3 Beat egg white; brush over dough. Combine sugar and cinnamon; sprinkle over tops. Bake at 425° for 15-18 minutes or until golden brown. Remove from pans to wire racks. Serve warm. **Yield:** about 1-1/2 dozen.

—*Martha Plassmeyer, St. Elizabeth, Missouri*

the history of scones

It's believed this Scottish quick bread originated between 1505 and 1515. Scones are named after the Stone of Destiny (or Scone), the place where Scottish kings were once crowned.

Oat Scones

Unlike other scones, this recipe instructs you to use a round biscuit cutter.

2 **cups all-purpose flour**
1/2 **cup packed brown sugar**
2 **teaspoons baking powder**
1 **teaspoon baking soda**
1 **teaspoon salt**
1/2 **cup shortening**
1-1/4 **cups quick-cooking oats**
3/4 **cup milk**

1 In a large bowl, combine the flour, brown sugar, baking powder, baking soda and salt. Cut in shortening until mixture is crumbly. Stir in oats and milk just until moistened.

2 Turn dough onto a lightly floured surface. Roll out to 3/4-in. thickness. Cut with a floured 2-1/2-in. biscuit cutter. Place 1 in. apart on an ungreased baking sheet. Bake at 375° for 15-20 minutes or until lightly browned. Serve warm. **Yield:** about 15 scones.

—*Barbara Chornoboy, Thunder Bay, Ontario*

Shaping Scones

Divide dough if directed by recipe. Shape dough into a circle about 1/2 in. thick. Cut into wedges with a sharp knife.

Apricot Scones

Cranberry Orange Scones

(Pictured on page 256)

Serve these cranberry-dotted goodies with the delicate orange butter.

- 2 cups all-purpose flour
- 10 teaspoons sugar, *divided*
- 1 tablespoon grated orange peel
- 2 teaspoons baking powder
- 1/2 teaspoon salt
- 1/4 teaspoon baking soda
- 1/3 cup cold butter
- 1 cup dried cranberries
- 1/4 cup orange juice
- 1/4 cup half-and-half cream
- 1 egg
- 1 tablespoon milk

GLAZE (optional):
- 1/2 cup confectioners' sugar
- 1 tablespoon orange juice

ORANGE BUTTER:
- 1/2 cup butter, softened
- 2 to 3 tablespoons orange marmalade

1 In a small bowl, combine flour, 7 teaspoons sugar, orange peel, baking powder, salt and baking soda. Cut in butter until mixture is crumbly. In a small bowl, combine cranberries, orange juice, cream and egg. Stir into crumb mixture until a soft dough forms.

2 Turn dough onto a floured surface; knead gently 6-8 times. Pat into an 8-in. circle. Cut into 10 wedges. Separate wedges and place 1 in. apart on an ungreased baking sheet. Brush with milk; sprinkle with remaining sugar. Bake at 400° for 12-15 minutes or until lightly browned. Remove to a wire rack.

3 Combine glaze ingredients if desired; drizzle over scones. Combine orange butter ingredients; serve with warm scones. **Yield:** 10 scones. *—Karen McBride Indianapolis, Indiana*

Apricot Scones

Traditional Devonshire cream (also called clotted cream) is made by slowly heating cream until it clots. The mock version in this recipe uses cream cheese and whipping cream.

DEVONSHIRE CREAM:
- 1 package (3 ounces) cream cheese, softened
- 1 tablespoon confectioners' sugar
- 1/2 teaspoon vanilla extract
- 1/4 to 1/3 cup heavy whipping cream

SCONES:
- 2 cups all-purpose flour
- 1/4 cup sugar
- 3 teaspoons baking powder
- 1/4 teaspoon salt
- 1/3 cup cold butter
- 1/2 cup chopped dried apricots
- 1/2 cup chopped pecans
- 1 teaspoon grated orange peel
- 1 cup plus 2 tablespoons heavy whipping cream, *divided*

Jam of your choice

1 For Devonshire cream, beat cream cheese, confectioners' sugar and vanilla in a mixing bowl until fluffy. Gradually beat in enough cream to achieve a spreading consistency. Cover and refrigerate for at least 2 hours.

2 For scones, combine the flour, sugar, baking powder and salt in a bowl. Cut in butter until mixture resembles fine crumbs. Add the apricots, pecans and orange peel. With a fork, rapidly stir in 1 cup cream just until moistened.

3 Turn dough onto a floured surface; knead gently 5-6 times. Divide in half; shape each portion into a ball. Flatten each ball into a 6-in. circle; cut each circle into eight wedges. Separate wedges and place 1 in. apart on an ungreased baking sheet. Brush with remaining cream.

4 Bake at 375° for 13-15 minutes or until a toothpick comes out clean. Remove from pan to a wire rack. Serve warm with Devonshire cream and jam. **Yield:** 16 scones (1 cup cream).
—*Robin Fuhrman*
Fond du Lac, Wisconsin

Apple 'n' Honey Scones

Round out a flavorful fall meal with these fruity scones. Wheat germ adds a little extra nutrition.

      2 cups all-purpose flour
    2/3 cup wheat germ
      2 teaspoons baking powder
      1 teaspoon ground cinnamon
    1/4 teaspoon baking soda
    1/4 teaspoon salt
    1/4 teaspoon ground nutmeg
    1/3 cup cold butter
      1 large tart apple, peeled and chopped
    1/2 cup milk
    1/4 cup honey
TOPPING:
      2 teaspoons wheat germ
      2 teaspoons sugar
    1/4 teaspoon ground cinnamon

1 In a large bowl, combine the flour, wheat germ, baking powder, cinnamon, baking soda, salt and nutmeg. Cut in butter until mixture is crumbly. Combine the apple, milk and honey; stir into crumb mixture just until moistened.

2 Turn dough onto a floured surface; knead gently 5-6 times. Gently pat into a 9-in. circle, about 1/2 in. thick. Combine topping ingredients; sprinkle over dough. Cut into eight wedges. Separate wedges and place 1 in. apart on a greased baking sheet. Bake at 400° for 15-18 minutes or until lightly browned. Remove from pan to a wire rack. Serve warm. **Yield:** 8 scones.
—*Bernadette Colvin, Houston, Texas*

Double Orange Scones

Orange butter adds the perfect finishing touch to each hearty bite.

      1 cup all-purpose flour
      1 cup whole wheat flour
      3 tablespoons sugar
  2-1/2 teaspoons baking powder
      2 teaspoons grated orange peel
    1/4 teaspoon salt
    1/3 cup cold butter
    1/3 cup milk
      1 egg
    1/2 cup chopped mandarin oranges, well drained
Additional sugar
ORANGE BUTTER:
    1/2 cup butter, softened
      2 tablespoons orange marmalade

1 In a small bowl, combine the flours, sugar, baking powder, orange peel and salt. Cut in butter until mixture is crumbly. Combine the milk and egg; add to crumb mixture. Stir in oranges just until moistened.

2 Turn onto a floured surface; knead gently 10 times. Pat into a 6-in. circle; sprinkle with additional sugar. Cut into eight wedges; separate wedges and place 1 in. apart on a greased baking sheet. Bake at 400° for 15-20 minutes or until golden brown. Remove from pan to a wire rack.

3 For orange butter, beat butter and marmalade in a small mixing bowl until fluffy. Serve with warm scones. **Yield:** 8 scones.
—*Margaret Frayser*
Linton, Indiana

Double Orange Scones

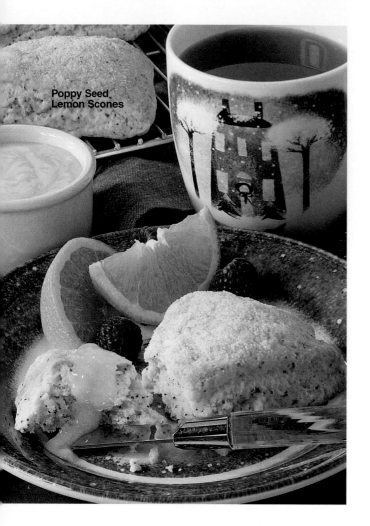

Poppy Seed
Lemon Scones

1/3 **cup cold butter**
3/4 **cup milk**
2 **tablespoons lemon juice**
Additional sugar

1 In a heavy saucepan or top of a double boiler, beat eggs and sugar. Stir in the butter, lemon juice and peel. Cook and stir over low heat or simmering water for 15 minutes or until mixture reaches 160° and is thickened. Cover and refrigerate until chilled (may be stored in the refrigerator for up to 1 week).

2 For scones, combine the flour, sugar, poppy seeds, baking powder, baking soda and salt in a bowl. Cut in butter until the mixture resembles fine crumbs. Combine milk and lemon juice; stir into crumb mixture just until blended (dough will be soft).

3 Turn dough onto a floured surface; knead gently 6 times. Shape into a ball. Pat dough into an 8-in. circle; cut into eight wedges. Separate wedges and place 1 in. apart on a greased baking sheet. Sprinkle with additional sugar. Bake at 425° for 12-15 minutes or until lightly browned. Remove from pan to a wire rack. Serve warm with lemon curd. **Yield**: 8 scones (1-1/2 cups lemon curd).

—Linda Murray
Allenstown, New Hampshire

Poppy Seed Lemon Scones

You'll love the appealing look and delicate texture of these lightly sweet scones. They're wonderful served warm with homemade lemon curd for breakfast or with a salad for lunch.

LEMON CURD:
2 **eggs**
1 **cup sugar**
6 **tablespoons butter, melted**
1/4 **cup lemon juice**
2 **tablespoons grated lemon peel**
SCONES:
2 **cups all-purpose flour**
1/4 **cup sugar**
1 **tablespoon poppy seeds**
2 **teaspoons baking powder**
1/2 **teaspoon baking soda**
1/4 **teaspoon salt**

Buttermilk Scones

Dried currants are tiny seedless raisins from sun-dried black Corinth grapes. They're similar in appearance to raisins but smaller.

1 **cup all-purpose flour**
2 **tablespoons plus 1/2 teaspoon sugar,** *divided*
1 **teaspoon baking powder**
1/8 **teaspoon baking soda**
1/4 **cup cold butter**
1/3 **cup buttermilk**
3 **tablespoons dried currants** *or* **raisins**
1/4 **teaspoon grated lemon** *or* **orange peel**
1/8 **teaspoon ground cinnamon**

1 In a small bowl, combine the flour, 2 tablespoons sugar, baking powder and baking soda. Cut in butter until mixture is crumbly. Stir in the buttermilk, currants or raisins and lemon peel until a soft dough forms.

2 Turn dough onto a lightly floured surface; knead gently 5-6 times or until no longer sticky. On a lightly greased baking sheet, pat dough into a 5-in. circle, about 3/4 in. thick. Score the top, making six wedges.

3 Combine cinnamon and remaining sugar; sprinkle over dough. Bake at 375° for 23-25 minutes or until golden brown. Remove from pan to a wire rack. Break into wedges. Serve warm. **Yield:** 6 scones.

—Ruth LeBlanc, Nashua, New Hampshire

Heart-Shaped Cheese Scones

When you set out a plate of these golden scones flecked with bits of cheddar cheese, everyone will know you've put your heart into your baking. If you don't have a heart-shaped cutter, use a round one instead.

    2 cups all-purpose flour
    2 tablespoons sugar
    3 teaspoons baking powder
    1 teaspoon salt
  1/4 teaspoon baking soda
1-1/2 cups (6 ounces) shredded cheddar cheese
    1 egg
  1/2 cup sour cream
  1/4 cup vegetable oil
    3 tablespoons milk

1 In a large bowl, combine the flour, sugar, baking powder, salt and baking soda. Stir in cheese. In a small bowl, combine the egg, sour cream, oil and milk. Make a well in the center of dry ingredients; stir in egg mixture just until moistened.

Heart-Shaped Cheese Scones

2 Turn dough onto a floured surface; knead gently 10-12 times. Pat out to 1/3-in. thickness. Cut with a floured 3-in. heart-shaped cutter. Place 2 in. apart on a greased baking sheet. Bake at 425° for 15-20 minutes or until golden brown. Remove from pan to a wire rack. Serve warm. **Yield:** about 1 dozen. *—Edna Hoffman Hebron, Indiana*

Gingerbread Scones

Moist Gingerbread Scones are a delight to share at Christmastime.

    2 cups all-purpose flour
    3 tablespoons brown sugar
    2 teaspoons baking powder
    1 teaspoon ground ginger
  1/2 teaspoon baking soda
  1/2 teaspoon salt
  1/2 teaspoon ground cinnamon
  1/4 cup cold butter
  1/3 cup molasses
  1/4 cup milk
    1 egg, *separated*
    Sugar

1 In a large bowl, combine the flour, brown sugar, baking powder, ginger, baking soda, salt and cinnamon. Cut in butter until mixture is crumbly. In a small bowl, combine the molasses, milk and egg yolk until smooth; stir into the crumb mixture just until moistened.

2 Turn dough onto a floured surface; knead gently 6-8 times. Pat into an 8-in. circle; cut into 12 wedges. Separate wedges and place 1 in. apart on a greased baking sheet. Beat egg white until frothy; brush over scones. Sprinkle with sugar. Bake at 400° for 12-15 minutes or until golden brown. Remove from pan to a wire rack. Serve warm. **Yield:** 1 dozen.

—Reverend David Bostedt Zephyrhills, Florida

savory
Yeast Breads
rise to any
occasion

Herbed Oatmeal Pan Bread
(p. 287), Rosemary Orange
Bread (p. 295) and Icebox Butterhorns (p. 305) are
just a taste of this chapter's homemade goodies that
round out casual as well as special-occasion meals.
From lovely loaves and mouth-watering rolls to
sourdough delights and bread machine favorites, this
chapter offers a variety of savory breads.

the basics of Yeast Breads

*Y*east breads, rolls, pretzels, biscuits and more can be made completely from scratch, can start with convenience products such as frozen bread dough or hot roll mix and can be made in a bread machine for even more convenience.

They can be savory (like the recipes in this chapter) or sweet (like the recipes featured in the Sweet Yeast Breads chapter beginning on page 328).

All yeast breads are divided into the two following basic categories: kneaded yeast breads and batter yeast breads.

- Kneaded yeast breads are usually mixed, kneaded, allowed to rise, shaped, allowed to rise again, then baked. The rise times may be shortened or one may be eliminated if quick-rise yeast is used. Bread machine breads are also kneaded breads.

- Batter breads aren't kneaded. Rather, ingredients are beaten, allowed to rise once or twice, then baked. Batter breads have a coarser texture and rugged crust.

The ingredients you use in bread making will affect the texture, density and crust. Lean breads (like French bread) are made with yeast, flour, water, salt and a minimal amount of sugar to produce a dense, chewy bread with a crisp crust.

Rich or short breads (like Brioche) are made with fat such as butter or shortening, eggs and/or milk to produce a tender bread with a soft crust. For more information on ingredients and how they affect bread, see the Common Baking Ingredients on pages 13 through 18.

secrets for successful yeast breads

- Use butter, stick margarine (with at least 80% oil) or shortening. Do not use light or whipped butter, diet spread or tub margarine.

- Measure ingredients accurately, using the measuring tools and techniques suggested on pages 8 and 9.

- Arrange the oven racks so that the bread will bake in the center of the oven.

- Preheat oven for 10 to 15 minutes before baking.

- When mixing dough, always start with a minimum amount of flour until dough reaches desired consistency (soft, sticky, stiff or firm).

- Knead dough only until it does not tear easily when stretched.

- Let dough rise in a warm (80° to 85°) draft-free area. Proper rising helps in the development of the bread texture.

- Use aluminum pans with a dull rather than shiny or dark finish. Glass baking dishes and dark finishes will produce darker crusts.

- To allow for good air circulation while baking, leave at least 1 in. of space between pans and between pans and sides of oven.

- Use a kitchen timer and test for doneness at the minimum recommended baking time. Bread is done when it is golden brown and sounds hollow when tapped on the bottom. Or, insert an instant-read thermometer in the thickest part of the loaf. The bread is done when the thermometer reads 200°.

- Remove breads from pans and cool on wire racks. Let breads cool for at least 20 minutes before slicing. Use a serrated knife and a sawing motion when cutting.

problem-
Solving pointers for Yeast Breads

If this happens to your yeast bread:	This could be the reason:
Bread did not rise well or did not rise at all.	Yeast was not fresh. Next time, proof the yeast (see page 288).
	Liquid was too hot and killed the yeast.
	Dough was kneaded too much or not enough.
	Oven temperature was too low.
Bread is heavy and coarse.	There's too much liquid or not enough flour in dough.
	Next time, use a lower-gluten flour such as whole wheat, rye or oat.
	Dough was allowed to rise too long.
	Oven temperature was too low.
Bread is dry and crumbly.	Too much flour was used.
	Dough was allowed to rise too long.
Bread is doughy on the bottom or has a slightly gummy texture.	Bread was underbaked.
	Bread stayed in the pan too long after baking.
Loaf sinks in the center.	Dough rose too long during the second rise time in the pan.
Bread has large holes.	Dough was not kneaded enough.
	Air was not compressed out of the dough during shaping.
Bread crumbles when cut.	Too much flour was used.
	Dough was kneaded too much or not enough.
	Dough was allowed to rise too long or not long enough.
	Oven temperature was too high.
Bread has a yeasty taste.	Dough had too much yeast or rose too long.

Traditional Mixing Method for Yeast Bread

1. In a saucepan or microwave, heat liquid to 110° to 115°. Use a thermometer to check the temperature. Measure liquid and place in a large mixing bowl. Add active dry yeast; stir until dissolved.

2. Add sugar, salt, fat, eggs (if using) and about half of the flour. Beat with an electric mixer or by hand until smooth.

3. Gradually stir in enough of the remaining flour by hand to form a dough of the consistency stated in the recipe. The amount of flour depends on the humidity in the air.

Savory loaves

Home-Style Yeast Bread

Everyone will like the tender texture and slightly sweet taste of this homemade bread. The dough also makes heavenly rolls.

3 packages (1/4 ounce *each*) active dry yeast
2 cups warm water (110° to 115°)
1 cup sugar
1/2 cup butter, melted
1-1/2 teaspoons salt
2 eggs, beaten
7-3/4 to 8-1/4 cups bread flour

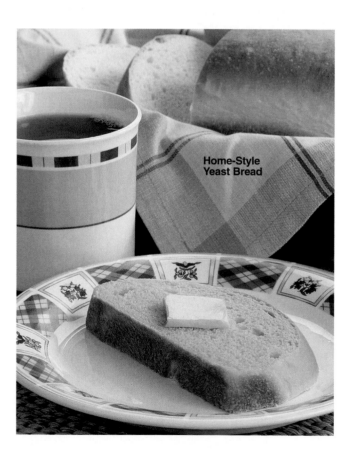

Home-Style Yeast Bread

1 In a large mixing bowl, dissolve yeast in warm water. Add the sugar, butter, salt, eggs and 4 cups flour; beat until smooth. Stir in enough remaining flour to form a soft dough.

2 Turn onto a floured surface; knead until smooth and elastic, about 6-8 minutes. Place in a greased bowl, turning once to grease top. Cover and let rise in a warm place until doubled, about 45 minutes.

3 Punch dough down. Turn onto a heavily floured surface; divide into thirds. Shape each portion into a loaf. Place in three greased 9-in. x 5-in. x 3-in. loaf pans. Cover and let rise until doubled, about 45 minutes.

4 Bake at 350° for 25-30 minutes or until golden brown. Remove from pans to wire racks to cool.
Yield: 3 loaves.

—*Launa Shoemaker*
Midland City, Alabama

English Muffin Bread

Slices of this traditional batter bread are terrific when toasted and slathered with butter.

- **6 cups all-purpose flour**
- **2 packages (1/4 ounce *each*) active dry yeast**
- **1 tablespoon sugar**
- **2 teaspoons salt**
- **1/4 teaspoon baking soda**
- **2 cups warm milk (120° to 130°)**
- **1/2 cup warm water (120° to 130°)**
- **Cornmeal**

1 In a large mixing bowl, combine 3 cups flour, yeast, sugar, salt and baking soda. Add milk and water; mix well. Stir in remaining flour (batter will be soft). Do not knead.

2 Sprinkle three greased 8-in. x 4-in. x 2-in. loaf pans with cornmeal. Spoon batter into prepared pans; sprinkle cornmeal on top. Cover and let rise in a warm place until doubled, about 45 minutes.

3 Bake at 400° for 20-25 minutes or until golden brown. Remove from pans to wire racks to cool. **Yield:** 3 loaves. —*Donna Meyer, Dayton, Ohio*

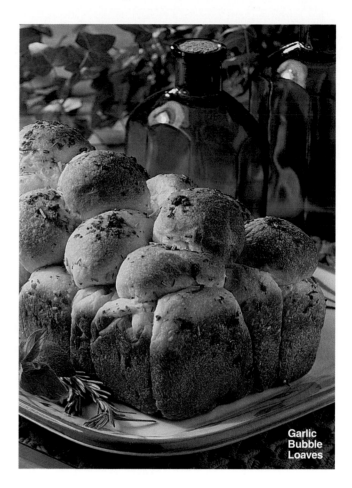

Garlic Bubble Loaves

Garlic Bubble Loaves

Complete your next spaghetti dinner with this eye-catching loaf. Family and friends will have fun pulling off each rich and buttery piece.

- **2 packages (1/4 ounce *each*) active dry yeast**
- **1/4 cup warm water (110° to 115°)**
- **2 cups warm milk (110° to 115°)**
- **2 tablespoons sugar**
- **1 tablespoon shortening**
- **2 teaspoons salt**
- **6-1/4 to 6-1/2 cups all-purpose flour**
- **1/2 cup butter, melted**
- **1 tablespoon dried parsley flakes**
- **2 teaspoons garlic powder**

1 In a large mixing bowl, dissolve yeast in warm water. Add the milk, sugar, shortening, salt and 2 cups flour; beat until smooth. Stir in enough remaining flour to form a soft dough. Turn onto a floured surface; knead until smooth and elastic, about 6-8 minutes. Place in a greased bowl, turning once to grease top. Cover and let rise in a warm place until doubled, about 1 hour.

2 Punch dough down. Turn onto a lightly floured surface; divide into fourths. Divide each portion into 12 pieces. In a shallow bowl, combine the butter, parsley and garlic powder. Shape each piece of dough into a ball; dip into butter mixture. Place in two greased 9-in. x 5-in. x 3-in. loaf pans. Pour any remaining butter mixture over dough. Cover and let rise until doubled, about 30 minutes.

3 Bake at 375° for 35-40 minutes or until golden brown. Cool for 10 minutes. Remove from pans to wire racks. Serve warm. **Yield:** 2 loaves. —*Lynn Nichols, Bartlett, Nebraska*

Bread
with a friend makes any meal a feast.

Kneading, Shaping and Baking Yeast Bread

1. Turn dough onto a lightly floured surface; shape into a ball. Fold top of dough toward you. With palms, push with a rolling motion away from you. Turn dough a quarter turn; repeat motion until dough is smooth and elastic. Add flour to surface only as needed.

2. Place the dough in a bowl greased with butter, oil or nonstick cooking spray. Turn dough over to grease the top. This prevents the dough from drying out while rising. Cover with a clean towel or plastic wrap.

3. Place covered dough in a warm draft-free area (80° to 85°) until dough has doubled.(Place covered bowl on the top rack in a cold oven with a pan of steaming hot water underneath. Or turn your oven to its lowest setting for no longer than 40 to 50 seconds. Turn off and let dough rise in the oven.)

4. Press two fingers 1/2 in. into the dough. If the dents remain, the dough is doubled in size and ready to punch down.

5. To punch dough down, make a fist and push it into the center. Gather the dough to the center and shape into a ball. Place on a floured surface.

6. Divide the dough if the recipe directs; shape into balls. Roll each ball into a 12-in. x 8-in. rectangle. You will hear air bubbles "popping" as you roll the dough.

7. Dust off any loose flour that might cling to the dough. Beginning at the short end, roll up each rectangle firmly. If it's too loose, you'll see air pockets when the bread is cut. If it's too tight, the bread will crack while baking.

8. Pinch seam and each end to seal. Place seam side down in a greased pan; cover with a towel and allow to double in size in a warm draft-free area.

9. When dough has doubled, remove towel; place pans several inches apart in the center of the preheated oven.

10. When bread is golden brown, test for doneness by carefully removing loaves from pans and tapping the bottom crusts. If it sounds hollow, the bread is done. If the bread is browning too fast and it's not done, tent with foil and continue baking. Unless recipe directs otherwise, immediately remove breads from pans. Cool completely on a wire rack.

Crusty French Bread

What we think of as French bread in America is actually called a baguette in France. It has a lighter texture than Italian bread and is shaped into a long narrow loaf.

  1 package (1/4 ounce) active dry yeast
1-1/2 cups warm water (110° to 115°), *divided*
  1 tablespoon sugar
  2 teaspoons salt
  1 tablespoon shortening, melted
  4 cups all-purpose flour
Cornmeal

1 In a large mixing bowl, dissolve yeast in 1/2 cup warm water. Add the sugar, salt, shortening and remaining water; stir until blended. Stir in flour until smooth. Do not knead. Cover and let rise in a warm place until doubled, about 1 hour.

2 Punch dough down. Turn onto a floured surface; divide in half. Cover and let rest for 10 minutes. Roll each portion into a 10-in. x 8-in. rectangle. Roll up jelly-roll style, starting with a long side; pinch seam to seal. Sprinkle greased baking sheets with cornmeal. Place loaves seam side down on prepared pans. Sprinkle tops with cornmeal. Cover and let rise until doubled, about 45 minutes.

3 With a sharp knife, make five diagonal cuts across the top of each loaf. Bake at 400° for 20-30 minutes or until lightly browned. Remove from pans to wire racks to cool. **Yield:** 2 loaves. —*Christy Freeman Central Point, Oregon*

Crusty French Bread

Herbed Oatmeal Pan Bread

(Pictured on page 280)

This beautiful golden pan bread is especially good with a steaming bowl of homemade soup. The oats in the dough and Parmesan topping give it a distinctive flavor.

1-1/2 cups boiling water
  1 cup old-fashioned oats
  2 packages (1/4 ounce *each*) active dry yeast
1/2 cup warm water (110° to 115°)
1/4 cup sugar
  3 tablespoons butter, softened
  2 teaspoons salt
  1 egg
  4 to 4-3/4 cups all-purpose flour
TOPPING:
1/4 cup butter, melted, *divided*
  2 tablespoons grated Parmesan cheese
  1 teaspoon dried basil
1/2 teaspoon dried oregano
1/2 teaspoon garlic powder

1 In a small bowl, combine boiling water and oats; cool to 110°-115°. In a large mixing bowl, dissolve yeast in warm water. Add the sugar, butter, salt, egg, oat mixture and 2 cups flour; beat until smooth. Stir in enough remaining flour to form a soft dough.

2 Turn onto a floured surface; knead until smooth and elastic, about 6-8 minutes. Place in a greased bowl, turning once to grease top. Cover and let rise in a warm place until doubled, about 45 minutes.

3 Punch dough down. Press evenly into a greased 13-in. x 9-in. x 2-in. baking pan. With a very sharp knife, cut diagonal lines 1-1/2 in. apart completely through dough. Repeat in opposite direction, creating a diamond pattern. Cover and let rise until doubled, about 1 hour.

4 Redefine pattern by gently poking along cut lines with knife tip. Brush with 2 tablespoons melted butter. Bake at 375° for 15 minutes. Meanwhile, combine Parmesan cheese, basil, oregano and garlic powder. Brush bread with remaining butter; sprinkle with cheese mixture. Bake for 5 minutes. Cover loosely with foil; bake 5 minutes longer. Serve warm. **Yield:** 8-10 servings. —*Karen Bourne, Magrath, Alberta*

Golden Sesame Braids

With a crisp crust and tender inside, these
loaves will be gobbled up in a hurry.
Slices also make great sandwiches.

   2 **packages (1/4 ounce** *each*) **active dry yeast**
1/2 **cup warm water (110° to 115°)**
1-1/2 **cups warm milk (110° to 115°)**
  1/4 **cup shortening**
  1/4 **cup sugar**
    1 **tablespoon salt**
    3 **eggs**
7-1/2 **to 8 cups all-purpose flour**
TOPPING:
    1 **egg**
    1 **tablespoon cold water**
    2 **tablespoons sesame seeds**

1 In a large mixing bowl, dissolve yeast in warm water. Add the milk, shortening, sugar, salt, eggs and 4 cups flour; beat until smooth. Stir in enough remaining flour to form a soft dough.

2 Turn onto a floured surface; knead until smooth and elastic, about 6-8 minutes. Place in a greased bowl, turning once to grease top. Cover and let rise in a warm place until doubled, about 1 hour.

3 Punch dough down. Turn onto a lightly floured surface; divide in half. Divide each portion into thirds. Shape each piece into a 12-in. rope. Place three ropes on a greased baking pan and braid; pinch ends to seal and tuck under. Repeat with remaining dough. Cover and let rise until doubled, about 45 minutes.

4 Beat egg and cold water; brush over braids. Sprinkle with sesame seeds. Bake at 350° for 30-35 minutes or until golden brown. Remove from pans to wire racks to cool. **Yield:** 2 loaves.　　—*Barbara Sunberg*
Camden, Ohio

Golden
Sesame Braids

proofing yeast

To make sure active dry yeast (not quick-rise yeast) is alive and active, you may first want to proof it. Here's how:

Dissolve one package of yeast and 1 teaspoon sugar in 1/4 cup warm water (110° to 115°). Let stand for 5 to 10 minutes. If the mixture foams up, the yeast mixture can be used because the yeast is active. If it does not foam, the yeast should be discarded.

Braiding Breads

1. Arrange three ropes of dough lengthwise on a greased baking sheet, so they are almost touching. Starting in the middle, loosely bring the left rope under the center rope. Bring the right rope under the new center rope and repeat until you reach the end.

2. Turn the pan and repeat braiding.

3. Press each end to seal and tuck ends under.

Herbed Whole Wheat Bread

A blend of dill, parsley and sage dresses up ordinary wheat bread. The flavor pairs well with a poultry dinner.

1 medium onion, chopped
3 tablespoons vegetable oil
2 packages (1/4 ounce *each*) active dry yeast
1/2 cup warm water (110° to 115°)
1 can (12 ounces) evaporated milk
1/2 cup minced fresh parsley
3 tablespoons sugar
1 teaspoon salt
1/2 teaspoon dill weed
1/4 teaspoon rubbed sage
3/4 cup cornmeal
2 cups whole wheat flour
1-3/4 to 2-1/4 cups all-purpose flour

1 In a skillet, saute onion in oil until tender; cool. In a large mixing bowl, dissolve yeast in warm water. Add the milk, parsley, sugar, salt, dill, sage and onion mixture; mix well. Add cornmeal; mix well. Stir in whole wheat flour and enough all-purpose flour to form a soft dough.

2 Turn onto a floured surface; knead until smooth and elastic, about 3-5 minutes. Place in a greased bowl, turning once to grease top. Cover and let rise in a warm place until doubled, about 1 hour.

3 Punch dough down. Turn onto a lightly floured surface; divide in half. Shape each portion into a loaf. Place in two greased 9-in. x 5-in. x 3-in. loaf pans. Cover and let rise until doubled, about 30-45 minutes.

4 Bake at 350° for 30 minutes. Cover loosely with foil. Bake 15-20 minutes longer or until golden brown. Remove from pans to wire racks to cool. **Yield:** 2 loaves.
—*Barbara Glover, Port St. Lucie, Florida*

Potato Bread

This bread's firm crust is reminiscent of old-fashioned breads. Using some of the potato cooking water provides even more flavor.

1 medium potato, peeled and diced
1-1/2 cups water
2 packages (1/4 ounce *each*) active dry yeast
1/2 cup warm water (110° to 115°)
1 cup warm milk (110° to 115°)
2 tablespoons butter, softened
2 tablespoons sugar
2 teaspoons salt
6-1/2 to 7-1/2 cups all-purpose flour
Additional all-purpose flour

1 Place potato and water in a saucepan; cook until very tender. Drain, reserving 1/2 cup liquid. Mash potatoes (without adding milk or butter); set aside.

2 In a large mixing bowl, dissolve yeast in warm water. Add the milk, butter, sugar, salt, 4 cups flour, potatoes and reserved cooking liquid; beat until smooth. Stir in enough remaining flour to form a stiff dough.

3 Turn onto a floured surface; knead until smooth and elastic, about 6-8 minutes. Place in a greased bowl, turning once to grease top. Cover and let rise in a warm place until doubled, about 1 hour.

4 Punch dough down. Turn onto a lightly floured surface; divide in half. Shape each portion into a loaf. Place in two greased 9-in. x 5-in. x 3-in. loaf pans. Cover and let rise until doubled, about 30 minutes.

5 Sprinkle loaves lightly with additional flour. Bake at 375° for 35-40 minutes or until golden brown. Remove from pans to wire racks to cool. **Yield:** 2 loaves.
—*Martha Clayton, Utopia, Texas*

Potato Bread

the basics of batter breads

- Batter bread is beaten with an electric mixer to help develop the gluten faster and give the bread a better texture. Because these breads are not kneaded, it is important to beat them until the batter comes away from the bowl and appears to be stringy.

- Stir in the remaining flour with a sturdy wooden spoon until you have a stiff batter. Since less flour is used for batter breads, it forms a batter rather than a dough and is stickier than a kneaded dough.

- If a recipe directs you to stir the batter after the first rising, stir it enough to bring it down to the original volume.

- Most batter breads are spooned or spread into a baking pan or dish. Push batter evenly to the edge of pan or into corners with a rubber spatula. Some batter breads can be shaped.

- Follow the directions given for rising in each recipe. Batter breads rise until doubled or almost doubled—they don't rise to the top of the pan. If left to rise too long, they may fall during baking.

- Batter breads are best served the day they are made.

Maple Oat Batter Bread

This moist, hearty bread has a terrific mix of grains and maple flavor. Batter breads are so appealing because they require no kneading.

1-1/4 cups warm milk (120° to 130°)
   1 cup quick-cooking oats
1/4 cup butter, softened
   1 package (1/4 ounce) active dry yeast
1/4 cup warm water (110° to 115°)
1/3 cup maple syrup
1-1/2 teaspoons salt
   1 egg, lightly beaten
3/4 cup whole wheat flour
   2 cups all-purpose flour
Additional oats

1 In a large mixing bowl, combine the milk, oats and butter; cool to 110°-115°. In a small bowl, dissolve yeast in warm water; add to the oat mixture. Add the syrup, salt, egg, whole wheat flour and 1 cup all-purpose flour. Beat on low speed for 30 seconds; beat on high for 3 minutes. Stir in remaining all-purpose flour (batter will be thick). Do not knead.

2 Sprinkle additional oats into a greased 1-1/2-qt. baking dish. Spoon batter into dish. Cover and let rise in a warm place until doubled, about 50 minutes.

3 Bake at 350° for 40-45 minutes or until golden brown. Cool for 10 minutes before removing from pan to a wire rack. **Yield:** 1 loaf.
—Denise Frink
Henderson, Iowa

Cheese Batter Bread

This bread has a unique flavor and will become a family favorite. Slices pair well with soup and chili.

   1 package (1/4 ounce) active dry yeast
   1 cup warm chicken broth (110° to 115°)
   1 tablespoon butter

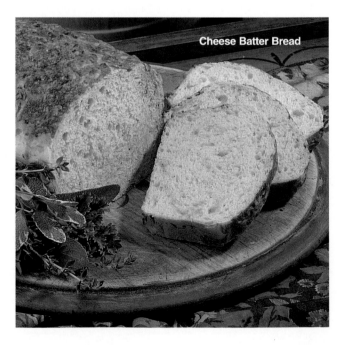

Cheese Batter Bread

  2 tablespoons sugar
1/2 teaspoon salt
1/2 teaspoon poultry seasoning
  1 egg
  3 cups all-purpose flour
1-1/4 cups finely shredded cheddar
      cheese, *divided*
Onion salt, optional

1 In a large mixing bowl, dissolve yeast in warm broth. Add the butter, sugar, salt, poultry seasoning, egg and 1 cup flour; beat until smooth, about 1 minute. Add 1 cup cheese and the remaining flour; stir for 1 minute. Do not knead. Cover and let rise in a warm place until doubled, about 30 minutes.

2 Stir batter down, about 25 strokes. Spread evenly into a greased 9-in. x 5-in. x 3-in. loaf pan. Cover and let rise until doubled, about 20 minutes. Top with the remaining cheese. Sprinkle with onion salt if desired. Bake at 375° for 25-30 minutes or until golden brown. Remove from pan to a wire rack. Serve warm. **Yield:** 1 loaf. —*Shirley Ramsey, Wymore, Nebraska*

Rosemary Focaccia

This classic Italian flat bread rivals any store-bought focaccia. Serve slices as a side dish or snack.

  2 medium onions, chopped
1/4 cup plus 3 tablespoons olive oil, *divided*
1-1/2 teaspoons active dry yeast
1/2 teaspoon sugar
1-1/2 cups warm water (110° to 115°), *divided*
1/2 teaspoon salt
  3 to 4 cups all-purpose flour
  2 tablespoons snipped fresh rosemary *or* 2
      teaspoons dried rosemary, crushed, *divided*
Cornmeal
Coarse salt

1 In a skillet, saute onions in 1/4 cup oil until tender; cool. In a large mixing bowl, dissolve yeast and sugar in 1/4 cup warm water; let stand for 5 minutes. Add 2 tablespoons oil, salt, 2 cups flour and remaining water. Beat until smooth. Stir in enough remaining flour to form a soft dough.

Rosemary
Focaccia

2 Turn onto a floured surface; knead until smooth and elastic, about 6-8 minutes. Add onion mixture and half of the rosemary; knead 1 minute longer. Place in a greased bowl, turning once to grease top. Cover and let rise in a warm place until doubled, about 40 minutes.

3 Punch dough down. Turn onto a lightly floured surface; divide in half. Pat each portion flat. Cover and let rest for 5 minutes. Sprinkle two greased baking sheets with cornmeal. Stretch each portion of dough into a 10-in. circle on prepared pans. Cover and let rise until doubled, about 40 minutes.

4 Brush with remaining oil. Sprinkle with coarse salt and remaining rosemary. Bake at 375° for 25-30 minutes or until golden brown. Remove from pans to wire racks. **Yield:** 2 loaves. —*Debra Peoples Calgary, Alberta*

storing yeast breads

Cool unsliced yeast bread completely before placing in an airtight container or resealable plastic bag. It will stay fresh at room temperature for 2 to 3 days. Bread with cream cheese or other perishable ingredients should be stored in the refrigerator.

For longer storage, freeze bread in an airtight container or resealable plastic bag for up to 3 months.

Light Rye Sandwich Loaves

This bread may also be shaped into two round loaves. Place on two greased baking sheets that have been sprinkled with cornmeal.

4 to 4-1/2 cups all-purpose flour
2-1/2 cups rye flour
1/3 cup packed brown sugar
2 packages (1/4 ounce *each*) active dry yeast
1 tablespoon grated orange peel
2 teaspoons salt
1/2 teaspoon fennel seed *or* aniseed, crushed
2-1/4 cups water
1/4 cup shortening
1-1/2 teaspoons molasses
Cornmeal
Melted butter

1 In a large mixing bowl, combine 2 cups all-purpose flour, rye flour, brown sugar, yeast, orange peel, salt and fennel seed. In a saucepan, heat the water, shortening and molasses to 120°-130°. Add to dry ingredients; beat until smooth. Stir in enough remaining all-purpose flour to form a soft dough.

2 Turn onto a floured surface; knead until smooth and elastic, about 6-8 minutes. Place in a greased bowl, turning once to grease top. Cover and let rise in a warm place until doubled, about 1-1/4 hours.

3 Punch dough down. Turn onto a lightly floured surface; divide in half. Shape each portion into a loaf. Sprinkle two greased 8-in. x 4-in. x 2-in. loaf pans with cornmeal. Place loaves in prepared pans. Cover and let rise until doubled, about 45 minutes.

4 With a sharp knife, make three shallow slashes across the top of each loaf. Bake at 375° for 30-35 minutes or until golden brown. Remove from pans to wire racks. Brush with melted butter. Cool. **Yield:** 2 loaves.   —*Katie Koziolek, Hartland, Minnesota*

Basic Pizza Crust

Store-bought pizza crusts and boxed mixes just can't compare to homemade. The ingredients can be easily doubled.

1 package (1/4 ounce) active dry yeast
1 cup warm water (110° to 115°)

Rapid Mixing Method for Yeast Breads

1. In a mixing bowl, combine flour (about 2 cups), the sugar, active dry or quick-rise yeast, salt and any seasonings.

2. In a saucepan, heat the liquid ingredients (water, milk, honey, molasses and butter or oil) to 120°-130°. Add to dry ingredients and beat just until moistened.

3. Add any eggs; beat until smooth. Gradually stir in enough of the remaining flour to form a dough of the desired consistency. The amount of flour will vary with the humidity in the air.

2 tablespoons vegetable oil
1 teaspoon sugar
1/4 teaspoon salt
2-1/2 to 2-3/4 cups all-purpose flour
Cornmeal
Pizza toppings of your choice

1 In a large mixing bowl, dissolve yeast in warm water. Add the oil, sugar, salt and 1-1/2 cups flour; beat until smooth. Stir in enough remaining flour to form a firm dough. Turn onto a floured surface; cover and let rest for 10 minutes.

2 Roll dough into a 13-in. circle. Sprinkle a greased 12-in. pizza pan with cornmeal. Transfer dough to prepared pan, building up edges slightly. Do not let rise. Bake at 425° for 12-15 minutes or until browned. Add toppings; bake 10-15 minutes longer. **Yield:** 1 pizza.
        —*Beverly Anderson, Sinclairville, New York*

Stromboli

Stromboli

This specialty sandwich, which originated in Philadelphia, features pizza dough wrapped around savory ingredients like cheese, herbs, meat and sausage.

       1 **package (1/4 ounce) active dry yeast**
1-1/3 **cups warm water (110° to 115°)**
   1/4 **cup vegetable oil**
   1/2 **teaspoon salt**
       4 **to 5 cups all-purpose flour**
FILLING:
1-1/2 **pounds ground beef**
       3 **tablespoons prepared mustard**
     12 **slices American cheese**
     12 **slices hard salami**
   1/2 **pound thinly sliced deli ham**
       4 **cups (16 ounces) shredded mozzarella
          cheese**
Vegetable oil
Oregano to taste

1 In a large mixing bowl, dissolve yeast in warm water. Add the oil, salt and 2 cups flour; beat until smooth. Stir in enough flour to form a soft dough.

2 Turn onto a lightly floured surface; knead until smooth and elastic, about 10 minutes. Place in a greased bowl, turning once to grease top. Cover and let rise in a warm place until doubled, about 45 minutes. Meanwhile, in a large skillet, cook beef over medium heat until no longer pink; drain and set aside.

3 Punch dough down. Turn onto a lightly floured surface; divide in half. Roll each portion into a 15-in. x 12-in. rectangle. Spread mustard lengthwise down half

of each rectangle; layer with American cheese, salami, beef, ham and mozzarella. Fold plain half of dough over filling and seal ends well. Brush with oil; sprinkle with oregano. Bake at 400° for 25-30 minutes or until lightly browned. Cool slightly; cut into 1-in. slices. **Yield: 2** loaves (about 8 servings each).
— *Erma Yoder*
Millersburg, Indiana

baking yeast breads at high altitudes

High altitude (over 3,000 feet) affects bread baking because the lower air pressure allows the yeast to rise 25 to 50 percent faster, and the drier air makes the flour drier. If the dough over-rises, the results might be a heavy, dry loaf or misshapen or collapsed loaf. Make these adjustments when baking bread at high altitudes:

- Start checking the dough halfway through the recommended rise time to see if it has doubled. If the dough has over-risen, punch it down and allow it to rise again.

- Use about a third less yeast. If a recipe calls for one package of active dry yeast (2-1/4 teaspoons), you would need to use about 1-1/2 teaspoons.

- Add flour slowly when mixing the dough and use only enough to make the dough easy to handle. If the dough is sticky, use greased rather than floured hands for kneading.

- Oil the dough and cover with greased plastic wrap to prevent it from drying out while using.

- Check doneness a few minutes before the minimum recommended baking time. Tent with foil if it's browning too quickly.

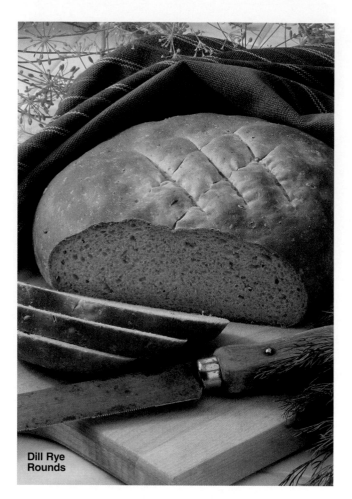

Dill Rye Rounds

2 Turn onto a floured surface; knead until smooth and elastic, about 6-8 minutes. Place in a greased bowl, turning once to grease top. Cover and let rise in a warm place until doubled, about 45 minutes.

3 Punch dough down. Turn onto a lightly floured surface; divide in half. Shape each portion into a ball. Place on two greased baking sheets. Cover and let rise in a warm place until doubled, about 35 minutes.

4 With a sharp knife, make several shallow slashes across the top of each loaf. Bake at 375° for 30-35 minutes or until golden brown. Remove from pans to wire racks to cool. **Yield:** 2 loaves. *—Betty Pittman Letts, Iowa*

Making Slashes on Top of a Loaf

Slashing or scoring the top of a bread loaf allows steam to vent and helps prevent cracking. It also gives the bread a decorative appearance.

With a sharp knife, make shallow slashes across top of loaf. For a more interesting look, make slashes in a crisscross pattern.

Dill Rye Rounds

If your family is not a big fan of rye, reach for this recipe that calls for only 1-1/2 cups of rye flour. It adds delicious flavor without being overpowering.

3-1/2 to 4 cups all-purpose flour
1-1/2 cups rye flour
  1/2 cup nonfat dry milk powder
   2 packages (1/4 ounce *each*) active dry yeast
   2 teaspoons sugar
   1 teaspoon salt
   1 teaspoon caraway seeds
   1 teaspoon dill seed
   1 teaspoon dill weed
1-3/4 cups water
   2 teaspoons shortening

1 In a mixing bowl, combine 2 cups all-purpose flour, rye flour, milk powder, yeast, sugar, salt, caraway seeds, dill seed and dill weed. In a saucepan, heat water and shortening to 120°-130°. Add to dry ingredients; beat until smooth. Stir in enough remaining all-purpose flour to form a soft dough.

Rustic Whole Wheat Bread

Looking to get a little more fiber into your diet? Try this wonderful whole wheat bread.

   5 to 5-1/4 cups all-purpose flour
   2 cups stone-ground whole wheat flour
   2 packages (1/4 ounce *each*) active dry yeast
   1 tablespoon sugar
   1 tablespoon salt
2-1/2 cups water
   1 tablespoon butter
Yellow cornmeal
   1 egg white
   1 tablespoon cold water

1 Combine the flours. In a large mixing bowl, combine 3 cups flour mixture, yeast, sugar and salt. In a small saucepan, heat water and butter to 120°-130°. Add to dry

ingredients. Beat on low speed for 30 seconds; beat on medium for 3 minutes. Stir in enough remaining flour mixture to form a soft dough.

2 Turn onto a floured surface; knead until smooth and elastic, about 6-8 minutes. Place in a greased bowl, turning once to grease top. Cover and let rise in a warm place until doubled, about 1 hour.

3 Punch dough down. Turn onto a lightly floured surface; divide in half. Cover and let rest for 10 minutes. Roll each portion into a 15-in. x 12-in. rectangle. Roll up jelly-roll style, starting with a long side; pinch seam to seal and turn ends under to form a smooth loaf. Sprinkle two greased baking sheets with cornmeal. Place loaves seam side down on prepared pans. With a sharp knife, make slashes every 2-1/2 in. in the top of each loaf. Cover and let rise until doubled, about 1 hour.

4 Beat egg white and cold water; brush some over loaves. Refrigerate remaining mixture. Bake at 375° for 20 minutes. Brush again with egg white mixture. Bake 15-20 minutes longer or until golden brown. Remove from pans to wire racks to cool. **Yield:** 2 loaves.

—*Roseann Loker, Colon, Michigan*

1 package (1/4 ounce) active dry yeast
3/4 cup warm water (110° to 115°)
3/4 cup orange juice
2 tablespoons honey
1 tablespoon vegetable oil
1 tablespoon minced fresh rosemary *or* 1 teaspoon dried rosemary, crushed
2 teaspoons salt
1 teaspoon grated orange peel
3-3/4 to 4-1/2 cups all-purpose flour
1 egg white, lightly beaten
Whole peppercorns and small rosemary sprigs, optional

1 In a large mixing bowl, dissolve yeast in warm water. Add the orange juice, honey, oil, rosemary, salt, orange peel and 2 cups flour; beat until smooth. Stir in enough remaining flour to form a soft dough. Turn onto a floured surface; knead until smooth and elastic, about 6-8 minutes. Place in a greased bowl, turning once to grease top. Cover and let rise in a warm place until doubled, about 1 hour.

2 Punch dough down. Turn onto a lightly floured surface; roll into a 15-in. x 10-in. rectangle. Roll up jelly-roll style, starting with a short side; pinch edges to seal. Shape into an oval. Place seam side down on a greased baking sheet. Cover and let rise until nearly doubled, about 30 minutes.

3 Bake at 375° for 20 minutes. Brush egg white over loaf. Place peppercorns and rosemary sprigs on top if desired. Bake 25 minutes longer or until browned. Remove from pan to a wire rack to cool. **Yield:** 1 loaf.

—*Deidre Fallavollita, Vienna, Virginia*

Rosemary Orange Bread

Rosemary Orange Bread

(Also pictured on page 280)

Rosemary is the perfect herb to pair with homemade bread. Here it subtly combines with orange.

Italian Bread

Years ago in Italian villages, bread was baked only once a week. So they made the loaves a little bigger to last for 7 days.

2 packages (1/4 ounce *each*) active dry yeast
3 cups warm water (110° to 115°), *divided*
3 tablespoons sugar
3 tablespoons shortening
1 tablespoon salt
1 egg
8 to 9 cups all-purpose flour, *divided*
Melted butter

1 In a large mixing bowl, dissolve yeast in 1/2 cup warm water. Add the sugar, shortening, salt, egg, remaining water and 4 cups flour; beat until smooth. Stir in enough remaining flour to form a soft dough. Turn onto a floured surface; knead until smooth and elastic, about 6-8 minutes. Place in a greased bowl, turning once to grease top. Cover and let rise in a warm place until doubled, about 1 hour.

2 Punch dough down. Turn onto a lightly floured surface; divide in half. Shape each portion into a loaf. Place seam side down on greased baking sheets. With a sharp knife, make four shallow diagonal slashes across the top of each loaf. Cover and let rise until doubled, about 1 hour.

3 Bake at 350° for 37-42 minutes or until golden brown. Remove from pans to wire racks. Brush with melted butter. Cool. **Yield:** 2 loaves. —*Virginia Slater West Sunbury, Pennsylvania*

Sausage Calzones

In these pizza turnovers, Italian sausage combines with ricotta, Parmesan and spinach.

1 package (1/4 ounce) active dry yeast
1/2 cup warm water (110° to 115°)
3/4 cup warm milk (110° to 115°)
2 tablespoons olive oil
1-1/2 teaspoons salt
1 teaspoon sugar
3 to 3-1/4 cups all-purpose flour
1 pound bulk Italian sausage
1 package (10 ounces) frozen chopped spinach, thawed and squeezed dry
1 carton (15 ounces) ricotta cheese

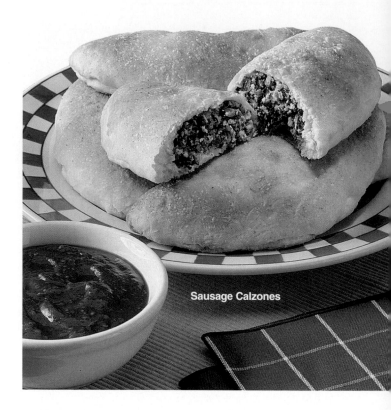
Sausage Calzones

1/2 cup grated Parmesan cheese
1 tablespoon minced fresh parsley
1/8 teaspoon pepper
2 tablespoons cornmeal
Additional oil
1/2 teaspoon garlic salt
1-1/2 cups pizza sauce, warmed

1 In a large mixing bowl, dissolve yeast in warm water. Add the milk, oil, salt, sugar and 2 cups flour; beat until smooth. Stir in enough remaining flour to form a soft dough.

2 Turn onto a floured surface; knead until smooth and elastic, about 6-8 minutes. Place in a greased bowl, turning once to grease top. Cover and let rise in a warm place until doubled, about 1 hour. Meanwhile, in a large skillet, cook sausage over medium heat until no longer pink; drain. Stir in the spinach, cheeses, parsley and pepper; set aside.

3 Punch dough down. Turn onto a lightly floured surface; divide into six pieces. Roll each piece into an 8-in. circle. Top each with 2/3 cup filling. Fold dough over filling; pinch edges to seal. Sprinkle greased baking sheets with cornmeal. Place calzones on prepared pans. Brush tops lightly with oil; sprinkle with garlic salt. Bake at 400° for 20-25 minutes or until golden brown. Serve with pizza sauce. Refrigerate leftovers. **Yield:** 6 calzones. —*Janine Colasurdo, Chesapeake, Virginia*

Cornmeal Mini Loaves

This recipe makes six miniature loaves that can be baked, cooled and tucked into your freezer. To reheat, wrap in foil and bake at 400° for 15-20 minutes.

       2 packages (1/4 ounce *each*) active dry yeast
       1 cup warm water (110° to 115°)
       1 cup warm milk (110° to 115°)
   1/2 cup shortening
   1/2 cup sugar
       2 eggs
       2 teaspoons salt
       1 cup cornmeal
       6 to 6-1/2 cups all-purpose flour
   Additional cornmeal

1 In a large mixing bowl, dissolve yeast in warm water. Add the milk, shortening, sugar, eggs, salt, cornmeal and 4 cups flour; beat until smooth. Stir in enough remaining flour to form a soft dough.

2 Turn onto a floured surface; knead until smooth and elastic, about 6-8 minutes. Place in a greased bowl, turning once to grease top. Cover and let rise in a warm place until doubled, about 1 hour.

3 Punch dough down. Turn onto a lightly floured surface; divide into six pieces. Shape each piece into a 6-in. oval loaf. Sprinkle two greased baking sheets with cornmeal. Place three loaves 3 in. apart on each prepared pan. Cover and let rise until doubled, about 30 minutes.

4 With a sharp knife, make three shallow diagonal slashes across the top of each loaf. Bake at 400° for 15-20 minutes or until golden brown. Remove from pans to wire racks to cool. **Yield:** 6 loaves.
                    —*Ellen Govertsen, Wheaton, Illinois*

Milk-and-Honey White Bread

Honey adds special flavor to this traditional white bread.

       2 packages (1/4 ounce *each*) active dry yeast
   2-1/2 cups warm milk (110° to 115°)
   1/3 cup honey

   1/4 cup butter, melted
       2 teaspoons salt
       8 to 8-1/2 cups all-purpose flour

1 In a large mixing bowl, dissolve yeast in warm milk. Add the honey, butter, salt and 5 cups flour; beat until smooth. Stir in enough remaining flour to form a soft dough.

2 Turn onto a floured surface; knead until smooth and elastic, about 6-8 minutes. Place in a greased bowl, turning once to grease top. Cover and let rise in a warm place until doubled, about 1 hour.

3 Punch dough down. Divide in half; shape each portion into a loaf. Place in two greased 9-in. x 5-in. x 3-in. loaf pans. Cover and let rise until doubled, about 30 minutes.

4 Bake at 375° for 30-35 minutes or until golden brown (cover loosely with foil if top browns too quickly). Remove from pans to wire racks to cool. **Yield:** 2 loaves.
                    —*Kathy McCreary, Goddard, Kansas*

Milk-and-Honey White Bread

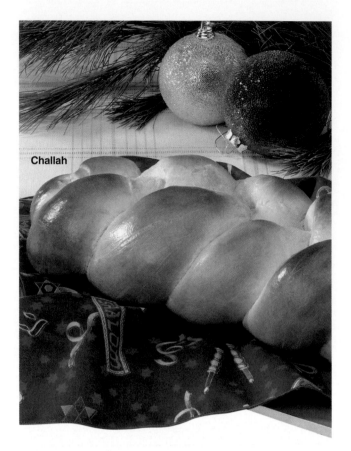
Challah

Challah

This traditional Jewish bread is often called egg bread because it uses more eggs than most. The attractive golden color and delicious flavor make it hard to resist.

    2 packages (1/4 ounce *each*) active dry yeast
    1 cup warm water (110° to 115°)
1/2 cup vegetable oil
1/3 cup sugar
    1 tablespoon salt
    4 eggs
    6 to 6-1/2 cups all-purpose flour
TOPPING:
    1 egg
    1 teaspoon cold water
    1 tablespoon sesame *or* poppy seeds, optional

1 In a large mixing bowl, dissolve yeast in warm water. Add the oil, sugar, salt, eggs and 4 cups flour; beat until smooth. Stir in enough remaining flour to form a firm dough.

2 Turn onto a floured surface; knead until smooth and elastic, about 6-8 minutes. Place in a greased bowl, turning once to grease top. Cover and let rise in a warm place until doubled, about 1 hour.

3 Punch dough down. Turn onto a lightly floured surface; divide in half. Divide each portion into thirds. Shape each piece into a 15-in. rope. Place three ropes on a greased baking sheet and braid; pinch ends to seal and tuck under. Repeat with remaining dough. Cover and let rise until doubled, about 1 hour.

4 Beat egg and cold water; brush over braids. Sprinkle with sesame or poppy seeds if desired. Bake at 350° for 30-35 minutes or until golden brown. Remove from pans to wire racks to cool. **Yield:** 2 loaves.

Butternut Squash Bread

Squash gives the loaves a pretty golden color. One pound of squash yields about 1 cup mashed.

    2 packages (1/4 ounce *each*) active dry yeast
1/2 cup warm water (110° to 115°)
1-1/4 cups mashed cooked butternut squash
    1 cup warm milk (110° to 115°)
    2 eggs
1/3 cup sugar
1/3 cup butter, melted
    1 teaspoon salt
    7 to 7-1/2 cups all-purpose flour

1 In a large mixing bowl, dissolve yeast in warm water. Add the squash, milk, eggs, sugar, butter and salt; beat well. Gradually add 3-1/2 cups flour, beating until smooth. Stir in enough remaining flour to form a soft dough.

2 Turn onto a floured surface; knead until smooth and elastic, about 6-8 minutes. Place in a greased bowl, turning once to grease top. Cover and let rise in a warm place until doubled, about 1 hour.

3 Punch dough down. Turn onto a lightly floured surface; divide into thirds. Shape each portion into a loaf. Place in three greased 8-in. x 4-in. x 2-in. loaf pans. Cover and let rise until doubled, about 30 minutes.

4 Bake at 375° for 25-30 minutes or until golden. Remove from pans to wire racks to cool. **Yield:** 3 loaves.
                              —Agnes Miller, Marshall, Illinois

Dilly Bread Ring

This batter bread requires no kneading, so even novice bakers will find it easy.

        2 packages (1/4 ounce *each*) active dry yeast
      1/3 cup warm water (110° to 115°)
      1/3 cup warm milk (110° to 115°)
        6 tablespoons butter, softened
      1/3 cup sugar
        2 eggs
        1 cup (8 ounces) sour cream
        2 tablespoons minced fresh parsley
        1 to 2 tablespoons dill weed
        2 teaspoons salt
    1-1/2 teaspoons minced chives
    4-1/2 cups all-purpose flour

1 In a large mixing bowl, dissolve yeast in warm water. Add the milk, butter, sugar, eggs, sour cream, seasonings and 3 cups flour. Beat on low speed for 30 seconds; beat on high for 3 minutes. Stir in remaining flour (batter will be sticky). Do not knead. Cover and let rise in a warm place until doubled, about 1 hour.

2 Stir dough down. Spoon into a greased 10-in. tube or fluted tube pan. Cover and let rise until nearly doubled, about 45 minutes.

3 Bake at 375° for 30-35 minutes or until golden brown (cover loosely with foil if top browns too quickly). Cool for 10 minutes before removing from pan to a wire rack. **Yield:** 1 loaf.   —*Natercia Yailaian
Somerville, Massachusetts*

Cheesy Flat Bread

With its pretty color and cheesy topping, this buttery bread is delicious with soup. Kids can help press out the thawed bread dough and sprinkle it with cheese.

      1 loaf (1 pound) frozen bread dough, thawed
      3 tablespoons butter, softened
      2 tablespoons finely chopped onion
      2 to 3 teaspoons paprika
    1/2 teaspoon garlic powder
    1/2 teaspoon dried oregano *or* basil
      1 cup (4 ounces) shredded cheddar cheese

Pat dough onto the bottom and up the sides of a greased 14-in. pizza pan or 15-in. x 10-in. x 1-in. baking pan, forming a crust. Spread with butter. Sprinkle with onion, paprika, garlic powder and oregano. Prick crust several times with a fork; sprinkle with cheese. Cover and let rise in a warm place for 30 minutes. Bake at 375° for 20-25 minutes or until golden brown. **Yield:** 8 servings.

—*Sue Burton, Frankfort, Kansas*

**Dilly Bread
Ring**

Whole Wheat Braids

*A hearty loaf of bread completes any fall meal.
Braiding the dough makes a pretty presentation.*

3 packages (1/4 ounce *each*) active dry yeast
3 cups warm water (110° to 115°)
1/2 cup sugar
3 eggs
1/3 cup vegetable oil
1 tablespoon salt
5 cups whole wheat flour
4 to 4-1/2 cups all-purpose flour

1 In a large mixing bowl, dissolve yeast in warm water. Add the sugar, eggs, oil, salt and whole wheat flour; beat until smooth. Stir in enough all-purpose flour to form a soft dough.

2 Turn onto a floured surface; knead until smooth and elastic, about 6-8 minutes. Place in a greased bowl, turning once to grease top. Cover and let rise in a warm place until doubled, about 1 hour.

3 Punch dough down. Turn onto a lightly floured surface; divide into nine pieces. Shape each piece into a 14-in. rope. Braid three ropes together; pinch ends to seal and tuck under. Place in three greased 8-in. x 4-in. x 2-in. loaf pans. Cover and let rise until doubled, about 30 minutes.

4 Bake at 350° for 40-45 minutes. Remove from pans to wire racks to cool. **Yield:** 3 loaves.
—Suella Miller, Lagrange, Indiana

Anadama Bread

*This Early American recipe from New England
features an interesting combination
of cornmeal and molasses.*

1/2 cup water
1/4 cup cornmeal
1/2 cup molasses
2 tablespoons butter
1 package (1/4 ounce) active dry yeast
1/2 cup warm water (110° to 115°)
1 teaspoon salt
3 to 3-1/2 cups all-purpose flour

1 In a small saucepan, bring water and cornmeal to a boil. Reduce heat; cook for 2 minutes or until mixture thickens, stirring constantly. Remove from the heat; stir in molasses and butter. Cool to 110°-115°.

2 In a large mixing bowl, dissolve yeast in warm water. Add the cornmeal mixture, salt and 2 cups flour; beat until smooth. Stir in enough remaining flour to form a soft dough.

3 Turn onto a floured surface; knead until smooth and elastic, about 6-8 minutes. Place in a greased bowl, turning once to grease top. Cover and let rise in a warm place until doubled, about 1 hour.

4 Punch dough down. Turn onto a lightly floured surface; shape into a loaf. Place in a greased 9-in. x 5-in. x 3-in. loaf pan. Cover and let rise until doubled, about 1 hour.

5 Bake at 375° for 25-30 minutes or until browned (cover loosely with foil if top browns too quickly). Remove from pan to a wire rack to cool. **Yield:** 1 loaf.

**Whole Wheat
Braids**

Cheesy Italian Bread

Romano cheese adds a little more flavor to plain Italian bread. This goes so well with an Italian meal or alongside a big bowl of soup.

      1 **package (1/4 ounce) active dry yeast**
1-1/4 **cups warm water (110° to 115°)**
      2 **tablespoons sugar**
      1 **teaspoon garlic salt**
  1/2 **teaspoon salt**
  1/2 **cup grated Romano cheese**
      3 **to 3-1/2 cups all-purpose flour**
Cornmeal

Cheesy Italian Bread

1 In a large mixing bowl, dissolve yeast in warm water. Add the sugar, garlic salt, salt, cheese and 2 cups flour; beat until smooth. Stir in enough remaining flour to form a soft dough. Turn onto a floured surface; knead until smooth and elastic, about 6-8 minutes. Place in a greased bowl, turning once to grease top. Cover and let rise in a warm place until doubled, about 1 hour.

2 Punch dough down. Turn onto a lightly floured surface; divide in half. Shape each portion into a 14-in. loaf. Sprinkle an ungreased baking sheet with cornmeal. Place loaves on prepared pan. Cover and let rise until doubled, about 45 minutes.

3 Brush loaves with water. With a sharp knife, make three diagonal slashes about 1/2 in. deep in each loaf. Fill a 13-in. x 9-in. x 2-in. baking dish with 1 in. of hot water; place on the bottom rack of oven. Place pan with loaves on middle rack. Bake at 400° for 20-25 minutes. Remove from pan to a wire rack to cool. **Yield:** 2 loaves.
—Cookie Curci-Wright
San Jose, California

Multigrain English Muffin Bread

There's no need to knead this dough, which bakes into a hearty nutty-tasting bread with the texture of English muffins.

      1 **package (1/4 ounce) active dry yeast**
1-1/4 **cups warm water (110° to 115°)**
  1/3 **cup whole wheat flour**
  1/3 **cup quick-cooking oats**
  1/3 **cup toasted wheat germ**
      1 **tablespoon sugar**
  3/4 **teaspoon salt**
      2 **cups all-purpose flour**
  1/4 **cup cornmeal**

1 In a large mixing bowl, dissolve yeast in warm water. Add the whole wheat flour, oats, wheat germ, sugar, salt and 1-1/4 cups all-purpose flour; beat until smooth. Stir in enough remaining all-purpose flour to form a soft dough. Do not knead. Place in a greased bowl, turning once to grease top. Cover and let rise in a warm place until doubled, about 1 hour.

2 Punch dough down. Turn onto a lightly floured surface; shape into a loaf. Sprinkle half of the cornmeal into a greased 9-in. x 5-in. x 3-in. loaf pan. Place loaf in prepared pan; sprinkle with remaining cornmeal. Cover and let rise until doubled, about 30 minutes.

3 Bake at 400° for 30-35 minutes or until golden brown. Remove from pan to a wire rack to cool. **Yield:** 1 loaf.
—Carol Forcum, Marion, Illinois

Swiss-Onion
Bread Ring

Cheddar Chili Braid

Hot roll mix gives you a head start when preparing this savory bread. Make it with a big pot of chili and serve thick warm slices for "dunking".

- **1 package (16 ounces) hot roll mix**
- **1 cup warm water (120° to 130°)**
- **2 eggs**
- **2 cups (8 ounces) shredded cheddar cheese**
- **2 tablespoons canned chopped green chilies, drained**
- **2 tablespoons grated Parmesan cheese**

1 In a large bowl, combine contents of roll mix and yeast packet; stir in water, one egg, cheddar cheese and chilies. Turn onto a floured surface; knead until smooth and elastic, about 5 minutes. Cover and let rest for 5 minutes.

2 Divide dough into thirds. Shape each portion into a 14-in. rope. Place ropes on a greased baking sheet and braid; pinch ends to seal and tuck under. Cover and let rise in a warm place until doubled, about 30 minutes.

3 Beat remaining egg; brush over dough. Sprinkle with Parmesan cheese. Bake at 375° for 30 minutes or until golden brown. Remove from pan to a wire rack. **Yield:** 1 loaf.
— *Katie Dreibelbis*
State College, Pennsylvania

Swiss-Onion Bread Ring

With the ease of refrigerated bread dough, this tempting cheesy bread has delicious down-home goodness. You'll find it crisp and golden on the outside, rich and buttery inside.

- **2-1/2 teaspoons poppy seeds, divided**
- **2 tubes (11 ounces each) refrigerated white bread dough**
- **1 cup (4 ounces) shredded Swiss cheese**
- **3/4 cup sliced green onions**
- **6 tablespoons butter, melted**

1 Sprinkle 1/2 teaspoon poppy seeds into a greased 10-in. fluted tube pan. Cut the bread dough into 40 1-in. pieces; place half in prepared pan. Sprinkle with half of the cheese and onions. Top with 1 teaspoon poppy seeds; drizzle with half of the butter. Repeat layers.

2 Bake at 375° for 30-35 minutes or until golden brown. Immediately invert onto a wire rack. Serve warm. **Yield:** 1 loaf. — *Judi Messina, Coeur d'Alene, Idaho*

Irish Bread

Unlike traditional Irish Soda Bread, this version calls for yeast, giving it a slightly different texture.

- **2-1/2 to 2-3/4 cups all-purpose flour**
- **3 tablespoons sugar**
- **1 package (1/4 ounce) active dry yeast**
- **1/2 teaspoon salt**
- **1/2 teaspoon baking soda**
- **1 cup warm buttermilk* (120° to 130°)**
- **2 tablespoons butter, melted**
- **3/4 cup raisins**
- **Additional all-purpose flour**

1 In a large mixing bowl, combine 2 cups flour, sugar, yeast, salt and baking soda. Combine buttermilk and butter; gradually add to dry ingredients, beating well. Stir in enough remaining flour to form a soft dough.

2 Turn onto a lightly floured surface; knead in raisins until dough is smooth and elastic, about 6-8 minutes. Place in a greased bowl, turning once to grease top. Cover and let rise in a warm place until doubled, about 1-1/2 hours.

3 Punch dough down. Turn onto a lightly floured surface; knead about 15 times, forming a smooth round ball. Place on a greased baking sheet. Press dough down to form an 8-in. circle. Cover and let rise until doubled, about 45 minutes.

4 Sprinkle dough lightly with additional flour. With a sharp knife, make a 4-in. cross about 1/4 in. deep on top of loaf. Bake at 350° for 30 minutes or until browned. Remove from pan to a wire rack to cool. **Yield:** 1 loaf.　　　—*Martha Glenn, Enid, Oklahoma*

*Editor's Note: Warmed buttermilk will appear curdled.

Special Savory Loaves

Tomato soup beautifully colors the dough, while herbs, tomatoes and cheese provide lots of flavor.

　　2 packages (1/4 ounce *each***) active dry yeast**
1-1/3 cups warm water (110° to 115°)
　　1 can (10-3/4 ounces) condensed tomato soup, undiluted
　1/4 cup olive oil
　1/2 teaspoon salt

6-1/4 to 6-3/4 cups all-purpose flour
FILLING:
　　1 cup minced fresh basil
　1/2 cup minced fresh parsley
　1/4 cup minced garlic
　1/2 cup olive oil
　　2 large tomatoes, thinly sliced
　1/2 cup grated Romano cheese
TOPPING:
　　1 egg white, lightly beaten
　　2 tablespoons sesame seeds
　　1 tablespoon cracked black pepper
　1/2 teaspoon garlic salt
　1/2 teaspoon crushed red pepper flakes

1 In a large mixing bowl, dissolve yeast in warm water. Add the soup, oil, salt and 3 cups flour; beat until smooth. Stir in enough remaining flour to form a soft dough.

2 Turn onto a floured surface; knead until smooth and elastic, about 10 minutes. Place in a greased bowl, turning once to grease top. Cover and let rise in a warm place until doubled, about 1 hour. For filling, combine the basil, parsley, garlic and oil in a bowl; let stand for 30 minutes.

3 Punch dough down. Turn onto a lightly floured surface; divide in half. Roll each portion into a 16-in. x 12-in. rectangle. Spread filling over dough to within 1 in. of edges. Cover with tomatoes; sprinkle with cheese. Roll up jelly-roll style, starting with a long side; pinch seams to seal and tuck ends under.

4 Place loaves on greased baking sheets; brush tops with egg white. Combine the sesame seeds, pepper, garlic salt and red pepper flakes; sprinkle over loaves. With a sharp knife, cut four 1/2-in. slits on top of each loaf. Cover and let rise until doubled, about 30-45 minutes.

5 Bake at 350° for 40-45 minutes or until golden brown. Cool on a wire rack. Serve warm. **Yield:** 2 loaves. —*Alanna Petrone Terryville, Connecticut*

Special Savory Loaves

Rolls, Buns & beyond

Dinner Rolls

2 Turn onto a floured surface; knead until smooth and elastic, about 6-8 minutes. Place in a greased bowl, turning once to grease top. Cover and let rise in a warm place until doubled, about 1 hour.

3 Punch dough down. Turn onto a lightly floured surface; divide in half. Divide each portion into 12 pieces. Shape each piece into a ball. Place in two greased 13-in. x 9-in. x 2-in. baking pans. Cover and let rise until doubled, about 30 minutes.

4 Bake at 375° for 20-25 minutes or until golden brown. Lightly brush with melted butter if desired. Remove from pans to wire racks. Serve warm. **Yield:** 2 dozen. —*Anna Baker, Blaine, Washington*

Shaping Plain Rolls

Divide dough into equal pieces as recipe directs. Shape each piece into a ball, pulling edges under to smooth top. Place 2 in. apart on greased baking sheets. For pan rolls, place eight balls in a greased 9-in. round baking pan or 12 balls in a greased 13-in. x 9-in. x 2-in. baking pan.

Dinner Rolls

A basic roll like this can be served with dinner or used for small appetizer sandwiches. Either way, it's a recipe you'll come to rely on.

 2 **packages (1/4 ounce *each*) active dry yeast**
 1/3 **cup plus 1 teaspoon sugar, *divided***
 1/2 **cup warm water (110° to 115°)**
1-1/4 **cups warm milk (110° to 115°)**
 1/2 **cup butter, melted and cooled**
1-1/2 **teaspoons salt**
 2 **eggs, beaten**
 6 **to 6-1/2 cups all-purpose flour**
Additional melted butter, optional

1 In a large mixing bowl, dissolve yeast and 1 teaspoon sugar in warm water. Add the milk, butter, salt, remaining sugar, eggs and 3 cups flour; beat until smooth. Stir in enough remaining flour to form a soft dough.

Green Onion Potato Rolls

The mild green onion flavor of these tender rolls appeals to all. Keep the ingredients on hand to bake up a batch on a moment's notice.

4-1/2 **to 5-1/2 cups bread flour**
1-1/4 **cups mashed potato flakes, *divided***
 3 **tablespoons sugar**
 2 **packages (1/4 ounce *each*) active dry yeast**
 2 **teaspoons salt**
 2 **cups milk**
 1/2 **cup butter**
 4 **to 6 green onions, sliced**
 2 **eggs**
All-purpose flour

1 In a mixing bowl, combine 1-1/2 cups bread flour, 1 cup potato flakes, sugar, yeast and salt. In a saucepan, heat the milk, butter and onions to 120°-130°. Add to dry ingredients; beat until moistened. Add eggs; beat on medium speed for 3 minutes. Stir in enough remaining bread flour to form a soft dough.

2 Turn onto a surface floured with all-purpose flour; knead until smooth and elastic, about 8-10 minutes. Place in a greased bowl, turning once to grease top. Cover and let rise in a warm place until doubled, about 45 minutes.

3 Punch dough down. Cover and let rest for 15 minutes. Turn onto a lightly floured surface; divide into 24 pieces. Shape each piece into a ball. Dip each ball into remaining potato flakes. Place in a greased 13-in. x 9-in. x 2-in. baking pan. Cover and let rise in a warm place until doubled, about 30 minutes.

4 Bake at 375° for 25-35 minutes or until golden brown. Remove from pan to a wire rack to cool. **Yield:** 2 dozen.   —*Louise Beaulieu, Monticello, Maine*

Icebox Butterhorns

(Pictured on page 281)

These beautiful golden rolls just melt in your mouth! People will be impressed when these appear on your table.

2 packages (1/4 ounce *each*) active dry yeast
1/4 cup warm water (110° to 115°)
2 cups warm milk (110° to 115°)
1/2 cup sugar
1 egg
1 teaspoon salt
6-1/2 cups all-purpose flour
3/4 cup butter, melted
Additional melted butter

1 In a large mixing bowl, dissolve yeast in warm water. Add the milk, sugar, egg, salt and 3 cups flour; beat until smooth. Beat in butter and remaining flour (dough will be slightly sticky). Do not knead. Place in a greased bowl, turning once to grease top. Cover and refrigerate overnight.

2 Punch dough down. Turn onto a lightly floured surface; divide in half. Roll each portion into a 12-in. circle. Cut each circle into 12 wedges. Roll up wedges from the wide end and place pointed side down 2 in. apart on greased baking sheets. Cover and let rise in a warm place until doubled, about 1 hour.

3 Bake at 350° for 15-20 minutes or until golden brown. Immediately brush tops with melted butter. Remove from pans to wire racks to cool. **Yield:** 2 dozen.
—*Judy Clark, Elkhart, Indiana*

Spoon Rolls

The batter for these rolls may be refrigerated overnight. The next day, simply spoon the batter into muffin cups for homemade rolls in no time.

1 package (1/4 ounce) active dry yeast
2 cups warm water (110° to 115°)
1/2 cup butter, melted
1/4 cup sugar
1 egg
4 cups self-rising flour*

1 In a large mixing bowl, dissolve yeast in warm water. Add the butter, sugar and egg; beat well. Stir in flour until thoroughly combined (batter will be soft). Cover and refrigerate overnight.

2 Spoon batter into greased or paper-lined muffin cups. Bake at 375° for 25-30 minutes or until golden brown. Remove from pans to wire racks to cool. **Yield:** 16 rolls.   —*Oma Rollison, El Cajon, California*

***Editor's Note:** As a substitute for *each* cup of self-rising flour, place 1-1/2 teaspoons baking powder and 1/2 teaspoon salt in a measuring cup. Add all-purpose flour to measure 1 cup.

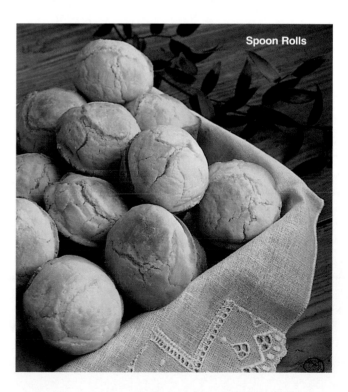
Spoon Rolls

Brioche

These classic French rolls (pronounced BREE-osh) are rich in butter and eggs. The unique shape resembles a muffin.

3-1/2 **cups all-purpose flour**
1/2 **cup sugar**
2 **packages (1/4 ounce** *each***) active dry yeast**
1 **teaspoon grated lemon peel**
1/2 **teaspoon salt**
2/3 **cup butter**
1/2 **cup milk**
5 **eggs**

1 In a large mixing bowl, combine 1-1/2 cups flour, sugar, yeast, lemon peel and salt. In a saucepan, heat butter and milk to 120°-130°. Add to dry ingredients; beat until moistened. Add four eggs; beat on medium speed for 2 minutes. Add 1 cup flour; beat until smooth. Stir in the remaining flour. Do not knead. Spoon into a greased bowl. Cover and let rise in a warm place until doubled, about 1 hour. Stir dough down. Cover and refrigerate overnight.

2 Punch dough down. Turn onto a lightly floured surface. Cover with a bowl; let rest for 15 minutes. Cut one-sixth from the dough; set aside. Shape remaining dough into 12 balls (about 2-1/2 in.); place in well-greased muffin cups. Divide reserved dough into 12 small balls (about 1 in.). Make an indentation in the top of each large ball; place a small ball in each indentation. Cover and let rise in a warm place until doubled, about 1 hour.

3 Beat remaining egg; brush over rolls. Bake at 375° for 15-20 minutes or until golden brown. Remove from pan to a wire rack to cool. **Yield:** 1 dozen.

—*Wanda Kristoffersen, Owatonna, Minnesota*

Brioche

Making Brioche

1. Shape dough into equal numbers of large and small balls (about 2-1/2 in. and 1 in.)

1.

2. Place large balls in greased muffin cups. Using the end of a wooden spoon handle, make a deep indentation in the center of each large ball.

2.

3. Place a small ball in each indentation.

3.

Chili Cornmeal Crescents

Shaping Crescent Rolls

Roll a portion of the dough into a 12-in. circle. Cut into 12 wedges and roll up, beginning at the wide end. Place pointed side down 2 in. apart on greased baking sheets. Curve ends to form crescent shape.

Chili Cornmeal Crescents

These unique rolls are tender, light and delicious, with a bit of chili tang. For a fun change of pace, use blue cornmeal.

      1 package (1/4 ounce) active dry yeast
1-3/4 cups warm water (110° to 115°)
1-1/2 cups cornmeal
   1/3 cup sugar
      1 egg
      2 tablespoons olive oil
      1 tablespoon chili powder
      1 teaspoon salt
      4 to 4-1/2 cups all-purpose flour

1 In a large mixing bowl, dissolve yeast in warm water. Add the cornmeal, sugar, egg, oil, chili powder, salt and 2 cups flour; beat until smooth. Stir in enough remaining flour to form a soft dough.

2 Turn onto a floured surface; knead until smooth and elastic, about 6-8 minutes. Place in a greased bowl, turning once to grease top. Cover and let rise in a warm place until doubled, about 1 hour.

3 Punch dough down. Turn onto a lightly floured surface; divide in half. Roll each portion into a 12-in. circle. Cut each circle into 12 wedges. Roll up wedges from the wide end and place pointed side down 2 in. apart on greased baking sheets. Curve ends to form a crescent shape. Cover and let rise until doubled, about 30 minutes.

4 Bake at 375° for 20 minutes or until browned. Remove from pans to wire racks to cool. **Yield:** 2 dozen.   *—Marion Lowery, Medford, Oregon*

Garlic Parmesan Rolls

Just four ingredients are all you need to make fresh-from-the-oven dinner rolls that are dripping with butter and cheese!

      1 loaf (1 pound) frozen bread dough, thawed
      6 tablespoons grated Parmesan cheese
      1 teaspoon garlic powder
   1/2 cup butter, melted

1 Cut bread dough into 16 pieces; shape each piece into a ball. Place on a floured surface; cover and let rise in a warm place for 10 minutes. In a bowl, stir Parmesan cheese and garlic powder into butter. Using a spoon, roll balls in butter mixture. Arrange loosely in a 9-in. round baking pan. Cover and let rise in a warm place until doubled, about 30 minutes.

2 Bake at 375° for 10-15 minutes or until golden brown. Warm leftover butter mixture; when rolls are baked, pull them apart and dip again. Serve warm. **Yield:** 16 rolls.   *—Loretta Ruda, Kennesaw, Georgia*

Accordion Rye Rolls

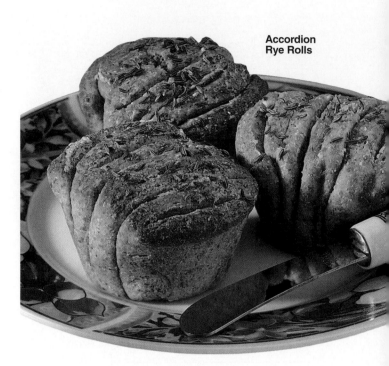

Accordion Rye Rolls

These rolls will make anyone like rye bread. Although you conveniently make the dough ahead, bake them right before serving so they're hot and fresh.

    2 packages (1/4 ounce *each*) active dry yeast
  1/2 cup warm water (110° to 115°)
1-1/2 cups warm milk (110° to 115°)
  1/4 cup molasses
    4 tablespoons butter, softened, *divided*
    1 tablespoon sugar
    1 tablespoon plus 1/2 teaspoon salt, *divided*
    3 to 3-1/2 cups all-purpose flour
2-1/2 cups rye flour
Vegetable oil
    1 egg white
    2 teaspoons caraway seeds

1 In a large mixing bowl, dissolve yeast in warm water. Add the milk, molasses, 2 tablespoons butter, sugar and 1 tablespoon salt. Add 2 cups all-purpose flour; beat until smooth. Stir in rye flour and enough remaining all-purpose flour to form a soft dough.

2 Turn onto a floured surface; knead until smooth and elastic, about 6-8 minutes. Place in a greased bowl; turn once to grease top. Cover and let rest for 20 minutes.

3 Punch dough down. Turn onto a lightly floured surface; divide into four portions. Roll out each portion into a 14-in. x 6-in. rectangle. Brush with the remaining butter.

4 With dull edge of a table knife, score dough widthwise at 2-in. intervals. Using those marks as a guideline, make score marks widthwise across the dough. Fold dough accordion-style back and forth along creased lines. Cut folded dough into 1-in. pieces. Place each piece cut side down in a greased muffin cup. Brush with oil. Cover loosely with plastic wrap. Refrigerate for 4-24 hours.

5 When ready to bake, uncover dough and let stand at room temperature for 10 minutes. In a small mixing bowl, beat egg white until stiff peaks form; brush over dough. Sprinkle with caraway seeds and remaining salt. Bake at 375° for 20-25 minutes or until lightly browned. Remove from pans to wire racks. **Yield:** 2 dozen.
—*Alyson Armstrong
Parkersburg, West Virginia*

Making Accordion Rolls

1. Roll dough into a 14-in. x 6-in. rectangle. Brush with butter. With the dull edge of a table knife, score dough widthwise at 2-in. intervals.

2. Fold dough accordion-style back and forth along crease lines.

3. Cut dough into 1-in. pieces. Place each piece cut side down in a greased muffin cup.

Parker House Rolls

These tender rolls were created at Boston's Parker House Hotel in the 1870s. The folded shape makes them unique.

2 packages (1/4 ounce *each***) active dry yeast**
1 teaspoon plus 6 tablespoons sugar, *divided*
1 cup warm water (110° to 115°), *divided*
1 cup warm milk (110° to 115°)
2 teaspoons salt
1 egg
2 tablespoons plus 2 teaspoons vegetable oil
5-1/2 to 6 cups all-purpose flour
3 tablespoons butter, melted, optional

1 In a large mixing bowl, dissolve yeast and 1 teaspoon sugar in 1/2 cup warm water; let stand for 5 minutes. Add the milk, salt, egg, oil and remaining sugar and water. Gradually add 2 cups flour; beat until smooth. Stir in enough remaining flour to form a soft dough.

2 Turn onto a floured surface; knead until smooth and elastic, about 6-8 minutes. Place in a greased bowl, turning once to grease top. Cover and let rise in a warm place until doubled, about 45 minutes.

3 Punch dough down. Turn onto a lightly floured surface; divide in half. Roll out each portion to 1/3-in. or 1/2-in. thickness. Cut with a floured 2-1/2-in. round cutter. Brush with butter if desired. Using the dull edge of a table knife,

make an off-center crease in each roll. Fold along crease so the large half is on top; press along folded edge. Place 2 in. apart on greased baking sheets. Cover and let rise until doubled, about 30 minutes.

4 Bake at 375° for 10-15 minutes or until golden brown. Remove from pans to wire racks to cool.
Yield: about 2-1/2 dozen.   *—Sandra Melnychenko*
Grandview, Manitoba

Forming Parker House Rolls

Roll out to 1/2-in. thickness. Cut with a floured 2-1/2-in. biscuit cutter. Brush with melted butter. Using the dull edge of a table knife, make an off-center crease in each roll. Fold along crease.

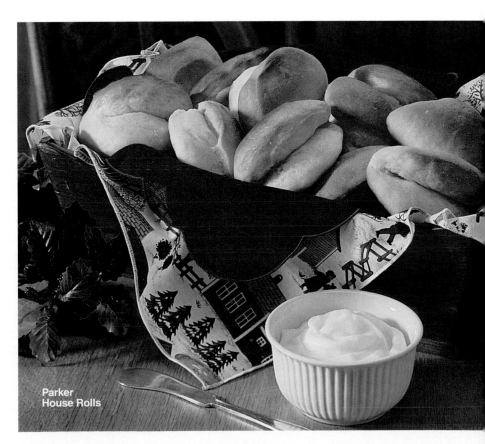

Parker House Rolls

Making Herbed Bread Twists

1. Roll dough into a 12-in. square. Spread butter mixture to within 1/2 in. of edges. Top with cheese. Fold dough into thirds.

2. Cut dough widthwise into 24 strips.

3. Twist each strip twice; pinch ends to seal.

Herbed
Bread
Twists

2 Fold dough into thirds. Cut widthwise into 24 strips. Twist each strip twice; pinch ends to seal. Place 2 in. apart on greased baking sheets. Cover and let rise in a warm place until doubled, about 40 minutes.

3 Beat egg and water; brush over dough. Sprinkle with sesame seeds. Bake at 375° for 10-12 minutes or until light golden brown. Remove from pans to wire racks. **Yield:** 2 dozen.
—*Deb Stapert*
Comstock Park, Michigan

Herbed Bread Twists

A blend of herbs and a special shape dress up ordinary frozen bread dough in this unbelievably easy recipe.

1/4 cup butter, softened
1/4 teaspoon *each* garlic powder, dried basil, marjoram and oregano
1 loaf (1 pound) frozen bread dough, thawed
3/4 cup shredded mozzarella cheese
1 egg
1 tablespoon water
4 teaspoons sesame seeds

1 In a small bowl, combine butter and seasonings. On a lightly floured surface, roll dough into a 12-in. square. Spread with butter mixture to within 1/2 in. of edges; sprinkle with mozzarella cheese.

Best-Ever Breadsticks

Present these long and thin breadsticks in a tall clear glass alongside an Italian favorite like lasagna or spaghetti.

3 to 3-1/4 cups all-purpose flour, *divided*
1 tablespoon sugar
1 package (1/4 ounce) quick-rise yeast
1 teaspoon salt
3/4 cup milk
1/4 cup water
1 tablespoon butter
1 egg white
1 tablespoon cold water
Coarse salt

1 In a large mixing bowl, combine 1-1/2 cups flour, sugar, yeast and salt. In a saucepan, heat the milk, water and butter to 120°-130°. Add to dry ingredients; beat just until moistened. Stir in enough remaining flour to form a stiff dough.

2 Turn onto a lightly floured surface; knead until smooth and elastic, about 6-8 minutes. Place in a

greased bowl, turning once to grease top. Cover and let rise in a warm place until doubled, about 30 minutes.

3 Punch dough down. Pinch off golf ball-size pieces. On a lightly floured surface, roll into pencil-size strips. Place on greased baking sheets 1 in. apart. Cover and let rise for 15 minutes.

4 Beat egg white and cold water; brush over bread-sticks. Sprinkle with coarse salt. Bake at 400° for 10 minutes or until golden. Remove from pans to wire racks. **Yield:** about 1-1/2 dozen. —*Carol Wolfer*
Lebanon, Oregon

Shaping Breadsticks

Divide dough into 2-1/2-in. balls. Roll each ball back and forth with both hands until they are shaped into 10-in. x 1/2-in. ropes.

Caption: Multigrain Buns

Multigrain Buns

Delicious with a meal or to make a sandwich, these light and tasty rolls have a super nutty flavor.

> **2 packages (1/4 ounce *each*) active dry yeast**
> **3 cups warm water (110° to 115°)**

> **1-1/2 cups whole wheat flour**
> **1 cup old-fashioned oats**
> **1 egg**
> **1/4 cup sesame seeds**
> **1/4 cup salted sunflower kernels**
> **1/4 cup vegetable oil**
> **3 tablespoons butter, softened**
> **2 tablespoons sugar**
> **1-1/2 teaspoons salt**
> **1 teaspoon caraway seeds**
> **1/2 teaspoon white vinegar**
> **5-1/2 to 6 cups all-purpose flour**
> **1 egg yolk**
> **2 tablespoons cold water**
> **Additional oats**

1 In a bowl, dissolve yeast in warm water. Add the whole wheat flour, oats, egg, sesame seeds, sunflower kernels, oil, butter, sugar, salt, caraway seeds, vinegar and 2 cups all-purpose flour; beat until smooth. Stir in enough remaining flour to form a soft dough.

2 Turn onto a floured surface; knead until smooth and elastic, about 6-8 minutes. Place in a greased bowl, turning once to grease top. Cover and let rise in a warm place until doubled, about 1 hour.

3 Punch dough down. Turn onto a lightly floured surface; shape into 18 round balls. Roll each ball into a 4-1/2-in. circle. Place on greased baking sheets. Cover and let rise until doubled, about 45 minutes.

4 Beat egg yolk and cold water; brush over buns. Sprinkle with additional oats. Bake at 350° for 20 minutes or until golden brown. Remove from pans to wire racks to cool. **Yield:** 1-1/2 dozen. —*Josie Drzewicki, Spirit River, Alberta*

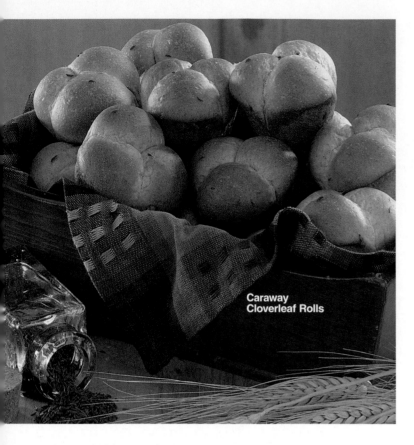

Caraway Cloverleaf Rolls

2 teaspoons caraway seeds
1-1/2 teaspoons salt
3-1/2 to 4 cups all-purpose flour

1 In a large mixing bowl, dissolve yeast in warm water. Add the whole wheat flour, sugar, oil, caraway seeds, salt and 2 cups all-purpose flour; beat until smooth. Stir in enough remaining all-purpose flour to form a soft dough.

2 Turn onto a floured surface; knead until smooth and elastic, about 6-8 minutes. Place in a greased bowl, turning once to grease top. Cover and let rise in a warm place until doubled, about 1 hour.

3 Punch dough down. Turn onto a lightly floured surface; divide in half. Divide each portion into 36 pieces. Shape each piece into a ball; place three balls in each greased muffin cup. Cover and let rise until doubled, about 30 minutes.

4 Bake at 375° for 15-18 minutes or until golden brown. Remove from pans to wire racks to cool. **Yield:** 2 dozen.
—*Ruth Reid*
Jackson, Minnesota

Caraway Cloverleaf Rolls

It takes a little more time to shape these cloverleaf rolls, but the pretty presentation is worth it, especially for special occasions.

2 packages (1/4 ounce *each*) active dry yeast
1-1/2 cups warm water (110° to 115°)
1 cup whole wheat flour
1/2 cup sugar
1/2 cup vegetable oil

Shaping Cloverleaf Rolls

Divide dough into 1-1/2-in. balls. Make each ball smooth by pulling the edges under. Place three balls smooth side up in each greased muffin cup.

Flaky Croissants

These croissants may be a little time-consuming, but for holidays and other special occasions, it's worth the extra effort.

2-1/2 to 3 cups all-purpose flour
1 tablespoon sugar
1 package (1/4 ounce) active dry yeast
3/4 teaspoon salt
1 cup warm water (120° to 130°)
1 tablespoon shortening
1 cup cold butter, cubed
1 egg, beaten

1 In a large mixing bowl, combine 1 cup flour, sugar, yeast and salt. Add water and shortening; beat on medium speed for 2 minutes. Add 1/2 cup flour; beat 2 minutes longer. Stir in enough remaining flour to form a soft dough.

2 Turn onto a floured surface; knead until smooth and elastic, about 6-8 minutes. Place in a greased bowl, turning once to grease top. Cover and let rise in a warm place until doubled, about 45 minutes. Punch dough down. Cover and refrigerate for 2 hours.

3 Turn dough onto a lightly floured surface; roll into a 15-in. x 10-in. rectangle. In a small mixing bowl, beat cold butter until softened but still cold. Spread a fourth of the butter over dough. Fold dough into thirds, starting with a short side. Turn dough a quarter turn. Repeat rolling, buttering and folding three times. Wrap in plastic wrap. Refrigerate overnight.

4 On a floured surface, roll the dough into a 14-in. square. With a sharp knife, cut into quarters. Cut each quarter diagonally in half, forming two triangles. Roll up triangles from the wide end; place with pointed end down 2 in. apart on a greased baking sheet. Curve ends to form a crescent shape. Cover and refrigerate for 20 minutes.

5 Brush with egg. Bake at 425° for 13-18 minutes or until golden brown. Remove from pan to a wire rack. **Yield:** 8 croissants.
—Pam Butler
Branson, Missouri

Yogurt Yeast Rolls

People will snap up these fluffy golden rolls in a hurry whenever you take them to a potluck. It's a nice contribution since rolls are easy to transport and one batch goes a long way.

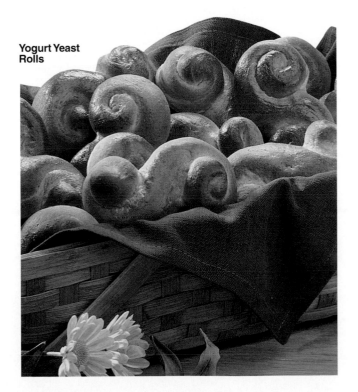

Yogurt Yeast Rolls

1-1/2 cups whole wheat flour
3-1/4 cups all-purpose flour
   2 packages (1/4 ounce *each*) active dry yeast
   2 teaspoons salt
1/2 teaspoon baking soda
1-1/2 cups (12 ounces) plain yogurt
1/2 cup water
   3 tablespoons butter
   2 tablespoons honey
Additional butter, melted

1 In a large mixing bowl, combine whole wheat flour, 1/2 cup all-purpose flour, yeast, salt and baking soda. In a saucepan over low heat, heat yogurt, water, butter and honey to 120°-130°. Add to dry ingredients; beat well. Beat on medium speed for 3 minutes. Stir in enough remaining all-purpose flour to form a soft dough.

2 Turn onto a floured surface; knead until smooth and elastic, about 6-8 minutes. Place in a greased bowl, turning once to grease top. Cover and let rise in a warm place until doubled, about 1 hour.

3 Punch dough down. Turn onto a lightly floured surface; divide into 2-in. balls. Roll each piece into a 10-in. rope. To form S-shaped rolls, coil each end of rope toward center in opposite directions. Place 3 in. apart on greased baking sheets. Cover and let rise until doubled, about 30 minutes.

4 Bake at 400° for 15 minutes or until golden brown. Brush tops with melted butter while warm. Remove from pans to wire racks to cool. **Yield:** 2 dozen.
—Carol Forcum, Marion, Illinois

Forming S-Shaped Rolls

Divide dough into 2-in. balls. Shape each ball into a 10-in. rope. On a greased baking sheet, coil each end in opposite directions until it touches the center and forms an S-shape.

Pretzels with Cheese Dip

Chewy and golden brown, these soft pretzels are the best by far. Pair them with a warm cheese dip for a special snack.

1 package (1/4 ounce) active dry yeast
1 cup warm water (110° to 115°)
2 tablespoons butter, softened
1 tablespoon sugar
1/2 teaspoon salt
2-3/4 cups all-purpose flour
4 cups water
2 tablespoons baking soda
Coarse salt
8 ounces process cheese (Velveeta), cubed
1 package (3 ounces) cream cheese, cubed
1 to 2 tablespoons milk
Prepared mustard

1 In a large mixing bowl, dissolve yeast in warm water. Add the butter, sugar, salt and 2 cups flour; beat until smooth. Stir in enough remaining flour to form a soft dough. Cover and let rise in a warm place for 20 minutes.

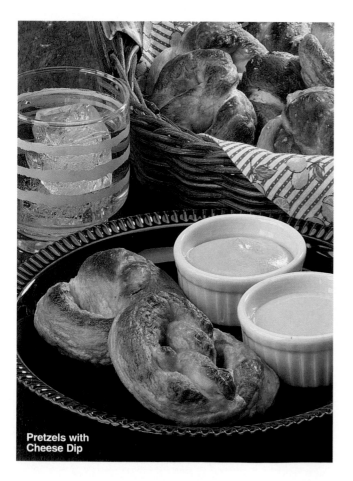

Pretzels with Cheese Dip

Forming Pretzels

1. Roll each piece of dough into a 15-in. rope and taper the ends. Shape rope into a circle with about 3 in. of each end overlapping.

2. Twist ends where they overlap.

3. Flip the twisted ends over the circle; place ends around edge and pinch under.

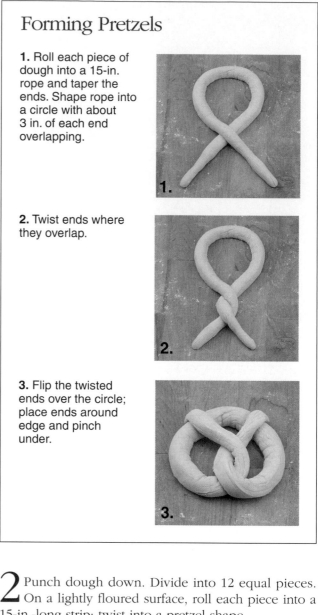

2 Punch dough down. Divide into 12 equal pieces. On a lightly floured surface, roll each piece into a 15-in.-long strip; twist into a pretzel shape.

3 In a large nonaluminum saucepan, bring water to a boil; add baking soda. Drop two pretzels into water; boil for 1 minute. Remove with a slotted spoon; drain. Place on a greased baking sheet; sprinkle with coarse salt. Repeat with remaining pretzels. Bake at 475° for 10-12 minutes. Remove from pan to wire rack.

4 For dip, combine cheeses in a microwave-safe bowl. Microwave on high for 2-3 minutes or until melted, stirring occasionally. Stir in milk. Serve pretzels with the cheese dip and mustard. **Yield:** 1 dozen pretzels and 1-1/4 cups dip.
—*Shannon Cooper*
South Gibson, Pennsylvania

2 Turn onto a lightly floured surface; knead gently 6-8 times. Roll out to 1/2-in. thickness; cut with a floured 2-1/2-in. biscuit cutter. Place on lightly greased baking sheets. Brush tops with butter. Bake at 450° for 10-12 minutes or until golden brown. Serve warm. **Yield:** 2-3 dozen. —*Nancy Parker, Seguin, Texas*

Editor's Note: No rising time is necessary before baking these biscuits. The dough can be rerolled. Warmed buttermilk will appear curdled.

Golden Carrot Buns

These rolls have a nice flavor...folks usually don't guess that carrots are one of the ingredients!

    4 cups sliced carrots
    2 eggs, beaten
    1 cup warm water (110° to 115°), *divided*
    2 packages (1/4 ounce *each*) active dry yeast
  3/4 cup vegetable oil
  1/2 cup sugar
    1 tablespoon molasses
    2 teaspoons salt
8-1/2 to 9 cups all-purpose flour

1 Place carrots in a saucepan and cover with water; cook until tender. Drain and cool slightly. Place carrots in a blender or food processor. Add eggs and 1/2 cup warm water; cover and process until smooth.

2 In a large mixing bowl, dissolve yeast in remaining water. Add the carrot mixture. Stir in the oil, sugar, molasses, salt and 5 cups flour; beat until smooth. Stir in enough remaining flour to form a soft dough.

3 Turn onto a floured surface; knead until smooth and elastic, about 6-8 minutes. Place in a greased bowl, turning once to grease top. Cover and let rise in a warm place until doubled, about 1 hour.

4 Punch dough down. Turn onto a floured surface; shape into 48 balls. Place 2 in. apart on greased baking sheets. Cover and let rise until almost doubled, about 1 hour.

5 Bake at 350° for 18-20 minutes or until browned. Remove from pans to wire racks to cool. **Yield:** 4 dozen. —*Katharine Groine, Altona, Manitoba*

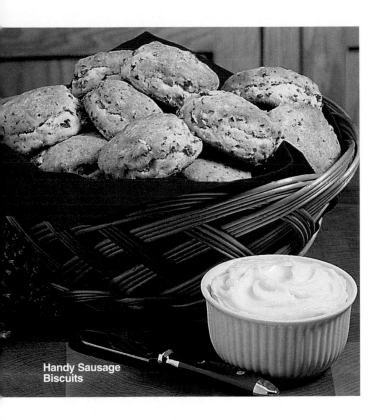

Handy Sausage Biscuits

Handy Sausage Biscuits

These are similar to old-fashioned biscuits made from scratch but even better, thanks to the addition of tasty browned sausage.

    3/4 pound bulk pork sausage
  2-2/3 cups all-purpose flour
      2 tablespoons sugar
  1-1/2 teaspoons baking powder
    1/2 teaspoon baking soda
    1/2 teaspoon salt
    1/2 cup shortening
      1 package (1/4 ounce) active dry yeast
    1/4 cup warm water (110° to 115°)
      1 cup warm buttermilk (110° to 115°)
Melted butter

1 In a skillet, cook sausage over medium heat until no longer pink; drain well and set aside. In a bowl, combine the flour, sugar, baking powder, baking soda and salt; cut in shortening until mixture is crumbly. Stir in sausage. In another bowl, dissolve yeast in warm water; add buttermilk. Stir into sausage mixture just until moistened.

Homemade Bagels

Instead of going to a bakery, head to the kitchen and surprise your family with homemade bagels. For variation and flavor, sprinkle the tops with cinnamon-sugar instead of sesame and poppy seeds.

1 teaspoon active dry yeast
1-1/4 cups warm milk (110° to 115°)
1/4 cup butter, softened
2 tablespoons sugar
1 teaspoon salt
1 egg yolk
3-3/4 to 4-1/4 cups all-purpose flour
2 quarts water
Sesame *or* poppy seeds, optional

1 In a large mixing bowl, dissolve yeast in warm milk. Add the butter, sugar, salt, egg yolk and 1 cup flour; beat until smooth. Stir in enough remaining flour to form a soft dough.

2 Turn onto a floured surface; knead until smooth and elastic, about 6-8 minutes. Place in a greased bowl, turning once to grease top. Cover and let rise in a warm place until doubled, about 1 hour.

3 Punch dough down. Turn onto a lightly floured surface; divide into 12 pieces. Shape each piece into a ball. Push thumb through the center to form a 1-in. hole. Stretch and shape dough to form an even ring. Place on a floured surface. Cover and let rest for 10 minutes; flatten rings slightly.

4 In a large nonaluminum saucepan, bring water to a boil. Drop bagels, one at a time, into boiling water. Cook for 45 seconds; turn and cook 45 seconds longer. Remove with a slotted spoon; drain well on paper towels.

5 Sprinkle with sesame or poppy seeds if desired. Place 2 in. apart on greased baking sheets. Bake at 400° for 20-25 minutes or until golden brown. Remove from pans to wire racks to cool. **Yield:** 1 dozen.
　　　　　—*Rebecca Phillips, Burlington, Connecticut*

Homemade Bagels

Shaping Bagels

1. Shape dough into balls. Push your thumb through the center of the dough, forming a 1-in. hole.

1.

2. Stretch and shape dough to form an even ring.

2.

Caraway Rye Rolls

These tender yeast rolls require no shaping. Simply spoon the batter into muffin cups and bake.

- **2 packages (1/4 ounce *each*) active dry yeast**
- **1/2 cup warm water (110° to 115°)**
- **2 cups warm small-curd cottage cheese (110° to 115°)**
- **1/2 cup sugar**
- **2 eggs**
- **2 tablespoons caraway seeds**
- **2 teaspoons salt**
- **1/2 teaspoon baking soda**
- **1 cup rye flour**
- **3 to 4 cups all-purpose flour**

1 In a large mixing bowl, dissolve yeast in warm water. Add the cottage cheese, sugar, eggs, caraway seeds, salt, baking soda, rye flour and 1 cup all-purpose flour; mix well. Stir in enough remaining all-purpose flour to form a sticky batter. Do not knead. Cover and let rise in a warm place until doubled, about 1 hour.

2 Stir batter down. Spoon into well-greased muffin cups. Cover and let rise until doubled, about 35 minutes. Bake at 350° for 18-20 minutes or until golden brown. Cool for 1 minute before removing from pans to wire racks. **Yield:** 2 dozen. —*Dot Christiansen Bettendorf, Iowa*

2 Turn onto a floured surface; knead until smooth and elastic, about 6-8 minutes. Place in a greased bowl, turning once to grease top. Cover and let rise in a warm place until doubled, about 1-1/2 hours.

3 Punch dough down. Turn onto a lightly floured surface; divide into four pieces. Cover three pieces with plastic wrap. Divide remaining piece into 12 balls. To form knots, roll each ball into a 10-in. rope; tie into a knot and pinch ends together. Repeat with remaining dough. Place rolls on greased baking sheets; brush with butter. Cover and let rise until doubled, about 20-30 minutes.

4 To serve immediately, bake at 375° for 15-18 minutes. To freeze for later use, partially bake at 300° for 15 minutes. Remove from pans to wire racks to cool; freeze. Reheat frozen rolls at 375° for 12-15 minutes or until browned. **Yield:** 4 dozen. —*Jayne Duce Raymond, Alberta*

Forming Knot-Shaped Rolls

Divide dough into 3-in. balls. Roll each ball into a 10-in. rope; tie into a knot. Tuck and pinch ends under.

Freeze-and-Bake Knots

Almost any occasion's right for these handy rolls. You can keep them in the freezer for Sunday meals and for company...they never fail to taste fresh.

- **2 packages (1/4 ounce *each*) active dry yeast**
- **1-1/2 cups warm water (110° to 115°)**
- **2 teaspoons plus 1/2 cup sugar, *divided***
- **1-1/2 cups warm milk (110° to 115°)**
- **1/4 cup vegetable oil**
- **4 teaspoons salt**
- **7-1/2 to 8-1/2 cups all-purpose flour**

Melted butter

1 In a large mixing bowl, dissolve yeast in warm water. Add 2 teaspoons sugar; let stand for 5 minutes. Add the milk, oil, salt, remaining sugar and 2 cups flour; beat until smooth. Stir in enough remaining flour to form a stiff dough.

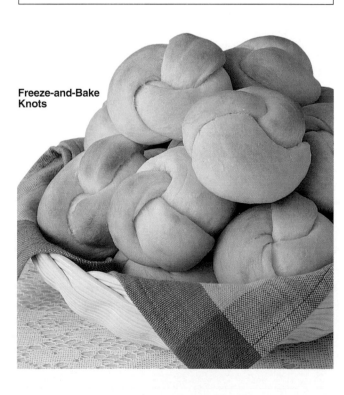

Freeze-and-Bake Knots

Sourdough breads

secrets for successful sourdough starters

- Starters contain acid that can react with metal, so only prepare sourdough starters in nonmetallic bowls. Be sure to use a large bowl since the starter will significantly increase in volume and may overflow a small bowl.

- If you don't use the starter immediately, stir it and transfer it to a clean glass, ceramic or plastic container. Cover loosely and store in the refrigerator. Always bring the starter to room temperature before using. This will take 2 to 12 hours. The longer it stands at room temperature, the more tangy it will be.

- To use, stir the starter and remove the desired amount. Bring to room temperature if refrigerated, and use in the recipe as directed. Replenish the starter with equal amounts of flour and water to restore the volume; stir. (For example, if 1/2 cup starter was removed for a recipe, combine 1/2 cup all-purpose flour and 1/2 cup warm water. Stir into starter.) Let the replenished starter stand in a warm place (80° to 90°) for 12 to 24 hours or until light and bubbly. Stir starter; cover loosely and refrigerate.

- If you don't use any starter within 2 weeks, you will need to nourish it to keep it active. To nourish, remove half of the starter and share with a friend or discard. Transfer remaining starter to a large nonmetallic bowl. Add equal parts of all-purpose flour and warm water. Let stand in a warm place (80° to 90°) for 12 to 24 hours or until light and bubbly. Stir starter and transfer to a clean storage container; cover loosely and refrigerate.

- If used and replenished or nourished at least once every 2 weeks, the starter should remain active indefinitely.

- Discard a starter if it develops an offensive odor, changes color or becomes slimy or stringy, which means it's spoiled. Sterilize the storage container before using it for a new batch of starter.

Sourdough Starter

Sourdough breads have a unique tangy flavor, which is achieved from the use of a yeast starter. A portion of the starter is used to make bread, and the remaining starter is replenished to use another day.

1 package (1/4 ounce) active dry yeast
2 cups warm water (110° to 115°)
2 cups all-purpose flour

1 In a 4-qt. nonmetallic bowl, dissolve yeast in warm water; let stand for 5 minutes. Add flour; stir until smooth. Cover loosely with a clean towel. Let stand in a warm place (80°-90°) to ferment for 48 hours; stir several times daily (the mixture will become bubbly and rise, have a "yeasty" sour aroma and a transparent yellow liquid will form on the top).

2 Use starter for your favorite sourdough recipes. The starter will keep in the refrigerator for up to 2 weeks. Use and replenish or nourish at least once every 2 weeks. Refer to the Secrets for Successful Sourdough Starters at left. **Yield:** about 3 cups.
— *Delila George, Junction City, Oregon*

Sourdough French Bread

These loaves rival any found in stores and can be made with relative ease.

1 package (1/4 ounce) active dry yeast
1-3/4 cups warm water (110° to 115°)
4-1/4 cups all-purpose flour
1/4 cup Sourdough Starter (recipe above)
2 tablespoons vegetable oil
2 tablespoons sugar
2 teaspoons salt
CORNSTARCH WASH:
1-1/2 teaspoons cornstarch
1/2 cup water

1 In a large mixing bowl, dissolve yeast in warm water. Add the flour, Sourdough Starter, oil, sugar and salt; mix well. Turn onto a floured surface; knead gently 20-30 times (dough will be slightly sticky). Place in a greased bowl, turning once to grease top. Cover and let rise in a warm place until doubled, about 1 to 1-1/2 hours.

2 Punch dough down. Turn onto a lightly floured surface; divide in half. Roll each portion into a 12-in. x 8-in. rectangle. Roll up jelly-roll style, starting with a

Sourdough French Bread and Honey Wheat Sourdough Bread

long side; pinch ends to seal. Place seam side down on two greased baking sheets; tuck ends under. Cover and let rise until doubled, about 30 minutes.

3 With a sharp knife, make four shallow diagonal slashes across the top of each loaf. In a small saucepan, combine cornstarch and water until smooth. Cook and stir over medium heat until thickened. Brush some over loaves. Bake at 400° for 15 minutes. Brush loaves with the remaining cornstarch wash. Bake 5-10 minutes longer or until lightly browned. Remove from pans to wire racks to cool. **Yield:** 2 loaves.

—Delila George, Junction City, Oregon

Honey Wheat Sourdough Bread

Honey adds a slightly sweet taste to this bread, which nicely complements the tangy sourdough.

- **1 tablespoon active dry yeast**
- **1 cup warm milk (110° to 115°)**
- **3 tablespoons butter, softened**
- **2 tablespoons honey**
- **2 tablespoons molasses**
- **2 cups Sourdough Starter (recipe on opposite page)**
- **3 tablespoons wheat germ**
- **1 tablespoon sugar**
- **1 teaspoon baking soda**
- **1 teaspoon salt**
- **1 cup whole wheat flour**
- **3-1/4 to 3-3/4 cups all-purpose flour**
- **Vegetable oil**

1 In a large mixing bowl, dissolve yeast in warm milk. Add the butter, honey, molasses, Sourdough Starter, wheat germ, sugar, baking soda, salt, whole wheat flour and 2 cups all-purpose flour; beat until smooth. Stir in enough remaining all-purpose flour to form a soft dough.

2 Turn onto a floured surface; knead until smooth and elastic, about 6-8 minutes. Place in a greased bowl, turning once to grease top. Cover and let rise in a warm place until doubled, about 1 hour.

3 Punch dough down. Turn onto a lightly floured surface; divide in half. Shape each portion into a loaf. Place in two greased 8-in. x 4-in. x 2-in. loaf pans. Cover and let rise until doubled, about 1 hour.

4 Brush loaves with oil. Bake at 375° for 25-30 minutes or until browned. Remove from pans to wire racks to cool. **Yield:** 2 loaves. *—Evelyn Newlands Sun Lakes, Arizona*

Sourdough Ham Crescent Rolls

Sourdough Ham Crescent Rolls

These eye-appealing crescent rolls are loaded with ham and hard-cooked eggs. They're a terrific main course for a ladies' luncheon.

  2 packages (1/4 ounce *each*) active dry yeast
1/2 cup warm water (110° to 115°)
  1 cup warm milk (110° to 115°)
  1 cup Sourdough Starter (recipe on page 318)
1/2 cup vegetable oil
1/4 cup sugar
  2 teaspoons salt
  5 to 5-1/2 cups all-purpose flour
FILLING:
  2 cups finely chopped fully cooked ham
  2 hard-cooked eggs, chopped
  1 small onion, chopped
**1/2 cup condensed cream of mushroom soup,
    undiluted**

1 In a large mixing bowl, dissolve yeast in warm water. Add the milk, Sourdough Starter, oil, sugar, salt and 2 cups flour; beat until smooth. Stir in enough remaining flour to form a medium-stiff dough.

2 Turn onto a floured surface; knead until smooth and elastic, about 6-8 minutes. Place in a greased bowl, turning once to grease top. Cover and let rise in a warm place until doubled, about 1 hour.

3 Punch dough down. Turn onto a lightly floured surface; divide into four pieces. Roll each piece into a

12-in. circle; cut each into eight wedges. Combine the filling ingredients; spread over wedges. Roll up from the wide end and place with pointed side down 2 in. apart on greased baking sheets. Curve ends to form a crescent shape. Cover and let rise until doubled, about 45 minutes.

4 Bake at 375° for 12-15 minutes or until golden brown. Remove from pans to wire racks. Serve warm. Refrigerate leftovers. **Yield:** 32 rolls.   *—Jean Graf
Albany, Oregon*

Country Crust Sourdough Bread

Brushing the top of these baked loaves with melted butter gives them a beautiful golden color.

  2 packages (1/4 ounce *each*) active dry yeast
1-1/4 cups warm water (110° to 115°)
  1 cup Sourdough Starter (recipe on page 318)
  2 eggs
1/4 cup sugar
1/4 cup vegetable oil
  1 teaspoon salt
  6 to 6-1/2 cups all-purpose flour
Melted butter

1 In a large mixing bowl, dissolve yeast in warm water. Add the Sourdough Starter, eggs, sugar, oil, salt and 3 cups flour; beat until smooth. Stir in enough remaining flour to form a soft dough.

2 Turn onto a floured surface; knead until smooth and elastic, about 6-8 minutes. Place in a greased bowl, turning once to grease top. Cover and let rise in a warm place until doubled, about 1 hour.

3 Punch dough down. Turn onto a lightly floured surface; divide in half. Shape each portion into a loaf. Place in two greased 8-in. x 4-in. x 2-in. loaf pans. Cover and let rise until doubled, about 45 minutes.

4 Bake at 375° for 30-35 minutes or until golden brown. Remove from pans to wire racks. Brush with butter. Cool. **Yield:** 2 loaves.   *—Beverley Whaley
Camano Island, Washington*

Bread Machine recipes

secrets for SUCCESS with bread machines

- Before beginning, carefully read your bread machine owner's manual.

- All liquid ingredients should be at room temperature (70° to 80°). This includes water, milk, yogurt, juice, cottage cheese, eggs and applesauce.

- Measure ingredients accurately, using the measuring tools and techniques suggested on pages 8 and 9 before adding to your machine. Then add in the order suggested by your bread machine manufacturer.

- For best results, use bread flour.

- While either active dry yeast or bread machine yeast can be used in bread machines, bread machine yeast is a little finer, which allows for better dispersion during mixing and kneading. For 1 cup of flour, it is generally recommended to use 3/4 teaspoon of active dry yeast or 1/2 teaspoon of bread machine yeast.

- Check dough after 5 minutes of mixing. The dough should feel smooth, soft and slightly tacky. If it's moist or sticky, add 1 tablespoon of flour and check again after a few more minutes of mixing. If it's dry and crumbly, add 1 tablespoon of liquid, then check again.

- Recipes containing eggs, milk, sour cream, cottage cheese and other dairy or perishable products should be baked immediately and not placed on a "timed-bake" cycle.

Golden Honey Pan Rolls

Using your bread machine to make the dough saves about 2 hours compared to the traditional method. The rich buttery taste of these honey-glazed rolls will be popular with your family and friends.

1 cup warm milk (70° to 80°)
1 egg
1 egg yolk
1/2 cup vegetable oil
2 tablespoons honey
1-1/2 teaspoons salt
3-1/2 cups bread flour
2-1/4 teaspoons active dry yeast
GLAZE:
1/3 cup sugar
2 tablespoons butter, melted
1 tablespoon honey
1 egg white
Additional honey, optional

1 In bread machine pan, place the first eight ingredients in order suggested by manufacturer. Select dough setting (check dough after 5 minutes of mixing; add 1 to 2 tablespoons of water or flour if needed).

2 When cycle is completed, turn dough onto a lightly floured surface. Cover and let rest for 15 minutes. Divide into 24 pieces; shape each piece into a ball. Place 12 balls each in two greased 9-in. square baking pans. Cover and let rise in a warm place until doubled, about 30 minutes.

3 For glaze, combine sugar, butter, honey and egg white; drizzle over dough. Bake at 350° for 20-25 minutes or until golden brown. Brush with additional honey if desired. **Yield:** 2 dozen. —*Sara Wing Philadelphia, Pennsylvania*

Editor's Note: If your bread machine has a time-delay feature, we recommend you do not use it for this recipe.

Golden Honey
Pan Rolls

problem-Solving pointers for Bread Machines

If this happens when using your bread machine:	This could be the reason:
Bread is lumpy or dough appears dry.	Dough is too dry. Add a little more water during the kneading cycle.
Dough is sticky and won't form a ball or appears too wet.	Dough is too moist. Add a little more flour during the kneading cycle.
Bread has a mushroom top.	Water was too warm.
Bread has an underbaked, gummy center.	Dough was too moist.
Top is sunken.	Too much yeast or liquid and/or not enough flour was used.
Bread rose too high or overflowed pan.	Next time, reduce the amount of yeast slightly and remember to add the salt.

Home-Style White Bread

- 2 tablespoons sugar
- 2 tablespoons nonfat dry milk powder
- 3 cups bread flour
- 2 teaspoons active dry yeast

In bread machine pan, place all ingredients in order suggested by manufacturer. Select basic bread setting. Choose crust color and loaf size if available. Bake according to bread machine directions (check dough after 5 minutes of mixing; add 1 to 2 tablespoons of water or flour if needed). **Yield:** 1 loaf (about 1-1/2 pounds). —*Yvonna Nave, Lyons, Kansas*

Home-Style White Bread

Serve this basic white bread with butter and jam. Or use slices to assemble your favorite sandwiches.

- 1 cup water (70° to 80°)
- 2 tablespoons butter, softened
- 1 teaspoon salt

2 When cycle is completed, turn dough onto a lightly floured surface. Cover and let rest for 15 minutes. Roll or pat to 1/2-in. thickness. Cut with a floured 2-1/2-in. biscuit cutter. Place in a greased 15-in. x 10-in. x 1-in. baking pan. Cover and let rise in a warm place until almost doubled, about 40 minutes.

3 Bake at 375° for 10-15 minutes or until golden brown. For glaze, combine confectioners' sugar and enough orange juice to achieve a drizzling consistency; drizzle over warm biscuits. Sprinkle with chopped cranberries if desired. **Yield:** about 1-1/2 dozen.
—Debra Fulenwider, Colfax, California

Editor's Note: If your bread machine has a time-delay feature, we recommend you do not use it for this recipe.

Cranberry Biscuits

Cranberry Biscuits

These yummy breakfast biscuits combine the texture and nutrition of potato rolls and the taste of orange-cranberry bread.

- 1-2/3 cups warm milk (70° to 80°)
- 2 eggs
- 3 tablespoons butter, softened
- 3/4 cup mashed potato flakes
- 1/4 cup sugar
- 2 teaspoons salt
- 1-1/4 teaspoons ground cinnamon
- 1 teaspoon grated orange peel
- 4 cups bread flour
- 1 tablespoon active dry yeast
- 1 cup dried cranberries
- ORANGE GLAZE:
- 1 cup confectioners' sugar
- 2 to 3 tablespoons orange juice
- 3 tablespoons chopped dried cranberries, optional

1 In bread machine pan, place the first 10 ingredients in order suggested by manufacturer. Select dough setting (check dough after 5 minutes of mixing; add 1 to 2 tablespoons of water or flour if needed). Just before the final kneading (your machine may audibly signal this), add cranberries.

Herbed Tomato Bread

Slices of this moist bread are terrific when eaten alone, with Garlic Chive Spread or when used to make grilled cheese sandwiches.

- 1/2 cup plus 2 tablespoons warm milk (70° to 80°)
- 1 can (6 ounces) tomato paste
- 1 egg
- 2 tablespoons olive oil
- 1/2 teaspoon salt
- 2 tablespoons minced fresh parsley
- 1 tablespoon sugar
- 2 teaspoons dried minced onion
- 1/2 teaspoon garlic powder
- 1/2 teaspoon dried tarragon
- 3 cups bread flour
- 2-1/4 teaspoons active dry yeast
- GARLIC CHIVE SPREAD:
- 1/2 cup butter, softened
- 1 tablespoon minced chives
- 1 garlic clove, minced

In bread machine pan, place the first 12 ingredients in order suggested by manufacturer. Select basic bread setting. Choose crust color and loaf size if available. Bake according to bread machine directions (check dough after 5 minutes of mixing; add 1 to 2 tablespoons of water or flour if needed). In a small bowl, combine the spread ingredients. Serve with bread. **Yield:** 1 loaf (1-1/2 pounds) and 1/2 cup spread.
—Sherry Letson, Trinity, Alabama

Editor's Note: If your bread machine has a time-delay feature, we recommend you do not use it for this recipe.

Work is the yeast that raises the dough.

converting recipes for use in bread machines

Converting a traditional yeast bread recipe for the bread machine will require some experimentation on your part. We've included some pointers to help get you started.

First, determine the size of your bread machine. Look at the recipes that came with your bread machine and note the amount of flour and liquid called for in most of those recipes. The chart below gives a general guideline for the ratio of ingredients for bread machines yielding 1 pound, 1-1/2 pound and 2 pound loaves.

- Flour includes dry ingredients such as any type of flour, oats, cereal and cornmeal. Liquid includes milk, water, yogurt, sour cream, applesauce, eggs (1/4 cup liquid per egg), cottage cheese, etc. Sugar includes other sweeteners such as honey, molasses or brown sugar. Fat includes shortening, butter, margarine and oil.

- It's best to start with a bread recipe you are familiar with and have successfully made. Once you've mastered those familiar recipes, look for other bread recipes that use the amount of flour needed for your bread machine. Or, look for a recipe that makes two loaves and can be easily divided in half. Divide all the ingredients in half. When recipes give a range of flour, always start with the lower amount.

- Avoid sourdough recipes, recipes that require refrigerating the dough or recipes with a high ratio of fat. These types of recipes won't be successful in the bread machine.

- For breads with topping or fillings as well as ones that require special shapes or rolls—just mix, knead and proof the dough in the bread machine. Punch the dough down, fill and/or shape. Then follow the original recipe to finish the bread.

- Add ingredients to the bread pan in the order your manufacturer recommends. Check the dough after 5 minutes of mixing. Add 1 to 2 tablespoons of flour or liquid if necessary.

- Make notes on your recipe for reference. If it wasn't quite right, make an adjustment in one ingredient and try again.

Bread machine size	Flour by cups	Liquid by cup	Active dry yeast by teaspoons	Sugar by tablespoons	Salt by teaspoons	Fat by teaspoons
1 pound	2 to 2-1/2	2/3	1-1/2	2	1	4
1-1/2 pounds	3 to 3-1/2	1	2-1/2	3	1-1/2	6
2 pounds	4 to 4-1/2	1-1/3	3	4	2	8

Cranberry Nut Bagels

Do you love homemade bagels but not the time commitment? This convenient recipe lets you prepare those delicious baked goods in a lot less time.

     1 cup plus 2 tablespoons water (70° to 80°)
     2 tablespoons sugar
     1 teaspoon salt
 1-1/4 teaspoons ground cinnamon
   1/4 cup quick-cooking oats
     3 cups bread flour
 2-1/2 teaspoons active dry yeast
   3/4 cup dried cranberries
   1/4 cup chopped pecans
     2 quarts water
TOPPING:
     2 tablespoons brown sugar
     1 teaspoon ground cinnamon

1 In bread machine pan, place the first seven ingredients in order suggested by manufacturer. Select dough setting (check dough after 5 minutes of mixing; add 1 to 2 tablespoons of water or flour if needed). Just before the final kneading (your machine may audibly signal this), add the cranberries and pecans.

2 When cycle is completed, turn dough onto a lightly floured surface. Cover and let rest for 15 minutes. Divide into eight balls. Push thumb through the center of each ball to form a 1-in. hole. Stretch and shape dough to form an even ring. Place on a floured surface. Cover and let rest for 10 minutes; flatten rings slightly.

3 In a large nonaluminum saucepan, bring water to a boil. Drop rings, one at a time, into boiling water. Cook for 45 seconds; turn and cook 45 seconds longer. Remove with a slotted spoon; drain well on paper towels.

4 Combine brown sugar and cinnamon; sprinkle over bagels. Place 2 in. apart on greased baking sheets. Bake at 375° for 20-25 minutes or until golden brown. Remove from pan to a wire rack to cool. **Yield:** 8 bagels.   —*John Russell, Greentown, Indiana*

Pumpernickel Caraway Bread

This rich dark bread has an old-fashioned homemade taste that's oh-so-satisfying. Made with molasses and caraway seeds, it's moist and flavorful.

   3/4 cup water (70° to 80°)
     2 tablespoons molasses
 4-1/2 teaspoons butter
     1 teaspoon salt
     1 cup bread flour
   2/3 cup rye flour
   1/3 cup whole wheat flour
     2 tablespoons cornmeal
     5 teaspoons baking cocoa
 4-1/2 teaspoons sugar
     3 teaspoons nonfat dry milk powder
     1 teaspoon caraway seeds
   1/4 teaspoon instant coffee granules
 1-1/2 teaspoons active dry yeast

In bread machine pan, place all ingredients in order suggested by manufacturer. Select basic bread setting. Choose crust color and loaf size if available. Bake according to bread machine directions (check dough after 5 minutes of mixing; add 1 to 2 tablespoons of water or flour if needed). **Yield:** 1 loaf (1 pound).

—*Lorraine Darocha, Berkshire, Massachusetts*

Pumpernickel Caraway Bread

Sour Cream Lemon Bread

Sour Cream Lemon Bread

Serve slices of this light and tender bread with a creamy lemon spread for an early-morning treat or late-night snack that's simply dreamy.

- 1/4 cup sour cream
- 2 tablespoons lemon juice
- 2 to 3 tablespoons warm milk (70° to 80°)
- 2 tablespoons butter, softened
- 1 egg
- 2 teaspoons grated lemon peel
- 2 tablespoons sugar
- 1 teaspoon salt
- 1/4 teaspoon baking soda
- 2 cups bread flour
- 1-1/2 teaspoons active dry yeast

LEMON SPREAD:
- 1 package (3 ounces) cream cheese, softened
- 1/4 cup confectioners' sugar
- 1 tablespoon lemon juice
- 1 teaspoon grated lemon peel

1 In a measuring cup, combine sour cream and lemon juice. Add enough warm milk to measure 1/2 cup. In bread machine pan, place the sour cream mixture, butter, egg, lemon peel, sugar, salt, baking soda, flour and yeast in order suggested by manufacturer. Select sweet bread setting. Choose crust color and loaf size if available. Bake according to bread machine directions (check dough after 5 minutes of mixing; add 1 to 2 tablespoons of water or flour if needed).

2 In a small mixing bowl, combine the spread ingredients; beat until smooth. Serve with bread. Store in the refrigerator. **Yield:** 1 loaf (1 pound) and about 1/2 cup spread. *—Barbara Strickler, Syracuse, Indiana*

Editor's Note: If your bread machine has a time-delay feature, we recommend you do not use it for this recipe. If your bread machine does not have a sweet bread setting, follow the manufacturer's directions using the basic setting.

Jalapeno Bread

Ordinary sandwiches become extraordinary when made with slices of this pretty corn-flecked loaf. For a milder chili taste, use green chilies in place of the jalapenos.

- 1/2 cup water (70° to 80°)
- 1 tablespoon butter, softened
- 1 tablespoon sugar
- 1 teaspoon salt
- 1/2 cup whole kernel corn
- 2 tablespoons chopped jalapenos *or* green chilies
- 1 teaspoon chopped fresh cilantro
- 2 cups bread flour
- 1/3 cup cornmeal
- 1-1/2 teaspoons active dry yeast

In bread machine pan, place all ingredients in order suggested by manufacturer. Select basic bread setting. Choose crust color and loaf size if available. Bake according to bread machine directions (check dough after 5 minutes of mixing; add 1 to 2 tablespoons of water or flour if needed). **Yield:** 1 loaf (1 pound).
—Lola Gangwer, Burgoon, Ohio

Editor's Note: If your bread machine has a time-delay feature, we recommend you do not use it for this recipe.

Three-Seed Bread

This hearty whole wheat bread is chock-full of sunflower kernels and poppy and sesame seeds. It rivals any gourmet bakery bread.

- 2/3 cup plus 2 teaspoons water (70° to 80°)
- 1 tablespoon butter, softened

1 tablespoon honey
2 tablespoons sesame seeds
2 tablespoons sunflower kernels
2 tablespoons poppy seeds
3/4 teaspoon salt
1 cup bread flour
1 cup whole wheat flour
3 tablespoons nonfat dry milk powder
2 teaspoons active dry yeast

In bread machine pan, place all ingredients in order suggested by manufacturer. Select basic bread setting. Choose crust color and loaf size if available. Bake according to bread machine directions (check dough after 5 minutes of mixing; add 1 to 2 tablespoons of water or flour if needed). **Yield:** 1 loaf (about 1 pound).

—*Melissa Vannoy, Childress, Texas*

Apricot Nutmeg Bread

Slices of this fruity bread are good for breakfast when toasted and spread with strawberry jam. Nutmeg complements the apricot flavor in this golden soft-textured loaf.

1 cup water (70° to 80°)
3 tablespoons vegetable oil
1 teaspoon lemon juice
2 tablespoons plus 1-1/2 teaspoons brown sugar
1 teaspoon salt
2-1/4 teaspoons active dry yeast
3 cups bread flour
1 tablespoon plus 1-1/2 teaspoons nonfat dry milk powder
1 cup chopped dried apricots
3/4 teaspoon ground nutmeg

1 In bread machine pan, place the first eight ingredients in order suggested by manufacturer. Select sweet bread cycle. Choose medium crust color and loaf size if available. Bake according to bread machine directions (after 5 minutes of mixing, check dough; add 1 to 2 tablespoons of water or flour if needed).

oven temperatures for baking bread

The oven temperature for bread baking varies according to the ingredients used to make the bread.

- Generally, leaner breads (made with flour, water and yeast) are baked at 400° to 425°. Richer breads (made with more fat and eggs) are baked at lower temperatures.

- Breads made with less than 1/2 cup sugar are generally baked at 375° and breads with more are baked at 350°.

- A loaf of bread can bake from 25 to 45 minutes. The baking time depends on the size and shape of the loaf and the temperature of the oven.

2 Just before the final kneading (your machine may audibly signal this), add apricots and nutmeg. **Yield:** 1 loaf (1-1/2 pounds).

—*Anna Kinney*
Farmington, New Mexico

Editor's Note: If your bread machine does not have a sweet bread setting, follow the manufacturer's directions using the basic setting.

Apricot Nutmeg Bread

Beckon your brood with Sweet Yeast Breads

If it's hard to entice your clan out of bed early in the morning, head to the kitchen and pop some sweet breads or rolls into the oven! Before long, sleepyheads will clamor to the kitchen for such mouth-watering goodies as Apple Ladder Loaf (p. 335) and Sticky Buns (p. 346).

the basics of Sweet Yeast Breads

$\mathscr{S}$weet yeast breads fall into two basic categories: sweet loaves and sweet rolls. The dough can be made by hand or in a bread machine.

- Sweet breads include fruit-filled breads and a variety of coffee cakes.

- Sweet rolls refer to fruit-filled rolls, sticky buns, cinnamon rolls, doughnuts, kolachkes and individual Danishes.

For general information on baking yeast breads (including success with bread machines), refer to the Savory Yeast Breads chapter beginning on page 280.

vanilla glaze recipe

Add a sweet finishing touch to coffee cakes, sweet rolls and many other breads with a flavorful Vanilla Glaze. Follow this easy recipe:

For 1/2 cup glaze, combine 1 cup confectioners' sugar and 1/4 teaspoon vanilla extract in a bowl. Add 1 to 2 tablespoons milk to achieve desired consistency.

Sweet breads & Coffee cakes

Pineapple Cheese Braids

Folks will be pleasantly surprised by this bread's pineapple filling. If you're in a hurry, you can use canned pie filling.

  2 packages (1/4 ounce *each*) active dry yeast
  1 cup warm water (110° to 115°)
1/2 cup butter, softened
  5 tablespoons sugar
  2 eggs
1/4 teaspoon salt
4-1/4 to 4-1/2 cups all-purpose flour
PINEAPPLE FILLING:
  1 can (8 ounces) crushed pineapple, undrained
1/2 cup sugar
  3 tablespoons cornstarch
CREAM CHEESE FILLING:
  2 packages (8 ounces *each*) cream cheese, softened
1/3 cup sugar
  1 tablespoon lemon juice
1/2 teaspoon vanilla extract
ICING (optional):
  1 cup confectioners' sugar
  2 to 3 tablespoons milk

1 In a large mixing bowl, dissolve yeast in warm water. Add the butter, sugar, eggs, salt and 2 cups flour; beat on low speed for 3 minutes. Stir in enough remaining flour to form a soft dough.

2 Turn onto a floured surface; knead until smooth and elastic, about 6-8 minutes. Place in a greased bowl, turning once to grease top. Cover and let rise in a warm place until doubled, about 45 minutes.

3 For pineapple filling, combine the pineapple, sugar and cornstarch in a small saucepan. Bring to a boil. Reduce heat; cook and stir until thickened. Cool. In a mixing bowl, combine the cream cheese filling ingredients; mix well.

4 Punch dough down. Turn onto a lightly floured surface; divide in half. Roll each portion into a 15-in. x 9-in. rectangle. Place on greased baking sheets. Spread the cream cheese filling lengthwise down the center third of each rectangle. Spread the pineapple filling on top.

5 On each long side, cut 1-in.-wide strips about 3 in. into center. Starting at one end, fold alternating strips at an angle across filling; seal ends. Cover and let rise for 20 minutes.

6 Bake at 350° for 25-30 minutes or until golden brown. Remove from pans to wire racks to cool. If desired, combine icing ingredients and drizzle over braids. Store in the refrigerator. **Yield:** 2 loaves.
—*Shirley Kensinger, Roaring Spring, Pennsylvania*

Braiding a Filled Bread

1. Roll dough into a rectangle; place on a greased baking sheet. Spread filling down center of rectangle. On each long side, cut 1-in.-wide strips, about 1/2 in. from the filling.

2. Starting at one end, fold alternating strips at an angle across filling. Seal ends.

Pineapple Cheese Braids

Fruited Swedish Tea Ring

These tasty "wreaths" are wonderful gifts from the kitchen at Christmastime.

>   1 cup chopped candied fruit
> 1/2 cup raisins
> 2/3 cup packed brown sugar
> 1/4 cup butter, melted
>   1 teaspoon grated orange peel
> 1/2 teaspoon ground cardamom

DOUGH:

>   2 packages (1/4 ounce *each*)
>   active dry yeast
> 1/3 cup sugar, *divided*
> 1-1/4 cups warm water (110° to 115°), *divided*
>   2 eggs
> 1/4 cup shortening
> 1-1/2 teaspoons salt
> 4-1/4 to 4-3/4 cups all-purpose flour

ICING:

>   1 cup confectioners' sugar
>   1 tablespoon lemon juice
>   1 tablespoon milk

Candied cherries, optional

1 In a bowl, combine the first six ingredients. Cover and refrigerate. In a small bowl, dissolve yeast and 1 teaspoon sugar in 1/4 cup warm water; let stand for 5 minutes. In a large mixing bowl, stir remaining water and sugar until dissolved. Add the yeast mixture, eggs, shortening, salt and 3 cups flour; beat until smooth. Stir in enough remaining flour to form a soft dough.

Fruited Swedish Tea Ring

2 Turn onto a floured surface; knead until smooth and elastic, about 6-8 minutes. Place in a greased bowl, turning once to grease top. Cover and let rise in a warm place until doubled, about 1 hour.

3 Punch dough down. Turn onto a lightly floured surface; divide in half. Roll each portion into a 16-in. x 9-in. rectangle. Sprinkle fruit mixture over each rectangle to within 1/2 in. of edges.

4 Roll up jelly-roll style, starting with a long side; pinch seam to seal. Place seam side down on greased baking sheets; pinch ends together to form a ring. With scissors, cut from outside edge two-thirds of

Shaping a Coffee Cake Ring

1. Roll into a rectangle. Spread filling evenly over dough to within 1/2 in. of edges. Roll up jelly-roll style, starting with a long side; pinch seam to seal.

2. Place seam side down on greased baking sheets; pinch ends together to form a ring.

3. With scissors, cut from outside edge to two-thirds of the way toward center of ring at 1-in. intervals.

4. Separate the cut pieces slightly, twisting each individually to allow filling to show.

the way toward center of ring at 1-in. intervals. Separate strips slightly; twist to allow filling to show. Cover and let rise until doubled, about 1 hour.

5 Bake at 350° for 20-25 minutes or until golden brown. Cool on wire racks for 20 minutes. For icing, combine the confectioners' sugar, lemon juice and milk; drizzle over warm rings. Decorate with cherries if desired. **Yield:** 2 tea rings. —*Betty Murray*
Hamiota, Manitoba

Shaping a Pan Bread

To easily shape a round loaf of bread, place ball of dough in a greased 9-in. round baking pan. Flatten into a 6- or 7-in. circle.

Hawaiian Sweet Bread

Pineapple juice lends to the slightly sweet flavor of this delicious bread. The recipe makes three loaves, so you can keep one for yourself and offer the others as gifts from the kitchen.

    7 to 7-1/2 cups all-purpose flour
 3/4 cup mashed potato flakes
 2/3 cup sugar
    2 packages (1/4 ounce *each*) active dry yeast
    1 teaspoon salt
 1/2 teaspoon ground ginger
    1 cup milk
 1/2 cup water
 1/2 cup butter, softened
    1 cup pineapple juice
    3 eggs
    2 teaspoons vanilla extract

1 In a mixing bowl, combine 3 cups flour, potato flakes, sugar, yeast, salt and ginger. In a saucepan, heat the milk, water, butter and pineapple juice to 120°-130°. Add to dry ingredients; beat just until moistened. Beat in eggs until smooth. Beat in vanilla. Stir in enough remaining flour to form a soft dough.

2 Turn onto a floured surface; knead until smooth and elastic, about 6-8 minutes. Place in a greased bowl,

turning once to grease top. Cover and let rise in a warm place until doubled, about 1 hour.

3 Punch dough down. Turn onto a lightly floured surface; divide into thirds. Flatten into a 6- or 7-in. circle. Place balls of dough in three greased 9-in. round baking pans. Cover and let rise until doubled, about 1 hour.

4 Bake at 375° for 20-25 minutes or until golden brown (cover loosely with foil if top browns too quickly). Remove from pans to wire racks to cool. **Yield:** 3 loaves. —*Ruthie Banks, Pryor, Oklahoma*

Fruit 'n' Nut Bread

Keep frozen bread dough on hand during the holidays so you can bake this favorite in brisk fashion!

 1/2 cup chopped pecans
 1/2 cup raisins
 1/2 cup chopped dates
 1/2 cup halved candied cherries
    2 teaspoons orange juice
    1 loaf (1 pound) frozen bread dough, thawed
    1 tablespoon butter, melted
GLAZE:
 1/2 cup confectioners' sugar
    1 tablespoon orange juice
    1 tablespoon butter, melted
 1/8 teaspoon grated orange peel
Pecan halves

1 In a small bowl, combine the pecans, raisins, dates, cherries and orange juice; set aside. Shape bread dough into a ball. Turn onto a floured surface; roll out to about 1 in. thick.

2 Spread pecan mixture over dough; fold over and knead well until the fruit and nuts are evenly mixed into dough. Shape into a flattened ball; place on a greased baking sheet. Brush with butter. Cover and let rise until doubled, about 1 hour.

3 Bake at 375° for 20-25 minutes or until golden brown. Remove from pan to a wire rack to cool. For glaze, combine the confectioners' sugar, orange juice, butter and orange peel. Spread over bread. Top with pecan halves. **Yield:** 1 loaf. —*Mary Hansen*
St. Louis, Missouri

Making a Flower-Shaped Coffee Cake

1. Divide dough into thirds and roll each piece into a 12-in. circle. Place one on prepared pan. Brush with a third of the butter. Sprinkle with a third of the filling. Repeat layers.

2. Pinch around edges to seal. Carefully place a glass in center of circle. With scissors, cut from outside edge just to the glass, forming 16 wedges.

3. Remove glass; twist each wedge five to six times. Tuck edges under.

Maple Nut Coffee Cake

This flower-shaped coffee cake is actually quite easy to make. The impressive presentation makes it great to serve guests.

> 1 package (16 ounces) hot roll mix
> 3 tablespoons sugar
> 3/4 cup warm water (120° to 130°)
> 1 egg
> 1 teaspoon maple flavoring
> 1/2 cup butter, melted, *divided*

FILLING:
> 1/2 cup sugar
> 1 teaspoon ground cinnamon
> 1/2 teaspoon maple flavoring
> 1/3 cup chopped walnuts

GLAZE:
> 1-1/2 cups confectioners' sugar
> 1/4 teaspoon maple flavoring
> 1 to 2 tablespoons milk

1 In a large bowl, combine contents of hot roll mix and sugar. Stir in the water, egg, maple flavoring and 6 tablespoons butter; mix well.

2 Turn onto a floured surface; knead until smooth and elastic, about 2-3 minutes. Place in a greased bowl, turning once to grease top. Cover and let rise in a warm place until doubled, about 45-60 minutes.

3 Punch dough down. Turn onto a lightly floured surface; divide into thirds. Roll one portion into a 12-in. circle; transfer to a greased 12-in. pizza pan. Brush

Maple Nut Coffee Cake

with some of the remaining butter. Combine sugar, cinnamon and maple flavoring; add nuts. Sprinkle a third of the filling over butter. Roll out second portion of dough into a 12-in. circle; place over filling. Brush with butter; sprinkle with a third of the remaining filling. Repeat with remaining dough, butter and filling.

4 Pinch dough around outer edge to seal. Place a small glass in center. Cut from outside edge just to the glass, forming 16 wedges. Remove the glass. Twist each wedge five to six times. Tuck edge under. Cover and let rise until doubled, about 30-45 minutes.

5 Bake at 375° for 20-25 minutes or until golden brown. Remove from pan to a wire rack to cool. Combine glaze ingredients; drizzle over warm coffee cake. **Yield:** 1 coffee cake. —*Rosadene Herold Lakeville, Indiana*

Apple Ladder Loaf

(Also pictured on page 329)

This pretty filled bread makes a nice breakfast pastry or—with a scoop of ice cream—a lovely dessert.

  2 packages (1/4 ounce *each*) active dry yeast
1/4 cup warm water (110° to 115°)
1/2 cup warm milk (110° to 115°)
1/2 cup butter, softened
1/3 cup sugar
  1 teaspoon salt
  4 eggs
4-1/2 to 4-3/4 cups all-purpose flour
FILLING:
1/4 cup butter, softened
1/3 cup packed brown sugar
  2 tablespoons all-purpose flour
1-1/4 teaspoons ground cinnamon
1/2 teaspoon ground nutmeg
1/8 teaspoon ground allspice
  4 cups thinly sliced peeled tart apples
ICING:
  1 cup confectioners' sugar
1/4 teaspoon vanilla extract
  1 to 2 tablespoons orange juice

1 In a large mixing bowl, dissolve yeast in warm water. Add the milk, butter, sugar, salt, eggs and 2 cups flour. Beat on low speed for 3 minutes. Stir in enough remaining flour to form a soft dough.

Apple Ladder Loaf

2 Turn onto a lightly floured surface; knead until smooth and elastic, about 6-8 minutes. Place in a greased bowl, turning once to grease top. Cover and refrigerate for 1-2 hours; punch down. Cover and refrigerate overnight.

3 Punch dough down. Turn onto a lightly floured surface; divide in half. Roll each portion into a 12-in. x 9-in. rectangle. Place on greased baking sheets. Spread with butter. For filling, combine the brown sugar, flour, cinnamon, nutmeg and allspice in a large bowl; add apples and toss to coat. Spoon down the center third of each rectangle.

4 On each long side, cut 1-in.-wide strips about 3 in. into center. Starting at one end, fold alternating strips at an angle across filling; seal ends. Cover and let rise for 45-50 minutes or until nearly doubled.

5 Bake at 350° for 30-40 minutes or until golden brown. Remove from pans to wire racks. Combine icing ingredients; drizzle over warm loaves. Serve warm or at room temperature. Store in the refrigerator. **Yield:** 2 loaves. —*Norma Foster, Compton, Illinois*

Heart-Shaped Coffee Cake

You'll love to make this pretty coffee cake for anniversaries and Valentine's Day.

        2 packages (1/4 ounce *each*) active dry yeast
    1/4 cup warm water (110° to 115°)
      1 cup warm milk (110° to 115°)
    3/4 cup butter, melted, *divided*
      2 eggs, beaten
    1/4 cup sugar
      1 teaspoon salt
 4-1/2 to 5-1/2 cups all-purpose flour
FILLING:
    1/4 cup butter, melted
    1/2 cup sugar
    1/2 cup finely chopped walnuts
      2 teaspoons ground cinnamon
ICING:
      2 tablespoons butter, softened
      2 cups confectioners' sugar
      1 teaspoon vanilla extract
      5 to 6 tablespoons milk

1 In a mixing bowl, dissolve yeast in warm water. Add milk, 1/2 cup butter, eggs, sugar, salt and 2 cups flour. Stir in enough remaining flour to form a soft dough. Turn onto a floured surface; knead until smooth and elastic, about 6-8 minutes. Place in a greased bowl, turning once to grease top. Cover and let rise in a warm place until doubled, about 1 hour.

2 Punch dough down. Turn onto a lightly floured surface; cover and let rest for 10 minutes. Divide in half. Roll each portion into a 15-in. x 10-in. rectangle. Brush with remaining butter. Combine filling ingredients; sprinkle over each rectangle to within 1/2 in. of edges.

3 Roll up jelly-roll style, starting with a long side; pinch seams to seal. Fold each roll in half with seams touching, making top half 1-1/2 in. longer than bottom half. Transfer to a greased baking sheet. Starting at the folded end, cut lengthwise down the middle with scissors to within 1-1/2 in. of open ends. Turn each side so that the cut side is up. Shape into a heart. Tuck heart point under. Cover and let rise until doubled, about 30 minutes.

4 Bake at 350° for 15-20 minutes or until golden brown. Remove from pans to wire racks to cool. For icing, in a small mixing bowl, cream the butter, sugar and vanilla; add milk. Drizzle over hearts. **Yield:** 2 coffee cakes. —*Norma Hammond, Leland, Iowa*

Heart-Shaped Coffee Cake

Making a Heart-Shaped Coffee Cake

1. Roll dough into a 15-in. x 10-in. rectangle. Brush with melted butter. Spread filling to within 1/2 in. of edges. Roll up jelly-roll style, starting with a long side; pinch seams to seal. Fold roll in half with seams touching, making top half 1-1/2 in. longer than bottom half. Place on a greased baking sheet.

2. Starting at the folded end, cut lengthwise down the middle with scissors to within 1-1/2 in. of open ends.

3. Turn each side so that the cut side is up and shape into a heart. Tuck pointed end of heart under.

Old-Fashioned Stollen

Stollen is a traditional German Christmas yeast bread. The fruit-filled loaf topped with a confectioners' sugar icing and candied cherries has a shape resembling a giant Parker House roll.

2	packages (1/4 ounce *each*) active dry yeast
1/2	teaspoon plus 1/2 cup sugar, *divided*
1/2	cup warm water (110° to 115°)
1	cup warm milk (110° to 115°)
3/4	cup butter, softened
1-1/2	teaspoons salt
2	eggs
2	egg yolks
6-1/4 to 6-3/4	cups all-purpose flour, *divided*
1/2	teaspoon ground cardamom
1/2	cup raisins
1/2	cup diced citron *or* mixed candied fruit and peel
1/2	cup sliced candied cherries

Additional butter, melted

ICING:

1	cup confectioners' sugar
5 to 6	teaspoons milk

Blanched whole almonds and additional candied fruit

1 In a large mixing bowl, dissolve yeast and 1/2 teaspoon sugar in warm water; let stand for 5 minutes. Add the milk, butter, salt, eggs, yolks, remaining sugar and 2 cups flour; beat until smooth. Stir in the raisins, citron, cherries and enough remaining flour to form a soft dough.

2 Turn onto a lightly floured surface; knead until smooth and elastic, about 6-8 minutes. Place in a greased bowl, turning once to grease top. Cover and let rise in a warm place until doubled, about 1-1/4 hours.

3 Punch dough down. Turn onto a lightly floured surface; divide into thirds. Roll each portion into a 10-in. x 6-in. oval; brush with melted butter. Fold one long side over to within 1 in. of the opposite side; press edges to seal. Place on greased baking sheets. Brush with butter. Cover and let rise until doubled, about 45 minutes.

4 Bake at 375° for 25 minutes or until lightly browned. Remove from pans to wire racks to cool. For icing, combine confectioners' sugar and milk; spread over bread. Decorate with almonds and fruit. **Yield:** 3 loaves.

—*Linda Hinners, Brookfield, Wisconsin*

Old-Fashioned Stollen

3 Turn onto a floured surface; knead until smooth and elastic, about 6-8 minutes. Do not let rise. Roll into an 8-in. square. Remove top sheet of waxed paper from butter mixture; invert onto center of dough. Peel off waxed paper. Fold plain dough over butter layer; fold widthwise into thirds. Roll into a 12-in. x 6-in. rectangle. Fold into thirds. Repeat rolling and folding twice. Wrap in waxed paper; refrigerate for 30 minutes.

4 On a lightly floured surface, roll dough into a 24-in. x 5-in. rectangle. In a small mixing bowl, beat almond paste and remaining butter until smooth. Spread lengthwise down the center of dough. Fold dough over filling to cover; pinch seam to seal. Place on a greased baking sheet. Shape into a pretzel. Flatten lightly with a rolling pin. Cover and let rise in a warm place until doubled, about 1 hour.

5 Brush egg white over dough. Sprinkle with cookie crumbs and almonds. Bake at 350° for 20-25 minutes or until golden brown. Carefully remove from pan to a wire rack to cool. **Yield:** 1 kringle.   *—Lorna Jacobsen*
Arrowwood, Alberta

Danish Kringle

Danish Kringle

This traditional Scandinavian yeast bread has flaky layers of tender dough flavored with almond paste. The unique sugar cookie crumb coating adds the perfect amount of sweetness.

 8 tablespoons butter, softened, *divided*
1-1/2 to 2 cups all-purpose flour, *divided*
 1 package (1/4 ounce) active dry yeast
 2 tablespoons warm water (110° to 115°)
1/4 cup warm half-and-half cream (110° to 115°)
 2 tablespoons sugar
1/4 teaspoon salt
 1 egg, beaten
1/2 cup almond paste
 1 egg white, beaten
1/4 cup sugar cookie crumbs
 2 tablespoons sliced almonds

1 In a small mixing bowl, cream 6 tablespoons butter and 2 tablespoons flour. Spread into an 8-in. x 4-in. rectangle on a piece of waxed paper. Cover with another piece of waxed paper; refrigerate.

2 In a large mixing bowl, dissolve yeast in warm water. Add the cream, sugar, salt and egg; beat until smooth. Stir in enough remaining flour to form a soft dough.

Peach Flip

This recipe is a little less time-consuming than most because the dough only needs to rise once.

 2 packages (1/4 ounce *each*) active dry yeast
1/2 cup warm water (110° to 115°)
1/2 cup plus 2/3 cup sugar, *divided*
3/4 cup butter, softened, *divided*
1/2 cup warm milk (110° to 115°)
 2 teaspoons salt
 3 eggs
 5 to 5-1/2 cups all-purpose flour
 1 cup peach preserves
 1 cup chopped pecans
 2 teaspoons ground cinnamon

1 In a large mixing bowl, dissolve yeast in warm water. Add 1/2 cup sugar, 1/2 cup butter, milk, salt, eggs and 2-1/2 cups flour; beat until smooth. Stir in enough remaining flour to form a stiff dough.

2 Turn onto a floured surface; knead until smooth and elastic, about 6-8 minutes. Place in a greased bowl, turning once to grease top. Cover and let rise in a warm place until doubled, about 1-1/4 hours.

3 Punch dough down. Turn onto a lightly floured surface; divide in half. Roll each portion into a 21-in. x 13-in. rectangle. Spread each with the remaining butter to within 1/2 in. of edges. Spread 1/4 cup preserves over butter. Combine the pecans, cinnamon and remaining sugar; sprinkle over preserves.

4 Roll up jelly-roll style, starting with a long side; pinch seam to seal. Place seam side down on greased baking sheets; curve to form a crescent shape. With a sharp knife, make a lengthwise slash a third of the way through the center to within 2 in. of each end. Spoon 1/4 cup preserves into each roll.

5 Bake at 350° for 25-30 minutes or until golden brown. Remove from pans to wire racks to cool. Store in the refrigerator. **Yield:** 2 loaves.
— *Helen Millhouse, Piqua, Ohio*

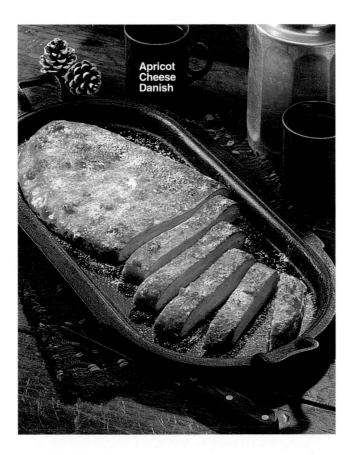

Apricot Cheese Danish

Apricot Cheese Danish

It's easy to offer your family a fresh-from-the-oven morning treat with this recipe. You mix it up at night, then just roll it out and bake the next morning.

---

  1 **package (1/4 ounce) active dry yeast**
1/4 **cup warm water (110° to 115°)**
  3 **tablespoons sugar**
1/2 **cup butter, softened**
  2 **eggs**
1/2 **cup sour cream**
1/4 **teaspoon salt**
  3 **cups all-purpose flour**
FILLING:
  2 **packages (8 ounces** *each***) cream cheese, softened**
1/2 **cup sugar**
  2 **egg yolks**
  2 **teaspoons vanilla extract**
1/4 **cup apricot preserves**
Confectioners' sugar

1 In a large mixing bowl, dissolve yeast in warm water. Add the sugar, butter, eggs and sour cream. Gradually add salt and 2 cups flour; beat until smooth. Stir in all of the remaining flour (dough will be soft and sticky). Place in a greased bowl. Cover and refrigerate overnight.

2 Punch dough down. Turn onto a lightly floured surface; knead 2-3 times. Divide in half. Roll each portion into a 16-in. x 10-in. oval; place on greased baking sheets.

3 For filling, combine the cream cheese, sugar, egg yolks and vanilla in a large mixing bowl; beat until smooth. Spread 1-1/4 cups over each oval to within 1 in. of edges. Fold longest side over filling; pinch edges to seal. Cover and let rise in a warm place until doubled, about 1 hour.

4 Bake at 375° for 20-22 minutes or until golden brown. Remove from pans to wire racks to cool. Spread preserves on top. Dust with confectioners' sugar. Store in the refrigerator. **Yield:** 2 loaves.
— *Florence Schafer, Jackson, Minnesota*

Cinnamon Raisin Bread

Two kinds of raisins are swirled into each slice of this heavenly bread. Use leftovers to make French toast.

- **2 packages (1/4 ounce *each*) active dry yeast**
- **1/3 cup warm water (110° to 115°)**
- **1 cup warm milk (110° to 115°)**
- **1/2 cup sugar**
- **6 tablespoons butter, softened**
- **2 eggs, lightly beaten**
- **1-1/4 teaspoons salt**
- **5-1/2 to 6 cups all-purpose flour**
- **FILLING:**
- **1-1/3 cups raisins**
- **1-1/3 cups golden raisins**
- **1 cup water**
- **1/3 cup apple juice *or* cider**
- **1 tablespoon ground cinnamon**
- **1 egg, beaten**

1 In a large mixing bowl, dissolve yeast in warm water. Add the milk, sugar, butter, eggs, salt and 2 cups flour; beat on medium speed for 2 minutes. Stir in enough remaining flour to form a soft dough.

2 Turn onto a floured surface; knead until smooth and elastic, about 6-8 minutes. Place in a greased bowl, turning once to grease top. Cover and let rise in a warm place until doubled, about 1 hour.

3 In a saucepan, combine the first five filling ingredients; bring to a boil. Reduce heat to medium; cook for 15-20 minutes, stirring occasionally, or until almost all of the liquid is absorbed. Remove from the heat; set aside.

4 Punch dough down. Turn onto a lightly floured surface; knead for 1 minute. Divide in half. Roll each portion into a 12-in. x 8-in. rectangle; brush with egg. Spread half of the filling over each rectangle to within 1/2 in. of edges. Roll up jelly-roll style, starting with a short side; pinch seams to seal. Place each loaf seam side down in a greased 9-in. x 5-in. x 3-in. loaf pan. Cover and let rise until doubled, about 1 hour.

5 Bake at 350° for 35-40 minutes (cover loosely with foil if top browns too quickly). Remove from pans to wire racks to cool. **Yield:** 2 loaves.   —*Joan Hutter Warnick, Rhode Island*

Chocolate Marble Bread

This is just the recipe for folks who think chocolate should be served at every meal! It will be the highlight of your breakfasts and brunches.

- **7 to 7-1/2 cups all-purpose flour**
- **1/2 cup sugar**
- **1 package (1/4 ounce) active dry yeast**
- **1 teaspoon salt**
- **2 cups milk**
- **1/4 cup butter**
- **2 eggs**
- **1/4 cup baking cocoa**
- **GLAZE:**
- **1 cup confectioners' sugar**
- **1 tablespoon milk**
- **1/4 cup chopped walnuts**

1 In a large mixing bowl, combine 3 cups flour, sugar, yeast and salt. In a saucepan, heat milk and butter to 120°-130°. Add to dry ingredients; beat until moistened. Add eggs; beat on low speed for 30 seconds. Beat on high for 3 minutes. Stir in enough remaining flour to form a soft dough.

2 Turn onto a floured surface; knead until smooth and elastic, about 6-8 minutes. Divide dough into thirds. Knead cocoa into one portion of dough (this may take

Cinnamon
Raisin Bread

Chocolate Marble Bread

Plum Coffee Loaf

A simple-to-make filling and hot roll mix make it easy to whip up this delicious bread on a moment's notice. People are pleasantly surprised to see plum in the filling instead of the more traditional apple or cherry.

      1 package (16 ounces) hot roll mix
      2 tablespoons butter, melted
      1 can (30 ounces) purple plums, drained, halved and pitted
  1/4 cup sugar
  1/4 teaspoon ground cinnamon
  1/8 teaspoon ground cloves
GLAZE:
      1 cup confectioners' sugar
  1/4 teaspoon almond extract
      1 to 2 tablespoons milk
  1/3 cup slivered almonds

5-6 minutes). Shape into a ball. Shape remaining portions of dough into one ball. Place each ball in a lightly greased bowl, turning once to grease top. Cover and let rise in a warm place until doubled, about 1-1/4 hours.

3 Punch dough down. Turn onto a lightly floured surface; cover and let rest for 10 minutes. Roll chocolate dough into a 20-in. x 10-in. rectangle; repeat with plain dough. Place chocolate layer on top of plain layer.

4 Roll up jelly-roll style, starting with a long side; pinch seam to seal. Cut into 20 slices; place in a greased 10-in. tube pan in about three layers. Cover and let rise until nearly doubled, about 30-40 minutes.

5 Bake at 350° for 40-45 minutes or until lightly browned. Immediately remove from pan to a wire rack to cool. For glaze, combine confectioners' sugar and milk; drizzle over bread. Sprinkle with walnuts. **Yield:** 1 loaf. —*Rosina Sacks, Copley, Pennsylvania*

1 Prepare hot roll mix and knead dough according to package directions. Place in a greased bowl, turning once to grease top. Cover and let rise in a warm place until doubled, about 30 minutes.

2 Punch dough down. Turn onto a lightly floured surface; roll into a 15-in. x 10-in. rectangle. Brush with butter. Place plums cut side down lengthwise down the center third of rectangle. Combine the sugar, cinnamon and cloves; sprinkle over plums.

3 Fold both long sides of dough over filling; pinch seam to seal and tuck ends under. Place a baking sheet on work surface next to the loaf. Carefully slide loaf onto baking sheet. With a sharp knife, make slashes 1 in. apart across top of loaf. Cover and let rise until doubled, about 30 minutes.

4 Bake at 350° for 20-25 minutes or until golden brown. Remove from pan to a wire rack. For glaze, combine confectioners' sugar, almond extract and milk; drizzle over warm loaf. Sprinkle with almonds. Cool. Store in the refrigerator. **Yield:** 1 loaf. —*Janet Snider, Kalamazoo, Michigan*

Apple Pull-Apart
Bread

2 Turn onto a floured surface; knead until smooth and elastic, about 6-8 minutes. Place in a greased bowl, turning once to grease top. Cover and let rise in a warm place until doubled, about 1 hour.

3 Punch dough down. Turn onto a lightly floured surface; divide in half. Cut each portion into 16 pieces. Pat or roll each piece into a 2-1/2-in. circle. Combine the apple, pecans, cinnamon and remaining sugar; place 1 teaspoonful in the center of each circle. Pinch edges together and seal, forming a ball. Dip in remaining butter.

4 In a greased 10-in. tube pan, place 16 balls seam side down; sprinkle with 1/4 cup apple mixture. Layer with remaining balls; sprinkle evenly with remaining apple mixture. Cover and let rise until nearly doubled, about 45 minutes.

5 Bake at 350° for 35-40 minutes or until golden brown. Cool for 10 minutes before removing from pan to a wire rack to cool completely. Combine icing ingredients; drizzle over bread. **Yield:** 1 loaf.
—Carolyn Gregory, Hendersonville, Tennessee

Apple Pull-Apart Bread

Drizzled with icing, each finger-licking "piece" of this bread has a yummy filling of apples and pecans. It's well worth the bit of extra effort.

  1 **package (1/4 ounce) active dry yeast**
  1 **cup warm milk (110° to 115°)**
1/2 **cup butter, melted, *divided***
  1 **egg**
2/3 **cup plus 2 tablespoons sugar, *divided***
  1 **teaspoon salt**
  3 **to 3-1/2 cups all-purpose flour**
  1 **medium tart apple, peeled and chopped**
1/2 **cup finely chopped pecans**
1/2 **teaspoon ground cinnamon**
ICING:
  1 **cup confectioners' sugar**
1/2 **teaspoon vanilla extract**
  3 **to 4-1/2 teaspoons hot water**

1 In a large mixing bowl, dissolve yeast in warm milk. Add 2 tablespoons butter, egg, 2 tablespoons sugar, salt and 3 cups flour; beat until smooth. Stir in enough remaining flour to form a stiff dough.

Walnut Cream Braids

A nutty cheese filling is tucked inside each bite of these pretty braided breads.

  1 **package (1/4 ounce) active dry yeast**
1/4 **cup warm water (110° to 115°)**
1/2 **cup butter, softened**
  2 **tablespoons sugar**
1/2 **teaspoon salt**
  1 **egg**
  2 **to 2-1/2 cups all-purpose flour**
FILLING:
  2 **packages (3 ounces *each*) cream cheese, softened**
3/4 **cup sugar**
1/2 **cup finely chopped walnuts**
Confectioners' sugar, optional

1 In a large mixing bowl, dissolve yeast in warm water. Add the butter, sugar, salt, egg and 1-1/2 cups flour; beat on low speed for 3 minutes. Stir in enough remaining flour to form a soft dough.

2 Turn onto a floured surface; knead until smooth and elastic, about 6-8 minutes. Place in a greased bowl, turning once to grease top. Cover and let rise in a warm place until doubled, about 1 hour. Meanwhile, in a small mixing bowl, beat the cream cheese and sugar; set aside.

3 Punch dough down. Turn onto a lightly floured surface; divide in half. Roll each portion into a 12-in. x 8-in. rectangle; place on greased baking sheets. Spread half of the cream cheese mixture down the center third of each rectangle. Sprinkle with walnuts.

4 On each long side, cut 1-in.-wide strips about 2-1/2 in. into center. Starting at one end, fold alternating strips at an angle across filling; seal ends. Cover and let rise for 30 minutes.

5 Bake at 375° for 15-20 minutes or until browned. Cool on wire racks. Dust with confectioners' sugar if desired. Store in the refrigerator. **Yield:** 2 loaves.
—*Jean Erickson, North Pole, Alaska*

Orange Cinnamon Bread

This citrusy cinnamon bread is a hit with anyone who has a sweet tooth. You can also make a loaf that's terrific for toasting by eliminating the glaze.

    2 packages (1/4 ounce *each*) active dry yeast
1/4 cup warm water (110° to 115°)
    1 cup milk
3/4 cup orange juice
    1 cup sugar, *divided*
    1 tablespoon grated orange peel

1-1/2 teaspoons salt
    1 egg
6-1/2 to 7 cups all-purpose flour
Additional water
    2 teaspoons ground cinnamon
GLAZE:
    1 cup confectioners' sugar
    2 tablespoons orange juice

1 In a large mixing bowl, dissolve yeast in warm water. In a saucepan, heat milk and orange juice to 110°; add to yeast mixture. Stir in 1/2 cup sugar, orange peel, salt, egg and 3 cups flour; beat until smooth. Stir in enough remaining flour to form a soft dough.

2 Turn onto a floured surface; knead until smooth and elastic, about 6-8 minutes. Place in a greased bowl, turning once to grease top. Cover and let rise in a warm place until doubled, about 1 hour.

3 Punch dough down. Turn onto a lightly floured surface; divide in half. Roll each portion into a 15-in. x 7-in. rectangle. Brush with water. Combine cinnamon and remaining sugar; sprinkle over dough to within 1 in. of edges.

4 Tightly roll up jelly-roll style, starting with a short side; pinch seams to seal. Place seam side down in two greased 9-in. x 5-in. x 3-in. loaf pans. Cover and let rise until doubled, about 1 hour.

5 Bake at 350° for 35-40 minutes or until golden brown. Remove from pans to wire racks to cool. Combine glaze ingredients; drizzle over bread. **Yield:** 2 loaves.
—*Cindy Anderson, Delhi, New York*

Orange Cinnamon Bread

Raspberry Coffee Cake

This fresh and fruity coffee cake looks elegant but is so simple to make, thanks to frozen bread dough.

- 1 loaf (1 pound) frozen bread *or* sweet bread dough, thawed
- 1 pint fresh raspberries
- 1/2 cup all-purpose flour
- 1/4 cup sugar
- 1/4 cup cold butter
- 1/8 teaspoon vanilla extract

GLAZE:
- 1/2 cup confectioners' sugar
- 3 to 4 teaspoons milk

1 On a lightly floured surface, roll dough into a 14-in. circle. Transfer to a greased 14-in. pizza pan. Build up edges slightly. Bake at 350° for 5 minutes. Sprinkle with raspberries. In a small bowl, combine flour and sugar; cut in butter and vanilla until mixture is crumbly. Sprinkle over berries.

2 Bake at 350° for 25-30 minutes or until golden. Cool on a wire rack. Combine glaze ingredients; drizzle over coffee cake. Store in the refrigerator. **Yield:** 1 coffee cake. —*Lisa Schulz, Madison, Wisconsin*

Chocolate Coffee Cake

Chocolate and cinnamon combine for a scrumptious filling in this tender coffee cake. For added sweetness, drizzle with Vanilla Glaze (page 330).

- 1 package (1/4 ounce) active dry yeast
- 1 cup warm water (110° to 115°)
- 3 tablespoons butter, softened
- 3 tablespoons sugar
- 1 egg, beaten
- 1 teaspoon salt
- 2 tablespoons nonfat dry milk powder
- 3 to 3-1/2 cups all-purpose flour

FILLING:
- 1 cup (6 ounces) semisweet chocolate chips
- 1/3 cup evaporated milk
- 2 tablespoons sugar
- 1/2 teaspoon ground cinnamon

TOPPING:
- 1/4 cup all-purpose flour
- 1/4 cup sugar
- 1 teaspoon ground cinnamon
- 1/4 cup cold butter

1 In a large mixing bowl, dissolve yeast in warm water. Add butter, sugar, egg, salt and milk powder; mix

Raspberry
Coffee Cake

well. Add 2 cups flour; beat until smooth. Stir in enough remaining flour to form a soft dough.

2 Turn onto a floured surface; knead until smooth and elastic, about 6-8 minutes. Place in a greased bowl, turning once to grease top. Cover and let rise in a warm place until doubled, about 1 hour.

3 For filling, combine the chocolate chips, milk and sugar in a small saucepan; cook and stir over low heat until smooth. Stir in cinnamon; set aside. For topping, combine the flour, sugar and cinnamon in a small bowl; cut in butter until mixture is crumbly. Set aside.

4 Punch dough down. Turn onto a lightly floured surface; roll into a 20-in. x 10-in. rectangle. Spread with filling. Roll up jelly-roll style, starting with a long side; pinch seam to seal. Place in a well-greased 10-in. fluted tube pan, with seam facing the inside of pan. Sprinkle with topping. Cover and let rise until doubled, about 30 minutes.

5 Bake at 350° for 45-50 minutes or until golden brown. Let stand for 10 minutes before inverting onto a wire rack to cool. **Yield:** 1 coffee cake.
—*Deborah Keller, Goose Creek, South Carolina*

Braided Cardamom Rings

Braided Cardamom Rings

Red and green candied cherries look so festive on top of these mouth-watering rings, which may be iced and served warm if desired.

> 2 **packages (1/4 ounce *each*) active dry yeast**
> 1/4 **cup warm water (110° to 115°)**
> 2-1/2 **cups warm milk (110° to 115°)**
> 3/4 **cup butter, softened**
> 1 **egg, beaten**
> 1 **cup sugar**
> 1-1/2 **teaspoons ground cardamom**
> 1/2 **teaspoon salt**
> 8-3/4 **to 9-1/4 cups all-purpose flour**
> **LEMON ICING:**
> 2 **cups confectioners' sugar**
> 3 **to 4 tablespoons milk**
> 1/4 **teaspoon lemon extract**
> **Red and green candied cherries, halved, optional**

1 In a large mixing bowl, dissolve yeast in warm water. Add the milk, butter, egg, sugar, cardamom and salt; mix well. Add 6 cups flour; beat until smooth. Stir in enough remaining flour to form a soft dough.

2 Turn onto a floured surface; knead until smooth and elastic, about 6-8 minutes. Place in a greased bowl, turning once to grease top. Cover and let rise in a warm place until doubled, about 1 hour.

3 Punch dough down. Turn onto a lightly floured surface; divide in half. Divide each portion into three pieces. Shape each into a 24-in. rope. Place three ropes on a greased baking sheet; braid. Form into a ring; pinch edges tightly together. Repeat with remaining ropes. Cover and let rise until doubled, about 30 minutes.

4 Bake at 350° for 30-35 minutes or until golden brown. Remove from pans to wire racks to cool. For icing, combine the confectioners' sugar, milk and lemon extract; spoon over rings, allowing icing to drizzle down the sides. Decorate with cherries if desired. **Yield:** 2 coffee cakes. —*Jo Learman, Caro, Michigan*

Sweet rolls

secrets for successful sweet rolls

- After punching down the dough, let it rest for 10 minutes. This allows the dough to relax, which makes it easier to roll out.

- Roll up dough firmly. If it's too loose, you'll see air pockets or large gaps when cut. If it's too tight, the bread will crack.

- A simple way to slice cinnamon rolls or sticky buns is to place a piece of unflavored dental floss or heavy-duty thread under the rolled dough, 1 in. from the end. Bring the floss up around the dough and cross it over the top, cutting through the dough and filling. Repeat at 1-in. intervals.

- Evenly space the cut rolls in the pan, leaving room around each to allow for the final rising.

Sticky Buns

Sticky Buns

(Also pictured on page 328)

It's impossible to eat just one of these soft, yummy sticky buns—they have wonderful old-fashioned goodness.

    2 teaspoons active dry yeast
1-1/4 cups warm water (110° to 115°)
    3 tablespoons butter, softened
    3 tablespoons sugar
    2 tablespoons nonfat dry milk powder
    1 teaspoon salt
    3 to 3-1/4 cups bread flour
FILLING:
  1/3 cup butter, softened
    1 tablespoon sugar
    1 teaspoon ground cinnamon

SAUCE:
  1/2 cup packed brown sugar
  1/4 cup butter
  1/4 cup corn syrup
  1/2 cup chopped pecans

1 In a large mixing bowl, dissolve yeast in warm water. Add the butter, sugar, milk powder, salt and 2 cups flour; beat on low speed for 3 minutes. Stir in enough remaining flour to form a soft dough.

2 Turn onto a floured surface; knead until smooth and elastic, about 6-8 minutes. Place in a greased bowl, turning once to grease top. Cover and let rise in a warm place until doubled, about 1 hour.

3 Punch dough down. Turn onto a lightly floured surface; roll into a 16-in. x 10-in. rectangle. Spread with butter; sprinkle with sugar and cinnamon. Roll up jelly-roll style, starting from a long side; pinch seam to seal. Cut into 12 slices; set aside.

4 In a saucepan, combine the brown sugar, butter and corn syrup; cook over medium heat until the sugar is dissolved. Stir in pecans. Pour into a greased 13-in. x 9-in. x 2-in. baking pan. Place rolls cut side down over sauce. Cover and let rise until doubled, about 1 hour.

5 Bake at 375° for 20-25 minutes or until golden brown. Cool for 3 minutes. Invert onto a serving platter. **Yield:** 1 dozen.
—*Dorothy Showalter*
Broadway, Virginia

Shaping Cinnamon Rolls and Sticky Buns

1. Roll dough into a rectangle. Spread or brush with butter; sprinkle with filling. Roll up, starting from a long end, and pinch seam to seal.

2. Slice into rolls. Place cut side down in a greased baking pan.

3. Cover and let rise until doubled. Rolls will begin to touch each other.

4. After baking, combine glaze ingredients if desired; spoon in a thin stream over warm rolls.

Blueberry Pinwheels

Juicy blueberries peek out from the swirls of these tender, flaky sweet rolls. A succulent sauce settles on the bottom of the pan.

      2 cans (5 ounces *each*) evaporated milk
      6 tablespoons butter, softened
      1 package (1/4 ounce) active dry yeast
  1/4 cup sugar
      1 teaspoon salt
      1 egg
  3-1/2 to 4 cups all-purpose flour
FILLING:
      3 tablespoons butter, melted
  1/2 cup sugar
  1-1/2 to 2 teaspoons ground cinnamon
      1 teaspoon grated lemon peel
      2 cups fresh *or* frozen blueberries*
GLAZE:
      1 cup confectioners' sugar
  1/2 teaspoon vanilla extract
      1 to 2 tablespoons water

1 In a saucepan, heat milk and butter to 110°-115°. In a large mixing bowl, dissolve yeast in warm milk mixture. Add the sugar, salt, egg and 2 cups flour; beat until smooth. Stir in enough remaining flour to form a soft dough.

2 Turn onto a floured surface; knead until smooth and elastic, about 6-8 minutes. Place in a greased bowl, turning once to grease top. Cover and let rise in a warm place until doubled, about 1-1/4 hours.

3 Punch dough down. Turn onto a floured surface; divide in half. Roll each portion into a 14-in. x 8-in. rectangle; brush with melted butter. Combine the sugar, cinnamon and lemon peel; sprinkle over each rectangle to within 1/2 in. of edges. Top with blueberries; press into dough.

4 Roll up jelly-roll style, starting with a long side; pinch seam to seal. Cut each roll into 12 slices. Place cut side down in two greased 13-in. x 9-in. x 2-in. baking pans. Cover and let rise until doubled, about 1-1/4 hours.

5 Bake at 375° for 20-25 minutes or until golden brown. Cool for 5 minutes. Combine glaze ingredients; drizzle over warm rolls. Cool in pans on wire racks. **Yield:** 2 dozen. *—Betsy Stoner, Elmira, New York*

*Editor's Note:** If using frozen blueberries, do not thaw.

Cranberry Sweet Rolls

Christmas morning will be sweeter than ever when you serve these festive rolls topped with a rich and creamy frosting. They rise nice and high and hold their shape. Plus, the tart cranberry filling is a nice change of pace from cinnamon rolls.

    3/4 cup sugar
    1/2 cup water
      2 cups fresh *or* frozen cranberries
      1 teaspoon grated orange peel
DOUGH:
      2 packages (1/4 ounce *each*) active dry yeast
    1/2 cup warm water (110° to 115°)
    1/2 cup plus 2 tablespoons butter, softened,
         divided
    1/2 cup milk
      2 eggs
    1/2 cup sugar
      1 teaspoon salt
      1 teaspoon ground cinnamon
    1/2 teaspoon ground nutmeg
  4-1/2 to 5 cups all-purpose flour
CREAM CHEESE FROSTING:
      1 cup confectioners' sugar
    1/2 of a 3-ounce package cream cheese, softened
    1/4 cup butter, softened
    1/2 teaspoon vanilla extract
    1/2 teaspoon milk

1 In a saucepan, bring sugar and water to a boil. Add cranberries; return to a boil. Boil, uncovered, for 20 minutes, stirring occasionally. Remove from the heat. Stir in orange peel; cover and refrigerate.

2 In a large mixing bowl, dissolve yeast in warm water. Add 1/2 cup butter, milk, eggs, sugar, salt, cinnamon, nutmeg and 3 cups flour; beat until smooth. Stir in enough remaining flour to form a soft dough.

3 Turn onto a floured surface; knead until smooth and elastic, about 6-8 minutes. Place in a greased bowl, turning once to grease top. Cover and let rise in a warm place until doubled, about 1 hour.

4 Punch dough down. Turn onto a lightly floured surface; roll into a 20-in. x 10-in. rectangle. Melt the remaining butter; brush over dough. Spread with cranberry filling to within 1 in. of edges. Roll up jelly-roll style, starting with a long side; pinch seam to seal. Cut into 15 slices. Place cut side down in a greased 13-in. x 9-in. x 2-in. baking pan. Cover and let rise until doubled, about 30 minutes.

5 Bake at 375° for 25-30 minutes. Cool for 5 minutes before removing from pans to a wire rack. In a small mixing bowl, combine frosting ingredients; beat until smooth. Spread over warm rolls. Store in the refrigerator. **Yield:** 15 rolls.

—Germaine Stank
Pound, Wisconsin

Cranberry
Sweet Rolls

Easy Apple Danish

This dough should be refrigerated for at least 2 hours. You can prepare it the night before and bake the rolls fresh in the morning as a special breakfast treat.

      1 package (1/4 ounce) active dry yeast
    1/4 cup warm water (110° to 115°)
      5 cups all-purpose flour
    1/4 cup sugar
      1 teaspoon salt
      1 teaspoon grated lemon peel
      1 cup cold butter
      1 cup warm milk (110° to 115°)
      2 eggs, beaten
FILLING:
      2 tablespoons butter, melted
  1-1/2 cups chopped peeled tart apples
    3/4 cup chopped walnuts
    1/3 cup sugar
  1-1/2 teaspoons ground cinnamon

GLAZE:
- 2 cups confectioners' sugar
- 3 tablespoons milk
- 1/2 teaspoon vanilla extract

1 In a small bowl, dissolve yeast in warm water. In a large bowl, combine the flour, sugar, salt and lemon peel; cut in butter until mixture is crumbly. Stir in the yeast mixture, milk and eggs by hand.

2 Turn onto a floured surface; knead about 20 times (dough will be slightly sticky). Cover and refrigerate for at least 2 hours.

3 Punch dough down. Turn onto a lightly floured surface; divide in half. Roll each portion into an 18-in. x 15-in. rectangle; brush with melted butter. Combine the apples, walnuts, sugar and cinnamon; sprinkle over each rectangle to within 1/2 in. of edges.

4 Starting with a short side, fold a third of the dough over filling; repeat with other side, making a 15-in. x 6-in. rectangle. Pinch seam to seal. Cut each into 15 slices. Twist each slice a few times; pinch ends together, forming a small circle. Place 2 in. apart on greased baking sheets.

5 Bake at 400° for 12-15 minutes or until golden brown. Remove from pans to wire racks. Combine glaze ingredients; drizzle over warm rolls. **Yield:** 2-1/2 dozen. —*Dorothea Ladd, Ballston Lake, New York*

Traditional Hot Cross Buns

Traditional Hot Cross Buns

These yeast rolls dotted with raisins and currants are traditionally topped with a white glaze in the shape of a cross and served at Easter.

- 2 packages (1/4 ounce *each*) active dry yeast
- 2 cups warm milk (110° to 115°)
- 1/3 cup butter, softened
- 2 eggs, lightly beaten
- 1/4 cup sugar
- 1-1/2 teaspoons salt
- 6 to 7 cups all-purpose flour
- 1/2 cup raisins
- 1/2 cup dried currants
- 1 teaspoon ground cinnamon
- 1/4 teaspoon ground allspice
- 1 egg yolk
- 2 tablespoons water
- Vanilla Glaze (recipe on page 330)

1 In a large mixing bowl, dissolve yeast in warm milk. Stir in the butter, eggs, sugar and salt. Combine 3 cups flour, raisins, currants, cinnamon and allspice; add to the yeast mixture and mix well. Stir in enough remaining flour to form a soft dough.

2 Turn onto a floured surface; knead until smooth and elastic, about 6-8 minutes. Place in a greased bowl, turning once to grease top. Cover and let rise in a warm place until doubled, about 1 hour.

3 Punch dough down. Turn onto a lightly floured surface; shape into 1-1/2- to 2-in. balls. Place 2 in. apart on greased baking sheets. With a sharp knife, make a cross on top of each roll. Cover and let rise until doubled, about 30 minutes.

4 Beat egg yolk and water; brush over rolls. Bake at 375° for 15-20 minutes or until golden brown. Remove from pans to wire racks to cool. Pipe glaze over rolls. **Yield:** 2-1/2 dozen. —*Barbara Jean Lull, Claremont, California*

Bear Claws

Bear Claws

You don't have to head to gourmet bakeries to indulge in this sweet pastry. This recipe lets you master rich flaky pastries at home.

- 1 **package (1/4 ounce) active dry yeast**
- 1/2 **cup warm milk (110° to 115°)**
- 2 **tablespoons sugar**
- 1 **teaspoon salt**
- 1 **egg, lightly beaten**
- 1-1/2 **cups plus 2 tablespoons all-purpose flour**

BUTTER MIXTURE:
- 2 **tablespoons all-purpose flour,** *divided*
- 3/4 **cup cold butter, cut into tablespoon-size pieces**

FILLING:
- 6 **tablespoons prepared almond filling** *or* **filling of your choice**
- 1 **egg, beaten**

GLAZE:
- 3/4 **cup confectioners' sugar**
- 2 **to 3 teaspoons water**

1 In a large mixing bowl, dissolve yeast in warm milk. Stir in the sugar, salt and egg; mix well. Add the flour all at once, stirring until mixed. Set aside.

2 For butter mixture, sprinkle 1 tablespoon flour on a work surface; place butter on surface and sprinkle with 1 teaspoon flour. Press and roll out with a rolling pin. Scrape butter from rolling pin and continue to work the butter until it forms a smooth mass without any hard lumps. Knead in remaining flour, working quickly to keep butter cold. Place butter mixture on a sheet of plastic wrap and shape into a small rectangle. Cover with another sheet of plastic wrap; roll into a 9-in. x 6-in. rectangle. Set aside.

3 Turn dough onto a floured work surface; roll into a 14-in. x 10-in. rectangle, with a 10-in. side toward the bottom. Unwrap butter mixture; place on dough 1 in. above bottom edge and 1/2 in. from each side edge. Fold top half of dough over butter and pinch edges to seal.

4 Turn dough a quarter turn to the right; sprinkle lightly with additional flour. Lightly roll into a 16-in. x 8-in. rectangle. Fold bottom third of rectangle up and top third down, as when folding a business letter, making a 5-1/2-in. x 8-in. rectangle (this is called one turn). Rotate dough a quarter turn to the right. Lightly roll into a 16-in. x 8-in. rectangle and again fold into thirds, finishing the second turn. Repeat rotating, rolling and folding two more times for a total of four turns. Wrap loosely in plastic wrap; refrigerate for 30 minutes.

5 Roll dough into a 12-in. square; cut square into three 12-in. x 4-in. strips. Spread 2 tablespoons filling down the center of each strip to within 1 in. of long edge. Fold lengthwise over filling and pinch seam to seal. Cut each strip into three pieces. With scissors, cut each piece four times from pinched seam to about 1/2 in. from folded side. Place 2 in. apart on greased baking sheets. Curve folded side slightly to separate strips and allow filling to show. Cover and let rise in a warm place until almost doubled, about 1 hour.

6 Brush with egg. Bake at 400° for 10-14 minutes or until puffy and golden brown. Remove from pans to wire racks. Combine glaze ingredients; brush over warm rolls. Cool. **Yield:** 9 rolls.

Shaping Bear Claws

1. Roll dough into a 12-in. square, then cut each square into three 12-in. x 4-in. strips.

2. Spread 2 tablespoons of filling down the center of each strip to within 1 in. of long edge. Fold lengthwise over filling; pinch seam to seal. Cut into three pieces.

3. With scissors, cut each strip four times, starting from pinched seam to about 1/2 in. from the folded side.

4. Place 2 in. apart on greased baking sheets. Curve folded side slightly to separate strips and show the filling.

Almond Apricot Logs

Almond Apricot Logs

This recipe makes 5 dozen delicious rolls, so bake and take them to your next potluck.

> 2 packages (1/4 ounce *each*) active dry yeast
> 1/3 cup warm water (110° to 115°)
> 1-1/2 cups warm milk (110° to 115°)
> 1/3 cup vegetable oil
> 1/2 cup sugar
> 2 eggs
> 2 teaspoons salt
> 2 teaspoons ground nutmeg
> 5 to 5-1/2 cups all-purpose flour
> 1-1/2 cups coarsely chopped dried apricots
> 1 cup chopped almonds
> **GLAZE:**
> 1-1/2 cups confectioners' sugar
> 1/2 teaspoon vanilla extract
> 2 to 3 tablespoons milk

1 In a large mixing bowl, dissolve yeast in warm water. Add milk, oil, sugar, eggs, salt, nutmeg and 2 cups flour; beat until smooth. Add apricots and almonds. Stir in enough remaining flour to form a soft dough.

2 Turn onto a floured surface; knead until smooth and elastic, about 6-8 minutes. Place in a greased bowl, turning once to grease top. Cover and let rise in a warm place until doubled, about 1-1/2 hours.

3 Punch dough down. Turn onto a lightly floured surface; cover and let rest for 10 minutes. Roll into a 15-in. x 12-in. rectangle. Cut into 3-in. x 1-in. strips. Place 1 in. apart on greased baking sheets. Cover and let rise until doubled, about 30 minutes.

4 Bake at 375° for 15 minutes or until light golden brown. Remove from pans to wire racks. Combine glaze ingredients; brush over warm logs. Cool. **Yield:** 5 dozen.
—*L. Kniffin, Hockessin, Delaware*

No-Fry Doughnuts

*These warm glazed doughnuts are
finger-licking good! They bake in the oven,
so there's no greasy mess to clean up.*

2 packages (1/4 ounce *each*) active dry yeast
1/4 cup warm water (110° to 115°)
1-1/2 cups warm milk (110° to 115°)
1/3 cup shortening
1/2 cup sugar
2 eggs
1 teaspoon salt
1 teaspoon ground nutmeg
1/4 teaspoon ground cinnamon
4-1/2 to 5 cups all-purpose flour
1/4 cup butter, melted
GLAZE:
1/2 cup butter
2 cups confectioners' sugar
5 teaspoons water
2 teaspoons vanilla extract

1 In a large mixing bowl, dissolve yeast in warm water. Add milk and shortening; stir for 1 minute. Add the sugar, eggs, salt, nutmeg, cinnamon and 2 cups flour; beat on low speed until smooth. Stir in enough remaining flour to form a soft dough (do not knead). Cover and let rise in a warm place until doubled, about 1 hour.

2 Punch dough down. Turn onto a floured surface; roll out to 1/2-in. thickness. Cut with a floured 2-3/4-in. doughnut cutter; place 2 in. apart on greased baking sheets. Brush with butter. Cover and let rise in a warm place until doubled, about 30 minutes.

3 Bake at 350° for 20 minutes or until lightly browned. Meanwhile, for glaze, melt butter in a saucepan. Add the confectioners' sugar, water and vanilla; cook and stir over low heat until smooth (do not boil). Keep warm. Dip warm doughnuts in glaze, one at a time, and turn to coat. Drain on a wire rack. Serve immediately. **Yield:** 2 dozen. —*Susie Baldwin, Columbia, Tennessee*

Fan Rolls

*When you're expecting busy days ahead,
this recipe comes in handy because the dough
can be made and refrigerated for up to 24 hours.*

3-1/4 cups all-purpose flour
1/4 cup sugar
1 package (1/4 ounce) active dry yeast
1 teaspoon grated lemon peel
1/2 teaspoon salt
1 cup milk
1/4 cup shortening
1 egg
FILLING:
2 tablespoons butter, softened
1/2 cup packed brown sugar
1/2 cup raisins
1 teaspoon ground cinnamon
Vanilla Glaze (recipe on page 330)

1 In a large mixing bowl, combine 1-1/4 cups flour, sugar, yeast, lemon peel and salt. In a saucepan, heat milk and shortening to 120°-130°. Add to dry ingredients; beat until moistened. Add egg; beat on high speed for 3 minutes. Stir in enough remaining flour to form a soft dough. Do not knead. Cover and refrigerate for 2-24 hours.

2 Let dough stand at room temperature for 10 minutes. On a lightly floured surface, roll dough into a 16-in. x 12-in. rectangle. Cut in half lengthwise; spread with butter. Combine the brown sugar, raisins and cinnamon; sprinkle down the center third of each rectangle. Fold one long side of dough over

No-Fry Doughnuts

filling, then fold the other long side of dough over, forming a 16-in. x 2-in. rectangle. Pat lightly to flatten.

3 Cut each rectangle into four 4-in. rolls. Line a baking sheet with foil and grease the foil. Place rolls seam side down 3 in. apart on foil. With scissors, cut five strips two-thirds of the way through each roll. Separate each strip slightly, curving to form a fan shape. Cover and let rise in a warm place until doubled, about 45 minutes.

4 Bake at 350° for 15-20 minutes or until lightly browned. Remove from pan to a wire rack to cool. Drizzle with glaze. **Yield:** 8 rolls. —*Christine Wahlgren Sandwich, Illinois*

Potato Doughnuts

Potato Doughnuts

For ease of preparation, the dough for these baked favorites is made in a bread machine. The cinnamon-sugar topping is irresistible.

- **3 medium potatoes, peeled and quartered**
- **1 cup warm milk (70° to 80°)**
- **2 eggs, well beaten**
- **3/4 cup shortening**
- **1/2 cup sugar**
- **1 teaspoon salt**
- **4-1/2 cups bread flour**
- **2-1/4 teaspoons active dry yeast**
- **TOPPING:**
- **3/4 cup sugar**
- **1-1/4 teaspoons ground cinnamon**
- **1/4 cup butter, melted**

1 Place potatoes in a saucepan and cover with water. Bring to a boil; cook until tender. Drain, reserving 1/4 cup cooking liquid; set liquid aside to cool to 70°-80°. Mash potatoes; set aside 1 cup to cool to room temperature. (Refrigerate any remaining mashed potatoes for another use.)

2 In bread machine pan, place milk, eggs, shortening, sugar, salt, bread flour and yeast in order suggested by manufacturer, adding reserved cooking liquid and mashed potatoes. Select dough setting (check dough after 5 minutes of mixing; some flour may remain on top; add 1 to 2 tablespoons water or flour if needed).

3 When cycle is completed, turn dough onto a lightly floured surface. Knead in an additional 1/4 to 1/2 cup flour if necessary. Roll out to 1/2-in. thickness. Cut with a floured 2-1/2-in. doughnut cutter. Place on greased baking sheets; cover and let rise until almost doubled, about 25 minutes.

4 Bake at 350° for 15-20 minutes or until lightly browned. Combine sugar and cinnamon. Brush warm doughnuts with butter; dip in cinnamon-sugar. **Yield:** about 2-1/2 dozen. —*Jill Shramek Smith, Nevada*

Editor's Note: If your bread machine has a time-delay feature, we recommend you do not use it for this recipe.

The optimist sees the doughnut; the pessimist sees the hole.

Fruit-Filled Kolachkes

Fruit-Filled Kolachkes

*Kolachkes are a small, flaky Polish pastry
made with sweet yeast dough and filled with
fruit, jam, poppy seeds or nuts.*

1-1/4 cups water (70° to 80°)
  1/2 cup butter, softened
    1 egg
    1 egg yolk
    1 teaspoon lemon juice
  1/3 cup nonfat dry milk powder
  1/4 cup mashed potato flakes
  1/4 cup sugar
    1 teaspoon salt
3-3/4 cups plus 3 tablespoons bread flour
    2 teaspoons active dry yeast
    1 can (12 ounces) apricot *or* raspberry filling
Additional butter, melted

1 In bread machine pan, place the first 11 ingredients in order suggested by manufacturer. Select dough setting (check dough after 5 minutes of mixing; add 1 to 2 tablespoons of water or flour if needed).

2 When cycle is completed, turn dough onto a lightly floured surface. Pat or roll into a 15-in. x 10-in. rectangle. Cover with plastic wrap; let rest for 10 min-

utes. Cut dough into 24 squares. Place a heaping teaspoon of filling in the center of each square. Overlap two opposite corners of dough over filling; pinch tightly to seal. Place 2 in. apart on greased baking sheets. Cover and let rise in a warm place until doubled, about 1 hour.

Shaping Fruit-Filled Kolachkes

1. Roll dough into a 15-in. x 10-in. rectangle. Cover with plastic wrap; let rest for 10 minutes. Cut dough into 24 squares.

2. Place a heaping teaspoonful of filling in the center of each square. Overlap two opposite corners of dough over filling; pinch tightly to seal.

3 Bake at 425° for 8-10 minutes or until lightly browned. Brush with melted butter. Remove from pans to paper towels to cool. **Yield:** 2 dozen.
—*Mary Pecinovsky, Calmar, Iowa*

Editor's Note: This recipe was tested with Solo fruit filling. If your bread machine has a time-delay feature, we recommend you do not use it for this recipe.

Bohemian Kolachkes

In Eastern Europe, a kolachke is typically shaped into a circle, which is a symbol of good luck, prosperity and eternity.

    2 packages (1/4 ounce *each*) active dry yeast
  1/2 cup sugar, *divided*
    2 cups warm milk (110° to 115°)
5-3/4 to 6-1/2 cups all-purpose flour
    4 egg yolks
    1 teaspoon salt
  1/4 cup butter, softened
    2 cups canned prune, poppy seed, cherry *or*
        lemon pie filling
    1 egg white, beaten

1 In a small bowl, dissolve yeast and 1 tablespoon sugar in warm milk; let stand for 5 minutes. In a large mixing bowl, combine 2 cups flour, egg yolks, salt, butter, yeast mixture and remaining sugar; beat until smooth. Stir in enough remaining flour to form a stiff dough.

2 Turn onto a floured surface; knead until smooth and elastic, about 6-8 minutes. Add additional flour if necessary. Place dough in a greased bowl, turning once to grease top. Cover and let rise in a warm place until doubled, about 1 hour.

3 Punch dough down. Turn onto a lightly floured surface; roll out to 1/2-in. thickness. Cut with a large glass or a 2-1/2-in. cutter. Place on greased baking sheets. Let rise until doubled, about 45 minutes.

4 Firmly press an indentation in the center of each roll; fill each with a heaping tablespoon of filling. Brush dough with egg white. Bake at 350° for 15-20 minutes or until rolls are light golden brown. **Yield:** about 2-1/2 dozen.   —*Maxine Hron, Quincy, Illinois*

Almond Croissants

These tender croissants are a little lighter than others. The subtle flavor of almond pairs well with a cup of hot coffee or a glass of cold milk.

    1 package (1/4 ounce) active dry yeast
  1/4 cup warm water (110° to 115°)
    4 cups all-purpose flour
  1/4 cup sugar
    1 teaspoon salt
    1 cup cold butter
  3/4 cup warm milk (110° to 115°)
    3 egg yolks
FILLING:
  1/2 cup almond paste
    1 egg white
  1/4 cup confectioners' sugar
EGG WASH:
    1 egg white
    1 tablespoon water
  1/4 cup sliced almonds

1 In a bowl, dissolve yeast in warm water. In a large bowl, combine the flour, sugar and salt. Cut in butter until mixture is crumbly. Add milk and egg yolks to yeast mixture; mix well. Stir into crumb mixture; mix well. Do not knead. Cover and refrigerate overnight.

2 Punch dough down. Turn onto a lightly floured surface; divide in half. Roll each portion into a 12-in. circle; cut each circle into eight wedges. In a small mixing bowl, beat filling ingredients until smooth. Spread over wedges; roll up from wide end. Place pointed side down 3 in. apart on ungreased baking sheets. Curve ends to form a crescent shape. Cover and let rise in a warm place for 1 hour (dough will not double).

3 Beat egg white and water; brush over crescents. Sprinkle with almonds. Bake at 350° for 15-20 minutes. Remove from pans to wire racks to cool. **Yield:** 16 rolls. —*Patricia Glass, East Wenatchee, Washington*

Cherry Danish

These ruby-colored pastries will be the first to disappear from your brunch table. You can use apple pie filling with equally good results.

- 1 package (1/4 ounce) active dry yeast
- 1/4 cup warm water (110° to 115°)
- 1 cup warm milk (110° to 115°)
- 3/4 cup shortening, *divided*
- 1/3 cup sugar
- 3 eggs
- 1 teaspoon salt
- 1/4 teaspoon ground mace
- 1/4 teaspoon lemon extract
- 1/4 teaspoon vanilla extract
- 4 to 4-1/2 cups all-purpose flour
- 1 can (21 ounces) cherry pie filling

GLAZE:
- 1-1/2 cups confectioners' sugar
- 2 to 3 tablespoons milk
- 1/2 teaspoon vanilla extract
- 1/4 cup chopped almonds

1 In a large mixing bowl, dissolve yeast in warm water. Add the milk, 1/4 cup shortening, sugar, two eggs, salt, mace, extracts and 2 cups flour; beat until smooth. Stir in enough remaining flour to form a soft dough.

2 Turn onto a floured surface; knead until smooth and elastic, about 6-8 minutes. Place in a greased bowl, turning once to grease top. Cover and let rise in a warm place until doubled, about 1 hour.

3 Punch dough down. Turn onto a lightly floured surface; roll into a 24-in. x 16-in. rectangle. Dot half of the dough with 1/4 cup shortening; fold dough in half lengthwise. Dot with shortening and fold lengthwise into thirds. Dot with remaining shortening and fold widthwise into thirds.

4 Roll dough into a 16-in. x 15-in. rectangle. Cut into 8-in. x 3/4-in. strips; coil into spiral shapes, tucking end underneath the coil. Place on greased baking sheets. Cover and let rise until doubled, about 1 hour. Beat remaining egg. Make a depression in the center of each roll; brush with egg. Fill each with pie filling.

5 Bake at 375° for 15-18 minutes or until golden brown. Remove from pans to wire racks to cool. For glaze, combine the confectioners' sugar, milk and vanilla; drizzle over rolls. Sprinkle with almonds. **Yield:** 40 rolls.
—*Christie Cochran, Canyon, Texas*

Cherry Danish

Quick 'n' Easy Cinnamon Rolls

The delectable homemade taste of these cinnamon rolls will bring raves. With raisins and a light lemon glaze, these rolls are perfect for a special brunch.

    1 **loaf (1 pound) frozen bread dough, thawed**
    3 **tablespoons butter, melted**
1/3 **cup sugar**
    2 **teaspoons ground cinnamon**
    1 **teaspoon grated lemon peel**
1/2 **cup raisins**
GLAZE:
1/2 **cup confectioners' sugar**
    2 **tablespoons lemon juice**

1 On a lightly floured surface, roll the dough into a 14-in. x 10-in. rectangle. Brush with butter. Combine the sugar, cinnamon and lemon peel; sprinkle evenly over butter. Sprinkle with raisins.

2 Roll up jelly-roll style, starting with a long side; pinch seam to seal. Cut into 12 rolls. Place cut side down in a greased 11-in. x 7-in. x 2-in. baking pan. Cover and let rise until doubled, about 45 minutes.

3 Bake at 350° for 25-30 minutes or until golden brown. Cool for 10 minutes. Combine glaze ingredients; brush over rolls. **Yield:** 1 dozen. —*Gayle Grigg Phoenix, Arizona*

Morning Crispies

Morning Crispies

These large cinnamon-sugar pastries make quite an impression on the table. Every bite melts in your mouth.

    1 **package (1/4 ounce) active dry yeast**
1/2 **cup warm water (110° to 115°)**
    1 **cup warm milk (110° to 115°)**
    2 **cups sugar,** *divided*
1/2 **cup vegetable oil**
1-1/4 **teaspoons salt**
    2 **eggs**
1-1/2 **teaspoons lemon extract**
5-1/2 **to 6 cups all-purpose flour**
    6 **tablespoons butter, softened,** *divided*
    1 **tablespoon ground cinnamon**

1 In a large mixing bowl, dissolve yeast in warm water. Add the milk, 1/2 cup sugar, oil, salt, eggs, ex- tract and 2 cups flour; beat well. Stir in enough remaining flour to form a soft dough.

2 Turn onto a floured surface; knead until smooth and elastic, about 6-8 minutes. Place in a greased bowl, turning once to grease top. Cover and let rise in a warm place until doubled, about 1 hour.

3 Punch dough down. Turn onto a lightly floured surface; roll into a large rectangle, 1/4 in. thick. Spread with 2 tablespoons butter; sprinkle with 1/3 cup of the remaining sugar. Fold dough in half lengthwise; roll out to 1/4-in. thickness. Spread with 2 tablespoons butter; sprinkle with 1/3 cup sugar. Fold in half width- wise; roll out to 1/4-in. thickness. Spread with remain- ing butter; sprinkle with 1/3 cup sugar. Fold in half lengthwise; roll into an 18-in. x 10-in. rectangle. Com- bine the cinnamon and remaining sugar; sprinkle half over the dough to within 1/4 in. of edges.

4 Roll up jelly-roll style, starting with a short side; pinch seams to seal. Cut into 1/2-in. slices; place on greased baking sheets (four to six slices per sheet). Cover with waxed paper and flatten with palm of hand. Sprinkle with remaining cinnamon-sugar. Let stand for 30 minutes.

5 Bake at 400° for 12-15 minutes. Immediately remove from pans to wire racks to cool. **Yield:** about 1-1/2 dozen. —*Emily Goad, Franklin, Indiana*

storing coffee cakes & sweet rolls

- Cool coffee cakes and sweet rolls completely. Place in an airtight container or plastic bag; keep at room temperature for 2 to 3 days. Breads containing perishable items should be refrigerated.

- For longer storage, unfrosted sweet breads can be frozen for up to 3 months. Thaw at room temperature, then frost or glaze as desired.

Cranberry Almond Sweet Rolls

These sweet rolls feature tangy cranberries, crunchy almonds and vanilla chips.

- 1 package (16 ounces) hot roll mix
- 2 tablespoons sugar
- 1/2 teaspoon ground cinnamon
- 1/2 teaspoon ground ginger
- 1/4 teaspoon ground nutmeg
- 1 cup warm water (110° to 115°)
- 2 tablespoons butter, softened
- 1 egg, beaten
- 1 cup finely chopped fresh *or* frozen cranberries
- 1 package (10 to 12 ounces) vanilla *or* white chips
- 1 cup slivered almonds
- 1/4 cup confectioners' sugar
- 1/2 teaspoon lemon juice
- 3 to 4 teaspoons milk

1 In a large bowl, combine the contents of hot roll mix, sugar, cinnamon, ginger and nutmeg; mix well. Stir in the water, butter and egg to form a soft dough. Turn onto a floured surface; knead until smooth and elastic, about 6-8 minutes. Cover and let rest for 5 minutes.

2 Roll into a 15-in. x 10-in. rectangle; sprinkle with cranberries. Set aside 1/2 cup vanilla chips for glaze. Sprinkle almonds and remaining chips over cranberries.

3 Roll up jelly-roll style, starting with a long side; pinch seam to seal. Cut into 12 slices; place in a greased 13-in. x 9-in. x 2-in. baking pan. Cover and let rise in a warm place until doubled, about 30 minutes.

4 Bake at 375° for 18-20 minutes or until lightly browned. In a saucepan over low heat, melt reserved vanilla chips. Stir in the confectioners' sugar, lemon juice and milk. Drizzle over warm rolls. **Yield:** 1 dozen.
—*Marian Platt, Sequim, Washington*

Austrian Apple Twists

Austrian Apple Twists

The addition of apple makes these butterhorns stand out from all the rest. The recipe is actually quite easy to make because no rising time is needed.

- 1 package (1/4 ounce) active dry yeast
- 3 cups all-purpose flour
- 1 cup butter, softened
- 3 egg yolks, beaten
- 1 cup (8 ounces) sour cream
- 1/2 cup sugar
- 1/2 cup finely chopped pecans
- 3/4 teaspoon ground cinnamon
- 1 medium tart apple, peeled, cored and finely chopped

ICING:
- 1 cup confectioners' sugar
- 4 teaspoons milk
- 1/4 teaspoon vanilla extract

Finely chopped pecans

1 In a large mixing bowl, combine the yeast and flour. Add butter and mix well. Add egg yolks and sour cream; mix well. Shape into four balls. Place in separate resealable plastic bags or wrap in plastic wrap; refrigerate overnight.

2 On a floured surface, roll each ball of dough into a 9-in. circle. Combine sugar, pecans and cinnamon; sprinkle over each circle. Top with apple. Cut each circle into 16 wedges. Roll up wedges from the wide end and place pointed side down 2 in. apart on greased baking sheets.

3 Bake at 350° for 16-20 minutes or until lightly browned. Immediately remove from pans to wire racks to cool. For icing, combine the confectioners' sugar, milk and vanilla until smooth; drizzle over rolls. Sprinkle with pecans. **Yield:** 64 rolls.

—Kathy Bless, Fayetteville, Pennsylvania

Editor's Note: The yeast does not need to be dissolved in liquid, and no rising time is necessary before baking.

Butterscotch Crescents

With a coconut and pecan filling and a brown sugar frosting, these flaky rolls are loaded with flavor. Butterscotch pudding mix in the dough makes them nice and moist.

　1 can (12 ounces) evaporated milk
　1 package (3-1/2 ounces) cook-and-serve butterscotch pudding mix
1/2 cup butter, cubed
　2 packages (1/4 ounce *each*) active dry yeast
1/4 cup warm water (110° to 115°)
　2 eggs
　2 teaspoons salt
　5 to 5-1/2 cups all-purpose flour
FILLING:
　2/3 cup packed brown sugar
　2/3 cup flaked coconut
　1/3 cup chopped pecans
　1/4 cup butter, melted
　2 tablespoons all-purpose flour
FROSTING:
　1/4 cup packed brown sugar
　2 tablespoons butter
　1 cup confectioners' sugar
　2 to 3 tablespoons hot water, optional

Butterscotch Crescents

1 Set aside 2 tablespoons evaporated milk for frosting. In a saucepan, combine pudding mix and remaining milk until smooth. Bring to a boil over medium heat, stirring constantly. Remove from the heat; stir in butter until melted. Let stand until mixture cools to 110°-115°.

2 In a large mixing bowl, dissolve yeast in warm water. Beat in eggs, salt, 2 cups flour and pudding mixture until smooth. Stir in enough remaining flour to form a soft dough.

3 Turn onto a floured surface; knead until smooth and elastic, about 6-8 minutes. Place in a greased bowl, turning once to grease top. Cover and let rise in a warm place until doubled, about 1 hour.

4 Punch dough down. Turn onto a lightly floured surface; divide into thirds. Roll each portion into a 15-in. circle. Combine filling ingredients; spread 1/2 cup over each circle. Cut each circle into 12 wedges. Roll up wedges from the wide end. Place pointed side down 2 in. apart on greased baking sheets. Curve ends to form a crescent shape. Cover and let rise until doubled, about 45 minutes.

5 Bake at 375° for 15-18 minutes or until golden brown. Remove from pans to wire racks to cool.

6 For frosting, combine the brown sugar, butter and reserved evaporated milk in a saucepan. Cook and stir over low heat until smooth. Remove from the heat; stir in confectioners' sugar until smooth. Add water if needed to achieve desired consistency. Frost rolls. **Yield:** 3 dozen.

—Phyllis Hofer, De Witt, Iowa

Orange Knots

Orange Knots

These orange rolls are a little time-consuming to prepare, but they're worth the extra effort. They bake up featherlight with a sweet and tangy flavor.

2 packages (1/4 ounce *each*) active dry yeast
1/4 cup warm water (110° to 115°)
1 cup warm milk (110° to 115°)
1/3 cup sugar
1/2 cup butter, softened
1 teaspoon salt
2 eggs
1/4 cup orange juice
2 tablespoons grated orange peel
5-1/4 to 5-3/4 cups all-purpose flour
ORANGE ICING:
1 cup confectioners' sugar
2 tablespoons orange juice
1 teaspoon grated orange peel

1 In a large mixing bowl, dissolve yeast in warm water. Add the milk, sugar, butter, salt, eggs, orange juice, orange peel and 3 cups flour; beat until smooth. Stir in enough remaining flour to form a soft dough.

2 Turn onto a floured surface; knead until smooth and elastic, about 6-8 minutes. Place in a greased bowl, turning once to grease top. Cover and let rise in a warm place until doubled, about 1 hour.

3 Punch dough down. Turn onto a lightly floured surface; roll into a 16-in. x 10-in. rectangle, about 1/2 in. thick. Cut into 10-in. x 3/4-in. strips; roll lightly and tie into knots. Place on greased baking sheets; tuck ends under. Cover and let rise until doubled, about 45 minutes.

4 Bake at 400° for 10-12 minutes or until golden brown. Remove from pans to wire racks to cool. Combine icing ingredients; drizzle over rolls. **Yield:** 20 rolls.   —*Bernice Morris, Marshfield, Missouri*

French Crescent Rolls

*Layers of buttered dough result in
the richest sweet rolls you've ever tasted.*

    1 package (1/4 ounce) active dry yeast
  1/4 cup warm water (110° to 115°)
  3/4 cup warm milk (110° to 115°)
    1 egg
    2 tablespoons sugar
    1 tablespoon shortening
    1 teaspoon salt
2-1/2 cups all-purpose flour
    3 tablespoons butter, softened, *divided*
ICING:
1-1/2 cups confectioners' sugar
    2 tablespoons milk
    3 tablespoons butter
  1/2 teaspoon almond extract
  1/2 teaspoon vanilla extract
  1/2 cup chopped walnuts

1 In a large mixing bowl, dissolve yeast in warm water. Add the milk, egg, sugar, shortening and salt; mix well. Add flour; beat until smooth. Place in a greased bowl, turning once to grease top. Cover and refrigerate for at least 1 hour.

2 Turn dough onto a floured surface; roll to 1/4-in. thickness. Spread with 1 tablespoon butter. Fold corners to the middle and then fold in half. Wrap dough in waxed paper; chill for 30 minutes. Repeat rolling, buttering, folding and chilling steps twice.

3 Turn onto a floured surface; divide dough in half. Roll each portion into an 11-in. circle; cut each circle into eight wedges. Roll up wedges from wide end. Place pointed side down 2 in. apart on greased baking sheets. Curve ends to form a crescent shape. Cover and let rise in a warm place until doubled, about 30 minutes.

4 Bake at 400° for 10 minutes or until lightly browned. Remove from pans to wire racks. For icing, combine confectioners' sugar, milk, butter and extracts; spread over warm rolls. Sprinkle with nuts. **Yield:** 16 rolls.
—*Betty Ann Wolery, Joplin, Montana*

Sour Cream Twists

*Keep some of these terrific flaky twists in your freezer
to serve in a pinch at breakfast, lunch or dinner.*

    1 package (1/4 ounce) active dry yeast
  1/4 cup warm water (110° to 115°)
    3 cups all-purpose flour
1-1/2 teaspoons salt
  1/2 cup cold butter
  1/2 cup shortening
    2 eggs
  1/2 cup sour cream
    3 teaspoons vanilla extract, *divided*
1-1/2 cups sugar

1 In a small bowl, dissolve yeast in warm water. In a mixing bowl, combine flour and salt. Cut in butter and shortening until mixture is crumbly. Stir in the eggs, sour cream, 1 teaspoon vanilla and the yeast mixture; mix well. Cover and refrigerate overnight.

2 Combine sugar and remaining vanilla; lightly sprinkle 1/2 cup over a pastry cloth or work surface. Divide dough in half; put one portion back in the refrigerator. On the sugared surface, roll the other portion into a 12-in. x 8-in. rectangle. Sprinkle with about 1 tablespoon sugar mixture. Fold rectangle into thirds.

3 Give dough a quarter turn; repeat rolling, sugaring and folding two more times. Roll into a 12-in. x 8-in. rectangle. Cut into 4-in. x 1-in. strips; twist each strip two or three times. Place on chilled ungreased baking sheets. Repeat with the remaining dough and sugar mixture.

4 Bake at 375° for 12-14 minutes or until lightly browned. Immediately remove from pans to wire racks to cool. **Yield:** 4 dozen.
—*Linda Welch*
North Platte, Nebraska

Sour Cream Twists

Fanciful Creations
bring fun to the table

Important occasions like weddings, baby showers, birthdays and holiday dinners call for special dishes. Festive finales like Spring Bonnet Cookie Torte (p. 368) and Wedding Petit Fours (p. 366) with Chocolate Butterflies (p. 381) will be the main attraction on your table. Many of this chapter's whimsical treats are easy to do and don't require specialty pans.

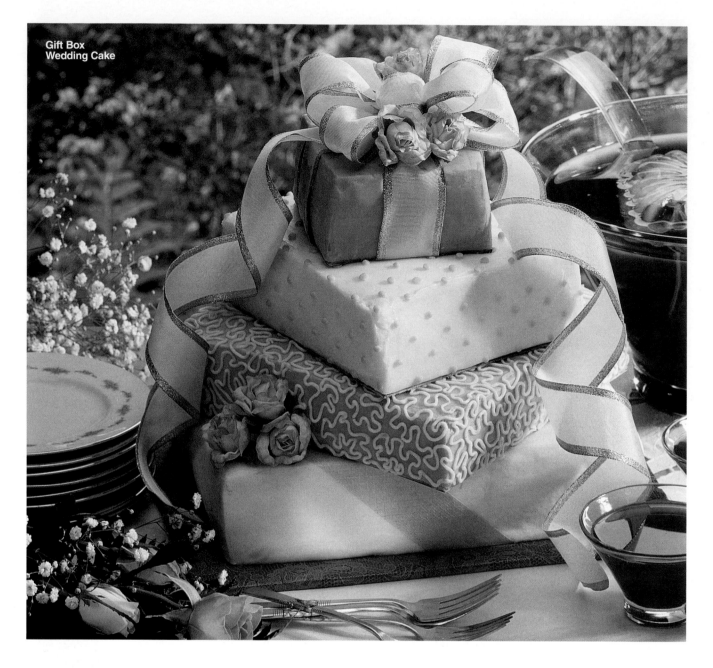

Gift Box
Wedding Cake

Gift Box Wedding Cake

*With the lovely cake "presented" here, you'll never
need to special-order one for a wedding (or an
anniversary) again! The recipe calls for pink icing,
but feel free to use the food coloring of your choice.*

1-1/3 cups poppy seeds, *divided*
   4 packages (18-1/4 ounces *each*) white
      cake mix
   1 package (3.4 ounces) instant lemon
      pudding mix

FROSTING:
1-1/2 cups butter, softened
  15 cups confectioners' sugar
  3/4 cup half-and-half cream
1-1/2 teaspoons vanilla extract
  1/2 teaspoon salt
Pink liquid *or* paste food coloring

1 Place 1/3 cup poppy seeds in each of four small
bowls; add the water called for in cake mix directions to each bowl. Soak for 1 hour.

2 Prepare cake batters according to package directions, using the poppy seed water. Bake in three greased and floured 13-in. x 9-in. x 2-in. baking pans and two 8-in. square baking dishes. Cool for 10 minutes before removing from pans to wire racks to cool completely. Prepare pudding mix according to package directions; refrigerate.

3 For frosting, in a large mixing bowl, cream butter and confectioners' sugar. Add the cream, vanilla and salt; beat on medium speed until light and fluffy, about 3 minutes. (Frosting may need to be made in batches.) Add food coloring to 4-1/2 cups frosting.

4 Cut a small hole in the corner of two pastry bags or heavy-duty resealable plastic bags; insert round pastry tip #3 in one bag and round pastry tip #5 in the other. Place 1/2 cup white frosting in the bag with tip #3 and 1/2 cup pink frosting in the bag with tip #5. Cover remaining frosting with a damp clean cloth until ready to use.

5 Trim two 13-in. x 9-in. cakes into 12-in. x 8-in. rectangles (see Fig. 1a); level tops (see Leveling Cake Layers on page 99). Cut an 8-in. x 2-in. strip off each, leaving two pieces (A). Cut each strip in half, forming four 4-in. x 2-in. pieces. Attach two 4-in. x 2-in. pieces together lengthwise with white frosting to form a 4-in. x 4-in. piece (see Fig. 1b); repeat with two remaining pieces and set aside.

6 Trim remaining 13-in. x 9-in. cake into a 12-in. x 7-in. rectangle (see Fig. 2); level top. Cut cake in half to form two 7-in. x 6-in. pieces (C); set aside. Level tops of 8-in. square cakes.

7 Each frosted layer of the cake consists of two cake pieces with lemon pudding filling in between. Place one piece A on a covered board; spread with pudding to within 1/2 in. of edges. Place second piece A on top; set aside. Repeat filling procedure for remaining layers (pieces B, C and 8-in. square cakes) and place on covered boards.

8 For bottom layer, frost piece A with 3-1/2 cups white frosting. If desired, attach a ribbon across the corners of piece A (as shown in photo on opposite page).

9 For second layer, frost 8-in. cake with 2-1/2 cups pink frosting. With prepared bag of white frosting, pipe a continuous string, curving up, down and around so strings never touch or cross on cake.

10 For third layer, frost piece C with 2 cups white frosting. With prepared bag of pink frosting, pipe dots 1/2 in. apart over entire cake. Frost piece B with remaining pink frosting. Add bow on top.

11 For bottom three layers, cut a 1/4-in.-diameter dowel rod into five pieces the height of each layer. Insert dowels 1-2 in. apart in center of each cake to support the next layer. Carefully stack layers on a large serving platter, working from largest cake to smallest. Decorate with ribbon and silk flowers as desired. Remove dowels before cutting each layer. **Yield:** 50 servings.

Editor's Note: Unfrosted cakes can be frozen for up to 6 months wrapped in foil. Frosting can be prepared 2 weeks ahead; store in refrigerator. Rewhip before spreading. Cake can be assembled 8 hours before serving.

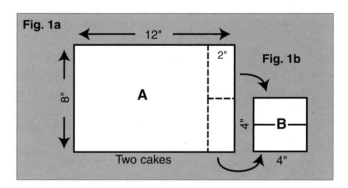

Fig. 1a — 12" — 8" — A — Two cakes — 2" — Fig. 1b — 4" — B — 4"

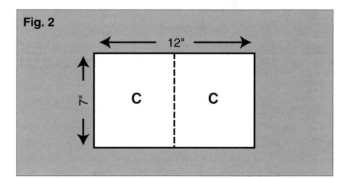

Fig. 2 — 12" — 7" — C — C

Wedding Petit Fours

(Also pictured on pages 362 and 363)

Prepare these bite-size cakes for any occasion by changing the shape and food coloring.

- 1 package (18-1/4 ounces) white cake mix
- 3 cups confectioners' sugar
- 1/4 cup water
- 3 tablespoons light corn syrup
- 2 tablespoons butter
- 1/2 teaspoon vanilla extract
- 1/4 teaspoon almond extract
- Food coloring, optional
- Chocolate Butterflies (page 381), optional

1 Line a greased 15-in. x 10-in. x 1-in. baking pan with parchment paper. Prepare cake batter according to package directions; pour into prepared pan. Bake at 350° for 18-24 minutes or until a toothpick inserted near the center comes out clean. Cool completely in pan on a wire rack.

2 Invert cake onto a large cutting board or work surface. Gently peel off parchment paper. Cut cake into hearts (or other desired shapes) with a 2-1/2-in. to 3-in. cookie cutter.

3 For glaze, combine the confectioners' sugar, water, corn syrup, butter and extracts in a mixing bowl; beat on low speed until sugar is moistened. Beat on high until smooth. Tint with food coloring if desired. Add 2-3 teaspoons of additional water if needed for desired consistency.

4 Place petit fours on a wire rack with a piece of waxed paper beneath. Spoon glaze evenly over top and sides, letting excess drip off. When glaze is dry, repeat with a second coat. Top each with a Chocolate Butterfly if desired. **Yield:** 1-1/2 dozen.

Glazing Petit Fours

Place a wire rack over a sheet of waxed paper. Arrange petit fours on rack, leaving space between each. Spoon glaze over the top and sides, allowing excess to drip off. When glaze is dry, repeat with a second coat.

Wedding Petit Fours

Booties 'n' Rattles Cake

This cake is easy to make and feeds a bunch. You can simply frost it, or follow the easy instructions here for an adorably adorned baby shower dessert.

- 6 eggs, *separated*
- 1-1/2 cups butter, softened
- 1-1/2 cups sugar
- 3 tablespoons grated orange peel
- 2 cups all-purpose flour
- 2 teaspoons baking powder
- 1/4 teaspoon salt
- 6 cups Easy Vanilla Buttercream Frosting (page 140)
- Pink and blue liquid food coloring

1 Let separated eggs stand at room temperature for 30 minutes. In a large mixing bowl, cream butter and sugar until light and fluffy. Add egg yolks and orange peel; beat well. Combine the flour, baking powder and salt; add to creamed mixture and mix well (batter will be thick). In a small mixing bowl and with clean beaters, beat the egg whites on high speed until stiff peaks form. Fold into batter.

2 Pour into a greased and floured 13-in. x 9-in. x 2-in. baking pan. Bake at 375° for 25-30 minutes or until a toothpick inserted near the center comes out clean. Cool for 10 minutes before inverting onto a wire rack to cool completely. Transfer cake to a large platter or covered board (about 15 in. x 12 in.).

3 Place 3/4 cup frosting each in two small bowls; tint one pastel pink and one pastel blue. Set aside 2-1/2 cups white frosting for trim and border. Cover and set bowls aside. Frost cake with the remaining white frosting.

4 Using dental floss or a sharp knife, mark a straight line lengthwise down the center of cake. Mark an additional lengthwise line on each side of the center line, dividing cake into four equal sections. Mark four lines widthwise, dividing cake into a total of 20 squares.

5 For booties, cut a small hole in the corner of a pastry bag or heavy-duty resealable plastic bag. Insert round pastry tip #8; fill bag with pink frosting. In alternating squares, pipe an elongated dot, raising up at one end to form the heel.

6 For rattles, use another pastry bag, round tip #8 and blue frosting. In each empty square, pipe one large dot and one small dot, leaving 3/4 in. between. Use round pastry tip #2 and blue frosting to pipe a line connecting the dots.

7 For trim, use a third pastry bag, round tip #2 and reserved white frosting. Pipe a bow and trim on each bootie and a bow on each rattle.

8 Use star pastry tip #20 and white frosting to pipe rows of shells (see Shell Border on page 142) on top of the straight lines. Pipe a row of shells around top and bottom edges of cake. **Yield:** 20 servings.
—*Mary Cicio, Youngwood, Pennsylvania*

Editor's Note: Use of a coupler ring will allow you to change tips easily for different designs.

Decorating the Booties 'n' Rattles Cake

1. For booties, use round tip #8 and pink frosting to pipe an elongated dot, raising up at one end to form the heel.

2. For rattles, use round tip #8 and blue frosting to pipe one large dot and one small dot, leaving 3/4 in. of space between. Use round tip #2 to pipe a line to connect dots.

3. For trim, use round tip #2 and white frosting to pipe a bow and trim on each bootie and a bow on each rattle.

Booties 'n' Rattles Cake

Spring Bonnet Cookie Torte

Spring Bonnet Cookie Torte

(Also pictured on page 362)

Unlike other hat-shaped desserts, this one is fashioned from crisp cookies. A dreamy creamy filling holds the layers of cookies together and serves to soften them at the same time, making it a cinch to slice. Add silk flowers to the torte's brim as in the photo above.

  3/4 **cup butter, softened**
1-1/2 **cups sugar**
    2 **eggs**
  3/4 **teaspoon vanilla extract**
    3 **cups all-purpose flour**
1-1/2 **teaspoons baking powder**
  3/4 **teaspoon salt**
Additional sugar
FILLING:
    1 **cup vanilla** *or* **white chips**
  1/4 **cup half-and-half cream**

    1 **cup heavy whipping cream, whipped**
    1 **teaspoon vanilla extract**
FROSTING:
  1/2 **cup butter, softened**
  1/2 **cup shortening**
    4 **cups confectioners' sugar**
    2 **tablespoons heavy whipping cream**
    1 **teaspoon almond extract**
Pink *or* **red liquid** *or* **paste food coloring**

1 In a large mixing bowl, cream butter and sugar until light and fluffy. Beat in eggs and vanilla. Combine the flour, baking powder and salt; add to creamed mixture and mix well. Form seven balls, using 1/4 cup of dough for each. Form three balls, using about 1/2 cup of dough for each. Cover and refrigerate for 1 hour.

2 Sprinkle each ball with additional sugar and place each one between two sheets of waxed paper. Roll smaller balls into 6-in. circles. Roll larger balls into 9-in. circles. Remove top sheet of waxed paper and invert circles onto ungreased baking sheets. Remove waxed paper; prick cookies with a fork.

3 Bake at 350° for 8-10 minutes or until edges are lightly browned. Carefully loosen cookies and place on paper towels to cool.

4 In a small heavy saucepan or microwave, melt chips with half-and-half; stir until smooth. Cool to room temperature. Combine whipped cream and vanilla; fold into melted mixture.

5 To form bonnet brim, layer 9-in. cookies on a large platter or covered board (about 15 in. square), spreading 1/2 cup filling between layers. For crown, spread 1/4 cup filling on the bottom of one 6-in. cookie and center cookie on top of the 9-in. layer. Layer remaining 6-in. cookies, spreading 1/4 cup filling between layers. Refrigerate overnight.

6 For frosting, in a large mixing bowl, beat butter, shortening and sugar on low speed until blended; beat on high for 5 minutes. Reduce speed to medium. Gradually add cream and extract, beating until smooth. Set aside 3/4 cup; tint remaining frosting pink.

7 Spread pink frosting over top and sides of cookies. Cut a small hole in the corner of a pastry bag or heavy-duty resealable plastic bag; insert star pastry tip #20. Fill bag with white frosting. Holding bag at a 45°

angle, form shell border at base of bonnet (see Making a Shell Border on page 142). Using the same tip, form a reverse shell border on top of bonnet.

8 Using another pastry bag, basketweave pastry tip #48 and white frosting, hold bag at a 45° angle to form a ribbed border at base of crown. Decorate with silk flowers on one side of bonnet. Tie a piece of ribbon into a bow and place on opposite side of bonnet. **Yield:** 8-10 servings.

Cookie Burgers

You may have to install a drive-thru window in your kitchen after family and friends sample these playful treats from the Hershey Kitchens! The "buns" hold a "patty" of deliciously creamy cocoa icing on a bed of green-tinted coconut "lettuce".

> 1 package (17-1/2 ounces) sugar cookie mix*
> 2 drops yellow food coloring, optional
> 1-1/2 cups peanut butter chips, chopped
> 3/4 cup flaked coconut
> Green liquid food coloring
> FILLING:
> 1/2 cup butter, softened
> 2-2/3 cups confectioners' sugar
> 1/2 cup baking cocoa
> 1/4 cup milk
> 1 teaspoon vanilla extract

1 Prepare cookie dough according to package directions; add yellow food coloring if desired. Stir in peanut butter chips. Shape into 1-1/4-in. balls; place 2 in. apart on ungreased baking sheets. Flatten slightly with a glass. Bake at 375° for 9-10 minutes or until lightly browned. Remove to wire racks to cool.

2 Place coconut in a plastic bag; sprinkle 5-6 drops green food coloring into bag and shake until color is evenly distributed.

3 In a small mixing bowl, cream butter until smooth. Add the confectioners' sugar, cocoa, milk and vanilla; beat until smooth. Spread over the bottoms of half of the cookies; sprinkle with coconut. Top with remaining cookies and gently squeeze together. **Yield:** about 22 sandwich cookies.

*Editor's Note: You may substitute your favorite sugar cookie recipe for the cookie mix; just add the yellow food coloring if desired and the peanut butter chips.

Cookie Burgers

Kitty Cat Cupcakes

Kitty Cat Cupcakes

These fine feline treats are so simple to assemble. Kids will be clamoring to help decorate!

    2/3 cup shortening
1-3/4 cups sugar, *divided*
      4 eggs, *separated*
2-1/2 cups all-purpose flour
2-1/2 teaspoons baking powder
    1/2 teaspoon salt
      1 cup orange juice
      1 cup flaked coconut
FROSTING:
1-1/4 cups sugar
    1/4 cup water
    1/4 cup light corn syrup
      1 egg white
    1/8 teaspoon salt
    1/2 cup miniature marshmallows (about 50)
    1/2 teaspoon vanilla extract
Assorted M&M's
      1 piece red shoestring licorice, cut into 3/4-inch
        pieces
Chocolate sprinkles
About 9 vanilla wafers
      2 cups flaked coconut, toasted

1 In a large mixing bowl, cream shortening and 1-1/2 cups sugar until light and fluffy. Add egg yolks; mix well. Combine the flour, baking powder and salt; add to creamed mixture alternately with orange juice, beating well after each addition.

2 In a small mixing bowl and with clean beaters, beat egg whites on medium speed until soft peaks form. Gradually beat in the remaining sugar, a table-spoon at a time, on high until stiff peaks form. Fold into creamed mixture along with coconut.

3 Fill paper-lined muffin cups two-thirds full. Bake at 350° for 15 minutes or until a toothpick comes out clean. Cool for 10 minutes before removing from pans to wire racks to cool completely.

4 For frosting, combine the sugar, water, corn syrup, egg white and salt in a heavy saucepan. With a portable mixer, beat on low speed for 1 minute. Continue beating on low over low heat until frosting reaches 160°, about 12-18 minutes. Pour into a large mixing bowl; add marshmallows and vanilla. Beat on high until stiff peaks form, about 5 minutes. Frost cupcakes.

5 Arrange M&M's for eyes and nose, licorice for mouth and sprinkles for whiskers. For ears, cut vanilla wafers into quarters with a serrated knife; place two on each cupcake, rounded side down. Sprinkle with coconut. Refrigerate until serving. **Yield:** about 1-1/2 dozen. —*Doris Barb, El Dorado, Kansas*

Editor's Note: A stand mixer is recommended for beating the frosting after it reaches 160°.

Butterfly Cupcakes

Herald the arrival of spring with a platter of these eye-catching cupcakes bursting with lemon pie filling.

    3/4 cup butter, softened
    3/4 cup sugar
      3 eggs

Butterfly Cupcakes

1 teaspoon vanilla extract
2 cups self-rising flour*
1/2 cup milk
1 can (15-3/4 ounces) lemon pie filling
40 pieces red *and/or* black shoestring licorice (2 inches)

1 In a large mixing bowl, cream butter and sugar until light and fluffy. Beat in eggs and vanilla. Add flour to creamed mixture alternately with milk, beating well after each addition.

2 Fill greased muffin cups half full. Bake at 350° for 15-20 minutes or until a toothpick inserted near the center comes out clean. Cool for 10 minutes before removing from pans to wire racks to cool completely.

3 Cut off the top fourth of each cupcake; cut the slices in half. Spoon 1 tablespoon pie filling onto each cupcake. Place two halves upside down on top of filling for wings. Insert two pieces of licorice for antennae. **Yield:** 20 cupcakes.

—*Adeline Piscitelle, Sayreville, New Jersey*

*Editor's Note: As a substitute for *each* cup of self-rising flour, place 1-1/2 teaspoons baking powder and 1/2 teaspoon salt in a measuring cup. Add all-purpose flour to measure 1 cup.

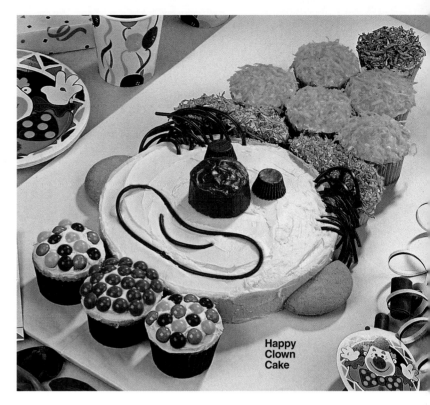

Happy Clown Cake

Happy Clown Cake

Children of all ages will find this fun-filled cake irresistible! To serve, first pass out the cupcakes, then cut up what's left.

1 package (18-1/4 ounces) yellow cake mix
1 cup flaked coconut, *divided*
Yellow, blue, green and red liquid food coloring
1 package (5 ounces) red shoestring licorice
1 can (16 ounces) vanilla frosting
2 miniature peanut butter cups
1 package (2.17 ounces) Skittles bite-size candies

1 Prepare cake batter according to package directions. Fill 12 paper-lined muffin cups two-thirds full. Pour remaining batter into a greased 9-in. round baking pan. Bake cake and cupcakes according to package directions. Cool for 10 minutes before removing from pans to wire racks to cool completely.

2 Place 1/2 cup coconut in a plastic bag; sprinkle 5-6 drops of yellow food coloring into bag and shake until color is evenly distributed. Repeat with 1/4 cup coconut and blue coloring, then with remaining coconut and green coloring. Reserve one licorice piece for mouth; cut remaining pieces into 2-in. to 3-in. pieces for hair.

3 Frost round cake with vanilla frosting; place on a large platter or covered board (about 22 in. x 15 in.). Press peanut butter cups upside down in place for eyes. Form long licorice piece into mouth and press into frosting (insert a small piece for smile if desired).

4 Remove liner from one cupcake and cut the top off. Cut the top in half again and press into sides of frosted cake for ears. Tint 2 tablespoons of frosting with red food coloring; frost bottom half of cupcake and press in place for nose.

5 Frost all remaining cupcakes. Remove liners from two cupcakes and cut in half; sprinkle with green coconut. Press flat sides against top of cake to form hat brim. Sprinkle five cupcakes with yellow coconut and one with blue coconut; stack in a pyramid on top of brim to make the hat.

6 Push ends of small licorice pieces into frosting for hair. Place remaining cupcakes at bottom of cake to make a bow tie; decorate those cupcakes with Skittles. **Yield:** 16-20 servings.

Fish-Shaped Cakes

Create a trophy-size treat with these tropical fishes. With a cake mix, some 9-inch round pans and a sharp knife, you can land your own school of sweet fish in no time!

  1 **package (18-1/4 ounces) lemon cake mix**
1/2 **cup milk**
  2 **teaspoons grated lemon peel, *divided***
  1 **teaspoon coconut extract**
  1 **package (3.4 ounces) instant coconut cream *or* lemon pudding mix**
  1 **carton (8 ounces) frozen whipped topping, thawed**
1/3 **cup confectioners' sugar**
Red, yellow, green and blue liquid food coloring
  2 **black jelly beans**
  9 **slices fresh lemon**
  2 **cups flaked coconut**

1 Prepare cake batter according to package directions, replacing 1/2 cup water with milk. Add 1 teaspoon lemon peel and coconut extract. Pour batter into two greased and floured 9-in. round baking pans.

2 Bake at 350° for 28-30 minutes or until a toothpick inserted near the center comes out clean. Cool for 10 minutes before removing from pans to wire racks to cool completely.

3 Prepare pudding according to package directions; add remaining lemon peel. Cut cakes into large and small fish (see illustration below). Split each fish into two horizontal layers; spread pudding on bottom layers and replace tops.

4 Place fish on a large platter or covered board (about 22 in. x 16 in.). Combine the whipped topping and confectioners' sugar; set aside 1 tablespoon. Use remaining frosting to frost top and sides of each fish.

5 On each large fish, place three separate drops of red food coloring on the top third, three drops of yellow on the middle third and three drops of green on the bottom third. Starting from top edge of fish, use the tip of a spoon to form scales and blend colors into frosting.

6 For eyes, form a 1-in. oval on each large fish with reserved frosting. Place a jelly bean in the center of oval. For small fish, blend one color of food coloring into frosting to make solid-colored fish.

7 Cut four lemon slices in half; place two halves in the center of each large fish for fins. Push rounded edges of one slice into the back of small fish for tails. Cut remaining slices into quarters; place one or two on the bottom of each large fish for fins and two slices on each side of small fish for fins.

8 Place coconut in a plastic bag; sprinkle 3-4 drops of blue food coloring into bag and shake until color is evenly distributed. Sprinkle coconut around fish to resemble water. Store in the refrigerator. **Yield:** 12 servings.

—*Margaret Pache, Mesa, Arizona*

Decorating the Fish-Shaped Cakes

Place three drops of red food coloring on the top third of the cake, three drops of yellow on the middle third and three drops of green on the bottom third, spacing out the drops along the cake. Using the tip of a spoon and a half swirling motion, blend coloring into frosting while making the scales.

Fish-Shaped Cakes

pastry tip #7. Fill bag with batter. On a greased baking sheet, pipe 3 dozen 2-in.-long S shapes for the swan necks, making a small dollop at the end of each for head. Bake at 400° for 5-8 minutes or until golden brown. Remove to wire racks to cool.

3 For swan bodies, drop remaining batter by 36 level tablespoonfuls 2 in. apart onto greased baking sheets. With a small icing knife or spatula, shape batter into 2-in. x 1-1/2-in. teardrops. Bake at 400° for 30-35 minutes or until golden brown. Cool on wire racks.

4 Meanwhile, prepare pudding according to package directions for pie filling; chill.

5 Just before serving, cut off top third of swan bodies; set tops aside. Remove any soft dough inside. Spoon filling into bottoms of puffs. Top each with a small amount of jam if desired. Cut the reserved tops in half lengthwise to form wings; set wings in filling. Place necks in filling. Dust with confectioners' sugar; serve immediately. **Yield:** 3 dozen.
—*Carole Davis, Keene, New Hampshire*

Swan Cream Puffs

These pretty pastries can be prepared a day in advance, then stored at room temperature in an airtight container. Fill just before serving.

  1 **cup water**
1/2 **cup butter**
1/4 **teaspoon salt**
  1 **cup all-purpose flour**
  4 **eggs**
  2 **packages (3.4 ounces** *each***) instant vanilla pudding mix**
  2 **tablespoons seedless raspberry jam, optional**
Confectioners' sugar

1 In a heavy saucepan over medium heat, bring water, butter and salt to a boil. Add flour all at once; stir until a smooth ball forms. Remove from the heat; let stand for 5 minutes. Add eggs, one at a time, beating well after each addition. Beat until smooth and shiny.

2 Cut a small hole in the corner of a pastry bag or heavy-duty resealable plastic bag; insert round

Making Swan Cream Puffs

1. To make swan necks, pipe batter into 3 dozen 2-in. long S shapes onto greased baking sheets, making a small dollop at the end of each for the head. Bake as directed.

2. To assemble cream puffs, cut off the top third of swan bodies. Remove any soft dough inside. Cut tops in half lengthwise to form wings. Fill bottoms of puffs with pudding. Place necks and wings in filling.

Buggy Gal Cake

Buggy Gal Cake

*A delectable chocolate buttermilk cake
forms the base of this cute confection.*

   1 cup shortening
   2 cups sugar
   1 cup buttermilk
   2 eggs
2-1/2 cups all-purpose flour
  1/2 cup baking cocoa
   1 teaspoon baking soda
   1 teaspoon salt
   1 cup water
FROSTING/DECORATING:
  1/4 cup butter, softened
  1/4 cup shortening
  1/2 teaspoon vanilla extract
   2 cups confectioners' sugar
   4 to 5 teaspoons milk
Red paste food coloring
   **1 tube (4.25 ounces) black frosting (about 1/4
     cup)**
   2 vanilla *or* white chips
  12 chocolate-covered peppermint patties
   2 pieces black shoestring licorice (2-1/2 inches)

1 In a large mixing bowl, cream shortening and sugar until light and fluffy. Beat in buttermilk and eggs. Combine the flour, cocoa, baking soda and salt; add to creamed mixture alternately with water, beating well after each addition.

2 Pour into a greased and floured 4-qt. ovenproof bowl. Bake at 350° for 80-90 minutes (covering with foil halfway through baking time) or until a toothpick inserted near the center comes out clean. Cool for 10 minutes before removing from bowl to a wire rack to cool completely.

3 For frosting, cream butter, shortening and vanilla in a large mixing bowl. Gradually beat in confectioners' sugar and enough milk to achieve a spreading consistency. Tint with red food coloring. Set aside 3 tablespoons frosting.

4 Place cake on a serving platter. Frost with remaining frosting, leaving an 8-1/2-in. x 6-in. x 6-in. triangle of cake unfrosted. Frost triangle with some of the black frosting.

5 Fill a heavy-duty resealable plastic bag with remaining black frosting; cut a small hole in corner of bag. Pipe a line from the tip of the triangle over top of cake to the other side, creating wings. With the same frosting, outline triangle edge. For the eyes, pipe a 1/4-in. black dot on the flat side of each vanilla chip; position chips on black triangle and press gently into frosting.

6 Randomly place peppermint patties over red frosting for ladybug's spots; press down gently. Fill another plastic bag with reserved red frosting; cut a small hole in corner of bag. Pipe a smile under eyes. Insert licorice pieces above eyes for antennae. **Yield:** 12-16 servings.   *—LaVonne Hegland, St. Michael, Minnesota*

Sweet Stars Cake

*Three ingredients are all you need for this dazzling
dessert perfect for a Fourth of July celebration.*

  1 package (18-1/4 ounces) chocolate cake mix
  1 can (16 ounces) vanilla frosting
  1 package (5 ounces) Fruit Roll-Ups

1 Prepare and bake cake according to package directions, using two greased and floured 9-in. round baking pans. Cool for 10 minutes before removing from pans to wire racks to cool completely.

2 Place bottom cake layer on a serving plate; spread with some of the frosting. Top with second layer; spread frosting over top and sides of cake.

3 Unroll Fruit Roll-Ups. Cut one blue, one green and one red star with a 2-3/4-in. star-shaped cookie cutter. Place on top of cake. Cut remaining Roll-Ups with a 2-in. star-shaped cookie cutter. Place a yellow star in the center of each large star. Arrange remaining stars on top and sides of cake. **Yield:** 12 servings.

—*Flo Burtnett, Gage, Oklahoma*

Sweet Stars Cake

Susie Sunshine Cake

Fresh fruit garnishes provide the fun final touches on this light citrus cake.

- 1 package (9 ounces) yellow cake mix
- 1 carton (8 ounces) frozen whipped topping, thawed
- 1 teaspoon grated lemon peel
- 1 teaspoon grated orange peel
- Red and yellow liquid food coloring
- 2 medium lemons, sliced and halved
- 2 medium oranges, sliced and halved
- 2 fresh blueberries
- 1 large fresh strawberry

1 Prepare and bake cake according to package directions, using a greased and floured 9-in. round baking pan. Cool for 10 minutes before removing from pan to a wire rack to cool completely. Transfer to a 12-in. to 14-in. serving plate.

2 In a bowl, combine whipped topping and lemon and orange peels. Frost top and sides of cake. Place

drops of red and yellow food coloring randomly over frosting. With a spatula, blend colors randomly.

3 Alternate lemon and orange slices around base of cake to form rays. Add two orange slices and blueberries for eyes. Slice the strawberry; use two center slices for the mouth, placing them on the cake with straight edges touching. Store in the refrigerator. **Yield:** 6 servings.

Decorating Susie Sunshine Cake

1. Place drops of red and yellow food coloring randomly over the frosted cake.

2. Blend colors randomly over frosting with a spatula.

Susie Sunshine Cake

Blooming Breadsticks

Instead of baking ordinary breadsticks, why not fashion refrigerated breadsticks into these blooming beauties? With just the right amount of seasoning, they pair well with a variety of meals.

- **1 tube (11 ounces) refrigerated breadsticks***
- **1/4 cup butter, melted**
- **1 teaspoon dried parsley flakes**
- **1/2 teaspoon garlic powder**
- **1/2 teaspoon Italian seasoning**
- **Additional parsley flakes**
- **Sesame seeds**

1 Unroll dough and separate into 12 breadsticks. Adjust the length of each breadstick to 6 in. For each flower, cut one breadstick into 1-in. pieces and another breadstick into one 4-in. piece and two 1-in. pieces.

2 For stem, twist 4-in. piece twice and place on a greased baking sheet. For leaves, pinch one end of two 1-in. pieces; place on each side of stem and pinch to seal. Roll one 1-in. piece into a ball; place 1 in. above stem for flower center. For petals, pinch one end of remaining five pieces; position with sides touching flower center and other petals.

3 In a small bowl, combine butter, parsley, garlic powder and Italian seasoning; brush over dough.

Sprinkle parsley on stem and leaves. Sprinkle sesame seeds on flower center. Bake at 375° for 10-12 minutes or until golden. **Yield:** 6 servings.

*Editor's Note: This recipe was tested with Pillsbury refrigerated breadsticks.

Baby Chick
Cookies

Baby Chick Cookies

When you serve these cookies, you won't hear a peep from guests—they'll be too busy gobbling up the sweet treats!

- **1-3/4 cups all-purpose flour**
- **1/2 cup plus 1 tablespoon butter, softened**
- **1/3 cup sugar**
- **3 egg yolks**
- **12 drops yellow food coloring**
- **TOPPING:**
- **3 egg whites**
- **1 teaspoon ground cinnamon**
- **1 teaspoon lemon juice**
- **Dash salt**
- **3/4 cup sugar**
- **1-3/4 cups finely ground almonds**
- **2 ounces white candy coating**
- **2 drops yellow food coloring**
- **1 drop red food coloring**

1 In a large mixing bowl, combine the flour, butter, sugar, egg yolks and food coloring. Beat on medium speed for 2 minutes. Knead 3-4 times to form a ball. On a floured surface, roll out dough to 1/8-in. thickness. Cut with a 2-1/2-in. to 3-in. chick-shaped cookie cutter. Place 1 in. apart on greased baking sheets.

Blooming
Breadsticks

2 In a small mixing bowl and with clean beaters, beat egg whites, cinnamon, lemon juice and salt on medium speed until soft peaks form. Gradually beat in sugar, 1 tablespoon at a time, on high until stiff peaks form. Fold in almonds. Place 2 teaspoons of topping on each chick, spreading to cover all but the beak and feet.

3 Bake at 375° for 12-14 minutes or until lightly browned. Cool completely on wire racks.

4 In a small heavy saucepan or microwave, melt candy coating; stir until smooth. Stir in yellow and red food coloring to make orange; spread on beak and feet of each chick. **Yield:** about 4 dozen.

—*Phyllis Madonna, Cleveland, New York*

Teddy Bear Rolls

These cute rolls would be a nice addition to a "Teddy Bear" party. Their oven-fresh goodness is so appealing.

- **2 packages (1/4 ounce *each*) active dry yeast**
- **1 cup warm water (110° to 115°)**
- **1 cup warm milk (110° to 115°)**
- **2 tablespoons sugar**
- **2 tablespoons vegetable oil**
- **1 egg**
- **1 teaspoon salt**

- **5-1/2 to 6-1/2 cups all-purpose flour**
- **About 20 raisins**
- **White frosting**
- **HONEY BUTTER:**
  - **1 cup butter, softened**
  - **1/4 cup honey**
  - **1/4 cup confectioners' sugar**

1 In a large mixing bowl, dissolve yeast in water. Add the milk, sugar, oil, egg, salt and 4 cups flour; beat until smooth. Stir in enough remaining flour to form a soft dough.

2 Turn onto a floured surface; knead until smooth and elastic, about 6-8 minutes. Place in a greased bowl, turning once to grease top. Cover and let rise in a warm place until doubled, about 1 hour.

3 Punch dough down. For each bear, shape a 2-in. ball for the body. Add a 1-1/4-in. ball for the head and six 1/2-in. balls for ears, arms and legs. Place 2 in. apart on greased baking sheets. Cover and let rise until doubled, about 20 minutes.

4 Bake at 400° for 17-20 minutes or until golden brown. Cool on wire racks. Add raisins for eyes, anchoring with a dab of frosting. Add a frosting smile.

5 In a small mixing bowl, beat honey butter ingredients until fluffy. Chill. Serve with rolls. **Yield:** about 10 rolls (1-1/4 cups butter).

—*Annette Ellyson*
Carolina, West Virginia

Teddy Bear Rolls

Peppermint Candy Cookies

Peppermint Candy Cookies

These buttery mint treats practically melt in your mouth. Plus, bright food coloring gives them a lively look for wintertime parties.

1-1/4 cups butter, softened
3/4 cup confectioners' sugar
2-1/2 cups all-purpose flour

1/2 teaspoon salt
1/2 teaspoon peppermint extract
Green and red paste *or* gel food coloring

1 In a large mixing bowl, cream butter and confectioners' sugar until light and fluffy. Add the flour, salt and extract; mix well. Divide dough into fourths. Tint one portion green and one red; leave the remaining portions plain.

2 Divide each portion into thirds; shape each into a 6-in. log. Flatten into triangular logs, bending the top of one point slightly (to give finished cookies a pinwheel effect). Assemble one large roll by alternating three green and three plain logs. Wrap in plastic wrap. Repeat with red and remaining plain dough. Refrigerate for 4 hours or until firm.

3 Unwrap dough and cut into 1/4-in. slices. Place 2 in. apart on ungreased baking sheets. Bake at 375° for 8-10 minutes or until edges are golden brown. Cool for 1 minute before removing to wire racks.

4 Cut 6-in.-square pieces of cellophane or plastic wrap to wrap each cookie; twist ends securely or tie with a ribbon. **Yield:** about 4 dozen.
— *Gloria McKenzie, Panama City, Florida*

Shaping Peppermint Candy Cookies

1. Shape each piece into a 6-in. log. Flatten into triangular logs, bending the top of one point slightly.

2. Assemble one large roll by alternating three green and three plain logs. Repeat with red dough and remaining plain dough.

Roly-Poly Santas

Tuck these fanciful Santas onto every gift cookie tray you make...they're guaranteed to be a hit.

1 cup butter, softened
1/2 cup sugar
1 tablespoon milk
1 teaspoon vanilla extract
2-1/4 cups all-purpose flour
Red paste food coloring
Miniature chocolate chips
FROSTING:
1/2 cup shortening
1/2 teaspoon vanilla extract
2-1/3 cups confectioners' sugar, *divided*
2 tablespoons milk, *divided*

1 In a large mixing bowl, cream butter and sugar until light and fluffy. Add milk and vanilla; mix well. Add flour and mix well. Remove 1 cup dough; add red food coloring. Shape white dough into 12 balls, 3/4 in. each, and 48 balls, 1/4 in. each. Shape red dough into 12 balls, 1 in. each, and 60 balls, 1/2 in. each.

2 Place 1-in. red balls on two ungreased baking sheets for the body of 12 Santas; flatten to 1/2-in. thickness. Attach 3/4-in. white balls for heads; flatten to 1/2-in. thickness. Attach four 1/2-in. red balls to each Santa for arms and legs. Attach 1/4-in. white balls to ends of arms and legs for hands and feet. Shape remaining 1/2-in. red balls into hats (see photo on opposite page). Add chocolate chip eyes and buttons.

3 Bake at 325° for 12-15 minutes or until set. Cool for 10 minutes; carefully remove from pans to wire racks (cookies will be fragile).

4 For frosting, in a small mixing bowl, beat shortening and vanilla. Gradually add 1-1/3 cups confectioners' sugar; add 1 tablespoon milk. Gradually add remaining sugar and milk.

5 Cut a small hole in the corner of a pastry bag or heavy-duty resealable plastic bag; insert round pastry tip #3. Fill bag with frosting. Pipe a band of icing on hat, cuffs at hands and feet, and down the front and at bottom of jacket. Use star pastry tip #16 to pipe beard and pom-pom on hat. **Yield:** 1 dozen.
—*Mrs. Andrew Seyer, Oak Ridge, Missouri*

Editor's Note: Use of a coupler ring will allow you to easily change tips. Remaining dough may be shaped into balls and baked.

Meringue Stockings

Stocking-shaped meringues hold tangy cranberry and sweet cream cheese fillings. They're a festive addition to any Christmas cookie tray.

  3 egg whites
  1/4 teaspoon cream of tartar
  1/4 teaspoon vanilla extract
  3/4 cup sugar
CRANBERRY FILLING:
  1 cup sugar
  2 tablespoons cornstarch
  1 cup cranberry juice
 1-1/2 cups fresh *or* frozen cranberries
CREAM CHEESE FILLING:
  2 packages (3 ounces *each*) cream cheese, softened
  1 cup confectioners' sugar
  1 teaspoon vanilla extract
  1 cup heavy whipping cream, whipped

  32 to 48 small mint leaves
  8 dried cranberries, halved

1 Place egg whites in a small mixing bowl; let stand at room temperature for 30 minutes. Add cream of tartar and vanilla; beat on medium speed until soft peaks form. Gradually beat in sugar, 1 tablespoon at a time, on high until stiff peaks form.

2 Line a baking sheet with parchment paper. Spoon meringue into 16 mounds on paper. Using icing spatula, shape each into a 4-1/2-in. stocking. Bake at 300° for 35 minutes. Turn oven off and do not open door; let meringues dry in oven for 1 hour. Remove from the oven and cool on baking sheet. When meringues are completely cooled, remove from parchment paper and store in an airtight container at room temperature.

3 For cranberry filling, combine the sugar, cornstarch and cranberry juice in a saucepan until smooth. Stir in cranberries. Bring to a boil; cook and stir for 2 minutes. Reduce heat. Cook until berries pop, about 5 minutes. Mash; cool.

4 For cream cheese filling, in a small mixing bowl, beat the cream cheese, confectioners' sugar and vanilla. Fold in whipped cream. Cut a small hole in the corner of pastry bag or heavy-duty resealable plastic bag; insert star pastry tip #18. Fill bag with cream cheese filling. Pipe filling in a 1-in. band at the top of each stocking; pipe filling to form heel and toe of stocking.

5 Spread 4-1/2 teaspoons cranberry filling in the center of each stocking. Add mint leaves and dried cranberries for the holly decoration on cuff of stocking. **Yield:** 16 servings.

Meringue Stockings

Chocolate Garnishes

Chocolate garnishes add a special touch to desserts. These garnishes can be made from either chocolate or candy coating. (In this section, the terms are used interchangeably.)

Most of these garnishes call for melted chocolate. Here's how:

Break or chop large pieces of chocolate. This gives it more surface area and it will melt more evenly. Melt in a heavy saucepan over low heat and stir until smooth. (High heat will scorch and ruin the chocolate.) Small amounts of water will cause chocolate to seize. So make sure the pan and spoon are dry.

To melt in the microwave, heat semisweet chocolate at 50% power. Heat milk chocolate and vanilla or white chocolate at 30% power. Stir during melting and don't overheat.

Cutouts. Melt 1 cup chips—semisweet, milk, vanilla or white—and 1/4 teaspoon shortening (do not use butter, margarine or oil).

Line a baking sheet with aluminum foil (shiny side up) or waxed paper. Smooth the foil or paper so there are not any wrinkles or bumps, which would make the chocolate uneven.

Pour melted chocolate onto foil or paper; spread with a spatula so the chocolate is about 1/8 in. thick. Let stand at room temperature until firm.

Using sharp metal cookie cutters, cut out desired shapes. (See photo.) Carefully lift off shapes with a metal spatula.

The chocolate scraps my be remelted and used to coat fruit or whole nuts for additional garnishes.

Curls. Using a vegetable peeler, peel off curls from a solid block of chocolate. (See photo above left.) Allow curls to fall gently onto a work surface or plate in a single layer. If you get only shavings, try warming the chocolate slightly.

1.

2.

Hearts and Arrows. Trace the design several times on a piece of paper. Place the paper on a baking sheet and cover with waxed paper.

Melt semisweet, milk, vanilla or white chocolate. The amount of melted chocolate needed depends on the number of garnishes you are making. Fill pastry bag or resealable plastic bag with melted chocolate. Cut a small hole in the bottom corner of bag. The more detailed the design, the smaller the hole in the bag should be. But remember, when finished, thicker designs will be sturdier and easier to remove.

Following traced designs, pipe chocolate onto waxed paper. (See photo 1.) Refrigerate until the chocolate is firm, about 15 minutes.

Just before serving, carefully remove the hearts with a metal spatula. (See photo 2.) If designs are not to be used immediately, store in a cool dry place in a covered plastic container until needed.

Edible Clay. Melt 10 oz. chocolate or white candy coating. Stir in 1/3 cup light corn syrup. If using white candy coating, you can divide between different bowls and tint with various liquid or paste food coloring. Spread on a sheet of waxed paper to 1/3-in. thickness. Let stand, uncovered, at room temperature for 2-3 hours or until dry to the touch. Remove clay from waxed paper and gather into a ball. Wrap tightly in plastic wrap; let stand overnight. Use immediately or store for up to 2 weeks.

To use, unwrap clay and knead until pliable but not soft. Roll between sheets of waxed paper to 1/8-in. thickness. Cut into desired shapes with a sharp knife or cookie cutters. Carefully lift up shapes with a spatula.

Butterflies. Melt about 10 oz. white candy coating.

Trace pattern (at right) onto tracing paper. Place butterfly pattern on a flat surface. Arrange wooden spoons with handles 2 in. apart. Place a 4-in. square of waxed paper directly over the pattern.

Cut a small hole in the bottom corner of a pastry bag or heavy-duty resealable plastic bag. Insert round pastry tip #4 if desired or pipe candy coating directly from the bag. Fill bag with some melted candy coating.

Pipe chocolate over the pattern, carefully tracing the butterfly outline. (See photo 1). Continue with the inside design, then pipe the body and antennae. If mistakes are made when tracing over the pattern with chocolate, or if chocolate begins to harden while tracing, simply start over. Remove chocolate from bag before remelting. To fix broken wings or antennae, "glue" them back on with melted chocolate.

Immediately pick up the edges of waxed paper and place the completed butterfly between the spoon handles with the wings resting against the handles. (See photo 2.) This will create the curve of the wings. Repeat, lining up the butterflies down the length of the handles. Remove butterflies from waxed paper by carefully peeling away the waxed paper.

If butterflies are not to be used immediately, store in a cool dry place in a covered plastic container. Place butterflies on cakes, cupcakes or petit fours while frosting is still moist. This will help secure them in place.

Leaves. Wash 10 to 12 lemon, rose or mint leaves and set aside until completely dry. Melt 1/2 cup chips—semisweet, milk, vanilla or white—and 1/4 teaspoon shortening (do not use butter, margarine or oil).

With a new small paintbrush, brush melted chocolate in a thin layer on the underside of each leaf. (See photo 1.) Refrigerate until set, about 10 minutes. Apply a second layer of melted chocolate; chill for at least 15 minutes or overnight. Gently peel leaf from chocolate. (See photo 2.)

If leaves are not to be used immediately, store in a cool dry place in a covered plastic container until needed.

Chocolate Almond Pinecones. Divide one 7-oz. tube almond paste into six equal portions. Form each into a cone shape, about 1-1/2 in. tall and 1 in. in diameter. Beginning at the base, insert pointed end of sliced almonds (4 ounces total) into paste to resemble a pinecone. (See photo 1.)

Melt 1-1/4 cups chips—semisweet, milk, vanilla or white—and 1 tablespoon shortening (do not use butter,

margarine or oil). Stir until smooth. Insert a toothpick into the bottom of each pinecone. Holding over a bowl, spoon melted chocolate over pinecone. (See photo 2.)

Use another toothpick to spread the chocolate to completely cover. Place on a wire rack over waxed paper; let stand until firm. (See photo 3.)

Use immediately or store in an airtight container at room temperature for several weeks.

Alphabetical Listing of Recipes

Refer to this index for a complete listing of all the recipes in this book.

General Recipe Index

This index lists every recipe by food category and/or major ingredient, so you can easily locate them.

396 Index

Reference Index

*Use this index as a guide to the many helpful hints and step-by-step instructions throughout this book.
Also see the Baking Basics chapter for more reference information.*